HINDUISM

Hinduism ❁ Past and Present

AXEL MICHAELS

Translated by Barbara Harshav

PRINCETON UNIVERSITY PRESS

Princeton and Oxford

First published in Germany under the title *Der Hinduismus: Geschichte und Gegenwart*

Published by Princeton University Press, 41 William Street,
Princeton, New Jersey 08540
In the United Kingdom: Princeton University Press, 3 Market Place,
Woodstock, Oxfordshire OX20 1SY

LIBRARY OF CONGRESS CATALOGING-IN-PUBLICATION DATA

Michaels, Axel.
[Hinduismus. English]
Hinduism: past and present/Axel Milchaels; translated by Barbara Harshav.
p. cm.
Includes bibliographical references and index.
ISBN 0-691-08952-3—ISBN 0-691-08953-1 (pbk.)
1. Hinduism. I. Harshav, Barbara. II. Title.
BL1202.M53 2003
294.5—dc21 2003045972

British Library Cataloging-in-Publication Data is available

This book has been composed in Adobe Caslon and Veljovic

Printed on acid-free paper. ∞

www.pupress.princeton.edu

Printed in the United States of America

1 3 5 7 9 10 8 6 4 2

Contents

RELIGION AND SOCIETY

FROM DESCENT TO TRANSCENDENCE

Illustrations

Tables

Preface

This book treats Hinduism from the perspective of Indology and religious studies. But, since the religion of nearly 700 million people and roughly three thousand years of history can hardly be compressed into a few hundred pages, it should be said immediately what readers may and may not expect: My view is oriented toward a Hinduism that is traditional but still practiced, not toward a modernized, Western-influenced Hinduism. I look at the village and only minimally at the city. Literature, art, mythology, or philosophy are treated only peripherally; parallels to Buddhism and Jainism are disregarded. I would like to offer an analysis of the socioreligious aspects of Hindu society, but not of Indian society. Therefore, expectations of salvation are accorded more attention than illiteracy rates or political parties.

Despite these constraints, I try to grasp "the whole" of Hinduism in its difference and uniqueness. Such an aspiration can be no more than an attempt: One individual cannot cope with the diversity of Hinduism and the magnitude of India.

Recent publications in Indology and anthropology seem to put an end to antiquated customs in representations of Hinduism. I shall cite only a few examples: The entity of castes has often been treated in an unreflected way and without any anthropological background. Classes (*varṇa*) are still defined according to racial instead of cultural criteria of division. The disproportionate importance of asceticism is accepted, and an exoticism of horror with relation to India is generally seen: The subjects of dowry murder, widow-burning, or casteless people are in great demand, but a complex society can be understood only if the sociocultural context is taken into account. Conceptions of after-death reality are represented almost only from a Brahmanic-Sanskritic perspective; the equally important folk religious aspects and anthropological components, on the other hand, are neglected. Theistically, the notion of god assumes one-sided ideas: Talk of "Śaivism" or "Vaiṣṇavism" is rarely thought through; the term *henotheism,* worship of one god in a polytheistic milieu, coined by the religious scholar and Indologist Max Müller (1823–1900), is still used, even though it misses the mark. In rituals, the assumption is too often based on normative texts instead of practice; and this represents a disproportionate focus of books about Brahmanic-Sanskritic rituals. The extraordinary significance of astrology for Hindu religious life is usually underestimated or overlooked. In the ways to salvation, heroism is not adequately taken into account.

Considering all these factors, it is time to reinforce one form of Indology that represents a link between anthropology and text-Indology, but not at the expense of philological Indology. I call this approach "ethno-Indology." This does not mean examining modern India or its tribes and ethnic groups, but rather including materials from religious studies and anthropology. From the Indological aspect, contemporary Hinduism is often seen as a confirmation that the past still works in the modern age. It usually forms the stylish dessert after a traditional menu. The basis of classical Indological analyses and descriptions, like a rite of passage, are historical situations, deduced from written texts, usually complemented with a few comments about the present. In this book, I have taken the opposite way, first looking at contemporary practice in order to understand it by means of historical text material.

Even though Indology has supplied material for many religious and sociological theories about sacrifices, gifts, ritual, polytheism, purity and impurity, and kingship, the authors of these theories—George Dumézil, Edward Burnett Tylor, Marcel Mauss, Henri Hubert, Louis Dumont, Max Weber, Arthur M. Hocart, and others—were not Indologists. Although I will also concentrate essentially on India, I intend this book as a preliminary study of a comprehensive theory of ritual, which I hope to be able to present someday.

The canon of subjects keeps turning out to be a problem, especially in German-speaking universities: Indology usually does not feel adequate for field study, but rather for the textual legacy; moreover, it still concentrates on old India and raises its voice only imperceptibly in discussions of cultural theory. South Asian anthropology, on the other hand, too seldom includes Brahmanic-Sanskritic texts, even though these are still used in many rituals and are bases of an influential and modern ideology of society. I have tried to fill these gaps by linking anthropological study results with Indological findings. Thus, I have not striven for completeness, but rather have tried to develop general and theoretical considerations from concrete cases for which I have occasionally resorted to my own publications. In this English translation I have not tried to take account of the literature published since 1998.

This book introduces examples and, at the same time, presents a study of rituals and the formation of socioreligious identity. It seeks to introduce both the subject of Hinduism and also a specific, habitual thinking and feeling. The chapters in Part I lay the theoretical, historical, and literary foundations. Parts II and III are self-contained, but they are oriented toward a theory explained in summary in the concluding section. At the beginning of each section, I usually give references to literature that represents a detailed or fundamental treatment of the subject. For the same reason, I have drafted the bibliography as a comprehensive list of anthropological and Indological sources; its focus is the literature of religious and social studies that has appeared in recent decades,[1] which—as I said—is much too briefly considered in the usual representations of Hinduism.

All Indian terms stem from the Sanskrit or are otherwise noted. I have tried to introduce Sanskrit terms only when they seem unavoidable and untranslatable to a certain extent. I have used standard editions of Sanskrit texts, and, unless otherwise indicated, I have quoted the standard English translations referred to in the notes. If no translation is listed in the notes, Barbara Harshav supplied the English translation from my German translation. The tables summarize details that are not always clarified in the text. Almost without exception, the notes contain bibliographic information, not substantive points or discussion.

I am grateful to Niels Gutschow for his views of and about India. Thanks to Albrecht Wezler for reading the manuscript even though he had limited time; he still proposed many important suggestions and improvements. I thank Michael Witzel for help in questions of detail in Vedic material. I am also grateful to Atul Agarwala, Parameshwara Aithal, Martin Gaenszle, Jörg Gengnagel, Thomas Lehmann, Burkhard Schnepel, and Annette Wilke for reading parts of this book, for discussions, and for valuable hints. Thanks to Barbara Harshav for her meticulous and excellent translation; Srilata Raman Müller for reading the translation and suggesting many improvements; Madeleine B. Adams for her careful copyediting, and, last but not least, Brigitta van Rheinberg for her intelligent guidance of the English edition through the press. Above all, I thank my beloved wife, Annette, who has helped me to look at life, but whose own life was taken too early.

Pronunciation of Indian Words

Cities and well-known persons of recent history are written in their Anglicized form; on the other hand, gods and shrines are written in the internationally common transcription of Sanskrit, Hindī (H.), Nepālī (N.), or Tamil. This transcription oriented to Devanāgarī writing enables a precise pronunciation, in which two rules are especially to be observed.

1. A line over a vowel indicates its length: *bh**ū**ta* pronounced like the English "mood"; both *e* and *o* are always long.
2. An S (ś,ṣ) is pronounced like the English "sh," when it is provided with an additional sign: ***ś**āstra* like ***sh**āstra* and *mokṣa* like *mok**sh**a;* without a diacritical mark, it is always a sharp (dental) S.

In addition, the following rules of pronunciation apply:

C like the English *ch: cakra* like **ch**urch
J like the English *j: jātrā* like **j**ungle
Y like the English *y: yogī* like **y**ogurt
V like the English *v: Viṣṇu* like **v**ine.

A dot under a consonant (except *ṃ*) indicates retroflex pronunciation, i.e., with the tongue bent back.

A dot or a tilde over an N (*ṅ, ñ*) and a dot under an M (*ṃ*) indicate the conformed nasalization of the succeeding consonants (see the English "end").

A dot under an R (*ṛ*) is often pronounced *ri* (*mahāṛṣi* as "Mahā**ri**shi").

An H behind a consonant is a clearly strengthening aspiration of the consonant (see the English "**T**ea").

THEORETICAL AND HISTORICAL FOUNDATIONS

1. Theoretical Foundations

IS INDIA DIFFERENT?

Introductory books on Hinduism often begin with a caveat: India is much too complex geographically, ethnically, linguistically, and religiously to allow any definitive statements to be made about it. Everything must be taken with a grain of salt. Millions of gods, a thousand castes, hundreds of languages and dialects. As a matter of fact, Hinduism is not a homogeneous religion at all, but is rather a potpourri of religions, doctrines and attitudes toward life, rites and cults, moral and social norms.[1] For every claim, the reader should be aware "that the opposite could, more or less justifiably, be asserted."[2] Thus images chosen to represent Hinduism are similar: an impenetrable jungle, an all-absorbent sponge,[3] a net ensnaring everything,[4] an upside-down banyan tree with countless roots growing from the branches to the earth.

In light of such metaphors, many have agreed with Johann Wolfgang von Goethe: "I am by no means averse to what is Indian, but I am afraid of it because it draws my power of imagination into formlessness and deformation." Goethe wrote this on December 15, 1824, in a letter to August Wilhelm Schlegel, one of the founders of German Indology, thus clearly moving away from his original enthusiasm for India expressed in his famous verse: "Would thou include both Heaven and earth in one designation / All that is needed is done, when I Sakontala[5] name" (translated by Edgar Alfred Bowring).

But it is not that Hinduism lacks form. What it does lack is a form of religion that we have become accustomed to in monotheism: There is neither *one* founder of the religion nor *one* church nor *one* religious leader. Nor is there *one* holy book or *one* doctrine, *one* religious symbol or *one* holy center. As a result, no one binding religious authority could emerge. Nevertheless, what threatened Goethe's power of imagination is precisely what fascinates many people today. Belief that stones or trees have souls (animism, pantheism) co-exists here with the belief in the highest gods. The monotheistic worship of one God is just as possible as the polytheistic or demonic worship of many gods, demons, and spirits. A god-excluding monism exists alongside dualism, materialism, and agnosticism. Religiosity is performed in ritualistic (Brahmanism, Tantrism), devotional (Bhakti), spiritual-mystical (asceticism, Yoga, meditation) and heroic modes. A strict puritanical ritualism encounters wild, inebriated cults and blood sacrifices. There is a commandment not to harm living creatures, the *ahiṃsā*, but there are also animal sacrifices and traces of human sacrifice. Nothing seems to be generally accepted, not even the doctrine of Karma, of retribution through reincarnation, which, according to Max Weber, constitutes "perhaps the only dogma of Hinduism." Yet all these forms of religion are practiced quite peacefully alongside one another. One might almost say that religious postmodernism is realized in India: Anything goes.

What makes it possible for India to endure so many contrasts and contradictions and to absorb so many alien elements? Is it tolerance or ignorance? Is there an implicit form of religion and religiosity here whose extensive peaceful toleration of Otherness can serve as a model for the multicultural and multireligious problems of the present? Is it a worldview whose boundless claim to pervasiveness forms a countermodel to the delimiting rationality of the West? Can we sing a Hindu hymn in "praise of polytheism" against the malaise of monotheism?[6] Do we find here a fluid, amorphous, soft, possibly "female"[7] culture, society, or religion, as opposed to a Western, hard, rigid, "male" culture, society, or religion? Is the Indian a *homo hierarchicus* rather than a *homo aequalis?* Is Indian society a holistic rather than an individualistic culture?

If we raise these issues, we have to fear the subsequent question: Do Indians or Hindus really think, feel, and act differently from other people? Leaping over our own cultural shadows requires walking a tightrope between exalting and taking over another culture and religion, to avoid either establishing the West as a generally valid standard or idealizing other religions.

According to Hans-Georg Gadamer, "understanding" means understanding differently. It can be realized only in oneself, not delegated; it is achieved neither through mindless empathy nor through emotionless thought, neither through esoteric subjectivity nor through exoteric objectivity. On the face of it, great differences between India and the West must be acknowledged, which is one reason why Hinduism usually constitutes the paradigmatic *other* religion in comparative studies of religion: where men are not considered equal, where India is hierarchical, where families, clans, and subcastes are valued higher than the individual, where India is ascetic and world-denying, where alongside proof of worth through work, "proof" of worth through idleness has a higher value in some cases. Liberty, Equality, Fraternity—these ideals of the French

Revolution and foundations of Western constitutions and human rights—are not the highest values of society in traditional India. India, it seems, really is different.

I would like to develop the following argument to attempt to understand the cause of such serious differences: There are three large groups of religion that still exist and are practiced today, according to the criteria of antiquity, number of followers, and the characteristics of a high culture (e.g., a written literature, a common language, ruling classes, professional priesthood). These are the Abrahamic-monotheistic religions of Judaism, Christianity, and Islam; Buddhism; and the Hindu religions.[8] It can hardly be doubted that the Abrahamic religions (especially Christianity and Islam) and Buddhism are the most widespread in world history. East and west of India, many religions have declined or been absorbed by Christianity, Islam, and Buddhism. But Hinduism has resisted the other world religions even though it was hard pressed by their missionary or universalist claims. How could that happen? Neither power politics nor geographical factors alone can account for this, since even though Buddhism arose in India itself and was emphatically promoted politically by Emperor Aśoka, it ultimately could not succeed in its homeland. Therefore, there must be some internal criteria that constitute the special "force" and form of the Hindu religions.

The Identificatory Habitus

I refer to the cohesive force that holds the Hindu religions together and makes them resistant to foreign influences as "the Identificatory Habitus," and I ascribe an outstanding value to it because it is linked in special ways to the descent, the origin of the individual, which is crucial to salvation in India. The Identificatory Habitus, descent, and salvation or immortality are thus key notions of my understanding of the Hindu religions. Unlike Max Weber, in his 1921 study of Hinduism, and Louis Dumont (whose *Homo Hierarchicus* of 1966, despite all criticism, is unsurpassed as a comprehensive socioreligious analysis of India), I do not focus primarily on caste, the individual, or ritual purity, but rather on the extended family as a descent group that has been much more resistant to modern influences than the norms of hierarchy and purity.[9] By descent, I do not mean only biological or natural origin, but also a fictive descent, based on soteriological identifications or substitutions that have to do with salvation. But, like Dumont, I see traditional Hinduism as a countermodel to the Western world, where the individual has priority, where the self is preferred to the not-self, where freedom *in* the world is more important than liberation *from* the world.

Religions are characterized mainly by the paths of salvation they offer, because this is how they answer the first and last questions: Where do I come from? Where am I going? Religion is man's answer to the awareness of his mortality: "Not miracle, but death is belief's 'favorite child,'" said Ernst Bloch in 1964 in a conversation with Theodor W. Adorno.[10] The religious concepts of salvation and the afterlife embody the order whose maintenance is the highest duty of the individual—even at the expense of his own interests or even his life. Orders are justified with reference to service to the holy worlds, which are in other places and at other times, and are inhabited by gods, spirits, and the dead, but not by men. The basic problem is: How can man know about those worlds, when everything he can possibly say about them is grounded in the here and now? Religious concepts have a lasting influence on the conduct of life when they deal with these final questions that are also binding on the community.[11] In the Hindu religions, the social order is largely determined by identifications indicating the systems of kinship and community life, originally derived from sacrificial rituals and then transferred to lineage.

In the following chapters I try to elaborate what is meant by the Identificatory Habitus before I finally return to a systematic evaluation of the concept. It is one, but not the only characteristically Indian way of thinking, feeling, and communicating, and is thus encountered by everyone who has dealt with India. Three examples which, at first glance, seem totally unrelated, express this attitude: (1) Every Western visitor to Germany is amazed by the Volkswagen factory in Wolfsburg, but the reaction of an Indian was: "I think that car factories are the same all over the world." (2) The Olympic Games challenge many countries to high athletic achievements; yet, in the hundred-year history of the Olympic movement, India has won only fifteen medals, most of them in field hockey, two each in track and field and tennis, and one in wrestling—and this in a nation of almost a billion inhabitants. Neither poverty nor climate nor the lack of political encouragement of sports can explain this phenomenon, because smaller and poorer countries constitute counterexamples. The explanation that physical activity was low-caste in India and thus regarded negatively is hardly convincing either. An Indian friend asked about this indifference to athletic competition once said: "For us, it doesn't count if someone is the best or not!" (3) A Nepali, asked if he was a Hindu or a Buddhist, answered: "yes!" All these answers may be imagined with a typical Indian gesture: the head slightly bent and softly tilted, the eyelids shut, the mouth smiling.

What do these examples have in common? The first quotation is a paraphrase of the Hindi saying, "All goddesses [or mothers] are one" (the title of a book by Stanley Kurtz, which will be discussed later).[12] The second example may illustrate that, in India, individual achievement is not valued highly. And the third demonstrates that contrasts and tensions are endured more easily in India than can be accommodated by an analytical mind. Behind all that I see the Identificatory Habitus at work: the establishment of an identity by equating it with something else, a habitus inherent in both the philosophical nondualism of the Vedānta and in the method of substitution in sacrificial rituals or asceticism, with which the caste system "works," which illuminates the multiplicity of the gods as much as it does the monotheism of India. It is still necessary, however, to prove and substantiate that such a way of grasping and shaping the world prevails in India and to account for why it has been and still is so successful.

"Habitus" is a notion introduced by Max Weber and brought to the fore in recent years by the French sociologist and ethnographer Pierre Bourdieu.[13] It denotes culturally acquired lifestyles and attitudes, habits and predispositions, as well as conscious, deliberate acts or mythological, theological, or philosophical artifacts and mental productions. *Pace* Bourdieu, I assume that the patterns of behavior of the individual in a society are fixed to a large extent. But the habitus of social activity emerging from these is not innate; rather "it ensures the active presence of past experiences, which, deposited in each organism in the form of schemes of perception, thought and action, tend to guarantee the 'correctness' of practices and their constancy over time, more reliably than all formal rules and explicit norms."[14] These cognitive, normative, and aesthetic models constitute the "social sense" people use to orient themselves in a culture. Bourdieu even talks of "the automatic certainty of an instinct" and relates the social sense to physical forms of expression, ways of speaking, or manners.[15] With this concept, he gets away both from voluntaristic notions that claim that the individual in a culture exercises free thought and free will, or that thought and action can be considered isolated from the social context, on the one hand; and from a social-science determinism or materialism that maintain that the collective or (economic) reality determines the individual, on the other. In a certain respect, Pierre Bourdieu takes up Durkheim's notion of "total social facts" (*fait sociaux totales*), which Durkheim describes as "every way of acting, fixed or not, capable of exercising on the individual an external constraint."[16]

Bourdieu's notion of habitus proves to be productive precisely in the context of the Hindu religions. In them, collective, family-related habits stubbornly resist all intention to change because they are acquired, learned, and shaped in early childhood, and are part of a "cultural memory" with almost independent processes of memory and tradition, as Jan Assmann has explained.[17] Not that cultural habits are unchallenged, but they are such strong norms that even occasional violations do not alter their widespread acceptance.

"Social sense" (Bourdieu) and "cultural sense" (Assmann) are parts of the shaping of cultural identity. They contribute to the sense of community and the "we" feeling of a culture, which is based on a "stock of common values, experiences, expectations, and interpretations,"[18] but also on rituals, myths, proverbs, or gestures. Identity formation implies drawing boundaries, and this often leads to erecting images of the enemy. Religious identity, for example, uses instruments of faith, initiations, or canonization to facilitate this process. Such walls clearly separate "in" and "out" from one another and exclude the alien element. It is indeed characteristic of the Hindu religions that they almost never erect these walls. Even the Hindu initiation, as I try to show, can be substituted. Since Hindu religions presuppose such an identificatory principle of equality, they are "disturbed" by fewer oppositions and dichotomies. They do not need exclusions, as it were, because the Other is always one's own. Since they assume a basic unity, separation for them can mean harmony: maintaining a tension that is basically not a tension at all. The other god can remain the other god because he is basically one's own. From this perspective, the phrase often heard in India—"all the same"—signifies not a lack of conceptual acuity or an exaggerated need for leveling, but rather a code of Hindu religious identity and a basic form of the Identificatory Habitus.

The concept of habitus has the advantage of not reducing the "whole," on the one hand, while preventing an overemphasis on details, the places, the historical uniqueness, on the other.[19] It thus counters a favorite objection against comprehensive analyses of Hinduism, that they cannot encompass the multiplicity of India because they want to know either too much or too little: too much because they see one single thought prevailing everywhere; too little because, for the sake of particular principles, there is much they overlook.

In general, the method of wanting to structure societies according to principles or laws has fallen into disrepute because of Postmodernism. Principles are considered dogmatic, reductionist, and essentialist. They seem to avoid historical change and are immune to cultural influences. They might seem attractive as cultural metaphors, but those are basically naïve masculine fantasies of omnipotence that attempt to comprehend a world that is incomprehensible because something new is always appearing beyond the aptly described horizon. They admit no anomalies, conflicts, or interests. Postmodern critics object that there can be no bird's-eye view for understanding how people organize their lives and for censuring them for deviating from the norms of the old legal texts, the Dharmaśāstras. Wanting an overall view is Western, Christian, masculine, and imperialistic. It is considered unseemly to try to cram the multiplicity of reality into a prefabricated (spiritual) harmony, a plan of God, or a law of nature, in which the welfare of the collective (the whole, the system) is valued more highly than the interest of the individual, where the viewpoint of the other is judged higher than one's own. In relation to India, Louis Dumont and Max Weber provide outstanding examples of such holistic analyses of Indian society, in which people (in this case, Hindus) almost always appear as passive instruments of impersonal structures, but not as agents. Yet, according to the new methodological trend, cultures (and thus people) have no principles, no goals, no secret plans, no (inner) core, only an infinite number of variations. Culture is life and life is disorder.

In the case of India,[20] there is something to be said for such formulations. Goethe was not the only one who was struck by the formlessness mentioned earlier. Indeed, Postmodernism looks as if it could have been created for India because it makes no attempt to produce *one* order, construct *one* principle, where—perhaps—there is none. (The difference between this and Western religious Postmodernism is that, in India, people are not subject to any "heretical imperative"—from the title of Peter Berger's book on religion in pluralistic society[21]—and so do not have to "choose" their religion.)

Not everything in India exhibits this diversity; the country also has a superregional normative, obligatory social order for many classes. That is, in countless texts, Brahmans have written and prescribed social rules. Thus, analyses of India quite often maintain that Brahmanic norms are the rules of this society. But it was not hard to see that Indian society did not "function" according to the will of the Brahmans, that these rules have always been followed only by a few. Nevertheless, several analyses fuel the suspicion that the Brahmans had at least formulated the ideals of Indian society. Such rigid, Brahman-centric approaches are no longer tenable. This concerns an elite culture that did indeed influence the sociocultural sense of social groups by setting norms and creating literature that granted identity. But, as shown primarily by ethnological research, this process ideologically also raised one specific group above the others. In other words, the Brahmans placed themselves "above" and thus affected the other classes of the population "below." At any rate, the claim that a society or culture must be ordered or centered along the axis of a single dominant religion is misleading not only in relation to India: In the West, too, several religions have coexisted at the same time (currently, e.g., Christianity, Buddhism, Islam, new religions, "secular" religions, and all sorts of esoteric forms of religion). But even if Brahmanic ideas have turned out to be limited as general social norms, there is a sense of social behavior specific to India. To determine what this is requires not only textual research but also field research.

Hence, for some years now, attention has shifted from philological cultural studies to the living streets and squares. As Bourdieu puts it, diversity is no longer epiphenomenal, and thus peripheral, but central. The private has become just as important as the public, sensibility as valuable as sense. Experiencing and participating are methodologically as valuable as reading. The individual is no longer merely the insignificant case study or the illustration of general rules: The subjective is considered objective. The messy, the chaotic, the incidental are to be collected. Context is superior to text. The everyday now counts almost more than Sunday, when there is preaching. The house is all at once an important place, and not only the temple, the palace, or the marketplace. The everyday is no longer considered only as the sphere of life of small chores, but as the counterworld of women, farmers, or artisans.

In this book, however, Indian everyday life is understood not as the world of the lower classes, nor will there be an attempt to rehabilitate underprivileged groups or to display the material culture of kitchen or bedroom, farm or workshop.[22] Instead, I would like to establish a theoretical connection between textual and normative ideas and less clearly articulated ways of life. Renouncing such a theoretical fusion of the everyday and the counterworld would mean using truisms or—as Ernest Gellner puts it—"unexamined theories."[23] But getting lost in the odds and ends of daily life, the details of village studies and philology, or in the decentralization of Postmodernism would ultimately result in confusion and helplessness about what it "all" means.

The insistence that no statement should be made about India as a whole, that the area should be circumscribed historically and regionally, is justified because only such an approach can lead to precise arguments based on the critical evaluation of sources. But regional history and the history of daily life are embedded in the theoretical discourse of historiography, which has its own subject matter, but not its own methodology.[24] Hence, despite all necessary concentration on the specific, now and then one must go to "the whole" and build a rickety house with as much room as possible. The house exists as uneasily among the ruins of Modernism as in the fragmentary outlines of Postmodernism. Despite such great restrictions, however, those theories that go beyond their limited subject matter are still fascinating. The village studies of the American anthropologist Gloria Goodwin Raheja or the British anthropologist Jonathan Parry, or the ritual studies of the Dutch Indologist Jan Heesterman, to pick three influential examples, are relevant not only for understanding the villages of Pahansu or Kangra, or the special problems of the Vedic sacrifice. In their details, they also encompass "the whole," and are therefore pathbreaking. In this sense, all (good) religious study is also, *pace* Hayden White, the philosophy of religion, as Hans G. Kippenberg has noted correctly.[25]

I have suggested understanding the Identificatory Habitus as part of the social meaning in Hinduism. I am aware that this represents a (Western, male) construct ordering "the whole," which cannot be found so easily in India. Therefore, it should be clarified: The Identificatory Habitus expresses *my* working understanding of India in two words, it is the common denominator of *my* concerns with various subjects, but it is not a theory that claims a validity independent of those to whom it is addressed. In its explicit subjectivity, the theory of the Identificatory Habitus cannot be refuted, but it can be rejected. In Kantian terms, it is an æsthetic judgment, not a rational judgment and certainly not a moral judgment. My factual statements can be refuted or proved empirically false, as can the argumentative links I establish. Much can be criticized, perhaps everything; but the theory itself can only be rejected. The theory does not attempt to give an objective total picture or portrayal of Hindu culture and society. That is not possible. Yet it does try to promote a way of looking at India that is not simply fragmentary.

It is strange that classical theories are always attacked and yet manage to endure. Everyone knows that Freud and Marx have proven to be fundamentally wrong, but that has not prevented the success of their theories. Many factual errors have also been pointed out in the theories of Max Weber and Louis Dumont.[26] Yet they clearly got "something right." They introduced a way of seeing that had an impact in part because it says more about the West than about India: in Weber about the emergence of capitalism, in Dumont about hierarchy and individuality. Thus, theories in cultural studies are clearly successful when they reflect their material in the mood of the time in a way that need not have anything to do with the subject matter of the study. Max Weber did not need India for his thesis about the emergence of capitalism from the spirit of Protestantism; he had already developed the thesis and "only" supported it with comparative studies. Thus, theories in cultural studies are often remote from reality. They produce a multiple reality, but they do not reproduce it. And yet, cultural theories are "right" only when they are more than projections or wild fantasies. In reflecting on the present and their own culture, they also have to encompass the Other. Whether they succeed in this, however, is not only a matter of a convincing argument, but also of æsthetics.

In a certain respect, the Identificatory Habitus is only old wine in new bottles. Indian society has repeatedly been defined as holistic, encompassing the opposites, inclusive, integrative, producing similarities—by Max Weber, Louis Dumont, Paul Hacker, Jan Heesterman, McKim Marriott, Sudhir Kakar, Brian K. Smith, and others. They have all emphasized another soul, structure, way of thinking, or code with regard to India. They have all tried to grasp the "essence" of India. The danger of constructing and imagining such a personal India—the main criticism of Ronald Inden[27]—is certainly not to be denied, nor is the danger of seeing this other India as a deviation from the

West or drawing an overly harmonious image of India: Women or Untouchables see the alleged solidarity of the caste system less harmoniously than Dumont does.[28] But anyone who intends to avoid completely the danger of Orientalism, and thus the construction of a counterworld, starts from the premise that cultures exist independent of perspectives on them. Such objectivity is not possible because human relations between fellow men or with gods—which is what cultural analyses are about—can be perceived only when they are based on classifications, institutions, and relations. Such relations do not exist atomistically, but are made and thought out: internally and externally, by the persons affected and by those who describe them. Objectivity consists of (a) not basing conclusions on individual cases, but on making statements that apply to the majority and the average case; (b) getting as close as possible to the conceptual framework of the analyzed contexts so that those who are described can accept it; and (c) allowing change in one's own thinking. For—to cite Gadamer again—understanding means: understanding differently. Hindus are only Hindus when they are different from Christians or Muslims or atheists—whether they're admired or detested. Or, more simply: If someone is a Hindu, he is different; if he is not different, he is no more a Hindu than I am a Christian or a Western atheist. But who is really a Hindu among the Indians? This term is already a test case for the fundamental considerations with which I began.

WHAT IS HINDUISM?

What traditions can be called "Hindu" is controversial both inside and outside India.[29] As we have seen, scholars of India often say that one must have an encyclopedic knowledge to be able to bring the variety of Hinduisms into one coherent system. At best, precise statements are possible only with regard to a temporally or regionally circumscribed area. Others lament the lack of a conceptual clarity that also poses a temptation to compare incongruent elements. And some maintain that Hinduism, as a coherent religion, is a Western construct: "Today, without wanting to admit it, we know that Hinduism is nothing but an orchid cultivated by European scholarship. It is much too beautiful to be torn out, but it is a greenhouse plant: It does not exist in nature."[30]

Legislators can hardly indulge in such hesitant thoughts. In cases of conflict, they have to know and decide if they are dealing with a Hindu or not. Thus, according to the Hindu Marriage Act of 1955, an Indian is a Hindu if he does not belong to another religion.[31] It was not the Indians who came up with this adroitly evasive definition, but the British. In 1881, for the second ten-year census, the government official and anthropologist Denzil Ibbetson told how he determined religious affiliation: "Every native who was unable to define his creed, or described it by any other name than that of some recognised religion or of a sect of some such religion, was held to be and classed as a Hindu."[32] This suggests that, until recently, Indians did not call themselves Hindus. In fact, the term *Hindu* is a foreign appellation[33] used initially by the Persians for the population living on the Indus River (linguistically derived from the Sanskrit *sindhu,* meaning river or sea). With the penetration of the Muslims into Sindh (711–712 A.D.), the word came to be used for the non-Muslim population. The Europeans followed this practice. Thus, in about 1830 A.D., the description of a population (all non-Muslims) became the description of a religion, "Hinduism," but it did not exist as a unity in the consciousness of that population.

Such a viewpoint might also be familiar to Western traditions. Religions do not depend absolutely on the differentiating view of foreign religions. Polemics crave simplification. Until the eighteenth century, for Christians, there were practically only Jews, "Mohammedans," and the one distorting, offensive descriptive division of Christian and Pagan.[34] In 1711, the missionary Bartholomäus Ziegenbalg titled his substantial book on Tamil Hinduism *Malabarisches Heidentum* (Malabar Paganism), and until the late Middle Ages, India stood for one of three parts of the world—along with Europe and Africa. People talked of several Indias; talk of *India Major* and *India Minor* can be traced back to the fourth century; and Columbus, as is well known, wanted to discover the sea route to one of these fabled Indias of antiquity. And at the end of the eighteenth century in France, along with Voltaire's *Candide* and Rousseau's *La Nouvelle Hêloise,* in 1770, Guillaume Ragnay and Denis Diderot published *Histoire Philosophique et Politique des êtablissements et du commerce des Europêens dans les deux Indes,* the greatest bestseller, even though the authors hardly wrote about India, but rather presented a critical debate regarding colonialism.

Hinduism and Hindu-ness

Is Hinduism in fact a Western construct, as these examples suggest? First, it should be asked how the Indians themselves have described their religion(s). The answer is baffling: Previously, while most of them mentioned their caste or ethnic group when they were asked about their belief, religious self-consciousness has changed under European influence. Since the early nineteenth century, at least the English-speaking classes see themselves as Hindus. And it was partly for anticolonial motives that they saw themselves as a unity in order to hold out against the missionary Christians and the Muslims who were allegedly favored by the British.

In present-day India, there are even tendencies to distinguish oneself radically and sometimes by force from the West and from Islam by constructing a Hindu political identity. Spokesmen for that are radical Hindu groups such as the strong *Bharatiya Janata Party* (Indian People's Party, BJP); the *Rashtriya Svayamsevak Sangha* (National Volunteer Corps, RSS), founded in 1925 and repeatedly banned, with several million trained paramilitary members; the *Vishva Hindu Parishad* (World-Hindu-Council, VHP), which has existed since 1964; and the *Shiv Sena* (Army of Shiva), a tightly organized right-wing affiliate of the BJP.

All these organizations want either to strengthen or revive Hindu-ness (*hindūtva*).[35] The term goes back to the book of that name by Vinayak Damodar Savarkar, a radical freedom fighter, who was imprisoned by the British in 1910. Sarvarkar distinguished between a Hindu Empire (*hindūrāṣṭra*), a territorial and political or nationalist definition, and Hindu-ness (*hindūtva*), a genealogical and national definition: "a Hindu means a person who regards this land of Bharatvarsha (the Indian subcontinent) from the Indus to the Seas, as his Fatherland as well as his Holyland."[36] This is a geographical, genealogical, and religious definition with an adroit solution: Sikhs, Jains and Indian (more precisely, South Asian) Buddhists are Hindus, but not Christians, Muslims, or other Buddhists, for whom either Bharatavarsha is neither a fatherland (Westerners and East Asian Buddhists) nor a holy land (Christians and Muslims).

Aside from exceptions and recent developments, Hinduism does not pursue any missionary activity, as per this definition. The widespread fear of foreigners in India and especially of proselytizing religions such as Islam or Christianity is always being stoked by Hindu fundamentalist groups. It is especially lamented that even though there are converted Hindus, conversion to Hinduism is not possible. Because of that and because of the polygamy of the Muslims, a constant attenuation of Hinduism is forecast.

Such a Hinduism is, first of all, understood as a national Hindu-ness: Accordingly, one is a Hindu if one was born in India and behaves like a Hindu, if one does not identify oneself publicly as a Christian or a Muslim. Belief is secondary to behavior. M. S. Gowalkar, who led the *Rashtriya Svayamsevak Sangha* from 1940 to 1973, could even speak of "Hindu Muslims." "Hindu by culture, Muslim by religion," adds D. Gold.[37] Others speak of "Christian Hindus." Such arguments are directed primarily at political goals: national identity, improvement of power positions, and chances of election. But what Hinduism is as a religion neither Gowalkar nor other such emphatic Hindu politicians can say.

Even at the second world Hindu conference organized by *Vishva Hindu Parishad* in February 1979 in Allahabad, which was again devoted to the question of definition, representatives of various Hindu groups, castes, or religious trends could not unite on genuine common grounds. Nevertheless, a Six-Point Code for all Hindus was developed: anyone who recites prayers (*sūryapraṇāma* and *prārthana*), reads the Bhagavadgītā, worships a personal chosen deity (*mūrti,* literally: "statue, image of god"), uses the holy syllable *Oṃ,* and plants the Tulasī or Tulsī plant (*Oscium sanctum,* "basil") may call himself a "Hindu."[38] But this is clearly a superficial definition, and colored by Vaiṣṇavism (because of the Tulsī plant associated with this god).

Religion and Dharma[39]

The difficulties of defining Hinduism reside in a term analogous to *religion,*[40] which is often used normatively or strategically in order to defend one's own belief against others. Thus, the esoteric or the sectarian is denied the title *religion,* religion is separated from magic or superstition, certain kinds of science are disqualified with the designation *religion. Religio* in Latin denotes "conscientiousness," "fear," and "obedience" toward gods as well. The early Christians in Rome called both their own faith and the pagan cults *religio;* only later was the Christian faith elevated to *vera religio* (true religion), and not until the Enlightenment did *religion* become a generic term for religions. So, when we speak of "religion," we already have a preconception. This includes a notion of a personal god (which is why there is a continuing controversy about whether early, "godless" Buddhism is a religion) or an idea of the sacred, which is otherworldly and is revealed, manifested, and incarnated in this world. Non-Western languages are not familiar with the term *religio.* In Arabic, *islām* (from the verb *aslama,* to be intact, sacred, hence the participle *Muslim*) is an equivalent for *religion* just as much as the word *dīn* (practice, custom, law);[41] in the Greek *eusebeia* (awe of god), but also *latreia* (service and reward), *therapeia* (worship, service), or *sebas* (sacred fear);[42] in Old High German *ē* or *ēwa* (divine law, order, hence in New High German, *Ehe,* marriage).

Many Hindus, especially the intellectual upper class, call their religion *sanātana dharma* (eternal Dharma),[43] and *dharma* is also the term that usually appears in comparative treatises on the definition of religion. Dharma, related etymologically to the Latin *firmus* (solid, strong) and *forma* (form, shape), is what holds the world together and supports it, the eternal (*sanātana*) law, the "order in consummation."[44] The Dharma applies to humans and animals, but also to elements; it includes natural and structured order, law and morals in the broadest sense. Dharma is life ritualized according to norms and rules, which ultimately depend less on an internal participation than on proper behavior derived from the Veda. Thus Dharma includes domestic rites and ceremonies, daily and life-cycle "sacraments" (*saṃskāra*), rites of sin and atonement, the whole area of civil and criminal law, constitutional law and common law, normative and ritual regulations about caste, age, sacrifices, pilgrimages, vows, ritual gifts, and so on. "The ten points of duty are patience, forgiveness, self-control, not stealing, purification, mastery of the sensory powers, wisdom, learning, truth, and lack of anger," says the *Laws of Manu,* the Mānavadharmaśāstra, but that is only one of many definitions. The Dharma can be said to be a religion of law without a codified law, whose most frequently cited sources are the Veda, tradition (*smṛti*) and good custom (*sadācāra, śiṣṭācāra, śīla*).

Even though the Dharma is not always understood theistically, and even though it does not rely on a divine creator, the term comes close to current notions of "religion." Yet there is one essential difference between it and a monotheistic concept of religion: Dharma is a relative term, always referring to special circumstances. The Righteous (*dharma*) and the Unrighteous (*adharma*) do not go around saying, "Here we are!" Nor do gods, Gandharvas, or ancestors declare, "This is righteous and that is unrighteous," explains an old legal text.[45] There are various Dharmas, according to sex, age, and origin. There is talk of regional Dharma (*deśadharma*), extended family Dharma (*kuladharma*), personal Dharma (*svadharma*), the Dharma of women (*strīdharma*) or the Dharma of animals (*paśudharma*). A lot of common law appears there, but little natural law and no common morality: "Better a man's own duty, though ill-done, than another's duty well-performed."[46] The decision about the right Dharma lies with the elders, Brahmans, and scholars, and they judge according to different rules, even though they are to strive for consensus.[47] Thus, there can be a Dharma of killing for warriors and butchers, of stealing for the castes of thieves, or of adultery for prostitutes,[48] even though the Brahmans consider only high-ranking social groups capable of adhering to Dharma. The relation between Dharma and salvation is that everyone who acts in accordance with his Dharma may hope for and even count on a better reincarnation, to a certain extent. Georg Wilhelm Friedrich Hegel commented correctly on Dharma: "If we say that courage is a virtue, the Hindoo says that courage is a virtue of the Kshatriyas (warriors)."[49]

The relativity of Dharma in Hinduism marks a definite difference between it and Buddhism, as Richard Gombrich emphasized:[50] "I do not see how one could exaggerate the importance of the Buddha's ethicisation of the world, which I regard as a turning point in the history of civilisation."[51] In fact, Brahman ethics relates to a large extent to the position of birth, that is, to one's own Dharma. On the other hand, the Buddha, according to Gombrich, ethicizes not only the act, but also the intention. Instead of proper behavior, he demanded proper motivation to a certain extent. But intention can no longer be understood as relative. In Buddhism, an intention is good or bad, whether one is a Brahman or a casteless person. Thus, the relativity of the Dharma is the special feature of Hinduism that should be grasped. It is possible only because the individual social groups tacitly agree that ethics or Dharmas can be mutually exchanged. In other words, the principle of the relativity of the Dharma is higher than a claim to absoluteness. This principle, as will be shown, is expressed as a social sense in patterns of thought as well as in customary forms of behavior.

The Dharma in its relativity explains the versatility of Hinduism, but it does not define it as religion, since it is accepted conceptually only in certain Brahman-influenced circles. The same holds for other concepts that are always cited to define the "religion" of Hinduism. Robert Charles Zaehner's influential 1962 book, *Hinduism,* begins with the assertion: "*Brahman—dharma—moksha—samsara—karma:* these are the key concepts of classical Hinduism."[52] But, in the first section of Mircea Eliade's equally impressive monograph on Yoga, we read: "Four basic and interdependent concepts, four 'kinetic ideas,' bring us directly to the core of Indian spirituality. They are *karma, māyā* [illusion], *nirvāṇa* [release], and *yoga.*"[53] But those terms are also important for Buddhism and Jainism. Moreover, their selection is limited: *veda* (sacred knowledge) is lacking, as are *bhakti* (devotion), *pūjā* (divine service), *yajña* (sacrifice), and *avatāra* (incarnation.)

Thus, definitions of Hinduism tend to be lengthy and ramified. It cannot be otherwise because—as Heinrich von Stietencron in particular has often shown[54]—in India, we are dealing with various religions that belong to one geographically definable cultural space, influence one another, and sometimes overlap, but that often differ considerably from one another in their founders, holy writings, doctrines, divine worlds, rituals, languages, historical conditions, and supporters. Only when there is a convergence of several of these criteria, however, can a religious community be recognized and a religion defined—regardless of whether one speaks of the development of religions, their individual or social effects, or their nature, or classifies them phenomenologically, symbolically, or theoretically.[55] In any case, in terms of history and religion, Judaism, Christianity, and Islam have more in common with each other than the religions of Indian tribal groups and Brahmanism or the reform Hinduism in the big cities.

Nevertheless, Hinduism is counted as one of the world religions. With more than 663 million followers, it even forms the third largest religious denomination—after Christianity (1.67 billion) and Islam (881 million) and before Buddhism (312 million) and Judaism (18.4 million). But these 1995 estimates are controversial and still rely on the British census method, that is, they count all religions as Hinduism that cannot win acceptance as another acknowledged religion of India. For a long time, it was also common practice to explain traditions based mainly on Brahman Sanskrit texts as the "foundation" of Hinduism, and everything else as deviations or modernizations. Particularly in the early colonial period, religious events that often seemed strange (the marriage of children, the burning of widows) and objects (so-called idols) were explained by Brahmans who were expert in written and oral sources. Thus the impression emerged that the religion of this priestly class was the reference point for all other religions in Southern Asia.

This appears especially in the evaluation of the status of the Veda for definitions of Hinduism.[56] These texts were first handed down orally, and were later fixed in writing. The Indologist and scholar of religion Brian K. Smith defines it thus: "Hinduism is the religion of those humans who create, perpetuate, and transform traditions with legitimizing reference to the authority of the Veda."[57] No doubt, the Veda plays an important role for Brahmans and population groups that employ Brahman priests or live in an area dominated by Brahmans. It is considered a source of revealed truth that is a source of religious merit, and all other sacred knowledge as well as moral behavior (according to *dharma*) can be derived from it. Finally, the Veda is considered by many non-Brahman classes as exemplary, so that other texts are also called Veda. The Nāṭyaśāstra, a kind of "textbook of dances," is named the fifth Veda, even though professionally, in the old texts female dancers (*naṭī*) are also prostitutes and certainly do not belong to Brahman circles.[58] Most Indians today merely pay lip service to the Veda and have no regard for the contents of the texts; or else they learn it only symbolically or condensed in the form of the Gāyatrī hymns.[59]

The authority of the Veda is also often disputed. Buddhism, Jainism, Sikhism, and other Indian religions owe their identity not least to separation from the Veda and from the Brahmans. Other religious groups, which are not recognized as independent religions, also reject the Veda, even though they worship the gods of the Vedic and Hinduistic pantheon.[60] A song addressed to Kṛṣṇa is thought to bring a hundred times more merit than a Vedic sacrifice. Thus, the authority of the Veda can hardly be called a touchstone of being Hindu, as Brian K. Smith attempts to show.[61] According to his definitions, for example, the saints Kabīr and Rāmānandī (see table 4) may not be called

Hindu, for they neither acknowledge the Veda nor accept Brahmans as religious authorities.

It is certainly exaggerated to represent Hinduism as a delusion, but there *is* Hinduism as a habitus and a socioreligious system of meaning with differing positions. Thus, it should always be clearly indicated which groups of persons or which trend of the Hindu religion is meant. Of course, Christianity also has more variety than commonality: Early Christianity, ascetic monasticism, Mariolatry, papal and sacramental Catholicism, reformed Protestantism, free-church Christianity, evangelism, liberation theology, feminist theology—all these trends and movements are so distinct that commonalities can hardly be recognized. Nevertheless, they all appeal to *one* founder (Jesus), *one* text (the Bible), *one* name of the religion (Christianity), and *one* symbol (the Cross). For the religions of so-called Hinduism such agreements cannot be determined. In India, one talks of paths (*mārga*), doctrines (*mata, vāda*), philosophies (*darśana*), or traditions (*saṃpradāya*) that are different, but equal in principle, rather than of one common religion. But most Indians (including Christians) have no problem belonging to or following various "paths" at the same time. Therefore, the individual cults, sects, philosophies, and theistic systems are not different religions—as von Stietencron portrayed them[62]—but rather cognitive systems or socioreligious institutions of a society that has reached an understanding in principle about the interchangeability and identity of the systems of belief. A "Hindu" can be a Brahman ritualist in the life-cycle ritual, an Advaitin philosophically, a devotionalist (Bhakta) in terms of practice, and a Gaṇeśa-worshipper in his popular religion. "Privately, he can be a tantric worshipper of the gods, and a Śaiva, and Vedic in his social intercourse," as a well-known poem puts it.[63] Or, like many Newar subcastes in Nepal, he can be a Hindu and a Buddhist at the same time.[64] This regular identification of various forms of belief is the special feature of so-called Hinduism!

Thus, Hinduism can be delineated not so much by its doctrines as by its religious practices and organizations, and this is true from the start: Brahmans who became Buddhists did not change their social status or usually their religious status either.[65] The primary principle of Indian religiosity is not to be sought in beliefs, doctrines, or rituals, but rather in the socioreligious organization. Thus, if there is a common feature for all of India, it is the caste system. Of course, this is rejected by Reform Hindus or Hindu "sects," but these groups too are mostly organized according to the same norms: a restriction of the possible candidates for marriage by genealogical criteria and, to a lesser extent, professional restrictions. Even if social groups themselves are not organized as castes, the majority treats them as such. Even tourists form a kind of caste in the system of categories of many Indians: the Mlecchas. Indians can adhere to various socioreligious systems, but can belong to only one caste or subcaste. Thus, one can normally become a Hindu not as an individual, by conversion, but rather through a process relating to the entire social group.[66] So, one is Hindu primarily by birth, not by a profession of faith; one can believe anything and yet call himself a Hindu. Even for a Christian or Muslim woman who marries a Hindu, circumventing this rule is possible only with the help of the Identificatory Habitus. American followers of Hare-Krishna sects are barely allowed into previously existing Hindu temples; but in India they may build their own Krishna Temple and call themselves Hindus.

Even on the "dogmatic" side, belonging to a Hindu religious community is linked with traits of birth. This is explained in a text from the second half of the eleventh century, the Somaśambhūpaddhati. This Śaiva ritual text includes a conversion ritual (*liṅgoddhāra*), with which one becomes a follower of Śiva and attains salvation. In this ritual, the essential thing is to obliterate the traits (*liṅga*) acquired through previous Karma at birth from followers of non-Śaiva religious traditions or schools, by wiping out all merit accumulated in past births through the consecration (*dīkṣā*). The list of non-Śaiva religious traditions includes Buddhists, Jains, followers of the Vedas, Bhagavān or Viṣṇu worshippers, Śāktas, astrologers (Jyotiṣa), Pāśupatas, materialists (Cārvāka), Vedāntins, and followers of other philosophical schools of thought.[67] As Heinrich von Stietencron has explained,[68] this list is remarkable in three respects: (1) Buddhism and Jainism are not treated differently from other schools of thought; (2) Śaivism, Vaiṣṇavism, and other so-called "Hindu" groups do not appear together as *one* community; (3) religious and philosophical schools of thought are not separated.[69] There are only various paths (more or less related to birth) that lead to salvation.

So, "Hinduism" is nothing more than a collective term for certain religions, religious communities, and socioreligious systems that fulfill the following five criteria: (1) they emerged or spread on the South Asian subcontinent; (2) their social organization is characterized essentially by special rules of descent and marriage (the so-called caste system); (3) Vedic-Brahmanic values, rituals, and myths dominated (originally); (4) a manifestation of Śiva, Viṣṇu, Devī, Rāma, Kṛṣṇa, or Gaṇeśa is worshipped as god or divine force, or is at least not explicitly rejected; (5) an Identificatory Habitus prevails, closely connected with a salvation linked to descent, derived from the ancient Indian sacrifice, but which has broken with that to a large extent. I am aware that this is a tepid definition. Yet, definitions do not conclude the work, but constitute a summary and a program. Thus, in what follows, this definition is to be tested against empirical material. Of course, because of this definition, special attention must be directed to the socioreligious and Vedic-Brahmanic aspects.

Hindu Religions and Hindu Religiosity

Examined closely, Hinduism consists of three Hindu religions and four forms of Hindu religiosity, which can occur in all Hindu religions. (For the sake of simplicity, I shall use the term *Hinduism* from now on for the totality of the Hindu religions and their religious forms.) The main criterion for defining the first group is the question of whether membership or affiliation based on socioreligious criteria can be discerned. Only then do I speak of a "Hindu religion," while the forms of Hindu religiosity include modes of religious activity in the Hindu religions. I call the first two Hindu religions "basis religions"; the third category includes founded religions. By "basis religion," I mean the fact that from birth on, one out of every nine Indians belongs to at least one, but usually both these Hindu religions, even if he doesn't practice religion (like most Europeans and North Americans who are born into Christianity but are not observant). Belonging to a religion is seldom a question of choice, and the "imprinting" of a definite religious type happens early in life; Indian scholars were aware of this when they described origin based on birth as an essential feature (*liṅga*) of the school of thought—as shown by the previously discussed Somaśambhūpaddhati texts. On the other hand, membership in one of the founded religions is usually a matter of choice. One belongs to them as an alternative or in addition to the basis religion; only in exceptional cases is one born into them.

1. Hindu Religions

1.1. *Brahmanic-Sanskritic Hinduism:* a polytheistic, ritualistic, priestly religion that has spread over almost all of South Asia, centered on extended family domestic rituals and sacrificial rituals and an appeal to a corpus of Vedic texts as an authority. This religion is the center of nearly all discourse on Hinduism (including the present one) for two reasons: (1) it fulfills many common criteria for the definition of "religion": "canonical" texts (Veda), a unifying, sometimes holy language (Sanskrit), visible membership (the sacred thread), a common priesthood (Brahmans); and (2) in many regions of India, it is the dominant religion into which the non-Brahman population groups strive to assimilate. Because of its extensive and uniform textual traditions, many common features can still be discerned in domestic rituals (birth, initiation, marriage, death), worship of supreme gods (especially Śiva, Viṣṇu, Devī, Rāma, Kṛṣṇa, Gaṇeśa, or a manifestation of them) in house and temple, pilgrimages, holidays, vows, food, the holiness of the cow, and others. Yet, none of these elements is exclusive to Brahmanic-Sanskritic Hinduism, since almost all Hindus, even Brahmans, also belong to another religious community or practice the rituals and holidays of at least one more religion, which is distinctive only because it usually has non-Brahman priests. These are:

1.2. *Folk religions and religions of social communities* (subcastes, castes, tribes); *Hindu folk or tribal religions:*[70] polytheistic, sometimes animistic religions with an emphasis on the locality, community, caste-inclusive celebrations or forms of worship, and predominantly countless oral texts in the local language. In many cases, these religions have their own priests, most worship only regional deities (in the village or among a subcaste—*kuladevatā, grāmadevatā;* e.g., Khandobā, Aiyanār, Pīg̃āmāī), whose myths of origin are linked with the place of worship, and their own pantheon, which usually also includes spirits or deified heroes. Humans can often be possessed by these gods or spirits. From the perspective of Brahmanic-Sanskritic Hinduism, the forms of worship are considered impure in many cases, and so the folk religion is quite often in tension with Brahmanic Hinduism. In the so-called folk Hinduism,[71] folk forms of Brahmanic-Sanskritic Hinduism are usually combined with aspects of folk religions.

1.3. *Founded religions:* usually ascetic, often anti-Brahmanic, occasionally proselytizing, salvation religions with monastic communities and a basic corpus of texts of the founder. Buddhism, Jainism, and Sikhism were such founded religions, but they withdrew from the authority of the Veda and the Brahman priests so early and so clearly in terms of organization by shaping their own canon that they were able to mold an identity as separate religions.

Three distinct subgroups can be defined by form of organization and geographical sphere of influence:

(1.3.1) *Sectarian religions:*[72] for example, Vaiṣṇava sects (Śrīvaiṣnava, Pāncarātra, Rāmānandī, Nāga, Tyāgī, among others), Śaiva sects (Daśanāmī, Nātha, Pāśupata, Kāpālika, Aghorī, among others).

(1.3.2) *Syncretically founded religions:* Hindu-Islamic (Sikhism with Udāsīs, Kabīrpanthīs), Hindu-Buddhist (Newar-Buddhism), and Hindu-Christian mixed religions like the (ethical) Neohinduism (Brahmo Samāj, Ārya Samāj, Rāmakṛṣṇa, and Vivekānanda, Śrī Aurobindo, Theosophical Society, and other, or even Hindu-influenced religious forms of Christianity (Dalit theology) and Islam (Kabīr or Indian Sufism partially influenced by Yoga).

(1.3.3) *Founded, proselytizing religions, "Guru-ism":* religious groups originating in India, but also widespread in the West, founded by charismatic persons (Gurus) with a corpus of esoteric writings of the Gurus predominantly in English: Maharishi Mahesh Yogi and Transcendental Meditation, Satya Sai Baba and the Satya Sai Federation, Bhaktivedanta Swami Prabhupada and

ISKCON, Guru Maharaj Ji and the Divine Light Mission, Rajneesh Chandra Mohan and the Sannyasi movement in Poona, etc.

Dividing Hinduism into three Hindu religions is a categorization found in India itself. It corresponds with the subdivision of ritual practices into Vedic (*vaidika*), village and folk religions (*grāmya*), and sectarian (*āgama* or *tantra*).[73] The following religious forms, on the other hand, are oscillating strands of religious activity, but are not religions.

2. Forms of Hindu Religiosity

2.1. *Ritualism:* frequently lavish rituals, usually performed with the assistance of priests. Alongside the Vedic-Brahmanic domestic and sacrificial ritualism, which includes high and low traditional temple ritualism and caste ritualism, forms of Tantrism must also be included.

2.2. *Spiritualism:* intellectualistic, sometimes atheistic salvation doctrines, whose main objective is one's own individual liberation, without necessarily requiring solid religious organizational forms or rituals, but often a guiding spiritual teacher (Guru). This form of religion is characteristic, for example of Advaitavedānta, Kashmir Śaivism, Śaivasiddhānta, Neovedānta, and modern, esoteric Guruism, as well as some sorts of Tantrism.

2.3. *Devotionalism:* usually a pastoral, rapt, often mystical worship of a god (and his female consort) with songs and mythological texts. This form of religion, practiced by nearly all castes and especially by women, does not demand sacrifice, ritualism, or knowledge, so much as heart, poetry, musicality, or dance. Priests are not necessarily required for the encounter with god. This form of religion is found mainly in Bhakti religiosity, Kṛṣṇaism (the sects of Nimbārka, Viṣṇusvāmi, Rādhavallabhī, Mahānubhaus), or the festive celebration of many ceremonies as divine games (*līlā, khela*).

2.4. *Heroism:* a polytheistic form of religiosity rooted in militaristic traditions, with deification upon the death of the hero, special death cults (including widow-burning), and features of martyrdom, rituals of robbery (marriage by abduction), plundering, or war, public celebrations, and a manifestly heroic ethos and code of honor (*vīrya*) whose sources are often the Mahābhārata or Rāmāyaṇa epics. Examples of this are Rāmaism, the religious orders of militant Yogis, or parts of political Hinduism. The deifying worship of Gurus also fits in here when the latter are extolled more for their (alleged) heroism than for their teachings.

Hindu forms of religiosity and Hindu religions do not exist in an unalloyed form. Sometimes the differences are even smaller than the common features.

Thus, both Bhakti religiosity and Tantric ritualism, in their emphasis on a devoted proximity to god, are forms of devotionalism, and thus they grant the aspect of god's grace a similarly large scope; but Tantric ritualism maintains the tension between Śiva and Śakti, which Bhakti devotionalism seeks to resolve.[74] Or "self-surrender, asceticism" (*tyāga*) is an important criterion of piety in Hindu religions, which is commonly to be found in Tantric ritualism, Bhakti devotionalism, and epic heroism. Consequently, asceticism and piety are in all above-mentioned forms of Hindu religiosity.

These forms of Hindu religiosity were also differentiated within India. Thus the first three forms (2.1–3) are the three classical paths (*mārga*) to salvation acknowledged by Brahmans as equivalent, that is, the path of action and of sacrifice (*karmamārga*), the path of knowledge (*jñānamārga*), and the path of (devotional) participation (*bhaktimārga*); these must be joined by a path of honor and heroism (*vīryamārga*). The concept of "Tantra" is also used in India as a ritualistic form of religiosity within Hinduism and Buddhism, but not as a term for religion. It is typical for the relativity of the paths to salvation of Hindu religions that no one way of salvation has been accepted as strictly obligatory—as, for example, the path of internal purification in Buddhism (Pāli *visuddhimagga*).

The forms of religiosity can also be applied to the social segments of the classes of a Brahmanic social order. Thus, ritualism and spiritualism belong to the world of priests and ascetics, between whom a certain tension exists—as we shall see. In ancient Indian terminology, both forms of religion were ascribed to the realm of the *brahman,* the absolute, embodied by the Brahmans and the priestly aristocracy, the devotionalism of the common people (*viś*) embodied by the businessman (*vaiśya*), and the heroism of the world of political and military rule (*kṣatra*) to the class of the Kṣatriyas.[75] From the Brahmanic perspective, there is only *one* valid hierarchy:[76] *brahman, kṣatra, viś,* after which the status of peasant and slave does not even occur. But the forms of religiosity are not corporate forms of religion. Spiritualism is found among merchants as well (and perhaps even more), just as there is heroism among Brahmans.

With all the love for order and classifying, Indians do not see these boundaries as exclusive. There are few struggles between devotionalists and heroists over the right form of divine worship. They are considered equal in principle. One reason is that, for most Hindus, the highest is an emptiness to be filled, to which there are several exchangeable and basically equal paths; otherwise, it would not be the highest.[77] This highest, whether God or the absolute, can be stretched or compressed so that it includes everything or everything is contained in it. Thus, for example, the goddess Kālī can be worshipped without any problem as a frightening goddess with a thrust-out and blood-smeared tongue or as a concerned, gracious mother, or can be adored as a loving consort.[78]

Great and Little Hinduism

Alongside the classifications mentioned above, the division of Hindu religions according to criteria of geographical spread, theistic orientation, forms of tradition, or their historical emergence is possible and meaningful. The distinction, for example, between great and little traditions is customary. "Great (or high) Traditions" are understood as Sanskritic, Brahmanic, largely homogeneous Hinduism that extends over all of South Asia (thus, Hindu Religion 1.1 and parts of 1.3 according to the previous classification); on the other hand, folk religions (1.2) and sects are interpreted as "Little Traditions." This distinction goes back to two influential social scientists. In 1952, M. N. Srinivas separated "Sanscritic Hinduism" or "All-India and Peninsular Hinduism" from regional and local, village Hinduism; and two years later, Robert Redfield introduced the distinction between "Great" and "Little Traditions."[79] Such a distinction is also found in traditional India, where there is a separation between "shastric" (referring to the *śāstra,* the Vedic-Brahmanic doctrine) and "laukik" (referring to *loka,* this world) or between a superordinate Dharma and a local Dharma (*dharma* and *deśadharma, mārga* and *deśī*).[80] The disadvantage of such divisions is that very different criteria for classifying "Great" or "Little" traditions are used: caste (high-caste and low-caste Hinduism), language (Sanskrit and folk languages), regional spread (city and village or supra-regionality and regionality), or religion (high religion and popular religion, high gods and local gods). But only the Brahmanic-Sanskritic Hinduism can really claim the title of "Great Tradition," when it is used to establish common notions of a high culture (standard texts, priesthood, supreme gods, etc.).

Such notions often rely on a more or less veiled nineteenth-century evolutionism, when it was assumed that religions undergo a maturing, which includes purging them of irrationality and demonism. Typologies of religion are seldom free of evolutionary thinking and belief in progress, including Social Darwinist thought, which maintains that the "better" religion drives out the "worse," or—vice versa—an original "pure" form of religion becomes "impure" through historical development (the theory of decadence). Georg Wilhelm Friedrich Hegel's *Religious History as the Unfolding of Spirit,* Gotthold Ephraim Lessing's *The Education of the Human Race,* and Auguste Comte's *Introduction to Positive Philosophy* are famous examples of the evolutionist philosophies of history, which find their counterparts in the ethnological theories of Edward B.

Tylor, Hubert Spencer, James George Frazer, and Pater Wilhelm Schmidt. Even Max Weber is not free of evolutionist notions, and assumes that rational economic behavior drives out magic and even religion; or, where this has not been the case, as in India and China, economic development has been impeded.

The currently widespread notion that religion is a preliminary stage to a rational, scientific worldview, with more freedom, is also a form of evolutionism. But these kinds of evaluations are anachronistic, basically lagging behind the Enlightenment and Romanticism. With Johann Gottfried Herder and even more with Friedrich Schleiermacher, it was possible to discover parallels in the history of religions and to emphasize the unique qualities of individual religions and forms of religion. Christianity's claim to absoluteness could become open to dispute. The critique of natural religion (*religio naturalis*), a religion of reason, which forms the basis of all individual religions, also rejected the doctrine of stages of religions and religious forms (yet allowing the emergence of religious studies), even if Herder saw the childhood of mankind realized in India, and thus encouraged the Romantics' sentimental image of India, which is still in evidence today.

Hence, the paradigm of great and little traditions is problematic if it interprets religious parallelism as evolutionism. But superstition does not give way to belief, "magic" to religion, spirits to gods, textless religions to text-based religions. These forms of religion still exist beside one another. The high or great tradition of Sanskritic Hinduism is by no means the older, higher, or purer form of religion. It is just as "demonic," "magical," and textless as the little tradition of popular Hinduism is theistic, religious, and textual. Despite all differences, both levels should not be understood as separate religions, but rather as variants that presuppose and complement one another in a constant process of expansion and dynamism.[81] The extent of the distortion that overemphasizes the textual aspect may be measured by the notion of an Indian writing a description of Christianity using only biblical exegesis.

Thus, Sanskritic Hinduism and Hindu folk religion are in a constant process of adaptation and demarcation. This elucidates the process of Sanskritization first described by M. N. Srinivas.[82] Non-Brahman population groups accept the customs of Brahmanic-Sanskritic Hinduism (vegetarianism, cow worship, etc.) in order to attain a higher status. But this process is not one-sided. If a previously non-Hindu divinity acquires a Sanskrit name and is worshipped according to a purely Brahmanic ritual, this can happen from "below," in order to enhance the status of the divinity in question and its circle of worshippers (Sanskritization, Kṣatriyasization, Brahmanization), or from "above," in order to take in a population group and a cult (inclusivism).[83] There are also cultural processes leading to the expansion of the Brahmanic-Sanskritic religion into non-Brahman communities, the parochialization[84] (communalism), regionalization, popularization, and trivialization of Sanskrit Hinduism, or politicization and Westernization. In all cases, mixtures have taken place whose result can be understood only from the assumption of two base religions (1.1 to 1.2 in the classifications above). It is these cultural processes of social dominance and dynamics that characterize Hinduism more than its doctrines or practices.

The division of Hindu religions by gods (e.g., Vaiṣṇavism, Śaivism, Śāktism)[85] emphasizes theistic forms of worship. *Henotheism* is a controversial term coined by Max Müller (1823–1900), one of the founders of religious studies as an academic discipline and a highly respected Veda scholar of his time. It refers to the preferred worship of a single divinity in a polytheistic context. Aside from the fact that there is hardly any polytheism without henotheism, it is unwarranted to limit henotheist variants only to Śiva, Viṣṇu, and the goddess. In terms of religious dissemination, we can also talk about Kṛṣṇaism, Gaṇeśaism, or Rāmaism. The same is true for the worship of prominent regional gods. It is also questionable whether the simple preference for Śiva in certain sects (e.g., Pāśupatas or Liṅgāyats) and in certain stories of the gods is enough to classify them as a common religious trend, even as Śaivism.

A division of Hindu religions by texts (Vedism, Brahmanism, epic Hinduism) is meaningful only if there is a simultaneous recognition of the danger that the canonic, written portion is usually valued more highly than the unwritten. Therefore, in part, Jainism and Sikhism, with their canonic writings, have been granted the status of separate religions, even though they originally had essentially no more adherents than the sects of the Rāmānandis. Moreover, since the Veda was not fixed in writing for a long time, it may be better to talk of canonic texts instead of writings. The excessive emphasis on text-based religions, a result of the theological and exegetical tradition of Christianity and its respect for philology, can be properly understood only if we have the philosophical systems and traditions of teaching in mind. Yet, the Hindu religions rely as much on written texts as on oral traditions, which have begun to be studied only recently, and on a religious practice that is hardly reflected in texts.

Continuity and Change

Even though the Hindu religions constantly change and intersect in these processes, it is appropriate to combine them into epochs. For even if each occurring religious form has a lasting effect, quite often even to the present,

Hindu religions and Hindu religiosity change with every new period in a way that goes beyond a simple expansion of their pantheon or a shift in ideology. We can speak of a paradigm change that determines every successive epoch by heralding new conceptions of life and the world, new gods, goals of salvation, forms of worship, or priests.

Despite all the invoked continuity, this religious change does not originate only in the whim of the Brahmans, but usually has socioeconomic, historical, political, climatic, or geographic causes. The history of religions, which neglects such changes and concentrates only on the history of ideas, tends to underestimate historical transitions and revivals and to avoid the problem of dating. Indeed, it turns out that, even the comparatively widely accepted divisions of epochs of European history with its tripartite division into ancient, medieval, and modern history, by overestimating the short-lived political and military history of events, cannot appropriately grasp the *long-term* effects of certain social and even everyday religious structures; but creeping changes of religions can be understood and dated historically. What matters in the religious history of India are not only the big events or hard, comparatively well-documented facts (e.g., changes of regimes, landowning, war, and temple building), but also soft, symbolic facts (e.g., symbolic wills and testaments, changes in values, styles). This is the only way that history can be grasped, which does not get much attention because it is overwhelmed or neglected by the great Sanskritic tradition: the history of women, the peripheral and illiterate population, as well as the history of everyday life or non-Brahman norms and notions of value.

Epochs are delineations to sort historical material for a specific purpose. They also encourage us to misjudge developments that are inconvenient to our argument, and are thus also always pre-judgments. Hence, the division of Indian history into ancient, medieval, and modern is a projection of the European scheme onto Indian circumstances,[86] which underestimates other, equally significant caesuras, such as the rise of Buddhism or the influence of Islam. For this reason alone, periodizations should not be rigid. But they do not exist without a reason: The influences of Muslim or British hegemony in India are unmistakable and mark momentous cleavages, even in terms of religion.

Yet, even politically and economically decisive events, such as the decline of the Mughal empire or the distinctive influence of Islam in North and South India, do not always entail serious and sweeping religious change. Instead, in times of crisis, religious structures hold their own. Therefore, subtle periodizations of historians are useful only in a limited way for the specific periodizations in religious history discussed here.

The history of religions must try to link religious changes to historically significant events, even if reliable dating is hardly possible for large periods in the history of India. Text datings are uncertain because information about authors is lacking or is legendary. Inscriptions—with the exception of the Aśokan inscriptions—are only moderately productive for the history of religions. And for Hinduism, until the Gupta time, there are few archaeological or art historical objects, and even if these become more extensive, the relation between objects and texts is extremely problematic to establish. Moreover, the problems of dating in Hindu folk religions are nearly insoluble because there is no periodization for them. Finally, even ironclad changes in the history of religions appear tentative because of the great distances and regional power constellations. For example, Bhakti devotionalism emerged in the sixth to seventh centuries in the south, but appears in the north only with a "delay" of a few centuries. Or: in Nepal, burning widows was legally forbidden only in 1927, a century later than in India.

It is no accident that the fundamentally ahistorical history of mentalities has fallen into disrepute in European historiography. But, for India, the thesis of a long-term, almost unchangeable Hinduism is still maintained.[87] In most cases, change is always seen as coming from outside: from the Indo-Aryans, Muslims, British, tourists. As frequently asserted, without any solid proof, the culture of the Indus valley perished not from internal causes, but because it could not withstand a supposed superiority of tribes speaking an Indo-Aryan dialect. The racist undercurrent in this theory of the superiority of the Aryans (*ārya*) originates in the nineteenth century. But this immigration thesis can explain neither the great socio-ritual and material differences between the cultures in the west (Indus valley) and the Ganges plain nor the continuing existence of the Dravidian language remnants in the north.[88] It is conceivable that instead of these, an indigenous, Dravidian culture in the north did not fall victim to an assumed genocide, but rather assimilated the language and culture of the immigrant tribes by a slow process of acculturation and infiltration that has not yet been studied.[89] Nor was Buddhism driven out of the land of its emergence, even if in many places it was dealt a deathblow by Muslim conquerors.

Such a perspective can be partially traced back to the uncritical acceptance of the Brahmanic thesis of a holistic society and an eternal, always renewed sociocosmic order, which is without beginning and without end (*anādi*).[90] The Identificatory Habitus understands history mainly as repetition and extension of what is always the same and is thus interested less in breaks and epochal boundaries; it mitigates the "fear of history," as Mircea Eliade[91] has called the ephemerality of events.

Thus, there is continuity in India over long but not unbroken periods. The following quotation could be contemporary, but it comes from the Persian traveler in India al-Bīrūnī (973–1048): "They call them *mleccha,* i.e., impure, and forbid having any connection with them, be it by intermarriage or any other kind of relationship, or by sitting, eating, and drinking with them, because thereby, they think, they would be polluted. They consider as impure anything which touches the fire and the water of a foreigner; and no household can exist without these two elements."[92] This shows how the criterion of purity with regard to conjugality and commensality is preserved throughout the epochs. The same is true of asceticism or the cyclical understanding of time and nature. Vedic elements, for example, are also preserved in the life-cycle rites of passage. Nevertheless, the differences between Hinduism and the Vedic religion are greater than their common features. It is even more meaningless to state that, since prehistoric times, goddesses, Śiva, the phallus, or the tree were objects of cult worship in India,[93] when the only source for the assumed tree worship is the image of a man kneeling before a tree on an Indus valley seal.[94]

It is just as problematic to see change as evolutionary. Between *brâhman* as the highest principle and the god Brahman (usually, the nominative form Brahmā is used), there is a linguistic relationship and a historical sequence, but when Gustav Mensching talks of the "development from a first stage of material related power to the immaterial, purely spiritual absolute being,"[95] he grants a higher rank to the spiritual, which superseded the earlier, more primitive forms of religion. This shows the evolutionism and theological rationalism of the nineteenth century mentioned above, which devalues the religious experience vis-à-vis knowledge (of God). We still read that the Brāhmaṇa texts reflect a magical image of the world, which was superseded by the allegedly philosophical perspective of the Upaniṣads, as if there were not still a "magical" image of the world alongside a "philosophical" one in India. History, even the history of religions, has no destination. Only the people who want to see history in a specific way have destinations.

2. Historical Foundations

EPOCHS IN THE HISTORY OF RELIGIONS[1]

I divide the development of the Hindu religion into six epochs and fourteen historical periods (see table 1). These include basic political, social, or economic changes, inasmuch as they affect religious changes.

First Epoch: Prevedic Religions (until ca. 1750 B.C.)[2]

The historical material of these epochs originates in Neolithic and Chalkolithic settlements all over the subcontinent and in all cultures of the original inhabitants of India, the Mundas and Dravidas, as well as the highly developed urban cultures of Harappa, Mohenjo-Dara, and other settlements in the area of the Indus River and the outlying areas often called Harappa or the Indus Valley civilization.

All that is preserved from the early Stone Age settlements are stone weapons as well as painted and unpainted Ochre-Colored Ware (OCW), or Ochre-Painted Pottery, OPP) with copper and bronze ornaments. Practically nothing is known about religious life. However, it is known that corpses were burned. The worship of mother deities and trees is generally accepted, but is not proved. The religions of the early Stone Age cultures at the mountains on the border with Persia and Baluchistan were characterized by hunting, but from about 3000 B.C. also by agriculture, perhaps occasionally even with an agricultural surplus, as indicated by evidence of a voluminous grain storage, and by keeping herds of cattle, sheep, or goats.

The Indus Valley culture (ca. 2500–1500 B.C.) had developed complex urban arrangements of up to 40,000 inhabitants, irrigation systems, houses and fortresses of baked, standard-shaped bricks, as well as paved, right-angled streets. They probably relied on a corporate social order led by theocratic elites. We

TABLE 1
Epochs of Religious History

First epoch	To 1750 B.C.	Prevedic Religions
Second epoch	1750–500 B.C.	Vedic Religions
	1750–1200 B.C.	Early Vedic Period
	from 1200 B.C.	Middle Vedic Period
	from 850 B.C.	Late Vedic Period
Third epoch	500 B.C.–200 B.C.	Ascetic Reformism
Fourth epoch	200 B.C.–1100 A.D.	Classical Hinduism
	from 200 B.C.	Preclassical Hinduism
	from 300 A.D.	Golden Age
	from 650 A.D.	Late Age
Fifth epoch	1100–1850 A.D.	Sects of Hinduism, Islamic-Hindu syncretism
Sixth epoch	From 1850 A.D.	Modern Hinduism
	from 1850 A.D.	Neo-Hinduism
	from 1950 A.D.	Missionary Hinduism

can assume that they had trade relations in the Middle East and the present-day Gujurat. Divinities are most likely portrayed on pictographic seal inscriptions and terra-cottas. Certain structures such as the so-called College of Priests in Mohenjo-Daro allow us to infer the existence of a widespread priesthood. A portable altar was found in Taxila. The deciphering of the Indus writing,[3] which has not yet been done, affords hope for a greater decoding of this epoch. Until then, not even the identification of some famous images is certain: The interpretation of the image of a person possibly sitting on a throne, surrounded by animals on a steatite seal from Harappa as Śiva or Paśupati ("Lord of the Animals")[4] is still speculative, as is the identification of countless representations of (possibly pregnant) women or female clay figures as mother goddesses. But it can be supposed that animism, demonic cults, fertility cults, and the worship of natural forces and mother goddesses determined the religiosity of this culture, even if these aspects have been obscured by subsequent stages of the Hindu religions and can be filtered out only with difficulty.[5]

Second Epoch: Vedic Religion (ca. 1750–500 B.C.)

From about the middle of the second millennium before Christ, various tribal groups of Indo-Iranian cattle nomads from Central Asia or the Near East penetrated the northern Punjab, in incursions that were sometimes peaceful and sometimes belligerent. They called themselves *ārya* ("Aryans," literally "the hospitable," from the Vedic *ārya,* "homey, the hospitable")[6] but even in the Ṛgveda, *ārya* denotes a cultural and linguistic boundary and not only a racial one. Since they could breed horses, it is assumed that they came from Central Asia. Because they possessed horse- and ox-drawn chariots and carts, as well as copper and later iron weapons,[7] the Āryas were probably superior to the natives in northern and middle India. But it is not certain whether the decline of Indus Valley culture is in fact to be ascribed to the Āryas or to environmental damage such as overgrazing or epidemics. The further penetration of the Āryas into northwest India and later the Ganges plain as well as the slow transition of those seminomads to a settled form of existence—first corrals of wagons, then settlements, and finally radial villages with temporary ramparts—ensued in several stages.[8]

The immigration thesis has been challenged in recent publications[9] with the arguments that (a) none or hardly any specific settlements of the Āryas can be proved; (b) skeletal remains indicate no phenotypically distinct features of Āryas as opposed to so-called non-Āryas, thus indicating that Ārya is not a biological or racial demarcation (the light skin pigmentation of the northern Indians has nothing to do with Āryan origin, since east of India, light skin pigmentation also existed without such racial or linguistic associations);[10] (c) the language of the Indus Valley seal was already Indo-European;[11] (d) the painted gray ceramic (see below) and iron can be proved already in the First Epoch.[12] For these reasons, the so-called migration theory should be revised to take account of the premise that the culture of the Āryas relied on slow processes of acculturation. This position has been adopted by some Indian scholars partly for political motives, to be able to reject the thesis of "Western" foreign influence on India.

One problem remains that cannot be ignored for linguistic and archaeological reasons: that from about 1750 B.C. a new culture emerged and spread from the northwest, which is called "Vedic" because of its texts, but it cannot be known precisely which cultural and historical changes are brought in by these "interlopers." The Finnish historian Asko Parpola in particular has indicated the obvious discontinuities between the cultures of the Āryas and of the Indus Valley inhabitants. Thus, in the excavations of Indus Valley culture, neither horses nor wagons were found, while they are mentioned frequently in the Ārya texts. The iconographic discontinuities on the seals and earthenware are also clear. Moreover, Parpola sees indications that the language of the steatite seals belongs to the Dravidian language group (currently including Tamil, Kannarese, Telugu): for example, the retroflexive sounds of Sanskrit are not to be found in other Indo-European languages.

The dispute among the various theories about the origin and extraction of the Āryas will go on for a long time. In any case, theories of a massive invasion, of a cultural or even racial superiority of the Āryas over the resident population are untenable. Even the hostile Dāsas or Dasyus, who are occasionally described as "dark" or "dark-skinned" in the Ṛgveda,[13] were probably not indigenous to the Indus Valley, but Indo-Aryan tribes who had immigrated before the Vedic Āryas. It is not said that they worshipped false gods, but rather that they worshipped the gods falsely.

The center of the early Vedic period (ca. 1750–1200 B.C.) is in northwest India (Indus Valley, Panjab, the Kuru district, Madura, Mahāvṛṣa, etc.). Knowledge of this period is based essentially on Books I to IX of the Ṛgveda[14] and ancient Iranian sources, for the Āryas left astonishingly little evidence for archaeology. The oldest strata of the Ṛgveda are not familiar with rice culture, tigers, elephants, or apes; there is a single mention of the Ganges;[15] there are no words for bricks, writing, or iron in these texts; there are no cities, the Vedic *grāma* (in classical Sanskrit: "village") is still "wandering pastoral tribe" (Wilhelm Rau). Countless struggles took place among the Āryas themselves and with the original inhabitants, for many hymns talk of a struggle of the gods with dark, demonic Dāsas, and one of the main gods is Indra, who is also a god of war. The pantheon (see table 16), which is clearly akin to the gods of the ancient Iranians and the Greeks as well, knows gods as personifications of nature, deified moral principles, and deified forces and demons, but only a few "personal" gods emerge, as characteristic of Hinduism. Sacrifice took place in the open or in simple sacrifice huts[16] with changing sacrificial altars. In these sacrifices on altars layered with clay bricks, the preparation of the hallucinogenic somage drink[17] played a great role for the gods and priests. Animal sacrifices and cattle sacrifices were customary, and there were cyclical celebrations of the full or new moon. Corpses were customarily burned, yet burial mounds with urns were also common.[18] The priesthood was probably not hereditary; hymns were memorized in priestly lineages and their mode of chanting was learned. Magic played a conspicuous role in religious life.

In the middle Vedic period (ca. 1200–850 B.C.), which is recorded primarily in Ṛgveda X,[19] the mantras of the Yajurveda and the older Brāhmaṇa texts, the Āryas are already found in the upper Ganges valley (Pañcāla, Kuru, in what is now western Uttar Pradesh). This is evident in the textual allusions and the gradual advance of the Painted Gray Ware (PGW) typical of middle Vedic culture, which was produced with iron. Thus, the tribes became increasingly settled. A type of rule appeared that centered on a leader and a professional stratification of priests (Brahmans), warriors, shepherds and farmers, and craftsmen, with the original inhabitants as enslaved classes. The first forms of government also emerged. In the hierarchical order, tribal chieftains and competing priests ruled the people of the community (*viś*). The clans and tribes of the Vedic Indians, still linked by kinship, struggled for hegemony; the great battle in the Mahābhārata epic on the Kurukṣetra battlefield is considered a late testimony of such a struggle.

An increasingly ritualized mode of sacrifice and a magic worldview were typical of the form of religion.[20] Sacrifice became a single sequence of substitutions and identifications. Vedic polytheism did live on, but new gods were added. Belief in one or several creator gods appeared. While gods in the early Vedic time were persuaded to help with prayer or sacrifice, the priests now induced the gods to obey the laws to which the sacrifice and the world order were subject. This knowledge was possessed only by the priests, who declared themselves divinity on earth and the personification of the *brâhman* and called themselves *brāhmaṇas* (Brahmans). They became powerful by charging fees for sacrifices and by their protected position in tribal life, and their office became hereditary; genealogies became necessary. But movements of solitary ascetics, originating both inside and outside the community of Vedic Āryas, seriously criticized the ritualized way of life.[21]

In the late Vedic period (ca. 850–500 B.C.), the Indo-Aryans invaded the lower Ganges plain (Videha, the present-day northern Bihar). The tribal struggles for hegemony went on, but the system of centralized monarchies (*janapada*) led by a king (*rājan*) and a limited military and administrative machinery, whose main task was to collect taxes and supervise small tributary rulers, also appeared. The professional stratification became consolidated as a social order in the Varṇa system. Interregional trade increased. Money was minted, but coins were without writing. A new pottery gradually appeared, the Northern Black-Painted Ware (NBPW), which was a luxury item and was thus spread by trade.

In the early Upaniṣads, we find a philosophic epistemological monism based on a philosophy of nature in which—as in early Buddhism—life is suffering, and consequently the focus is on thoughts of salvation, the doctrine of the identity of the cosmos with the individual soul (*Brahman-ātman* doctrine) and belief in reincarnation. The mythical and allegorical interpretation of the sacrifice is valued more highly in these ascetic circles than the actual performance of ritual. Henceforth, there are two paths to salvation: the path of sacrifice (with Veda study for the Brahmans) and the path of renunciation; but not until the next epoch do those ideas, first propounded hesitantly in the secret teachings (Upaniṣads), become widespread.

Third Epoch: Ascetic Reformism (ca. 500–200 B.C.)

From about 500 B.C., Black-Painted Ware (BPW) is used in northern India and the eastern regions where the waves of immigration occurred. The existence of several village settlements in the Ganges belt can be proved. Iron plows from this time have not been found so far, but iron implements may have been necessary[22] to clear the fertile but wooded land of the lower Ganges plain and make it arable. The knowledge of techniques important for rice growing, sowing, planting, and harvesting, as well as canalization, drainage, and terracing also emerged. With the new techniques and improved ecological conditions, and possibly with new tools, an agrarian surplus emerged. According to tradition, this led first to the sixteen great kingdoms (*mahājanapada*) with urban centers (Pāṭaliputra, Kauśāmbī, Ayodhyā, Vaiśālī, Campā, Kapilavastu, Avanti, and others). The appearance of writing was probably connected with the formation of centers, for progression from the local collection of duties by harvest tax collectors to the creation of central tax officers responsible for long-term registrations is possible only with the introduction of bookkeeping and a corresponding training of elites.[23] The hegemonies of Magadha (560–325 B.C.) in the eastern Ganges plain and the Mauryan empire (321–181 B.C.) in north and central India made the strongest impact. These empires knew interregional trade routes, had a self-confident merchant class, a division of labor in (hereditary?) professions, a complex administrative machinery, and the limited transition from a barter economy to a money economy. The manorial system with serfs and slaves, whose protection was ensured against enemy raids,[24] was common, but the territorial mapping of the empires was done only by a network of mutual obligations and kinship relations.

In terms of the history of religions, it is important that, for the first time, work was liberated and thus loose associations of workers could be formed instead of firm kinship communities.[25] Oligarchies, cities, and mainly trade "produce" individualism. Max Weber also saw the urban elite as decisive for individual and religious rationalization. "Like Jainism, but even more clearly, Buddhism presents itself as a product of the time of urban development, of urban kingship and the city nobles," he begins his study of Buddhism.[26] The Brahmans did continue to hold a monopoly of sacrifice as the path to salvation, but economic changes allowed the growing criticism of the brahmanic mode of sacrifice to assume a previously unknown form: Ascetic reform movements no longer remained limited to a local sphere of influence. Buddhism and Jainism, whose organization was initially hardly distinguished from other ascetic reform movements (e.g., the Ājīvikas),[27] are the best examples of that. It is noteworthy that the big ascetic groups not only had interregional monastic structures, but also sought supporters among tradesmen and merchants, and expanded as a result. From the start, Buddhist monks had to beg, preach, and regularly (biweekly) form into a loose monastic group. Thus, they could not withdraw like other ascetics, as forest-dwellers, living on food they gathered themselves, and striving only for salvation in strict self-discipline; for, according to legend, this was the way the historical Buddha tested the limits of endurance and dismissed it as unsuitable. Buddhist and Jaina monks needed society, and because of the changed socioeconomic relations, society could tolerate and care for the monks.

Exactly why the ascetic reform movements were so successful, why this far-reaching change in the worldview occurred which saw life as suffering and preached escapism, is obscure. Perhaps it was the depth of the thought itself, spread by the rising use of writing, or perhaps famine and economic problems also played a role; in any case, the texts do mention poverty and situations of crisis (*āpad*) remarkably often. It may also have been only a reaction to the new urban culture: The village Brahmans with their ritualism were considered conservative and had to conform to the aristocratic culture of the cities. Henceforth, the "village" Brahman competed with the "city" Brahman, occasionally the Brahman was even forbidden to enter the city,[28] until the cities themselves were criticized and the ascetics moved into the wilderness. The ascetic reform movements emerged in the cities and fled from them.

From India to Central Asia, for a long time Buddhism was at least the politically favored religion. Archaeological monuments—such as the Stūpa of Bharhut (170–160 B.C.), the archways of Sanchi, the caves of Ajanta (first century B.C.), the Aśoka inscriptions or the Buddhist relics on the Silk Road—until the first century A.D. are predominantly Buddhist, even if we must keep in mind that these stone objects of worship give a one-sided picture of the religious landscape, since hardly any statues made of unfired clay or wood survive, and many objects were destroyed during the later Islamic conquests.

Yet, Brahmanism lived on, as did popular Hinduism, as evidenced by the countless accompanying figures (e.g., *yakṣa*) on Buddhist reliefs. Emperor Aśoka (ca. 273–236 B.C.), with his moral rigor, proclaimed in many firm edicts, may have become unreasonable, often using his centralized administrative structures to suppress popular customs and cults. There were also later influences of Greeks, Scythians, and Kushanas (both Central Asian nomads), Parthians (Grecophile, Iranian nomads), and finally Huns. Between 327 and

325 B.C., Alexander the Great advanced as far as the Indus Valley. On Kushana coins—the Central Asian Kushanas dominated northern India from about 78 (the beginning of the Śaka era) until 230 A.D.—representations of Hellenistic, Iranian, and Indian deities or rulers are found, in some cases alongside one another. The many north Indian kingdoms had acknowledged Greek or Scythian overlords. Syncretic cultures developed, mainly in the northwest, where people lived according to Iranian mores, Buddhist religion, and with Greek art. Thus, the epoch of upheaval is also a time of religious eclecticism and the counterreaction to foreign rule. The Hindu religious capacity to conform and accept influences of foreign religions was certainly formed at this time and in contact with these various external cultures. The Identificatory Habitus developed beyond its roots in sacrificial ritual to become a prevailing social etiquette.

Fourth Epoch: Classical Hinduism (ca. 200 B.C.–1100 A.D.)

At the time of upheaval, many elements of the Vedic religion were lost, and so India's influences show up in other cultures, which relied on maritime trade relations with the Roman Empire, Central Asia (from the second century on the old caravan roads, from the seventh century, Tibet), and Southeast Asia (from the first century A.D., Malayan Peninsula, then until the fifth century, Cambodia, South Vietnam, Indonesia, and Burma). This Indianization and partly also Hinduization of other religions took place without military conquests and is therefore considered one of India's historical achievements by the Indologist Wilhelm Rau.[29]

The legacy of the Vedic religion in Hinduism is generally overestimated. The influence on the mythology is indeed great, but the religious terminology changed considerably:[30] all the key terms of Hinduism either do not exist in Vedic or have a completely different meaning. The religion of the Veda does not know the ethicized migration of the soul with retribution for acts (*karma*), the cyclical destruction of the world, or the idea of salvation during one's lifetime (*jīvanmukti; mokṣa, nirvāṇa*); the idea of the world as illusion (*māyā*) must have gone against the grain of ancient India, and an omnipotent creator god emerges only in the late hymns of the ṛgveda. Nor did the Vedic religion know a caste system, the burning of widows, the ban on remarriage, images of gods and temples, Pūjā worship, Yoga, pilgrimages, vegetarianism, the holiness of cows, the doctrine of the stages of life (*āśrama*), or knew them only at their inception. Thus, it is justified to see a turning point between the Vedic religion and Hindu religions.

Preclassical Hinduism (ca. 200 B.C. to 300 A.D.) begins with the collapse of the Mauryan Empire and extends to the beginning of the Gupta rule. It comes at the time of the spread of Buddhism and Jainism and religious eclecticism, thus in the third epoch. Characteristic of this age is the gradual restoration of Vedic-Brahmanic Hinduism. Perhaps because of the loss of religious orientation, people remembered the Brahmanic legacy and collected what suited transfiguration of the old tradition. It is typical that the compilation of the two great epics (Mahābhārata and Rāmāyaṇa) occur in this early age of Hinduism, even though the events recorded in them refer to a much earlier time.

Thus, early Hinduism relies not only on acculturation or ascetic reform movements, but also on a restoration. Brahmans, as high priests or advisors, were increasingly summoned to courts that sought to preserve or revive the Vedic religion. Hence, despite social mixtures with the previous inhabitants, the ancient Indian tradition was able to preserve its identity. The exclusive character of the Brahmanic sacrifice religion was indeed challenged, but the claim to an exclusive religion with a social system based on descent and criteria of ritual purity was preserved. The religious independence also depended on Sanskrit, which could be revived at least in the courts as a *lingua franca,* even though Buddhists and Jainas were already composing their works in vernacular languages. It became a courtly fashion to employ poets and scholars who could compose their verses in Sanskrit.

Most of the aristocratic dynasties were completely dependent on the king, who alone dispensed sovereignty. But there were also republican forms of rule. The historical Buddha belonged to such a republican lineage: the Śākyas. When there was a religious change at the top, this was done according to the Reformation principle of the territorial system of *cuius regio, eius religio* (the religion of a territory is the religion of the ruler) among the masses and the dependent regions. Theistic conceptions in which certain high gods still received supreme power in the polytheistic pantheon corresponded to the feudal ruling orders. Gods are kings, as kings are gods. A religiosity of grace was also favored, in which the high gods—like the kings—determined fate according to their will, but unlike the prevailing religion of the second Vedic epoch, were not subject to powers whose workings are hidden or known only to initiated priests. Brahman priests explain the pastoral divinities of local cults as manifestations of their respective supreme deity and thus accept them into the Vedic-Brahmanic, and now Hindu pantheon. Ascetic reform movements also worship the gods of the Vedic-Hindu pantheon, for example, the Śaiva Pāśupatas or the Vaiṣṇava Bhāgavatas.

Furthermore, the decline of the Vedic gods and the rise of deities that are not mentioned or are barely mentioned in the Veda, especially Śiva and Viṣṇu or their manifestations, is to be observed. The worship of goddesses and even the deification of the Buddha Śākyamuni in Mahāyāna Buddhism (from the first century B.C.) also follows such theistic developments. What scope this worship assumed is hard to say. In the area around Mathurā (from about 100 B.C.), there was a center of Vaiṣṇavism, at other places were coins of the Kushana dynasty with representations of Śiva, but such isolated indications of Hindu deities are not sufficient to get a picture of the scale of divine worship. At any rate, in temples, these gods were hardly addressed, for Buddhist Stūpa buildings, rock caves, or monasteries still dominate in terms of art history.

Only with the beginning of the Gupta rule, the penultimate large empire of northern India, does classical Hinduism achieve its so-called "golden age" (ca. 320–650 A.D.), until it suffers a considerable downfall with the collapse of the Harṣa empire (647 A.D.). The external and structural changes are substantial: trade with distant and luxury goods (ivory, gems, spices, precious woods); an extended, sometimes safe traffic network with inns, ferries, caravan routes, and walled cities; artisan guilds (*śreṇi*) for potters, metal workers, and carpenters; production of royal articles (arms, gold and silver items); usually a royal monopoly of mines, salt, or forest use. The centralization of power also appears in a sacralization of rule in divine kingdoms, territorial sovereignty over defense and taxes as well as feudalism, collection of duties and taxes (25 percent harvest duties are not rare). The economy is characterized by slave labor, market supervision, standardization of measures, weights, and coins, and capital formation with the possibility of reinvesting earned income. In addition, standard legal procedures and a general rationalization of the law developed, along with a general spread of literacy with schools and centers of scholarly erudition (*maṭha, saṃgha, ghaṭika*). It is a epoch when science, the arts, and crafts revived almost everywhere in India.

One sign of the reinforcement of the Brahmans is that kings heaped gifts on them and gave them land. Thus, the priests also became well-to-do landowners. Their increased valuation corresponded to the devaluation of Śūdras and women. Child marriage was common, as was burning widows and the ban on remarriage. And the taboo of cattle slaughter was also carried out.

In the late Gupta age, the first Hindu temples emerged—the Durgā Temple in Aihole and the Viṣṇu Temple in Deogarh—with pointed towers (*śikhara*) as cult centers, where a main deity was worshipped in the sanctuary, and other deities were worshipped in the niches, towers, or smaller outbuildings. Government temples, which frequently managed extensive estates, rapidly amassed great wealth. As a result, pilgrimages started because the monumental buildings attracted the masses. The Brahmans still harbored some distrust for the graphic depiction of the gods and against pilgrimages. Even at the end of the Gupta time, the iconographic language of Hinduism was hardly distinguished from that of Buddhism or Jainism. The temples are also an expression of the feudal system. Deities are treated as lords: Buildings are palaces; priests are servants who wake the gods, clothe them, entertain them in palatial style, and put them to bed at night; temple musicians or female dancers—including temple prostitutes—provide entertainment for the god, supported by poets, who compose panegyrics, and artisans who create images. Hindu worship (*pūjā*), which also emerged at this time, connects ancient Indian forms of entertaining important guests with courtly ceremony.

The late time of classical Hinduism in north India (ca. 650–1100 A.D.) began with the collapse of the Harṣa Empire. Harṣa (606–647 A.D.) had been able to unite the regions of Bengal, Bihar, and Malwa into a big empire. After him, only regional, struggling, or loosely bound surrounding dynasties with countless vassal states emerged. The big kingdoms in the east included the Pālas (770–1125), in the west and north the Gurjara-Pratiharas (seventh to tenth centuries), in the southwest the Rashtrakutas (752–973), in the Dekkhan the Calukyas (seventh to eighth centuries), in the south the Pallavas (seventh to eighth ceturies) and Colas (ninth century).

Lacking their own military power, the smaller kingdoms remained dependent on the protection of the larger kingdoms—a situation that has much in common with European feudalism. The vassal lords did retain their signs of sovereignty, but had to declare their dependence with oaths and duties. They remained owners of the fallow lands and the agriculturally cultivated areas. Tax-free gifts of land to monasteries, temples, and Brahmans (*brahmadeya*) were common; even whole villages were given away. Only the military received cash payments. Vassalage made extensive administrations largely superfluous. Rights to the use of land were often hereditary sinecures. Even though the king was the ruler, he was thus not always a direct ruler. The people showed loyalty to the feudal lord or vassal, to their lord and patron. The great king was remote, was exalted and deified. As for him, he built imperial temples as centers of pilgrimage to reinforce his religious legitimation as defender of order and thus the religious necessity of loyalty: Bhubaneswar in Orissa (eighth to ninth centuries), Ellūra in Bombay (eighth to ninth centuries) and Mahābalipuram in the south (seventh century) were the first such centers of pilgrimage, followed by Tanjore (eleventh century), Konarak (thirteenth century), Vijayanagara (sixteenth century), Madurai (seventeenth century), and many others. Note the segmentation and polycentric division of power. This was the time in the history of India when regionalization and political inconsistency were clearly manifested.

The disintegration of the big empire brought visible changes of religiosity: The lack of a political hegemony also contributed to religious regionalization and religious rivalry. Local cults (*deśī*) were enhanced, as were regional languages; once again Brahmanic ritualistic Hinduism sailed against the wind. This change appeared primarily in the preference of gods that were declared to be manifestations of Viṣṇu and Śiva. Along with them came rural, devotional movements and occasional non- or anti-Brahman founder religions, Śaivaism, Vaiṣṇavism, Bhakti, and the so-called Tantrism; these "typical" Hindu trends matured in this late time of classical Hinduism. On the other hand, sectarian groupings were only at the beginning of their development.

Even in the heyday of classical Hinduism, there was a struggle of the religious movements for recognition by the feudal lords. Whoever succeeded in getting his deity accepted as the tutelary deity of the state, even "lodging" it in one of the big temples, could expect recognition. After the Gupta time, the process of reevaluating local deities increased even more, probably under the influence of southern Indian itinerant preachers. Thus, a locally worshipped boar god became a manifestation of Viṣṇu (Varāha). Hero gods such as the Brahman Paraśurāma also became manifestations of Viṣṇu, and an historical figure in western India was also worshipped as a god. His name was Kṛṣṇa-Vāsudeva, and he may have been the leader of the Bhāgavata sect, which is proved in the first century B.C. and which operated in Mathurā between the fourth and sixth centuries. But a flute-playing shepherd god also amalgamated in Kṛṣṇa. Countless local deities also merged in Viṣṇu, Śiva, or the goddesses. At the same time, Buddhism was increasingly driven out of its land of origin.

The wandering ascetic Śaṃkara, who was active sometime between 650 and 800 (traditionally 788–820) and probably came from Malabar, had a special impact. Against Brahmanic ritualism and Buddhism, he preached a radical monism: the Advaitavedānta doctrine. Śaṃkara is considered the founder of various ascetic groups, but the historical proof of that is not certain.

The intensive process of religious assimilation begins with the epoch of classical Hinduism and has lasted until the present. Remarkably, from the tenth to eleventh centuries, a more emphatic Brahmanic conservatism spread. Aside from its syncretic variants, the Vedic-Brahmanic Hindu religion is now concerned with itself. The old works are constantly commented on, and there is no original thinking added, but no dogmatic orthodoxy is developed either. There is occasional talk of the rigidity of classical Hinduism. This is not completely unjustified, although unmistakable changes can be cited in the religious landscape. But much more important is the question about why the Vedic-

Brahmanic Hindu religion could be so immune to all kinds of external influences. Clearly, the old values were adhered to in a restoration to withstand the new and sometimes threatening influences.

Fifth Epoch: Sects of Hinduism (ca. 1100–1850 A.D.)

The penultimate epoch of Hinduism is already influenced by Islam and Christianity. Unlike religions indigenous to India, these monotheistic religions could hardly be assimilated by Hindu religions, because of their antipathy to the caste system, and because they could better assert their own religious structures within their own political or economic superiority. Thus, despite a good deal of intermingling, foreign religions remained foreign. It is also typical that already with Pāśupatas and Bhāgavatas, not to mention Buddhism and Jainism, there had been precursors of ascetic groups that went back to one founder, but most of the other similar religious communities were established only from the eleventh century on, often under the influence of Islam (see table 4). These changes in religious history are expressed in an Islamic-Hindu and Christian-Hindu syncretism.

The Islamic-Hindu syncretism developed between 1100 and 1700. In 1206, Kutb-ud-Din Aibak, a former slave of Mohammed of Gor, who had repeatedly penetrated north India in the twelfth century, founded the sultanate of Delhi. Thus, Islamic rule was established, first over northern India, and from the middle of the fourteenth century, over southern India, too. At first the Vijayanagara Empire in the south was not affected; Orissa and Nepal were not Islamized either. The superiority of the Islamic conquerors certainly relied on better weapons, primarily firepower, a stronger cavalry—India itself was barely familiar with horse breeding—and greater experience of war. The introduction of silver coins and the creation of cogent administrations, land grants to officials, and the patronage of special intermediate castes (like the Kayasthas, a caste of scribes) guaranteed their supremacy for centuries. India itself could not repel the Moslems and might be Islamic today (like Pakistan, Bangladesh, and some parts of India), if the British had not contested Moslem rule.

Previous Greek, Iranian, Scythian, and other foreign rulers had made hardly any religious claims. On the contrary, they themselves were frequently influenced religiously, especially by Buddhism. Islam was different, interfering in religious life iconoclastically and with harsh persecutions. The result was to make Hindus revert to the old values or to go the way of isolation, to flee abroad or underground. But a great many religious movements and groups, even independently organized religions, adjusted and accepted Islamic notions, ideas, and forms of belief. Kabīr (1440–1518), equated Allah with Rāma, and

Nānak (1469–1539) established Sikhism, a religion with many Islamic influences.

But there was not a real Islamization of India, even though some low castes as a whole converted and thus laid the basis for present-day Islam in India. To the distress of radical Hindus, India presently provides a home for the largest group of Moslems after Indonesia. But for most, the differences between Islam and Hindu religions were too great, especially for the Moslems. They had a proselytizing religion that claimed to be egalitarian. They worshipped *one* book, *one* god, *one* prophet. For them, the Hindu religions must have seemed so chaotic and unholy that they didn't even bother to deal with them. Destruction of Hindu temples, compulsory marriages, and atrocities are frequently mentioned, but they give a distorted picture when they are the central focus. Political struggles are not necessarily religious struggles: Hindus fought in the armies of the Moslem rulers, just as Moslems fought for Hindu kings. In many regions, the Hindu religions were not bothered. Sanskrit texts continued to be written, but the traditional school and educational system was radically changed. Even in the Mogul epoch (1526–1857), Islamic influence remained limited to syncretic reformers, the courtly arts (music, dance, painting, and architecture), as well as the structures of administration and trade. Persian became the administrative language. The Sharī'a, Islamic law, was used only in limited cases. The obligation to pay duties was strictly enforced. The greatest religious influence was certainly exercised by Sufī saints, who communicated well with the followers of Bhakti saints, with their devotionalism and ideal of brotherhood.

As a counteraction to Islamic supremacy and as part of the continuing process of regionalization, two religious innovations developed in the Hindu religions: the formation of sects and a historicization which preceded later nationalism. The sects implied allegiance to religious, charismatic leaders or poet-saints (see table 4), without an organized following, as for example, Tulsīdas (about 1532–1623), Dādū (1544–1660), or Caitanya (1486–1533). These leaders composed devotional works in their respective vernaculars, which were established among the people as firmly as the anonymous Purāṇa literature. It is hard to say if the devotional internalization of religiosity represents a reaction to external pressures. On the other hand, saints and sometimes militant sect leaders, such as the Marathi poet Tukarām (1609–1649) and Rāmdās (1608–1681), articulated ideas in which they glorified Hinduism and the past. The Brahmans also composed increasingly historicizing texts, especially eulogies and chronicles of sacred sites (Māhātmyas), or developed a reflexive passion for collecting and compiling extensive collections of quotations on various subjects.

Sixth Epoch: Modern Hinduism (from ca. 1850)

The century from 1850 to 1950 is characterized by industrialization and a Christian-Hindu syncretism, which is usually called "Neo-Hinduism." In 1498, Vasco da Gama discovered the sea route to India; in 1510, Albuquerque became the Portuguese viceroy of India; in 1600, the British East India Company was established but in terms of religion, the Christian-European influences were not felt until much later, aside from the few islands of early Christianity in Kerala and Goa, and a few moderately successful missionaries. With the battle of Plassey (1757), the British achieved political and military control, first over Bengal, and from the mid-nineteenth century also over extensive parts of northern, central, and southern India. They started the industrialization of India, exported their educational system (in 1835, English became the official language of the administration and the court), and created a functional infrastructure with rapid construction of railroad networks (since 1853), roads, and canals. Within a very short time, India experienced an economic upturn and, because of the improvement of medical care, an enormous population explosion. Social unrest and—despite all economic success—famines were the results, but also the development of an interregional urban middle class, among whom the independence movement later started.[31]

In terms of religion, at first hardly anything changed. The British merchants initially pursued the strategy of staying out of religious controversies. Despite the encyclopedic thirst for knowledge, their intellectual contact was restricted to Brahman and Moslem administration officials. Until 1813, they did not allow any missionary societies into India. Only when protests increased in London against religious outrages such as widow-burning or child marriages, were there serious conflicts over religious issues. Discontent with the British colonial power also grew in India. Feelings of inferiority led to anti-British outcries and to a nostalgia for their own religious heritage. It is symptomatic that the Great Mutiny of 1857 ignited over a religious issue: When the rumor arose that the Enfield rifles were greased with cow or pig fat, Hindus and Moslems were so incensed that violent unrest erupted for months in many parts of India.

In Indian intellectual circles, an ethical reform Hinduism developed, which judged Hindu excesses (widow-burning, the caste system, and so on) on the basis of Christian influence, and aspired to a democratization of the Hindu religions without the priestly dominance of the Brahmans and supported by doctrines of intellectual liberation. Examples of this are the neo-Hindu reform movements of Brahmo Samāj (est. 1828), Ramakrishna (1836–1886), Śrī Aurobindo (1872–1950), the Theosophical Society (est. 1875), and Mahatma

Gandhi (1869–1948). On the other hand, Dayānand Sarasvatī (1824–1883) and the supporters of the Ārya Samāj (est. 1875) propagated an emphatically "Vedic" Hinduism, purged of harmful Western and Islamic influences. Western-influenced reform movements also emerged in Indian Islam, as in the Ahmadiya movement of the nineteenth century or in Buddhism through B. R. Ambedkar (1891–1956), who converted to Buddhism in 1956, along with hundreds of thousands of his mostly casteless followers.

With the independence of India (August 15, 1947), the period of the Christian-Hindu encounter ended and was replaced by pro-Hindu tendencies, but it is not yet clear what label this period will someday bear. The establishment of democracy, suppression of the last independent kingdoms, land reforms, legal secularization of the Indian Union, building industrialization in the Nehru epoch, eliminating supply shortages with the Green Revolution, organized mass tourism, and globalization have left traces in the religious image of the world, too. But it is especially the new media that have made lasting changes for people. Radio, cinema—India has the largest film production in the world—television, and video have led to a standardization, a politicization, and a brutalization of the Hindu religions, and the Internet has led to proselytizing. It is also obvious that in these media, the traditional mythology has been presented increasingly eroticized and heroized.

Moreover, recently, a Western-oriented and especially active proselytizing Hinduism has emerged, which I call "Guruism." The best-known representatives of that include Krishnamurti, Maharishi (Transcendental Meditation), Sai Baba, Bhaktivedanta, Swami Prabhupada, Balyogeshwar (Divine Light Mission), and Rajneesh (Sannyasis). Moreover, in recent years, a militant political Hinduism has developed centered on worship of Rāma, which culminated in 1992 in a violent conflict over the alleged birthplace of this god on the plot of land of a mosque in Ayodhya.

Thus, the epochs of the Hindu religions are connected with drastic historical changes: the advance and settlement of the Vedic Indians, the emergence of the first big empire and the creation of agrarian surplus, the decline of the hegemonic big empire and the polycentric regionalization, the Islamic and then the Western conquests. Every epoch registers new religions or previously unknown forms of religiosity: Vedism, Brahmanism, Buddhism, Jainism, revivalistic or reformist movements, theistic, sectarian, syncretic Hinduism. But, aside from the early Vedic religion, almost all religions and forms of religion have survived and thus the question arises as to what is the cohesive force of these Hindu religions that allows them to absorb so much and resist so much. This question was at the beginning of the epochization of the Hindu religions proposed here, and it is at the end. Indeed, we see the religious development of India as more differentiated now. Hinduism is not so much an impenetrable jungle as a mixed forest. The historical influences mentioned above and the regional variations considerably qualify talk of Hinduism as a uniform, continuous religion. But only the thorough examination of individual epochs and of themes will show whether the cohesive force I have called the Identificatory Habitus continues to survive behind the Hindu religions and their forms of religiosity.

RELIGIOUS LITERATURE

In India today, the constitution recognizes eighteen languages. Many of them approximately mark the boundaries of the states. The Indo-German linguistic group (ca. 82 percent) includes Hindi, Bengali, Punjabi, Marathi, Gujarati, Oriya, and Assamese; the Dravidian linguistic group (18 percent) includes Telugu, Kannarese, Malayalam, and Tamil. Some 42 percent of Indians have Hindi (with Hindustani and Urdu) as their mother tongue, followed by Bengali (16.5 percent), Telugu (8 percent), and Punjabi (6.5 percent). The other languages have less than 5 percent speakers. English—still indispensable in India for higher education and administration—can be spoken by only about 1.5–2 percent of the population. The linguistic distribution makes it clear that the demographic and linguistic core of the Hindu religions lies in the northern half of the Indian subcontinent. The significance of the Dravidian languages and regions may not be overlooked, but their impact should not be overestimated either. Sanskrit is not included among these living languages, even though it is still a spoken language in priestly and academic circles.[32] Yet, what is much more important is that, next to English, Sanskrit is the only language that is pan-regional. Accordingly, Sanskrit literature—especially in vocabulary, less in syntax—has had a greater effect on the vernacular literature than vice versa. The first written works in the vernacular were mainly adaptations of works of Sanskrit literature. Typically, the literatures of the vernacular emerged primarily in the epochs of upheaval and regionalization: for example, the Pāli canon of Buddhism and the religious literature from about the tenth to eleventh centuries.

In table 2, I have classified the essential religious writings of the five epochs.[33] In terms of texts, however, the problem of determining historical discontinuities is even greater than the problem of determining the socioeconomic or religious changes mentioned above. It is nearly impossible to date texts of certain genres (Saṃhitās, Brāhmaṇas, Upaniṣads, epos, Purāṇas, and Tantras) even approximately. The so-called dating in the secondary literature often varies by centuries. These mainly compiled works are handed down only orally

TABLE 2
Epochs of the Literatures of the Hindu Religions

Epochs	*Literary Changes*	*Linguistic and Stylistic Changes*
First epoch: pre-Vedic religions (to 1750 B.C.)	Seal inscriptions	?
Second epoch: Vedic religion (1750–500 B.C.)		
1750–1200 B.C.	Ṛgveda I–IX	Indo-Aryan languages (Vedic dialect)
From 1200 B.C.	Ṛgveda X, Sāmaveda, Mantras of Yajurveda, Atharvaveda, earliest Brāhmaṇa parts.	Verses and Mantras followed by Saṃhitā prose.
From 900 B.C.	Yajurveda prose, older prose Upaniṣads (Bṛhadāraṇyaka-Up., Chāndogya-Up., et. al.), Brāhmaṇas, Āraṇyakas, and possibly Śrautasūtras.	Brāhmaṇa prose.
Third epoch: Ascetic Reformism (500–200 B.C.)	Post-Buddhist, metrical Upaniṣads, Gṛhya-, Dharma-, and special Sūtras, grammar of the Pāṇini, Aśoka inscriptions, Pāli canon.	Epic, Sanskrit, Sūtra style, Pāli; writing.
Fourth epoch: Classical Hinduism (200 B.C.–1100 A.D.)		
From 200 B.C.	Mahābhārata, Rāmāyaṇa, Manusmṛti, early philosophical and scientific works.	Classical Sanskrit.
From 1 A.D.	Carakasaṃhitā, Mahābhāṣya, Brahmasūtra, Nāṭyaśāstra, Arthaśāstra (possibly earlier).	Prākrit, Apabhraṃśa

(continued)

TABLE 2
Epochs of the Literatures of the Hindu Religions (Continued)

Epochs	*Literary Changes*	*Linguistic and Stylistic Changes*
From 300 A.D.	Śāstras (science), Dharmasmṛtis, narrative literature, philosophical systems; Kāvya (poetry), drama, novels, Purāṇas, Tantras, and Āgamas.	Literality; court Sanskrit.
From 650 A.D.	Saṃnyāsa-Upaniṣads, commentaries on Śāstras, Smṛtis, and the philosophical systems, early sectarian literature (Śaṃkara), Āḻvars, collections of fairy tales (Kathāsaritsāgara), works of history (Rājataraṅginī).	Scientific "church" Sanskrit.
Fifth epoch: sect-Hinduism (1100–1850)	Sacred poetry, writings of sects (Yoga-, Saṃnyāsa-Upaniṣads), religious historiography (chronicles, Māhātmyas), encyclopedic compendia, Nibandhas	Vernacular sacred poetics; vernacular texts in verse; Persian as the language of officials.
Sixth epoch: Modern Hinduism (from 1850)		Vernacular prose, English.
From 1850 A.D.	Vernacular poetry, novels, dramas; Anglo-Indian literature; introduction of the printing press, pedagogic literature (textbooks).	
From 1950 A.D.	Comics, films, television, video, virtual media.	

for centuries before they are committed to writing and are constantly changed; as for their content, they are hardly concerned with realia that could make dating easier. Even the "Archimedes" point in the pre-Christian history of India, that is, the lifetime of Buddha, is not firm, according to recent studies: it well may be that Buddha Śākyamuni lived only in the middle of the fourth century B.C. instead of from 563–483 B.C., as is usually assumed.[34]

Unlike classical philology, most of the text material of India has not yet been critically edited. Often, no editions or only uncritical editions are available and dating the selected manuscripts is rather haphazard. Many texts have not yet been translated into Western languages. There are no complete translations or adequately critical editions of even the two great epics (Mahābhārata, Rāmāyaṇa). Although mostly written by the Brahmanic upper class, text editions and translations are still the most reliable means to advance the history of other population groups and the everyday structure of the Hindu religion as well. Philology is slow reading: Between the lines, in the history of the words is much that is unstated. Thus, philology is imperative for a culturally historical study of India. In any case, continued existence of inadequately analyzed sources does not mean that only future generations can reflect comprehensively about India. All texts are circumscribed by their time. Not even well-edited and translated texts are exempt.

Yet, the situation of literary history in India is not completely hopeless, for at least a relative chronology of texts is often possible. There are also works by authors that are easier to date. And there are also well-dated non-Indian sources: the Greek historians Hekateus (ca. 500 B.C.), Herodotus (483–431 B.C.), and especially Megasthenes, whose work, *Indica,* is handed down fragmentarily in the works of Strabo (63 B.C.–21 A.D.) and Arrian (second century A.D.); the Chinese-Buddhist pilgrims Fa-hsien (399–414), Hsuan-tsang (629–645), I-ching (671–695); the Moslem traveler in India al-Bīrūnī (973–1048); Christian traveling merchants or missionaries such as Roberto de Nobili (seventeenth century), Heinrich Roth (1652–1668), Bartholomäus Ziegenbalg (1706–1719) and others, not to mention the British scholars of the early time, whose pioneer achievements often form the basis of current knowledge of India.

Vedic Literature

Only undeciphered pictographic seal inscriptions have come down to us from pre-Vedic times.[35] The language used in them is not known. Thus, the history of Indian literature begins with the Vedas, as the ancient Indian collections of religious texts are called. The Veda, etymologically akin to "wisdom," is one of the oldest religious literatures in the world. Originally the texts were handed down only orally in priestly lineages and through a unique mnemonic technique; even today, there are priests who have committed them to memory. From about the fifth century A.D., individual texts were probably also recorded in writing, but were still considered esoteric priestly knowledge. Even in the modern age, some Brahmans remain skeptical about printing Vedic texts.[36]

Only the collections (*saṃhitā*), Brāhmaṇas, Āraṇyakas, and Upaniṣads, which contain the revealed wisdom of seers are considered Veda in the strict sense (see table 3). This group of texts is also called *śruti* ("the heard"), as distinct from the texts composed by men, which are called the *smṛti* ("the remembered"). These classifications, which date back to Max Müller, are often not tenable for linguistic and formal reasons: There is not only *one* collection at any one time, but rather several handed down in separate Vedic schools; Upaniṣads (so called "secret doctrines"; see chapter 5) are sometimes not to be distinguished from Āraṇyakas ("forest books"); Brāhmaṇas contain older strata of language attributed to the Saṃhitās; there are various dialects and locally prominent traditions of the Vedic schools.[37] Nevertheless, it is advisable to stick to the division adopted by Max Müller because it follows the Indian tradition, conveys the historical sequence fairly accurately, and underlies the current editions, translations, and monographs on Vedic literature.

The oldest collection is the Ṛgveda, the "wisdom consisting of verses (*ṛc*)," a collection of 1028 metrical hymns, sayings, and verses with more than ten thousand strophes, compiled in ten books. The tenth is considered the most recent linguistically, and Books II through VII constitute the core. The Ṛgveda is recited by "caller priests" (*hotṛ*), who invite the gods to the sacrifice. Therefore, the hymns are primarily invocations.

The Sāmaveda, the "knowledge of melodies" (*sāman*), sung by chanting priests or "singers" (*udgātṛ*), is identical textually with the Ṛgveda except for some seventy-eight songs, and is really a songbook, comparable to the biblical Psalms. In it, 1549 strophes (ca. 1800, if repetitions are included) of the Ṛgveda hymns are arranged from a liturgical perspective. These styles of chanting are of central significance for the liturgical support of the act of sacrifice.

The Yajurveda, the "knowledge of sacrificial sayings" (*yajus*), muttered by the ritually dominant "sacrificial priests" (*adhvaryu*), contains ritual instructions for the performance of sacrifices. The Yajurveda is handed down in several recensions: The collections of the Black (Kṛṣṇa) Yajurveda (Maitrāyaṇī-, Kāṭhaka-, Kapiṣṭhala-, and Taittirīya-Saṃhitā), along with the sacrificial sayings, contain some of the oldest prose sections in the world; they form the preliminary stages of the Brāhmaṇas (see below), and are interpretations of the sacrificial ritual. The obviously later White (Śukla) Yajurveda, preserved as

TABLE 3
Hindu Sanskrit Literature

		Śruti: Revelation (literally "the Heard"), Veda in the strict sense **Saṃhitā** (in parentheses: schools [*śākhā*])		
Ṛgveda (Śākala, etc.)	Sāmaveda (Jaiminīya, Kauthuma, Rāṇāyanīya)	Black Yajurveda (Maitrāyaṇī, Katha, Kapisthala, Taittirīya)	White Yajurveda (Vājasaneyi; Kāṇva and Mādhyandina-recension)	Atharvaveda (Paippalāda, Śāunaka = Vulgata)
		Brāhmaṇa and Āraṇyaka		
AitareyaBr, KauṣītakiBr	PañcaviṃśaBr, JaiminīyaBr, TāṇḍyaBr, ṢadviṃśaBr	KathaBr, TaittirīyaBr, Maitrāyaṇi-Saṃhitā	ŚatapathaBr	GopathaBr
		Upaniṣad		
AitareyaUp KauṣītakiUp	ChāndogyaUp KenaUp	MaitrāyaṇīUp, KathaUp, TattirīyaUp, MahānārāyaṇaUp, SvetāśvataraUp	BṛhadāraṇyakaUp, ĪśaUp	PraśnaUp MāṇḍūkyaUp

Smṛti: Tradition (literally: "the Remembered"), Veda in the broader sense **Vedāṅga** ("Limbs of the Veda") Śikṣā (phonetics), Vyākaraṇa (grammar), Nirukta (etymology), Chandas (meter), Jyotiṣa (astronomy, astrology), and Kalpa (ritual) Kalpa includes Śrautasūtra (sacrifice), Gṛhyasūtra (domestic ritual), Dharmasūtra (law and morals), special *sūtras* such as Śulvasūtra (geometry)				
ŚāṅkhāyanaŚrS, ĀśvalāyanaŚrS	DrāhyāyaṇaŚrS, JaiminīyaŚrS	MānavaŚrS, VādhūlaŚrS, YajñaŚrS, BaudhāyanaŚrS, ĀpastambaŚrS, VaikhānasaŚrS, HiraṇyakeśiŚrS, BhāradvājaŚrS	KātyāyanaŚrS	VaitānaŚrS
ŚāṅkhāyanaGS	KhādiraGS, GobilaGS, JaiminiGS, DrāhyayaṇaGS	MānavaGS, VārāhaGS, KāṭhakaGS (= LaugākṣīGS), BaudhāyanaGS, AgniveśyaGS, VaikhānasaGS, BhāradvājaGS, HiraṇyakeśiGS	PāraskaraGS	KauśikaGS
ĀśvalāyanaGS				
VāsiṣṭhaDhS	GautamaDhS	ĀpastambaDhS, Manusmṛti, Viṣṇusmṛti, BaudhāyanaDhS, Vādhūlasmṛti, VaikhānasaDhS, HiraṇyakeśiDhS	Yājñavālkyasmṛti	
		MānavaŚulvaS, BaudhāyanaŚulvaS, ĀpastambaŚulvaS	KātyāyanaŚulvaS	

(continued)

Table 3
Hindu Sanskrit Literature (Continued)

	Pariśiṣṭa ("Appendices") in almost all schools	
	Epics Rāmāyaṇa, Mahābhārata (with Bhagavadgītā, Harivaṃśa)	
	Sectarian and Theistic Literature Purāṇa, Stotra, Kathā Śaiva-Āgamas, Pāñcarātra-Saṃhitā, Hindu Tantras Saṃnyāsa-, Yoga-, and other late Upaniṣads Śaiva, Vaiṣṇava, and Śākta hymn literature	
	Sciences (Śāstra)	
Philosophy	*Legal Literature*	*Other Sciences*
Six systems:	Dharmaśāstra	Nītiśāstra (politics)
Sāṃkhya	Nibandha	Śilpaśāstra (architecture)
Yoga		Nāṭyaśāstra (dance, music)
Nyāya		Jyotiṣa (astronomy)
Vaiśeṣika		Vyākaraṇa (grammar)
Mīmāṃsā		Alaṃkāra (aesthetics)
Vedānta		Āyurveda (medicine)

Literature (Kāvya)
Kāvya (poetics, lyrics) Campū (novels) Art epics Nāṭaka (drama) Subhāṣita (lyric poetry) Fairy tales, fables Narrative literature
Commentaries, Compendia, Handbooks (Vidhi, Prayoga)
Historiography, Legends (Vaṃśāvalī, Sthalapurāṇa, Māhātmya)
Writings of Sectian Leaders, Modern Sanskrit Literature

Abbreviations: Br = Brāhmaṇa, DhS = Dharmasūtra, GS = Gṛhyasūtra, S = Sūtra, ŚrS = Śrautasūtra, Up = Upaniṣad.

Vājasaneyi-Saṃhitā in the editions of the Kāṇva and Mādhyandina schools, contain only the sacrificial utterances.

The Atharvaveda, the "knowledge of the [magic sayings of the] Atharvans [and Aṅgiras]" has 760 hymns, most of them metrical (about a sixth of the hymns are in common with the Ṛgveda), and primarily concerns protection against demons and disaster. Therefore, the Atharvaveda, handed down in two editions (Paippalāda and Śaunaka), is also described as a collection of magic spells. Even though some parts of the Atharvaveda are older than the Ṛgveda, for a long time it was not recognized as an authoritative collection. Later, the Atharvaveda was nominally ascribed to the high priest (*brāhmaṇa*).

The Vedic collection is followed by the Brāhmaṇa texts, prose texts with prescriptions for carrying out and explanations of the sacrificial ritual. Among the older Brāhmaṇas is the first part of the Aitareya-Brāhmaṇa, as well as the Kauṣītaki-Brāhmaṇa; the Jaiminīya-Brāhmaṇa, counted among the Sāmaveda, which is also called the fairy-tale book of ancient India; the Tāṇḍyamahā-Brāhmaṇas, which belongs to the Sāmaveda; and parts of the Taittirīya-Brāhmaṇa, which forms the continuation of the Taittirīya-Saṃhitā. The extensive Śatapatha-Brāhmaṇa, a part of the White Yajurveda ("Brāhmaṇa of the hundred paths") is more recent, as indicated by the fact that the eastern regions of India are already mentioned in the text. The concluding part of the Brāhmaṇas is formed by the Āraṇyakas ("forest books"), which contain those interpretations of the sacrificial ritual that must be learned outside the settlements because of their dangerous magic.

One part of the Āraṇyakas are the Upaniṣads, the so-called secret lore of ancient India, which conclude the Śruti. In these texts, which often have the form of disputations, there is a gradual transition from ritual to philosophy embedded in concepts derived from a philosophy of nature and based on the background of sacrificial ritual. The doctrine of reincarnation of the soul, the doctrine of the identity of individual souls (*ātman*) and the Absolute (*bráhman*), the ascetic ideal of life as a forest dweller, and so on, are first expressed here. There are texts where one seeks knowledge and asks about life and death. The older Upaniṣads include the Bṛhadāraṇyaka-, and Chāndogya-Upaniṣads, as well as the prose Taittirīya-, Aitareya-, Kauṣītaki-, and Kena-Upaniṣads. In general, the metrical Upaniṣads are considered later and post-Buddhist, as for example, the Kaṭha-, Īśa-, Mahānārāyaṇa-, Maitrāyaṇī-, and Śvetāśvatara-Upaniṣads. Even more recent are the countless composed Upaniṣads from about the eleventh century to the present (Saṃnyāsa-, Yoga-, Vedānta-, Śiva-, Viṣṇu-, and Śakti-Upaniṣads). Most of the older Upaniṣads are constantly commented on by learned religious leaders.

I have summarized the Vedic and post-Vedic literature (*śruti* and *smṛti*) in table 3. There the boundary between Śruti and Smṛti is clearer than that between Smṛti and the succeeding groups of texts. Sometimes, only the Vedāṅgas are counted as Smṛti, sometimes also the epics, Purāṇas, and occasionally even all post-Vedic Sanskrit literature are also included.

The Literature of the Ascetic Reformism

In linguistic terms, an epochal change began with the Āśokan inscriptions (dated 273/268–237/232 B.C.), when, for the first time in India, syllabic writing (Kharoṣṭhī and Brahmī)[38] and a middle Indian stage of language can be detected. Brahmī writing was probably even commissioned by Āśoka. Middle Indian, which has various linguistic stages, was also the language of Siddhārtha Gautama Śākya, the historical Buddha, and Vardhamāna Mahāvīras, the restorer of Jainism. Sanskrit changed in this epoch in that it became increasingly standardized on the basis of the grammar of the Pāṇini (see below).

Sūtras ("manuals") composed in a concise, nominal style, which explain and interpret, systematize and expand the Vedic sacrifice, also emerged. These texts, which are often incomprehensible without a commentary, are directly linked to the Śruti texts. They are still part of the Vedic literature, and traditionally classified as the so-called six limbs of the Veda (*vedāṅga*), but—even individual Śrautasūtras—are clearly more recent, that is, post-Buddhist. A large part of the Brāhmaṇas, Āraṇyakas, and Upaniṣads were also compiled at this time, even if the origins of these genres originated in the Vedic epoch. The Vedāṅgas were formative for the development of the indigenous science.

The Kalpasūtras dealt primarily with the sacrificial ritual. Since one of the topics concerning sacrifice is the duties for a religiously moral life, many Kalpasūtras deal with the normative regulations of the Brahmanic-Sanskritic Hindu religion. The Śrautasūtras treat the sacrifice ritual, supplemented by special sūtras such as the Śulvasūtras with geometrical rules for the layout of the sacrifice places. The Gṛhyasūtras concentrate on domestic rituals and duties, the Dharmasūtras on general moral and legal norms. The legal regulations of the Dharma books and compendia (Dharmaśāstra, Nibandha) were later added to the Dharmasūtras.

In connection with the interpretations of the Vedic rituals, countless local sciences were developed, some of them at a high level. The grammatical system (Aṣṭādhyāyī) of Pāṇini (about the fifth century B.C.) is one of them. That system allowed Franz Bopp to establish European comparative Indo-Germanic linguistics in the early nineteenth century. In 3996 formulae, consisting of a few syllables, Pāṇini had analyzed the language of the Sanskrit and thus discovered not only the smallest meaningful elements (prefixes, suffixes, infixes, verb roots), but also the vowel gradations that are important for the Indo-Germanic study of language. More recent is the Arthaśāstra, a textbook on governance of Machiavellian proportions, which is invaluable as a historical source primarily because it reflects the political and economic relations of the Mauryan period.

The Literature of Classical Hinduism

The epoch of classical Hinduism was the time when classical Sanskrit literature proliferated in all areas of thought. Sanskrit developed more and more into a scientific, courtly, and artificial language quite removed from the spoken language. Understanding it required training that could be acquired only in schools and private instruction run by the Brahmans. What was crucial was that the use of writing, even among the Brahmans, was now common. Style and vocabulary were so cultivated that they led to the emergence of several new genres.

Smṛti included the two great epics of India, the Rāmāyaṇa and the altogether more recent Mahābhārata, whose roots were no doubt in the previous epoch, but which were compiled in their current version only after the turn of the millennium. Both works handed down in verse contain a narrative framework, into which histories of the gods, sagas, episodes, legends, genealogies, treatises on morality and manners, legal instructions, and much more are inserted.

The Rāmāyaṇa ("Life of Rāma"), whose most widespread Sanskrit version with 24,000 couplets in seven books (*kāṇḍa*) is ascribed to the legendary seer Vālmīki, and deals with the fate of Rāma and his wife Sītā, who was kidnapped after a faithful marriage by the demon king Rāvaṇa and taken to Laṅkā (Ceylon), and was then freed with the help of the monkey leader Hanumān. Rāma unfairly suspects Sītā of adultery and banishes her. As a result, Sītā throws herself on a funeral pyre, but the god of fire (Agni) rejects her self-sacrifice, since he knows that Sītā is innocent. Reconciled, Rāma and Sītā return to Ayodhyā, and Rāma is crowned king. But Rāma still does not trust his now pregnant spouse. He has her taken off into the forest by his half brother Lakṣmaṇa, and there she gives birth to twins in the hermitage of the seer Vālmīki. When these children are grown up, Rāma recognizes himself in them and has Sītā called back. But now Sītā asks the earth goddess to take her in as a sign of her innocence, and she disappears in a furrow. Deeply troubled, Rāma continues to rule, but later abdicates in favor of his sons and assumes his divine form (again) as Viṣṇu. The motifs of courage and marital fidelity endorsed by the Rāmāyaṇa are respected by Indians even today. But, better known than the Sanskrit versions are the countless adaptations of the epic in the vernaculars, and a television series of the Rāmāyaṇa was a hit in the 1980s.

The Mahābhārata ("Great India"), with nearly a hundred thousand couplets in eighteen books (*parvan*), and the Harivaṃśa (a text about the life and adventures of Kṛṣṇa), which was later incorporated as a nineteenth book, is clearly more extensive than the Rāmāyaṇa and is ascribed to the seer Vyāsa. It is a report of a volatile, horrible struggle between the sons of King Pāṇḍu, the Pāṇḍavas (Yudhiṣṭhira, Bhīma, Arjuna, Nakula, and Sahadeva), and the sons of the blind Dhṛtarāṣṭra, the Kauravas (Duryodhana and others). The Pāṇḍavas first lose land and throne, but when Dhṛtarāṣṭra abdicates, he divides the land between his own children and the Pāṇḍavas. Duryodhana then wins the other half of the kingdom from the Pāṇḍavas in a dice game, and it is then agreed that the Pāṇḍavas can reclaim their kingdom after thirteen years. When the Kauravas do not keep their word, the Pāṇḍavas return with the help of Kṛṣṇa, the leader of the Yādavas. After a struggle of eighteen years, all the enemies of the Pāṇḍavas are vanquished. The five brothers and their common wife, Draupadī, a case of polyandry, finally move into the empire of the gods. Even though the frame story of the Mahābhārata is rather simple, the epic has an outstanding significance for Hindu heroism. The heroism of the Pāṇḍavas, the ideals of honor and courage in battle, are constant sources of treatises in which it is not sacrifice, renunciation of the world, or erudition that is valued, but energy, dedication, and self-sacrifice. The Bhagavadgītā, inserted in the sixth book (Bhīṣmaparvan), and probably completed in the second century A.D., is such a text, that is, a philosophical and theistic treatise, with which the Pāṇḍava Arjuna is exhorted by his charioteer, Kṛṣṇa, among others, to stop hesitating and fulfill his Kṣatriya (warrior) duty as a warrior and kill.

The Purāṇas ("Old Stories") are metrical Sanskrit texts, which contain myths, cosmologies, legends of saints, genealogies, law, science, and history. They are mainly concerned with divine order and thus contain sections on iconography, astrology, medicine, dance and music. The Purāṇas form the most important source of Hindu mythology. Most of them are already shaped by sectarian influences, and individual texts focus on one particular main god. According to Indian tradition, there are eighteen great (*mahāpurāṇa*) and countless small Purāṇas (*upapurāṇa*), since the numbers vary.[39] The Purāṇas emerged from the oral tradition, and a ritual and religious necessity to codify them or a need to keep them secret did not exist at first. As a result, many versions and manuscript variants circulate in India, which makes a precise dating or even a relative chronology nearly impossible. Individual sections of these texts are old, dating back to the Mauryan time, especially those that were probably composed in the area of Pāṭaliputra, present-day Patna, or Mathura; Purāṇas from the area of Kanauj are more recent. Nevertheless, the genre of the Purāṇas did not emerge before the Gupta period (ca. 320–500 A.D.).

The courts had contributed greatly to the promotion of dramas, poetry, belles lettres, and novels. Under the influence of educated Brahmans, polished aesthetic theories of art, music, poetry, and dance emerged, in which almost all details were normatively fixed in writitng. The collections of sayings, fables, or tales, such as the Tantrākhyāyika (third/fourth century?), the Pañcatantra (third–sixth century), or Hitopadeśa (nineth–eleventh century) owe their emergence partly to didactic purposes: They were intended to teach manners and mores to princes and young aristocrats. India's most famous poet, Kālidāsa, was probably active in the fifth century; most of the other great poets lived later: Daṇḍin, Māgha, Subandhu, Bāṇa, Bhāsa, Bhartṛhari, Bhāravi, and Bhaṭṭi (sixth or seventh century), Bhavabhūti (seventh/eighth century), Haricandra (nineth century), Bilhaṇa, Kṣemendra, Mammaṭa, and Bhoja (eleventh century). After the twelfth century, the more famous and significant poets are to be found in the vernacular.

A similar situation appears in the sciences. Here, too, there were amazing achievements early on. Pāṇini and the Arthaśāstra have already been mentioned, but there were also the grammarian Patañjali with his Mahābhāṣya (second century), the physician Caraka (first–second century?), and the Nāṭyaśāstra (second–third century?), a textbook of the arts, especially dance theater and music. The ancient Indians were particularly familiar with grammar, mathematics, astronomy, medicine, and metallurgy. Other great scientific and philosophical works that were the basis of many commentaries and subcommentaries were preserved only from about the fourth and fifth centuries. I will list only a few of the early authors and works: the philosophers Vātsyāyana (Nyāyabhāṣya, fourth century), Dignāga (Pramāṇasamuccaya, fourth century), Śabara (sixth century), Iśvarakṛṣṇa (Sāmkhyakārikā, fifth century), and Kumārila (Ślokavārttika, about 700 A.D.), the grammarian Bhartṛhari (fifth century), the mathematician Āryabhaṭa (fifth century), the lexicographer Amarasiṃha (Amarakośa, sixth century), the Kāmasūtra (fourth–seventh century). From the seventh century on, a genuine flood of works began that cannot be listed here, and which ebbed after about 1100, but—aside from some exceptions—the works lose originality.

In the area of legal texts, everything was codified in an extensive legal literature, the Dharmaśāstra. These contained instructions for everyday life, rites of passage, vows, rules for the monarchy, and much else. By the third century A.D. at the latest, the Dharmasmṛtis (Yājñavālkya-, Nārada-, and

Bṛhaspatismṛti, among others) were widespread; after the seventh century, no more independent legal texts were composed, but commentaries still were; Medhātithi, a commentator of the Manusmṛti, was an early scholar (tenth century); most of the others belong to the next epoch.

Whether religion, art, philosophy, or science, the Brahmans dominated them all. At least the religion handed down in the texts was a religion of the upper classes. In countless commentaries, change was justified or innovation was prevented with quotations from older religious texts, preferably the Veda. They gathered tales told throughout the land and created extensive collections of myths, folktales, fairy tales, or oral poems.

But the Brahmans were no longer the sole creators of a new category of religious writings. To an extent hardly to be overlooked, Purāṇas emerged in this period, along with hymns (*stotra, stava, gītā*), doctrinal treatises (*āgama*), tractates, manuals, and handbooks (*śāstra, sūtra, tantra*), commentaries (*bhāṣya, vyākhyā, prabandha, kārikā*) on the Upaniṣads and other works, eulogies (*māhātmya*), legends (*katha*), and ritual handbooks (*vidhi, prayoga, paddhati*). All these texts were formed to extracts (*sāra*), illuminations (*pradīpa, candrikā*), discussions (*nirṇaya*), collections (*saṃhitā, saṃgraha*), and so on.

Some of these texts were combined into literary genres according to textual or cultic similarities. The Tantras composed in Kashmir, Nepal, and Bengal are divided by sectarian affiliation into Śaiva-Āgamas (earliest from 400 A.D. or later),[40] Vaiṣṇava Pāñcarātra-Saṃhitās (earliest from the late Gupta time, usually between 600 and 850)[41] and Hindu Tantras (not before 800 A.D.);[42] in addition there are the Buddhist Tantras of the Vajrayāna system, Jaina Tantras, and the Saura Tantras to the sun (Sūrya), which have been lost. What is common to these texts is that they object to the Veda as (the sole) authority, stress the importance of ordination (*dīkṣā*), acknowledge the significance of spiritual practices (*sādhana*), and suggest that the sought-after deity can be realized through various means—e.g., through worship (*pūjā*), sacred diagrams (*maṇḍala, yantra*), or visualization.

Most of these texts are theistically oriented and are dedicated to the devotional glorification of Viṣṇu, Kṛṣṇa, Śiva, or individual goddesses. Cultic communities also formed in which these texts were composed, recited, and sung. These included the Vaiṣṇava Bhāgavatas (fourth–sixth century, possibly even earlier), who worshipped a deified hero of the Yādavas, Bhagavat ("the Sublime"); the ritualistic Vaikhānasas (from the third century?), who initially adhered to the Vedic tradition of the Black Yajurveda; the Pāñcarātrins (fifth–tenth century), who established classical Vaiṣṇava orthodoxy; and the movement of the Tamil Āḻvārs, who wandered around as itinerant priests in southern

India from the eighth century on. Śaiva communities included the ascetic Pāśupatas (from the first century A.D.?); the even more radical Kapālikas (from the sixth century?), who worshipped Śiva in his terrifying Bhairava aspect; the Śaivasiddhāntins (from the sixth century); and the Kashmiri Śaiva (from the tenth century). Śaṃkara (between 650 and 800 A.D., traditionally 788–820) was also considered the founder of a sect, but was more likely to have been an influential itinerant preacher.

The religious literature dedicated to the gods is clearly less exclusive and consists of hymns, panegyrics of local holy places, adaptations of epics, poetry, and collections of myths, composed primarily in Sanskrit at first, but then increasingly also in the vernacular.

The Literatures of the Hindu Sects

From the first century after the turn of the millennium, the creation of religious communities and the founding of sects increased. Before that, there had only been a few sects and a few poet saints, aside from the special development in southern India (particularly in Tamil Nadu). Thus it is striking that most of the sectarian writings—the first manuscripts come from the tenth century—were composed in the vernacular or were linked intensively with a local tradition and following. Kannarese, the southern Indian language of the Vīraśaivas, received royal patronage, as did Marathi in the Western Deccan. The saints and poets were generally not Brahmans either. Some of their texts express a vehement protest against the Veda. In table 4 (see also tables 19 and 24–25), I have gathered the more important founders of sects and their dates; it can be supplemented with a list of mostly metrical adaptations of Sanskrit religious literature, which would also show the trend of the vernacular literature.

In this period, the Brahmans became absorbed in their legacy, commented on the ancient writings, and thus developed dogmatics and systematics to a high art. Thus they advanced primarily in the areas of philosophy and science, while their creative force in poetics waned. They developed hardly any new forms of literary expression. Nevertheless, two groups of texts emerged in this period, which developed as a genre only after the turn of the millennium: compendia and historiography. In historiography, Kalhaṇa's Rājataraṅgiṇī (1148 A.D.) presents the first historiography oriented toward political reality. Moreover, Brahmans tried mainly to comprehend and glorify local history in chronicles (*vaṃśāvalī*) and legendary texts (*sthalapurāṇa, māhātmya, kathā*). Brahman scholars had proved their ability to collect and compile the Vedic

Table 4
Poet-Saints, Sect Founders, and Sects

Century	*Poet-Saint or Sect Founder*	*Sect*	*Language*
Seventh	Campan̲tar	Śaivasiddhānta	Tamil
	Tiruñāvukkaracu	Śaivasiddhānta	Tamil
Eighth	Cuntarar	Śaivasiddhānta	Tamil
	Nummāḻvār	Vaiṣṇava	Tamil
	Śaṃkara (650–800)	Śaivasiddhānta	Sanskrit
Ninth	Māṇikkavācakar	Śaivasiddhānta	Tamil
Tenth	Nāthamuni	Śrīvaiṣṇava	Tamil?, Sanskrit
Eleventh	Rāmānuja (1056–1137?)	Śrīvaiṣṇava, Śrīsampradāya	Sanskrit
Twelfth	Madhva (1199–1278)	Brahmā-Sampradāya	Sanskrit
	Nimbārka	Nimāvat, Sanakādi-Sampradāya	Sanskrit
	Basava (?–1168)	Liṅgāyat, Vīraśaivism	Kannada
	Nāmdev (1270-1350)	Vārkarī Panth (Kṛṣṇaite)	Marathi, Hindi
	Bilvamaṇgala	Viṣṇusvāmī (Kṛṣṇaite)	Sanskrit
	Jayadeva	Kṛṣṇaitic	Sanskrit
Thirteenth	Mukundarāja (ca. 1390–1400)	Vedānta with Nāthism	Marathi
	Mahānubhāva (Vaiṣṇava)		Marathi
	Cakradhāra Svāmī	Vārkarī Panth (Kṛṣṇaite)	Marathi
	Jñāneśvara	Kānphaṭā, Nātha (Śaiva)	
	Gorakhnāth (possibly earlier?)		

(continued)

Table 4
Poet-Saints, Sect Founders, and Sects (Continued)

Century	*Poet-Saint or Sect Founder*	*Sect*	*Language*
Fourteenth	Vallabha (1479–1531)	Vallabhācārī (Kṛṣṇaite)	Hindi
Fifteenth	Raidās	*nirguṇī* Sant	Hindi
	Mīrabāī (1488–1573)	Rādhā-Kṛṣṇaite	Rajasthani, Bhraj
	Rāmānanda	Rāmānandī (Rāmaite)	Bhāṣā
	Kabīr	Kabīrpanthī (*nirguṇī* Sant)	Hindi
Sixteenth Nānak (1469–1538)	Sikh (*nirguṇī* Sant)		Hindi
	Caitanya (1485–1533)	Gauḍīya Vaiṣṇavism, Caityanites, Vaiṣṇavas of Bengal Rāmaite	Bengali
	Tulsīdās (1532–1623)	Vārkarī Panth (Kṛṣṇaite)	Avadhī
	Eknāth (1533–1599)	Dādupanthī (*nirguṇī* Sant)	Marathi
	Dādū (1544–1603)	Kṛṣṇaite	Hindi
	Sūrdās (1583–1563)	Rādhāvallabhī	Hindi
	Harivaṃśa (ca. 1600)	(Kṛṣṇaite)	Hindi
Seventeenth	Tukārām (1568–1650)	Vārkarī Panth (Kṛṣṇaite)	Marathi
	Premānand (1615–1675)		Gujarati
	Mukteśvar (1599-1649)		Marathi
	Rāmdās (1608–1681)	Vārkarī Panth (Kṛṣṇaite)	Marathi
	Kina Rām	Aghorī (Śaiva)	Hindi

(continued)

TABLE 4
Poet-Saints, Sect Founders, and Sects (Continued)

Century	*Poet-Saint or Sect Founder*	*Sect*	*Language*
Eighteenth	Bhāratacandra (1712–1760)		Bengali
	Rāmprasād Sen (1718–1775)		Bengali
Nineteenth	Sahajānand (1780–1830)	Svāminārāyaṇa (Vaiṣṇava)	Gujarati
	Dayarām (1767–1852)		Gujarati
	Rāmmohan Rāy (1772–1873)	Brahmo Samāj	Bengali, English
	Dayānand Sarasvatī (1824–1883)	Ārya Samāj	Hindi, English
	Rāmakrishna (1836–1886)		Bengali

Hindi includes older stages of language such as Avadhī, Bhraj, etc.

literature. But only from the eleventh century on did they start the systematic arrangement of their knowledge, rearranging the older texts according to new criteria. These texts included Lakṣmīdharas Kṛtyakalpataru (ca. 1125–1150), Someśvaras Mānasollāsa (twelfth century), Hemādris Caturvargacintāmaṇi (thirteenth or fourteenth century), Raghunandana Bhaṭṭa's works (ca. 1510–1580), or Varāhamihiras Bṛhatsaṃhitā.[43] There were also significant commentators, including Sāyaṇa, the commentator on the Vedas (fourteenth century), and Kullūka, the commentator of Manu (between 1150 and 1300).

Characteristically, Sanskrit continued to develop as a literary language, as demonstrated by lavish and long nominal compounds (up to thirty-five parts) used along with old formal categories without any distinction of meaning. The middle Indian languages were considered and acknowledged, but were not yet used as living languages. The elite nature of Sanskrit can be seen particularly clearly in the fact that in drama, the high-placed characters often speak Sanskrit, whereas the lowly figures and women speak in regionally distinctive vernacular dialects.

Literatures of Modern Hinduism

In the mid-nineteenth century, India experienced another profound change of literary life: The British brought in the printing press. Previously there had been lithographic and mechanical printing, but book printing took place on a large scale only with the British occupation of large parts of southern Asia. In addition, English education became an issue of status and Indians increasingly wrote in this language and thus could have a direct impact on the West. Consequently, most writings of the neo-Hindu reform movements also appear in English, at any rate those of the missionary "Guruism" which were directed at the West. In the area of the vernacular, from the nineteenth century on, more prose poems have emerged. These include the works of the Hindi poet Hariścandra of Benares (1850–1885), the Bengali Bankim Candra Chattopadhyāya (1838–1894), and Rabindranātha Ṭhākur (1861–1941), known as Tagore.

After independence, print and electronic media (film, television, video, and recently the Internet) have emerged. Thus, popular Hinduism tends to become more standard, more populist, more graphic (comics), political, and radical, and more missionary, but the effects cannot yet be estimated. The trend is likely to be an increasing westernization and secularization.

The textual turning points in the history of the religious literature of India have by and large coincided with the historical breaks. The forms of Hindu religiosity are also connected with the epochal changes. Thus ritualism is rooted in the second ("Vedic") epoch, heroism and spiritualism in the third ("ascetic") epoch, devotionalism in the fourth ("classical") epoch, sectarian Guruism in the fifth ("sectarian") epoch, and a Christian-influenced moralism in the sixth ("modern") epoch. Nevertheless, it should not be ignored that, for lack of historically tangible evidence, Hindu popular religions do not fit this schematization, even though they have affected religiosity in all epochs. But only as a whole does a so-called Hinduism exist, emerging out of the conglomerate of religious and literary directions, trends, and movements. How was it possible for this pattern to hold together? For all that, there have always been states with functional specializations and thus great internal and external conflicts of interest. They should really have led to expulsion, amalgamation, and standardization. But this did not happen either. Smaller cults were absorbed, there was also the influence of foreign religions, and Buddhism was effectively expelled, but no centralization is to be noted. While canonized Buddhism expanded in the Far East and Islam occupied the Middle East and

North Africa, in the heart of the Orient—despite invasions and colonization, peacefully to a large extent, for there were no religious wars worthy of the name—a mixture of religions that have more differences than commonalities held its own. Or is there a structure that links these religions and constitutes their cohesive force?

RELIGION AND SOCIETY

3. Stages of Life and Rites of Passage

House, field, temple, palace, and wilderness—these are the places visited in this chapter. To this day, despite all modernization, house, field, and temple are still the most important places of Hindu life. More than 80 percent of the population of India lives directly or indirectly from agriculture, and people attend their temples almost every day. The maharajas and princes may have been stripped of power, so their palaces no longer form the political focus of their regions, but these places still represent the old grandeur. Finally, the wilderness is the counterpart of ordinary life: the dwelling place of the ascetics. But of all these places, the most important in the life of a Hindu is the house. The center of work and religion is a familiar house and courtyard.

This chapter concentrates on the social aspects of the Hindu religions. It may be objected that my emphasis on a specific social group, extended family, and descent assumes an ideal social order and overlooks social conflicts, divergent or strategic interests, and individual experiences in religions. But a search for what holds a society together internally or what is the cohesive force of the Hindu religions must be oriented toward coherence and not divergence. Religions are neither exclusively individual nor exclusively social phenomena, nor do they develop from the collective to the individual or vice versa; rather they are based on the question of how much community the individual needs and how much individuality the community grants him.[1] In this section, I shall try to determine how this mutual relation, which defines each religion, is constituted.

INITIATION[2]

Initiations are the clearest expression of membership in a religion. One is indeed a Hindu by birth, but not only by natural birth. For men, the second "authentic"[3] birth is being born in the Veda and out of the Veda, in the holy knowledge. "Mother and father only bring forth the (material) body," says a legal text.[4] Only through initiation is one a twice-born (*dvija*), only then was one a full member of the community of the Āryas in ancient India, only then is one a Hindu from the Brahmanic-Sanskritic point of view.

Origin is determined by birth. People need the help and solidarity of other people in their lives or at least for specific tasks such as harvesting, building a house, marriages, or funerals. In all traditional societies, the obvious form of group solidarity consists of family members. Kinship is thus a fundamental criterion of social ordering. Friends, professional colleagues, playmates, neighbors, and table companions are usually not related in modern Western societies, but they are in many traditional societies.[5] In Brahman-influenced India, "relatives" one doesn't even know, but who are part of a common kinship group, show up at weddings and funerals. *This* origin may be even more important for salvation than descent from one's parents. Occupation is often organized by *this* origin, which also determines the choice of marriage partners and the caste system. The ritual regarding *this* origin for male descendants is the Second Birth, the initiation.

In a Hindu initiation that follows the Dharma texts, the father must already have been initiated, thus the conversion of an individual to Brahmanic-Sanskritic Hinduism is almost excluded. A Brahmanic-Sanskritic initiation is not a confirmation. Unlike in Christianity, Buddhism, or Islam, the focus is not a profession of faith, but rather on obtaining the ritualized genealogically determined right to learn the Veda. Spiritual Brotherhood is thus less important than the ritual itself.

The Hindu religions are less dogmatic and more variable than almost any other religion. Keep in mind that there is no official dogma, no obligatory text, no church, no pontiff. In part because of this structure, the Hindu religions have absorbed many other religions (e.g., Buddhism, popular religions). And yet, they have been prevented from expanding because of genealogical and socio-ritual boundaries. Neither proselytism nor missionary activity is consistent with membership dependent on birth, even though it is precisely this biological origin that is supplemented by a ritual. But this ritual birth is much more than a rigid celebration of membership into a religious community. It is also a constant enactment of the method of substitution and identification with which Hindu religious thought and feeling operates.

The Salvational Goal of Initiation

In the early Vedic phase of the second epoch, the initiation was a consecration (*dīkṣā*)[6] into secret priestly knowledge, a privilege for those who had a calling and a voluntary act to a large extent for those who wanted to learn, mostly for the sons of priests. But Vedic texts also give evidence of the consecration of sons of other classes. It was even granted to women: Gārgī, who bested the seer Yājñavalkya in debate, wore the sacred hip cord, the sign of such a consecration.

But by the third ("ascetic") epoch, around 500 B.C., the formalized consecration (*upanayana*) became a means for all the higher classes to separate the Āryas vis-à-vis other population groups in India. This change marks one of the clearest socio-ritualistic separations of extended families. Various factors may have been responsible for this development: the transition to a settled life of the Āryas and the resulting problems of acculturation vis-à-vis the indigenous population; the related emergence of states; the defense of sinecures, prerogatives, and privileges; and the rise of superior technologies. Times of harsh distress (famine, epidemics), when the social order was shaken, must also be taken into account. In any case, many legal texts mention such instances of collective and individual distress (āpad).[7] Mingling with the resident population and their doctrines and religions also had to be regulated. Who was admitted for holy wisdom, sacrifice, and marriage, and who was not had to be determined. As acculturation between the Indo-Aryans and the other population groups progressed, the more clearly did specific classes need an externally visible demarcation. The Sacred Thread was to be their symbol of this boundary.

Anyone who did not get initiated was equated with the presumably non-Aryan, "defective"[8] Vrātyas or impure children and Śūdras, with outsiders, marginal groups, and enemies. That is, through birth everyone was a Śūdra, and only by celebrating Upanayana, i.e., birth in the Veda, did one become a Twice-Born.[9] The region where there were no initiated classes was the land of the barbarians (*mlecchadeśa*). A noninitiate could not take part in the Brahmanic rituals,[10] could not maintain the important domestic fire, could not take food with close relatives, and was allowed only limited participation in social life. Most important however, he was not available as a marriage partner. To the leading circles that employed Brahmanic priests, he was a social outcast.

By linking consecration with marriage, Hindu caste society was almost established. The ritual and normative ramifications are, by and large, only the consequence of this henceforth indissoluble and tense connection between individual salvation on the one hand and descent and matrimony on the other. Even in their negation, asceticism, this connection is still felt. Initiation now meant acceptance into patriarchal society and instruction in the study of the Veda—the literal meaning of Upanayana is "leading (to the teacher)" or more precisely "leading" (of the student by the teacher to his self)—along with initiation into his ritual sacrifice practice derived from that; and all this also meant the ability to marry. The youth becomes a member of a caste, an apprentice, entitled to perform sacrifice, and a candidate for marriage all at once. What was originally a consecration rite became a life-cycle rite of passage and a socio-ritualistic transformation in the system of norms of the specific extended families. Thus, this rite takes priority over all other rites of passage.[11] For the formation of Hindu identity, initiation is perhaps even more significant than the wedding,[12] for no son can be married without being initiated. All male Hindus who employ Brahman priests are initiated, but not all get married. Initiation is also indispensable for the right to perform death and ancestor rites.

It is not easy to determine how widespread initiation is in India today. For the subcastes who are aware of tradition and the (urban) middle class, it is still obligatory; but in the "lower" classes, it is hardly self-evident for the historical reasons cited, and it is partly even explicitly forbidden for them to be initiated by a Brahman priest. Nevertheless, these subcastes also often conduct comparable rituals, in which they imitate wearing the Sacred Thread (see below).

In the terminology of the native jurists, the transition between two phases of life is a *saṃskāra,* a life-cycle rite that places someone in the condition of salvation and perfection.[13] The tradition knows up to forty *saṃskāras;* those who are learned in scriptures focused particularly on twelve of them and at least three of these (initiation, marriage, death ritual) are obligatory for the Twice-Born (see table 5). *Saṃskāra,* formed from the same verbal root as "Sanskrit" (*saṃskṛta,* which literally means "the totally and (correctly) formed [speech]"), is usually translated as "transition rite," "rite of passage," or "sacrament," but these terms only partially convey its significance. What is crucial, as Brian K. Smith has emphasized,[14] is that with the *saṃskāras,* someone or something is made either suitable, appropriate, or equivalent (*yogya*) for a holy purpose—for example, as a sacrificial offering. The gods accept only what is appropriate for them, that is, something correctly composed and perfect.

Thus, a *saṃskāra* is not a divine punctuation or an esoteric mysterium (the Greek *mysterion,* "secret," corresponds to the Latin *sacramentum,* originally "oath of allegiance," at least since the time of Saint Augustine, the visible sign of another reality). Nor is a *saṃskāra* primarily the celebration of a phase of life, but is rather a ritual identification or substitution. That is, in the initiation, the son is equated with the father, the Veda, the sacrifice, the fire, and only because of such an identification can he participate in salvation and immortality. If this substitution is perfect (*saṃskṛta*), the rite works *ex opere operato,* through the action itself and the power of the ritual equivalence—with all its consequences: Thus, the Veda teacher is to be venerated more than the physical father,[15] because the Second Birth follows from the womb of the Veda and of

Table 5
Hindu Rites of Passage

Phase of Life	*Rite (*saṃskāra*)*	*Sanskrit*
Prenatal and rites of birth	Procreation, insemination	*garbhādhāna*
	Transformation of the fruit of love to a male fetus	*puṃsavana*
	Parting the hair of the pregnant woman	*sīmantonnayana*
	Birth	*jātakarma*
Childhood rites	Naming	*nāmakaraṇa*
	First outing	*niṣkramaṇa*
	First solid food	*annaprāśana*
	Tonsure	*cūḍākaraṇa*
	Ear piercing	*karṇavedha*
Puberty and adolescence	Beginning of learning	*vidyārambha*
	Initiation	*upanayana*
	Beginning of study	*vedārambha*
	First shave	*keśānta*
	End of study	*samāvartana*
Marriage rite	Wedding	*vivāha*
Death rites	Burning the corpse	*antyeṣṭi*
	[Burning the widow	*satī*]
	Ancestor ritual	*śrāddha**

*Srāddha rites are usually not considered part of the life-cycle Saṃskāras, but typologically they are part of them.

sacrifice, and not of the mother. This stipulation is the result of a ritualistic conception of paternity, of life itself, that is to be found in hardly any other religion.

Such a conception is so important for Brahmanic Hinduism because its image of the world is based on such chains of identification as the following: Veda/gods (immortality) = sacrifice = man (mortality); or "Now the sacrifice is the man."[16] In Middle Vedic texts, statements like the following are to be found: "The man who does not sacrifice is not yet born."[17] These chains of identification are part of a "magical grammar,"[18] which consists of expressive, ritualistic, and conjuring elements of language, styles, and speech acts. One example of such an element are etymologies that identify various linguistic terms with one another, like man with sacrifice. Since language pronounced in this world of sacrifice is at the same time reality, etymologies have serious repercussions.

The sentence of the Śatapatha-Brāhmaṇa cited above could also be read as: "The sacrifice (and thus the gods) does not exist if man does not maintain it." By equating the immortal sacrifice with mortal man, immortality itself could be salvaged only if man were also (to be considered) immortal; and this happened on the one hand in a substitution of the father by the son—"By descendants we achieve immortality"[19]—and on the other hand, through asceticism.[20] Both these steps contradict each other and yet are related attempts at a solution. For, absurd as the identifications may seem—in terms of religious studies—they are only one of many religious attempts to harmonize the desire for immortality with human mortality and the inevitability of death. Others would be Christology or the Buddhist doctrine of the non-self. There too, mortality and finiteness (Jesus or self and rebirth) become immortality and infinity (Christ or non-self and redemption) through religious transformations.

But such preserved "inconsistencies" are also an expression of a form of thinking in which consistency is not the highest goal. Respect for the sacred, spoken word is often too great in India to be able to make changes in a text in favor of logic. Moreover, one had to and wanted to live with secret assumptions of truth: The opinion of the other (school) exists alongside your own, even if it contradicts it. Nor is it always possible and meaningful to explain these inconsistencies with the compilatory nature of the work in which various ideas that are to be historically separated have grown together over time. With the process of substitution contradictions were easily explained as unities.

For the Hindu initiation, one of these "paradoxes" looks like this: The initiation is a *brahmasaṃskāra,*[21] the "perfection in *brahman* (the Absolute, Highest)" or the identification of the initiate with Brahman. This is the primary identification—with the result that whoever is the Brahman and is thus immortal does not need reproduction[22]—like the ascetic, which the initiate will become. On the other hand, the "eternal," immortal Brahman is bound to the obvious mortality of the individual, which casts doubt on the truth and thus the effectiveness of the primary identification. There is no striving for a "solution" to the paradox: Both progeny and asceticism can mean salvation.

The Second Birth

What is in the Sanskrit texts is certainly old, but is not outdated. The following description of a Hindu initiation illustrates how such chains of identification are still practiced. It is based on the Upanayana rite of the son of a comparatively well-to-do Nepalese family in Kathmandu.[23] The initiation was guided by a Brahman and was carried out according to a ritual handbook (*Vratabandhapaddhati*) of the Royal Academy of Nepal, which is based on the Gṛhyasūtra and Dharmaśātra texts.[24] In table 6, I have summarized the most important sequences of the ritual, and will elucidate more closely in the following.[25]

Pre-Rites

The age of initiation is given variously in most Dharmaśāstra texts, depending on social class: a Brahman (priesthood, scholar class) is to be initiated at the age of eight, a Kṣatriya (aristocracy, warrior class) at eleven, and a Vaiśya (merchant, farmer class) at twelve; the Śūdras (slaves, manual laborers, serfs) are not considered as Twice-Born. Age is calculated from the time of conception, not of birth. The instructions for age were more recommendations than rules, for legal scholars in the Vedic schools allowed exceptions: If a Brahman boy appeared eager to learn, he could undergo the Upanayana at the age of five.

In modern India, hardly anyone follows the age instructions of the legal texts. To save the high cost of such a celebration, many parents initiate several sons together or along with the sons of close relatives. Thus, a small child, who has just cut his teeth, stands in line with a boy who has already grown a beard. Occasionally, the initiation is put off until shortly before the wedding. The initiation is the inauguration of a student and a man: An early initiation age is advisable for schooling in Vedic knowledge and ritual, a late initiation age for the ceremonial transformation into the age of manhood and thus marriage.

Even if deviations from the written norm have always been common, the system as a whole is not arbitrary. On the contrary, the difference in the age of initiation marks the old class order of society of the second ("Vedic") epoch

TABLE 6
Course of a Hindu Initiation

Previous weeks

1. Preparations

Establishment of the initiation age.

Astronomical and astrological determination of the initiation time.

Invitation of friends and relatives.

Involvement of ritual specialists (priests, cooks, musicians, barbers).

Day before

*2. Pre-rites (*pūrvāṅga*)*

Ritual purification of the participants in the ritual: restoring the Sacred Thread, atonement for sins (*prāyaścitta*).

Ritual purification of the house (*gṛhaśāntipūjā*): recitation of texts (*Gṛhasāntipaddhati*), purification of the ground.

Worship of the gods, especially the clan or family deities (*kuladevatā*), appeal to and worship of ancestors (*śrāddha*), expulsion and satisfaction of spirits.

Preparation of the ritual place (*yajña, maṇḍapa*): measuring according to the dimensions of the son, erection of a canopy, rubbing the ground with cow dung and scattering Maṇḍalas, piling five fireplaces with unbaked bricks, preparation of the ritual articles.

*3. Tonsure (*cūḍākaraṇa*)*

Ritual preparation of the son (evening): binding the hair with the thorns of a porcupine or *ḍubo*-grass (*darbha*), worship of deities: the "Mothers" (Mātṛkā), Agni, Gaṇeśa, ancestors (Viśve Devāḥ, Pitṛ).

Vows of fasting and silence of the son for the night.

Main Day

Lighting of the Cūḍākaraṇa fire.

The son sits in the mother's lap and eats a meal with her.

Tonsure: cutting the first three locks of the son's hair by the house priest and the maternal uncle with a knife, on which a gold coin is pasted; shaving the hair of the head down to one lock of hair (*śikhā*) by the barber, accompanied by music. The cut-off hair is thrown into the Bāgmatī River.

Strengthening rites: rubbing the initiate with turmeric by the son's sister, bath of the son.

Gifts (*godāna,* literally: "cow gift") of money to the priests.

TABLE 6
Course of a Hindu Initiation (Continued)

*4. Initiation (*upanayana*)*

4.1. Inauguration of the ascetic

Donning of a yellow loincloth with a hip cord (*mekhalā*) and a shirt.

Donning of the Sacred Thread (*yajñopavīta*).

Supplying with an antelope fleece and a walking stick.

Recitation of texts (praise of gods) by the Brahman priests.

The priest pours water into the hands of the initiate and leads him to look into the sun and to climb onto a stone.

Lighting of the Upanayana fire: The son walks around all fires.

Worship of the planets (*grahapūjā*).

Supplying the initiate with a turban, shoes, and a sunshade.

4.2. Inauguration of the student (Veda instruction)

Acceptance of the initiate as a student in the form of a dialogue: obligation to take a vow of chastity and obedience to the teacher.

Ritual purification of the body (head, eyes, nostrils, limbs) by the son.

The house priest teaches the initiate the Sāvitrī hymn (Ṛgveda 3.62.10) under a blanket.

The initiate worships the house priest as a Guru: He touches his foot with his forehead, gives him a payment of sacrifice, etc.

4.3. Inauguration of the man (tending the fire)

Worship of the main fire with besom by the initiate.

The initiate pours clarified butter and grain into the Upanayana fire, and walks around all fires three times; acquisition of the right to maintain the domestic fire.

Recitation of Veda texts.

5. Study

*5.1. Beginning of study (*vedārambha*)*

Begging: The initiate begs with the maternal uncle for alms for the Guru from his mother, the relatives, and the guests, but not from his father.

Lighting and worship of the Vedārambha fire: symbolic beginning of the study of the Veda.

Ritual bath.

(continued)

TABLE 6
Course of a Hindu Initiation (Continued)

*5.2. Study (*deśāntara*)*
Initiate is given a bow and arrows by the priest.
Maternal uncle leads the initiate to the garden gate and right back.
The priest reads to the mother and son the *Deśāntarakathā*—a text that warns of the privations of studying in a distant land (*deśāntara*) and praises married life.
*5.3. End of study (*samāvartana*)*
Lighting and worship of the Samāvartana fire.
The son receives curds and other foods from the priest.
Ritual bath and tooth polishing: The initiate becomes one who is at the end of his study (*snātaka*).
Priest gives the son a white loincloth (*dhoṭi*).
Restoration of the Sacred Thread.
Initiate dons new, secular clothes, looks in the mirror.
6. Concluding Rites
Worship of the clan deity (*kuladevatā*) in the city quarter by the son and four relatives.
Burning of a coconut.
The mother's sisters and the maternal uncle sacrifice grain in a fire.
All participants look into the water of a pot (*kalaśa*).
Closing (*visarjana*): farewell of the gods, the priest ties a red wool string around the wrist of all the participants, payment of the sacrifice wage to the priest (*dakṣiṇā*).
Purification of the ritual place.

with its scholarly, military, and farming classes, a division reinforced once again by initiation. The desire for knowledge, physical strength, or wealth in livestock[26] roughly corresponds to these classes. There are class-determined gradations in the Dharma texts concerning the season of the initiation, the colors and fabrics of the initiation garment or the objects the boy is provided (see table 7).[27] By identifying the initiate with the qualities of the objects, these become his property. Thus, the bowstring as a hip cord (not to be confused with the Sacred Thread called *yajñopavīta* or Hindī *janeū*) and the tiger skin

TABLE 7
Class Distinctions in Initiation according to the Dharmaśāstras

Brāhmaṇa	*Kṣatriya*	*Vaiśya*
Youngest and oldest age		
8/16	11/22	12/24
Season		
Spring	Summer	Fall
Day of the week		
Sunday	Tuesday	Saturday
Skin (uttarīya, ajina)		
Black antelope	White gazelle, game, tiger	Brown goat or cow
Undergarment (vāsa)		
Reddish-brown or white linen or hemp	Red cotton or linen	Yellow wool
Sacred Thread		
White cotton	Red wool	Yellow linen
Waistband (mekhalā)		
Muñja-grass (*Saccharum Sara*)	Bowstring	Wool or hemp
Staff (daṇḍa)		
Palaśa or *Bilva* wood (*Butea frondosa,* aegle Marmelos); gives spiritual strength (*brahman, tejas*)	Fig tree (*nyagrodha, Ficus Indica*); gives physical strength (*ojas*)	*Badara* or *Udumbara* wood (*Zizyphus Jujuba, Ficus Glomerata*); gives nourishment (*ūrj*)
Height of the staff		
To the head	To the forehead	To the nostrils
Meter of the Sāvitrī verses (Ṛgveda 3.62.10)		
Gāyatrī: 8 syllables per metric foot	*Triṣṭubh:* 11 syllables per metric foot	*Jagatī:* 12 syllables per metric foot

not only bestow strength and courage on a Kṣatriya son, but also testify to his place in the system. Time, place, material, and words are determined for the individual by the forces that combine to make the order of the sacrifice or the whole. The age of the initiate is eight years old for a Brahman because the metrical foot (*pada*) for this class has a meter (*gāyatrī*) of eight syllables; by being identified with that, he is (not: he becomes) the Veda, which is the sacrifice, which is the world order, which is the Bráhman, which is immortal.

Thus, the Brahmanic Hindu initiation focuses not on the individual and his feelings, or his maturity or the inheritance of (profession-)specific knowledge or rights, but rather on his integration into a soteriological chain of identification, whose links are Veda and sacrifice, gods and forefathers. Only the time of the initiation is based on the personal horoscope of the initiate, which is valid only for the son. But this, too, mainly marks his position in a cosmological system that determines the individual more than his predispositions or acquired abilities. The position of the planets, seasons, and days of the week, even the numbers themselves, are forces and powers that must be used only with the help of specialists. Thus, the house priest usually brings an astrologer for the initiation, who determines in advance the favorable date by comparing the precise time of the son's birth with that suitable for the initiation, and calculates favorable times. Springtime months (Māgha, Phālguna, Caitra, Vaiśākha), when the sun is in the northern, propitious hemisphere, are considered favorable. "Impure" days are avoided, especially eclipses. What is crucial is the time specific to the individual, not a common time for all like Palm Sunday for Christian confirmation.

Even though student and teacher (in personal union with the priest) are the focus of the initiation, the rite is also an event, with which the family of the son demonstrates its social status. There are not many occasions on which a Hindu invites people to his house. Mutual invitations for meals are quite rare in the village milieu. People meet in the fields and markets, squares or tea stands, where they have a snack together at most. Moreover, even when people are formally invited to the initiation, the guests do not usually enter the house even if it is big enough, but rather remain in the party tent in the forecourt or garden.

The preparations for the important day must be meticulous and extravagant in order to impress the guests. Thus, weeks before the celebration, the father visits the Brahman high priest to go over the details. Not only must the course and date of the initiation be fixed, but other ritual specialists (cooks, barbers, musicians) must be involved and the materials for the ritual have to be acquired. Small companies supply all the equipment: party tent, chairs, tables, carpets, crockery, lamps, and so on. In the months considered auspicious for the initiation (or wedding), brown and gray tents with colorful lanterns and sparkling greeting signs are seen at many houses. Thus, the day of the initiation is indicated by an unusually large number of social contacts and meetings.

Whoever can afford it sends out printed invitations, frequently gold engraved. Those invited include relatives, dignitaries, or prestigious personages, as well as friends if they suit the rank and status of the host family. To reject an invitation is considered impolite, even disrespectful. Playmates or friends of the son can usually come only if their parents are also invited.

The initiation begins with ritual purifications, blessings, and appeasements. On the day before, the house priest (*purohita*) appears early in the morning for a ritual preparation of the son and the other participants in the event. He also purifies and blesses the house and calls on the gods for assistance. The house is not only the residence of the family, it is also the home of the ancestors, who remain dependent on the regular care of the survivors at least temporarily. With the death of the father, one ancestor, that is the great-grandfather, leaves the status of ancestor (*pitṛ*) and goes into heaven as a semi-divine transitional creature (*viśve devāḥ*), until he is reborn. But the father can then become the ancestor only when his first-born son is initiated, and has thus ritually entered his father's position. The father does die biologically, but in the socio-ritual sense he is replaced by the son. Thus the initiation is also an ancestor ritual, as many of its ritual sequences demonstrate.

As in all important family rituals, the father of the family also renews his Sacred Thread on the day before the initiation. It consists of nine cotton strands each with three knots, symbolizing among other things the link with the ancestors. The next day, the son also receives such a thread, the visible sign that he is a Hindu. Then, as the sacrificer, the father makes a formal resolution (*saṃkalpa*) without this the ritual would not be effective. In the speech, the father explicitly names his ancestors and links them with the time and place of the ritual. Hence, nothing is left to chance. Every step must follow the Dharmaśāstra rules, so that the whole ritual is withdrawn from everyday life and identified with that immortal realm of life where the initiate is to be brought.

So the initiation takes place in the garden or the forecourt, but in its meaning as a sacrificial ritual, the place of the ritual is the domestic fire, which obtains a special sacrificial position for the initiation. That is, the site of the sacrifice (*yajñamaṇḍapa*) is prepared on a square surface of ground in the front garden. First, two girls (virgins) break up the ground with a scythe on which a small gold coin has been pasted. Then, the house priest measures the place with the physical dimensions of the son: eight ulnas and one handspan squared. On this site, which is then smeared with reddish cow dung, the priest stacks five small fireplaces with unbaked bricks. Gold,[28] virgins, and the sacrificial fire are various signs or symbols of immortality, with which the initiate is identified.

The next steps also consistently emphasize this theme of immortality. As the sacrificer, the father of the family first paints a red mark (*ṭīkā*) on the forehead of the priest. Such a gesture is usually a sign of a higher ritual and frequently also a higher social rank. Thus the priest usually gives the *ṭīkā* to the layman, the older man to the boy, the Guru to the student. That the father now grants the *ṭīkā* to the priest recalls earlier, Vedic times, when the inauguration of the son was carried out by the father himself. The father puts the priest in place of himself, as it were. The teacher, the Veda scholar, becomes the father (and Sāvitrī, the personification and condensation of the Veda, becomes the mother): "They call the teacher the father because he gives the Veda," says the *Laws of Manu.*[29]

The following episode illustrates that this ritual father is "immortal." The priest-father hands the physical father a gold ring, called the "ring of the Kuśa grass" in Nepal (*kuśāuṃti,* in Nepal). The Kuśa grass (*poa cynosoroides Retz*) is an attribute of Brahmā, the creator god and the personification of the eternal *brāhman* principle, with which the Brahman sees himself identified by virtue of his knowledge of Veda. This ring is bound into the son's hair on the evening of the previous day and holds apart that plait (*śikhā*) that will not be cut off later because it represents the paternal line and thus the link to the ancestors. A special ritual (*śrāddha*) is then devoted to these ancestors, which is carried out together by the father of the family and the priest.

Finally, the priest worships various deities, especially Gaṇeśa, who removes obstacles, the mother goddesses (Mātṛkā), and the clan or house gods. Liberally scattering black grains of sesame, he appeases the spirits of the house by following a handbook that guarantees the peace of the house (Gṛhaśāntipaddhati), and reciting from it now and then. He also asks the gods to be indulgent toward mistakes committed in the course of the initiation. Through an appeasement ritual (*prāyaścitta*), previous offenses, which could still exercise a harmful influence, are removed. With incense (*dīpa*), fire (*homa*), and water in the form of a ritual jug (*kalaśa*), the place is purified and the participants in the ritual are also ritually purified.

By incorporating the ancestors in these preliminary rites, asking the gods for blessings, and driving out the spirits, right at the beginning of the initiation the participants in the ritual and especially the initiate secure that world from which there is no way back in salvation, no rebirth, and whose objective is the goal of the ritual—as baptism is understood as rebirth to eternal life and in the Holy Spirit.

Tonsure

An important ritual begins on the eve of the initiation, which according to most Dharmaśāstra texts, should have taken place at the age of one, three, or five; that is, the first ritual tonsure (*cuḍākaraṇa, kaula*).[30] But, today, in most cases this tonsure, in which the boy's hair is shaved off down to a small remnant, is carried out shortly before the Upanayana rite. First the priest parts the hair of the initiate (which has been washed) with three thorns of a porcupine, each of which has to have three white stripes. He ties each of these bristles into three bundles with twenty-seven stems of the evergreen Kuśa grass and wraps them in a yellow cotton cloth, along with a powder made of various medicinal plants (*sarvauṣadhi*), as well as Kuśa and ṣubo grass, curds, unshelled and unbroken grains of rice (*akṣatā*), and sesame and barley seeds.

The number three and its force not only stands for the divine trio of Brahmā, Viṣṇu, and Śiva, it also stands for the three debts (*ṛṇa*) that man owes to the gods, the primordial seers as the fictional genealogical patriarchs, and the ancestors, particularly the last three generations. The other components of the bundle are to bless and safeguard the act. Thus, rice is a sign of fertility and also purity, for only undamaged grains of rice can be used with all unshelled and broken grains sorted out and discarded beforehand. The ṣubo grass (Sanskrit, *darbha*) stands for invulnerability and immortality: According to old folk beliefs, this evergreen does not wilt because it received a drop of nectar (*amṛta*, literally "[drink of] immortality").

The priest worships and consecrates the three bundles with incense, water, grains of rice, coins, and rose petals. Then he ties the son's hair into them. All night long, the initiate may neither eat cooked rice nor speak. Cooked rice and speech are signs of social contact, which, in this vulnerable time of transition, is to be avoided as much as possible.

The next day, the day of the actual initiation, begins with the continuation of the tonsure rite. While the priest pours clarified butter and rice into the main fire on the place of sacrifice with a big sacrifice spoon, the son sits in his mother's lap. At the astronomically determined auspicious time, the father or often the maternal uncle cuts the first three locks of hair. He uses a razor on which a piece of gold has been pasted and recites a Veda verse that prays the razor not to hurt the son: "*Oṃ*, in your name, be amiable! Your father is hard iron. Do not wound in any case!"[31] Then, without soap, but with a lot of water, the barber shaves the head bald in a few minutes, except for the small tail of hair on the back of the head (*śikhā, cūḍā*). While little boys often cry during this process, musicians from the caste of the barbers play drums and shawms. As often in festivals and rituals, music announces transitional events. In this case it is the son's passage from the world of the mother to the world of the father, expressed symbolically and graphically by the contrast between the mother's lap and the razor. What this change means for the son's development will be discussed in detail later.[32]

The tonsured hair, now considered impure, is taken to the nearest river in a basket woven of leaves, which is also to make sure no one uses the hair to bewitch the initiate. With his bald head, the son now looks visibly different. Embarrassed, he keeps stroking his bare skin. It is not the last time in his life that his head will be shorn. At the death of his father and of his mother, on the anniversary of his father's death, sometimes also at the beginning of a sacrifice, this will happen to him again. Even today in Nepal, when the king dies, all male subjects are still expected to shave their heads. But these days men are less willing to shave their heads. When Indira Ghandhi's corpse was cremated in 1984, many orthodox Hindus considered it scandalous that her son Rajiv lit the fire unshorn.

A tuft of hair (*śikhā*) is almost always left unshorn. Many Hindus consider this *śikhā* the sign of the paternal line.[33] According to Hindu belief, during the cremation of the male corpse, the individual soul escapes from the body through the crown of the head and begins its journey to the forefathers. In Indian medicine, this spot is also considered the site of the center of life,[34] probably because the fontanelle, the gap in the bones in the infant's skull, the "sovereign (of the body)"—the meaning of fontanelle—is an especially vital and at the same time a fatally vulnerable part of the body. Cutting the *śikhā* means severing the patrilinear "umbilical cord," keeping the ancestors in their deplorable in-between state, unable to get to heaven. In ancient India, the tuft of hair was a clear sign of distinction between Brahman subcastes or schools.[35] Some wore it on the right, others on the left. Today, two variants of it have remained: a northern Indian (small tuft of hair) and a southern Indian (a shock of hair on the back of the head as wide as a hand).

Hair defines people. Whether long or short, it is an expression of social conformity and affiliation. Hairstyle and beards, along with clothing, show who you are. Cutting off hair completely is often a signal of leaving the everyday world and its conforming hairstyles. Many life-cycle rituals are seen as a withdrawal from everyday life, work, and repetition.[36] Monks and ascetics shave their hair or, the opposite, let it grow without ever cutting it. In fact, the initiates become ascetics for a brief time. Yet, unlike most of those who renounce the world, they keep a lock of hair.

Opinions differ about the significance of this tuft of hair and the Sacred Thread. Christian missionaries refused baptism if the converts would not also cut off the *śikhā*,[37] seeing the latter as a crucial sign of Hinduism. For the

Twice-Born themselves, the *śikhā* was a visible proof of the right to sacrifice: "A head without a *śikhā* is impure," said the legal scholars, meaning that a ritual act, carried out by a man without this lock of hair, was incomplete. Anyone who cut it off inadvertently had to undergo an act of penance to be accepted back into the caste or the extended family.[38]

Since the lock of hair, like the Sacred Thread, increasingly came to be identified with the right to sacrifice, ascetic criticism of the Vedic sacrificial ritual as the only path to salvation was granted a striking means of expression. Those who renounced the faith needed only to have their heads shaved completely and cut up the Sacred Thread.[39] Not only did one resist such externalities—"Knowledge is his [the ascetic's] tuft of hair,"[40] says an Upaniṣad—it was also considered ripping off the tie to the ancestors deliberately and almost literally, in order to avoid the paradox of the mortality of the immortality of the sacrifice. And finally, the tuft of hair signified the acknowledgment of social class distinctions as a prerequisite for spiritual salvation. Buddhism also criticized the mediating role of the Brahmans for individual salvation and thus Buddhist monks shave their heads completely. Even in the separate world of Nepalese Newar Buddhism, a Buddhism almost devoid of monasticism and with a caste social structure,[41] boys have their tuft of hair cut off at their consecration, even though the other parts of the rite are based on the Hindu initiation.

Buddhists and many Hindu ascetics—Vaiṣṇava ascetics, however, do not undergo this radical tonsure—thus are in total opposition to those with socially conforming hair.[42] In the tonsure itself, separation (shaving) and connection (tuft of hair) are achieved at the same time. This is not because an emotional or social crisis has to be overcome, as maintained in many analyses of such rites of passage that follow Arnold van Gennep or Victor Turner, but because the old principle and paradox of sacrifice mentioned above comes into use and has a (re)solution: The regenerative conceptualization of salvation as an eternal sacrifice, borne by the salvation-oriented legacy of the Brahmans and the Twice-Born, needs the tuft of hair that symbolizes the continuity of the paternal line for its survival. Only then is the preservation of the sacrifice guaranteed. But if the sacrifice is genealogically dependent, it is exposed to the danger of mortality, of tearing away from the paternal line. This problem is avoided by the ritual father-son identification, which tries to eliminate the biological side of the succession. But if this identification is possible, procreation is no longer needed to achieve salvation; one can seek and realize the latter in oneself. Here the way to asceticism is already indicated.

Consequently, the Brahmanic Hindu initiation is a new becoming and the means of attaining immortality: "[being] free from old age and death,"[43] as the

Laws of Manu says. A new becoming means severing, discarding, shaking off, washing off the old. But as soon as the new emerges, it is already the new old. The more radical opposition is constituted by the completely different. Initiation wants the upheaval it simultaneously prevents. Therefore, the initiate is deprived of the old hair, but not completely. Attaining immortality by mortality cannot be thought consistently. Furthermore, the solution a person chooses in the awareness of his mortality and in the fantasy of his immortality does not depend in Hinduism only on a thin strand of hair.

Natural Birth, Ritual Birth, New Birth[44]

From the time of the tonsure until his new birth from the Veda, in terms of ritual, the initiate is an embryo who requires special protection. A number of stages in the ritual can thus be seen as rites of strengthening and protecting this newborn. "The man who does not sacrifice is not yet born." The sentence of the Śatapatha-Brāhmaṇa also applies here, for only the initiated is entitled to take part in or exercise the domestic sacrificial rituals and marriage and death rites. In fact, in the Brahmanical Hindu initiation, birth processes are even portrayed. Mircea Eliade's general observation that initiations often represent a *regressus ad uterum* also applies to ancient Indian times.[45] Thus, the Atharvaveda says that the guide in the consecration (*dīkṣā*) takes the adept in the womb: "The teacher, taking [him] in charge (*upa-nī*),[46] "makes the Vedic student an embryo within; he bears him in his belly [*garbham antaḥ,* literally: "in the womb"] three nights."[47]

The Upanayana[48] also begins with the statement that the naked boy should be dressed only in a loincloth rubbed with a paste of turmeric (*curcuma*) like a newborn, often by his sisters, if they are still virgins. According to Ayurvedic theories of nutrition, turmeric is recommended for curing diseases of the womb.

Beforehand, partly in the morning, partly during the initiation itself, the boy has a final meal with his mother. During the meal, he sits on her lap (fig. 1), even as an adolescent or even older. Once more, he returns to the well-protected place of his childhood. After the initiation, other norms will apply to him.[49] Then, he may no longer eat with his mother,[50] and in traditional families this regulation is maintained.

After washing off the ritual turmeric "placenta," the boy puts on a yellow loin cloth (*kaupīna*) and a knee-length garment of the same color. These "innocent" fabrics, which the priest gives the initiate, have no seam, thus have not been in the hands of the tailor, who is considered partly impure. The son receives the garment from the priest, formally requesting that he accept him

(a)

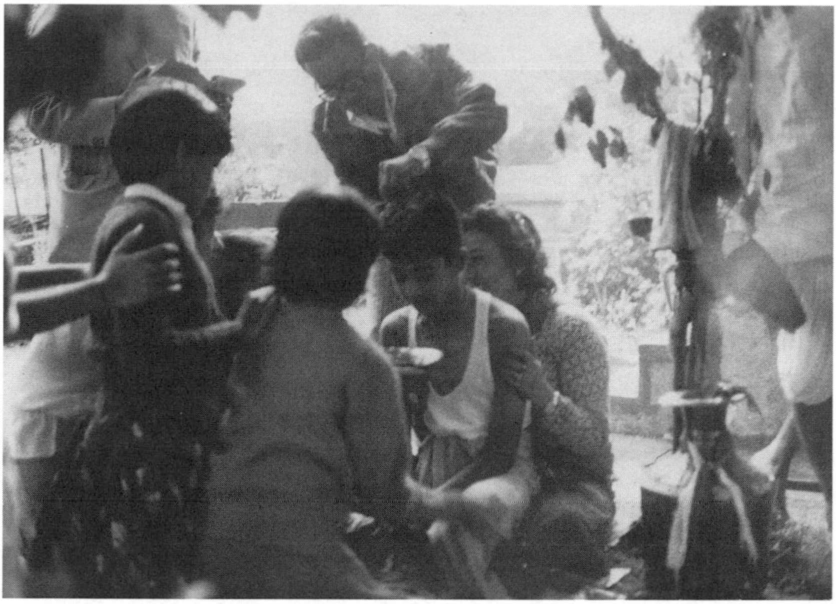

(b)

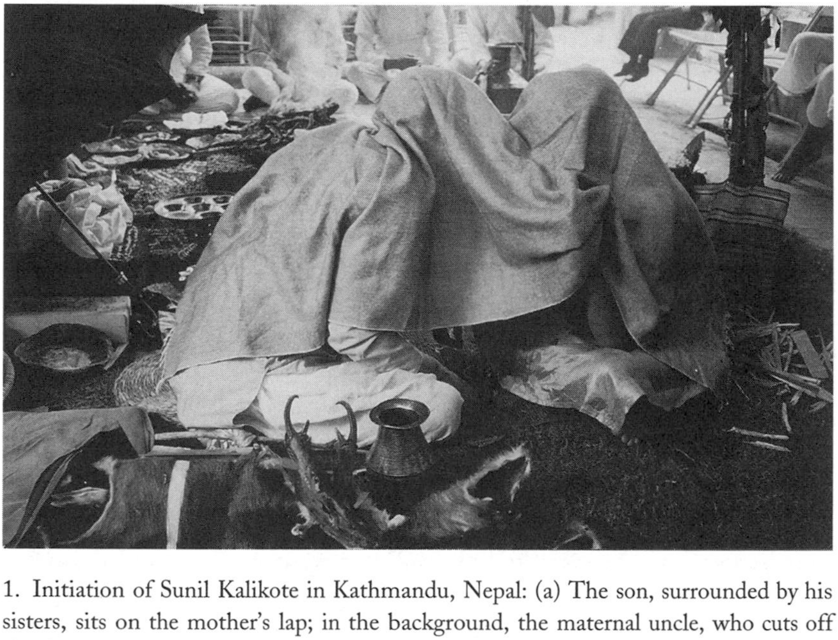

1. Initiation of Sunil Kalikote in Kathmandu, Nepal: (a) The son, surrounded by his sisters, sits on the mother's lap; in the background, the maternal uncle, who cuts off the first locks of hair. (b) Under the cover, the high priest whispers the Gāyatrī verse, the condensation of the Veda, to the son. *(continued)*

(c)

1. (continued) (c) The son leaves his parents' house as an ascetic for a few minutes in order "to study abroad." In the background, the mother, the maternal uncle (with eyeglasses), and another priest. Photographer: A. Michaels, 1983–1984.

as a student, saying: "I have come hither in order to study [literally: to walk] the *bráhman*."[51]

The new birth also signifies a ritual substitution of the parents—with far-reaching consequences: The ritual father can be younger than his "son,"[52] marriage with the teacher's daughters is considered incestuous,[53] and sexual relations with the teacher's wife is considered one of five mortal sins (*mahāpātaka*) along with murder of a Brahman, alcoholism, robbery, and relations with those who have committed such crimes.[54] Ritual parentage almost excludes natural parents. In Christianity, too, marriage to a godfather or godmother was forbidden, just as nuns and monks were not allowed to be godparents. Spiritual parentage is not consistent with natural parentage. By maintaining a distance from natural parentage, spiritual parentage acquires a higher legitimation in the religious training of the children. Biological, natural parentage is linked with deadly forces; according to Indian ideas, birth is an impure process which poses an obstacle to the realization of immortality.

Even in ancient Indian conceptions of propagation and birth, it is clear that the male seed that swells in the womb "for immortality"[55] forms the whole body.[56] Heinrich von Stietencron has correctly noted here: "In his son, the father lives on himself, avoids death, and, if the chain of descent continues, becomes immortal."[57] The father's seed comes into the woman, where it becomes the embryo and is reborn—and the ancient Indians were not the only ones who thought of procreation this way.[58]

Most legal scholars assume that the rite of insemination (*garbhādhāna;* literally: "putting in the fruit of the womb," see table 5) is meant for the fetus (*garbha*), but not for the womb (*kṣetra*).[59] In any case, here, too, the ritual primacy of procreation comes before the biological conditions. Adoption and Leverite marriage[60] are thus comparatively unproblematic, but mainly begetting itself becomes an almost unnatural act. "When a person has intercourse according to the procedure of *garbhādhāna* he establishes in the wife a foetus that becomes fit for the reception of the Veda."[61] Among other things, this ritual form of begetting allows the man to approach the woman only on specific days between the fourth and sixteenth day of the menstrual cycle, at night, after a bath and an appeal to the gods.[62] Radical legal scholars regarded sexual relations performed at any other time as abortion, since, in their view, the male semen already represents the fetus.[63]

Thus, procreation becomes almost male self-regeneration.[64] The self-born, origination from oneself (*svayambhū*), becomes the ideal. According to this view, the mother can indeed influence the shape of the embryo, but hardly adds anything to it. She simply delivers it. Therefore, in a soteriological sense, biological propagation was considered unsatisfactory and imperfect, because the male self or the semen could be influenced. The male semen is the whole vitality, which only swells "to immortality," as the Śatapatha-Brāhmaṇa says.[65]

Hence, only the ritual of new birth is a redeeming birth. Those who have not done it are not yet born for the sacrifice.[66] On the other hand, the Twice-Born are ritually perfect, i.e., "immortal." The legal scholars speak derisively of "Brahmans only by origin" or of "Brahmans only through family relations," or of the only Once-Born.[67]

Ritual birth, initiation, on the other hand, is a birth in sacrifice, which itself may not die: "He thereby consecreates him (the sacrificer) after death, and causes him to be born from out of it, and he is delivered from that death. And the sacrifice, indeed, becomes his body."[68] The ritual propagation thus identifies the individual with the sacrifice, the Veda, salvation, and immortality. "The one who knows will neither be born nor does he die; he comes from nowhere, is not anybody. Unborn, solid, eternal, original is he; he doesn't die when the body dies"—this is how the Kaṭha-Upaniṣad (2.18) formulates immortality, which can be achieved through knowledge and ritual identifications.[69] For this, the initiate must fulfill the criteria of equivalence, so he must be immortal himself. The biological, mortal stain must be eliminated. Hence, the symbolism of birth is almost a hindrance, for the issue is basically an elimination of birth and thus also new birth, the disappearance of birth, the liberation from birth.[70] Thus, initiation is not a transformation, but rather a construction of something that was not there before:[71] "Man is born into a world made by himself."[72] He must be being (*sat*) instead of non-being (*asat*), light instead of dark, pure instead of impure, truth instead of untruth, immortality instead of mortality.[73] Through repeated ritual identifications, he is "made" all those.

In a limited sense, the concept of the Second Birth is aimed against woman, for the ritual birth created by man devalues the birth from the womb.[74] However, this is true only from the point of view of sacrifice ritualism, because, at the same time, in the world of women, which was barely perceived or grasped ritually or textually by men, natural birth is still highly valued. Popular religious ideas of (re)birth or the protection of the newborn, respect for pregnancy and delivery, and admiration of motherhood are to be found in fairy tales and myths, vernacular poems and literature, but not in the austere sacrificial texts.

The Sacred Thread[75]

The Sacred Thread (*yajñopavīta,* Hindī: *janeū*) also refers to the birth processes. It is the new umbilical cord, which binds the initiate to the Veda and the sacrifice. The time of awarding this Thread, its production, its material, its number of threads and knots, the way it is worn, the occasions of its renewal, the philosophical and symbolical interpretations—all that varies in the late Vedic texts from one class to another, one school to another, one text to another. In the early Vedic time, those who were involved in the sacrifice seem not yet to have worn a sacrificial Cord permanently, but only at specific sacred occasions. Nor do the texts show that the terms *yajñopavīta* or *upavīta*—expressions that originally denoted only donning something—already meant the Sacred (Sacrificial) Thread itself; for example, they might refer to strips of antelope hide or a cloth, both of which were thrown over the left shoulder, like the Roman toga.

Wearing the Sacred Thread is still optional in the Dharmaśāstras. The Āpastamba Dharmasūtra says that the Twice-Born should wear a cloth over the upper torso or a Thread of Kuśa grass, which can assume the function of this cloth.[76] Most of the older Gṛhyasūtras, however, are silent on the subject of the Sacred Thread, and even the later Gṛhyasūtras invoke no Vedic sacrificial sayings (*mantra*) for the ritual donning of the Sacred Thread during the consecration of the youth.[77] But, from the third epoch on, at the latest, it was stipulated that the Thread was to be given during youth, woven of cotton by Brahman virgins or widows, wound by Brahmans in three strands of nine threads each, made to fit the length of the body of the initiate (precisely: ninety-six times the width of his four fingers), and should usually be worn over the left shoulder and under the right arm.[78] If it is too long and reaches the lower body, impurity threatens.

The Thread itself does not mean much. As a kind of belt, there is evidence for it in India from the ancient Iranian[79] and early Vedic time and in many other cultures; it is a favorite metaphor of cohesion. It recalls the terms *guideline, red thread, connecting thread, canon,* or the Indian equivalents *sūtra* and *tantra*—denoting both texts and threads. So, its meaning depends on the particular interpretation. In the high tradition, the nine threads of the Thread stand, among other things, for eight deities (Oṃkāra, Agni, Nāga, Soma, Pitaraḥ, Prajāpati, Vāyu, and Sūrya) and the sum of all gods; its three strands stand for the three Vedic collections of texts or for three of the four stages of life[80] and classes (*varṇāśrama*), for the three obligations (*ṛṇa*) man has toward seers, ancestors, and gods,[81] for the divine triad of Brahmā, Viṣṇu, and Śiva, or for the three basic qualities (*guṇa*—which also means literally "thread, cord") of primordial matter (*prakṛti*); the knots usually stand for the row of ancestors (*pravara*).

But, despite this rich symbolism, the girding is completely ritualistic: An understanding of the ritual and the sacrificial sayings or an internal participation is not demanded; even the mentally ill are given the Sacred Thread if they are born into the class of the Twice-Born. Through such relations, the initiate is literally bound into purity and ritually protected from impurity—e.g., from women and casteless people, neither of whom receives a Sacred Thread. Hence, during impure or inauspicious activities, the Thread must be renewed or its way of being worn must be changed—as after illicit sexual relations, in the death ritual, or in defecation. Twice-Born people who are very traditional are expected not to take a step without the Thread and always to carry a replacement.

The Sacred Thread has become the symbol of the Hinduism of the Twice-Born to such an extent that even social groups who do not use Brahman priests have such a Thread bestowed on them.[82] Even ascetics, who reject almost everything the Thread symbolizes, have quite often sought a substitute for it.[83] For example, they spoke of an internal Thread, which distinguishes the truly wise from others: "Cutting his hair together with the topknot, let a wise man discard his external string. As his string let him wear the supreme and imperishable Brahman."[84]

From the start, the social function of the Thread was extensive. It was a status symbol, used by the upper classes to delineate themselves. Under no circumstances could it be given to those who had become outcasts, to marginal groups of Āryas, the indigenous population, or the Vrātyas.[85] It was a cohesive force in a society that saw its religious and social identity endangered by increasing acculturation, because languages, skin colors, clothing, and professions were blending and changing. At a time of upheaval, in the third ("Ascetic") epoch, an ideal of social segregation also developed. The Identificatory Habitus helped maintain this ideal. Anyone who wore the Sacred Thread belonged to the category of those who were entitled to sacrifice and thus to the economic, social, and often also religious ruling stratum. No wonder that the Sacred Thread was imitated by other population groups as a desirable status symbol.

But most of all, the Thread was the sign of the right to pursue either of the equally worthwhile paths of knowledge (Veda) and action (sacrifice). In the subsequent ritual section of the initiation, both possibilities are staged as exemplary for the initiate: In constant alternation, he is ascetic, student, and householder.

Consecration of the Ascetic, Consecration of the Student, Consecration of the Man

The Sacred Thread is a central part of the initiation today, but it not the only thing the initiate receives. A hide and a walking stick are obviously connected with asceticism. The hide—originally different according to class (see table 7), today usually an antelope hide—was the preferred garment of the forest dweller and ascetic. The stick[86] is a sign of ascetic wandering and the authority gained by renunciation; at the same time, it serves for self-protection. Other objects presented to the young man[87] are to grant him dignity and strength: an umbrella,[88] symbol of the sky and the king, or a turban and wooden shoes, signs of dignity and sovereignty.

Thus equipped, the initiate is almost ready to receive the Veda and the right to sacrifice. But more rites are needed to bless this act. The forces of the elements are necessary for purification and strengthening, and thus the priest pours water into the boy's hands, appeals to the sun as a witness, and worships the stars to eliminate every bad influence. The initiate also steps on a rock to demonstrate his future steadfastness. All this happens while the five fires burn, and Brahman priests read Vedic texts and thus guarantee that every act of the house priest is secured through the recitation of a Vedic verse. Word and deed form a performative unity; only together are they ritually effective, as a vow can only be valid with words spoken aloud, the gesture of the raised fingers, and in the presence of witnesses.

Then begins the acceptance as a student and the initiation in the Veda. This takes place in the form of a dialogue in which the priest among others gives the words and the student answers:

Priest Say: "Oṃ, I have come for studentship (*brahmacarya*)."
Initiate Oṃ, I have come for studentship.
Priest Say: "I am a student (*brahmacārin*)."
Initiate I am a student.

With this exchange of words, the acceptance is complete. The initiate has become a student.[89] *Brahmacārin* literally means someone who walks to the *brahman,* that is, to the Veda or the absolute, mainly the Brahman student, but it also means chastity and thus an ascetic life. *Brahmacarya* is also the first of the four stages of life in the traditional Āśrama system, which arose at the end of the second epoch (see table 8). After scholarship comes the phase of householder (*gṛhastha*) with the establishment of the family, and then a two-stage retreat to asceticism, first as a forest dweller (*vānaprastha*), then as a wandering ascetic (*saṃnyāsa*). As Moritz Winternitz and Patrick Olivelle have shown,[90] the Āśramas were originally theological concepts of equally valid life-styles, which an adult male could feel compelled to follow all his life. Lifelong scholarship (*naiṣṭhika brahmacārin*) and the direct transition from the phase of the student (*brahmacārin*) to that of the wandering ascetic (*saṃnyāsin*) were possible, but were the exception. But from the late third epoch, these paths became a theological ideal of successive stages of life with specific tasks and life goals (*puruṣārtha*), which succeeded mainly in integrating asceticism into the stages of life.[91]

As soon as the student is accepted, the priest teaches the student a Veda verse, the Gāyatrī, and later also called "Sāvitrī" because of the deity praised in it: *tat savitur vareṇyaṃ bhargo devasya dhīmahi. dhiyo yo naḥ pracodayāt.* "We meditate on that shining light of the divine *Savitṛ* [i.e., the Sun]; may he stimulate our thoughts."[92]

The priest sits in the north and has the student in the east repeat the verse (*mantra*) syllable after syllable and metric foot after metric foot. This takes place under a blanket, shielded from the public (see fig. 1b). Even though the Veda has long been accessible in print and translation, its esoteric, secret transmission is expressed here once again. At the same time, this retreat mirrors the ritual process of birth itself, but here the natural mother is replaced by the Sāvitrī hymn.[93]

TABLE 8
The Traditional Brahman Stages of Life and Goals of Life

*Stages (*āśrama*) and Their Persons*	*Tasks*	*Entrance Rite*	*Classical Life Goals (*puruṣārtha*)*
brahmacarya (brahmacārin)	Study, chaste scholarship	Initiation (*upanayana*)	
gṛhastha (gṛhastha)	Paterfamilias, professional life, establishing a family	Marriage (*vivāha*)	Material welfare (*artha*), sexual satisfaction (*kāma*), socioreligious fulfillment of duty (*dharma*)
vānaprastha (vānaprasthin)	Forest dwelling with maintenance of the domestic fire		
saṃnyāsa (saṃnyāsin)	Renunciation without domestic fire, wandering	"Death ritual" (*antyeṣṭi*); *praiṣa* appeal, ordination	Liberation, deliverance (*mokṣa*)

The teaching of this mantra is the beginning of the Veda study. Only later did another rite (*vedārambha*) involving the fire sacrifice, begging alms for the teacher, and the ritual bath develop. But, in fact, studying the text has become unnecessary for most initiates unless they want to be priests or scholars. For, according to ancient rules, at least twelve years of study is stipulated.[94] According to tradition, the Gāyatrī verse is also a condensation of the Veda: Prajāpati himself, the creator god, was supposed to have "milked" the three Vedas and formed the Gāyatrī out of the three metric feet.[95] Today this verse is practically the only one that remains important for most initiates—comparable to the confirmation text in Christianity that substitutes for knowledge of the Bible. In orthodox families, the Vedic verse is recited every day at the morning ritual (*saṃdhyā*).[96] Absence from the parents' house, the time sacrificed in study, and the social prestige of training in the Veda and for the priesthood—both highly respected and derided as unworldly—still make the traditional study of Veda not exactly attractive. For ritual reasons, moreover, it was not necessary to learn all collections of the Veda. Nevertheless, the Brahmanic Hindu initiation did preserve the old culture of teaching and learning because, even if Vedic knowledge is not learned, it has to be acquired. The initiation does not grant the acquisition of skills, but rather it grants the right to knowledge of the Veda and thus to the sacrifice.

Because this right applies both for priests and for initiated laymen, there is a twofold interpretation of the meaning and stages of the individual parts of the ritual: From the perspective of the priests and Brahmanic scholars, the Upanayana is primarily the beginning of professional education; from the perspective of the other Twice-Born, it is a symbolic identification with the Veda, in which the content of the texts is less important than the acquired right to maintain the domestic fire. Just as an oath on the Bible does not require knowledge of the Bible to corroborate the truth of a statement, so the condensation of knowledge of the Veda in the Sāvitrī hymn is sufficient as a substitute for the whole.[97] And yet, the Brahmanic Hindu initiation is the beginning of education, for from now on, caste norms must be learned and followed.

The right to study the Veda was thus also a social demarcation. The right to hear the Veda was withheld from the impure lower social classes—knowledge (Veda) is power: "A priest [Brahman] should never, even in extremity, forge Vedic or sexual bonds with those people who have not been purified [by initiation]."[98] Thus, not to be allowed to study the Veda also meant not to be able to achieve purity.

Because of the tension between ritual and natural parenthood, various claims become apparent to the adolescent. By becoming able to make his own decisions, he confronts the question of his future way of life: Should he study his father's profession, should he study the Veda with a foreign teacher and (as a Brahman) become a scholar (*śrotriya*), should he establish his own home and family or follow the ascetics passing through the village? Even today, these problems are still dramatized in the course of the initiation: Priests and parents woo the youth, and study, ascetic begging, or the sacrificial fire move in and out of the foreground.

Studenthood[99] implies subordination to the teacher, deferentially holding his feet, bringing him firewood, collecting alms for him. The Veda teacher was godlike.[100] Studenthood meant no playing, singing, dancing, or laughing, but sleeping on the floor, accepting the teacher's punishments without complaint. And yet this studenthood was clearly attractive. However, in most cases, economic conditions did not allow the son to devote himself to the study of Veda and thus drop out of the labor force; but at the end of the second epoch, there was religious freedom of choice in the cities, at least for the higher strata, who profited from the earned surplus, thus mainly among the aristocracy and wealthy merchants. There are the beginnings of religious freedom and individualism. In any case, in the urban centers, the first voluntary groups, sects, and religious communities, including Buddhism, emerged. They were based on a freedom to be able to choose between religious offers. This freedom was the greatest challenge for the exclusive Vedic religion.[101] This freedom of choice probably contributed to reshaping the ancient Indian sacrificial consecration (*dīkṣā*) of that time into an initiation for classes.

In the "rite of the foreigner" (*deśāntara,* literally: "moving to another country"),[102] the conflict between asceticism and profession, wilderness and home, alms and sacrificial fire, escape from the world and acceptance of the world, is also expressed playfully. In modern initiation celebrations, the son sometimes leaves the house, equipped with the tools of wandering: staff, hide, bow, and arrow (see fig. 1c). He explains that he wants to go to Benares to study the Veda there for twelve years. But his mother points out the dangers and troubles of life abroad. She asks him not to violate his obligations to others. Instead, she praises home and family life, and promises him a bride. But the son prefers to woo Sarasvatī, the goddess of the arts and sciences, as a bride. Only when the game threatens to become serious[103] and the son sets out on the road does his maternal uncle hold him back.

This scene concludes the Brahmacarya, the time of chastity and study of Veda. What follows is the ritual part of the "return home" (*samāvarta, samāvartana*), which is composed of rites of affiliation, in van Gennep's terminology. It is the formal conclusion of scholarship and the resumption of family life. One last time, the initiate feeds his teacher's fire and showers him with gifts. Historical (priestly!) documents keep mentioning cows, gold, and land. Rice, grains, fruits, money, and an umbrella—a royal symbol of status and protection—are usually given. Brahmanic priests today frequently have great collections of umbrellas.

Then the initiate bathes. The initiation is obviously the identification with the Veda and the sacrificial fire, from which a certain force understood as fire is derived, which the ascetic preserves as an internal fire (*tapas*). The end is consequently a cooling down, a bath (*snāna*). As soon as the sacrifice is extinguished, and the boy has bathed and clad himself in secular clothing, the initiation is consummated, even though minor concluding rites follow. The son is then a "Bathed One" (*snātaka*) and has also become a marriageable member of his extended family, possessing the right to sacrifice.

In the Hindu initiation, what is confirmed is neither common religious affiliation nor acceptance into a community, but rather—*ritually:* the son's Brahmanic-Sanskritic right to maintain a family domestic fire; *psychologically:* the son's maturity, his adulthood or manhood (ability to marry); and *socially:*

the coherence and status of a family unit. Thus, only in a limited sense is the Hindu initiation a life-cycle rite of adolescence, which ceremonially commemorates the change to a new stage of life (but also ritually concludes the coming of age). It has little to do with coming into one's majority, and even less to do with finding one's identity or coping with a crisis of adolescence. At any rate, the Western stages of life of childhood, youth, and adulthood only inadequately mark the subtle human maturing and aging processes.[104] As Philippe Ariès has shown and as Indian material confirms, "childhood" is not just a biological phase; it is more a cultural product. Only after the Renaissance did Europeans see the child not just as a small adult, but rather as a creature with its own thoughts and feelings. And youth, puberty, or adolescence became the focus of attention only in the twentieth century. In ancient India, these phases of life were not conceptually delineated.

The Hindu initiation is full of ritual equivalents: The son is identified with the Veda,[105] the sacrifice, the father, and the paternal line; he receives a new self; he is born as an I-less I, which is identical with the Brahman and immortality, expressed in the evergreen Kuśa grass, the gold, or the virgin. Above all, natural parentage is replaced by a ritual one. These identity equivalents are the bases of all sacrificial ritual practice and theology—so much that they are usually taken for granted, without the sense of sacrifice and salvation aspects always being present for all those involved. In terms of doctrine, the initiation is a release from individualism aimed at incorporating the individual into immortality, making him equivalent with it. But an initiation has to do with individuals and actors, not with special ritual beings. The danger in rituals conceived as normative and textual is that reality is seen as an imperfect realization of an ideal. It is assumed that rituals have to proceed by plan according to rules. But such rituals exist only in the minds of those who codify the ritual rules: priest-theologians and scholars. Standardized rituals are also an expression of habits that are thought and felt, done and experienced, that are acquired, learned, and shaped in a culture; and thus introduced deliberately, they can be molded tactically, combatively, jokingly, or playfully. With the cultural sensory apparatus acquired in their childhood, most of the participants know what is permitted and what is not, what is good or bad, beautiful or repulsive. Using the authors of ritual books as the only witnesses is like using traffic laws to describe traffic.

CHILDHOOD AND SOCIALIZATION

Only in childhood is it possible to "change" cultures. Later, boundaries remain; later, one remains a foreigner. Culture is mainly custom and habit, and, like one's mother tongue, is acquired in childhood. Proverbs like: "What little Hansie doesn't learn, big Hans never learns"—and oral wisdom like: "Give me another mother and I'll give you another world" (Augustine)—confirm worldly experience and psychological, pedagogical, or neurobiological knowledge, that the cognitive model of a culture is stamped in childhood. Religions, too, rely not so much on individual experiences or on innate feelings—like a *sensus numinosus* (Rudolf Otto)—but rather on behavioral patterns acquired and learned in childhood.

A study of childhood in other cultures has to break away from many Western notions. As Hartmut von Hentig explains in the foreword to the German edition of Philippe Ariès's *Centuries of Childhood,* childhood in the West today is the complete opposite of childhood in traditional societies: With television and urbanization, childhood in the West is not only increasingly disappearing (Neil Postman), but is to a large extent focused pedagogically on the future, planning for a world that applies to children later, but not now. Childhood, therefore, is mostly deficient and full of problems, which have to be solved by knowledge, teaching, and training as early as possible. Children are often told that the world they live in is not (yet) right. Childhood in the West, therefore, is basically alien to life: Learning is distinct from experience, education is education with peers, and more and more adults do not have hands-on experience with children. Childhood for the masses in India is different: It is a life with many children of all ages, in an extended-family community, with relatively little school instruction. How do these differences affect the understanding of the world?

Psychological analyses of childhood based on the nuclear family are often based wholly on the relative ego strength of the individual and tend to see other forms of society in which the nuclear family is not the norm as pathological,[106] by underestimating the strengths of family cohesion. Max Weber's methodical individualism, as well as Louis Dumont's transcendental holism—to some extent the obverse—illustrate that the actual dynamic grouping in India, that is, the extended family, is underestimated. Neither individual nor caste is India's driving social force, but rather the extended family. Western economic theories recognize individuals and business units, but not families.[107] Individuals are paid salaries; individuals work, buy, and sell. Just as housework is seldom included in economic calculations because it is not subject to market rules, so the family as an economic and social agent in India is not perceived or is perceived only negatively. Such thinking maintains that strong family cohesion leads to unprofitable parceling of the family property, low mobility, nepotism, and a lack of initiative. But the Indian extended family is basically a company with capital, production of goods, distribution of labor, hierarchical corporate organization, bookkeeping, reserves, and social security, but also with a market value, as is clear in marriage negotiations. The cohesion of this "company," its corporate identity, is attained, among other things, through childhood.

However, in the traditional legal literature of India, childhood hardly appears; so we must depend on indirect sources and field studies. In Sanskrit texts, the first years of life are divided into separate phases: Childhood (*kaumāra*) ends at the age of five, boyhood (*paugaṇḍa*) at ten, adolescence (*kiśora*) at fifteen; then begins youth (*yauvana*).[108] Or: "A child is called infant [*śiśu*] till the teeth are cut; till the tonsure ceremony he is called a child [*bāla*]; a boy [*kumāra*] till the *kuśa* girdle is put [at the *upanayana*]."[109] But these instructions are more schematic than reflected in real life.

For most legal scholars, children are ritually impure.[110] Only a few childhood rites are treated briefly in the Dharmaśāstra: the naming, the first outing, the first solid food (see table 5). This is because Indian children in their early years are mainly in the care of mothers and sisters, but are not in the world of the men who wrote the Sanskrit texts. Only with the initiation do the legal texts become more eloquent. It is also the end of childhood. But, the silence about childhood in the Sanskrit texts should not mislead us into ignoring this phase of life in the analysis of processes of socialization. Other sources must be substituted to give a picture of how children are raised in India. Ethnographic studies and biographies are especially useful.[111] I begin with observations from everyday life which are confirmed by a comprehensive literature about childhood and socialization in India, and try to comprehend the situation of women and mothers before I return to the initial questions about the relationship between Hindu religions and Indian personality.

I will attempt to describe the "normal case" of Indian childhood. This may be seen as an idealization, perhaps a romanticization, and counterexamples may be thought of with childhood exposure and killing, child slave labor, deliberate crippling for begging, deficient care during sickness, and the high rate of child mortality. I am not ignoring all these, but for me they are exceptions. To look only at the repulsive extremes is a negative variant of exoticism. For the structure of social relations in a society, the normal case is relevant; but the special case can contribute to an elucidation. The normal case, however, is not known empirically, but is a theorem, an abstraction, and a simplification, an ideal type as defined by Max Weber, a social fact as defined by Emile Durkheim. All empiricism is theoretical in this sense, a reflection about reality. Thus, the individual case also stands for a theory. But the average individual case turns subjectivity into a critical subjectivity, generalizes the individual, brings us down to earth, prevents the bird's-eye view that sees the life of people and their everyday activity in miniature.

The Early Years[112]

Children in India are little maharajas. Even if they often grow up in bitter poverty, they hardly lack emotional care. "Treat your son in the first five years like a maharaja, in the next ten as a friend, then as a slave," says a popular proverb.[113] Compared to Western standards, small children are spoiled and pampered, even if their life is not a bed of roses. They are seldom punished with beatings; impudence is forgiven and smiled at. The wild, tyrannical childhood of the god Kṛṣṇa is a favorite motif, represented in sugary form on colorful posters. Even though the chubby-cheeked child Kṛṣṇa (Bālakṛṣṇa) steals clarified butter, unties calves, or defecates in the middle of the house, his parents do not get angry with him, but are glad "about [his] wildness, which frightens the pedagogues of bourgeois Europe."[114]

Children are seldom left alone. They are always in the arms of their own mothers, other mothers, or children of siblings. They are present at work, at celebrations and assemblies, or in the cinema, the bazaar, and on trips; they are seldom sent away because they might disturb. It is not the child who has to conform to the adults, but rather those who take care of the child. Indian parents do not especially want to be models for their children; at any rate, they estimate their influence as negligible. The child is not a *tabula rasa* who needs good parents and a beneficial environment to be able to develop, but is rather an autonomous divine creature "with 'innate' psychic dispositions from its previous life,"[115] who must be cared for, but not educated.

Thus, children are not urged to be independent. Whereas children in the West are confirmed in their individual strength very early ("You can already do that by yourself!"), Indian children rarely hear such sentences. It is not laudable to be able to do something by yourself, but rather to be able to do something with others. It is not the individual capacities of the child that are encouraged, but rather his relationships with other family members.

The slow weaning from the maternal breast also leads to solidarity. Indian children are not weaned until they are two or three years old, sometimes even later. Whenever they shout, they receive the breast, but more reluctantly as they grow older. So, weaning does not take place suddenly, as can be read repeatedly, but gradually.[116] The mother obstinately pushes the child to other members of the family. This conveys to him that he is mature enough to eat with the other children rather than lying by himself at his mother's breast. A child who can run and talk, but is not yet weaned, is even considered selfish.

The child is pampered accordingly by his older siblings. He is still given the breast, but the child is clearly made to sense the displeasure in his milieu.

The difference in observations of weaning may seem small, but is considerable. The message for the child is not as in the West: away from the mother, to strengthening the ego ("You can, you may eat all by yourself; you don't have to be fed anymore!"), but rather away from the mother, to the community of the family group ("You may eat with the others," "You get something to eat when you do this or that for us"). Stanley Kurtz has correctly criticized a Western psychology fixated on the ego for not perceiving this fine but momentous distinction.[117] It is momentous because it is not the egotistic interest that is praised, but rather the group welfare. "The family is everything, the individual is nothing," an informant tells the American author Margaret Cormack[118] and thus gets to the heart of a pedagogical maxim of India. So, whereas in the West, according to Kurtz, the child matures by learning to tolerate and sublimate frustrations, in India, he is strengthened by small gibes to grow up by renouncing on his own the primary oral needs and dependence on the mother.[119]

In general, children in India are not praised as often as in the West. It is even considered explicitly improper to praise a child, even an infant, in his presence. This would not only draw the attention of the evil spirits to the offspring, but would also make him arrogant and addicted to admiration. Too much love, love in general, harms the child. What he needs is care and punishment for selfishness. Thus, very early, a social and family interest is the focus of togetherness. Self-interest can often be articulated only by retreating from the group, through asceticism.

Closeness to the family is physical. Babies and small children are rubbed with oil and massaged every day; they run around naked or dressed only in little shirts, and are hardly urged to cleanliness by their parents.[120] It is mainly the sibling children who are annoyed by the small child, if he cannot relieve himself. Thus, the child feels isolated when he does not conform to group pressure.

The Indian psychoanalyst Sudhir Kakar, whose 1978 book *The Inner World: A Psycho-analytic Study of Childhood and Society in India* caused a sensation, emphasizes particularly the symbiosis in Indian childhood with the mother: "An Indian mother tends to indulge her child's wishes absolutely, either for quiet, a change of diaper, his need for sleep or company. Moreover, she tends to continue this kind of care far beyond the time when the child is capable of independence in many areas."[121] According to Western psychoanalytic standards, such a long symbiosis with the mother would lead to a weakly differentiated ego and would favor a narcissistic personality structure.[122]

Parentage and the "Oceanic Feeling"

Since the father does not intervene until late in the child's development, the impression may arise that Indian men have weak superegos. In fact, the father does not become involved in the upbringing of the child, especially the son, until relatively late—when the boy is about five years old—that is, in matters of learning and following caste restrictions and prohibitions. This transition is felt by the sons as harsh, occasionally traumatic: "The liberality the child is granted during his early years is constantly cut back. Now value is placed on good behavior and nice manners. The child is often beaten when he disturbs. And the older he becomes, the harder the beatings become," writes Shyama Charan Dube in a monograph on Indian village life.[123] Kakar endorses this view: "The most impressive indication of this change is the contrast between the early more or less unlimited and benevolent leniency and the new, inflexible demand for absolute obedience and adjustment to family and social rules."[124] Ultimately, fathers are the guarantors of the good reputation of the family, which is preserved or improved through his personal characteristics and by the ritual purity of the extended family.

Kurtz criticizes the widespread view that the transition into the world of the father takes place abruptly for the sons and thus is harsh. Instead, he assumes a gradual transition.[125] But there is still a contrast between an indulged early childhood and the stricter period of youth. As we have seen, in the initiation, the separation of the son from the mother and sisters and the assumption of responsibility for him by the men (priest, father, uncle) is ritualized.

Vis-à-vis the son, the father tends to be emotionally withdrawn. He is not strict, but remote, almost inaccessible. He expects subordination and obedience; the son expects direction, but not closeness. In the father's presence, the son is cautious, silent, and passive. There is hardly any rivalry. Despite the most extensive mythological literature in the world, Oedipal myths are rare in India.[126] More commonly, the father kills the son (as, for example, in the myth of the birth of Gaṇeśa, the son of Pārvatī and Śiva, who received his elephant head because his father had decapitated him in rage at Pārvatī's wish for children). The son is respectful and quite shy toward the father. He does not address him by his first name. Often he greets him by touching his feet, an unclean part of the body. The son eats only after the father, does not smoke in his presence, speaks only when he is asked to do so. Women relate similarly to men, or young people to older respected persons. What is noteworthy in these patterns of behavior acquired in childhood but retained until old age[127] is that respect is expressed to a large extent by avoiding contact, the so-called "respect avoidance." Too much physical and emotional proximity would level the status distinction. In Indian men, this socialization frequently leads to a yearning for an ideal, charismatic authority, a Guru, who shows you the way if you trust him completely. Young Indian scholars occasionally begin their work with the words: "To my Father the God."[128]

Sukhir Kakar also analyzes the significance of the birth of a child, primarily a son, for the self-esteem and social position of the mother. He starts with the observation that the Hindu woman finds a proper recognition in her husband's family only with the birth of a son. As a daughter, the woman, as we will see, is almost unwelcome at birth; as a daughter-in-law in her husband's family she is more tolerated than liked at first. Frequently, there are problems with the mother-in-law and other women in the new extended family. But when she bears a son, she attains respect and esteem. Then the mother is sometimes considered even more worthy of respect than the father.[129] Thus, says Kakar, a special relation emerges between mother and son: On the one hand, she needs him for her identity and self-respect; on the other hand, at an unconscious level, she makes him responsible for her dependency and her disappointment at having to leave her own family. Affection and aggression are blended in this ambivalence. The mother attaches her children to her because she feels endangered by the separation from the child. Thus, the son also develops ambivalent feelings toward the mother. On the one hand, he sees her as the good mother, who allows him to have a nearly infinite basic trust in the world and his fellow man, as well as a self-love that is unusual in the West; on the other hand, he is afraid of the wicked, devouring, castrating mother, so that he is quickly offended and anxious about the punishment for breaking away, while feeling incapable of assuming responsibility.[130]

A few examples from everyday life demonstrate how these patterns are expressed: Separations from the family are nearly impossible (except through asceticism or escape). Illnesses often "accompany separations from family ties, the compulsion to individual decisions at the cost of the group feeling, and healing them depends to a large extent on the reproduction of the 'oceanic' equilibrium."[131] The establishment of one's own household is almost always fraught with conflict. Individualism and egoism are disapproved. Personal privileges must be shared. Anyone who travels abroad is busy for days buying gifts for countless close and distant relations so they can participate. Kakar thinks that the individual devotes himself to the group in order to avoid the anxiety of individualization. He also says that in India, "the individual functions as a member of a group rather than on his own."[132] Kakar thus confirms the priority of the family over the individual, but with a negative conclusion: The group is valued higher because individualization is beset with anxiety.

On the other hand, Kurtz posits the family group as the foundation and positive reference point of child-rearing. Thus, he sees separation from the mother and the recourse to the family group as evidence of maturity—and not escape, as Kakar does. Kurtz substitutes the shaping of an "ego of the whole" for the Western ego-formation.[133] Therefore, for Kurtz, motherhood is also essentially function and relation. The mother does not give her child love in a Western sense (a special emotional care, emphasis on the mother-child dyad), but rather fills his need for care and warmth. This can be replaced with comparative ease because the personal relation between mother and child is not so important as the family relations. Kurtz talks of multiple motherhood,[134] by which he means also the child's other maternal reference persons: the grandmothers, aunts, sisters-in-law, older sisters, who all have a much higher value in the development of the child than in the West because of their proximity in the household. The child does not need *the* mother, but rather a mother. Thus, it is always observed[135] that the physical mother does not fondle her child when the mother-in-law or grandmother is present. Unlike in the West, these have a prerogative in caring for the child; they are often more "motherly" than the mother herself. The same is true for the father. In certain regions of northern India, a son calls his grandfather "papa," but calls his father "older brother."[136] Moreover, in an Indian extended family, nonbiological children are taken in either temporarily or permanently: adopted children, foster children, orphans and wards, or domestic help. The social and economic situation of India promotes this kind of mutual support and care. But hardly anyone thinks it damages the child emotionally if he grows up apart from his mother. Thus, in India, it is not motherhood or multiple motherhood or fatherhood that is primary, but rather more or less caring modes of behavior, which are assumed by several interchangeable reference persons.[137] Motherhood and fatherhood can be replaced to a large extent. Here the relationship of biological and ritual parentage during the initiation is repeated emotionally: "All the mothers are one" (the title of Stanley Kurtz's book) is a developmental psychological variant of the Identificatory Habitus.

Kakar is credited with having shown the connection between individual socialization and Hindu images of the world.[138] Thus, he has primarily interpreted escapist tendencies as a regressive wish for the unspoiled symbiosis with the mother. This lifelong wish to merge applies not only to sons, but also to daughters. Yearning for the mother is a topos of novels, films, and biographies, and in the southern Indian Tamil Nadu, it is an established idiom (Tamil *ammāvai tēṭi*).[139] In India, as we know, an active conquest of the world is represented as a wrong karmic path and a deception. The objective of many meditative and yogic practices is to dissolve ego boundaries instead of consolidating them, as in the West. In the West, stability is determined by ego boundaries, which are constantly tested. In India, one tries to abolish the contrasts between internal and external, subject and object. Contemplative ascetics who are renouncers, who deny the world, are admired, but not successful, active, autonomous, and worldly people, as in the West. The ascetics have a preconscious, preverbal, sensitive, and intuitive, or—in Freud's terminology[140]—an "oceanic" access to the internal world instead of the external one, and thus a higher, liberating truth. This is why Gurus, seers, fortune-tellers, and palm readers have such a great influence in India. The West is concerned with liberation in the world; India is also concerned with liberation from the world.

Sigmund Freud is supposed to have said that a person feels good and is psychologically healthy if he can love and work, if he receives satisfaction and confirmation. In fact, Western society is shaped by the yearning for love and the need for self-confirmation through (paid) work. Both these needs assume individualization, at least in modern Western industrial societies. It is different in India. There, too, there is yearning for love and the wish to be acknowledged through achievement, but a comprehensive well-being, even happiness, also appears in patterns of relations that are harmonious if they are balanced. Maintaining a belligerent tension in these relations is thus considered just as harmonious as friendly cooperation and togetherness. It is not the individual who is the focus, but his relationship within a group. It is not an individual god that is interesting, but rather groups or throngs of gods, a god and his consort, a god and his antagonist, twin gods or hierarchies of gods. The person is interesting not so much as an individual, but rather in his function as father or mother, brother or sister, husband or wife, uncle or aunt, member of a subcaste or neighbor. It is not the author of a text that is important, but his scholarship in a teacher-student sequence (*paramparā*). From early on, the countless terms of relationships are impressed on children; they are the first words they learn.

Margaret Trawick has called these patterns of relating, among other things, "mirroring/twinning," "complementation/dynamic union," "sequential contrast," or projection and introspection. They are not limited only to psychological aspects, but, for example, also worked out as stylistic features of Tamil literature.[141] The Identificatory Habitus also appears in such a striving for a correlative balance, by which the tension in favor of the status quo is maintained in accordance with the Hindu soteriological maxim that change is death, and the unchangeable on the other hand is immortality. In the initiation, the Identificatory Habitus makes common descent equal to that of individual descent; in childhood, it makes the individual equal with the family. Thus, to overstate the case, childhood in India is an extensive deindividualization and therefore a complete and "perfect" (*saṃskṛta*) socialization.

Sacred Fatherhood[142]

In terms of ritual, what shapes the "oceanic" feeling acquired in children psychologically is the identification of the son with the Veda, the sacrificial fire, and the father, as expressed by the initiation. As we have seen, the initiation ultimately achieves the integration of the son into the family. He is identified with the Veda, the sacrifice, and thus with immortality. He wants to be worthy of the high, ascetic claim to study the Veda and sets out for Benares for this purpose. But his maternal uncle brings him back, reminds him to fulfill his duty to his progeny, and promises him a bride. Even if the ascetic path of the individual represents a higher goal of deliverance, it is more mature, as the priest says explicitly during the initiation, to deny this path and integrate back into the family group, to get married and beget children. For the son, the initiation ultimately grants him the right to marriage and inheritance. The son is the liberator of the father; he carries on his life work and takes care of him in illness, in old age, and after his death. Through the son, the father achieves immortality, as has been said since the epoch of the Vedic religion: "In your son you are reborn; that, o mortal, is your immortality."[143] This sentence is to be understood both experientially and ritually.

That is, the father passes on to the son not only his life and professional experience; he not only bequeaths his material property, he also bequeaths a sacral legacy: the duty to maintain the domestic fire and to provide for the ancestors. To study the Veda for the seer, to carry out the fire sacrifice for the gods, (to get married) and beget sons for the father—those are the three obligations the son has had from time immemorial,[144] right from birth, and which must be fulfilled. The married Twice-Born regularly has to make five major sacrifices: a fire sacrifice to the gods, self-study of the Veda, donation of food and water for the forefathers, hospitality toward people, and feeding (*bali*) all creatures, demigods, and spirits (*bhūta*).[145] Thus, birth inevitably means having obligations and being woven into a network of duties. In the Śatapatha-Brāhmaṇa, man is even born as "obligation" (*ṛṇa*).[146]

The domestic fire is part of the Vedic sacrificial fire, which was considered extraordinarily effective as early as the second epoch, for the gods were fed through the fire. Only the Brahmanic priests knew how to stack the fire and knew its salvational efficacy. This knowledge was the Veda. The priests identified themselves with the knowledge. They not only had the knowledge, they were the knowledge, they embodied it. This may have been the most momentous identification in the history of the Hindu religions. Thus, when the father died, he did not pass on the knowledge to his son, but rather put him in his place, and thus, deindividualized, he lived on in him. His legacy—in the Śatapatha-Brāhmaṇa was: "You are *brahman,* you are the sacrifice (*yajña*), you are the sphere to live (*loka*)!"[147] The son repeats these sentences and thus makes them irreversibly effective. "He who has no son, has no sphere to live."[148]

From about the middle of the second ("Vedic") epoch, sacral fatherhood was passed on by repeating the legacy; or better, the father was ritually replaced by the son: "The father is the same as the son, and the son is the same as the father."[149] In the sacral sense, then, he was no longer the father of the family, and he could, for example, become an ascetic. "If the father recovers his health, he should live under the authority of his son"[150] or he should wander (as a mendicant), says one of the Upaniṣads.[151] But the father hadn't died: In the ritual-sacral sense, he could not die because he was replaced. The immortality of the Veda could not be endangered by biological death. Thus, the sacral father could also be younger than the son.[152]

In the second epoch, these injunctions applied to Brahmans, whose name expresses the personification of the *brahman,* which is also the abbreviated Veda. Only the Brahmans could receive the knowledge, the Veda, from the seers of prehistoric times. These seers were considered the original ancestors of those clans (*gotra*), who had heard the secret knowledge of deliverance from the gods. Another name for this knowledge is *śruti* ("the heard"). What is crucial is that the knowledge of deliverance is passed on from generation to generation, from father to son, by replacing the biological father-son sequence with a ritual father-son identification.

Thus the hereditary class became the prerequisite and also the obstacle to achieving deliverance. In an early Upaniṣad, the teacher asks the student about his *gotra,* before he shares his knowledge with him (this is also one of the first proofs for this institution as a kinship group).[153] But because the ritual birth was more important than natural birth for receiving the knowledge, descent could also be substituted. This is why the teacher can wind the Sacred Thread on the son as a student, even if the son is not from the suitable class. Applying the Identificatory Habitus to genealogy in this way produces serious consequences, particularly in two areas: asceticism and the kinship system.

Since the father-son identification was not linked to natural fatherhood, deliverance could also be realized in oneself: as a self-sacrifice. Criticism of asceticism is increasingly expressed as fear of losing the son, which would endanger the continuation of the paternal line.[154] Note further that the three obligations to the seers, forefathers, and gods apply only to the firstborn son. *Manu* says of him that he was born because of the Dharma (*dharmaja*);[155] the other sons, on the other hand, are born out of lust (*kāmaja*). Only when the firstborn son died did they take over his duties. They were bound to the sacrificial ritual of the father-son identification, particularly to the ritual of remembrance (*śrāddha*), only in case of emergency and therefore they had greater religious freedom. That may be the reason for the various forms of Hindu religiosity.

The Karma doctrine, which appeared from the third ("Ascetic") epoch on and became widespread during the fourth epoch, also influenced the ritual father-son substitution.[156] The idea of the father living on in the son—"A son, the wise say, is the man himself born from himself," says Śakuntalā in the Mahābhārata[157]—is supplemented and partially replaced by the idea of an individual soul, whose continuation is influenced by its own acts, by Karma.

The effects of this on the kinship system (see below) mainly concern the possibility of replacing descent and fatherhood. If the knowledge of deliverance had remained limited to the Brahmans, there would have been a lack of clients for the profession of hereditary priesthood from the second ("Vedic") epoch on. Thus, on the one hand, the knowledge had to be able to be transmitted. This was done by the Brahmanic priests ritually transmitting their fictional ancestors to the members of other classes. Thus, the other two upper classes, the aristocracy and the warriors (Kṣatriyas), as well as the merchant class and the common people (Vaiśyas), could be consecrated as "Brahmans" and learn the Veda. On the other hand, the genealogical construction of the knowledge of deliverance was not given up. Therefore, the Brahmans reserved the right to teach the Veda. Only Brahmans could be teachers (*ācārya*). Being an Ācārya was no longer an expression of knowledge and dignity, as in early Vedic times, but had become hereditary. The privileged position of the Brahmans was legitimated only by this hereditary right to knowledge. At the same time, kinship was basically no longer a prerequisite for deliverance.

The emphasis on descent and its ritual substitution appears not only in asceticism, but also in marriage: With the possibility of transferring descent, women who came from other kinship groups could be integrated into this strict linear system without endangering the exclusivity of the knowledge of deliverance. As the teacher is a "father" to the student, so for the wife, the husband becomes her "father." For deliverance and immortality are possible only through the (fore)fathers; hence descent. Typical of these connections is that the teacher recites to the student in the rite of consecration almost the same words the bridegroom recites to the bride: "To me alone thou shalt adhere. In me thy thoughts shall dwell. Upon me thy veneration shall be bent. When I speak, thou shalt be silent."[158]

WEDDING AND MATRIMONY[159]

At a wedding, the perspective of the West tends to focus on the bridal couple. But in a traditional marriage, man and wife do not come together simply to establish a family; descent groups also come together, who try to preserve their purity and dignity; economic units change, for one family loses an able-bodied member (and a mouth to feed), the other gets one; and "strangers" become relatives, who forge a new bond of solidarity and mutual aid. Thus, marriage also has to do with the distribution of goods, labor rights, and duties or privileges. The other purposes of a marriage bond, including domesticity ("setting up a household"), legalizing sexuality, and producing progeny, are within this network of relations. Love in India—where it is a feeling expressed more conventionally than spontaneously[160]—is not the predominant motive for marriage. Romantic love may appear after the wedding, but can also emerge in a secondary marriage or in an extramarital relation. If a married couple feel that they love each other, they occasionally celebrate their wedding anniversary privately, by giving or granting each other something special: a trip, a watch, or just a visit to the movies.

If the development of the wedding as an institution is traced from the early European Middle Ages or from ancient Rome to today,[161] it becomes clear that a marriage bond does not always require the public expense of a wedding. Freer and more short-lived forms of unions sometimes fill the same purpose: "silent" or "blind weddings," concubinage, prostitution, adoption, or free marriages such as the Germanic "natural marriage" (*Friedelehe*), from which "kith" comes (see the idiom "kith and kin"). Only since the ninth century has marriage been considered God-given, as a mystery, a sacrament; only then did the idea of marriage as indissoluble or of marriage as an epiphany of the bond between Christ and the Church appear. Previously, there was often only the *benedictio,* the blessing of an already consummated marriage, including the already begotten children, *per matrimonium subsequens*—even today the legal formula for the legitimation of children born out of wedlock. Marriage was essentially a domestic act, it remained at that time "in the area of chamber and bed."[162] Divorces were possible for both sides. Christianity hardly assumed control of the wedding; it was more interested in asceticism, in priestly celibacy. Unmarried clerics were preferred to married lay people—a view that persists to this day in the Catholic Church. But the looser the marriage bond, the more uncertain were the relevant agreements. Religious marriage rituals considered equal to baptism, the Eucharist, and the ordination of priests can be dated only from the second Lateran Council (1139); and the marriage had to be concluded in the presence of a clergyman only since the Council of Trent

(1445–1463); but even today, marriage is the only sacrament that the bridal pair bestow upon themselves. Until the sixteenth century, the wedding mass took place outside the doors of the churches; only since the seventeenth century has there been a written record of it; and only since 1869 did civil marriage with government notification become necessary to forestall any potential obstacles to marriage. The principle of consent became accepted in time: The marriage vows became the marriage ceremony. Thus, at the latest, the relation between man and woman became the focus and the nuclear family was preferred to kindred and clan. With the Reformation came the reevaluation of marriage, but it also had an institutional character, linked with new moral views of the relations between the sexes. Not until the eighteenth century were love, sexuality, and marriage combined, and thus the cornerstone of the dissolution of marriage was also laid: If love is reduced or slips to the only basis for marriage, there is no necessity to maintain it, not even—with ultimate consistency—because of the children.

Premarital sexuality, progeny born out of wedlock, and the dissolubility of marital relations seem especially problematic and thus more in need of regulation the more the public is affected by it and the more alliances intervene in the network of economic and social relations. It then requires a consensus about the relationship and the legitimacy of offspring as heirs. Because of this, in contrast to the usual custom in Brahmanic-Sanskritic Hinduism, several parts of the ritual of the Hindu wedding are almost public: the wedding procession, the manner in which it is greeted at the edge of the village, the common meal, the loudspeaker announcement of the entering guests and their gifts. The wedding itself is a public act: a relation concluded before all eyes *ante portas.* Or vice versa: In the West, the significance of the bond of the couple through a wedding is diminished because the criterion of the publicity and control of relations has dropped off because marriage is no longer necessary to guarantee property, livelihood, and reproduction (the government is a substitute), because children and marriage no longer require one another, because the division of labor (domestic and professional work) has fallen off, because modern antiritualism against formalization turns away from high ideals of relations (fidelity, love). These days, people often get married only because of the children, that is, only when the relationship is no longer a private matter. Everything else—life insurance, inheritance, status reevaluation, motives of salvation—has become increasingly secondary for getting married.

In India, too, there still are freer forms of partnership which are not announced through a formal, public act like a wedding.[163] The (not quite so free) self-choice (*svayaṃvara*), in which the father invites a circle of candidates and the daughter places a garland of flowers on her chosen one as a sign of her desire to marry, is currently still practiced sometimes as a purely formal subrite in the official marriage ritual. The episode of "Nala and Damayantī" in the Mahābhārata is famous, but even there, the bride is given to the bridegroom by the father, after she has chosen him herself. In the legal texts, self-choice hardly appears. There are clues that in the fourth ("Classic") epoch, three forms of marriage were still practiced alongside one another: marriage with a dowry (Brahmanic), robbing the wife among Kṣatriyas, and buying the wife among common people. But the first form was carried out extensively, probably for status reasons. In a classical division, eight forms of getting married are distinguished from the beginning of the fourth epoch.[164]

Even *Manu* is unambiguous concerning the question of which of the forms of marriage listed in table 9 applies to which class, but leaves no doubt that only the first four are permitted for the Brahmans and the Brāhma form preserves the most religious merit. Typically, *Manu* justifies this with a genealogical point of view: A son of such a marriage wipes out the obligation of twenty-one previous and future generations. Only through sacrifice and Veda are marriages consecrated, only these preserve salvation. Other forms of marriage must be legitimated later by fire.[165] At the center of the wedding, then, is also the act of circling the domestic fire seven times.

The Wedding[166]

For Hindu women, there is no real initiation, only a few Brahmanic-Sanskritic childhood rites, but no celebration of the first menstrual period and no puberty rites.[167] The wedding is their initiation. This sumptuous fete is the most festive event in the life of a Hindu, celebrated with many guests in their best clothing and costly jewelry. No expense is spared to demonstrate the status of the host. I turn now to the wedding but will return subsequently to the relation between fictional and natural descent and its effects on the situation of the woman in marriage.

The woman is often married in her early youth.[168] Until the end of the nineteenth century, child marriages—originally a Brahmanic custom, but then adopted by other castes—were widespread and have not yet disappeared today. In 1860, the lowest marriage age for girls was set at ten, in 1891 at twelve, raised to fourteen in 1929. Today it is eighteen for the bride and twenty-one for the groom. Ritually, marriage cannot be dissolved.[169] Divorces are legally possible, but are seldom carried out. Separations occur, but are frowned upon and are possible for a woman only if she is taken back by her own family. The man can remarry, the woman only in certain subcastes. If the marriage is childless, the man can take another wife. There is isolated polygamy in the

Table 9
The Eight Classical Forms of Marriage

Name	*According to . . .*	*Type of Marriage*
Brāhma	the god Brahmā	The daughter is given as a gift to a worthy scholar of Veda of good character.
Daiva	the gods	Like Brāhma, but the father of the bride is a sacrifice priest.
Ārṣa	the seer (*ṛṣi*)	Like Brāhma, but the father of the bride receives a bull and a cow.
Prājāpatya	the Prajāpati, the "lord of creation"	Like Brāhma, but the proposal of marriage comes from the bridegroom.
Āsura	demonic nature (*asura*)	A purchased marriage, purchase of a wife, condemned by the legal texts because of the bride price (*śulka*).
Gāndharva	the Gandharva demons or the Gandharva tribe in the Himalayas	Marriage for love without parental consent, in which man and woman join together out of mutual passion; practiced in Kṣatriya circles; today popular in films.
Rākṣasa	"devil marriage"	Robbery marriage, is practiced infrequently, recommended by *Manu* (3.24) for the warrior nobility.
Paiśāca	a death demon (*piśāca*)	Rape, sleeping with an unconscious or inebriated woman.

south and in the Himalayas. The secondary marriage is often not publicly acknowledged, resulting in problems for the children of such marriages. Thus, the patrilinear "stress" on descent resides in the first marriage; in the other forms of marriage, there is a greater flexibility in the choice of partner and in the issue of remarriage.[170]

Marriage is arranged. Love matches are not frequent. Bride and bridegroom are chosen by the fathers and presented to the marriage partners, who can meet a few times, mostly under the supervision of relatives, and thus get to know each other. Marriage has always been a compulsory and occasionally an emergency association; it is also a sacrifice association.[171] The initiative for the marriage arrangement usually comes from the bride's side. The criteria for a good choice have been established since the third ("Ascetic") epoch[172] according to rules of kinship and caste, clan and village exogamy, and subcaste endogamy (see below), according to age, education, character, health, beauty, skin color, and especially important, the stars: No marriage would be concluded without consulting them previously; the written horoscope is examined in a matching ceremony. Advertisements for marriage partners in newspapers include details about caste, skin color, education, and astrological signs.

There are many wedding customs and they are full of regional variations. The marriage is a combination of rites of separation, affiliation, fertility, and protection. In table 10, I have summarized the course of a wedding in Rajasthan and supplemented the account with other sources.[173] The wedding was based on a Brahmanic manual,[174] but, as usual, it includes many popular religious and local elements. Common to all forms of weddings are: the giving of the bride (as *dāna*, "gift"), the grasping of hands (*pāṇigrahaṇa*, or *dextarium iunctio*) or presenting of rings, Vedic sayings, walking around the fire, seven (common) steps (*saptapadī*), and going home (*vivāha*, the current expression for the whole wedding).

The Daughter as Gift[175]

"Daughter, son-in-law, and their children, these three are not part of the family," says a northern Indian proverb. The daughter is considered one's own (Hindī *apnī*), but also from the beginning as the other (*dūsrī*), as one who is to be given away. She is married off to another family, if possible a family with higher status or standing. She moves into her husband's house and acquires his family and subcaste name; among Twice-Born men, she often acquires his fictional ancestors. In a series of rituals, the daughter is given by her own kinship group to another one. In most parts of India, marriage is thus patrilinear and patrifocal. The exchange of gifts between the marriage parties begins

TABLE 10
Course of a Hindu Wedding

Months Before
1. Preparations
Selection of the bridegroom according to the local rules of clan and village exogamy as well as subcaste endogamy and other criteria (*guṇaparīkṣā*).
Determination of the marriage age, time of the wedding, dowry, etc.; "matching ceremony": examination of the horoscope (*patrikā*).
Selection of ritual specialists (priest, potter, barber, musicians, cooks, etc.).
Inviting the wedding guests.
Weeks or Days Before
*2. Betrothal (*vāgdāna*) in the bridegroom's house*
One year to a few days before the wedding: The father of the bride gives a formal promise of marriage (Hindī *roka*).
Handing over of a ring to the bridegroom.
Exchange of gifts (clothing, fruit) or the dowry (bed, money, household implements, electronic equipment, etc.).
The father of the bride presses a forehead mark (*tilak*) on the bridegroom.
A Few Days Before (in some cases on the wedding day)
*3. Pre-Rites (*pūrvāṅga*) sometimes in the house of the bride and bridegroom*
Worship of ancestors, spirits, and gods in both houses.
Horoscope (*lagnapatrikā*): determination of auspicious times for the wedding ritual in the house of the bride, ceremonial handing over of this note to the bridegroom in his house.
Bringing of earth (*mṛdāharaṇa*): Mothers of both families fetch earth and clay, escorted by the wife of the barber.
Embellishing hands (H. *mehaṃdī*): The hands of the bride are rubbed with henna and ornamented in the presence of relatives.
Worship of Gaṇeśa (*Gaṇapatipūjana*): installation and worship of Gaṇeśa in both houses.
Banquet (H. *bindaurā*): In both houses, the relatives are fed.
Gifts (H. *pasīh bharnā*): Guests fill both hands of the bride or bridegroom with coconuts and other gifts.
Oil rubbing (H. *tel caṛhānā*): Worship of the goddess Śītalā, for three, five, or seven days; bride and bridegroom are rubbed with oil mixed with earth and grains. After that, annulment of the wedding is no longer possible.

Table 10
Course of a Hindu Wedding (Continued)

Arm ring (H. *kaṃganā*): A band with a conch, a ring, and iron is bound around the bridegroom.

Fetching pots (H. *bāsan*): The mothers and other women fetch clay pots from the potter.

Main Day

4. Preparations in the bride's house

Preparing the site of the wedding (*maṇḍapa*): A canopy and platform are set up in the bride's house.

Piling a fireplace (*vedi*) under the canopy of the bride's house.

*5. Wedding procession (*vadhūgṛhagamana*)*

Worship of the ancestors and domestic gods in both houses.

Solemn reception of the relatives of the mother of the bride (H. *moṣāḷā*): The mother's brother worships and feeds his sister and her relatives under the canopy.

Departure (H. *nikāsī*): The bridegroom's oil is washed off (H. *tel utārnā*); he bathes, is honored, is clad in new garments, and often is covered with a veil. The bridegroom's party proceeds with music and vehicles (wedding coach or auto; never on foot!) to the temple, then to the bride's house; the bridegroom often rides a mare for the last part.

*6. Reception of the procession (*madhuparka*)*

Greeting of the wedding procession at the edge of the village and mutual reverence shown by applying forehead marks.

Small gifts for the bridegroom's group, escort to the prepared guest accommodation (H. *barāt*).

Honoring the bridegroom: The father of the bride gives him (and his male relatives) a forehead mark, washes his feet, and gives him clothing, coconuts, money, and other gifts.

Conveying the horoscope (*lagnapatrikā*) from the bridegroom's father to the bride's father, opening by the priest.

Washing of the oil off the bride, donning of the wedding garments and the jewelry.

*7. Wedding (*vivāha*)*

The wedding procession moves to the area of the bride's house.

Reception under an arch (*toraṇa*), exchange of garlands, giving of a water jug, escort to the ritual place: The bridegroom sits down on the platform.

Honoring the bridegroom by the bride's parents.

(continued)

Table 10

Course of a Hindu Wedding (Continued)

The bride is led in, takes a seat on the right side of the bridegroom.

Giving of the bride (*kanyādāna*) at the astrologically auspicious moment: Formal decision (*saṃkalpa*) by the bride's father; he places his daughter's right hand in the bridegroom's right hand, assisted by the priest (*pāṇigrahaṇa*).

A cloth or band is bound around the bridegroom and the bride.

Lighting (*caturthīkarma*) their own new domestic fire (H. *bhaṃvar, pherā;* Skr. *agnipradakṣiṇā* or *pariṇayana*) and walking around it seven times while reciting Vedic sayings (*mantra*).

Seven Steps (*saptapadī*): The bridegroom leads the bride seven steps to the north on piles of rice: The marriage is complete.

Consecration (*abhiṣeka*) of the bride with water by the priest, honoring and giving gifts to her, first by her maternal uncle (*māmā*), honoring the bridal couple by the bride's parents with foot-washing.

Appeal to the stars as witnesses (*saptarṣimaṇḍala*).

Rites of dispersal: parting from the gods, payment of sacrificial fee to the priests, dispersal of the ritual place.

Splendid and sumptuous banquet; common meal of the bridal couple at which the wife eats from her husband's plate.

Return of the bridal couple to their accommodations (*barāt*).

Following Days

---

8. Rites of consolidation

Breakfast for the son-in-law in the bride's house.

Ritual teasing of the son-in-law by the bride's siblings, play between husband and wife.

Changing seats (H. *pher-pāṭṭā*): Escorting the wife to the left side of the husband by the maternal uncle.

Circumambulation of a bed (H. *pālkācār*): Walking around the bed seven times on the ritual place by bride and bridegroom.

9. Parting (H. vidā*)*

Ritual parting of the bridegroom's party on the day after the wedding.

Ritual smashing of a coconut: At the temple on the way back, the man must smash a coconut with one blow.

Table 10
Course of a Hindu Wedding (Continued)

10. Rites in the husband's house
Three-day stay of the wife in the husband's house while observing various vows (*trirātravrata*), e.g., a vigil and the chastity of man and wife.
Lighting the domestic fire (*caturthīkarma*): see above, no. 7.
Viewing the wife (H. *muṃh dikhāī, vadhūdarśana*): Women look at the face of the wife, which was previously veiled, and honor her with gifts.
Ceremonial return of the wife, usually escorted by the brother, to her parents' house.

at the betrothal and continues after the wedding. The bride's side has to provide a bigger share than the groom's, and demands for gifts can also continue after the wedding. The dowry is negotiated. A modern manual written for the Indian middle class recommends the following gifts for a wedding in the Punjab: sweets and fresh fruit or canned fruit for the family of the bridegroom; cash ("501 to 11,001 or more Rupees"), clothing, gold chains, and wristwatches for the bridegroom; a sari, a gold chain, and earrings for the mother-in-law of the bride; a sari and a gold chain for the sister-in-law; clothing and cash for the father-in-law, brother-in-law, and sisters-in-law, as well as their children; cash for all close relatives of the bridegroom (particularly paternal and maternal uncles); video recorders, air conditioners, and refrigerators for the family of the bridegroom.[176] Lavish weddings can still be read about. In 1995, the prime minister of Tamil Nadu, J. Jayalalitha, distributed more than ten million U.S. dollars for her stepson's (!) wedding, which was attended by two hundred thousand guests served by six thousand cooks. In the wealthy strata of Indian cities today, weddings are produced like film scenes with much glamour and electronic glitter. All legal attempts to stem the giving and taking of dowries have so far been unsuccessful. Whether the dowry represents an auspicious inheritance (*strīdhana*) is controversial, even in the family: There are constant debates over whether the wedding jewelry belongs to the wife or to the husband.

Even if the demanded gifts can strain the means and possibly ruin the family of the bride, they imply more than enrichment. The gifts are to be propitious, bring the bridal couple blessing, and allow a good, fertile marriage. Fruits, coconuts, dried dates, nuts, gold (and money), bracelets, but also a forehead mark (*tilak*) from the father of the bride to the bridegroom, are to strengthen the bridal couple. For the same reason, the bride, and in some cases the bridegroom, too, are oiled, rubbed with earth and henna, washed, adorned, crowned with garlands, and dressed expensively. This is almost a necessary part of every ritual, whether initiation or coronation.

What is remarkable and especially typical for northern India is the inequality in the exchange of gifts at the wedding celebrations. For all intents and purposes, only the bride's side gives gifts. In many regions, it is even explicitly forbidden for the bridegroom's party to give anything in return. And the father of the bride occasionally may not even eat cooked food in the bridegroom's house because that evokes the suspicion of an exchange or payment.[177] Ever since the fourth ("Classic") epoch, the bride herself is considered such a gift if the father gives her in a definite ritual segment (*kanyādāna,* gift of a "virgin" or "daughter") to her future husband. In the ritual sense, he "sacrifices" his daughter for religious merit,[178] for in return he obtains the "blessing" of the higher extended family. Representing his extended family, he also obtains standing and prestige. If the father does not give the daughter away as a virgin, disaster threatens: The daughter is impure or casteless (*śūdrā, vṛṣī*). The institution of child marriage arose out of anxiety about not marrying off the daughter before her first menstrual period, and the fear of impurity and loss of standing for the whole family. The early promise of marriage given long before the wedding, and in terms of ritual, almost as solid as marriage, probably occurred for the same reason.

That this "lopsided" exchange of gifts came about at the latest from the fourth epoch on has to do with the hierarchic structure of the gift, which I will discuss more precisely in chapter 4. But here I shall say only that, unlike gifts among equals or in the act of exchange, the religious gift (*dāna*) does not obligate a material gift in return. A gift produces religious merit for the giver only if it is given without expectation of a gift in return. What he then obtains is an invisible merit, unlike the profit or gain in secular gifts.[179] To avoid the appearance of a secular purchase, *Manu* stipulates that no bride price may be accepted; otherwise, it would be prostitution.[180] Thus the hierarchy of the gift is established from the outset. The giver has a lower status than the receiver. This applies both to the one who gives a woman and the one who takes her.

The one who gives a woman has a lower status because, in sacral terms, the woman forms a "breach" in the (partrilinear) line of descent. She is integrated into the fictional descent of the husband as a stranger. Thus, a problem similar to adoption arises,[181] and in fact, both rituals are alike. This is quite clear in the determinations of descent in marriage negotiations.

Kinship, Alliance, and Descent

According to Brahmanic ritualistic ideas, marriage is essentially a control of reproduction. It is considered "abortion" if one does not have sexual relations with one's wife when she is most likely to conceive or when the wife prevents sexual intercourse. A woman may even leave a man if he is impotent because her definition as a "field" (*kṣetra*) of propagation is not fulfilled.[182]

Marriage has always had to be with one's peers in the social hierarchy above and below as well as inside and outside specific social groups and neighborhoods to which each marriage partner belongs. The Brahmanic marriage system is isogamous, endogamous, exogamous, and hypergamous at the same time: The class (*varṇa*) is isogamous; class, caste, and subcaste are endogamous; extended family and clan are exogamous; the extended family is hypergamous. Isogamy and endogamy were (and perhaps still are) the most important. One should marry within one's class and subcaste.[183] Within the classes, there are no hierarchies: No Brahman or Kṣatriya is higher or lower than another Brahman or Kṣatriya solely because of his class. And the obligation to marry outside one's kinship group, extended family, and village still enforces no hierarchy in the choice of a partner. It is from the third ("Ascetic") to the fourth ("Classic") epoch that hierarchy comes into play through the various forms of marriage:[184] the hierarchical structure of the gifts (*dāna*) and the conception of the marriage as such a gift (*kanyādāna*) reinforce the hypergamous structures in the marriage system.[185] Thus, a higher and purer status is ascribed to the one who takes the woman than to the one who gives the woman.

The choice of male and female candidates for marriage is, therefore, a difficult business, primarily because the boundaries of kinship are not firm. Kinship is a human concept, not a natural law that commands or forbids the intermingling of blood or human classes. Because humans create their own rules for it, those rules can be changed. Thus, every marriage is an opportunity to clarify who belongs to one's kinship group, from whom one may expect (unpaid) help, whom one considers one's peers. Uncertainty about belonging to other kinship often exists, too. The caste name or the place of residence is not much help either. These questions are discussed, at the latest, when the list of wedding guests is drawn up.

Social status is not absolutely firm either, but is ascribed and thus is always relational. The parties to the marriage must reach a consensus over its definition. This also applies to kinship boundaries, hence ultimately for the question of when a marriage is considered incestuous. Even if the hierarchical relations are acknowledged by everyone in the same way, a logical problem would arise between the one who takes a woman and the one who gives her: Those who claim the highest status would find no one to take a woman and those at the bottom find no one to give a woman. In fact, in certain castes, this problem has led to killing female babies right after birth,[186] so as not to lose the claim to the highest status. But such incidents are the exception, since every high or low subcaste still considers others as higher or lower and thus excluded or accepted as candidates for marriage.

Moreover, since the fourth ("Classic") epoch (beginning even earlier, according to some estimates),[187] two systems of kinship have been coordinated, which weaken overly rigid criteria of hierarchy: The genealogical, fictional Gotra system and the blood kinship Sāpiṇḍya system of acknowledged kinship relations.[188] The introduction of these regulations is coterminous with other drastic changes affecting the women in the upper classes: child marriage, the ban on remarriage, the exclusion from sacrifice and the right of inheritance, as well as an increase of widow-burning. The fourth epoch was shaped by the formation of states and kingdoms with hierarchical power structures and a commensurate measure of subordination. Family changes reflect this situation. As the king is the leader of the community, so the paterfamilias presides over the extended family.

Gotras were originally sacrificial communities in which blood kinship was not obligatory. Because of the obligation to appeal to the head of the clan during the sacrifice, the male members of a Gotra were more or less compelled to preserve not only the names of the forefathers, but also a group identity that favored the formation of an exclusive clan system. From the end of the second epoch, Gotras are patrilinear clans or tribes, who call on a common ancient ancestor, one of seven or eight seers (*ṛṣi*), and draw their names from him: e.g., Jamadagni, Gautama, Bharadvāja, Atri, Viśvāmitra, Kaśyapa, and Vasiṣṭha, as well as Agastya.[189] According to this fictional kinship system, a man and woman may not marry if the same ancient ancestor appears in their paternal lines. So if someone is of the Vāsiṣṭhagotra, belonging to the line of descent of the seer Vasiṣṭha, he cannot marry a woman whose father also has this fictional descent. In reality, there are not only seven Gotras, but hundreds of exogamous units, which are also subdivided, according to Vedic schools (*śākhā*), the Veda collections (*saṃhitā*), or even totemic criteria[190]—but what is crucial is that even in these exogamous patrilinear ranks of ancestors, called *gaṇa* ("band, clan") or *pravara* (line of ancestors), the name of a legendary progenitor occurs. With the Dharmaśāstra texts, thus until the third or fourth century A.D., Gotra exogamy was widely accepted; from the fifth ("Sectarian") epoch on, it is nearly obligatory.[191] The Gotra or Pravara system was legally banned according to the Hindu Marriage and Divorce Act of 1955, but still prevails in the Brahmanic-Sanskritic classes. What is usually emphasized here is the modified Four-Gotra Rule, which forbids marriage if two of the eight Gotras of the partners overlap, that is, one's own paternal line overlaps that of the mother and both grandmothers.

According to Brahmanic legal literature, violations against the Gotra system and marriages between classes had serious consequences:[192] a man became casteless and so did his progeny, he destroyed the heavenly living space of the ancestors, was despised, and was threatened with hell. Despite all problems, despite all new legal bans, this exogamous marriage system has been preserved to this day, primarily in northern India. Whole castes earn their living by maintaining and recording genealogies (*vaṃśāvalī*). Non-Brahman Twice-Born men acquire such an ancestor, usually that of the house priest, and thus obtain access to the Veda. For belonging to a Gotra is indispensable for performing the Vedic-Brahmanic sacrifice. Only then is the identificatory link to the Veda revelation guaranteed. In non-Brahmanic circles, too, the Gotra system is thus imitated in order to participate in its high goal of salvation.

The Gotra system is strictly patrilinear: At birth, a woman acquires the Gotra of her father; when she marries, occasionally even at the betrothal,[193] she receives the Gotra of her huband. In parts of northern India, the married daughter is no longer considered a blood relative.[194] Gloria Goodwin Raheja reports that, for the inhabitants of the village she studied, married women lose their "physical" relationship (Hindī *śarīr kā saṃbandh*) after marriage and subsequently have only an indirect (kinship) relation (*rista*) to their own families.[195] The woman thus loses her "ancient ancestors" or those of her father. When she dies, her husband's relatives perform the death rites; if her own parents die, she must not include them in the ancestor worship. The ideas of blood kinship deviate considerably from Western views, for in India, it is generally assumed that blood is inherited only through the father, but is not intermingled.[196] And, as we have seen, because of norms of purity, intermingling is to be avoided. The extended families, therefore, attempt to generate themselves and keep foreign influence as minimal as possible.[197] In alliances, intermingling is certainly unavoidable. It is ritually circumvented by declaring the new part of the relationship as one's own and denying the "foreignness" as much as possible.

Traditionally, the blood relationship Sāpiṇḍya rule excludes marriage bonds in direct ascending and descending lines in the paternal line to the seventh generation and in the maternal line to the fifth generation. *Piṇḍa* denotes rice balls, which are central in the death ritual and are a sign of kinship proximity. Thus, relatives in a Sāpiṇḍya relation are to fast or be ritually purified in case of death or birth. But this Sāpiṇḍya rule is usually practiced only until the third generation on both maternal and paternal sides.[198]

Consequently, a Gotra is an exclusive (fictional) criterion of kinship, for Gotras cannot and may not overlap in a marriage made according to these rules. On the other hand, the individual can be part of several Sāpiṇḍya relations, including one that incorporates the maternal kinship line. Belonging to the Gotra is relatively unambiguous, even if it cannot be named by everyone. In cases of doubt, consulting the household priest or a glance in the personal birth horoscope helps. Moreover, along with the Sacred Thread, Gotra affiliation is a sign that one belongs to the group of the Twice-Born. On the other hand, the Sāpiṇḍya system is more open and variable. The boundaries of kinship or who is suitable as a marriage partner must always be discussed. Here there is a much greater uncertainty about what should be done. The elders in the village, genealogists, and often even barbers must be consulted.

Through the Gotra system, extended families form a common, pan-Indian social group, even though the members often do not know one another, hardly have anything to do with one another, and often live far away from one another. What is noteworthy is that the Gotra system continues to exist even when everything in the Hindu religions changes or is unsteady. The norms of purity and hierarchy deviate so much from one another that they exist only as strategies of delineating extended families. But the criterion of patrilinear descent of the Gotra system remains—at least among the Twice-Born—and even resists modern influences. An Untouchable may become a minister or a film star, he can achieve wealth, influence, and respect; but in the village it will still be hard for him to marry off his daughter to a traditional-minded Brahman or Kṣatriya. He lacks a Gotra, the ritual identification with the Vedic seers and thus the soteriologically crucial identification with the Veda.

Why do two families let their son and daughter marry if neither emotional nor economic reasons are decisive? When neither of the two decides this him- or herself and the families have nothing directly to do with one another? There appears to be only one conclusive answer: The pure patrilinear descent is the surviving, integrative principle of Brahmanic Hindu society, because only thus is the Brahmanic path to salvation substantially opened. Marriage endangers this strictly patrilinear path to salvation; it can be integrated only by ritually denying the matrilinear aspects.

The Situation of the Woman[199]

What effect does the patrilinear and patrifocal dominance have on the condition of the woman in marriage? As soon as the woman leaves her parents' house when she gets married, it becomes apparent that the new life will be quite different. The beginning of marriage is often described as a pure tragedy for women, but their situation also has other, less dramatic sides, as new studies and field studies show. Women in India are often inconspicuous, surrounded by silence. Often, in scholarly literature or in journalism, they are noticed only when there is something spectacular: a virgin who is worshipped as a goddess; a maiden who is married off in childhood; a widow who allows herself to be or is immolated. But this exotic perspective too easily loses sight of the fact that it is precisely women in India who uphold traditions, not as architects of historically significant temples, and seldom as authors or artists, but in their everyday practices, their religious life, their language, their songs,[200] and their lifestyle,[201] which is formative of the cultural habitus.

At the ritual parting of the daughter from her parents' house, songs are often sung which refer to the crucial change. Thus, one refrain is: "Dear girl, today you've left your father's house, today you've become 'other' (*parayi*). The streets in which you spent your childhood have today become *parayi*."[202] In fact, not only has her own parents' house become foreign, but the new one is not yet familiar. In her new family, the woman is initially considered an outsider and has to adapt to adult family structures. In the kitchen and household, she is ruled by her mother-in-law, who ostentatiously wears the key ring on her sari as a sign of her domestic power—with the keys to the storeroom, the safe, and the chambers of the heads of the family. Often, the daughter-in-law has to do the unpleasant work in the house or field: mow grass, fetch water or wood, collect cow dung and mix it with straw to make cowpats. She is expected to obey her mother-in-law, help her, rub her with oil and massage her, and comb her hair.

The young wife usually endeavors to do everything right; she strives for recognition and affection, for she has learned to be obedient and her everyday life now is no different from her previous life. She knows that she is now responsible for the welfare (*saubhāgya*) of her husband and the family. She goes to the temple, she fasts, she worships the gods in the house on behalf of her husband, she makes sure that their life is blessed and protected. Up to a certain rank, the husband is even dependent on her to behave like that, which gives her some feeling that she is needed. She also knows that things will be better for her as she grows older and as soon as she bears a son. Someday, she will be in charge of the house. She also knows that tensions and conflicts are part of family life, and even make up its harmony. At any rate, there is no alternative, for without family ties, the woman in India can hardly survive. Too clearly before her eyes are the nightmares of women widowed young or repudiated, who eke out a living as day laborers, beggars, or prostitutes. She lives with the other women in her own neighborhood, where she acquires her own prestige. At first she may encounter skepticism and distrust, and she may be suspected if misfortune befalls the husband or if something in the household is missing, and she may be mocked for the amount of her dowry; but in time, this sneering and abuse subsides.

(a)

2. (a) Wedding of Ishwor Joshi and Sahan sila Maskey in Bhaktapur, Nepal: For the bride, marriage also means the pain of parting; she is held by a sister-in-law. Photographer: N. Gutschow, 1994.

In the early years, she can hardly count on her husband, even though, as the Dharma texts say, she is to worship him as a god. They don't know each other; they ignore one another but try cautiously to get close to one another. In recent times, the honeymoon has been adopted by well-to-do families. The husband is usually still young, inexperienced, and uncertain, and may not show his feelings for his wife in the presence of his parents and elders. If they are lucky, the couple live in their own badly sound-proofed room and are usually in the company of others. They do not talk much with one another, do not eat together, hardly go out together, do not travel together. But even though the young wife may feel lonely, may yearn for her own relatives, she usually does not have the feeling of being treated unjustly. Only in recent years has this view changed, particularly among the urban middle class.

In public, the wife walks behind the husband, carries his things, covers her face with the sari, not only to avert looks but also to attract them. She behaves modestly, timidly, and bashfully, but also gracefully and occasionally even becomes playful. Even as a maiden, she was taught to be withdrawn and not to be loud, not to speak with male relatives or strangers, not to make violent

(b)

2. (continued) (b) Mock wedding (*ihi*) in Bhaktapur, Nepal: two girls who are married to the *bel* fruit, which represents the god Viṣṇu. Photographer: A. Michaels, 1983–1984.

movements, not to gesticulate, not to walk too fast. The decent body language of Indian women is in stark contrast to Western manners. Timidity and shyness are considered signs of good character, propriety, and contentment.[203] Publicly, the wife represses any manifestation of sexual desire, which would be considered detrimental to an old ideal of fidelity,[204] as embodied (for men) by Sītā, the wife of the god Rāma,[205] who courageously resisted all lascivious advances of the demon Rāvaṇa. And to a large extent the wife is seen as the property of the husband. Even the illegitimate children he himself did not beget "belong" to him, like the fruit of his field.[206]

In any case, this ideal of a wife often applies only to public behavior. Alongside it is another image of a wife that violates the myth of the patient Asian wife. For example, the Indian saying, "A wife who is modest and shy will always be hungry," challenges an obsequious attitude. And if women are asked today if Sītā is their ideal, they may often deny it laughingly, even if strangers or men are present.[207] In women's songs and sayings, there is self-conscious, provocative, and occasionally frivolous language.

Yet the situation of the married woman is still a subject of complaint, not only from a Western perspective, but also from that of Indian women themselves. Indeed, the facts indicate a striking discrimination against the female sex. "Those who have sons walk free from sorrow"—this saying of the Aitareya brāhmaṇa can still be heard.[208] "Drums are played upon the birth of a boy, but at my birth only a brass plate is beaten," says a north Indian folk song.[209] Discrimination against the woman begins with the currently common amniocentesis, which tells the sex of the fetus before birth. Ultrasound clinics and laboratories are accessible almost everywhere, advertising brazenly with slogans such as "Better 500 Rupees today than 500,000 tomorrow [for the dowry]." The methods have changed, but even today, there are attempts to influence the sex of the fetus and to prevent the birth of a girl. This is done with prayers and rites, as literally in the Puṃsavana (see table 5): "To produce a son," combinations of herbs and nutritional adjustments are employed,[210] and procreation is to take place according to astrological criteria, when the moon is in a male constellation.[211] Modern methods are more "effective," and their results can be proven statistically. In 1901, for every thousand males, there were 963 females; in 1991, it was only 927. And there are great regional variations: In the states of Punjab, Haryana, Rajasthan, and Uttar Pradesh, the portion of women is under 850; on the other hand, Kerala has a female surplus of 1040, which is probably due to the better educational system there and the system of matrilinear kinship. Moral reservations about this practice are found mainly in the upper middle class and among intellectuals. Moreover, large-scale, official abortion campaigns and politically organized family planning advertise on walls with sayings like "A small family is a happy family" (Hindī *choṭā parivār—sukhī parivār*).

Discrimination against women, especially among the lower classes,[212] appears in various ways: Sons are breastfed first. Girls are chronically underfed or malnourished more than boys. Girls are brought to the hospital less frequently and die more often than boys. Even murders of female babies are not rare, even though women are to be respected according to the Dharmaśāstras and may not receive the death penalty, unlike men.[213] Many women reach their maximum weight at the age of sixteen. During pregnancy they often gain only half as much weight as women in the West. Mortality from puerperal fever is high. Women have drastically fewer chances for education and attend school and university less. Women are raped, sexually molested, humiliated, and beaten. They are often exposed helplessly to the tyranny or alcoholism of their husbands. They must tolerate concubines and their children. During menstruation, they may not go to the temple, prepare food, or bathe in the river. They have to work more and are paid less. There are always sensations in the press about dowry murders, in which a wife is killed by her husband or his family because her dowry is too small, so that he can remarry and collect a new dowry. Usually the murder is concealed as an accident—a sari caught fire during cooking—or is declared a suicide. Often, the mother-in-law is either the perpetrator or an accomplice. The percentage of undetected crime is high; charges are seldom brought. Between 1979 and 1983, 2,273 cases of alleged or actual dowry murders were recorded; in only twelve cases were there convictions. But consciousness of a punishable offense is growing. In 1990, 4,836 official dowry murders were publicized.

In marriage, the young wife is initially isolated, confused, desperate, and homesick for her parents' house. All her life, she internalizes the conflict between her parents' house and her husband's house. The wedding can be a trauma for her.[214] This longing for her own parental family is often heard in songs, mixed with the disappointment that her parents have given her away too soon or at all, that the dowry was too small, that the husband is not the right one. In general, she may often return to her parents' house, sometimes she may even bear her first child there, but precisely because of that, she is suspected of not really belonging to the family she has married into. However, literature about the fate of women often has ironic undertones, and therefore—as Gloria Raheja says—particular attention must be paid to whether the plaintive songs are sung in her own or in the strange new family.[215]

In the Brahmanic-Sanskritic and patriarchal view, the woman is considered the alien element threatening the ideal of the cohesion of the autarchic, self-regulating extended family. She is needed for its survival, for the continuity of the paternal line, but is feared as a subversive force who urges her husband to break with his parents, to establish his own household, and not to fulfill his duties as son, brother, grandson. The ideal of the paternal line is its purity, which would best be preserved by celibacy. In fact, the high ideal of asceticism contrasts with the sexuality of the woman, which is felt as menacing. The widespread fear of nocturnal emissions among Indian men may also be an expression of this ambivalence: Semen is the means of propagation—even in a figurative sense, its healing force is conjured up in the talk of the seed (*bīja*) of knowledge concerning salvation—yet it should not go out of the man. Even the old highly honored seers, as countless myths tell, were dissuaded from asceticism and their spiritual goals by their wives, and thus the struggle between asceticism and sexuality is a recurring topos of Indian literature.

Indeed, the woman is not only a wife. She is also a daughter, a sister, and usually a mother. As the title of a book by the American anthropologist Lynn Bennett (1983) correctly implies, she is not only "a dangerous (or endangering) wife," but is also "a sacred sister." Bennett talks of a patrifocal (Brahmanic-Sanskritic) perspective, in which the woman is seen as a danger to the purity of the paternal line, but also of a filiafocal model, in which the daughter is in the foreground. From the beginning, daughters are to be given away, married off, but they can bring prestige to the father and protection to the brother. Here is the root of a special, often described brother-sister relationship in India, which is expressed in its own celebrations and protection rituals.[216] Husbands are indeed "higher" than their own fathers-in-law, but "lower" than the father-in-law of the sister, who is married off to a "higher" family. In a certain respect, as part of her new extended family, the sister is above her father and brothers. Thus, not only is the social discrimination against women to be noted, but also the question of why the married woman is treated in a way that does not correspond to the image of woman as experienced and learned. Part of the answer is in the high ideal of the purity of patrilinear descent—and its ambiguity. The woman is a danger to this ideal, but is also its only guarantee. So there is also a matrifocal perspective, on which patrilinear descent feeds and which leads to a high appreciation of the woman as mother.

According to Brahmanic-Sanskritic doctrine, on the one hand, women must compensate for their congenital impurity; on the other hand, in the minds of many men, women also constitute a special force and power, the dynamic part of the cosmos, life-giving energy. They are so much this (divine) force (*śakti*) that, as Indian men occasionally say, they don't need any ritual. They frequently call their wives "my government" or "my goddess." Because women have this Śakti, they can be deified healers, strong politicians such as Indira Gandhi, or brave gang leaders such as Phoolan Devi. Because of their Śakti, there is also a heroic women's religiosity. Women also care for the auspiciousness of the house as men do for the "purity" and prestige of the paternal line. Women practice divine worship, meet for devotional chanting in the temple, and preserve myths and legends by telling them to their children. Women especially often keep the vows (*vrata*) strictly—mainly fasts—primarily to safeguard the health of their spouse and children.

Thus, for the woman, marriage is not only a sacrifice. By entering the higher extended family, the daughter is also a source of prestige and dignity for her own parents. For ages,[217] the woman has been considered a necessary other half of the man (according to the legal texts, an unmarried man is incomplete); yet in terms of kinship, the patrilinear, patriarchal, and hierarchal structures do predominate. But that is the Brahmanic-Sanskritic view, which has dominated the analysis of marriage in India, and almost always leaves a misogynistic aftertaste.

The goddesses also reflect the various images of women:[218] in the marriage between Viṣṇu and his subordinate, obedient goddess Lakṣmī (or Śiva and Pārvatī, or Rāma and Sītā), who is always portrayed smaller in iconography; in the erotic, nearly equal love between Kṛṣṇa and Rādhā; as well as in the competing relation between Kālī and the visibly subordinate Śiva lying at her feet. In Brahmanic ritualistic religiosity, the first type of image predominates; in devotionalism, the second; and in heroism, the third. In popular religions, the strong female sides of the goddess myths are preferred: Pārvatī, Rādhā, or Sītā hardly receive the epithets Devī (goddess) or Mātā (divine mother), but rather Kālī or Durgā.[219] Certain goddesses are not merely the other half of the man, but have a force that cannot be controlled even by marriage.

The woman in India can hardly forsake the field of tension between humiliation and super-elevation. Tolerated as a daughter, loved as a sister (of the brother), feared as a spouse, worshipped as a mother (of a son)—that is the fate of many Indian women. But only from the patrifocal and male-centered perspective. The matrifocal perspective is perhaps much more positive: She is deified as a virgin, loved as a daughter and sister (of the brother), needed and respected as a wife, strengthened and venerated as a mother (of a son), and eventually honored as a grandmother.

DEATH AND LIFE AFTER DEATH[220]

When people die, they become ancestors, forefathers, heroes, ghosts, or demons, but not dead, not without "life." What they become depends on the manner of death, on the relationship between the deceased and the survivors, as well as on the kinship, temporal, and spatial distance to the deceased. But the dead do not "live" forever; their memory fades, they die through the *damnatio memoriae* of the living,[221] through a re-death in the next world.

Eschatologies, that is, doctrines of the end of things and of the next world, treat this relation between the living and the dead in a twofold way: On the one hand, heaven and hell form the counterworld to this one; on the other hand, they are a projection of the human mind, of human wishes and fears. Thus, the next world is always also in this one. One of the most controversial subjects in theology and religious studies concerns the question of how much eschatological notions influence action, how people in this world orient their actions according to hopes and fears of the next world, and thus how far such otherworldly counterworlds influence ethical and moral maxims and life "strategies of success." This is relevant for an analysis of society since notions of the next world generally reflect highly respected goals of the society. The latent threat of living the wrong life, paid for after death, affects socially virtuous behavior. The incentive to prove oneself in life thus continues to exist—in Max Weber's famous thesis—even if the belief that God will examine one's life after death lapses and one's life is not lived *in maiorem Dei gloriam,* but rather extremely selfishly.

In the following section, I concentrate on the Brahmanic death ritual (*antyeṣṭi*)—a ritual for and with the dead—ancestor worship (*śrāddha*), widow-burning (*satī*), rebirth, and the commandment not to injure living organisms (*ahiṃsā*), which is not a death ritual but a ban on killing. First I describe these rituals and try at the conclusion of this section to demonstrate the links between death rituals, conceptions of after death, and descent.

The Brahmanic Ritual of Dying and Death[222]

In table 11, I have summarized the most important events of the Brahmanic ritual of dying and death.[223] In Arnold van Gennep's terminology, it is a mixture of separation and aggregation rites, which can also be found in the death ceremonies of other cultures: For death which is threatening, there are *omina;* the dying person must accept death, must not resist, and must be ritually prepared; death is feared, its power, its return; often there is a special path of death for the corpse, almost a kind of secret path, so that the deceased cannot easily find his way back; the path of the dead after cremation is uncertain and dangerous; the deceased is dependent on the help and nourishment of the survivors; as in the Roman Catholic ritual of death, there are thus provisions for his journey, accompanied by prayers and blessings, laying out, and a kind of wake, anointing or embalming the corpse, a funeral procession, special clothing for the dead and for the survivors, a gathering for the dead, sprinkling the corpse with water, death knells, a death meal, and a period of mourning.

But the differences between the Brahmanic-Sanskritic death ritual and Christian blessings are also clear: The former entail no confession, no written obituaries (only recently have these appeared among the urban middle class), no charitable acts (donations to the needy), no funeral meals right after the burial, no dirges, and no ceremony like the Eucharist with a funeral sermon and a eulogy of the deceased. Generally, there is no grave, no memorial ritual, no votives. The deceased disappear from the field of vision as individual persons: No picture, no tombstone recalls them. And yet they are constantly

Table 11
Course of a Hindu Death Ritual

Days Preceding the Expected Death
1. Ceremonies of dying
The dying person is laid on the floor.
Ceremony of expiation of the father (is subsequently carried out by the son).
Drops of water are poured into the mouth of the dying person with Tulasī leaves.
An oil lamp is lit at the head of the dying person.
Relatives sing and pray.
A cow is given to a Brahman or others (this subritual sometimes takes place later).
Day of Death
2. Rites in and of the house
Laying the deceased out on the floor with the head toward the south.
Washing, anointing, wrapping the corpse in a shroud.
Sacrifice of six of the first sixteen dumplings (*piṇḍa*).
Circulation of the news of the death.
3. Death procession
Transporting the corpse to the cremation grounds: The corpse is carried out of the house feet first; the firstborn son leads the funeral procession, followed by the corpse and finally the relatives (*sapiṇḍa*); the lament is spread *Rām nām satya hai* ("Rāma's name is the truth").
At the cremation grounds, the feet of the corpse are placed in the Ganges.
Relighting of the domestic fire at the cremation grounds (the fire is brought from the house in a bowl).
4. Corpse burning
Ritual purification of the cremation grounds (*śmaśāna*).
The pyre is stacked by a special subcaste.
Laying out the corpse on the pyre.
Lighting the fire: at the head of a man, at the feet of a woman; the head mourner wears the Sacred Thread over the right shoulder instead of the left.
Cracking or smashing the skull of the corpse with a bamboo rod, which marks the ritual time of death: The soul leaves the body through the opening of the skull (*brahmarandhra*).
Fanning the wind, scattering sesame seeds, pouring water on the corpse (libation of water).

(continued)

Table 11
Course of a Hindu Death Ritual (Continued)

5. Rites at the cremation grounds
Bath of the head mourner.
Walking around the corpse.
Smashing an earthenware pot.
Stone worship with sesame water and dumplings (partially repeated on the following days).
Return home: without looking around, with purification rites at the threshold, chewing *nim* wood.
Rites on the First to the Thirteenth Day after the Death
6. Ritual purifications
Navaśrāddha: Worship of a grass doll on odd days.
Gathering of the bones (*asthisañcayana*), sometimes carried out right after the burning: The bones or ashes are scattered in the river and/or hung in a clay pot in a Śami tree.
*7. Restitution of the dead (*sapiṇḍīkaraṇa*)*
on the tenth (or eleventh) day:
The remaining ten of the first sixteen dumplings (*piṇḍa*) are sacrificed (*sapiṇḍikaraṇa*).
Sajjādāna: The cooking utensils, money, bed, and clothing of the deceased are given away to death priests, along with grain for a year.
Shaving and ritual bath of the head mourners.
Cow offering (*vṛṣotsarga*): (symbolic) release of a bull, touching a bull, a cow, or gold.
on the eleventh to the thirteenth day:
Ekoddiṣṭaśrāddha: presenting the second sixteen dumplings, invitation and feeding of Brahmans.
Sapiṇḍīkaraṇa (usually on the twelfth day): binding of the *preta* with the *pitaraḥ;* the third sixteen dumplings (*piṇḍa*) are composed.
Worship of Gaṇeśa.
New clothing for the head mourners.
Common meal with relatives and neighbors.

TABLE 11
Course of a Hindu Death Ritual (Continued)

Other Post-Death Rites
8. Memorial rites
Period of impurity (*aśauca*): graduated according to degree of kinship, age, sex, some fasting, sleeping on the floor, eating only during the day, eating no salt, and so on.
Monthly and yearly Śrāddhas: sesame and barley water, worship of dumplings as ancestors, praising and foot-washing of Brahmans.
(Impure) gifts for Brahmans.

present as forefathers and ancestors. It is these distinctions that deserve special interest because they explain why descent and ancestor worship in India have such a great significance for ideas of salvation and thus for Hindu religions in general.

According to Brahmanic ritual understanding, as expressed in the Garuḍapurāṇa,[224] one of the widespread texts on the death ritual, from the sixth to eleventh centuries, death is not a sudden event. It is a process and a transformation (see tables 12–13), which is to be prepared for. As in the Second Birth, the initiate is made progressively "perfect" (*saṃskṛta, saṃskāra*) for the study of the Veda, so in the rite of passage from life to death, the deceased must also be ritually immortalized. Thus, a Brahmanic-Sanskritic ideal exists that the dying person should have "died" ritually before death, if possible, by becoming an ascetic, for example, and thus relieving the survivors of caring for ancestors. Many Śaiva ascetics have a death ritual performed for themselves by lying on a pyre during the consecration: Release during life implies "death" during life. By accepting asceticism, the Saṃnyāsa (see table 8), in old age or performing this step even on his death bed in the so-called sick-asceticism (*āturasaṃnyāsa*), the Twice-Born frees the survivors from the pressure of caring for ancestors. During one's lifetime, one can also have a death ritual (*kāmyavṛṣotsargaśrāddha*) performed on oneself, if one has no children.

In the Hindu religions, the deceased (*preta,* literally: "the one who passed away") is seen as a restless soul, who initially has no room to live and has to be freed from its state of being dead in order to reach the world of heaven. Thus, most of the rite is a death convoy. The offerings are useful for the deceased in the Next World.[225] The corpse is immediately placed on the floor, which is smeared with cow dung. Even the dying person should be laid on the floor, for heaven is for the gods, earth for men and animals, but in the in-between space spirits dwell. Kuśa grass and gold coins should also be put on the body's orifices, especially the mouth, and the body should be weighted with a black stone or ammonite (*śālagrāma*) so that the soul will not fly away before it is ritually prepared for the journey. We have already encountered Kuśa grass and gold coins in the initiation, where they clearly represent immortality and the everlasting. According to the Garuḍapurāṇa, Kuśa grass emerged from Viṣṇu's hair, and it can also be read that this grass—like priests, Vedic mantras, the sacrificial fire, or basil (*tulasī*)—never loses its effectiveness.[226] If no corpse is available, because the dead person is missing, for example, a doll of Darbha grass is substituted. In big cities, it is becoming increasingly popular to have the corpse burned in a crematorium and to perform the death ritual at a holy place (such as Gokarṇa or Rāmeśvaram) with the ashes or the remains of the bones.

The dead person is carried out through a back door, feet first, wrapped in new, white cloths, dipped in holy water. He is placed on a bamboo bier and carried to the cremation grounds on a special death path, through special city gates, usually in the south. At the cremation grounds, the corpse is put with his feet in the water, which is considered Ganges water and thus liberating. The cremation grounds are occasionally hierarchically ordered: For the Untouchables there are special burning sites, and at the Paśupatinātha Temple in Kathmandu a platform is constantly reserved for the royal family. The domestic fire is brought along in a bowl. Women may not take part in the funeral procession. The corpse is burned on the same day on a pyre stacked with sandalwood and Palāśa wood (*Butea frondosa*), or at least one that contains some boughs of these. On the pyre the head points to the north. The fire is cooled with water offerings to soothe the agony of the dead person.[227] There is to be no weeping; otherwise the dead person has to absorb tears and mucus against his will. Only at home may feelings be expressed. There, nim leaves are often chewed: that is, the bitter taste of this plant (*Melia Azadirachta L.*) recalls the bitterness of death.[228]

In the cracking or shattering of the skull, the thumb-sized individual soul (*puruṣa*) escapes.[229] It is the place of the tuft of hair (*śikhā*) on the fontanelle, or the so-called "Brahma hole" (*brahmarandhra*), which already had a central significance in the initiation as a sign of the paternal line. Through spiritual or meditative powers, the ascetic can let the soul escape through this place, which is why only he and not his physical shell survives. Moreover, in popular belief it is held that in bad people, the soul escapes through other bodily orifices, such as the anus.[230] Right afterward, the individual soul must be cared for by putting out jugs filled with food for it, for example. Clay jugs are a constant ritual element in the death cult; sometimes they are shattered like the

3. Dogs warm themselves in the ashes of a pyre in the Paśupatinātha Temple in Deopatan, Nepal. Photographer: A. Michaels, 1983–1984.

skull, even though they are understood as the place of the deceased; and sometimes they are set out or hung up for the support of the deceased.[231] Bones or ashes are also gathered in them,[232] and scattered in the Ganges or occasionally taken on a pilgrimage to places that are especially suitable for ancestor rituals, such as Gayā in northern India.

Ritually, cracking or smashing the skull is the most important time of death. Afterward, a time of impurity (*aśauca, mṛtakasūtaka, sūtaka*)[233] begins for the survivors. This lasts from ten to thirteen days, requires various purification measures, and is "contagious." Therefore, in condolence calls, no food is served; a death meal takes place only later. The period of impurity is marked by a significant absence of the Veda and Vedic rituals for the one performing the sacrifice, as purity (*śuddhi*) is given by the presence of the Veda. Therefore, those affected by *aśauca* may not go to the temple or recite the Veda for at least ten days. Often, statues of gods in the house are also taken out. In the period of impurity, if the son must perform a ritual, this impurity is explicitly abolished temporarily.[234] According to the legal texts, only a few persons cannot be polluted or can be polluted only for a short time; these include ascetics, Brahmans who maintain a sacrificial fire, and occasionally the king.[235]

The degree of impurity for the survivors depends on the class as well as the kinship and spatial proximity to the deceased. Usually it is the patrilinear relatives who are strongly affected, especially the chief mourners, who perform the death rites, usually the firstborn son, or the brother, husband, wife, or mother. During this time, they are treated almost as Untouchables. One may not accept food from them, they may not shave at first, and they get their hair shorn on the tenth to the thirteenth day at the latest. Widows smash their bracelets, remove their jewelry, and no longer wear cinnabar strips in their hair part. Brothers living in the household and all male relatives of the male line are also affected, and even the most distant relatives perform only a brief ritual purification at the news of the death. According to the Garuḍapurāṇa,[236] the period of mourning for Brahmans is ten days, for Kṣatriya twelve, for Vaiśya fifteen, for Śūdra a month. In-laws are less polluted: for Sāpiṇḍya members rarely ten days, for other members three days; for other members of the Gotra, a bath is enough.

At any rate, impurity is to be understood ritually in the death ritual. It has little to do with the emotional relation to the deceased. If a father is expelled from the subcaste, no death rites for him may be performed; consequently, no one can be polluted by this death. The same applies to ascetics. And at the death of her parents, a daughter is less impure than at the death of her husband's parents, in the southern Indian Havik Brahmans, for example, only three as opposed to eleven days.[237]

Death works a serious change on the whole extended family and since every change is a deviation from the ideal of the unchangeable purity of an extended family, similar criteria apply to birth, initiation, and weddings.[238] Thus, the Garuḍapurāṇa says: "Through conception men are devastated after death, but without a physical body he cannot find salvation."[239] In Indian systems, birth and death are so closely connected that a virgin can mean immortality, and, on the other hand, a fertile woman can also mean death.

In the death rituals, death priests, house priests, and the oldest son assume the most important tasks. The goal is the ritual composition of a body for the deceased to allow him to reach the forefathers and ancestors. This is done ritually with dumplings or balls (*piṇḍa*)—ideally a mixture of barley flour, ses-

4. Ancestor ritual (*śrāddha*) in Benares: Two brothers "feed" the deceased parents, grandparents, and great-grandparents with dumplings (*piṇḍa*). Photographer: N. Gutschow, 1992.

ame, water, sugar, milk, yogurt, honey, and clarified butter; but often only a mixture of rice flour and water or milk. This ritual body first consists only of wind (*vāyuśarīra*), then is as big as a thumb (*liṅgaśarīra*), and finally is the size of a forearm (*yātanāśarīra,* literally: "a suffering body"), and thus allows him to reach the forefathers and the ancestors (fig. 4). "Bound by the sacrificial dumpling" (*sapiṇḍa*) is a sign of kinship, which is also taken into account at birth, and in determining endogamy and exogamy and in the Bengali right of inheritance (*dāyabhāga*): Anyone who is allowed to carry out the *śrāddha* has the right to inherit.[240] Typically, the woman is to eat piṇḍas during the ritual insemination (*garbhādhāna,* see table 5), because of the idea that rice grains correspond to male semen.[241] Sāpiṇḍya relatives form a common body because one is linked by forefathers (seven generations on the paternal side and five on the maternal side).[242] The acceptance of the deceased into the community of the ancestors (*sapiṇḍīkaraṇa*)[243] is completed in several rituals that can extend over a year (see table 12).

Among many Twice-Born men, three series of sixteen Piṇḍas are offered, always accompanied by Vedic sayings, except for the first sixteen.[244] Of the

Table 12
The Path to the Ancestors

	Living (manusya)	*Deceased* (preta)	*Dead* (preta)	*Forefathers* (pitṛ)	*Ancestors* (viśve devāḥ)
Time span	Birth or begetting until death	1–10 or 13 days after death	Until 1 year	3 generations	Until rebirth
Body	Coarse material body with all senses (*sthūaśarīra*)	Fine material, thumb-sized (wind) body without a mouth (initially *vāyuśarīra*, then *piṇḍaśarīra*, *liṅgaśarīra* or *puruṣa*)	Fine material, forearm-sized body with nail-sized mouth orifice (*yātanāśarīra*)	Anthropomorphic pleasure-loving body (*bhogadeha*, *-śarīra*)	Heavenly body (*divyadeha*)
Location	Earth	At the house or cremation place	On the journey to the Next World	Heaven or hell (Grave): god of death (Yama) decides	Heaven (*svarga*, *pitṛloka* or hell (*naraka*)

Group membership	Extended family	Individual	Individual	Forefatherhood	Ancestorhood
Śrāddha		*navaśrāddha ekoddiṣṭaśrāddha*	*sapiṇḍīkaraṇa, nārāyaṇabali*	*saṃyojanaśrāddha* (yearly or monthly)	
Veda recitation	Offered from the Second Birth	No Veda sayings (from the head mourner)	Veda sayings obligatory	Veda sayings obligatory	Veda sayings offered
Notes		In certain kinds of deaths, a direct way to the forefathers is allowed through *nārāyaṇabali*			After a time appropriate to Karma, rebirth follows
Results if the ritual is not performed		Becomes a spirit (*bhūta*)	Becomes a spirit (*bhūta*)	Falls into hell (*pātakin, patita*)	Falls into hell (*pātakin, patita*)

first sixteen dumplings (*malina ṣodaśī*), which are considered impure, six are placed in the following sites: at the place of death, at the door of the house of death, at the first crossroads, at the place where the bier stopped, on the corpse, on the cremation grounds, and at the spot where the remnants of bone are gathered.[245] Thus the first dangers that threaten the deceased—earth, gods, and spirits—must be placated.

As soon as death occurs, the domestic fire is extinguished and no food is cooked until the day after the cremation. The first food after the day of death is often a kind of milk rice which must be prepared without salt. In many cases, a plate woven of leaves is placed for the deceased. At the head of the company of mourners sits the head mourner. He mixes his rice with the portion for the deceased and then places five pieces on the plate of the deceased; his fellow diners each place a piece on this plate.[246] If the norms of commensality are recalled, this procedure is amazing: Son and (deceased) father mix their food, as if they were one person.

According to the legal texts, the remaining ten Piṇḍas of the first series are to be offered in the next ten days, while invoking the deceased. But usually they are offered together on the tenth day at a river or a watering place, in a southern direction, and again with Kuśa grass. Through them, the dead person receives a new body, for the ten dumplings stand for the following parts of the body: (1) head; (2) eyes, nose, and ears; (3) neck, arm, and breast; (4) navel, sexual organs, and arms; (5) hips, legs, and feet; (6) internal organs; (7) veins; (8) nails, teeth, and body hair; (9) semen; and (10) hunger and thirst.[247] This composition corresponds to Ayurvedic ideas of the development of the embryo and the formation of the fetus in the mother's womb.

On the tenth day, the chief mourner is shaved, bathes, and receives a new Sacred Thread. Prior to that, he is not to shave, cut his nails, or comb his hair; he is to sleep only on the floor, have no sexual intercourse, and wear no shoes or sewn garments. He is to cook his food by himself on a separate fire. Here, too, the son is identified with the father: During the ritual, the son is often the deceased.

On the eleventh day, a bull is to be branded and released (*vṛṣotarga*),[248] but this is seldom practiced either. On the other hand, the ritual of cow-giving (*godāna*) is still common. On his dangerous and extremely painful journey to the ancestors,[249] the deceased comes to a kind of hell river of blood and excrement that flows between the earth and the realm of the death god Yama. The cow is to help him get across the river. This ritual is usually practiced so that, while reciting Vedic sayings, the death priest holds a cow's tail and a leaf of basil, and the son grips the hand of the death priest. Once again, the son acts as a representative of the deceased.

Still on the eleventh day, and occasionally also on the twelfth day, the second series of sixteen Piṇḍas (*ekādaśa ṣoṣaśī*) is offered. Fifteen dumplings are meant for the gods, one for the deceased (*puruṣa*). Ideally, Brahmans are to eat the dumplings. On the same day, a death priest, the Mahābrāhmaṇa, and in a few subcastes, the house priests, too, consume the favorite food of the deceased or milk rice with a part of the ground-up bones of the dead person. But he takes this food only reluctantly and with constant demands for money and gifts, for it is considered hard to digest.[250] That is, the death priest thus removes the impurity and evil of the deceased. Ultimately, he is driven out of the house, sometimes with stones. When the king dies in Nepal, a special priest must even eat a piece of the corpse's brain; he is then given generous gifts and expelled from the country, which he may never again enter.[251]

The third set of sixteen Piṇḍas (*uttama ṣoḍaśī*) are no longer presented by the impure death priest, but by the pure house priest. Actually, they should be distributed throughout the year of mourning, but in fact this ritual takes place, if at all, as a preliminary rite for the Sapiṇḍīkaraṇa,[252] with which the arrival of the deceased among the ancestors is celebrated. In the process, the chief mourner divides one of the Piṇḍas, which is somewhat lengthened, into three parts, mixes gold and Kuśa grass in these parts, and blends the whole thing with three Piṇḍas, which represent the father, the grandfather, and the great-grandfather. Here too, Brahmans take the dumplings as representatives: Three represent the forefathers (*pitaraḥ*), two the ancestors (*viśve devāḥ*), one the deceased (*preta*). This is the crucial moment, when the deceased, abandoning his former name, is brought into the band of forefathers (*pitaraḥ*), forms an eating community with them, and is no longer a helpless outsider, as a Preta.[253] United with the other deceased, the dead person can now live on his own and is provided with a divine body (*divyadeha*). At the same time, the father of the great-grandfather moves into the band of the generalized, half-divine forefathers (*viśve devāḥ*).[254] So, whether one reaches this place depends not only on one's own Karma and one's own acts, on blame or merit, but also on if and how the descendants perform the death and ancestor rituals.

The rest of the dumplings are given to cows or thrown in the river. The crows also always get a part. As scavengers, they have allegedly been linked with the cult of death since ancient times.[255] Thus, people believe that the soul of the deceased sits in birds that circle the house. If a crow does not eat the thrown-out dumpling, this is interpreted as a bad sign. Crows are also considered immortal because they are supposed to have drunk from the nectar of immortality and allegedly no one has ever seen a dead crow.

On the twelfth or thirteenth day, Brahmans must be given presents and entertained again (*brāhmaṇabhojana*),[256] even though they reluctantly accept the offered meal. Relatives and neighbors are also invited to the meal. In the Dharma texts it is very important that the Brahmans are immaculate. *Manu* lists countless persons (priests and guests), who may not be invited because they are either impure or practice impure professions or are of frivolous character.[257] Ascetics are preferred guests. The meal forms the conclusion of the dying and death rituals and the especially impure period; it demonstrates the reintegration of the mourning family into the community, even though for another year, countless observances must be followed. Thus, during this time, for example, one may not hold a wedding. Thirteen days after the death, at the latest, the house of the deceased returns to normal. Then the clothes are given to the laundry, the house is ritually purified with cow dung, and the earthenware utensils are renewed.

To a large extent, the Brahmanic ritual of death and dying is a gradual removal of impurity and mortality as well as the new creation of a body in the next world. Death-bringing vital energy is still attributed to the deceased, for which he needs room to live and a body. If he had no vital energy, he would not have to be reborn and therefore would not have to die again. But he also leaves behind or transmits this death-bringing energy to the survivors, who must protect themselves and the deceased mainly by the purifying force of water, fire, and cremation, but also cremation in the stomach by digesting, as Jonathan Parry interprets the many feedings during the death ritual.[258] Comparably, the eternal, immortal forces (Brahman, Kuśa grass, basil, gold, fire offerings, Veda) can neutralize and filter the death-bringing vital energy. But, despite all ritual measures of caution, they cannot completely dissolve or remove it. The deceased also retains a remnant of it, which lets him become the almost deified ancestor, but also leads to his rebirth.

Ancestor Worship

The dead person is a sacrifice to the fire (*agni*) and the god Agni, who—according to a widespread notion—carries him to heaven and the world of the forefathers (*pitṛloka*) with the smoke. As long as the deceased have not yet found their place as forefathers, they are potentially dangerous, powerful dead and are mainly wandering around hungry.[259] But, as ancestors, the dead are sometimes seen on a level with the high gods—ancestors and gods once lived together, it says in one place[260]—partly in a separate class (with Vasus, Rudras, Ādityas).[261] In any case, they have a semidivine status. Thus, the place of the forefathers is a kind of heaven, not the heaven of the gods (*svarga*), but not the earthly world of humans (*bhūloka*) or of spirits (*antarikṣa*) either.

Table 13
Processes of Deification

<table>
<tr><td colspan="2">Rebirth</td><td rowspan="3">Liberation
(mokṣa)</td></tr>
<tr><td colspan="2">↑
HEAVEN</td></tr>
<tr><td>Viśve Devāḥ</td><td>Hero (vīra), Satī</td></tr>
<tr><td>Great great grandfather
or -mother
Great grandfather or -mother
Grandfather or -mother
Preta</td><td rowspan="2">↑
Heroic, violent, or premature death or suicide; widow-burning
↓</td><td rowspan="2">↑
Ritual or spiritual "death"</td></tr>
<tr><td>↑
Normal Death
↓</td></tr>
<tr><td colspan="2">Spirits (piśāca, bhūta; piśācī, ḍākinī)
HELL
Yama's Underworld
↓</td><td rowspan="2"></td></tr>
<tr><td colspan="2">Rebirth</td></tr>
</table>

Therefore, Brahmanic-Sanskritic death rituals are processes of deification (see table 13). Only after a year, as we have seen, do the dead achieve the semidivine status of the Pitaraḥ. The plural of this word means "forefathers, forebears," but also "great-grandfathers," as the seven ṛṣis of prehistory are sometimes considered; in the singular (*pitṛ*), it typically means (and is etymologically related to) "father." Father and forefather, thus, are seen ritually on the same level with the son, as was already seen clearly in the initiation.

The dead remain in the status of ancestors for only three generations, then they move up to the rather vague groups of heavenly creatures (*viśve devāḥ;* literally: "all gods"),[262] and as such they are worshipped only collectively and deindividualized. The three generations of the deceased form a ladder with rising status, but decreasing proximity to the survivors. With every new death, the deceased moves closer to heaven. "A man wins worlds through a son, and he gains eternity through a grandson, but he reaches the summit of the chestnut horse through the grandson of his son."[263] Therefore, sons are important for the salvation of one's own soul; only they can perform the rituals. Consequently, in Sanskrit, the son (*putra*) is described as someone who saves the father from hell. In contrast, the living man has obligations to seers, ancestors, and gods.

The close relationship between gods and ancestors (*viśve devāḥ*) is constantly reestablished.[264] They are both considered deities (*devatā*), but there are marked differences in the ancestor rituals.[265] Thus, while invoking the gods, the Sacred Thread is laid on the left shoulder; while invoking the ancestors, on the right shoulder; with the gods, the preferred number is even; with the ancestors, it is odd; the gods get grains of barley or rice, the ancestors sesame seeds (whose significance in the death cult is still to be studied—recall the "open sesame" of the Thousand and One Nights); the one performing the sacrifice looks east with the gods, south with the ancestors; the form of the sacrificial place (*maṇḍala*) is square in the one case, round in the other. But here, too, when a ritual counterworld is constructed, the ancestors are associated with the gods, only because they too have a heavenly body (*divyadeha*).

The dead—either forefathers, ancestors, or *viśve devāḥ*, not to mention the spirits of the dead—are ubiquitous in India. No domestic ritual is carried out without their getting their share. Often, they are worshipped every day. In a certain respect, they are even more dangerous than the gods: They are closer to the house, they are dissatisfied, they always demand respect. Only the ascetic, who has paid his debt to the gods, ancestors, and men, is free of the pressure of the deceased.

If the deceased does not die a natural death, if he is killed in a traffic accident, in a crime, or as a youth, but also if the death rituals are not performed or are carried out incorrectly, then he is threatened with remaining a Preta[266] or restless spirit (*bhūta, piśāca;* with women: *ḍākinī, piśācī*). The Sanskrit word, for a deceased person *preta,* is often used in new Indian idioms together with a word for spirit: *bhūt-pret.* These spirits can also be the unpacified dead, not only the ritually escorted dead.[267] As was described above, as long as their *sapiṇḍīkaraṇa* ritual has not yet been performed, that is, for a maximum of one year, Pretas have only a fine material thumb-sized body without a mouth. They have awareness and feelings, but no accompanying bodily organs. Like the survivors, they are in a marginal situation, full of ambivalence, pollution, weakness, and low vitality. They are hungry and—because of their internal heat (*tejas*)—thirsty; they hang around the house of the survivors, envy them their life, and want to inflict illnesses on them.[268]

The heroic death[269] and ritual suicide (see below) are not "bad deaths." There is a difference whether one commits suicide out of despair—the Jainas called that a childish death (*bālamaraṇa*)—or if one fasts to death, throws himself before the chariot of the god, has oneself burned as a widow, or is killed in battle. In a way, these dead circumvent the long way of the ancestors to heaven; they achieve it immediately as deified heroes or heroines. In the popular religions, those who died violently can also signify a source of salvation; countless temples and local shrines are devoted to them. And even though the heroic death is rooted in Kṣatriya circles, Brahmans have also acknowledged it as a liberating death. There is a special Brahmanic death ritual (*nārāyaṇa-bali*)[270] for direct deification, without the long road through forefatherhood, which is also used for those who cannot have the normal death rituals because they are missing, for example.

Children, ascetics, lepers, those inflicted with smallpox, and those who died of snakebite are not cremated, but are buried or thrown in the river,[271] either because their death is already a divine one (thus, in smallpox, the smallpox goddess Śītalā takes possession of the patient), or because—like children and ascetics—they are outside of ritual life, which begins with the Second Birth and ends with thc Brahmanic ritual of dying and death. As long as only a little Karma is accumulated, it needs only a little ritual, as the Garuḍapurāṇa says.[272] Children who die young still use up their bad remnant of Karma. Therefore, they must not be cremated as fire offerings, but are buried. Until what age this applies is variable: Many think until the child cuts teeth, others until the twenty-seventh month[273] or the third year, while still others until the tonsure (*cūḍākaraṇa*) or even the initiation. Ascetics are also buried, but at their consecration they are already considered "dead"; their souls have escaped during their lifetimes. And unmarried girls receive no death offerings either.[274]

The temporal and kinship distance to the dead person affects the frequency and intensity of ancestor worship. It can be observed that common death ceremonies increase the farther back in time the death is and the more faded the memory of the deceased. Again, textual and ethnographical material indicates a great latitude in the matter of ancestor worship (*śrāddha*), which has thus far been largely overlooked by Indologists and anthropologists.[275] Ancestor worship can be summarized in three types:[276]

- Rituals of dying, death for, and ancestor worship of the currently deceased: This includes the death rituals (*antyeṣṭi*), which are performed in the first thirteen days (summarized in table 11); the individual death offering (*ek-oddiṣṭaśrāddha*) on the eleventh day after the death; the death transformation ritual (*sapiṇḍīkaraṇa*) on the twelfth day or precisely one year after the death, which makes the deceased into a forefather; and memorial ancestor rituals (*pārvaṇaśrāddha, aṣṭakaśrāddha*) carried out monthly and particularly yearly on the anniversary of the death.

- Periodic—e.g., daily, monthly, or yearly—ancestor worship for those who died in the preceding year, usually the three forebears on the father's side (and sometimes on the mother's side), to be offered only by the male offspring, especially on determined junction days (the *parvans*), such as the new or full moon, or at an eclipse. These rituals are worship of a specific, named group of deceased persons.
- Common worship of all ancestors on certain holidays (Pitṛpakṣa, Sora Śrāddha, New Moon of the month of Bhādrapāda) or in the domestic ritual. This is a collective ritual for a generalized, "anonymous" class of ancestors.

The common term for ancestor worship, *śrāddha,* which is derived from a religious attitude referred to as early as the second ("Vedic") epoch (*śraddhā*),[277] indicates—even in the opinion of Brahmanic legal scholars[278]—various parts of rituals, three of which are especially important: the fire offering (*homa*), the rice balls or dumplings (*piṇḍa*), and feeding the Brahmans; in addition, gifts to Brahmans (*dāna*) and worship (*pūjā*) of the gods, especially Viṣṇu as a savior in death, are significant subrituals. In popular parlance, Śrāddha denotes both death rituals and ancestor rituals,[279] even though death rituals are considered impure, whereas ancestor rituals are not. Accordingly, in the legal texts and in popular notions, there is also some uncertainty about whom the offerings and sacrifices apply to or what meaning they have. Thus there are instructions that the food is meant for the Brahmans themselves or that these represent the forefathers or ancestors. Thus, the Piṇḍas are sometimes considered provisions for the journey for the dead, sometimes as part of his body in the next world. The uncertainty about the status of the survivors also involves uncertainty about his future: Will he get to heaven, has he earned it? A certain text helps by protecting him in all cases: Piṇḍas and other food that are given in fire are for the gods or for the deceased as a future demigod; Piṇḍas given to the Brahmans are for the status as forefather; and those that are thrown on the floor or dumplings offered to the crows are in case he goes to hell (*naraka*).[280]

Uncertainty about the meanings in the ritual of death and ancestors does not mean that those involved in them are unable to achieve clarity. Rather, rituals are expressions of the fact that there can be no clarity. Life-cycle transition rituals are thus, on the one hand, always meaningful, for there are reasons for them and an obligatory formal resolution (*saṃkalpa*), which makes the ritual effective (see table 20) and confirms the intention in clear words. On the other hand, ritual acts are meaningless and rigid because something else can also be done and often is done: series of acts from other rituals are always substituted.

Even though an astonishing continuity of death rituals is thus indicated from the second ("Vedic") epoch to the present,[281] a significant change of meaning has also taken place. Whereas in the Vedic-oriented death ritual, the focus is on the way to the ancestors and reaching heaven or immortality, ever since the third ("Ascetic") epoch, the idea of a repeated reincarnation has appeared, along with the fear of a return of the dead and of hell in popular religious and Purāṇic concepts of afterlife. Whether the dead person goes to an intermediate realm or is reborn right after death, whether he becomes an ancestor or a deindividualized soul-body, whether life in this world affects life after death, or whether the last thoughts at the moment of death do so, all these considerations and differing ideas are hardly harmonized. Thus, in the Brahmanic-Sanskritic death ritual, various conceptions of afterlife are mixed, which leaves the way of the dead person as it must be: an uncertain path.

Widow-Burning and Religiously Motivated Suicide[282]

That the wife dies after the death of her husband, including voluntary death by fire, exists not only in India. It has also been found among the Slavs and Germans, among the Thracians, and at first among the Greeks.[283] But only in India has widow-burning been practiced over such a long period among so many groups of the population, and been discussed in such detail by traditional scholars. Yet, rarely is a subject so freighted with prejudice. For example, widow-burning was only seldom carried out in fact among the general population, and in no class was it accepted without reservation.

In Indian legal literature, widow-burning is usually called *sahamaraṇa* and *sahagamana* ("dying with" or "going [to death] with") or *anumaraṇa* (literally: "[the widow] dying after"), according to whether the widow had herself burned with her spouse or later. During the time of British rule over India, widow-burning was known primarily as *satī* (or as it was Anglicized, "suttee"). This is a participle of the verbal root as ("to be") and really means the "good, true, pure (wife)." So, in Sanskrit, *satī* is not only widow-burning, but also the wife who has herself burned—like the goddess *Satī,* a consort of the god Śiva, who throws herself onto a sacrificial fire as a sign of her fidelity to her husband.

Let us first establish a few facts about the history and procedure of widow-burning: In the written sources of the second ("Vedic") epoch, widow-burning does not appear, but the possibility of a remarriage of the widow does. Only from the third epoch[284] are there rare indications in the texts, but there is much more evidence of widows living on. According to inscriptional evidence, widow-burning is first proved in Nepal in 464 A.D. and in India in 510 A.D., and there are countless *satī* commemorative stones from the eleventh century. Only a few late authors of legal texts (from the fifteenth century) are determined supporters of widow-burning, but there are also several opponents among them. Despite numerous ritual texts on widow-burning, it is seldom glorified. In the fifth ("Sectarian") and sixth ("Modern") epochs, there are clear epidemic outbreaks of widow-burning, mainly as a reaction to foreign rule. But, as for the total population, it was always only a few women who exposed themselves to the torture. In India, widow-burning was finally forbidden only in 1829 by Lord William Bentinck, and almost a century later in Nepal.[285]

Widow-burning probably was originally a custom of war, which focused on the protection of honor and wife. In any case, such an assumption is plausible with reference to Greek travel reports and from early inscriptions.[286] The lack of references in early Brahmanic literature also supports the conclusion that widow-burning was widespread mainly among the aristocracy and perhaps also in a few tribes. Indeed, widow-burning did not remain limited to these circles. Brahmans also practiced this custom—as it may be euphemistically termed.

According to the legal texts, widow-burning should take place voluntarily, without persuasion, anesthesia, or force. Small children or other husbands should not suffer from the decision of the widow. Therefore, a minimum age is established and it is stipulated that a mother with a small child may not have herself burned, nor may a pregnant woman. One should try to dissuade the widow from her intention. Clearly, the Brahmans mainly sought to safeguard the "purity" of it, to make widow-burning appropriate to the goddess Satī, and to protect it from abuse. Ritually, the widow is dead when she makes and expresses the decision—the *intentio solemnis* (see table 20)—and reinforces it by a ritual bath or by breaking her bracelets, a symbol of her status as a married woman. As soon as the pyre is kindled, she can be returned to society, mainly to her original commensual community, only through ritual countermeasures. A ritual decision, reinforced by fire and water, is irreversible. Therefore, withdrawal from widow-burning and remarriage are almost excluded. The whole thing is based, among other things, on the belief in a unity of speech or speech and act. In Nepalese Deopatan, a gate, the so-called *satīdvāra* (fig. 5),[287] brings this ritual threshold literally before your eyes: In the past, if widows went through this gate, they could not come back anymore. Even today, it is said of a few old beggar women that they had jumped out of the fire and therefore could no longer return to their families.

Widow-burning may have emerged as an analogy to the hero's death or even as part of it and may have been advocated by the Brahmans as a deifying kind of death. Hardly anything is known about this development. But as a ritualized self-killing, it soon encounters among the Brahmans another, completely different attitude, both toward self-burning as well as toward the deifying death, that is, the concept of a second life, which we have already en-

5. The "Gate of the Widow(-Burnings)" (*satīdvāra*) in Deopatan, Nepal: Widows previously announced their intention to have themselves burned by going through this gate. Photographer: A. Michaels, 1983–1984.

countered in the initiation and which assumes a death of the first life. Against this background, there was always the religiously motivated suicide, which was not to be imagined outside the logic of the sacrifice. Thus, the idea of voluntary death by fire fell on fertile ground in Brahmanic circles, and typically, this kind of suicide found recognition among the Brahmans, even though there is evidence of other deifying kinds of death in the war castes as well as in individual tribes.

As demonstrated earlier, in marriage the wife can only be brought into the patrilinear system through a ritual identification: She receives the fictional descent, the Gotra, of her husband. Thus, marriage is considered the initiation of the woman. One result of this combination is that, at the death of her husband, the wife is also ritually dead. If she undergoes her own cremation (*sahagamana*) with the death of her husband, she gets neither her own fire nor her own death ritual: Man and wife are a ritual unit. Only if she delays being burned (*anugamana*) does she also "die" ritually. This strong emphasis of the paternal line had to be at the expense of the woman. Physically, the widow lives on, but ritually and often socially, she dies with the husband. She loses authority and prestige in the extended family, becomes a problem to be taken care of, is sometimes harassed by male relatives, has no rights to a large extent, and is dependent on her oldest son. She must let herself be blamed for her husband's death and may not remarry. The life of a widow is full of privations: She must be chaste, cut her hair short, and wear only white garments and no jewelry. If she is still a young widow, she may face the threat of being called a witch, being disowned, or ending as a beggar or a prostitute.

In this oppressive social discrimination, it may sound cynical to talk about religious motives of a widow-burning, about love of her husband, the hope for a better rebirth, or the intention to attain the dignity of a worshipped saint. And yet, in certain cases, widow-burning was clearly more than a way out dictated by necessity. Even today in India, women still retain the prestige of Satīs. In the much-respected self-burning of Roop Kunwar, a young woman from Rajasthan, it was mainly women who demonstrated by the thousands in 1987 for their right to widow-burning, even though women's groups also organized counterdemonstrations.

The mode of death also shows that widow-burning is not always compelled by social circumstances. The widow who poisons or hangs herself is not a Satī and does not become one. India has almost always condemned suicide, not because it violates god's will, but because it offends Brahmanic norms: On the one hand, achieving the Sāpiṇḍya community is possible only if the father or mother has previously died;[288] youthful suicide usually breaks down this sequence. On the other hand, suicide means harmful Karma. But India did allow religiously motivated suicide and especially voluntary death by fire (*agnipraveśa*). Men are also honored who throw themselves before the wheels of procession carts as in the Jagannātha festival in eastern Purī, tumble off rocks and into holy rivers, or starve to death. Against this background, it is no wonder that women also sought a deifying death. For them, widow-burning could become a means to give a holy meaning to life through a "heroic" death by fire. The ascetics supplied a model for religious suicide: A few sects practice escaping from society by ascending to a pyre, which is, of course, not lit. Naturally, the limits of these parallels are that the ascetic could and should leave home voluntarily, but not the widow; and that, for the ascetic, internal motives were to have been decisive to change one's life, while for the widow, it is the "external" occasion of the death of the spouse and a certain pressure of expectation of the family.

Thus, India did not generally condemn religiously motivated ritual suicide, but the Brahmans clearly emphasized other paths to salvation: the ritualistic path of good deeds, religious devotion to a god, and above all liberating spiritual knowledge. In popular religion, the heroic death, including religiously motivated suicide, is highly regarded and those who die like that are usually deified. In the Brahmanic spiritual form of religion, suicide, even religiously motivated, but Karmic to a large extent because it presumes passion (*rāga*) and the willingness to injure (*hiṃsā*), is followed by rebirth and new suffering.

The Ban on Killing and Ahiṃsā[289]

A general right to life is to be found in India as rarely as a general ban on killing. Right[290] in India is often customary right and tradition (*ācāra*), with great distinctions between subcastes and regions. On this issue, the legal texts are not standard either. There is an extensive protection of life in the form of an injunction not to harm living creatures (*ahiṃsā*), but there is also an injunction to kill (in war, hunting, and sacrifice), capital punishment, killing in self-defense, ritual self-killing, as well as the expulsion of the old.

The injunction regarding Ahiṃsā developed within the nomadic cattle cultures of the second ("Vedic") epoch, to protect the stock of the cowherds. The cow has always been worshipped in India.[291] Its special position can be seen even in ancient Iranian and early Vedic sources. Affluence was equated with the stock of cows, just as the Italians derived *pecunia* from *pecus* ("cattle"), which was initially an indication of the extent of property in cattle before it became an expression for money. Welfare was synonymous with cow blessing. But the cow was also a sacrifice animal. Beef was consumed because sacrifice was not merely killing and did not mean taking life, but giving new life.

The Vedic religion was based on the principle[292] that life is possible only through force (*hiṃsā*) against others, since everything is created only for sacrifice. An early part of the Mahābhārata says: "Animals and men, trees and foliage yearn for heaven, and there is no heaven except through sacrifice."[293] The whole thing was refined in the detailed sacrificial theory of the Brahmans. At the end of the second epoch, however, Ahiṃsā thought burgeoned. It allows for a comprehensive ban on killing and results in vegetarianism. It is the time when the immigration of the Indo-Aryans into the northern and middle Ganges plain came to an end, thus completing the transition from the previous seminomadic life to a settled existence. Instead of big cattle herds, the individual cow was now emphasized as an animal for pulling carts and plowing. Other factors relating to this change include, in abbreviated form: year-round agriculture, the emergence of the first kingdoms, the right to inherited real estate, the expansion of trade, and the development of a permanent and caste-stratified social order. In this time, which was also turbulent for religion, an opposition grew against the elite Brahmanic sacrifice and priestly class; reform religions such as Buddhism and Jainism appeared, which opposed both killing and sacrificing animals.

One result of these ethnic, social, and religious changes or combinations was that the exclusive sacrifice ritual of the Brahmans was weakened and life was increasingly ethicized. At the end of a lengthy procedure, sustained by internal Brahmanic debates and by processes influenced externally, was the emergence of the possibility of internalizing the sacrifice, that is, the possibility of producing the magical effect of the sacrifice without priests, through the secret knowledge of ritual equivalences and ascetic self-sacrifice. According to *Manu,* "A sacrifice that consists of chanting ['*Oṃ*' and the verse to the sun-god] is ten times better than a sacrifice performed in accordance with the rules,"[294] but it is a hundred times better if the sacrifice is silent, and a thousand times better if it is carried out only mentally. Just as the sacrifice is based on force (*hiṃsā*), so its negation must lead to Ahiṃsā. The opposition to Brahmanic religion and social order objected to its central element: the dominance of sacrifice and its most important sacrificial animal, the cow.

But internalization of the sacrifice did not lead to a general vegetarianism; aside from exceptions such as Emperor Aśoka (274–232 B.C.), that was and still is an ascetic ideal that could be emulated by status-seekers. Yet, cow worship came only a good thousand years later, in the middle of the fourth ("Classical") epoch. Reinforced mother god cults probably played a crucial role in that. And only from the eleventh century was the cow understood as a uniting symbol of Hinduism, clearly delineated from Islam.

At no time, however, was the right to life a general ethical maxim. Such a formulation is hardly found in Brahmanic legal texts. As we have seen, life and death in the Hindu religion are ambiguous. Death is the end of the "natural" physical life, but not the end of every life. Life is also in inanimate objects, in elements or plants. But there is also the idea of various bodies of humans and the connected idea of various lives. The boundary between death and life is more fragile in India than in the West.

Karma and Rebirth[295]

The ancestors, as noted earlier, live on in various forms after death. How is the cult of ancestors, so strongly rooted in the life of the Hindus, consistent with the equally "typical" Indian concepts of Karma, reincarnation, and liberation? Doesn't the idea that the soul of the deceased forms a new birth contradict the cult of ancestors, including the deification of widows and other religious heroes? In fact, various concepts of the afterlife are blended in India, for which two fundamental notions of time are effective: linear time (experienced in the process of aging) and cyclical time (experienced in the regenerative processes of nature).[296] Based on these, the following concepts of the afterlife can be elaborated:

1. An intermediate realm of the soul: a temporary stopping area, which is dangerous in principle, where the survivors can still influence the deceased, and vice versa. This concept especially links notions of ancestors and spirits. The intermediate realm of the soul is a transitory boundary area and is therefore not always the same as:

2. Heaven and hell. The Vedic notion of eternal life in heaven,[297] understood as a world of inextinguishable light, or of the sun, or as the seat of the gods, is an old one. It corresponds to the notion of a hell or an eternal darkness, where the punishing flames burn or where one falls into a pit. These places are sought by a vital kind of soul, which still has thought (*manas*) and will. Only a lack of life energy (*asu, ojas*) distinguishes the dead from the living. The texts of the Brahmanic Hindu religion of the fourth epoch paint visions of heaven and hell in various ways.

3. Re-death (*punarmṛtyu*):[298] Because of the remaining vital energy or the remnant of vitality of the deceased, there is life and death in the next world as well as a consumption of religious merit, but especially the possibility of damnation, a trap and a wretched period, until re-death, an old idea in India. Therefore, even heaven is not necessarily the place of immortality; gods do not live forever either.

4. The multiple embodiment of the soul: The distinction common for Westerners between a physical and a mental world is not obvious in India. Instead, there have always been—as hinted in the Ṛgveda—ideas of various forms of the material, which is contrasted to an indistinguishable world that is nether mental nor physical. These thoughts are fully formed in the Sāṃkhya system, according to which the soul has at least two bodies:

(a) A coarse material body (*sthūlaśarīra*), which consists of a mixture of the coarse elements (earth, water, fire, air/wind, and ether), three liquids (gall, mucus, wind), and seven basic components (liquid, blood, flesh, fat, bones, marrow, and semen). This body is visible and decays after death.

(b) A subtle material body (*vāyuśarīra, sūkṣmaśarīra, liṅgaśarīra*) or the soul covering, which consists of subtle material or air. This soul body is invisible and is cast off only in deliverance. It wanders through the intermediate realm and assumes various bodies in rebirth in coarse materials.

These notions of the body, which are to be found particularly in the death and ancestor ritual, are linked with cyclical conceptions, as they are advanced in the doctrine of the recurring unfolding of the world or in the constant regeneration of nature, and with the idea of retribution for acts in the ideas of the transmigration of the soul and reincarnation.

5. Reincarnation and Karma: In the Ṛgveda, we do not yet find the doctrine of the transmigration of the soul, or a fateful repeated retribution for acts committed. But from the end of the second epoch, the idea arose that the kind of place in the next world or the future location of the individual soul depends on acts in the earthly life. At first, this was hardly ethicized: The good or wise came to the eternal world of the gods, the bad or ignorant through the rain went back into the food chain and to a new life.[299] With the early Upaniṣads (ca. 800–600 B.C.), diverse and incoherent speculations about the transmigration of the soul appeared, which were expanded into a ramified system in the legal texts and Purāṇas. Only with these texts do we find the concept of the repeated transmigration linked with desires for deliverance from the eternal cycle of rebirth (in the possibility of a nonhuman re-embodiment as plants or animals) and a continuous ethicization of retribution for acts in the form of catalogues of new existences. Thus, the doctrine of Karma is a theodicy, an explanation of the suffering and unjust earthly world as a result of previous acts, and an eschatology, a doctrine of liberation. Both doctrines do not belong together in every case, and countless other explanations for fate exist alongside them:[300] Gods with independent divine acts (*divyakriyā, daiva, bhāgya*), personalized time (*kāla*), death as an independent force (*mṛtyu, antaka,* the god Yama), or nature (*prakṛti*) can have influence independent of previous or present acts of the person in this world and the next, and thus help explain fate. The widespread notion that fate in India is considered deterministically and fatalistically is thus wrong.

6. Liberation: the subtle material, transmigrating body, which assumes various forms and existences—as seen under point 4—must be separated from an immaterial, formless, immortal "state of the soul," which is identical with the Absolute. Already in the late Vedic epoch, after death there was consequently the way to immortality and the way to re-death and rebirth. What was crucial for this was overcoming re-death by knowledge. The Brāhmaṇa texts often say: "He who knows this achieves immortality." Proper knowledge was more than the proper act, in which the proper knowledge can sometimes appear only through the ritually proper act. Proper knowledge or the proper act can liberate and thus produce immortality. For all others, there is only the eternally recurring mortality.

Mortality and Immortality[301]

Thus, in the Hindu religions, the dead are benign or malicious spirits, forefathers, ancestors, deified heroes, demigods, gods, or the redeemed; and they can return as plants, animals, or humans. It seems that in Brahmanic Hinduism, the greater the deification of the dead, the less the individuality of the deceased. In Brahmanic ancestor worship, the deceased become "depersonalized," timeless essences, basically at death, but after a year and three generations at the latest. In popular belief, on the other hand, there is also the notion of a single, irreversible death; and deification has a great deal to do with a violent, unnatural mode of death.

Indeed, death is not the end of any life, but rather a change from one form of existence into another. A spiritual body remains. Only when it is completely "deindividualized," when it is identical with the Absolute, is it really "dead," that is, without return. In Upaniṣad and Vedāntic terminology, mortality is Ātman-lessness,[302] when the Ātman (the individual soul) is identical with the *brahman* (the All or Absolute); this forms another counterworld to life. Death leads to rebirth; otherwise gods such as Rāma would have avoided their harsh fate and would not have come into the world, as the Garuḍapurāṇa says.[303] Anything that changes, that alters is eternally mortal. Kāla means both "time" and "death" in Sanskrit. As Ernst Cassirer says: "It is not immortality, but mortality that must . . . be 'proved.' "[304] Death leads to re-death, but not to the end of life, for the spiritual body is always seeking new existences.[305]

The pyre burns away the impurity of the coarse body, as many people believe, bearing the spiritual body to heaven. The death priest eats up the impurity of the dead.[306] But the dead always remain in the realm of mortality through the possibility of rebirth, even as demigods (Viśve Devāḥ). Through their life itself, they have accumulated death-bringing forces. The older they were, the more they had accumulated. When one is still young, there need be only a few rituals.[307] Only timelessness or immutability is eternal, and the preferred means to achieve these are ritual and spiritual identifications with what is not subject to change and therefore to time.

In the popular Hindu religions, these are achieved in the deification of heroes (who, however, can also be reborn); in the Brahmanic-Sanskritic Hindu religion, they are the sacrifice, ritual identification, and the notions of deliverance. Typically, in deliverance there is no individuality. Individuality produces death and re-death. The final salvation is not a place the soul body can reach. Nothing that belongs to this world or the other world can be eternal and everlasting. Ancestors are also reborn; only ascetics and heroes (with qualifications) are not. Life and death presume becoming and passing, constant change. In all this, a goal of salvation may be seen: the eternal return. But in addition, there has always been another notion of salvation: deliverance through dissolving without return. "What is sought is not salvation to an eternal life, but to the everlasting tranquillity of death," says Max Weber.[308] But he adds: "The basis of this salvation-striving [for Buddhism] was not any sort of 'satiety' with the 'meanness of life,' but satiety with 'death.' "

These notions of salvation have many effects on the cult of death: It has many variants, corresponding to the various forms of Hindu religiosity. But, on the whole, it is not surprising that the Brahmanic-Sanskritic Hindu religion has hardly any places of death worship, no photos, tombstones, death masks, or the like. Such individual worship of the dead implies a debasement of the deceased. As learned in childhood and socialization, ritualized in the Second Birth, practiced at the wedding, based in determinations of fictional descent, also in and after death, the individual is equated if possible with immortality by the Identificatory Habitus. Again this implies the radical elimination, if possible, of the biological, of becoming and passing away. Therefore, in the death ritual, the individual becomes the sacrifice, which always was and does not die, becomes the deindividualized ancestor through the father-son identification, as the ascetic is himself the sacrifice and therefore immortal. Death—in the extreme Brahmanic view—is not fate, but rather inability, error in ritual, or the incapacity to take the ascetic path and thus achieve immortality in one's lifetime.

4. The Social System

SOCIAL STRATIFICATION

The Indian family is usually a big family that lives and eats together, and shares work and property. It has common traditions, worships its own clan or family god, and maintains ritual and economic relations with certain families and professional groups, especially household priests, barbers, agricultural workers, and latrine cleaners. The family cultivates barter or market relations with other family groups in the village; I call these "extended families." The dominant groups in the traditional Indian village are generally landowners[1] (Rajputs, Kshetri, Marhatta, Nair), priests (Brahmans), astrologers (Joshi), healers (Vaidya), scribes (Kayasththa), and merchants (Baniya, Shrestha). Rank and status among builders (Jat, Kurmi, Gujar), cow herders (Ahir), goldsmiths (Sonar), carpenters, potters, brickmakers (Kumhar), blacksmiths (Lohar), barbers (Nai), launderers (Dhobi), weavers, and tailors are controversial and dependent on many local factors. Oil pressers (Teli), liquor brewers, basket weavers, butchers and leatherworkers (Mehar), tanners or knackers, street sweepers or latrine cleaners (Camar) are often considered impure and casteless. Many of these so-called Untouchables—called "Harijans" (Children of God) by Mahatma Gandhi, but increasingly now "Dalits" ("the destroyed, oppressed")—now work as day laborers in the field or in road construction. Ascetics (Bairagi) also live temporarily in the village; their status depends on their education and the spiritual abilities ascribed to them. There are seldom more than twenty to twenty-five professional groups in the village.

This network of religious and economic connections is typical of Indian villages or village groups. It is commonly called a caste system, a social network, which is termed the soul or "girding" of Hinduism.[2] Pauline Kolenda correctly indicates that before there were castes, there were only clans and tribes; but with the castes, a system of specific functions divided by professions and a ritualized distribution of labor arose. Yet, when this perspective of the professions specific to castes ceases (increasingly since the sixth "Modern" epoch, primarily in the cities), smaller or larger kinship groups, whose significance is shown primarily in marriage negotiations, emerged from castes. In the caste system, too, the determining and surviving feature is therefore descent. Thus, in the central question, raised by Louis Dumont[3] and which I also address, of why the opposition of purity and impurity affects hereditary groups and not individuals, the significance of descent is examined more closely than it has been in the past. The caste system will have "had its day" only when the fictional and substitutive rules of descent and the patrilinear system of marriage are no longer practiced.

But what is really a caste or the caste system? I will first trace the meaning of the word *caste* and the origin of caste society, then structure the social groupings and their segmentation in India, and finally examine the strategies of socioreligious delineation in domestic life.

The Caste Society[4]

It is often assumed that Hindu society consists of many hierarchically ordered, professionally structured castes, into which the individual is born and to which he belongs all his life, with hardly any possibility of professional change or mobility.[5] However, there is no agreement about the nature, scope, and manifestations of castes. What is written in the standard work on society in India by the American social scientist David Mandelbaum, who studied the ethnographic literature until the end of the 1960s, sounds almost like a surrender. The term *caste* is used for so many social units—endogamous groups, a category of such groups, a system of social organization—that it is almost better to give it up altogether.[6] A few social scientists have even almost denied the existence of such a social system.[7] The whole thing is a problem of social stratification, status, the power structures, and propertied classes that have risen in history, but not of caste. The caste system is basically a feudal structure, not very different from medieval conditions in Europe. Others claim that ideological notions of caste led to creating social realities instead of understanding them. In the British colonial bureaucracy, such groupings had to be incorporated into a system that was generally impracticable even for the British. Since a defined caste ranking was linked with privileges, there was an outright courting of higher classifications.[8]

Lack of conceptual clarity favored extremes. What was not called *caste*? Nearly every social grouping in India had to suffer for it: classes, clans, sects, tribes, professional groups, and folk communities. These distinctions are meaningful only when the criteria separating them are enumerated. And those are, first, origin (descent), marriage connection (connubium), professional and eating ties (commensality); add to those place of residence, language community, common lifestyles, family or clan deities, clan or tribal history, and the sense of belonging together.

But does this mixture need its own term? There is one convincing reason not to use the word *caste* uncritically: It is not an Indian word! If you use it, you have to be able to say what you mean. Otherwise you are seeking a phantom or constructing a society that does not really exist.[9] The fact that we have grown accustomed to the word does not justify its use. Words such as *race* or *primitive people* can no longer be used innocuously either. Do we want to use the word *caste* to maintain the notion that there is another type of human: a *homo hierarchicus,* who is deranged about norms of purity and rules of marriage? It would be conceivable, because men are quite often treated simply as collective objects of fixed ideas, as in studies of race. Two questions arise: Where does the word *caste* come from? Why has it been so triumphant?

It is generally assumed that the word *caste* is of Portuguese origin and comes from the Latin *castus* ("chaste, the unadulterated").[10] Yet, the use of this word in reference to India was quite different from the start.[11] For example, the Portuguese Barbosa writes in 1516 A.D. about the king of Calcutta that he had a thousand wives and they were from good families (*de boa caste*). In contrast, in 1561, in *Cendas da India,* the chronicler Caspar Correa talks of the *casta* of the Christians. In his *Colloquios dos Simples e Drogas e Cousas Medecinaes da India* (1563), Garcia mentions the *casta* of the cobblers. And in 1567, the Sacred Council of Goa uses the word as a synonym for "race, tribe" (*gentos*).

Thus, Julian Pitt-Rivers has denied that *caste* goes back to *castus* or the Portuguese *casta.*[12] He derives it from the Gothic *kasts,* which means "a group of animals," among other things. But Pitt-Rivers also reinforces a view that was often crucial for the use of *casta* instead of the already existing words for social groups, such as *tribe, class, nation, race,* or *clan*—that is, the purity of blood, hinted by *castus* ("chaste"). According to Pitt-Rivers, the purity of descent was not at first crucial for the usage; both *casta* and the English *caste* were used initially for castes and tribes, and there was also talk of a caste of mules.[13] But because of the bias of that time with respect to the purity of blood, it is not amazing that the word *casta* became synonymous with pure breeding and descent.[14] This view smacks of a tendency to accept purity of race and blood, and demands even greater caution.

The Portuguese and the English, as we know, were not the first to travel in India. What words did the Greek or Moslem conquerors have for the phenomenon of the so-called caste society? One of the first Greek reports comes from Megasthenes, who stayed in the court of Candragupta II in Pātaliputra, currently Patna, in about 300 B.C. Megasthenes's reports are handed down by many ancient authors, mainly by Arrian (ca. 95–175 A.D.) in his *Indikē.*[15] In this work, he talks of 188 "tribes" in India, as J. W. McCrindle translates the Greek word *meros;*[16] but a better translation would be "part [of the population]." In one place, Megasthenes also talks of seven *merē* (that is, sophists [= Brahmans?], farmers, shepherds, artisans, traders, soldiers, and officials and advisers), but he really means classes. In ancient historiography, it was common to divide the barbaric states into seven divisions. And al-Bīrūnī[17] speaks of the defense, teaching, and feeding classes, to which he assigns the Indian Varṇas and lines of descent.[18] Thus, in these early sources, the racial undertone that sounds in *casta* is clearly lacking.

Ostensibly, cultural anthropological evolutionism determined that the common Western term of segmentation did not catch on. The Europeans, led by the British, did not like to use the same words for their colonies that they used for civilized cultures. Like James George Frazer in his *Golden Bough,* Europeans thought that their culture represented the highest level of human development. People distinguished between primitives and hordes (e.g., the aborigines in Australia) and the somewhat more developed tribal cultures in Africa, South America, and Asia. The highest form of organization was states and nations, but they were reserved only for Europe. India, obviously, posed a problem for this classification. The segmentation was too diverse. Thus, a new social group was "discovered," the caste, which was seen as a closed corporation without the ability to form territorial states, comparable to the medieval guild.

Without a proper new noun, it was also hard to grasp the social delineations between dark-skinned and light-skinned members of the Indian population. But that in itself was seen as a reason for the emergence of the caste society. The dubious thesis was that castes had arisen because the immigrant, allegedly light-skinned Indo-Aryans, who did not yet know castes, could not prevail against the dark-skinned indigenous population and mingled with them; this thesis, based on the Brahmanic ideology of mixture, saw lawlessness (*adharma*) result if classes (*varṇasaṃkara*) intermingled, especially with those who were not Twice-Born.[19] Ever since the second epoch, Brahmans first propagated xenophobia against the dark Dasyus and Dāsas, and then against them as groups classified as impure. They considered the Caṇḍālas (knackers, leather workers) as bovine, on a level with the domestic pig or the dog.[20] They also placed Śūdras or Mlecchas (foreigners, barbarians) on the same level, along with animals and nonhumans.[21] Astrologers explained them as the offspring of the impure cobblers, and healers as the offspring of an illegitimate liaison between a Brahman and a Vaiśya woman.[22] An uncritical acceptance of such assertions for a social hierarchy comes from considering society only from the perspective of one social group. It is particularly bad when the racial argument is joined by another racism that claims that economic lethargy and a supposedly typical Indian apathy emerged only because of this mixture. Thus, the Indologist Hermann Oldenberg, who otherwise deserves respect, wrote in 1917: "In the luxuriant quiet of their new homeland, every Aryan, the brother of the most noble nations of Europe, mixing with the dark ancient population of India, increasingly assumed the characteristics of Hinduism, weakened by the climate . . . , and weakened by the idle enjoyments offered them by the rich land after an easy victory over inferior enemies, savages incapable of resistance, by a life which lacked great tasks, toughening suffering, strong and hard necessity."[23]

Once they were "discovered," the castes only had to be understood and recorded. Comprehensive ethnographical works, mostly titled "The Castes and Tribes of . . . ," indicate the collection mania of the colonial officials, who collected people almost like butterflies.[24] At that time, popular circus exhibitions toured Europe displaying people from distant countries. In the nineteenth century, ethnographic compendia and gazettes were often organized alphabetically. Yet, from 1901 on, when Herbert H. Risley (1851–1911) became Commissioner of the Census, a hierarchical system was introduced: Risley counted 2,378 castes and forty-three races, organized "by social precedence as recognized by native public opinion."[25] Risley was certainly not a racist in the meaning the word has acquired with German Nazism, but he was a racist in his predilection for anthropometry. He even drew up a law of caste organization, according to which, in the southern, Dravidian part of India, social status was in proportion to the width of the nose.[26]

As soon as caste became "typically Indian," it could be linked with all other distorting features ascribed to this country. It became the defining factor of Hinduism, its soul, its psychology—Risley even spoke of a "caste instinct"[27]—and it was contrasted with the West. An irrational muddle of castes, whose only structure seemed to be a rigid hierarchy, was then opposed to the clearly organized, centralized, or egalitarian Western social order. "It was impossible to shatter traditionalism, based on caste ritualism anchored in *karma* doctrine, by rationalizing the economy," wrote Max Weber,[28] who had studied Oldenberg as well as the ethnographic compendia. But were the travelers in India, the colonial officials, or the missionaries only fantasizing when they described the social reality of India? Is the caste system really only a fiction?

In 1990, Prime Minister Vishwanath Pratrap Singh announced that 27 percent of all public service positions were to be reserved for members of "backward castes." In itself, that would not have been sensational, for ever since the Indian constitution took effect on January 28, 1949, there have been such reservations for "registered castes and registered tribes" (Article 46).[29] Based on this article, there were soon quota regulations for government positions: 15 percent for the Untouchables, 7.5 percent for the Adivasis, members of India's 170 registered tribes. But the changes of 1990 went far beyond the old regulations. For the "backward castes" comprised 3,743 lower castes, more than half the Indian population, including basketmakers, barbers, blacksmiths, potters, and the populous farmer castes. No wonder this stirred protest. Middle-class students demonstrated, burned themselves in public, set fire to buses. They were worried about their future. Suddenly, they had become the minority.

No sooner had V. P. Singh announced the new rules than old conflicts erupted. In the newspapers and on the street, it was asked whether Buddhists (0.7 percent), Sikhs (1.1 percent), Christians (2.4 percent), or Moslems (11 percent) were not also minorities. According to the new regulation, hadn't Brahmans become a minority deserving protection? In Kerala, 90 percent of the population would then belong to disadvantaged groups. There was also talk of positive discrimination, because one first declared oneself and had to be registered as a minority, a "backward caste," in order to get the same chances as the others. Even the Harijans and Adivasis demonstrated against the government plan, for they saw their privileges endangered by more competitors.

The regulation of 1947 had not been much help. Corruption, lack of formal education, and low mobility meant that, despite legal provisions in the higher ranks of Category A of the Indian civil service, the Harijans and Adivasis represented only 8.5 percent and 2.3 percent, respectively. In the lower ranks, the quotas were better filled. What this means is that Untouchables became "government" street-sweepers, handymen, or kitchen helpers. There can be no question of social mobility or advancement for these disadvantaged groups. The spirit of the law was scarcely fulfilled, as the Supreme Court pointed out in a controversial decision. But if the caste system is a false belief, the Indians themselves adopted it long ago. It can no longer be denied as a form of the social organization of India.

Yet it is wrong to refer the caste system back to the Varṇa schema because then, in fact, the religious notions of the Brahmans are overestimated. As the French Indologist Robert Lingat notes, it is primarily Indologists who tend to see the effects of (Brahman) priests everywhere.[30] The tendency to want to explain the caste system from religious texts may be understandable for the early time, when one depended essentially on the legal texts and handbooks of the Dharmaśāstra. In the mid-nineteenth century, Max Müller tried to harmonize these two collections of material and establish the superiority of the Brahmans with respect to not only religion, but also society. In *Essai sur le régime des castes* (1908), which influenced Marcel Mauss, Emile Durkheim, and Louis Dumont,[31] Célestine Bouglé probably corrected this error by referring to religious, but not necessarily Brahmanic, mutual dependencies. Bouglé saw the connection of three features in the caste system as characteristic: the strategy of demarcation (*repulsion*), hierarchy, and hereditary professional specialization. The hereditary nature of professions could not be understood in "pure" economic terms and could only be justified on religious grounds. Only through religious ideas could a group be defined and classified hierarchically. By comprehending the caste as a religious institution,[32] Bouglé almost anticipated Durkheim's definition of religion: The belief system of Hindu society supported by the society—Dumont's "church" (French: *église*)—was its caste system. Since then, the thesis that the caste system could be asserted primarily because of religious ideas keeps reappearing.[33]

Yet, access to the caste system has changed since the 1950s; several studies have appeared since then that rely on observation.[34] Researchers lived in the village, took part in the life of the inhabitants, learned their languages. These village studies challenge a few theories about the caste system.[35] Some of the most important discoveries were: (1) Castes are not solid social groups, but rather cognitive concepts of social organization and hierarchy; (2) castes "function" as social systems only in a limited area; (3) dominant castes are not only Brahmans; (4) castes offer goods or services in a system of religious and economic exchange; (5) territorial points of view of the organization of mutual obligation (e.g., "little kingdoms") are very significant for the social system. Because of these discoveries, the aspects of centrality, economic dominance, and patronage are now emphasized instead of the religious origin of the caste system.

Segmentation

With the new ethnological discoveries, a smaller social group than the caste has increasingly become the focus of the social sciences: the family. Every society has its descent and kinship groups to which families belong. But what distinguishes India from the West are the size of the extended family understood as a unit and the fictionally substitutive determinations of descent. In the West, a family consists maximally of parents and siblings, the parents of the parents and possibly uncles and aunts and their children. Family size differs by region (more members in southern than in northern Europe) and denomination (more members in Catholic areas than in Protestant ones). Kinship as experienced also depends a great deal on personal predilections. But in every case, nuclear families or small extended families (possibly still with the paternal or maternal grandparents and a few other relatives) form the lived world and economic units—and this did not appear only in the modern age. In India, belonging to the family is different. First, it is extremely patrilinear (with the exception of southern India, particularly Kerala); the wife's parents and relations "belong to it" only to a very limited extent. Second, many more family members live, work, and reside together, not necessarily under one roof, but close to one another: the paternal parents and grandparents, the father's brothers and their families, and other patrilinear relations; in addition, there are employees, servants, and adopted and foster children. Thus, the nuclear family is not nearly as central as in the West.

But how does this extended family fit into other social categories such as class, caste, subcaste, or clan? There are at least five criteria for the definition of a social group: First, it is to have a comprehensible size, in which personal relations are possible. Second, it is to have external boundaries, so that members can be distinguished from outsiders. Third, its members are to develop common activities, at least temporarily. Fourth, there should be a we-feeling, a form of togetherness and belonging. And fifth, there should be a system of distribution of roles and status, which allows long-term, stable relations and not only ad hoc gatherings. In India, these criteria are best fulfilled by a social group I call an "extended family":[36] a broad circle of in-laws and blood relations, who meet regularly, work together, and practice religious rituals. Belonging to it is produced by common residence and descent with provable genealogical connecting links and through uniform distribution of roles and status—in other words, by the forms of demarcation from other extended families.

Such an extended family is also understood as part of a caste group (*varṇa*) and as a subcaste or a clan (*gotra*, literally: cow stall), and it includes the joint family as well as the extended and nuclear family. Thus, the crucial terms for the social segmentation of India are introduced (see table 14).[37] Since they are used interchangeably, they constantly contribute to confusion for both Western observers and Indians.[38] If an Indian asks another Indian about his caste (*jāti*), he usually wants to know his profession. If he knows this and nevertheless asks about caste, he generally wants to know the subcaste. If two Indians of the same subcaste ask each other about their caste, they possibly want to know the descent group. So the answer depends on the context and requires careful clarifications.

In the following section, I will define *my* use of this term. This may give the impression of essentialism, but that is specifically not intended, and so I emphasize at the start that social segments can be identified only through ascribed relations. The British anthropologist Edmund Leach correctly thought that castes did not exist per se, but rather that they could be seen only

Table 14
Social Segmentation

Social Groups	*Indian Terms*	*Relations, Functions, and Peculiarities*
Professional Class, Caste Groups	*varṇa* (also *jāti*)	Classical class order, order of professional classes, socioreligious ideology: Brāhmaṇa, Kṣatriya, Vaiśya, Śūdra
"Caste" professional groupings	*jāti*	Commonalities in professions, names, traditions; shaping of (political) caste organizations
Subcastes	*jāti*	Ditto, but circumscribed regionally and linguistically; sometimes endogamous upper limits
Clan, kinship group	*gotra, vaṃśa, kula, sāpiṇḍa;* Hindī: *kutumb, bhaibandh, khandan*	Genealogical-fictional criterion, especially relevant in marriage and kinship relations
Lineage		Blood kinship with provable connecting links
Extended family	*jāti;* Hindī: *birādarī;* Nepālī: *thar*	Close neighborly help in economic and religious matters, marriage arrangements, participation in death rituals because of being commonly affected by impurity, common lodging, and family deities, common festivals
Joint family		Similar criteria as in extended family, but also common property and household
Extended family or nuclear family	*parivāra*	Commensuality, child-rearing, care of ancestors, life-cycle rituals

Note: Gray indicates exogamous criteria.

in contrast to other castes, with whom the members were in a network of economic, political, and ritual relations.[39] For example, an Upadhyāya Brahman from Benares, a primary school teacher with a Western education, sees himself as an Indian when he watches a hockey game against Pakistan on television; as a Banarsī (inhabitant of Benares) when he travels to Delhi; as a Brahman when his (traditional) origin is asked; as a northern Indian Upadhyāya Brahman when he meets a southern Indian Nambudiri Brahman; as an Upadhyāya Brahman with the Vāsiṣṭha-Gotra (descent group) when he conducts marriage negotiations for his daughter; as the head of a family when there is a question of division of property. But never is he merely a Brahman! Never is he only a member of a caste! Such a characterization is meaningful only given the relations of the person in question. But then the Brahman can stand in several so-called caste or subcaste relationships. Therefore, table 14 serves only as an overview of the terms discussed, but should not tempt us to see subcastes, extended families, or Gotras in India as clubs whose membership can be easily identified. The very fact that the Indian terms overlap shows that each depends, in a dynamic and variable way, on contexts and relations, just as the actors in individual cases themselves see their membership in a social group and thus define these categories.

Varṇa ("class, caste-group," literally: "color")[40] is not a social group, but a classificatory unit that can be used for people as well as gods, animals, plants, or other things.[41] In reference to society, it is essentially an order of birth class (*varṇāśramadharma*)[42] and a division of social functions, but not a caste system. Since the end of the second epoch,[43] Varṇas have formed the traditional professional classes of teaching, defense, and nutrition, as well as property and slaves, thus the professional classes of the Brahmans (priests, intellectual nobility), Kṣatriyas (aristocracy, warriors), and Vaiśyas (merchants, farmers), as well as the commoners or Śūdras (servants, manual laborers). Beneath these are the Untouchables and the casteless. In the Arthaśāstra, the book of governance of Kauṭilya, the duties of the professional classes are established precisely: The Brahmans should study, teach, perform sacrifices for themselves and others, and give and receive gifts; the Kṣatriya should study, have sacrifices performed for themselves, give gifts, practice war, and defend; the Vaiśya should study, have sacrifices performed for themselves, breed cattle, and trade; the Śūdra should serve the Twice-Born as well as practice the professions of artisan and actor.[44] It is hardly tenable that the Varṇa order must be seen as an Indo-European tripartite division of social functions, as George Dumézil assumed.[45] Vaiśyas, Śūdras, Untouchables, or all three together are too interchangeable as respective remnant categories vis-à-vis Brahmans and Kṣatriyas.

The Varṇa categories are seen as the origin of the caste system in India and are traced back to Vedic and sometimes even pre-Vedic times. I cannot relate this discussion in detail here,[46] but can note a few facts. Practically nothing is known about the social system of the first "Pre-Vedic" epoch. Excavations do suggest professional specializations in the Indus Valley cultures, but conclusions about their social organization or even kinship relations are not possible. From the early Vedic period, there are several social classifications, which sometimes shaped the image of the world:[47] a bipartite division between the Indo-Aryans and the dark Dasyus and Dāsas; a tripartite division into Brahmans, Kṣatriyas, and slaves. In the late tenth book of the ṛgveda, in the so-called Puruṣa hymn,[48] the four-part division of the Varṇa system is obvious in the text, where the term *śūdra* appears for the first time. (The five-part division with the typically nameless Untouchables appears later.) In that Puruṣa hymn, the Varṇas are assigned to the body parts of a dismantled cosmic original man: "The Brahman was his mouth, the arms were made of Kṣatriya, his thigh of Vaiśya, and from his feet emerged the Śūdras."[49] In the middle Vedic period, the transition from tribal societies to small kingdoms occurred along with an increasing professional specialization:[50] The category of the exclusive professional groups or guilds was added to the social category of the class.

It is these economic differentiations that allow social segmentation. A caste system without an agrarian surplus is hardly conceivable. In the late middle Vedic period, certain administrative structures (competition for privileges in court, sinecures, rights to land use, bureaucracy) emerge. Declan Quigley correctly points out that the caste system does not function in the autarchic but still Hindu groups of the high regions of the Himalayas because such economic and political prerequisites are lacking.[51] This observation led Arthur M. Hocart to the generally correct but narrow thesis that without patronage (particularly monarchy) there is no caste system.

The Varṇa system has a social function, for it has always been used in India for a simplifying classification of social groups or individuals. It is cosmologically and mythologically justified, superregional, and based on birth status, but not on kinship: members of a Varṇa do not view each other as relatives. There are practically no sociologically ascertainable corporations or organizations of the Varṇas. Today, it is impossible to discern any clear common features in customs, professions, or rites of the individual Varṇas. Brahmans are scholars, soldiers, farmers, cooks, members of ascetic sects. Even as priests, they are employed in house, temple, or impure cremation places, and thus are so different from one another that they have practically no contact. The Varṇa system is thus predominantly a socioreligious ideology,[52] constructed not only for the "self-adulation" of the Brahmans, but designed mainly for their advantage. Anyone who accepts this interpretation, who makes the Varṇa order into the defined hierarchy of India, is arguing from the perspective of Brahmanic ideology.

The Varṇa system is also a Brahmanic ideology because it does not include the entire significance of important social groups—farmers, merchants, and artisans. The legal texts talk more about Varṇas than about subcastes. In the Varṇa system, the Vaiśyas have been something of an anomaly from the beginning.[53] In the middle and late Vedic texts, almost all the rest of the population belongs to this Varṇa; later it is mainly merchants and artisans. Yet the greatest differentiations have always been in this area, while the Brahmans and Kṣatriyas are relatively homogeneous groups. Today hardly anyone wants to be a Vaiśya, so that because of the self-classification in the Varṇas, the largest class according to profession—the Vaiśyas—has the fewest members in the census statistics. Merchants also had the strongest tendencies to turn to other religions (Buddhism, Jainism). The rigid Varṇa system is incompatible with the mobility of many merchants. So there is neither *one* hierarchy of the Varṇa system nor a Varṇa model applicable to all India. In southern India and parts of northern India, there are practically no Kṣatriyas; in many areas, there are no Brahmans. Thus, from the start, the Varṇa system is not even the attempt to comprehend social reality, but rather a method of interpreting reality with a definite goal.

That the Varṇa system has only a very limited use for describing the social strata of India has been seen early and often,[54] even by native legal scholars, who tried to maintain it despite all problems such as mixed marriages, polygamy, and adoption.[55] Nevertheless it is still used to divide the population of India. It has its own persistence, because every social classification uses such simplifications, standardizations, and idealizations: A professor who goes into politics, or a clergyman who carries on a flourishing trade in devotional objects to his own advantage, is no longer a "real" professor or clergyman in the eyes of many people.[56]

Thus, Varṇa is not a caste,[57] but a class of birth. But what is a caste? I designate as "caste"—in brief—a professional or ethnic group or, more precisely, a linguistic, ethnic, and religious supraregional, weakly endogamous social category, in which subcastes, clans, and extended families are made into one classificatory unit, whose similarities are mainly in profession, less in custom, mythology, and rite. In this sense, all blacksmiths (*lohar*) form a caste, if they practice the same profession, but there can also be Lohars who are not blacksmiths, and there are blacksmiths who are not Lohars. To use the definition of *lohar* meaningfully requires indicating whether it is the profession that is meant or something else. All millers belong to a common professional group, but no one will say that everyone named "Miller" forms a social group, that is, that those whose name is "Miller" establish a federation. But all millers do form a classificatory unit. The same is true in India; but there the family name is (still) also often the traditional indication of profession, which in the West forms an amusing exception, e.g., the millers who are actually named Miller. Caste names, moreover, can be names for tribes (for example, Gujars), sects (Giri), classes (Chetri), or titles (Shastri); they can arise from customs, professions, activities, settlements, or even nicknames.

If a northern Indian blacksmith is asked about his caste (*jāti*), he may say "Lohar," but he thus sees himself only vaguely in the category of all other blacksmiths who also call themselves "Lohar," just as the Millers in Ohio and Oregon are also usually connected only by name. Marriage relationships or other interactions do not necessarily exist between the individual social groups that bear the same (caste) name. Only since the sixth "Modern" epoch have there been common organizations, supraregional meetings, or celebrations in which subcastes amalgamate into a caste—usually for political purposes. "Caste" is thus the designation for a unit of people whose solidarity is constructed of common features. Consequently, "there is" as much a caste as there is a Varṇa.[58] In this limited sense, the caste system is in fact essentially a Western construct, for if we are talking of the caste of barbers, we can just as correctly talk of the professional group or—*pace* Hocart—the "ritual group" of the barbers and thus avoid a loaded word. The barbers in the south have almost nothing in common with their colleagues in the north except their profession: In the south, they are often also death priests and thus have an essentially more profound position; in the north, they are also marriage brokers or even assistants of the Brahmans.[59] How ideologically loaded is the word *caste* is shown by the stigmatizing term *casteless,* in which European caste thinkers join forces disastrously with the Brahmanic Varṇa hierarchy. If "caste" were a value-free category used only to understand and describe social groups, there ought not to be casteless people, just as there are no classless people.

Various social groups, for whom Western authors use terms like *caste, subcaste, clan, lineage,* or even *village,* are often denoted in India with only one word, that is, *jāti.*[60] The Sanskrit word *jāti,* derived from the verbal root *jan/jā* ("to be born") is partially synonymous with *varṇa* and is also used in the sense of the decadence of the once ideally realized Varṇa system mentioned above.[61] In Hindī, *jāti* has many more meanings: "descent," "birth," "race," "family," "genre," "species," "type," "state," "nation," etc. Thus, adopting this word can hardly solve the substantive or conceptual problems. Along with most authors, I use *jāti* in the sense of "subcaste,"[62] meaning a category like caste, but in an ethnically, linguistically, regionally, and religiously circumscribed sense: for example, all Bhandaris in Nepal. It may seem absurd to see a subsegment as central,[63] to talk of "subcastes" and avoid the word *caste*. But this manner of speaking seems to me justified primarily because, on the one hand, the discussion of India is inconceivable without the term *caste;* yet on the other hand, the term evokes holistic associations that, as I have tried to explain, have no foundation. The term *subcaste* breaks the uncritical use of the word *caste,* without giving it up altogether. Yet, subcaste is not to stand as "sub" to caste, but is to explain that it is possible only on a subordinated level, circumscribed regionally and contextually, to determine those relations that still allow us to talk of castes at all.

Subcastes often form the endogamous upper limit, but the criteria of endogamy require even more criteria (descendance, village-exogamy, etc.) to be effective: Members of subcastes often see one another as equal without necessarily entering into marriage relations or eating cooked food together. Subcaste relationships are always being reshaped by moving from one place to another, property distribution, or squabbles, by a change of profession or religious practices, by the conversion of non-Hindus to Hinduism or the conversion of Hindu population groups to Islam or Christianity. Members of subcastes often have the same language, name, and profession, and a common ethnic history. Many subcastes were previously tribes and became subcastes only through a gradual process of adjustment and increased relations.

Subcastes usually have exogamous clans (*gotra, birādarī, vaṃśa*), which can encompass several thousand members. By this I mean unilinear descent groups (in northern India usually patrilinear), whose genealogical connecting links are fictional and can hardly be listed except for a legendary patriarch. As seen above in the determinations of descent during marriage, individual clan segments or descent groups see themselves as equal with respect to the common patriarch, as a common (paternal) race (*gotra, vaṃśa*) or as a common family (*kula*). (Indian terms overlap here as in *varṇa* and *jāti.*) Therefore, a marriage within the clan is considered incest. Most clan segmentations are in the subcastes that are counted among the two higher classes (Brahmans and Kṣatriyas). Above all, ruling subcastes sometimes have written genealogies (*vaṃśāvalī*), marriage records, and texts with the legends of the origin of their clan. Frequently, they worship one or more common clan divinities and have common Brahman priests. Unlike the Varṇa system, the clan system intervenes more strongly in social reality through the rules of exogamy and thus forms a central internal delimitation criterion for the subcaste. Thus, the Nepalese

Śreṣṭha subcaste, which is characterized by a common Tibeto-Birmanic language and a common ethnic root, is segmented among other things by exogamous clans (Malla, Pradhān, Jośī, etc.): These segments sometimes recombine internally into hierarchical clan groups (Chatharīya Śreṣṭha, Pāñctharīya Śreṣṭha, etc.), but are usually understood externally as Śreṣṭhas.

Subcastes consist not only of clans, but also of exogamous lineages (*jāti, sāpiṇḍa*) and extended families. The difference between clan and lineage is that the genealogical-fictional clans play a role only in marriage connections, whereas blood kinship lineages—in the sense proposed here—are a group of families whose genealogical connecting links are remembered for several generations and who therefore maintain more or less close relations in everyday life.

I call a group with a common Gotra and lineage an "extended family,"[64] when several encounters occur between them in everyday life: for example, all Jośī Śreṣṭhas of the town of Dhulikhel and its neighboring villages. Such an extended family does not have common property, but does frequently have a common organization with a leader or a council that decides political, economic, and ritual questions such as the issue of a neglect of caste obligations (*kriyālopa*). Only the extended families can really control the members because caste-exclusion usually consists of avoiding contact with the person in question, not eating with him anymore, rejecting him as a candidate for marriage. Extended families meet for common celebrations and tend to agree about techniques of work, myths, rituals, customs, and behavior. There is economic exchange in the extended families through productivity and organizations that affirm solidarity, such as the death rituals. Under certain assumptions, members of an extended family can eat cooked food together; they form a food community. People know each other, even if sometimes only remotely, but there is a tangible feeling of kinship and belonging. From his extended family, a person obtains identity, pride, and self-awareness.

The extended family is divided into various extended and nuclear families that live under one roof or in close proximity. Therefore, spatial proximity often expresses kinship belonging too. If these extended families have common property and a common household, one also speaks of a joint family.[65]

In this social network, the individual is obligated primarily to his extended family. As the previous section on childhood showed, the child can only "realize" himself sometimes, according to Louis Dumont, when he abandons the network, when, for example, he becomes an ascetic. There is little latitude for personal predilections and tendencies. Whom the individual marries, what he studies and the work he does, where he lives, with whom he lives—all that depends not so much on his individual abilities and wishes, but on the norms of his extended family and his family.

For marriage connections and often also for profession, the extended family is central; for the everyday life of the household, nuclear and extended families are crucial. Here one cooks, eats, works, and sleeps. Here one sits with other family members every day, smokes the water pipe, jokes, quarrels—and talks about others in the village: who may do what or when, who may or—more important—may not practice what activity, who may eat with whom, who may take part in processions in what function, who may not enter the temple, who may or, more important, may not be where. Those are questions of everyday life in India; quite often, they concern purity and impurity.

One category has not been discussed in this section: class in a modern sense. This is because in India, it is only since the sixth "Modern" epoch began that membership in important social groups can be changed, and only conditionally, because it is connected with descent. Membership in a class in the modern sense, on the other hand, in principle goes beyond denominational, regional, racial, lineage, and generational criteria. Moving out of the working class into the bourgeoisie was difficult and rare, but it was possible through inheritance or property ownership, higher education, or participation in cultural activities. But this is nearly excluded in traditional India. Status and prestige may be changed, but not kinship membership in the central social groupings. No matter how rich a leather worker may be, his daughter might only be able to marry a Brahman who then would be seen as corrupt by others. Especially in decisions of marriage, social barriers still exist—to this day—and a large part of everyday activities consists of marking and constantly redefining these social boundaries of the extended family. Many forms of contact and mixing are thus seen as detrimental to status. People try to keep themselves and their extended family as pure as ever—that is, to protect it from impurity.

The collective social norms of subcastes and extended families can be seen as social boundaries. Cohesion of the extended family is quite obviously the focus. Its disintegration is counteracted, as will be shown below, for economic reasons and especially reasons concerning salvation. Extended families tend to protect themselves. But since it is a society defined by the division of labor, this is possible only to a limited extent. Therefore, social contact is the area governed by social norms. Despite their excluding tendency, these norms prove to be explicitly integrative. New groupings (professional groups, subcastes, religious communities, ethnic groups) can emerge and be incorporated with relatively few problems. This stabilizing capacity of the so-called caste system is always being rediscovered in amazement,[66] for it contradicts assertions that the caste system is static and does not allow any (economic) change.

The extended family defined by descent shapes the cohesion of Hindu society both internally and externally above and beyond economic change. Once again, Max Weber saw this clearly: The domestic cult of ancestors parallels the "patriarchal structure of the household, since only in a patriarchal structure is the home of central importance for the men." And "where the power and significance of the domestic cult and priesthood remain unimpaired, they naturally form an extremely strong personal bond, which exercises a profound influence on the family and the *gens* [one could also say *gotra*], unifying the members firmly into a strongly cohesive group. This cohesive force also exerts a strong influence on the internal economic relationships of the households. It effectively determines and stamps all the legal relationships of the family, the legitimacy of the wife and heirs, and the relation of sons to their fathers and of brothers to one another."[67] In my words, they have become a habitus.

SOCIAL CONTACTS

Since the end of the second "Vedic" epoch, Indian society has been characterized by the division of labor and professional specialization, in which mainly male members of an extended family have several contacts outside their kinship and subcaste groupings. As in all such societies, men come together to work with one another, exchange goods, offer and receive services, manage village or urban tasks (for example, to build roads, temples, or bridges), protect the community, make war, establish rights of the use of land, water, or roads, pay duties, or organize communal celebrations. The encounters and contacts in these social everyday contacts are the subject of this and the next section. Since it primarily concerns the subject of purity and impurity, the impression may arise that Indians are over-anxious about social contact, and so it is necessary here to preclude a widespread misunderstanding: Purity has little to do with cleanliness or hygiene; impurity has little to do with dirt. Purity and impurity are religious and ritual categories. Indians, Hindus, Brahmans, and Untouchables are just as clean as other people in similar walks of life!

I begin with a thesis: Pollution enters through temporal and spatial change, especially in contact with other people. On the other hand, avoiding change and contact is a goal of deliverance, attainable through the ascetic abolition of all boundaries or through the denial of boundaries by means of the Identificatory Habitus. My thesis, which goes back to Mary Douglas, Louis Dumont, and Marc Bloch, is based on the observation that change is also "dying," disappearance from existence. This applies to supplying food or moving to another house, as well as to new life (birth) and death.

In the framework of a theory of action and communication, as Pierre Bourdieu has presented, every communicative act is an "injury or a questioning of self-esteem," a "virtual dishonoring"[68] and a transgression of boundaries. Similarly, giving something—gifts, words, a greeting, or a look—to someone else is to expose oneself to him by giving him the possibility of a culturally and socially acceptable or unacceptable reply. The salvation ideal of no contact in the Brahmanic-Sanskritic Hindu religion grates against the socially demanded contact norms, as can be illustrated and proved with many examples from everyday life, even if it must be added that the variations are considerable and hardly any observation can be generalized. I limit myself to three examples: greeting, touching, and eating.

Greeting[69]

Dharma is "law and custom"[70] and thus, in Western eyes, frequently is simple etiquette. But it always concerns rules of cooperation, especially contact. The casual greeting is the most distant and shortest form of encounter, but it is contact and follows norms similar to those of marriage or eating together. For greeting also primarily concerns the bonds between giver and receiver, or, on the other hand, maintaining distance and thus marking a distinction in rank.

In Indian legal texts, rules of greeting occupy a great deal of space. They follow the same rules as the exchange of gifts. Indeed, the right to greet, gestures of greeting, forms of address, and the order of rank to be observed in greeting can vary according to class, age, race, profession, or situation; but the forms of greetings of the legal texts I am concentrating on here indicate not only the Brahmanic hierarchy, but also the effort to avoid pollution. For example, the greeting may be given only to a worthy recipient.[71] Not everyone may be greeted. An impure person is not to be greeted, nor is the verbal greeting of an impure person to be answered with words. The greeting is to be given in a respectful spirit, as an expression of deep respect to one who is of higher standing.[72] Greeting, accepting greetings, return greetings, and gestures of greeting are formalized. According to a Dharmaśāstra text,[73] while greeting, one should stand up; the formal greeting varies according to class and prestige, and the formula for greeting also varies according to the relationship between the greeter and the greeted. One should either touch the greeted one with the hands on the feet or with the *añjali* gesture (fig. 6), by placing the hands flat on one another, or with a raised right hand—always graded according to criteria of rank. Or the Brahman should greet the Kṣatriya with *añjali* at ear level, the Vaiśya at chest level, the Śūdra at stomach level.[74] Verbal forms of greeting are also stipulated precisely.

Strangers, enemies, murderers, menstruating women, running people, drunks,

6. Members of a clan of Jyāpu farmers greet their divinity, represented by a stone in the field near Bhaktapur, Nepal. Photographer: N. Gutschow, 1986.

eating people, yawning people, and others are not to be greeted.[75] The danger of disaster and pollution is inherent in these greetings, partly because they are in a fleeing or transient situation. A Brahman must not greet Kṣatriyas and Vaiśyas first. On the other hand, it says that even a ten-year-old Brahman is a father with respect to a hundred-year-old Kṣatriya and is to be greeted by him first.

At least a gestured return greeting is demanded in every case, even from Brahmans. When one is greeted, one should return the greeting or stand up. Otherwise, one goes to hell.[76] Anyone who does not reply to the greeting of a Brahman will be reborn as a tree at the cremation place, where vultures and crows gather. And it also says that one shares disaster (*pāpa*) with the greeters if one does not return the greeting. The obligation (*dharma*) to return a greeting exists even with a casteless Caṇḍāla, who is to be greeted in return with "have a drink" (*piba surāḥ*). In view of its function to express peacefulness, cutting off a greeting is generally equal to an act of violence, an aggression, an insult; greeting and replying to a greeting are peacemaking gestures.[77]

Direct physical contact in greeting or in showing respect especially requires rules. Touching the feet is a sign of reverence by self-imposed pollution, the respect pollution, as Edward Harper has called it.[78] The handshake was not a usual greeting in India and has appeared only through Western influence. But conferring a forehead mark (*ṭīkā*), usually a red dot, is widespread. This gesture of blessing is a significant feature of the purity and higher rank of the one granting the blessing.[79] Here too, the purer gives the impure *grosso modo* the Ṭīkā, the higher-ranking one the lower-ranking one, the older the younger, the man the woman. Thus, a little girl who is worshipped as the goddess Kumārī in the annual Indrajātrā celebration grants the king the Ṭīkā, while the king presses the forehead sign on certain selected soldiers, officials, and subjects.

Ascetics avoid contact with normal people to a large extent. Ideally, they do not greet, occasionally not even the gods, in order to demonstrate their equality of rank: According to the tradition of Nepal chronicles, the ascetic priest Nityānanda first refused to bow to two statues of gods, even though he had been required to do that by king Śivasiṃhamalla (ca. 1578–1619); but when he did bow, the statues shattered, whereupon the king could still prevent him from bowing to Paśupati, the tutelary deity of Nepal.[80]

Thus, the danger in greeting resides in what is given, what produces contact: the hand, the word, the gesture, the look. Greeting is not only words. It concerns a world in which speech and names acquire a subtle quality. And if something is given, the obligation exists to return the gift, which creates dependence and can thus pollute.

Touching[81]

The body receives and excretes. "We should expect the orifices of the body to symbolize its specially vulnerable points," notes Mary Douglas.[82] All liquid excretions—sweat, saliva, semen, blood, especially menstrual blood, excrement—but also hair, fingernails, and toenails[83] can be polluting if someone else comes in contact with them. At any rate, the extent of the pollution is again dependent on status, age, race, and the kinship proximity of the persons in question. Therefore, excretions are impure because they are an expression of a visible, biologically physical process, hence a change. And the stickier, the more consistent, and the more adhesive they are, the more impure:[84] jam on the kitchen table is "dirtier" than bread crumbs.

Pollution is contagious. Therefore, it is not only the individual body that is polluted, but, under some circumstances, also the whole extended family.[85] If, among the southern Indian Havik Brahmans, a man first touches a menstruating woman and then touches someone else, the latter must also bathe and put on new garments. The pollution becomes extinct only from the fourth contact person.[86] This is certainly an extreme example, but in the case of death, the whole extended family is afflicted with impurity, by degrees. Just as pollution can be passed on, religious merit (*puṇya*) can also be transmitted: The

7. Paṇḍā priest in Benares: A client puts the morning forehead mark (*ṭīkā*) on himself after a bath in the Ganges; the priest may only give it to those of lower rank. Photographer: N. Gutschow, 1992.

wife who goes to the temple every morning brings back Puṇya for her husband and family.

Therefore, a pollution of the body is not a question of personal feelings, such as disgust, but rather the violation of the norms of an extended family and the position of the individual in it. The Western dualistic separation between material and spiritual, substance and attribute, does not fit India. Emotional qualities such as sorrow, hatred, and love are understood almost as substances, as material and usually also "spiritual." What the body excretes is part of the essence and nature of the individual.

What pollutes is consequently a substance or a quality that cannot be separated from its originator or bearer. Dust and sweat on feet are not impure in principle, but only depending on the person in question. If a younger person touches the feet of an older person, if a woman touches the feet of her husband, if a pilgrim touches the feet of a statue of a god, this is a sign of subordination and respect. And even when a person has ritually purified himself personally after a pollution he is still not pure for all other members of his subcaste. The status of purity of the extended family as a whole can only be elevated collectively, but not through the virtuous behavior of the individual.

Biological intervals imply extreme changes of the body and thus are extremely polluting. For example, menstruation: It is a common notion among the southern Indian Haviks[87] that red ants come into the house (not only to the polluted persons) if a family member touches a menstruating woman; there (and in other subcastes), a menstruating woman is isolated for days in a separate room without any contact. Or, for example, birth: According to the Dharmaśāstras,[88] the woman in childbirth is on the same level as corpse-bearers or dogs. Or, for example, death: For days, many relatives are polluted. But life-cycle turning-points such as initiation and marriage are also changes that require special purification. In them, the social body changes to a certain extent. A child becomes a Twice-Born, a virginal daughter becomes a wife. These are rites of passage in which the extended family changes because the family roles have to be redefined. Basically, simple change, time, an anomaly or inequality are all polluting. Unfamiliar temporal changes also pollute: an eclipse, the transition between day and night, the change of month and year.

All physical contact is potentially polluting. This does not apply only to sexual relations and married life. "Contact" even with the shadow of a distiller could make a traditional Brahman immediately take a ritual bath. In many regions, therefore, Untouchables[89] had to keep a suitable distance and live outside the village in some cases. Even their name is an expression of status: They are untouchable because they are impure and thus inferior. On the other hand, the right to touch children is not a sign of friendship or intimacy, but rather of social position. In the West, too, people do not want strangers touching their children, but this is a matter of preference. In India it is also a matter of relative status.

Eating[90]

The efforts of many subcastes to limit contact with other extended families can be observed particularly in eating. For, just as excretions can endanger a person, what he ingests forms him internally. Man, animals, food, animate and inanimate material are thus subject to the same categories and qualities (*guṇa*). Orality and morality belong together. This connection also forms the core of the notion of reincarnation. Pure food not only is an expression of an external status, but also makes one pure internally and morally.

The production of foodstuffs and not only their consumption can cast doubt on the status of purity. Distillers or butchers usually have a lower status than bakers or milkmen. But here too, individual status depends on local relations and extended families. In coastal regions, where people live from fishing, a fisherman has a higher position than in the interior. In the traditional Brahmanic view, farmers practice an impure activity because they work the soil and thus inevitably kill small living creatures. But where Brahmans are farmers themselves, this attitude changes.

Actually, hardly anything can be generalized with regard to commensuality. The age, status, and sex of the persons cooking, serving, and eating are to be taken into account just as much as the time and place as well as the cooking utensils and the foodstuffs themselves. Thus, the kitchen must be a separate area, protected from strangers, animals, and spirits. It is purified every day before and after eating, and is frequently also purified with cow dung. In Nepal, the kitchen is often not on the lower floor, but in the upper stories, where a trespasser would find it difficult to enter. Occasionally, when a stranger passes by, the housewife closes the kitchen door as soon as he approaches.

For even looking at food can pollute it. Therefore, not everyone may cook, in any case not menstruating women. On the other hand, Brahman cooks are in great demand. Eating is done only in a place (*cauka,* "square") just previously purified (among traditional Brahmans occasionally with cow dung). Thus, orthodox Brahmans occasionally change clothing, put on a piece of seamless cloth as a loin cloth, which has not even been touched by an impure tailor. One eats with the right hand; the left side of the body is considered impure, especially the left hand because it is used for cleaning after defecation.

Cooking utensils must also be pure. Wood and clay vessels are considered impure more often than metal utensils. Here consistency is crucial: Wood and clay cannot be cleaned as well, cannot be purified of pollution, and must therefore be thrown away.[91]

Foodstuffs are chosen by qualities of purity—though according to classifications that vary from one place to another. These concern not only the food, but also basic categories of experience, comparable to the Chinese Yin-Yang dichotomy. Thus, there is the distinction between what grows wild and what is cultivated, what grows in the ground and what grows on the ground, what is cooked and what is raw, what is boiled and what is roasted, foodstuffs prepared at home and food prepared elsewhere, or the separation between food and leftovers. Above all, foods touched by human hands are exposed to social restrictions. Cooked food has its original condition changed, and thus the status of the one who prepared it is to be considered. This is why fasting often means only not ingesting any prepared food or any cooked grains, the staple foods.[92]

The distinction between raw and cooked food and the resulting food taboos are widespread. Raw foodstuffs may be taken and eaten by almost everyone (since they are impure). Otherwise, there could be no trade in foodstuffs. Such foodstuffs are still "without contact," since they are not yet mixed with water,

TABLE 15
Nepalese Classification of Food into "Hot" and "Cold"

Food	*"Cold" (Nepalī* sardhi*)*	*"Hot" (*garam*)*
Vegetables	Beans, tomatoes, sweet potatoes, yams, cucumbers, pumpkin	Peppers, onion, garlic
Fruit	Pineapple, papaya, bananas, citrus fruits	Mango
Cereals	Cooked rice, threshed rice (Nep. *ciuro*), lentils, corn, nuts	Wheat, millet
Dairy products	Cow and water buffalo milk, buttermilk, yogurt	
Meat, eggs	Water buffalo, lamb	Mutton, chicken, goat, pigeon, fish, eggs
Fats	Clarified butter	Corn oil
Sweets	Honey	Sweets fried in oil
Alcohol, tobacco	Corn beer, millet beer, sour alcohol	Distilled alcohol, cigarettes

fat, or spices. Undiluted and uncooked milk as well as water is usually considered so pure that they can barely transport impurity. But even through the drinking vessel—made by human hands—that can change. Therefore, it is preferable to drink water out of your own hand.

The separation between "cold" and "hot" foods is also widespread (see table 15).[93] According to this, all grains cooked in water, especially cooked rice, but also milk, clarified butter, most fruits, honey, lentils, and many kinds of vegetables, are also "cold, raw" (Hindī *kaccā,* Nepālī *sardhi*). These stand for the clear, pure, "Brahmanic" qualities of abstinence, serenity, and gentleness. "Hot" (*garam*) foods, on the other hand, are vegetables or sweets (e.g., *laḍḍū, halvā*) fried in clarified butter (*ghī*) or oil, meat, eggs, onions, garlic, mangos, and vegetables that grow in the ground; they produce desire, courage, and aggression. Knowledge preserved in native medicine, the Āyurveda, and folk medicine makes sure that the food of both groups (cold and hot) is in balance.

This subdivision has effects on the ingestion of such foods. Thus, from a Brahmanic perspective, *kaccā* food cooked in water is to be taken only in your own house and only when it is prepared under the specific stipulations of purity. *Pakkā* or *garam* food fried in clarified butter, however, can also be eaten outside the house, in some cases even if it is prepared by those of inferior rank. For this reason, at public celebrations, one sees many stands with fruit and fried snacks, but fewer snack bars with cooked food.

Vegetarianism[94] is usually the sign of a self-proclaimed high status, since the Brahmanic view considers consuming meat impure. This is connected with the ideal of Ahiṃsā discussed above, of not wounding living creatures. But note that the Ahiṃsā is observed more by Vaiśyas and women than by other classes and by men.[95] It is a clear, externally demonstrable sign of a status of purity that is not acquired by birth; consequently, it is popular as a means of improving one's status of purity. This is also true for the ban on remarriage of young widows, another means of "raising status" that is not dependent on birth.

Who may accept cooked food from whom? What was said above about weddings or greetings also applies here: The younger may accept cooked food from the elder, the wife from the husband, the inferior rank from the superior rank. Exceptions are weddings, when the bride's family entertains the higher-ranking groom's family; Brahman cooks, when they are hired by higher-ranking Brahmans; or temple feeding (fig. 8), when the food is seen as leftovers of the gods and thus all believers stand at the same level and eat next to one another. When the wife eats the leftovers of her husband or eats after him from his plate, that is also considered a sign of respect through deliberate pollution, as respect pollution.

Eating as an expression of social intercourse, the most popular form of togetherness in the West, hardly exists in traditional India. One is not invited to dinner. And if this does happen with a Western visitor, the guests frequently sit and eat separately from the host. Separation here is a sign of respect, not of distancing or disdain. Thus, nuances of status distinctions can be observed: If the host personally clears the plates with the leftovers, that can be an expression of respect for the guest. If he does not do that, but calls a servant, he may wish to demonstrate his superiority.[96]

Whether greeting, touching, or eating, the danger always lies in the social contacts the individual or the food is exposed to. There is a deep-rooted fear of becoming sick or dying because the food was bewitched, or because one was exposed to an evil look or an impure touch. This observation corresponds to the high ideal of avoiding contact. For this reason, fasting is also popular; among the Jainas, fasting to death, the complete avoidance of contact with (the producer of) foodstuffs, is even a means of deliverance. But, as we said,

8. Temple feeding in the Svāmī-Nārāyaṇa Temple of Ahmedabad: Deviating from the usual, believers of various subcastes take a common meal and thus express equality before god. Photographer: N. Gutschow, 1977.

these fears are not to be understood individually, but collectively. The specific permission and ban of social contacts creates the identity of an extended family and its subdivisions. Therefore, caste-exclusion also and primarily means lifting every contact: the exclusion of commensuality and connubiality.

Purity and Impurity[97]

These sections on greeting, touching, and cooking may give the impression that Indians are constantly preoccupied with protecting themselves against pollution, as if they saw in every contact a danger of pollution, as if they were all somewhat exaggeratedly preoccupied with simple externalities. This impression follows from my representation of the norms of social contact essentially from the Brahmanic perspective. And I must criticize myself for that, since the Brahmans along with the Indologists or the anthropologists influenced by Indologists have fallen prey to an obsession with purity, which distorts the reality of India.

Brahmanic norms of purity, naturally, do not come out of the blue. They are included in the legal texts and are widespread in the country. Most villagers still cook for themselves when they are traveling, not only for fear of spoiled food or because of expensive food in restaurants. Even decades ago, in Kashmir, soccer players underwent a ritual purification after they came in contact with the impure leather ball. And Europeans could serve canned food to Brahmans, while the same food was refused if it was made from scratch.[98]

Nevertheless, there are many counterexamples. Mobility and modernity in India today work against such strict adherence to Brahmanic norms of purity. How can there be factories or restaurants if people may hardly work and eat together? How can you know on a trip who cooked a dish? Must you therefore always cook for yourself or only accept fried food? How can you avoid physical contact on crowded buses or trains? By and large, modernization has been introduced without any problem. Pills are swallowed even if they have been made by Christians or Moslems. Autopsies led to an uprising in Calcutta in 1835, but not later. With the public water supply, there was at first a quarrel about the rights of use, but today it is hardly for ritual reasons. Cafeterias in factories, in the army, in the universities have encountered no resistance worthy of the name. Nevertheless, it must be observed that norms of purity do remain strict at home. Someone who eats next to someone else in the cafeteria does not necessarily sit down with him at the same table at home. Next to one another is not with one another. Thus, Hindu commensuality is primarily "sacramental" commensuality.

Brahmanic norms of purity are ideal notions which are seldom followed strictly, and those who do so are usually exposed to scorn. Edward B. Harper cited examples of that: the Brahman who always purifies himself ritually in the river after sexual intercourse, so everyone knows about his sexual life; or the Brahman widow who bathes even when she only hears the words "leather sandals."[99] Although extreme examples are illustrative of cultural ideals, an absolute determination of purity is not possible. There is a certain acceptance of specific criteria of purity such as the cow or Ganges water; and the Garuḍapurāṇa says[100] that Kuśa grass, fire, mantras, basil, priests, and cows never lose their effect. It is generally accepted that leather, death, or excretion produce impurity. But in between, there is no generally accepted hierarchy or scale. Even death priests and cremators are not equally impure. On the contrary, the latter can be Brahmans (although ones of low status), the former are considered Untouchables. A standard of purity for all India on the basis of characteristics is not possible because neither a single substance of purity nor generally accepted criteria of purity can be found. The rural subcaste of Kolis in north Indian Kangra is practically no different in its forms of life and activities from certain Rajput extended families in the same village; yet the Kolis are impure for the Twice-Born, but not the Kṣatriya Rajputs for the Kolis and other subcastes.[101]

Following Emile Durkheim and Marcel Mauss, Mary Douglas has correctly emphasized the cognitive aspects in the relativity of purity.[102] Ideas of purity serve to maintain cultural categories and ideals: Everything alien must be kept far away and isolated. "Dirt is material in the wrong place," says Mary Douglas. Sand is dirt on the kitchen floor, but not on the beach. "In short, our pollution behavior is the reaction which condemns any object or idea likely to confuse or contradict cherished classifications," she writes, about an article by Edward B. Harper.[103] In this sense, purity can be understood as an attempt to maintain the cultural categories and orientations that are acquired, handed down, and learned, even against new experiences and better knowledge. The public nature of cultural categories prevents a rapid revision. What the individual may see for himself as different for a long time is not yet generally accepted culturally. Nevertheless, the public must also come to terms with anomalies that occur and adjust its system of categories to keep up with the time.

Therefore, there can be a general standard of purity only in changing and altering delimitations of impurity. Purity is avoidance of impurity; impurity is loss of purity. Since a definition of purity and impurity that would be binding on all Hindu religions is not possible, the anthropologist McKim Marriott has proposed paying attention to the interactions between extended families.[104] Such a model assumes at least two persons. Who may touch whom, who may enter whose house, who may eat with whom, or who may marry whose daughter? From the forms of encounter and exchange, purity and impurity can be defined from their common features even as a social and ritual hierarchy of extended families and subcastes. The interaction model has four advantages, especially for ascertaining hierarchies, but it does not obviate the need to comprehend the system of categories, because only then can it be seen that refusing food concerns (ritual) impurity and not, for example, personal antipathies or local power relations.

In India, the problem resides in the multiplicity and changing acceptance of the systems of categories. This has already appeared in the various divisions of foodstuffs. But the criteria certainly can be standardized by a broad acceptance of Brahmanic values, the economic dominance of a subcaste as landowners, or the decrees of rulers. Thus, in the mid-nineteenth century the Nepalese prime minister and actual ruler Jaṅga Bahādur Rāṇā established an "official" hierarchy with a codex (Mulukī Ain) based on criteria of food and purity:[105] At the top are those who "wear the Sacred Thread" (various Brahman subcastes, Kṣatriyas, ascetics, and others), followed by "alcohol drinkers who cannot be enslaved" (including the ethnic Magar, Gurung, and Sunuwar), and "alcohol drinkers who can be enslaved" (Tibetans, potters, etc.); in the lowest two places are "impure but touchable subcastes" (butchers, tailors, or musicians, launderers, Moslems, and Western foreigners) and "Untouchables" (blacksmiths, tanners, tailors, street singers, knackers).

Obviously, the ruler of the heterogeneous population of Nepal wanted to introduce structure. So he classified the many ethnic groups relatively high, even though these groups were hardly familiar with a caste system. Indeed, in the same text, the traditional Varṇa model is also found. There is also a formulaic discussion of four classes (*varṇa*) and thirty-six subcastes (*jāt*), without saying which of the more than seventy subcastes belong to which Varṇa. But whenever there are concrete stipulations, acts of atonement, or rules of respect, there is a very precise differentiation between the individual subcastes and ethnic groups. Jaṅga Bahādur Rāṇā would not and could not give up using the Brahmanic Varṇa system, perhaps in order to authoritatively enhance the value of his codex. Thus, even within a relatively homogeneous and recent legal text, extremely variable criteria of purity (descent, Sacred Thread, alcohol, water, touchability) are applied.

As I have tried to show, the focus of life shaped by the Hindu religions is the extended family, whose identity and pride must constantly be tested by limiting or regulating social contact with other extended families. The identity of the extended family is determined essentially by being born into it. Marriage, profession, or social contact are thus influenced decisively by a criterion related to birth so that in traditional India, free choice of profession and spouse, equality of opportunity, and mobility are ideals that are valued less than the ideal of descent of the extended family. Quite often, in a conflict between extended family and job, the family is preferred despite crushing poverty; every personnel manager in India can sing a song about that. Nevertheless, in a stratified society with a division of labor, the autonomy of the extended family has its limits. An extended family can make an absolute claim, but can hardly enforce it. Thus, what is noteworthy for India is not only the great breadth of behavioral norms, but also the fact that these can exist alongside one another because of the relative autonomy of the extended families. Why traditional Indian society is nevertheless still analyzed as an especially hierarchical society and why such a view is only conditionally correct are the subjects of the following section.

RELIGIOUS AND SOCIAL HIERARCHY[106]

Along with the subject of purity, research on India has been mainly preoccupied and tangled up in the question of the social and religious hierarchy. Most social scientists have seen the Brahmanic model of society and its hierarchy as a binding or dominating order, not least because Western social theories prefer the aspect of solidarity: The Brahman is at the head, the others see him as their ideal. This Brahman-centric view—represented by Max Weber, Louis Dumont, and Jan Heesterman among others—has fallen into disrepute in recent years. It has been attacked violently by Declan Quigley, culminating in the statement that whoever sees the Brahmans as the highest caste will never understand how the caste system (and Hindu society) functions.[107] I will first criticize the Brahman-centric theory, then deal with the relation between religious and economic dominance, and finally reinforce the argument with the example of the gift.

Priests and the Supremacy of the Brahmans[108]

The Indologist Jan Heesterman begins his influential 1964 article, "Brahmin, Ritual, and Renouncer," with the words: "In Hindu society, the brahmin stands supreme."[109] The sociologist Louis Dumont (who preferred the term social anthropologist) followed Heesterman two years later with a similar statement: "The Brahmans, being in principle priests, occupy the supreme rank with respect to the whole set of castes."[110] Max Weber also spoke of "the pervasive and all-powerful influence of the Brahmans."[111]

Proofs for this Brahman-centric perspective were easy to enlist, especially from Sanskrit literature,[112] where the Brahman is sacrosanct and enjoys privileges, immunities, and tax exemptions. He is at the top of the scale of purity and sees himself as godlike. Many eulogies are devoted to Brahmans; gifts to Brahmans are always represented as auspicious; it says everywhere that other classes or subcastes have to serve the Brahmans. On the other hand, Brahmans are exempt from agriculture and trade, and should devote themselves mainly to studying the Veda. They may not be beaten and certainly not killed; they are not subject to the death penalty for capital crimes; on the street they have the right of way; they have special rights of greeting. They have these privileges because they are seen as purer than the rest of the population. Is the concept of purity a kind of conspiracy of the Brahmans against the rest of the population, as is constantly asserted? As Pandurang V. Kane says: "They could only succeed in influencing the other Varṇas by persuasion and their own worth."[113] But how did they manage to pull off this trick?

Kane and others see the superiority of the Brahmans in their high respect for the Veda or the ideal of poverty. This is countered by the notion that at least knowing the Veda is linked with a condition of birth and thus was not generally accepted. In general, Brahmans made sure that non-Brahmans did not challenge their privileges. Even if non-Brahmans behaved like Brahmans, they were not considered worthy to receive gifts (*dāna*). For Brahmans, behavior and manners alone make a Brahman, even if this position, the ethicization and internalization of Brahmanhood, have been accepted by all critics of Brahmans since the Buddha.[114]

Dumont[115] sees a reason for the socioreligious leadership of the Brahmans in the distinction between temporary and permanent impurity. For Dumont, all organic aspects of man are impure: birth, death, excretion, which make up "the irruption of the biological into social life."[116] But while organic pollutions strike ordinary men only temporarily, some professions deal with it permanently. The monthly period lasts only a few days; the launderer who does the laundry (while it is otherwise often washed in one's own house), always deals professionally with impurity. And the tanner, knacker, or drummer are impure because they are in constant contact with leather or the leather covering of their instruments; a well-known word for Untouchable, "Pariah," comes from the Tamil *paṟaiyaṉ* ("drummer"). So, in the Brahmanic system of categories of purity and impurity and the heredity of certain professions, Dumont sees a fixed point for the hierarchy of all of Hindu society.

Thus, according to Dumont, the organic, impure, transitory world and the inorganic, pure (and, I would add, immortal) world are in a complementary relationship: The purity of the one exists only because others remove impurity from it. Between the extremes—Brahmans on top and Untouchables on the bottom—it is difficult to order the social groups of a certain area hierarchically, but that does not change anything about the principle of the mutual dependence of purity and impurity.

However, according to Dumont, purity and impurity are not only complementary; but the pure also includes the impure. It is mainly this holistic statement that has been widely misunderstood. In a postscript to the German edition of his book, Dumont presents a succinct example:[117] in chapter 1 of the Book of Genesis, God created woman out of the rib of man. A piece is taken out of the originally sexless man, Adam, into which his own nature is breathed: Eve. This is also present in the language: *Homo* ("man") forms the gender-neutral opposite to animal or god, and means both man and woman; *homo* ("man," French: *homme*), on the other hand, is gender-specific and is the opposite of woman. *Homo* as a superordinate term also includes the subordinate opposite. Dumont illustrates this concept schematically, and I have supplemented it with the terms *pure* and *impure* (see figure 9).[118]

Thus, pure and impure are not only opposites, they are also in a hierarchic relationship to one another, which in its totality guarantees social cohesion and hierarchic order. Dumont keeps emphasizing that the West, with its egalitarian and individualistic thinking, is hardly in a position to see such a holistic concept

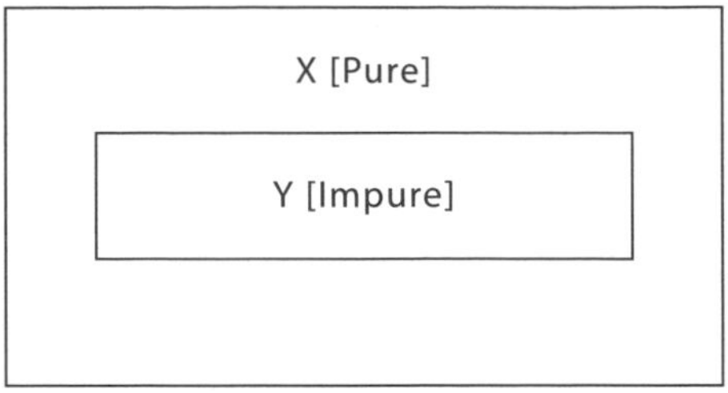

9. Relationship of purity to impurity according to Dumont.

of "encompassing the opposites," even though the hierarchy was similarly ordered in Plato's *Republic.*[119]

With this theory, Dumont proves himself a follower of Emile Durkheim, for whom religion—in brief—was the idealization of society (collective conscience). So, Dumont assumes "naturally, first that social organization and religion are in fact different things, then that religion represents a direct counterpart of social organization, purely and simply idealizing social relations and perhaps that is even its function."[120] He sees overarching norms as religion or the presence of transcendence in social life:[121] The Brahmans have the highest status because they ideally embody what society sees as its highest value. That means a clear separation of power and authority.[122] Kings and other rulers also subordinate themselves in terms of religion to the Brahmans. (In the abovementioned hierarchy arranged by a ruler, Jaṅga Bahādur Rāṇā, rulers are only in second place!) From this relationship between priest and king, Dumont infers a unique superiority of the spirit, which, unlike in Christianity—in the investiture conflict between the pope and the king—neither wants to nor can be political.

Several objections to this theory have been advanced.[123] In anthropology, detailed studies of villages have shown that the Brahman is not always at the top of the social scale,[124] that his influence wanes when he is in the minority,[125] and that there is considerable quarrelling and competition for the highest positions. Quigley says that Dumont saw Indian society as much too harmonious and thus ignored numerous conflicts.[126] Another objection against Dumont has to do with the various traditional professions and activities of the Brahmans: Brahmans are traditionally[127] ascetics (*saṃnyāsin, sādhu, yogin, svāmin, muni*), religious and secular teachers (*ācārya, guru, paṇḍita, śiṣṭa, śāstrī*), house priests (*purohita*), priests and advisors to the king (*rājpurohita*), temple priests (*pūjārī*), astrologers (*jyotiṣa*), healers (*ojhā*), pilgrim priests (*pāṇḍa*), and even potters[128] or death priests (*mahābrāhmaṇa*).[129] In this series of professions and

10. The Brahmanic pilgrim priest S. Vyās in Benares: Pilgrims begin at the throne of the priest with a vow to go around the city; they have themselves told the legends of the holy places. Photographer: N. Gutschow, 1991.

functions, increase of contact clearly reduces rank. A temple priest has a lot of contact with pilgrims and therefore the teacher-Brahmans are seen as higher-ranking (and do not allow temple priests to marry their daughters, even though both of them are Brahmans). The death priests, the "Untouchables" of the Brahmans, also have the added impurity of death. Finally, the priest also takes away impurity when he accepts gifts. He is a ritual specialist like the barber, the launderer, or the potter. Even Dumont calls him a special kind of Untouchable;[130] others call the Untouchables "anti-priests."[131] And thus, the one who rejects the gift is considered the purest Brahman: the ascetic. In the catalogue of the transfer of things, alms (*bhikṣā*) are not gifts (*dāna*).

Dumont is criticized for seeing only the Brahmans at the top of the socio-religious hierarchy. But not every priest is a Brahman nor is every Brahman a priest, as Dumont at least assumes.[132] Even a statement that Brahmans did not strive for worldly power is wrong: Brahmans were soldiers and kings.[133] And in popular Hinduism, it is the non-Brahman priests who have a prominent function.

Dumont fends off all these objections by referring to his concept of encompassing the opposites. Unlike Heesterman, for whom the ideal Brahman is the

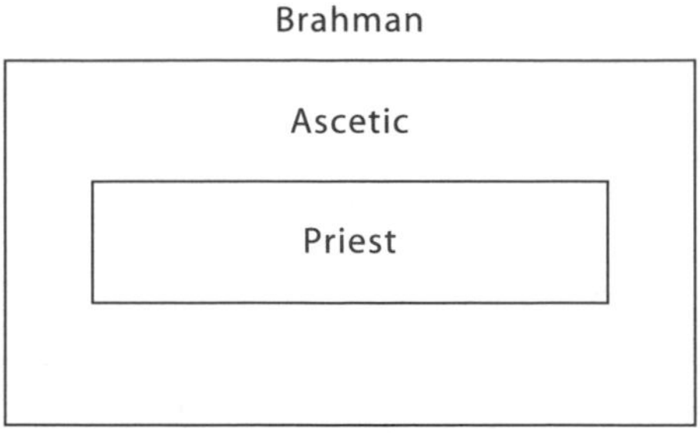

11. Relationship of Ascetic and Brahman priest according to Dumont.

ascetic because he keeps out of everything and thus forms an opposition to secular life, Dumont unites the Brahman as priest (in the world) and the Brahman as ascetic (outside the world) into a kind of "transcendent" Brahman who encompasses the whole (see Fig. 11), which is inside every Hindu to a certain extent, and with which the individual commits himself to the whole order: "[In India], separation and hierarchy of castes have meaning only because everyone knows tacitly that society is supported by the *mutual dependence* of the castes and consequently individual people in an order that constitutes the real meaning of human life. This is the core of the Hindu religion, while belief in spiritual beings and worship of the gods are basically only a secondary aspect."[134]

Hardly any criticism helps against the virtually religious a priori valuation in Dumont's theory. He is concerned not only with ideology before empiricism and religion before politics, but also with the holistic Brahmanic doctrine before empiricism and society. In fact, he "preaches" a holism that is clearly rooted in a critique of Western individualism and which he thus wants to be understood as a critique of Western society.[135] By not allowing any possibility of refutation—no critic thinks holistically enough for him—he almost becomes "the founder of a religion" at the boundary of the sociology of religion. However, it must be admitted that his inexhaustible insistence on the integrity of Hindu society touches on the crucial aspect of every analysis of Hinduism. For it is remarkable and unusual in the social history of mankind that many economic dependencies in India including slavery have so far been adhered to without compulsion, even though some of them were decidedly disadvantageous and have occasionally ruined extended families. Thus—as I try to explain—payment for service in ritual matters is essentially much smaller than on the market. There are hardly any combinations of extended families or uprisings against the dominant, sometimes exploitative subcastes, and few agrarian revolts.[136] But do all Hindus in fact know of the usefulness of this mutual dependency—as Dumont says—or only the Brahmans? And is there in fact only *one* order?

It may be thought that the economically dominant subcastes in the village are usually not Brahmans. What is denoted by dominant subcastes is every social group that is served by other subcastes in which the kind of service not only includes taking impurity (barbers, launderers), but also giving religious service (Brahmans).[137] Precisely because, in this relation, the Brahmans are the givers, according to the hierarchy of Hindu gifts (*dāna*), they are beneath the receivers, the dominant caste. According to this criterion, which goes back to Marriott's interaction theory, at the top are those who serve least, hence the landowners or the aristocracy. But since almost every subcaste has other subcastes who remove impurity and serve them, a star-shaped model in which every subcaste occupies the center once illustrates social dependencies better than a single linear, hierarchical model.[138] Even codified hierarchies, in which the Brahman or an ascetic or a Kṣatriya (king) is at the top, must not be self-contradictory since there can be various such hierarchies.[139]

In view of these objections, what remains of the superiority of the Brahmans and of Dumont's theory? Only various hierarchies, the "anything goes" of the Hindu religions mentioned earlier, their always underestimated formlessness? I don't think so. In my opinion, the basic misjudgment is that a social category has been confused disastrously with an ideological one. I am referring here to what I will explain more precisely in the concluding section of part 3: In the analysis of Hindu society, the Brahman has always been seen as the key, instead of the Identificatory Habitus that prevails in Hindu religions and society, which the Brahmans express explicitly in their social philosophy. The Brahman is not always at the top of the hierarchy; the evidence for that is convincing, and the Brahman texts are largely a goal-oriented ideology right from the start: Brahmans and Kṣatriyas together, as the Vedic texts say unequivocally, wanted to exploit the community (*viś*).[140] If only the Brahmanic-Sanskritic texts are examined, the norms of purity must in fact look like a conspiracy. But the dominance of textual scholarship in the history of religion and partly also anthropology should not blind us. Brahmans not only express high salvation goals, they also want to embody them. This implies combining the religious hierarchy with the social one. But it is precisely this link that has led to the misjudgment mentioned above. Only when the highest, generally accepted goals are detached from the group of people who propagate them especially is there a collective consciousness to which the overwhelming majority of society feels obligated.

Thus, the social position of the Brahmans has to be abstracted from them in order to grasp that position. This also applies for the concept of descent relating to birth, as illustrated in an episode in the Chāndogya-Upaniṣad.[141] The youth Satyakāma Jābāla comes to his mother with the wish to study the holy knowledge, the Veda. He asks her: "What race do I belong to?" Clearly, you had to be a Brahman in his time in order to study the Veda. But the mother answers that she doesn't know because she had had many men in her youth as a serving maid. Nevertheless, the son goes to the Brahman Hāridrumata Gautama and presents his wish. The Brahman asks him about his race and when Satyakāma Jābāla says that he doesn't know it, the Brahman says to him: "A non-Brahman cannot talk like that. Bring me firewood, my dear. I will lead you [to knowledge, i.e., accept you as a student and bind the girdle around you], for you have not deviated from the truth." Since this time at the latest, Brahmanhood and the Brahmanic ideal have been interchangeable. Notions of equality in the West often have a Christian origin (or at least have roots in Christianity), but not every claim to equality is therefore Christian. The Identificatory Habitus is Brahmanic (or has its roots in Brahmanic ideas), but, as a culturally dominant structure, it is not only Brahmanic. This can be extended in accordance with the changing relationship of religious and economic hierarchies.

Religious and Economic Centrality[142]

Difficult as it is to prove a criterion of purity, it is equally difficult to show an absolute hierarchy of Hindu society that refers to it. Instead, status markers such as profession, income, and property influence different models of strata. Next to religious authority, for example, stands economic and political power. McKim Marriott has given an example of that: Twice-Borns normally take no grain as a gift or payment from the impure leather workers; but if a member of this subcaste is hired by a Brahman for the harvest, this problem disappears. What is decisive here is not the status of purity, but rather the question of who serves whom.[143] Therefore, in questions of hierarchy, the relationship of the ritual sector to the subsistence sector must also always be determined. Usually, the system of these changing dependencies is called the Jajmānī system, whose name hints at the religious and ritual implications, because the term is connected with the verbal root *yaj* (to sacrifice) and its nominal form *yajamāna* (sacrifice-host, patron, a person who employs a priest to sacrifice for him).

The system can be described like this: A subcaste that is dominant in the village or the region receives goods and services—mainly because of ritual obligations, especially in rites of passage—from other subcastes, as from Brah-

12. Rice harvest in Bhaktapur, Nepal: The barber Tirtha Narain takes his share, for which he shaves the head of the farmer family on ritual occasions and cuts their toenails and fingernails. Photographer: N. Gutschow, 1987.

mans, barbers, potters, launderers, latrine cleaners, midwives, and others. In exchange, the patrons (*jajmān*) from the dominant subcastes give the serving subcastes grain, clothes, fodder, heating fuel, and other goods, cash, credit, or rights to land use. Even if a preference for an annual cash payment can be established,[144] the serving subcastes usually do not receive any regular salary, but rather a payment made according to traditional allowances or payment in kind. In a certain sense, noblesse oblige applies in these relations: The rich farmer subcaste, who often employ the Jajmāns, commit themselves to take care of the dependent subcastes.

Individual subcastes clearly dominate on the village level primarily because of the concentration of landowning. But also when one subcaste outnumbers the other subcastes, or has special political influence or an especially high ritual status, it can assume this supremacy. As Gloria G. Raheja has noted correctly, when an Indian is asked what kind of village he lives in, he often names the dominant subcaste there.[145]

But what is in question is whether impurity is also taken away in the so-called Jajmānī system, thus producing a socioreligious hierarchy. Many observers see that as the crucial foundation of the caste system,[146] and thus put priests, barbers, and launderers on the same level in relation to the patron. The services of priests and barbers are indeed different, but they occasionally receive the same gifts from the patron in rituals, are dependent on him, and respect his authority.[147] So in this case, centrality and economic power determine various hierarchies, but not religious authority, which is based on the "pure-impure" opposition.

Other authors doubt the existence of a socioreligious Jajmānī system and claim that it is a normal system of exchange of products, goods, and services.[148] In fact, it is striking that scholars first became aware of this system with William H. Wiser's monograph (1936) about the village of Karimpur (a fictitious name) in the southwest of the state of Uttar Pradesh. So, why it was not noticed before and was not comprehended by the traditional legal literature is a legitimate question.[149]

The confusion about this issue has a great deal to do both with the heredity of professions and the resulting monopoly and with the blending of ritual and economic activities. If a patron—an example from Pauline Kolenda[150]—is dissatisfied with his sweeper, who regularly cleans the latrines, he often cannot simply fire the man and look for a new sweeper. Instead he must appeal to the leader of the sweeper subcaste and try to get a replacement. In the same way, the sweeper can also present complaints against the patron through the leader of the subcaste. In this case, the link between patron and the sweeper subcaste is based more on the monopoly of the sweepers than on a traditional mutual obligation, and not at all on a socioreligious connection. Payment for agricultural service is similar.

The situation with barbers looks different. If these are called to the house of the patron in rituals, they receive gifts according to fixed, non-negotiated fees. So there is a clear distinction between whether the patron is shaved by a barber chosen by himself in his shop or brings him to his house for a ritual occasion. In the barbershop, market criteria apply, payment is in cash, and negotiation is possible to a certain extent. In the house of the patron, there is hardly any negotiation, payment is often made in kind, and there are traditional, inherited connections between the extended families. In rituals, the barber explicitly removes impurity, that is, the beard or the hair on the head. In his shop, these religious criteria hardly apply. Thus, the barber will also refuse to serve in rituals of extended families that are considered beneath him, while he would not impose this limitation on himself in his shop. But this lower classification of other subcastes and extended families is not produced solely by the removal of impurity, but also from the substantial standards applied to descent for marriage. In other words, barbers and launderers (and even Brahmans) remove impurity from the patron; but this alone does not explain why the barber is usually seen as more impure or lower than the launderer and thus does not enter into marriage connections with this subcaste.

Thus, the division of labor and economic exchange are structured both ritually and pragmatically. Exchange is regulated with measurable equivalents, usually money or goods in kind. The assessment of goods and services is based on criteria relating to goods, usefulness, and durability. The criteria of hierarchy derived from that are especially skills and abilities (the more difficult the work and the longer the training, the higher it is valued), as well as prestige or wealth acquired through achievement and success. In principle, economic exchange is symmetrical, since it is regulated by a measurable and quantifiable equivalent. In the ritual area, on the other hand, this symmetry is not achieved, since the equivalent for service of the subcastes is neither material nor measurable. That is, along with (material) reward (*dāna, dakṣiṇā*), they also receive religious merit (*puṇya*) for serving the patron. Their status then is not won or acquired by competition, achievement, and rivalry, but is assigned to them because of inherited rights and duties. The exchange of services for pay and religious merit is asymmetrical because, from the start, it does not assume an abstract equality of goods and services (and ultimately of people).

Therefore, neither with regard to economics nor religion can only *one* hierarchy or an all-prevailing dominance of the Brahman be established. Instead, it is reasonable to assume models of centrality that focus on one or another group, depending on the aspect. In this sense, it can even be said that Hindu society is less hierarchic than the theological state in the Christian Middle Ages. That is, not all Hindus feel obligated to *one* hierarchy—as Dumont claims—but rather there are several hierarchies, each delineated by extended families and subcastes, which—through the Identificatory Habitus—are seen as basically equal. The gift is another example.

Hierarchies of the Gift[151]

The refined Brahmanic legal theory of the gift (*dānadharma*), which Marcel Mauss dealt with in his famous study *The Gift*,[152] stipulated that the receiver of a religiously motivated gift (*dāna*)—for example, foodstuffs, especially rice, a cow, or a garment, but also money—may give nothing in return except religious merit. It would cancel the effect of such a gift if a measurable equivalent were possible as a return gift. In any case, religious merit (*puṇya*), a share of salvation and immortality, is given in return.[153] The consequences of such a construct are far-reaching: The recipients of the gift are in a lower position than the givers, since they assume impurity to a certain degree. Just because they are in a position to cope with, or, as the texts express it,[154] to digest, this impurity, they are considered the suitable recipients. The "logic" is that the recipient is lower than the giver because he assumes the impurity of the giver along with the gift; but the recipient is also higher than the giver because he can accept impurity. Before the gift, the giver is lower than the recipient because he hands over impurity; but through the gift, the recipient becomes lower than the giver because he is polluted by the gift. Thus, the hierarchy between giver and taker is turned upside down by the gift. Here a pattern is repeated that we have already encountered in the determinations of marriage, that is, in the concept of the bride as a gift. As a consequence, the recipient of a gift is not exactly happy about the gift, and the genuinely pure person, the ascetic, does not accept anything, not even alms, so as to exclude any reciprocity.

In his essay on the subject, Marcel Mauss advanced the idea that a gift contains the spirit of the giver (*esprit du don, Maori hau*), which obligates the receiver to give a gift in return. That is, the gift is only partly or only ostensibly relinquished. Hence, Mauss must have been amazed that there were clearly theories of the gift in which this "social fact" of reciprocity was excluded. He banished this amazement to an inconspicuous footnote that has been roundly criticized. He was faulted mainly for not understanding the soteriological aspect of salvation of the Indian exchange of gifts.[155] In the Brahmanic theory of gifts, it is crucial that the gift be completely relinquished so that it is not returned and thus no bond arises between giver and receiver. This is because, in some cases, the gift contains the impurity of the giver. The gift is a kind of sacrifice in which the gift or the impurity is destroyed, and the theory of the gift (*dānadharma*), as Jan Heesterman notes,[156] is a soteriology, the conversion of evil (*pāpman*) into salvation (*śrī*), but not a sociology of exchange. For that reason, no evidence of an obligation for reciprocity is found in the legal texts. Just because of that, a Dāna must be given to a worthy recipient,[157] for example, to a Veda scholar or an ascetic. Then, religious merit (*puṇya*) comes to the giver.

Indeed, the share of impurity in the gift should not be overestimated. A Dāna should be given mainly in a generous spirit, without regarding or speculating on the advantage or utility.[158] That is, a Dāna primarily produces a religious merit for the giver when it is given with the intention of Dharma: This merit is invisible, as the legal compendium says, unlike the utility of the merit (*dṛṣṭaphala*) in gifts given for secular motives.[159] Mutual credit does not form a Dāna, but rather a secular deal.

So, in the first instance, if the taker can be purified but not the giver, then the logic of this observation[160] dictates that there is a hierarchy between taker and giver and that the giver sometimes has a lower rank than the taker because he is the one who hands over the impurity. Because of this theory of gifts,

Brahman priests and scholars find themselves in a dilemma: On the one hand, they depend on gifts for their livelihood; but on the other, their higher rank is endangered by the impurity of the gift.

Some of these Brahmanic notions of the impurity in the gift can be explained by folk religious notions. Gifts to priests are usually connected with rites of passage or betrothals. Such rituals are frequently necessary to counteract a threatening or suffered disaster. The effect of this disaster is experienced partly as an adhesion with negative substances and qualities that one has to or wants to get rid of. Gloria G. Raheja has especially called attention to this distinction between impurity in the traditional Brahmanic sense (*aśauca*) and inauspiciousness (Hindī *nāśubh* or *kuśubh*).[161] Thus, Raheja adapted Dumont's separation between temporary and permanent impurity. She observed that the impurity that comes with birth, menstruation, or death is different from the impurity that comes, for example, through illness, danger, revolts, spirits, evil, or unfavorable constellations of stars. Whereas the first impurity breaks down in time and cannot be given away, the second form requires rituals in which gifts must be given to various recipients who are able to absorb this impurity, to dispose of it ritually, as it were.

In her field study, Raheja grasped an important point of view that is discussed only marginally in Brahmanic literature, but which is very significant in the everyday aspect of the Hindu religions. When members of extended families are afflicted with illness, crop failure, childlessness, quarrels, madness, etc., the balance is disturbed and must be restored. But the causes of these disturbances are attributed not only to the violation of the Brahmanic norms of purity, but perhaps more frequently to the reasons for disaster mentioned most often by Raheja (for example, unfavorable constellations), which are rooted more deeply in the popular belief.

The balance is thus restored by giving gifts, which bear impurity or misfortune, to others. One must get rid of them somehow,[162] preferably to recipients appropriate to the occasion or equivalent to the gift: a Brahman, a barber, a sweeper, an in-law, or simply someone passing by. So, giving away the gift does not so much establish a hierarchy as it strengthens the ruptured identity of the We-group, of the extended family. Typically, gifts are very seldom given within the family.[163] Gifts are only necessary when this identity can no longer be maintained with any other means.

As I have tried to show, the really crucial reason for the stability of the Hindu social system resides in the heredity of profession, which is bound partly with the endogamous and exogamous rules of marriage, which for their part are defined by determinations of descent and the expectations of salvation associated with them. The higher rank of the ascribed status of a social group can be explained only partly on the basis of the economic or religious dominance of subcastes and extended families. What is much more crucial is that an ideal relating to salvation is maintained bound up with substitutive descent, to be organized in social groupings so that the question of the absolute hierarchy—neither religious nor secular—did not have to be fought out. Just because there is such an Identificatory Habitus, which equates things even if they do not go together in Western eyes, can hierarchical orders, which sometimes contradict each other, such as the Varṇa and Jajmāni systems or the various gift hierarchies, exist alongside one another.

5. Religiosity

THE IDEA OF GOD AND THE PANTHEON

Gods are needed to explain the world and its emergence, the course of nature, evil, and the discrepancy between fate and merit: Why are there humans and animals, life and death, day and night? Why is there suffering, disease, injustice? Those are the questions that stories about gods and theology seek to answer. Hence, it is to gods that humans address ultimate questions in the myths and stories they tell each other to allay the fears that underly the questions. In Paul Feyerabend's provocative words,[1] today's science may well be the fairy tale we tell ourselves to avoid fear.

Many theories about the world of the gods can be reduced to the formula that the gods are like humans. In them gods are considered a projection of man, his fears and wishes for power, objectifications of the unconscious, archetypes, collective representations of the community, symbolizations of the highest human values. The world of the gods can be interpreted to individual taste in terms of religious psychology, religious sociology, or religious philosophy. Some say there is a god or gods or the sacred, which determines human thoughts and feelings. Others say it is men who think there is a god or gods or the sacred. Bertolt Brecht has reduced the difference between Substantialists and Functionalists in this old quarrel to a matter of punctuation: "Man proposes, God disposes" or "Man proposes: God disposes." There can never be a "winner." Every functionalist theory has to face the criticism of reductionism or determinism; every substantialist theory has to struggle with the criticism of irrationalism or dogmatism. The scholar of religion who thinks he can avoid the conflict by describing forms phenomenologically is no better off, for he himself must have an idea of god, the gods, or the sacred in order to be able to justify his field vis-à-vis psychology, sociology, or the humanities. There is no Archimedean point in the examination of your own or foreign worlds:

Everyone is director and audience at the same time, everyone is a hearer and a teller of myths. And without myths, as Odo Marquard says, it doesn't work for humans since "they fall prey to narrative atrophy."[2]

Do the remarks about the house in the preceding chapters also apply to the temple? Can the Identificatory Habitus be considered an important feature of the Hindu religions in this area, too? These are the questions I shall pursue in this chapter. I will discuss Vedic, epic, and Purāṇic mythology only peripherally, because in this book I am interested primarily in the *lived* religious world, thus in ritual, sacrifice, temple service, pilgrimages or celebrations, even if their meaning is often revealed only in myth.

Equitheism and Homotheism[3]

The pantheon of the second ("Vedic") epoch (see table 16)[4] consists of deified forces of nature, idolized moral and ethical principles, as well as potencies and powers that can pass to various personal gods and demons. Deities are often forces of nature: Indra is a god of "thunder" among other things, Agni is a god of "fire," Uṣas is a goddess of "sunrise." But the forces and phenomena of nature are restricted neither to a single deity nor in a single name. Indra, the god most often invoked in the ṛgveda, is also a god of "storm," the hurler of thunderbolts (*vajra*), god of war and ruler of the world. He is called "the powerful one" (*śakra*) or "lord of strength" (*śacīpati*). Depending on the myth, he is a friend, comrade, or king of men. But with all his versatility, he has one autonomous, immutable character, a "mythic substance" (Kurt Hübner)[5] or a "charisma" (Max Weber),[6] that appears in his analogies and identifications and that underlies all the diversity and uniqueness of his manifestations: Wherever a part of Indra is, there is all of Indra. This mythical substance is both idea and material, inner and outer, above (heaven) and below (earth).

Varuṇa is the god "true word" (Paul Thieme). He bases his rule on order and truth (*ṛta*), appearing as their power, among others. Among other things, he is the deification of an idea, an ethical principle, comparable to the Roman goddesses Victoria or Iustitia. Varuṇa also appears as ruler of the world, seated as a majestic ruler in the golden hall of heaven with a thousand gates and columns. The sun is his tool or his eye. But Varuṇa competes with Indra: Varuṇa is considered a self-ruler (*svarāj*), Indra as a world creator and ruler of all (*saṃrāj*); the former keeps the Ārya together, the latter defeats the enemy with his strength.[7]

The two gods might be thought to embody different forms of religiosity: Indra a heroic form, Varuṇa a spiritualistic or devotional form. But such a way of seeing would concentrate too much on gods as active, anthropomorphic

TABLE 16
The Vedic Pantheon

	Nature Gods, Deified Forces of Nature
Indra	Warrior, ruler, storm, thunder
Agni	God of "fire," divine priest, messenger of the gods, sacrifice (cf. Latin *ignis*)
Sūrya	God of the "sun"
Dyaus	God of "heaven" (cf. Greek *Zeus*)
Pṛthivī	Goddess "Broad Earth"
Maruts	Storm, thunder, bad weather; sons of Rudra, escort of Indra
Vāyu, Vāta	God "Wind," storm, thunder
Parjanya	Rain and downpour
Savitṛ	God "Sun," slave driver
	Gods of Order, Deified Moral and Ethical Principles
Varuna	God "True Word," water, cosmic order
Āditya(s)	Principles of the universe; various numbers, descendants of Aditi
Ṛta	"Law, order"
Mitra	God "Friend," contract
Bráhman	God "Form, Shape," holy formula, later the absolute
	Gods of Space
Rudra	"Screamer," heals and sickens, later epithet of Śiva; headquarters in the north, punisher of the gods
Viṣṇu	Strikes through the three worlds
Pūṣan	Guide, shepherd
	Creator Gods
Brahmā, Bṛhaspati	Sovereign
Viśvakarman	Architect
Tvaṣṭṛ	"Shaper," artist; son of Dyaus
Dakṣa-Prajāpati	Demiurge

(continued)

TABLE 16
The Vedic Pantheon (Continued)

	Deified Phenomena of Nature
Sītā	Goddess "Furrow"
Sarasvatī	River goddess
	Man-Gods
Puruṣa	"Man," primeval nature
Yama	Lord of the dead; first mortal
Manu	First "man," forefather
Ṛṣis	Seven "seers," patriarchs, priests
	Potencies and Powers
Soma	"Life sap," drink of immortality
Manyu	"Rage for Battle"
Ojas	Creative Power
Tapas	"Heat," fire, power, asceticism
Tejas	"Light," heat, perspicacity, energy
Māyā	Force of miracle
Takman	"Fever"
	Spirits and Demons
Apsaras	Water nymphs
Gandharvas	Demons, mainly in the empire of air or light
Rākṣasas	Evil spirits
Piśācas	Corpse demons
Vṛta	(Snake) demons
	Hostile Powers
Asura	Countergods
Dasyu, Dāsa	Foes of the gods, forces of darkness

individuals. Characteristic of the Vedic period, however, is that divine essences, substances, and forces can be shown in various ways. They assume human or animal form, but can also be inanimate or active forces, favorable or hostile. Sarasvatī, for instance, is a goddess in human form, but is also a divine river—like Gaṅgā, the Ganges, later on.[8] As persons or individuals, the gods are vaguely developed, but their activities are more important, even if only for a brief moment: Hermann Usener calls this phenomenon "*Augenblicksgötter*, momentary gods," referring to the world of the Greek gods. They hardly have any family life, kinship relations are unclear and changing: Uṣas is mother or lover of the sun; the goddess of prosperity (Śrī) appears as goddess "earth," but also as the consort of Viṣṇu or Agni; it is not known exactly whether the goddess Indrāṇī is independent or a consort of Indra. Gods appear in couples (Mitra-Varuṇa), as twin gods (Aśvins), and later in threes (*trimūrti*), from the ninth/tenth century in fives (*pañcāyatana:* Viṣṇu, Śiva, Gaṇeśa, Devī, Sūrya), in larger groups (Saptamātṛkā, Aṣṭamāṛkā, Navadurgā, ten *avatāras* Viṣṇu) or in whole troops (*gaṇa*). There are (as yet) hardly any hierarchies, no single sovereign, even if Indra, Varuṇa, Prajāpati, and Agni are prominent. But most of all, there are no differences "between spirit and material, animate and inanimate, human and inhuman, abstract and concrete, substances and qualities, procedures and states."[9] There is even some doubt about the existence of the gods.[10]

Thus, Martin Buber's question of whether God should be called "thou" or "it" remains unanswered for the ancient Indian. Both personifications and their opposite, "depersonalization" (Max Weber)[11] are ways of preserving charisma. Accordingly, *brahman* can be an abstract verbal formula and a divine person, a neuter or masculine noun. Similarly, in the fourth epoch, *śakti* can mean goddess and (female) power just as Śiva can be worshiped anthropomorphicallly as stone (Liṅga) and as syllable. *Cakṣas* (Eye) is not only the organ of sight, but also a god "ability to see," and the gods "fire" (Agni), "fever" (Takman), "agreement" (Mitra), or "fighting courage" (Manyu) also express such powers. "Sacrifice, individual acts of sacrifice, action, knowing, abilities, cosmic and religious dimensions, space, time, desire, anger, sleep, honor, friendship, truth, hunger, beauty, birth, age, death, ritual acts, sayings, poetic meters, in short everything that exists, that has a name (see, e.g., Atharvaveda 11.8), can be grasped as an independent reality, as a thing, talked about as a person, worshipped as a force."[12] Gods can strike with a thunderbolt, but also with a saying,[13] they can wrap and protect themselves in meter,[14] the sacrifice can assume the form of an antelope and simply run away, the house can tremble with fear when its owner comes back.[15] Theft, evil, truth, fame, strength can penetrate or abandon the body as substances.[16]

Forces and potencies are the central terms of the deities in this world. It is always necessary to produce or preserve identities and alliances. *Ojas,* for instance, was a creative, vital force, the life energy of gods, men, animals, and plants. Thus, the strength of a god could also be the same one that makes a tree grow: Indra—as the Śatapathabrāhmaṇa says—took the Ojas of the god Prajāpati and went off; this Ojas was the fig tree Udumbara, whose life sap is famous.[17] One was afraid of the forces and tried to protect oneself. One was afraid of contacts and contagions. The knife itself had the power to cut and kill, and not only the one who held it. In the initiation, the father or priest recites a verse of the Yajurveda that asks the knife not to wound the son when his hair is shorn. It was always necessary to humor the gods, forces, and potencies, to praise and extol them, to thank them or appease and court them. The social and economic situation of the second ("Vedic") epoch, when there was as yet no one higher power acknowledged by all tribes, is expressed in the warlike debates with hostile forces, in the forms of rule, in the alliances formed by the troops of gods, in the superior strength of natural forces, in the constant unrest of the gods.

Remnants of the ancient Indian religion that have survived since the second ("Vedic") epoch can be summarized in the following eight points.[18]

1. *The power of the powers:* Many ancient Indian powers have been preserved terminologically, even if their meaning has changed. This applies mainly for *tapas* and *tejas* (both mean "heat"), *ṛta* ("truth"), and *brahman* ("[sacred] word formula"). *Tapas* and *tejas* became basic terms of asceticism, *ṛta* became *dharma,* the moral and cosmic order of the world, *brahman* became the highest, the absolute. Other powers have been superseded or have lost their menacing aspects. But in all cases, knowledge of the effect of the powers remains crucial for salvation.

2. *Unity of multiplicity, multiplicity of unity:* Every divine aspect can be manifested in various ways: in divine qualities, but also in substances, objects, numbers, colors, sounds, periods of time, meters and much more. Therefore, the corresponding forms of representation and worship can be multiple without being various. The deity can have many forms, names, or bodies, with several arms, legs, and hands. It can be worshipped in its parts and ritual accessories, as well as in the diagrams, plants, animals, or stones ascribed to it. That is, a god—as defined by Kurt Hübner[19]—is worshipped as mythic substance. To some extent, the redness of a god, which can appear in gradual color shadings of red in entirely different things, is worshipped.

The attempts to seek the one in the many, the *one* god behind the many gods,[20] the *one* sacrifice behind the many sacrifices, are also early: by identifying the Ātman with the Brahman and identifying the *brahman* with god (*īśvara*), or in the devotionalism in the sight of the many gods in *one* god. In the Bṛhadāraṇyaka-Upaniṣad, when the seer Vidagdha Śākalya asks the seer Yājñavalkya how many gods there are, the latter answers: "Three thousand three hundred and six!" But, when Vidagdha repeats his question several times, it always becomes less: six hundred thirty, six, three, two, one and a half, one.[21] And in the Bhagavadgītā—a locus classicus—Arjuna can say to Kṛṣṇa, looking into his maw: "I see, Lord, in thy body all the Lords of Heaven and diverse hosts of beings, Lord Brahmā seated on his lotus-throne, and all the seers and snakes divine. . . . no end in thee, no middle, nor yet beginning do I see, O Universal Lord, O Universal Form!"[22] Images of swallowing and incorporating are generally preferred to illustrate the omnipotence of the god: Viṣṇu or Brahmā have the world inside themselves, let it out and swallow it back; the worlds are in them and they themselves are the world.

Since an all-encompassing claim cannot be made, there are several, equal accesses to powers and gods. Each preferred way does not exclude the others. A deity may be a chosen tutelary deity. But that does not give it a sole claim to one's allegiance. Therefore, ideas of false gods are rare. Whether this means tolerance or ignorance is an open question. Each believer worships his own god anyway in a kind of cryptic identification—Paul Hacker talks of "inclusivism" (see below, chapter 7): "Even those who are devoted to other Lords of Heaven, and sacrifice to them, possessed of faith—even they do sacrifice to me alone, but not as law ordains,"[23] says Kṛṣṇa in the Bhagavadgītā. The term *henotheism* coined by Max Müller, the monotheistic worship of a deity in a polytheistic ambiance, or *kathenotheism,* the worship of a god at a certain moment, does not grasp these connections adequately. *Homotheism* or *equitheism* are better terms, because they denote both the idea of god as well as the fundamental identificatory process.

3. *Featurelessness of the divine:* Despite the multiplicity of its representations, basically, the divine cannot be represented—this follows almost necessarily from the preceding point. The divine has no features (*nirguṇa*) and at the same time is full of features (*saguṇa*). Often, the "real" god is "contained" only in his highest, imperceptible form. All that can be perceived of him on earth is only a part of the whole. Only religious "virtuosos" such as seers, priests, or the enlightened have the ability to see the god as a whole. "The eye is truth, for the eye is indeed truth," says the Bṛhadāraṇyakā-Upaniṣad,[24] referring to a certain mental way of hearing and seeing. There are seers (*ṛṣi*) who have seen or heard (*śruti*) the knowledge, the Veda, and similarly the (mental, immaterial, ultimately objectless) view between believers and deity (*darśana*)

is also the crucial eye-contact into worship of the gods. But when the god reveals himself in his highest form, he "dies," loses his (personal) identity in favor of the unspeakable and unrepresentable, which he really is.

4. *The "apparent" nature of the divine:* Since the divine as a whole is not real, its parts—the gods, the manifestations—are only apparently divine. What is manifested is essentially an illusion (*māyā*). Indeed, many religions hold the view that the divinity of the world eludes the transitoriness of the world and thus cannot be visualized—in Islam and Christianity, for example, God cannot be represented visually—but in the Hindu religions, the deity can be represented infinitely. "For learned priests call one by many names," says the ṛgveda.[25] And therefore, the one or the divine can basically be represented infinitely—through serial identifications—because it really cannot be represented. This is why, in the Hindu religions, monotheism is basically considered disdainful of the divine since it presumes that one knows how the divine is manifested.

5. *Identity of god and man:* In the Hindu religions, not only is there a shaping of god according to the ideas of man, but there is also the shaping of man into god. As early as the Ṛgveda, gods are poets (*kavi*) and poets gods. This open boundary between god and man has meant that a man who makes himself into a "god" is identified with him in asceticism, that kings are considered manifestations of gods, that an actor who plays Rāma in the film is almost worshipped as the god Rāma himself. In the initiation, the boy is equated with a god and with the "body" of the Veda, the sacrifice and the priest or father.

6. *Materiality of the powers:* Since the divine is considered substantive or fine materiality, it can not only get lost, but can also cling, and in negative cases infect. Religious merit (*puṇya*) can be acquired, accumulated, and passed on, as from the wife to her husband. For example, many visitors of the Paśupatinātha temple in Nepalese Deopatan worship a figure named Virūpākṣa at the eastern exit of the sanctuary.[26] The statue of this deity stands up to its hips in a shaft full of mud and moves back and forth. According to an oral myth, Virūpākṣa is in this situation because he had committed incest with his mother. By giving Virūpākṣa half of the merit acquired by visiting the temple (*ardhadharmapūjā*), the believers—it is said—are to make it possible for him to get out of the hole over time.

Similarly, wrong action can mean a kind of harmful substance (e.g., *enas*) or desecration, which clings to the evildoer and brings him illness, misfortune, or poverty. Contact with an infected person is then infecting. Consequently, when someone commits a bad act, the whole family or even everyone who has had contact is affected. It is not only the individual who is responsible for disaster, but the community. Even gods can be affected by such evil: Thus, when Indra killed a Brahman, he was afflicted with this guilt, the substance "Brahman murder," until women were willing to remove this evil from him; therefore, it is said, women are impure every month. Defilements must and can be wiped out—independent of whether it is a happenstance, negligence, or a deliberate offense.

7. *Interdependence between men and gods:* Substances can not only change, they can also be used up. The same is true of divine powers and even of the gods, who are themselves (mythical) substances. Therefore they must be constantly maintained. They get their nourishment through sacrifices performed by men. The gods are not immortal; they themselves must try to win immortality through asceticism or through the drink called Soma. The gods are thus just as dependent on the favor of men as men are on the favor of the gods. The notion of substance presupposes a constant dependence between man and gods. Two important factors of religiosity in the Hindu religions have their roots here: worship of the gods (*pūjā*) with gifts (*dāna*) as hospitality and support, as well as the relatively strong position of man vis-à-vis the gods (see point 5, above). This means that men, especially priests, can even rise above the gods.

8. *Heaven and release:* Because men and gods are dependent on one another, but, on the other hand, because the eternal and immortal may not be dependent on anything, there is the idea of deliverance beyond heaven. In the Brahmanic-Sanskritic Hindu religion, release is beyond this world and the next world. Heaven (and hell) and earthly life are linked together in terms of fate; they are karmically connected in a cyclical, mutual relation, as in the notions of reincarnation. This is why gods and their worlds, even the various heavens—Vaikuṇṭha for Viṣṇu, Kailāsa for Śiva, etc.—are not necessarily the highest stage of release. Instead, the divine (immortality, eternity) is beyond god and man.

These points illustrate how much the early Vedic time shaped the later religious development: gods as impersonal forces, the substantive nature of these forces, the common features of the divine and its variability and diversity, polytheism, the proximity or identity of god and man. But these continuities should not lead us to overlook the discontinuities that form the basis of the division into epochs in table 1. Most of what characterizes the classical Brahmanic-Sanskritic Hindu religion is lacking in the early Vedic religion: self-liberation (*mokṣa*), reincarnation, vegetarianism, the goddess (Devī), temple cults, pilgrimages or vows (*vrata*), special forms of worship (*pūjā, bhakti,* etc.), as well as sects and their theistic texts. The concept of gods and the pantheon have also changed in many respects since the fourth ("Classical") epoch: There are greater specializations with respect to individual gods, an increased division of tasks in the pantheon (as in the trinity of Brahmā, Viṣṇu, and Śiva), clearer personifications and local linkages of the gods (the popular gods with their local traditions), as well as the emergence of an iconology and iconography of the gods.

In the West, the post-Vedic history of religion in India is often seen either as decadence or as progress. The Brāhmaṇa texts could demonstrate a rigid ritualism that had degenerated into a priestly religion and was devoid of the vitality of the Ṛgveda. On the other hand, with respect to the Upaniṣads, a development from religion to philosophy was discovered. For example, Hermann Oldenberg writes about the intermediate position of the Brāhmaṇas: "Here the compelling logic of primitive thinking no longer prevails; and on the other hand, the luminous freedom of the philosophic art of thought does not yet rule either. One turns away from the living, great gods of the old belief, but one has not yet discovered the silent glory of the powers in the Upaniṣads and later in the doctrine of Buddha that were to prevail over thinking and emotional life."[27] Oldenberg characterizes the Brāhmaṇas as a "region of the no-longer and the not-yet." And Moritz Winternitz writes of the Purāṇas, the divine texts of the fourth ("Classical") epoch, "As literary product they are no pleasant phenomenon. They are in every respect without shape and mass. . . . The wild confusion of the content and the measureless exaggerations [. . . it was] an inferior class of literates, belonging to the lower, uneducated priesthood."[28]

This undisguised evolutionism, whose notion of form is shaped by ancient and classical philology, is merely the recycling of the old complaints about the formlessness of India (see above, chapter 1). But ritualism, philosophy, or science are neither progress nor regress vis-à-vis religion or magic. Mythos is not dissolved by Logos. Such an analysis assumes the deficiency of the religious image of the world as opposed to the ideal of the scientific one. Thought, speech, or observation could then be considered deficient, incomplete, or prelogical. Mythos was false truth, science was still "pre-scientific science" (Oldenberg).

Ernst Cassirer rejected such a theory of deficiency by turning the relation of Mythos and history on its head: "It is not by its history that the mythology of a nation is determined but, conversely, its history is determined by its mythology—or rather, the mythology of a people does not *determine* but *is* its fate, its destiny as decreed from the very beginning. The whole history of the Hindus, Greeks, etc. was implicit in their gods. Hence, for an individual people as for mankind as a whole there is no free choice . . . by which it can accept or reject given mythical conceptions; on the contrary, a strict necessity prevails."[29]

In fact, where gods are powers and potencies, where the highest is thought of as multiple and the gods are not omnipotent, it is not subordination and obedience that are demanded, but rather usurpation and knowledge. Whoever has or knows the equivalent of what determines gods and men can achieve identification with the highest, whether this happens ritualistically, philosophically, or theistically. That is the general foundation for subsequent religious development in India, for the ritualism of sacrifice, the unity doctrine of the Upaniṣads, and even the Identificatory Habitus in the Hindu religions.

Therefore, the views of "there is only one god" and "all gods are one" are not so far from one another in the Hindu religions as has often been held. "Thou shalt not make unto thee any graven image" (Exodus 20:4) can also lead to the conclusion: Thou shalt not make only a single graven image. Hence, there is not *one* single word for god in Sanskrit, but many: *īśa/īśvara* ("ruler"), *bhagavat* ("elevated"), *prabhū* ("mighty"), *deva* ("god"), among others; the poet-saint Kabīr uses eighty-six terms for "god." But these terms are mostly used in contrast with other deities. Thus, Devas are the "deities of light, heavenly," as opposed to the forces of darkness and evil, such as the Asuras (who are still gods themselves in the most ancient layers of the ṛgveda; see Ahura Mazda in Iran) or the demonic Rākṣasas.

The consequences of this notion of god are tangible in popular religiosity all over. To use an example I have already cited (chapter 1), if a Newar in Nepal is asked if he is a Hindu or a Buddhist, he might simply answer "yes." To restrict oneself to one position, one god, would be a stingy perspective of divinity for him:[30] He can worship both Buddha and Śiva without getting into a conflict of belief. One does not want to fall out with the gods; for safety's sake; one prefers to worship several. Many pilgrims who attend celebrations at a temple scatter their gifts—flowers, rice seeds, cinnabar powder, or coins—around on all the shrines. Thus, even a hydrant can be gifted with something, simply because it has the phallic form of a Liṅga.

This oscillating and porous equitheism appears in all movements of the Hindu religions, as shown by the following four examples, each dealing with a special aspect: the relationship of Kṛṣṇa to Viṣṇu; Śiva and his sweetening; Gaṇeśa and the miracle; and the one and the many goddesses.

Viṣṇu, Kṛṣṇa, and the Centrality of the Gods[31]

It is widely held that two gods dominate the pantheon of the epic Purāṇic Hindu religion: Śiva and Viṣṇu. Whereas Śiva appears more as a wild, fearsome god—in many myths, he is the destroyer of the world—Viṣṇu has benevolent, mild, world-preserving features. The third god in the ancient Hindu divine triad, Brahmā, plays a rather subordinate role, although in the myths he is often the leader of the gods.

Unlike Śiva and his phallus-shaped Liṅga, Viṣṇu is rarely represented symbolically and abstractly, and then only as a black stone or ammonite (*śālagrāma*), which is considered his natural form (*svarūpa*), or by a stylized foot (Viṣṇupādaka). Yet, Viṣṇu appears more often in human or animal forms (see table 17), as a standing Nārāyaṇa with his attributes: a conch (*śaṅkha*), a discus or shotput (*cakra, sudarśana*), a lotus (*padma*), and a mace (*gadā*), as well as with a crown together with a diadem (*kaustubha*) and his accompanying animal, the mythical Garuḍa bird; or as Viṣṇu resting on the ocean or a snake (Ananta, Śeṣa), then called Anantanārāyaṇa or Śeṣanārāyaṇa, who, barely awake, lets a lotus emerge from his navel, from which Brahmā rises as the author of creation; or as a many-armed and many-headed Viśvarūpa ("All-Encompassing Form"), usually represented as a pyramid-shaped icon. Especially popular are his countless manifestations (*avatāra,* literally: "descent"), ten of which are considered classic: Thus he comes to the earth as a fish (Matsya), a tortoise (Kūrma), a boar (Varāha), Narasiṃha ("man-lion"), or in his tenth Avātara as the horse Kalkin in the destruction of the world. But Viṣṇu's "descents" are also figures in human form: dwarf (Vāmana), Paraśurāma, Rāma, Kṛṣṇa, and Buddha.

There are good reasons for seeing this sequence as an ascent (from water animal to land animal to man), but also as a descent, since in the division into the four ages of the world, the number of manifestations decreases. Kṛṣṇa worship has also been seen as a culmination, since the movement has incorporated historical figures such as Buddha or Kṛṣṇa and has privileged devotional religiosity, as opposed to other forms of religiosity, as a high point in Kṛṣṇa worship.[32] What interests me here is not so much these aspects as the following: How is it possible that a god can appear in so many ways? What really is Viṣṇu's relationship to his manifestations, for example, to Kṛṣṇa?[33]

The Bhāgavatapurāṇa says of Kṛṣṇa that everything else and everyone else emerged from him:[34] The seer, the patriarch (Manu), and his sons, men, are considered only partial manifestations (*kalā*) of Viṣṇu. In the Bhagavadgītā, too, Kṛṣṇa appears to the hesitant cart driver Arjuna in his all-encompassing, divine form.[35] The terms used here are illuminating: He talks of his birth (*janman*), emergence (*saṃbhava*), or creation (*sṛjana*); in other texts or places there is also talk of manifestation (*prādurbhāva*), abiding (*aśrita*), unfolding (*vibhāva*) or even descent (*avatāra*).[36] What is common to these notions is the featurelessness of divinity discussed above in point 3, the idea that a god can appear in various ways, but basically has no discernible manifestation visible

TABLE 17

Frequently Worshiped Deities of the Epic-Purāṇic Pantheon

1. High gods	**Brahmā** **Viṣṇu** (other names or manifestations: Dattātreya, Hari, Nārāyaṇa, Śeṣa-Nārāyaṇa, Viśvarūpa); Descents (*avatāra*): 1. Matsya (fish), 2. Kūrma (tortoise), 3. Varāha (boar), 4. Narasiṃha (man-lion), 5. Vāmana (dwarf), 6. Paraśurāma (Rāma with the axe), 7. Rāma, 8. Kṛṣṇa, 9. Buddha, 10. Kalkin **Śiva** (other names or manifestations: Bhairava, Dakṣiṇāmūrti, Maheśa, Naṭarāja, Nṛtyanātha, Rudra, Śadāśiva, Yogī, Liṅga) Rāma, Rāmacandra Kṛṣṇa, Kṛṣṇa -Gopāla, Bālakṛṣṇa, Gaṇeśa, Skanda (sons of Śiva)
2. High goddesses	Bhagavatī, Gaurī, Pārvatī, Lalitā, Umā (partners of Śiva) Lakṣmī, Śrī (partners of Viṣṇu) Sarasvatī, Sāvitrī, Gāyatrī, Vāc (partners of Brahmā and also partly Viṣṇu) Sītā (wife of Rāma) Rādhā (partner of Kṛṣṇa) Devī ("goddess"), other names or manifestations: Cāmuṇḍā, Chinnamastā, Durgā, Guhyeśvarī, Kālī, Kālikā, Mahiṣāsuramardinī, Śakti, Goddess groups: Aṣṭamāṛkā, Navadurgā, Saptamātṛkā, Yoginīs River goddesses: Gaṅgā, Yamunā
3. Folk deities	Folk gods and goddesses, village goddesses, local goddesses with countless names, partially identified with high gods—e.g., Aiyanār, Khandobā, Virūpākṣa, Vitthala
4. Guardians of the universe	Dikpāla, Kṣetrapāla; Vāyu, Kubera, Iśāna, Varuṇa, Indra, Nirṛta, Yama, Agni
5. Demigods of the epos	Arjuna, Bhīma, Bhīmasena (Bhīmsen), Hanumān, Lakṣmaṇa, Rāma, Yudhiṣṭhira, et al.
6. Heavenly gods	Sūrya (sun), Candra (moon, also Soma), planet gods (Śani, et al.)
7. Enemy gods, demons	Asura, Rākṣasa, Rāvaṇa, Hiraṇyakaśipu

(continued)

TABLE 17
Frequently Worshiped Deities of the Epic-Purāṇic Pantheon (Continued)

8. Divine animals and plants	Nandī (Śiva's mounts), Garuḍa (Viṣṇu's mounts), rats (Gaṇeśa's mounts), cow, elephant (Gaṇeśa), monkey (Hanumān), snake (Nāga), lion (Siṃha), horse (Kalkin); *bilva* tree, Tulasī (basil), lotus
9. Lower gods, spirits	Gaṇa, Apsara, Rākṣasa, Gandharva, Yakṣa, Bhūta, Preta, Piśāca

to man unless the latter has been initiated as Arjuna or has a visionary divine experience of god.[37]

In terms of the history of religions, these lists makes sense only in the aspect of multiple bodies or ostensible corporeality of gods or deified founders of religion. Christology and the three-body (Trikāya) doctrine in Buddhism are based on similar assumptions. In the Bhagavadgītā, Kṛṣṇa becomes a human creature, he occupies a human body; but, unlike normal mortals, he emerges on his own, so is *prima causa;*[38] he sires himself, so has a birth, but is unborn;[39] since he is not subject to the cycle of birth, he is not re-created. What is perceived as such is not his real form,[40] but rather—in concealed form—he permeates everything, as an indigenous etymology of "Viṣṇu" implies. Thus, he can cryptically be identified with everything.

Such theistic personifications of forces and potencies make identification in all directions possible and make the boundaries between man and god porous. Thus, for example, two different figures can also be incorporated in Kṛṣṇa: (1) the one mentioned by the grammarian Pāṇini[41] and Megasthenes, worshipped especially in the Mahābhārata, a heroic, presumably historic Kṛṣṇa-Vāsudeva, son of Vasudeva and Devakī, leader of the Yādavas of Dvāraka (present-day Dwarka) and the Bhāgavata sects; (2) the one found in the Harivaṃśa, a flute-playing, pastoral Kṛṣṇa-Gopāla from the region around Vṛndāvana (present-day Brindavan), who shows the features of the tribal population, is connected with the serpent cult, appears as a protector of cows, and reveals erotic aspects in his play with the Gopīs, the female cowherds. Both forms are combined by a general Brahmanization and also made into manifestations of Viṣṇu, although, under the influence of Bhakti religiosity, Kṛṣṇa-Gopāla has succeeded historically.

A similar process can still be observed today in the deification of local heroes or the equitheistic Sanskritization of local deities: First, there is a local hero, who becomes a demigod, often through his violent death, and after some time is worshipped in temples as a local god; identified as a manifestation of a high god, he moves up into the pantheon of the higher gods. In our day, an example of such a gradual rise is Mahatma Gandhi, and it is only a matter of time until his earthly manifestation is declared to be a descent of a high god. And when Tamils in Switzerland worship the Black Madonna (in Einsiedeln or in Köniz near Berne) as Kālī, despite the differences in the deifications, such a polyvalence of divinity can be seen.[42]

Consequently, since no god is raised to a supreme position, there can only be a relative hierarchy in the pantheon. What is true of the social hierarchy is repeated here: A better model is not hierarchy, but centrality.[43] Hence, the arrangement in table 17 is only a Brahmanic-Sanskritic version of several possible hierarchies, for even in a comparatively homogeneous local pantheon, it depends on which high god is in the center. Thus, for a few Vaiṣṇava traditions, Kṛṣṇa is a subordinate manifestation of Viṣṇu; but for others (see table 4) he is purely and simply the highest god—to such an extent that it is better to talk about Kṛṣṇaism instead of Vaiṣṇavism. Similar things can be said of Rāma. In the Purāṇas, "Viṣṇu" is not even the most common name; rather it is "Hari." Viṣṇu's centrality is based mostly on the Ten-Avatāra doctrine, and the common features of the Vaiṣṇava cult[44] are almost limited to the fact that there is a high god with distinct personal features (*saguṇa*), who preserves and protects the world and can manifest himself in various forms (*avatāra*).

In the everyday religious world, the high gods are often not the focus. That is, concerning the intensity of the worship of a god by the local population, even in a place like Deopatan in Kathmandu, which is shaped by a pilgrim's temple that dominates everything, the Paśupatinātha Temple, other deities are far more significant than the high divinity of the site of the pilgrimage. In Deopatan, this applies to certain goddesses, but also for Gaṇeśa, Bhairava, Virūpākṣa, and the Nevar Nāsadyaḥ (a remote form of Nṛtyanātha, the god of the dance, alias Śiva). Moreover, the time (normal day or festival day) determines which form of Hindu religiosity is in the foreground. In the Śivarātri celebration, Śiva-Paśupati is the focus for inhabitants of the city and for pilgrims; but on normal days, it is Gaṇeśa or the goddess of the quarter.

Śiva in the Great and Little Traditions[45]

Like Viṣṇu, Śiva is also a high god, who gives his name to a collection of theistic trends and sects: Śaivism. Like Vaiṣṇavism, the term also implies a unity which cannot be clearly found either in religious practice or in philosophical and esoteric doctrine. Furthermore, practice and doctrine must be kept separate.[46]

In sectarian and esoteric Śaivism, which usually requires a special initiation (*dīkṣā*), the Purāṇic Śiva and his mythology hardly play a role. Often, the philosophical tractates are embedded only formulaically in a dialogue between Śiva and Devī, which focuses on a transcendence of the personal Śiva and, at least in Kashmiri Śaivism, we have a monism whose spiritual goal is self-liberation (*mokṣa*) or the acquisition of special spiritual forces (*siddhi*). In the Śaiva philosophy and theology, Śiva is often synonymous with the abstract *śivatā* (feminine) or *śivatva* (neuter), both meaning "Śiva-hood," so Alexis Sanderson says correctly: "A Śaiva may well be a worshipper not of Śiva but of the goddess."[47] On the other hand, the epic-Purāṇic tradition of Śaivism (a variant of which is the Tamil Śaivasiddhānta) sees liberation as identification with the personal god Śiva. One wants simultaneously to be like Śiva (*sārūpya*), to worship him, to hope for his favor, and to have a seat in his heaven (Kailāsa; *sālokya*). Thus, it is necessary to distinguish between the sectarian, sometimes esoteric Śaivism, which has its own texts (Āgamas, Tantras) and in which the Vedic-oriented Brahmans are in the minority, and the epic-Purāṇic Śaivism, which is supported by a population influenced by Vedic-Brahmanism and popular religion (see table 18).[48]

In the epic-Purāṇic and popular religious Śaivism, Śiva (also called Maheśvara or Mahādeva, among others) is most often worshipped as *liṅga,* a phallus-shaped stone, which can also be represented anthropormorphically (in busts). And rarely does a Śiva temple lack his mounts, the bull Nandī, and his weapon, the trident (*triśūla*). In Indian classical myths, Śiva has a double nature: malicious and destructive as well as kindly and benevolent. Yet, in present-day India, Śiva is appealed to mostly as a peaceful god for help and assistance. The division of functions of the gods—Śiva as destroyer, Viṣṇu as preserver[49]—turns out even in Viṣṇu to be only conditionally valid, for Viṣṇu also appears as destroyer when he annihilates the demons as dwarf (Vāmana) or as man-lion (Narasiṃha), or in his manifestation as Paraśurāma, when he decapitates his mother Reṇukā at the behest of his father because of an alleged adultery. Nevertheless, in most representations of Hindu mythology, Śiva is given the role of the wild god. Thus, it is usually assumed that Śiva has taken on the features of the Vedic Rudra.

The alien god Rudra is indeed wild and dangerous, but he is also helpful and peaceful. At any rate, he is praised in only four hymns of the Ṛgveda,[50] where he appears as a god of storm and rain, with a black belly and a red back, clad in fur, and as a god who must be begged not to kill the cattle or steal the children, and to leave the clans in peace. Instead, he is to stay by himself in his region, the north. But quite early, he is also appealed to as a helper, a healer, a protector of cattle (Paśupati), if his name is to be uttered at all.[51] His double nature is also shown in the so-called Śatarudrīya hymn ("Hundred Names of Rudra"):[52] Here, he runs around the forest with long hair, clad in fur; and there

TABLE 18
Trends of Śaivism, Tantrism, and Śāktism

	Sectarian Śaivism	*Popular Śaivism*
Only ascetics	Ascetics and lay persons	Priests and mostly lay persons
Pāśupata, Aghorī, Daśanāmī (Nāga, Paramahaṃsa Daṇḍī), Gosai, Nātha, Yogī, Kānphaṭā, et al.	Nāyaṉārs, Liṅgāyat, Vīraśaiva, Sanskrit-Śaivasiddhānta **Tantrism** or tantric (Kāpālika) Śaivism, **Śāktism:** (a) worship of Śiva/Śakti (Krama); example: Guhyeśvarī, Kubjikā (b) Worship of Śiva as Bhairava or consort of the goddess (Trika or Kashmiri Śaivism); example: Kuleśvara/Kuleśvarī. (c) Worship of goddesses as *śakti* (Vidyāpīṭha, Śrīvidyā; Kaula, Kula, Yoginī cult); examples: Tripurasundarī, Kāmeśvarī, Lalitā	Popular religious, epic-Purāṇic Śaivism; Tamil-Śaivasiddhānta

are many of him (which hints at evil spirits),[53] but he is also identified with Agni and other predominantly benevolent deities.

The danger of Rudra is mainly that he is a god of the Other and is not integrated into the society of the Indo-Aryan tribes. The more this society collapsed in the second ("Vedic") epoch, the more peaceful Rudra/Śiva became—a process that begins with the Śvetāśvatara-Upaniṣad, in which Rudra is called "Śiva" (literally: friendly, dear) for the first time.

To what extent Śiva's origins are in fact to be sought in Rudra is extremely unclear. The tendency to consider Śiva an ancient god is based on this identification, even though the facts that justify such a far-reaching assumption are meager.[54] Nor may the worship of Śiva in the form of a phallus-shaped stone (*liṅga*) be regarded (as it usually is) as a sign of a primeval stone or fertility cult,[55] for there is no evidence for such great antiquity of the Liṅga cult. What is presumably the oldest Liṅga comes from the second or first century B.C. and is found in Gudimallam, in southeastern India; in texts, the Liṅga is first mentioned in the Mahābhārata.[56] Historically, the first evidence of Śiva worship is from the third ("Ascetic") epoch in the inscriptions and coins of the Kushanas, and the Śiva cult then becomes widespread in northern India first among the Guptas (ca. 300–550 A.D.), and in southern India only from the seventh century.

From the fourth ("Classic") epoch at the latest, Śiva must be linked to a porous notion of the godhead. For it turns out that, in the conception of Śiva, too, various ideas of god and spirit have come together, whose origins lack reliable sources and can be tracked down only sporadically. Thus, in the Śvetāśvatara-Upaniṣad, Śiva is a high god, origin of the cosmos, lord of everything, immanent in everything. There, he is addressed as Brahmā, Hara, the *one* god (*eka deva*), lord, (*īśa, īśāna*), Maheśvara, or great soul (*mahāpuruṣa*). This text is certainly an early indication of monotheistic tendencies. But there is no compelling reason for Śiva specifically to be in the center monotheistically and spiritually; in terms of the history of religions, it could just as well have been another god. The text—as R. G. Bhandarkar has correctly noted—is an early indication of the devotionalism (Bhakti), which is later linked primarily with the names of Viṣṇu and Kṛṣṇa. And there are also "descents" or Avatāras from Śiva—which are not as well known.[57]

From other perspectives and sources, Śiva appears quite early not as the most powerful god of a pantheon, but rather as an ascetic "outsider" or a Great Yogī, who resides in the Himalayas, is smeared with ashes, and holds a trident (*triśūla*) and an hourglass drum (*ḍamaru*), his long hair bound up. He wears a cobra or a chain of skulls as a necklace; in the middle of his forehead he has a third eye, with which he can destroy everything. Just as Rudra is excluded from the Vedic sacrifice, so Śiva is not invited to the great sacrifice of Dakṣa, his father-in-law. Furious about that, he destroys the sacrifice and cuts off the head of the Brahman Dakṣa. Therefore, he lives with the heavy sin of the murder of a Brahman and is thus the outsider par excellence.

The causes for Rudra's or Śiva's exclusion from the sacrifice and thus the society are varied: Rudra is above all a foreign, non-Aryan god; Śiva, on the other hand, is rejected because he is an ascetic. Most myths of Śiva show him as someone who voluntarily lives withdrawn, who does not want to know anything about others, who is sunk in asceticism or enjoys himself silently. And yet (or precisely because of that), he has a special, even erotic attraction. Śiva is both a chaste ascetic and an ardent lover. Mythologically, he manages what is not possible for men; he destroys Kāma, the god of erotic love, with his third eye, and experiences a thousand-year coitus with Pārvatī; or he seduces the wives of the seers, who castrate him for this by changing his phallus into the stone Liṅga. Śiva is potent and chaste, the ithyphallic ascetic, the god of the erotic (Kāmadeva) and the celibate Yogī. Thus, sexual potency and asexual power are blended in him; thus a paradox of asceticism is solved in him: Men are mortal and need sexuality to survive (in and through their children); gods are immortal and do not need sexuality; the man who wants to be a god, for example the ascetic, must have both potency and impotency.[58] Precisely as an ascetic, Śiva is a god of fertility, for by withholding his semen, he gathers fertility. Therefore, Śiva's asceticism (*tapas,* literally: "heat") is also creative force.[59]

Hence, Śiva is not only the wild man in the pantheon, the ash-besmeared "wearer of matted hair" (Jaṭādhara). He is also and increasingly the obedient husband of Pārvatī, and now and then even clearly subordinate to her. When the two of them are represented as Umāmaheśvara embracing each other intimately, along with the "sons" Gaṇeśa and Skanda or with Viṣṇu and Lakṣmī as "witnesses to a marriage," we have almost a normal family. Śiva—like most gods—unites contradictory aspects in himself. It is thus no accident that there are abundant representations of him with a double nature: As Hari-Hara, he is half Śiva, half Viṣṇu; as the androgynous Ardhanārīśvara, he is "half man, half woman," Śiva and Pārvatī at the same time. This is why it is a mistake to reduce Śiva to the function he has within the Hindu trinity, and even there only from a specific, presumably Vaiṣṇava perspective.

That is, even more than the wild destroyer, Śiva today is the gracious Śaṃkara ("the charitable one, redeemer") or Śaṃbhu ("the beneficent"). And when he is invoked and worshipped as Maheśvara or Mahādeva ("Great God"), when votive Liṅgas are erected in memory of deceased persons,[60] it is surely not the wild, destructive aspect of Śiva that is commemorated. Nor is Śiva only the mountain god (Girīśa), but is also the "lord of the universe" (Viśvanātha), the "citizen," whose preferred seat is Benares.[61] And, like Viṣṇu, Śiva is the protector: Only because, while escaping the cosmic whirlpool of the sea of milk, Śiva drank poison (Kālakūṭa), which dyed his throat blue (Nīlakaṇṭha), was Viṣṇu's creation of the world successful. And if Śiva had not brought Gaṅgā down on the world and trapped her in his topknot at the same time, the world would have been dried out or inundated. Even as cosmic Naṭarāja—Śiva in a circle of flames that symbolizes the cycle of the world (*saṃsāra*)—the god dances not only the dance of destruction, but also that of bliss (*ānandatāṇḍava*). Thus, with good reason, one can talk about the kindness of Śiva, which has led to saccharine-sweet contemporary conceptions of him. Even his wild appearance is no longer terrifying: In modern representations, Śiva mainly has charming features, similar to those of the childish Kṛṣṇa (Bālakṛṣṇa).

Even in so-called Tantrism (see table 18), Śiva has wild features only to a limited extent: Either Śiva is seen as pure consciousness—as in the so-called Kashmiri Śaivism (Trika), or a goddess (Guhyakālī, Kubjikā, Tripurasundarī) is worshipped instead of Śiva. In southern India—in the Śrīvidyā school, for example—she is quite often understood as benevolent: Hence, the "Tantric" benevolently worshipped Lalitā is especially popular. On the other hand, the Tantric worship of Śiva as the fearsome Bhairava or Svacchanda has been largely suppressed.

Finally, Śiva proves to be extraordinarily adaptable in religiosity, too, as illustrated by an example from Nepal. At the Piśācacaturdaśī celebration,[62] the "Black Fourteenth of the (corpse) Demons," shortly before the new moon in March/April, the ethnic groups of the Newar in Kathmandu clean the trash and debris out of the inner courtyard of the old city. Now and then, among the piles of rubbish, a small Liṅga or an unhewn stone appears, which is worshipped at night with mustard seeds, alcohol, meat, and garlic, and thus—in a Brahmanic view—with impure gifts. In the Nevārī language, this Liṅga is called "Lukumahādyaḥ," literally "hidden Mahādeva." Various myths and legends explain why Śiva had to hide in stinking piles of rubbish. The most widespread myth concerns a quarrel between Śiva and Pārvatī. A long time ago, it is told, Pārvatī took the form of Kālī or Bhagavatī and asked Śiva to ingest meat and alcohol as she did. To avoid this, Śiva changed into a demon, hid in a garlic field, and feasted on the garlic pods.

Such overlapping is typical for the Identificatory Habitus, with which an attempt is made to unite various deities and traditions mythologically. In this case, the tradition of the Newar, a population group with a Tibeto-Birmanic language, is linked with the Brahmanic-Sanskritic tradition of the Indo-Parbatīya population groups originating in India. In Nepalese chronicles, there is another version of the hidden Śiva: The Buddhists always threw their rubbish on Śiva-Paśupatinātha, the main Śaiva sanctuary of Nepal, some three kilometers northeast of Kathmandu, until Śaṃkara put an end to these goings on. Or it says that Śiva imposed almost impossible acts of penitence on a figure named Virūpākṣa, who had committed incest with his mother and led a bad life: For example, he was condemned to recite the thousand names of Śiva until he wore out a kind of iron rosary. Furious at this advice, Virūpākṣa pursued Śiva until the god could find shelter only under a heap of rubbish, where Buddha freed him on the day the mother deity ingested a lavish meal of meat.

Thus, it is no *single* hierarchy that is crucial for the image of a god in the Hindu religions, but rather a changing centrality. Nor is a specific form of religiosity limited to one deity, but rather every deity can be worshipped in various forms. The cultic worship of Śiva in the sects is another aspect of this (see below, chapter 7). For religious everyday life, the wandering (Śaiva) ascetics who spread the myths and doctrines are of primary significance, propagating esoteric or philosophical knowledge among the common people, even if they do not approve of or join ascetic practice. Like the other gods, Śiva remains an empty position which can be filled with almost unlimited aspects according to tradition, area, and form of religiosity.

Gaṇeśa and the Miracle[63]

The mythological and cultic incorporations are also particularly relevant in the case of Gaṇeśa, Śiva's unwanted son, whose very name indicates that countless more deities have amalgamated in this figure through identification processes: Gaṇeśa or Gaṇapati means "Lord of the troops (of pre-Hindu deities and essences)." The name is old, found even in the Ṛgveda,[64] and so is the Gaṇeśa cult, but Gaṇeśa, as an elephant-headed god with his attributes of an elephant driver stick, tusks, noose, bowl of sweets, and the rat as a mount can be found only from the fifth century A.D. The origins of this manifestation are unclear. Both totemic influences and military reasons for its emergence have been advanced.[65] In the foreground mythologically is the story that Pārvatī created her son by herself because Śiva as ascetic denied himself to her; when Śiva saw the child, he furiously cut off his head, but because Pārvatī grieved so badly, he promised to put the head of the first living creature who came along on the body of the child: This happened to be an elephant.

Gaṇeśa is not only the lovable, nibbling, elephant-headed god who is invoked especially for help in new enterprises; he is also worshipped in unhewn, rough stones, in which the trunk-shaped head is no longer to be discerned. In a district of Kathmandu, such a Gaṇeśa exists of a lump of rusty nails the inhabitants pound in when they have toothaches (fig. 13a). Clearly, in the course of Hinduization, pre-Hindu deities were enhanced by assuming prestigious names from the Sanskritic-Brahmanic Hindu religion. But the force of a deity is still more important for the worshippers than its name.

This was graphically illustrated on September 21, 1995, when a rumor suddenly arose that a statue of Gaṇeśa in a temple in Delhi was drinking milk with its trunk or tusk. The news spread like wildfire. Similar occurrences were soon heard from all parts of the country, long lines formed, everyone wanted to see the miracle of Gaṇeśa—like the bleeding statues of Mary in Italy, Poland, or Ireland. The phenomenon was confirmed even in Singapore, Hong Kong, London, and Hamburg. In Delhi, 120,000 additional liters of milk were sold on one day, and almost 60 percent of the population visited a Gaṇeśa

(a)

(b)

13. (a) Gaṇeśa in a quarter of Kathmandu: For toothache, a nail is pounded in. Photographer: A. Michaels, 1993. (b) Gaṇeśa as a neighborhood guard (*kṣetrapāla*) in Benares. Photographer: N. Gutschow, 1991.

temple at that time. Sober people immediately came up with a physical explanation: There was talk of a siphon effect and surface tension, of the principle of communicating pipes or secret suction machinery. What is noteworthy is that this hysteria erupted mainly in the big cities and among the middle class. Villagers hardly doubt the ability of the gods to work miracles, but this belief is an attitude that is not connected with a specific god and his abilities, but rather with the substantive nature of the divine, whose power is always only partially visible.

Wild and Mild Goddesses[66]

There are countless goddesses in India. The high gods have their consorts, spouses, and playmates (see table 17). Śiva's spouses—in their benevolent aspects—are, for example, Pārvatī ("Mountain Daughter"), Gaurī ("Golden"), or Umā. But Śiva's spouse can also appear wild and dangerous, like Kālī or Durgā, and then she is not very close to Śiva. Thus, for example, Durgā is usually represented as an independent goddess, who kills the buffalo demon Mahiṣa, who terrorized the world. Then—without Śiva in her retinue—she stands on the demon and pierces him with a long spear. It seems reasonable to suppose that a local goddess is incorporated here. Even today, local goddesses, who originally had no names in the high tradition and were Sanskritized only gradually, are worshipped in many small, inconspicuous places in southern India.[67] The justification for regarding these various goddesses as manifestations of a single goddess or of the female-cosmic energy (*śakti*) of Śiva is based mainly on the notion that the goddesses in India were themselves combined into groups and given a common point of reference. This appears as groups assembled in cosmic diagrams (*maṇḍala*), for example, the Nine Durgās (Navadurgā) or the Eight Mothers (Aṣṭamātṛkā).

Thus, among the goddesses, too, there is a contextual problem of identity. In the epic-Purāṇic pantheon, Sarasvatī—an independent river goddess even in the Vedic pantheon—is the goddess of the arts and sciences, and daughter or (!) wife of Brahmā or Viṣṇu. But she is also the spouse of Viṣṇu and in the Mahāyāna, she is considered a Buddhist goddess or a female creature of enlightenment (*bodhisattva*). Even though, in the epic-Purāṇic pantheon, Sarasvatī is usually represented with a book and Indian sounds as a lovable embodiment of science and art, she also appears in Tantric rituals, in which she is often called Dark or Blue Sarasvatī, as distinct from the White Sarasvatī; and then she is less a peaceful goddess than an independent Śakti.

In general, the wild and mild aspects of the gods are distinguished, even if these polarizations have recently fallen into disrepute and can be applied not only to the character of the goddesses, but also to the various forms of religion—such as the distinction between Brahmanic and popular Hinduism in Nepal.[68] Table 19[69] can only help to explain, but should not tempt us to construct polarities that overlook the polyvalent nature of the goddesses and gods.

The openness in principle by which a divinity can be identified with nearly everything can go so far that the identity of the goddess can hardly be ascertained, as can easily be seen in the goddess Guhyeśvarī, the "goddess of the secret":[70] In Nepal, Guhyeśvarī is worshipped near the Paśupatinātha Temple in completely different forms and under countless Brahmanic, Buddhist, and folk religious names. This makes her identity and function confused and contradictory: She is the spouse and wife of Śiva or Paśupatinātha, but she is also an independent goddess. She is the tutelary deity of Nepal, the favorite private goddess of many people, including the Malla kings, she forms one of sixty-four residences (*pīṭha*) of the Devī. She is a Buddhist *śakti* and a folk goddess with her own festival. Accordingly, she is manifested iconically as a vulva or an anus (*guhya*) in a hole in her temple, in a water jug, or as a sacred sword, but she is also represented anthropomorphically in a painting in her procession litter. Thus, like many other goddesses, Guhyeśvarī is wild and mild at the same time, carnivorous and vegetarian, Hindu, Buddhist, and folk religious; she is worshipped both by pure Brahmans and by Tantric priests or the lower castes; she is mobile and yet is rooted to her seat in a particular place.

But who is Guhyeśvarī "really"? Reducing the goddess to one aspect means not grasping her real nature. Classifying goddesses is usually done by arranging the individual names and forms of worship pertaining to them according to different historical stages or in connection with population groups.[71] Looking only at certain texts or building only on field observations produces a more or less complete picture. There is some reason to believe that Guhyeśvarī was originally a pre-Hindu deity, even if there are only speculations for it. But in her case, as in many other cases, it can no longer be determined who worshipped this deity, whether a local population wanted to enhance the status of their deity by using Sanskrit names, or whether followers of the great tradition wanted to take over local folk divinities. Important as the solution to this problem may seem, the issue of the origin of a deity does not solve the problem of its identity, for Guhyeśvarī has clearly preserved her various features.

"Identity" is a Western notion and is often also used in this connection as a psychological category. The strength or weakness of an identity is especially emphasized. It is considered strong when an individual is able to draw boundaries to delineate himself from others and can assert himself with regard to others, when he possesses special abilities and his own immutable character. According to such ideas, Guhyeśvarī has a weak identity. But in Nepal and

TABLE 19
Wild and Mild Goddesses

	*Mild (*saumya*) aspects*	*Wild (*ugra*) aspects*
Forms of Worship	*Pūjā, bhakti;* devotional and referred to the individual; the goddesses are to be entertained hospitably	(Animal)-sacrifices; ritualistic and communal; the goddesses are to be appeased
Times of worship	Depends on the personal horoscope, individually motivated oaths (*vrata*); by choice	Depends on fixed days of the calendar connected with the harvest cycle
Places of worship; territory	In houses, temples, and shrines; supralocal	Outside of settlements, open shrines; local
Kinship	The goddesses are married	The goddesses are unmarried and often have sisters, a mother, or grandmother
Offered foods	Fruit, sweets (*naivedya*); cooked	Alcohol, blood, eggs, meat; raw
Mobility	The goddesses are mobile, wander, and can manifest themselves almost everywhere; pilgrims go *to* them	The goddesses have fixed residences, are settled, rooted in the ground; pilgrimages go (in city processions) *with* statues of the goddesses
Celebrations	Are individualistic, referring to the individual, his clan or lineage	Are collective, referring to the community or several castes
Priests	Brahmans, "Vedic," superlocal, hereditary priesthood	Local, sectarian, "Tantric"; not necessarily hereditary priesthood, often from "lower" castes
Functions	Individual goals (*puṇya*), personal welfare, health, sons;—death, liberation	Common goals, welfare of the village, the settlement, harvest, rain;—life, fertility (creation and re-creation)
	Protection against personal illness and danger	Protection against epidemic diseases, failed harvests, earthquakes, evil spirits
	Protection through cosmic harmony	Protection through "magic" harmony (*maṇḍala, yantra*)
Features	Upward, peaceful, positive; benevolent, superior	Impure, fallen, raging, violent, negative; malevolent, low

14. Popular religious mural in Patan, Nepal: A worshipper of Chinnamastā, a manifestation of Śiva's divine power (*śakti*) pulls her husband as a dog to the goddess (to sacrifice him?). Photographer: A. Michaels, 1993.

India, she is considered a strong goddess precisely because she absorbs contradictions, because she basically has infinitely many identities and does not need any boundary lines. In sharp contrast to Western ideas of identity, the goddesses especially reflect that belief in the power of primary, preverbal, preconscious experiences of reality, which we have already encountered in the section on socialization (chapter 3). *All the Mothers Are One* is the title of Stanley Kurtz's book, which draws attention to multiple motherhood. In the same way, the Identificatory Habitus acquired in childhood also appears in reference to the deities, especially the goddesses: They are powerful *because* they can be identified with nearly everything.

ELEMENTS OF RELIGIOSITY

In the everyday religious life of India, the "profane" and the "sacred" are blended wherever you go. Gaṇeśa is invoked in a taxi, movie actors become living gods and goddesses, merchants adorn a picture of the goddess Lakṣmī with flowers and incense as soon as they roll up the tin shutters of their shop, the radio plays sacred chants, and a film version of the Rāmāyaṇa epic is broadcast on television with overwhelming success. The gods are omnipresent; there is a great need to care for them by oneself or with the help of priests. Fear of spirits, demons, ancestors, unfavorable constellations of stars, and the evil eye circulates. A certain "credulity" here is not to be overlooked. Often, there is a great tendency to believe in truth-tellers, palm readers, astrologists, medical quacks, gurus, or dream interpreters, as well as a wish for edifying histories of gods. Along with this lively everyday religiosity, there are also special religious occasions: festivals, pilgrimages, domestic rites. The following sections deal with this religiosity: first how words and looks form elements of the encounter with the god, prayer, the view (*darśana*) in ritual, as well as fundamental, recurrent ritual acts. General and exemplary ritualism, devotionalism, spiritualism, and heroism will then be discussed as the predominant forms of Hindu religiosity.

Prayer

In the Hindu religions, prayer is less observed as an expression of religiosity compared with rituals and celebrations.[72] In any case, a detailed study of this subject does not yet exist. Friedrich Heiler does consider Indian material in his monumental phenomenology of prayer, but he presents a typology that cannot be accepted because of its evolutionism. Thus, he talks of a lower and higher stage of prayer. To the lower stage, he assigns primitive and cultic prayer, naïve prayers as a kind of primeval form, ritual prayer, cult hymns, the literary poetry of hymns, and the philosophical ideal of prayer. His higher stage includes the creative prayerful piety of religious geniuses, which includes a mystical type (mystical prayer, Buddhist meditation), a prophetic type (prophetic prayer), the religious service congregational prayer, and—the highest stage—the legitimate and meritorious individual prayer. Heiler's differentiations of the forms of prayer, on the other hand, are useful. He distinguishes between *prayer* ("a living communion of the religious man with God, conceived as personal and present in experience, a communion which reflects the forms of the social relations of humanity"), *adoration* ("the solemn contemplation of the 'Holy One' as the highest good"), *devotion* ("the quiet, solemn mood of the soul, which is caused by the contemplation of ethical and intellectual, but especially of aesthetic and religious ['numinous'] values, whether of external objects or of imaginative conceptions dominated by feeling"), and *praying* ("to speak and to have intercourse with God").[73]

In most cases, prayer is in fact a "lively communication" with God, a linguistic contact with a god or goddess. Whether it concerns trade, praise, pleas, thanks, or cursing determines the form of address. Moreover, in the Hindu religions, there is also a special "form of prayer": the linguistic formulation of a holy syllable or a sacred utterance, which does not address a god, where the words have no meaning or a ritualistic meaning.

Even the Śatapathabrāhmaṇa says: "The speech conveys the sacrifice to the gods."[74] The Vedic Indians and their descendants were aware of the significance of speech from the start and placed great value on proper formulations and manner of expression, whether it concerned dialogues, invitations to a sacrificial meal, panegyrics, or desires for forgiveness or advice. For them, speech (Vāc) itself was a goddess.[75] In the fourth epoch, the form of direct address of a deity was usually typified in hymns of praise and supplication[76] (*stotra, stuti, stava,* and sometimes also *kāvya*), with which one prayed for liberation from rebirth, for support or grace, and more rarely for the fulfillment of concrete wishes. But these hymns and poems, alone or in a group, are not recited in a congregational service. Instead, they are used to seek direct encounter with a god and thus priestly formalism is declared a hindrance. In addition to the Stotra Hymns there are devotional songs and chants (*kīrtana, bhajana, vacana,* Hindī *satsang*), which were composed anonymously by poet-saints (see table 4). These texts are mainly sung, quite often accompanied by musical instruments, occasionally all night long. They are usually loud prayers, whose choice of words is fixed. The silent, freely formulated prayer, the private dialogue with a god, on the other hand, is less practiced. The gods want to be called upon audibly. From time to time, they have to be awakened with bells or the blowing of a conch.

Even though hymnic prayer is the most widespread form of invoking the gods, other religious aphorisms have become typical of India; these can be summarized under the rubric of "mantra,"[77] even though that category implies a simplification of many local terms (*brahman, stobha, bīja, kavaca, dhāraṇī, yāmala*). Mantras are irrevocably fixed syllables or word orders, which are ascribed a force that is occasionally felt as dangerous. They can usually be learned only after an initiation; therefore they can be passed on. Such word formulas are common in all forms of religiosity: in devotionalism as address by name (*nāmajapa;* see below), in ritualism as short quotations of the Vedic collections in domestic or Śrauta ritual, in spiritualism as meditative seed syllables (*bīja*), in heroism as a means of political power.

A controversial question is whether mantras have any meaning. The answer sometimes depends on whether they can be translated. Unlike hymns, mantras, especially the seed syllables, are generally untranslatable.[78] Thus, in normal speech, the mantras *svāha, hrīṃ,* or *aim* have no meaning, like the magic formula "abracadabra," but they do have a ritual or mystical function.[79] Mantras as quotations from Vedic texts, on the other hand, do have meaning. Mixtures of both forms are possible, as in the widespread mantra of *Oṃ tat sat* ("*Oṃ,* this is the being"). To be able to use the sacred substance of the mantras depends on (ritually correct) saying and hearing, not on understanding. In the Hindu view, this substance is the condensation of a comprehensive truth. Thus the Gāyatrī verse condenses a mantra of the Ṛgveda, the force and immortality of the whole Veda.[80]

Just as the whole can be condensed to one or a few words or phonemes, so compression can also happen in visual form, through gestures (*mudrā*), forms of sitting (*āsana*), or graphic representations (*yantra, maṇḍala*) of deities or powers. This always implies a space-time reification of a sacred substance, which can also be stretched again. The Gāyatrī mantra can become the goddess Gāyatrī, the holy syllable *Oṃ*—a combination of the sounds *a, u,* and *ṃ* (nasalization)—can be not only the Brahman, immortal and invincible, but also that force with which the god Brahmā and everyone who knows it becomes almighty: "Brahmā thought: 'Through which syllable can I fulfill all wishes, attain all worlds, gods, Vedas, sacrifices, tones, merits, living creatures, animate and inanimate?' He practiced asceticism and saw *Oṃ.*"[81] The syllable is again the substance of the whole, which is identified through secret chains of causation with sacrifice, the Veda, and immortality among other things.[82]

The meaning of words can recede into the background vis-à-vis such mystical and ritual identifications, as shown particularly in invocations and prayers consisting of names (*nāmajapa*).[83] The idea that a single name is not enough to grasp a god is quite widespread; it is found in the hundred names of Allah as well as in the Kabala or the litany to Mary. "In [the name of the god] rests the secret of divine plenitude; the diversity of God's names, the many names of the divine, indeed, the thousands of names, are a true indication of His omnipotence," notes Ernst Cassirer.[84] Extremely long name texts are typical of India; in them, 100 or 108, 300, 1,000, or 1,008 names of individual gods are listed in the form of hymns (*nāmastotra, nāmastuti, nāmavalī*), but a clear system of the order of the names is not often discernible in them. The multiplicity of names has to do with the notion of god and thus there is a widespread idea that a god can have many names or none, just as a god can have many forms and characteristics (*saguṇa*) or none (*nirguṇa*). By reciting the name texts, the multiplicity passes to the reciter. This is based on belief in the effect of language and, in the negative case, can also be used in curses or harmful magic. Even to utter the name of a god means to identify with the whole, the deity. As Annette Wilke has shown in a study of these texts,[85] what is important is the liturgically and ritually correct use, the proper emphasis and pronunciation, the proper number of names, and occasionally also the consecration through which the adept first learned the meaning of the secret names. But then the name of god is everything and it is widely believed that anyone who has the name of a god on his lips at the hour of death, like Mahatma Gandhi, is assured of heaven. It is no accident that funeral processions are announced—incidentally, ritual death follows biological death—by the Hindī saying *Rām nām satya hai* ("The name of Rāma is the truth").

The Hindu gods are not always present at fixed places; they have to be invoked,[86] and prayers and appeals by name are the favorite means for that. Indeed, the most widespread form of encountering the gods in the Hindu religions is not in words, but through the eyes.

Looks[87]

The mutual sight (*dṛṣṭi, darśana*) of believer and god is considered the central part of Hindu religious service (*pūjā*). As long as the statue of the god is not brought to life in a special rite (*prānapratiṣṭhā*),[88] it is inanimate. Thus the eyes or the pupils of the statue are not done by a painter (fig. 15), but rather by a priest, who animates the work, makes it "seeing," and this look is so strong that it forms the climax of the religious service. Folk religion notions of the evil eye are probably connected here with the general experience that the look in the eyes is evidence of truth. Thus, a term for philosophy is also *darśana* ("[proper] seeing").[89]

Fear of the evil eye is deeply rooted in India.[90] All living creatures, including plants, can be affected. Small children are especially in peril, and to protect them, a black or red thread is often wound around the ankle at the naming ritual (*nāmakaraṇa*);[91] the same thing happens in the *rakṣābandhana* ceremony in the fifth month of pregnancy.[92] It is also considered dangerous when food is polluted by the evil eye. It is striking that persons or animals who could be envious are often accused of the evil eye: pregnant women (because they envy children born healthy), widows, or hungry people.[93] In general, friends and relatives, even one's own mother,[94] tend to be accused rather than strangers.

One can defend oneself against the evil eye not only by threads, but also by amulets, sayings (mantras), or diagrams (yantras), talismans, rings, lights,

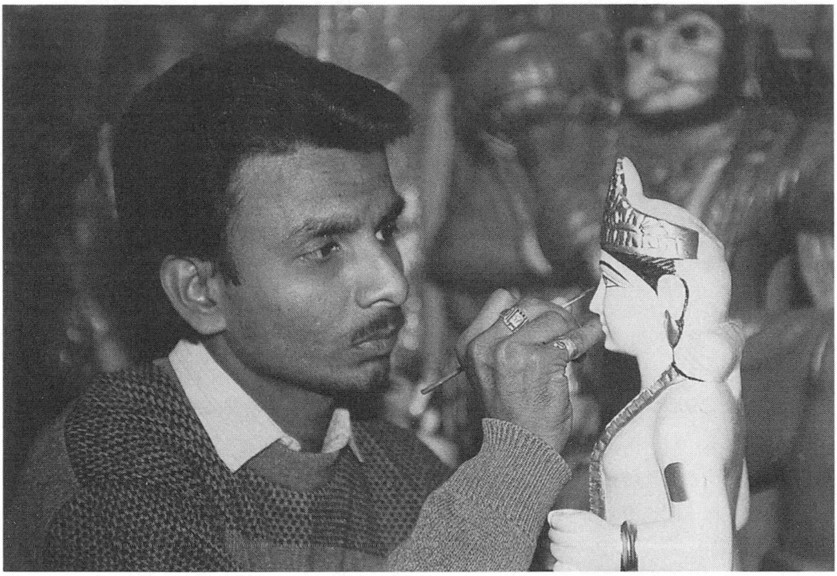

15. Enlivening of a statue in Benares: The painter paints the pupils of a divine figure (Sarasvatī) and thus enlivens it. Photographer: N. Gutschow, 1992.

or mustard seeds. Healers, exorcists, ascetics, or saints are ready to help. One protects oneself against spirits, demons, or restless souls in the same way. If illness, death, a financial loss, or a professional failure strikes, the cause is often seen as a lack of Darśana shown to gods, ancestors, or spirits. Protective paintings are also a favorite means of defense: Bodies, houses, especially thresholds, autos, and machines, but also cattle are often painted with eye motifs. If a rickshaw or truck driver adorns his vehicle with big, kohl-rimmed eyes, pictures of gods, and blessings, he does so not only to decorate it, but also to avert all dangers from outside. And if house entrances are painted accordingly, the malevolent forces will find no entrance here either. Foreign looks are not to strike the fragile, the open, the undelineated: the kitchen, where food could be polluted; the small child, who is not yet ritually protected; the woman, who could bring the family compound into disrepute.

Therefore, women should avoid the looks of others and pull the sari over their faces when they go in public. "Seeing is a kind of touching" (Diana Eck).[95] Sight is contact, in both the good and the bad sense. Like the greeting, it demands a response. The exchange of looks in the Indian dance can be learned as a separate language; in the Nāṭyaśāstra, thirty-six forms of looks are distinguished.[96] Anyone who looks away avoids contact, on the other hand. When women shyly avert their faces, it is considered a sign of courtesy and propriety and cannot be interpreted as coquetry. In many cases, one should not even look at the god, and many temples are structured to prevent a direct look at the main sanctuary.

Light drives out spirits, demons, and sinister looks. Thus, there is the widespread idea that electrification and street lighting have frightened off the spirits, and waving a light has always been a means of protection against the evil eye. In the Hindu religious service (*pūjā*), the deity is given light (*dīpa*). Clarence Maloney correctly asked to what extent the morning and evening light-waving ceremony (*ārati*) is connected with folk religious protection measures.[97] Often, the statue of the god in the temple is veiled. But when, during the Pūjā, it is allowed to be viewed while bells are tolled, tallow or oil lamps are waved. This beneficial look is considered the crucial moment of the encounter with the god; it is one of the most often cited motives for temple attendance.

Modern Indian languages have a saying that the look is given and taken (Hindī *darśan denā, darśan lenā*) and that this alone is sufficient as religious merit. So, Darśana is basically an exchange of looks,[98] as the look in the eyes can be the most intense experience in the encounter with another person. One takes Darśana from high-ranking people and gives it to low-ranking people. The offices of high-placed figures are sometimes packed with people whose only honestly admitted request is to take Darśana.

However, the looks of the gods can also destroy. Śiva (and his consort)[99] has a third eye, with which he burns the god of love, Kāma, to ashes.[100] The eye of the gods is mainly a symbol for vigilance, far-sightedness, and beauty, and often for sexuality and potency, too.[101] Many gods are all eyes, such as the goddesses Mīnakṣī ("Fish-eyed") or Kāmakṣī ("Pleasure-eyed"). Others (Rudra, Śītalā) have one hundred or one thousand eyes, with which they can see everything. Omnipresence and omnipotence are thus combined.

Finally, the eye as evidence of truth is held in high regard: The most reliable witness is the eyewitness (*sākṣin*),[102] and "Now, truth is sight."[103] But the eye is also suspicious. Someone who knows everything, like the gods, need no longer be able to see: Blindness can thus be higher insight. What is simply seen can be appearance, mirage, illusion. Thus, the criticism of the favorite part of Hindu worship of god, the exchange of looks, is expressed in philosophical illusionism: The god is basically featureless and formless (*nirguṇa, nirākāra*); the world is only an (optical) illusion (*māyā*), blindness, deception. True insight needs not sight, but rather knowledge and internal vision.

TABLE 20
The Five Components of Rituals

1. Causal Change
2. Formal Decision (*intentio solemnis*)
3. Formal Criteria of Acts Formalism (repetitiveness), publicity, irrevocability, "liminality"
4. Modal Criteria of Acts Subjective effect (*impressio*), public nature (*societas*), transcendence (*religio*)
5. Changes of Identity, Role, Status, Authority

Ritual Acts[104]

Words and looks are the most intense and frequent expressions of Hindu religiosity, but they are embedded in an abundance of other forms of worship and ritual acts: Brahmanic-Sanskritic domestic rituals (*karma, kriyā*), sacrifices (*homa, yajña, iṣṭi, bali*), celebrations (*utsava*), pilgrimages (*tīrthayātrā*), religious service (*pūjā, sevā*), oaths (*vrata*), meditations (*yoga, dhyāna*), heroic acts (*vīrya*), and many others. These ritual acts can be distinguished from everyday acts by five criteria, which I have summarized in table 20.

First, according to this scheme, rituals involve temporal or spatial changes, and life-cycle rituals refer to biological, physical, or age-related alterations or changes. It is mainly border crossings, alterations, and changes that entail rituals: house-warmings, examinations, beginning or ending work, change of day, year, and month, namings, birth, initiation, marriage, and death.

Second, a formal, usually spoken decision is required to carry out the ritual: an oath, vow, or pledge (*saṃkalpa*). The spontaneous celebration of a change is not a ritual. An initiation without Saṃkalpa has no effect.[105] I call this component *intentio solemnis*. What is controversial is precisely the intentionality of ritual acts.[106] Caroline Humphrey and James Laidlaw insist explicitly that ritual acts are "non-intentional" (even if not "unintentional"). But only the *intentio solemnis* makes an everyday or customary act into a ritual act. It singles out certain segments of acts and evokes awareness of the change. Therefore, a change of the level of language also usually takes place. In the ritual, water becomes ritual water, rice becomes ritual rice, a stone becomes the seat of the gods. All this is usually distinguished in language. Thus, in the Hindu initiation, water is called by the Sanskrit word *jala,* instead of the everyday

(Nepālī) *pāni;* and *mīṭhai* ("sweets") becomes *naivedya, phul* ("flowers") becomes *puṣpa, bati* ("light") becomes *dīpa, camal* ("rice") becomes *akṣatā.*[107]

Third, ritual acts must be (a) formal, stereotypical, and repetitive (and therefore imitable); (b) public; and (c) irrevocable; in many cases they are also (d) liminal (see below). So they may not be spontaneous, private, revocable, singular, or optional for everyone. Ritual acts are not deliberately rational; they cannot simply be revised to achieve a better or more economical goal. A sacred fire cannot simply be lit with a profane gas lighter. Therefore, formalism forms a central criterion in most definitions of ritual.[108] Ritualism as a form of religiosity is based primarily on this characteristic. Moreover, rituals cannot be private functions; they can be imitated. Publicity in principle in the sense of intersubjectivity—even if it concerns only a small secret circle of initiated specialists—is thus another formal criterion. Finally, rituals are effective independent of their meaning, *ex opere operato*; this means that they cannot be reversed. Girding makes the initiate a Twice-Born, even if he notes during the ritual that he would rather be a Moslem or a Christian—which, naturally, does not happen. That then requires a new ritual. Along with these three strict, formal criteria, many rituals also contain another one, which Victor Turner has described as "liminality" (from the Latin *limen,* "border"). He means the non-everyday and yet reversible, paradoxical, sometimes absurd and playful parts of rituals, especially in life-cycle border situations, such as the playful time of learning (*deśāntara*) during the initiation (see above, chapter 3).

Fourth, almost every ritual act takes place in an everyday context. But whether the act of "pouring water" is performed to clean or consecrate a statue is not to be decided solely on the basis of these external, formal criteria, but also depends on "internal" criteria relating to intentions. I distinguish three modal criteria of acts, which I call "Impressio," "Societas," and "Religio," and which can appear very distinct or weak in the ritual. By *Societas*—deviating from Turner, who uses the term *Communitas* in this connection—I understand all functions of a ritual referring to the community: solidarity, hierarchy, control, or establishment of norms. *Impressio* denotes the aspects of acts relating to individuals, such as alleviating anxiety, experiences or enthusiasm, desire and lack of it. *Religio* encompasses transcendental intentions relating to the other, higher, sacred world, which is called the "aura of factuality" in Clifford Geertz or the "numinous" in Rudolf Otto. With Religio, everyday acts acquire sublimity and the immutable, nonindividual, non-everyday is staged. This criterion is particularly controversial because, in a certain sense, by definition it links religion with ritual. But in definitions of ritual, it is just this link that is often questioned. Nevertheless, I mean that rituals without a portion of Religio, which is not to be equated with "religion," are not distinguishable from simple routines. Here, I follow Emile Durkheim's dictum that "the ritual can be defined only after defining the belief,"[109] which Bronislaw Malinowski adapted: "There is no ritual without belief."[110] In this sense, Religio is the awareness that the act in question is done because a transcendental value is attributed to it. In the great majority of cases, this is a theistic, demonic, or dynamic belief in supernatural beings or powers. But belief in some kind of elevated principle, such as the total order (Dharma) of a society or social group, is also sufficient. Every participant in the ritual does not need to have this belief, but Religio must be demonstrable in some place; usually it can be recognized in the *intentio solemnis.*

Fifth, a tangible change must take place with the ritual. For example, the participants in the ritual must acquire an ability they did not previously have or a new social status with social consequences: The initiate becomes a marriageable Twice-Born; a scholar becomes a candidate for an academic career with the Ph.D.; a nameless ship becomes a christened ship.

With these five components, a ritual can clearly be delineated from ceremonies, games, sports, routines, customs and practices, dramatizations, and other such events, without having to assume a theistic notion of religion or the often misleading distinction between profane and secular. A few examples illustrate this difference: Religio is usually lacking in sports; a rowing competition is not a ritual, but the annual regatta between Oxford and Cambridge may contain a small portion of Religio, the belief in one's own tradition-rich university as an expression of a high social status. Irrevocability and the liminal aspect of acts are lacking in routine; in customs and practices, the *intentio solemnis* is absent. Rituals have to demonstrate a formal, stereotypical portion, but this is to be separated from modal and intentional criteria. If a religious service fills those criteria, it is a ritual; but it can also be more or less devotional or formalistic. Consequently, I see ritualism as the overarching category that subsumes devotionalism, spiritualism, and heroism, and devote more space to it than to the other forms of religiosity. Only because in certain rituals devotional, spiritual, or heroic aspects are conspicuous do they appear as special forms of religiosity.

RITUALISM

Many religious acts are tinted with devotionalism, spiritualism, or heroism; but most of them are also ritualistic. If I delineate this mode as a separate form of religiosity, it is only because in many cases, the act is performed without a clearly discernable devotional, spiritual, or heroic background. The Lord's Prayer in Christianity can be recited or chanted silently, spiritually and meditatively, or very devotionally; but can also be a formal, "empty" ritual in which the content is less important than the form. Similarly, a Hindu divine worship service can be very rapt and devotional, or spiritual (*mānasikā pūjā*), or extremely formalistic, when it is performed by a paid temple priest without much internal sympathy. Only when these formal points of view predominate and are a large part of the prescribed ritual do I speak of "ritualism."

In this section, I discuss the examples of three frequently practiced or important types of ritual: the Brahmanic morning ritual (*saṃdhyā*), the Sanskritic and folk religious service (*pūjā*), and the (ancient Indian) sacrifice (*yajña, homa*). Rites of passage (*saṃskāra*), festivals (*utsava*), donations (*dāna*), pilgrimages (*tīrthayātrā*), or vows (*vrata*) have already been treated in chapter 3 or will be treated in the next chapter. "Tantric" and other rituals will not be discussed.

The Brahmanic-Sanskritic Morning Ritual[111]

Traditional Hindus, especially the so-called Twice-Born, begin the day with a series of rituals. Early in the morning, at dawn or before, flocks of believers can be seen at rivers or in temples invoking the gods and ancestors or driving away spirits by purifying themselves ritually. According to the legal texts, performing a morning and evening ritual—Saṃdhyā (*saṃdhyā-upāsana,* literally: "twilight, dusk")—is even a religious duty for the Twice-Born. This includes a ritual bath, breathing exercises, reciting the Gāyatrī hymns, certain ritual calls (*vyāhṛti*), worshipping the sun and gods, as well as driving out demons. There are, however, considerable variations in these rituals. Instead of rough generalizations, I shall concentrate in this section on summarizing a Saṃdhyā of 1987–1988 in Mithila (northern Bihar); it is based on the detailed description of Shinyo Einoo, which I supplement with my own observations of the bathing places of Benares (see table 21 and fig. 16).

A Twice-Born should get up before sunrise and begin the day auspiciously: Right after awakening, he should think of his tutelary deity or another deity, and look upon an image of the gods, a child, or at himself in the mirror. He should not gaze at inauspicious things, it is said[112]—no widow, no broom in the corner, no man with a red mustache, and so on. Before the ritual purification of the body, with which the real Saṃdhyā begins, comes the morning toilette. One asks the goddess Earth (Pṛthivī) for forgiveness for walking on her, washes one's mouth and face, and thins out the loin cloth (*dhoṭi*). Since most of the houses in the village have no toilet, one makes one's way to the fields to perform one's needs with a vessel of water. While defecating and

TABLE 21
The Brahmanic-Sanskritic Morning Ritual (*saṃdhyā*)

1. Washing (*snāna*)	8. Hand gestures (*mudrā*)
2. Breath control (*prāṇāyāma*)	9. Libations to gods, seers, and ancestors (*tarpaṇa*)
3. Washing the mouth (*ācamana*)	10. Libations to the sun (*sūrya-arghya*)
4. Ritual washing (*mārjana*)	11. Ritual dissolution (*utsarjana*)
5. Wiping out guilt substance (*aghamarṣana*)	12. Applying a forehead sign (*bhasma*)
6. Sun worship (*sūrya-upasthāna*)	13. Ritual conclusion (*saṃkalpa*)
7. Silent Gāyatrī recitation (*gāyatrījapa*)	14. Ritualistic physical postures and gestures (*nyāsa*)

urinating (which men also do squatting),[113] the Sacred Thread does not hang over the right shoulder, but around the neck and over the right ear through which one hears the Gāyatrī verses at the initiation,[114] and is therefore considered especially pure.

The ritual bath is clearly separated from hygienic physical purification by the formal decision (*intentio solemnis*), the recitation of the mantra, the use of certain ritual objects (spoon, *kuśa* grass, water jug), and by formal ritual acts. Thus, one form of the ritual purification occurs when holy water from a river (especially the Ganges), which is kept in a special sacred jug (*kalaśa*), is poured with a small sacred copper spoon over the ball of the right thumb and is then dribbled over the head and breast while reciting the following: "*Oṃ.* Be he pure, impure, or in any state whatever, he who thinks of the Lotus-Eyed One [namely, Viṣṇu] is pure both within and without."[115] This is followed by similar ritual washings. Because these are ritual acts, they can be substituted: instead of water, for example, clay from a holy river, dust from cows, or ashes can be used during illnesses.[116] The way of holding your fingers while dribbling water and washing the mouth (*ācamana*) is hardly arbitrary either. Instead, the right hand is divided into holy places assigned to gods (*tīrtha*),[117] which are used according to different and changing criteria. The tips of the three middle fingers and the ball of the thumb (*brahmatīrtha*) are used especially often. Ritual and profane washing can certainly be done together, as when the believer stands up to his hips in the river water and dives under several times to wash

16. Morning ritual with sun and Ganges prayer at Daśāśvamedhaghāṭ, Benares. Photographer: N. Gutschow, 1992.

himself. But it is always clearly delineated whether it is a ritual act or not. There is also a linguistic distinction between ritual (*mārjana*) and "profane" (*snāna, śauca*) washing.

Washing is combined with breath control (*prāṇāyāma*). This is done by blocking or opening alternate nostrils with the thumb and specific fingers. While inhaling or when both nostrils are pressed shut, the believer mentally recites the Gāyatrī verses. This also purifies him, for breath control is a kind of internal purification. So the Saṃdhyā produces an internal (*āntara*) and external (*bāhya*), mental and physical, spiritual and moral purity (*śauca*).[118]

A recurring part of the ritual is washing the mouth (*ācamana*), in which, while the bather is sitting, water is poured from a small vessel over the ball of the right thumb and the hand is then closed and placed on the right knee or leg. The following verse was then recited by the Brahman observed by Einoo in Mithilā: "May the sun, rage, and the lords of rage protect me from offenses that I commit in wrath. May the night destroy all offenses I commit at night in spirit with my words, with both hands, feet, stomach, or sexual member. Whatever evil is still in me, I now offer myself to the sun, born of immortality, to appear. *Svāha*."[119] With the ritual shout *svāha* ("salvation, blessing"), he shakes the water out of his hand and washes his mouth with fresh water. Then he repeats the whole thing in a similar form calling on the goddess Earth as well as the gods Brahmaṇaspati and Brahmā. Here at the latest, it becomes clear that the Saṃdhyā also represents an identification of the individual with immortality (Veda) or brahman. The believer separates himself emotionally and externally from all death-bringing concerns, from his individuality and singularity, and thus his mortality.

Next the participant washes himself again ritually (*mārjana*), by pouring the water in his left hand, and if possible dribbles drops over his face and head with "immortal"[120] *darbha* or *kuśa* grass, or else with the fingertips of the right hand, calling on the waters (plural!) and praying for strength or nourishment with a special mantra from the ṛgveda (10.90.1–3). This ritual is generally repeated twice. The mantras of the first section of the ritual deal with the cosmic creation.[121] Only by recreating himself anew every day is the participant equal to the Veda and thus immortality. These mantras are also repeated in the next part (*aghamarṣaṇa;* literally: "forgiveness for sins"); this time the water is in the closed right hand and is then thrown into a basin. With new water in the right hand on the right leg, he recites another verse. After an appeal to the sun (*sūrya-upasthāna*) with various gestures and sayings, the Gāyatrī verse is again recited silently (*gāyatrījapa*), again accompanied by various ritual gestures. What is crucial is that Gāyatrī now appears as a goddess: in the morning as a virgin and *śakti* of Brahmā, at noon as spouse and *śakti* of Śiva, in the evening as an old woman and *śakti* of Viṣṇu. The worship of the Gāyatrī—according to many legal scholars, the central part of the Saṃdhyā[122]—is done with twenty-five hand gestures (*mudrā*) and a muttered prayer.

This is followed by libations of water to the gods, seers, and ancestors. This ritual step can also be performed with river water. With the spoon or standing in the river using his hands, the actor scoops water; as he pours it out, he recites mantras to various gods. The same is done for the seers while the Sacred Thread hangs around his neck, but with the ancestors it is over his right shoulder and under his left arm. He offers the libation of water both to the deified ancestors (*viśve devāḥ*) and to the forefathers (*pitaraḥ*), invokes up to thirty-six deceased relatives on the paternal and maternal sides up to the fourth generation, each by name and clan (*gotra*), and concludes with the prayer: "*Oṃ*. You who were born in our family belonging to our Gotra, [but] dying without sons, drink the water I give you by wringing out my garment." Finally, the sun is once again worshipped (*sūrya-arghya*), now again with the Sacred Thread over the left shoulder. As is common in many rituals, the ritual place is formally dismantled and the gods are prayed to forgive any possible error. Thus ends the traditional Saṃdhyā.

Today, applying a sign of sect or caste (*ṭīkā, tilaka*)[123] on forehead and body is also part of the morning ritual. For that, too, there are countless prescriptions concerning the material used and the direction of the lines. Vertical lines usually indicate Viṣṇu and horizontal ones Śiva. Many believers apply the sign before the Saṃdhyā, but at the Ganges in Benares, some go to a pilgrim priest (*paṇḍa*) only after the morning ritual, obtain a mirror and cinnabar for the forehead mark (*ṭīkā*), and can oil and comb their hair.

The Saṃdhyā apparently emerged from an ancient sun cult and the Vedic Agnihotra ritual,[124] which was also to be performed morning and evening at twilight. But not much of this is still preserved in the Saṃdhyā. In the late phase of the second ("Vedic") epoch, the Agnihotra was mainly a milk offering to the fire, by which Agni or the sun was to be brought to life, along with the ritualized maintenance of the daily domestic fire and the worship of deities (*vaiśvadeva*). With the Gṛhyasūtras, at the latest (from the third epoch), the originally separate Vedic morning and evening rituals were still connected with the old Agnihotra. If originally only those who had in fact studied the Veda were allowed to carry out the Saṃdhyā, in time this ritual became obligatory for all male Twice-Born and was enriched with more ritual parts, especially the ritualization of the morning routines (bath, mouth-washing, etc.). The Saṃdhyā practiced today can thus be seen only conditionally as a Vedic ritual. Folk religious and devotional elements have acquired great importance. Thus, driving out spirits and demons, which has become a definitive component of the Saṃdhyā, has also influenced the evening temple service (*āratī, ārtī*).

Today, along with or as part of the Saṃdhyā, the worship of five divinities (*pañcāyatanapūjā*)[125] is also widespread in the room of the house where private cult worship takes place, mainly in the upper rooms of the house, quite frequently the bedroom. The head of the house sometimes attends to the deity, but more often it is the wife, and sometimes also the household priest (*purohita*). Usually, it is Viṣṇu, represented by a black stone or ammonite (*śālagrāma*); Śiva, represented in the form of a Liṅga; and an iconic form of Devī (often Durgā), Gaṇeśa, and Sūrya. The preferred deity is in the middle. Devī or Sūrya can also be replaced by a personal wish god (*iṣṭadevatā*). These deities are worshipped more or less lavishly with chanting, incense, flowers, light, rice seeds, and other things, often by women or even only by them. It is assumed that this five-god worship, which is evident from the sixth century on,[126] forms a link between the gods of five major sects: Śaiva, Vaiṣṇava, Śakta, Saura (sun worship), and Gāṇapatyas (Gaṇapati worship).

Many believers still go to a temple or a nearby holy place in the morning before they eat their first meal. Here, the gods, spirits, and ancestors are usually thought of by presenting a part of the rice dish to animals, primarily cows, chickens, crows, and ants. When the believer also has gifts granted to ascetics or beggars, he has fulfilled his obligation to do the five traditional daily sacrifices (*mahāyajña*), that is to the gods, seers, ancestors, animals, and humans.

The morning ritual is a blend of ritualist and devotionalist parts. Rites of purification and a ritual preparation for the day, the request for strength and support are central to it. In the process, the believer rids his body of death-bringing forces, identifies the parts of his body progressively with the Veda, and thus "eternalizes" himself internally and externally. But what was originally a predominantly ritual act became increasingly devotional through popular religious influences. The same is true of the Pūjā, which is currently the most common form of divine worship and the ritual center of the Hindu religions.

Divine Worship (*pūjā*)[127]

The daily or regular worship of one or several deities through invocations, offers of gifts, and ritual farewell is called *pūjā*. The etymology of this word is uncertain. It could have come from Tamil *pūcu* ("smear"), but as early as Vedic texts, the verb *pūj* is used in the sense of "worship";[128] although, in the same texts, no form of worship by smearing with dye or blood can be seen. Since this act is not central in the traditional Pūjā ritual either, the original meaning remains unclear.

The history of the Pūjā is rudimentary. There are no textual or archaeological indications that the Āryans of the second "Vedic" epoch worshiped gods in the form of statues. The first evidence of the Pūjā is found in early Gṛhyasūtras at the end of the second epoch; codifications of the ritual come only at the beginning of the fifth ("Sectarian") epoch. Nor is it clear how the Pūjā became the focus of the Hindu religions. Popular religious influences are probably to be advanced here.

The Pūjā is distinct from a Vedic sacrifice in that the food offerings in it are always vegetarian, while the sacrifice of animals in the Vedic and popular religious ritual have always been common. Moreover, the Vedic ritual is a priestly ritual, but the Pūjā can also be performed by lay people. Ancient Indians did know many forms of worship, which also occur in a classical Pūjā, especially in the ritual worship of a guest (*madhuparka* or *arghya*): offering a seat, washing the feet, bathing, feeding, offering lights, and other things; but these ritual acts are so general that they can be traced back to many religions. Yet, the anthropomorphic care and entertainment of a deity by waking, clothing, and offering flowers and food cannot yet be seen in the Veda.

Through a Pūjā the pious person seeks contact with the gods; he might call attention to himself with gifts and invocations to obtain their favor. But gods

17. Pūjā in Deopotan, Nepal: The goddess Vatasalā, worshipped tantrically, is evoked by a priest (in the foreground: bell and bowls), and is entertained, anointed, and decorated with an inflated intestine of a sacrificed animal as a necklace (*mālā*). Photographer: A. Michaels, 1983–1984.

are not the only ones who can be the focus of this ritual; Brahmans (at the end of every Pūjā), teachers (as on the *Gurupūrṇimā* day), virgins (*kumārīpūjā*), children (*baṭukapūjā*), cows and other animals, plants (Tulsī bush, the peepal tree), books (*Sarasvatīpūjā*), the earth (*bhūmīpūjā*), a water jug (*kalaśapūjā*), or stones (*śālagrāmapūjā*) can also be the focus. Moreover, the Pūjā can be performed only in spirit (*mānasikā pūjā*),[129] in which this form of it is often understood as a criticism of the externality and formality of the ritual. A Pūjā can be performed on any ritually purified place, for oneself (*ātmārtha*) or in the name of or on behalf of someone else (*parārtha*): The priest can do it for the lay people or the community, the wife for her husband and her children, subjects for the king, the king for the country. Everyone is entitled to do it, but if Vedic sayings are prescribed, only the Twice-Born are allowed to do it.

The procedure of a Pūjā varies according to the school, the region, and the time. There is an abundance of basic texts (Āgamas, Tantras, Saṃhitās) and ritual books (Nibandha), in which the details are established, of which the most detailed is the Pūjāprakāśa of Mitramiśra (1610–1640).[130] Below, I examine the sequence of a modern Pūjā for Paśupati ("Lord of animals"), a manifestation of Śiva, according to a Nepalese ritual text (Paśupatināthapūjāvidhi).[131]

As in the morning ritual (*saṃdhyā*), which also represents a form of Pūjā, the one officiating must prepare himself internally and externally and purify the ritual objects. If he has made the formal decision (*saṃkalpa*) for the Pūjā, he temporarily becomes a god himself, for only Śiva may worship Śiva, as the Śaivāgama texts emphasize; so he must identify with the deity internally and ritually.[132] The external purification consists of a bath, mouth-washing, donning new or freshly laundered clothes, renewal of the forehead mark; the internal purification (*ātmaśuddhi*) includes adopting a trusting attitude (*śraddhā*), mantras, immersion in meditation, and visualization. The result is shared with the deity in a worship of the mother/goddess, as for example: "I am dressing the Mother. I am at that time the Mother myself. . . . When I worship I forget myself. I become the goddess. She who is *Mā* [Mother] is me. There is no difference between *Mā* and me."[133]

According to the text, worship of Paśupati involves more than thirty standardized ritual acts, including sixteen gestures of respect (*upacāra*) which are often stipulated for a traditional Pūjā (see table 22).[134] But this series is not compulsory either, for one list is hardly like any other. The list can be expanded to up to 108 gestures of respect, for example by including "Tantric" parts of the ritual—for instance, finger gestures and physical poses (*mudrā, nyāsa*).[135] Abridgements are also common: The five gestures of respect (*pañcopacāra*) with anointing, flowers, incense, swinging lights, and feeding (see nos. 9–13 of table 22) are widespread.

Such a worship is a mixture of invoking, washing or anointing (*abhiṣeka*),[136] decoration, exaltation, offering, and entertaining. The deity is treated respectfully as an important guest or a king. The gods rejoice over the Pūjā and are thus graciously disposed toward the person. An essential component of a Pūjā are the gifts obtained by the organizer of the Pūjā. For his offering he obtains religious merit (*puṇya*) and indirect worldly advantage (*bhukti*), health, happiness, or wealth, but also a special form of favor of the deity (*prasāda*) or his protection (*śaraṇa*). In "material" form, the Prasāda consists of the return of

TABLE 22
The Sixteen Proofs of Respect (*upacāra*) of a Pūjā

1. Invocation (*āvāhana*)	9. Anointing (*gandha, anulepana*)
2. Installation (*āsana,* literally: seat, throne)	10. Flowers (*puṣpa*)
3. Washing the feet (*pādya*)	11. Incense (*dhūpa*)
4. Welcome (*arghya*)	12. Light (*dīpa*)
5. Mouth-washing (*ācamanīya*)	13. Feeding (*naivedya*)
6. Bath (*snāna*)	14. Greeting (*namaskāra*)
7. Clothing (*vastra*)	15. Circumambulation (*pradakṣiṇā*)
8. Fastening (*yajñopavīta*)	16. Dissolution (*visarjana*)

the offered foods—sweets, (cooked) rice, fruit, ashes (*vibbūtī*), flowers, etc.—by the priest or the contact with the liquid excretions of the god or Guru, his "sweat" or water used for washing his foot, for example.

By the believers eating what they themselves have offered the gods, a relationship is created between the believers and the god, which corresponds with the social position and its rules of commensality. In the process, it is not altogether clear whether the deity has eaten food according to the view of the believer or only consecrated it. The distinction is serious. If the deity took the food and "ate" it, the believer eats (impure) leftovers.[137] The believer thus expresses his submission to the god, just as many other services the priest or the believer perform are "impure" or subordinate activities: foot-washing, clothing, offering food, cleaning the temple or ritual place.

On the other hand, Christopher J. Fuller thinks that the Prasāda is not a return gift. Instead, through contact with the deity, the food is only transmuted; the deity does not "eat" it.[138] Moreover, in social life, it is a sign of higher rank to reject food, especially cooked rice. So, if the gods take food, they basically behave contrary to the fundamentals of the social hierarchy. Instead, the relationship between god and believer reflects the relationship between man and wife. The wife cooks for the man and explicitly eats his leftovers, thus demonstrating her subordination. So, what is expressed in the Prasāda is not the social caste hierarchy—for then the gods might not take anything, not even cooked rice—but rather marriage.

However, in the whole religious service, the god is treated as a living being, is awakened, dressed, spoken to, and even fed. Why should the last part of the ritual have the same function? Why should the god take the clothing, inhale the incense, see the light, but refuse (or be unable) to eat? Moreover, the Prasāda, which does not always consist of food, is usually given by the priest to the believer, whose high rank in a ritual (not social) context is determined beforehand. But most important is that the hierarchy between god and man is abolished through and in the Pūjā. Through purification, man himself becomes "godly." If the believer has also identified with the supernatural form of the deity, as Lawrence A. Babb points out, his excretions or leftovers are no longer impure, but rather—on the contrary—the purest substances: "What is filth to the world, is nectar to the awakened."[139] Babb has seen correctly that in essential parts, the Pūjā is also an identificatory process: By taking the Prasāda or excretions of the god into himself, the believer has an equal share of the highest substance and overcomes all worldly caste and kinship limits: "The result is the closest possible intimacy, tending toward identity, and any analysis not taking this into account is incomplete."[140]

Because the differences between god and believer as well as between believer and fellow believers are abolished to a great extent in the Pūjā, there are very few or no differences of rank in the distribution of the Prasāda: Everyone can receive Prasāda, independent of his social position. It is probably precisely because of this abolition of social and everyday boundaries that the Pūjā has become so popular. At any rate, contact with the deity in the Pūjā must not happen through the Prasāda. Strictly speaking, the acceptance of Prasāda is no longer even a part of the official ritual; in any case, it is seldom counted as a classical form of worship (*upacāra*). But—as Fuller indicates with the title of his book *The Camphor Flame,* and which I have shown above—the look of the deity is central, especially in the flame of the obligatory light (*dīpa*): The deity sees this light, is in it, and the believer encounters the deity by seeing the light too, by stretching his fingers over the flame, touching his eyes, and thus taking the deity into himself.

Despite the social experience, the Pūjā remains primarily a matter between the individual and the deity, even if the priest stands between. Only in rare cases is the Pūjā a communal religious service, in which the aspect of *societas* (see table 20) is the focus because the believers act in common. Even if many thousands of people come together to a Pūjā in celebrations or in the temple, each worships the deity all by himself or in the name of another. One reason for this individualization of the religious service is the ancient Indian sacrifice in which the identification of the individual with the sacrifice was so ritually consistent that it was completely separated from the community and ultimately became replaceable.

Sacrifice[141]

The sacrifice was seen as a gift, a transfer of power, or even as a kind of bribery (E. B. Tylor) on the basis of the binding *do ut des*[142] or *do ut possis dare* (G. van der Leeuw). It was interpreted either as producing a sacrificial community (W. R. Smith, E. Durkheim), as the staging of a primal event (A. E. Jensen) or a primal myth (R. Panikkar), or as an eruption and mastery of violence (R. Girard, W. Burkert, J. Heesterman). The rich and textually well-transmitted nature of (ancient) Indian sacrifice has provided material for many of these theories of sacrifice.[143] I concentrate here on another point of view: the soteriological chain of identification in the sacrifice.

In the Indian view, the sacrifice is mainly a fire sacrifice and a sacrifice meal. We have already encountered fire[144] as central to the life of the Brahman-influenced population in various guises: Among other things, the initiation is an entitlement and obligation to maintain the domestic fire; the morning ritual (*saṃdhyā*) goes back to the old daily fire offering (*agnihotra*), of which it is said that the sun does not rise if it is not lit every day;[145] at the wedding, the couple walks around the fire; at death, the body is cremated. Fire gives and takes. It takes foods and brings them to the gods; it takes impurity by burning it away; it banishes guilt substance. The beneficial force of fire is based on an old speculation:[146] Fire takes gifts and brings them with smoke to the sun; from there, rain falls, which makes vegetable food grow, which nourishes creatures.[147] This doctrine of the cycle of nature forms a religious foundation of the ancient Indian sacrifice and thus of much of the Brahmanic-Sanskritic ritual.

The benefit of the sacrifice is based to a large extent on substantive and ritualistic identifications of the sacrificer with the sacrifice.[148] If the sacrificer lights the sacrifice fire with a rubbing stick, he draws the sacrifice—ritually speaking—out of himself. The sacrifice is then his self (*ātman*), and the self is the sacrifice. Prajāpati, the supreme lord of the gods and the first sacrificer, creates the world by dismembering himself and putting himself back together in the sacrifice. Thus, becoming the self and creation come together insolubly in the sacrifice.

Jan Heesterman has shown that the key to understanding not only the sacrificial ritual but also the extreme individualism of the salvation doctrine in the Brahmanic-Sanskritic Hindu religion resides in this fundamental identification of sacrifice and self: "The sacrificer, being the sole and unchallenged master of his sacrifice, performs his *karman* in sovereign independence from the mortal world. This *karman* is his self. The sacrificial fire, established through his own *karman* is equivalent with his inner self. Independent from

18. Fire sacrifice (*homa*) during an initiation in Kathmandu: far right, the son with the Brahmanic domestic priest; middle, the fire; left, more Brahmans, who recite the Veda (see fig. 1). Photographer: A. Michaels, 1983–1984.

the mortal world it cannot but be immortal and inalienable. Hence, the inextricable junction of fire, self and immortality."[149] In fact, since the second "Vedic" epoch, fire has been a holy substance and force, not only fuel, heat, and smoke. It is everything that burns or is hot: sun, light, warmth, redness, breath, belly, rage, passion, and asceticism; it is altar and god (*agni* and Agni). It is also everything that is heated, cooked, roasted: "I am the [cooked] food," says the "fire" in the Taittirīya-Upaniṣad.[150]

I shall first give a brief overview of types of sacrifices and then will analyze the piling of the fire altar (*agnicayana*) as an example. This is necessary to demonstrate why the ancient Indian conception of sacrifice is so enduring in the ritualism of the Hindu religions and has affected many forms of Hindu religiosity.

Ancient India knew basically two types of sacrifice, one of which is more important today than the other: domestic sacrifice and "public" sacrifice. The domestic sacrifice was performed by the head of the house and his wife as well as with a (domestic) priest (*purohita, pūjāri*) under some circumstances; its textual basis is formed mostly by the Gṛhyasūtras; examples are the rites of passage (see table 5) or the morning and evening rituals. The "public" sacrifices, called Śrauta, may be carried out only by Brahman priests, who are usually appointed by a sacrificer. The textual foundations of the Śrauta sacrifice are formed by the Śrautasūtras; as an example, I deal below with the piling the fire altar.

Domestic and Śrauta sacrifices are categorized by the ritualists according to two points of view: (a) according to type or sacrificial offerings as with vegetable food such as milk, barley, rice, clarified butter, and others (*haviryajña, iṣṭi,* primarily the *agnihotra*), human sacrifices (*puruṣamedha*), animal sacrifices (*paśubandha, aśvamedha*), and sacrifice by pressing the divine drink Soma[151] (*agniṣṭoma*); (b) according to the occasion, as in new and full moon sacrifices (*darśa-pūrṇamāsa*), sacrifices linked with seasons, or trimester sacrifices at the beginning of spring, the rainy season, and the cooler season (*caturmāsya*) as well as coronation (*rājasūya*).

Unlike the life-cycle rites of passage, the Śrauta rituals[152] today are practiced more rarely or in very different form. They demand a precise knowledge of the texts, a great number of specialists, and a great many sacrifice materials. Central to them are at least three fire altars: The circular fire of the domestic altar (*gārhapatya*) in the west is the fire of the earthly world for cooking the offering, a rectangular fireplace in the east (*āhavanīya*) for cooking the sacrificial rice and to receive the food offering as a heavenly fire, and a semicircular fireplace in the south (*dakṣiṇāgni*) to protect from evil powers as a fire of the space between heaven and earth. In the middle the holy place (*vedi*) is set, on which the offerings are placed and on which sacrificer and gods meet. In animal sacrifice, a sacrifice stake (*yūpa*) is erected to tie the animal. Everything is measured and piled precisely according to specially developed geometric rules. As in piling the fire altar, altars could be large.

Of the countless aspects presented by the ancient Indian sacrifice, I will emphasize only two: the consecration and the meaning of the word. Sacrificers usually had to be prepared ritually for the occasion with a consecration (*dīkṣā*); they had to become godlike themselves because only then could the gods accept what came to them, because only then was immortality possible. Man is the sacrifice, the texts say several times, but also the gods are the sacrifice.[153] Thus, the sacrifice became the meeting place and center, an independent individual, indivisible because it worked only when one knew about identifications and equivalents and had been initiated into them. In the process, the syllables, words, meters, and way of reciting were granted a special function. The word was magically charged, so to speak, received sacred power. Every ritual act was effective only if the appropriate Vedic text was spoken by persons authorized to do so, in an unchanged formulation, in the proper intonation, with the proper meter: You could lose your son or break your arm if the meter was wrong.[154] The identification of the sacrificer with the sacrifice and the word was the most momentous of the identifications made in the Brāhmaṇa texts. It led to the internalization of the sacrifice, its separation from social life,[155] and finally with asceticism to the renunciation of the sacrifice. I shall come back to this later.

Occasions for sacrifice were numerous. They extended from concrete desires for cattle, sons, or health, through intentions to harm one's enemy or to redeem one's own guilt substances, all the way to wishes for salvation in the next world—and that meant primarily immortality or avoiding another death in the next world. Thus, in piling the fire altar (*agnicayana*),[156] the primary goal of the sacrificer is to fly to heaven and conquer the heavenly worlds.[157] Therefore, the basic form of the piled brick altar is the stylized shape of a bird; more precisely, a falcon (*śyena*).

How the equivalences that occupy the sacrificer are produced in detail for the sacrificer to achieve the desired results can only be hinted at here. First, note that although piling the fire altar lasts several days and has an extremely wide variety of forms, it is only one subordinate part of the Soma sacrifice. But, among other things, it has also acquired a special significance because it is linked with the enduring Indian doctrine of the Brahman-Ātman identity and the transmigration of the soul.[158] The architecture of the altar is a model of how the macrocosm is reproduced microcosmically: Whoever sacrifices creates the whole.[159] The falcon altar (*śyenacit*) measures 7 or $7^1/2$ human lengths (*puruṣa*).[160] The total number of bricks comes to 360, corresponding to the number of days in the lunar calendar. The basic measure of space is anthropocentrically related to the sacrificer; the basic measure of time is oriented to the year. In the individual layers, the sacrificer (*adhvaryu*) places several objects, always while reciting the appropriate Vedic verses or sayings (*mantra*): a lotus leaf, gold tiles, gold manikins, as well as a porous brick, a tortoise, a mortar and pestle, a fire bowl and (stylized?) heads of a man, a horse, a sheep, a cow, and a goat. The individual layers of the altar are piled according to precisely stipulated instructions of size with bricks in various patterns. Finally, a sacrificial fire is lit on the altar.

Through these ritual stipulations, intellectual presuppositions for the development of a general, abstract geometry are also given. Thus, surfaces had to be constructed and divided in given dimensions, were to be increased gradually and transformed because of changing brick shapes. The knowledge thus acquired led early—in the Śulvasūtra texts—to the formulation of abstract geometrical propositions, like those of Pythagoras. This is even more astonishing since the whole enterprise took place in an environment where new and almost arbitrary chains of identification of statements of reason were given so that axioms as in Euclidian geometry do not seem possible.

The varying identifications include spiritual and material things—a distinction that was not made in the second "Vedic" epoch. Nor was there a separation between object and symbol. Through this substantialism, the truth of the laws is carried out in the sacrifice, and is not just represented or symbolized. The sacrifice is the subjective *and* objective world order. The sacrifice is the whole world, on which man *and* gods depend.[161] Thus, the gods are both the sacrifice and the objects of the sacrifice, and vice versa. Similarly, in the sacrifice, the spoken word is the sacrifice, and vice versa. Abstractions not varying with situations seem not to be possible. But, this was achieved—and essentially through the principle of equality *similia similibus,* "the principle which permeates the whole cult"[162]—or by the "law of symbolic equivalence."[163]

In part this concerns a phenomenon that is called contagious or homeopathic magic in anthropology. Through family similarities—or equivalents—and identifications derived from them, a substitute or a part of the whole can necessarily be affected and something at a distance, too. As the whole genetic program is contained in an individual cell, so the sacrificer can be identified with the whole universe through the bird altar. Because the altar is built with the physical dimensions of the sacrificer, he thus—literally—becomes the measure of all things; and because all powers, such as the seasons, directions, meters, animals, and plants, are built into the altar, the sacrificer becomes the whole along with the altar. The gods are then administrators instead of bearers of the truth; they become partners to a contract, subject to the same laws as man. Thus, there is no thanks in ancient Indian sacrifices, only ritually determined reciprocity. And the gods themselves have to sacrifice! This is what is said in the Taittirīyasaṃhitā: "Prajāpati after creating creatures entered in affection into them; from them he could not emerge; he said, 'He shall prosper who shall pile me again hence.' The gods piled him; that is why they prospered; in that they piled him, that is why the piled (Agni) has its name. He who knowing this piles the fire altar (*agni*) is prosperous. 'For what good is the fire altar piled?' they say. 'May I be possessed of Agni,' with this aim shall the fire altar (*agni*) be piled; verily he becomes possessed of Agni."[164]

As early as this small text fragment, inner and outer, this world and the next, man and god, altar and god, language and act are constantly identified with one another. To succeed, you must only know about the proper equivalents. On the other hand, small errors lead to failure, and since this is almost never to be excluded, there is also an easy explanation of why a ritual does not bring the desired result. But, within certain limits, there is some leeway to see such equivalents and to carry out identifications. For example, in the fire altar, the limits are that the basic surface remains unchanged, that the dimensions correspond to the sacrificer, that his consecration was performed, and that the right Vedic verses were recited properly. Thus, a geometric standard of equality could come from a concept of "magical" equivalence. Therefore, the term *magical worldview* has only a limited application: The science of sacrifice is also a "science," and the logic of sacrifice is also a "logic." What is fundamental for this logic of sacrifice, as we said, is the identifications that mean salvation, because salvation happens (which may not be expected) in them (not through them).

Once again, the individual steps of identification that shape the Brahmanic-Sanskritic Hindu religion are: In ancient India, fire is the focus of social and religious life. It is hearth and site of sacrifice. With the Brāhmaṇa texts, the cult of fire sacrifice was established liturgically, and achieved an almost Copernican turning point in the nature of sacrifice: The sacrifice is identified with the sacrificer. At first the creator god Prajāpati was the sacrifice:[165] "The basis of the whole system is the identification of the sacrifice with Prajāpati."[166] Through the sacrifice Prajāpati is "all this" (*idam sarvam*) and much more.[167] But, basically, the sacrifice "needs" neither Prajāpati nor any other god, nor even men.[168] It exists for itself like a law of nature and is also dangerous for men. Anyone who knows that this sacrifice is dangerous, eternal, and immortal obtains immortality himself. This construction leads to the possibility that the sacrifice can be identified with knowledge (*veda*). The gods were the first who obtained knowledge, the sacrifice, and thus immortality. The sacrifice became their self (*ātman*).[169] At first the gods did not want to give knowledge to men. They felt pressured. But the seers discovered it and passed it on, not to everyone, however, but only to genealogically authorized ones. The consequence was that the chain of identification of sacrifice = knowledge = immortality = Prajāpati (gods) could be completed with the link of "man": Now the sacrifice is the man.[170] But, by his nature (birth), man is not the sacrifice, but only when he becomes the sacrifice, that is, when he is identified with it ritually: "Verily, unborn is the man insofar as he does not sacrifice. It is through the sacrifice that he is born; just as an egg first burst."[171] What comes next results from the initiation, which itself is a collection of identifications, including the obligation to perform the fire sacrifice (*agnihotra*) every day: "A twice-born man should always offer the daily fire sacrifice at the beginning and end of each day and night."[172] Anyone who does not light the fire anew every day is fallen (out of the caste), an outcast, with whom one may not eat (food cooked in the fire) and whom one may not marry.[173]

Thus, the initiation and the authorization to sacrifice are linked genealogically in order to keep the knowledge of the sacrifice within the circle of one's own kinship group and clan. Only by marriage is it possible to get into this closed chain of identification. But this also happens because the wife ritually loses her own descent and is identified with the husband, so that the following soteriological chain of identification is possible: sacrifice (salvation) = knowledge (Veda) = gods-[father (=wife) ⊃ son] = sacrifice.[174] Of course this chain can begin at every place and is hardly complete. And it should be emphasized again that the wedding and initiation concern ritualistic forms of religiosity whose spiritual variant is, for example, that these or similar chains of identification are performed internally.

DEVOTIONALISM AND THEISTIC TRADITIONS

Devotionalism is currently the most popular form of religiosity in India. It is connected with the term *bhakti* (literally: "participation, devotion, love"). This is also a form of encountering and adoring god that seeks closeness to a high god through devotional means. The Vedic sacrifice ritual was devotional only to a very small extent; Hindu folk religiosity has always been devotional. Thus, talk of the rise of Bhakti in the sense of a new form of religiosity or even of religion usually refers to the adoption of devotional elements into the Brahmanic-Sanskritic Hindu religion.

I will first sketch the historical development of Bhakti religiosity in its theistic orientations. Here, textual history and social or religious history are to be distinguished: A few poet-saints had only a small circle of adherents or had a predominantly literary effect; others, like Basava, the founder of the Liṅgāyat sects, evoked great social changes. In conclusion, I will discuss the aspect of grace.

Bhakti Movements[175]

Bhakti as a movement arose in southern India in the seventh century and spread into northern India from the twelfth and thirteenth centuries. Since southern India remained impervious to northern influences for a long time, certain parts of Bhakti religiosity can be understood as a thoroughly genuine contribution of southern India to the Hindu religions. Initially, in the Śaiva and Vaiṣṇava movements of southern Indian Bhakti religiosity, local gods were worshipped, who were increasingly declared to be manifestations of Viṣṇu or Śiva: Murukaṉ later became Skanda, Śiva's son; Tirumāl became a manifestation of Viṣṇu. In detail, the following theistic movements can be distinguished.

TABLE 23
Vaiṣṇava, Kṛṣṇaite, and Rāmaite Traditions

Viṣṇu as Main God	*Kṛṣṇa or Rādhā-Kṛṣṇa as Main Gods*	*Rāma and Sītā as Main Gods*
*Pāñcarātra-System	*Bhāgavata	Rāmānandī (Rāmānanda)
*Vaikhānasa	Nimbārkī	Nāgā, Tyāgī
Śrīvaiṣṇava	Viṣṇusvāmī	Tulsīdas
Viśiṣṭādvaita (Rāmānuja, Vedāntadeśika)	Vallabhacārī (*puṣṭimārga*) Gauḍīya (or Caityanites)	
Dvaita (Madhva)	Rādhāvallabhī	
	Sūrdās	
	Mahānubhāva	
	Bauls of Bengal	
	Svāmīnārāyaṇa	
	Hare-Kṛṣṇa movement	
	Vārkarī (Saguṇī) Pantha	
	(see table 24)	

Note: In parentheses: Main representatives (see table 4 for life dates and region)
* = extinct

The Vaiṣṇava tradition (table 23) goes back to twelve authoritative teachers (Āḷvārs) in the south and was developed further among others in the Śrīvaiṣṇava system. Its best-known representative is Rāmānuja (1056–1137), a Brahman, who represented an effectively modified monism (Viśiṣṭādvaita) and created countless ritualistic reforms in reference to temple service and divine worship. Rāmānuja belonged to one of four traditions (*saṃpradāya*) that constitute the Vaiṣṇava orthodoxy from a pan-Indian perspective: to the Śrī-Saṃpradāya. Madhva, alias Ānandatīrtha (1199–1278), who taught a dualism (Dvaitavedānta) according to which god and the individual soul constitute contrasting realities but only Viṣṇu is autonomous, founded the Brahmā-Saṃpradāya. Nimbārka, alias Nimbāditya (twelfth century), a Brahman from Kerala, founded the Sanaka-Saṃpradāya as well as the Nimāvat sect, which tried to unite monism and dualism in the system of Dvaitādvaita. Finally, in

TABLE 24
The Saints (Poet-Saints and Founders of Sects)

Nirguṇī Sants (emphasize the lack of qualities of god)	Vārkarī (Saguṇī) Panths (worship of Viṭhobā or Viṭṭhala as a form of Kṛṣṇa in south Maharashtra, especially Pandharpur
Kabīr	Jñāneśvara
Mīrabai	Namdev
Dādū Dayāl	Eknāth
Guru Nānak	In a limited sense: Rāmdās, Śivajī
Guru Amar Dās	
Sundaradās	

the thirtheenth century, Viṣṇusvāmi founded the Rudra-Saṃpradāya, which represented a Śuddhādvaita, an extreme monism. The difference between these positions is in the scholastic area; for the great mass of believers and their everyday religiosity, they were of secondary importance. For them, what was important was what god was worshipped in what form as the main god: Viṣṇu, Kṛṣṇa or Rādhā-Kṛṣṇa, or Rāma.

Kṛṣṇa and his love for the cowherd and companion Rādhā are the focus of the following cult groups: from the thirteenth century on, the cult group of the Vārkarī Panth ("Pilgrim path) in Maharashtra (see table 24), who saw their god Viṭṭhala or Viṭhoba as a manifestation of Kṛṣṇa, and in whose tradition are some poet-saints (Jñāneśvara, Nāmdev, Tukarām, Janābāi, Eknāth, etc.); the Vallabhacārīs in and around Mathura, who go back to the Telugu Brahman Vallabha (1479–1531) and worship Kṛṣṇa mainly as a youth (Bālagopāla or Bālakṛṣṇa); and the Gauḍīyās or Bengal Vaiṣṇavas, including Jayadeva (twelfth century) with his influential Gītagovinda ("Song of Kṛṣṇa"), Caitanya (1485–1533), and the Gosvāmī sects, are prominent. The Rāmāvats or Rāmānandīs, which are supposed to have been founded by Rāmānanda, allegedly a student of Kabīr, and which are in the tradition of Viśiṣṭādvaitin, pray mainly to the heroic god Rāma. The poet Tulsīdās (1532–1623) with his popular free rendering of the Rāmāyaṇa, the Rāmcaritmānas ("Ocean of the Acts of Rāmas"), had a significant influence.

The Nirguṇī Sants ("Saints")—including Kabīr, Dādū, and Nānak (1469–1538), the founder of Sikhism—form a special, loosely organized group, influenced by Islam, for whom god has no qualities (*nirguṇa*).[176]

Devotionalism that refers to Śiva (see table 18) is problematic. While the popular Purāṇic Śaivism is full of devotional parts, the later Śaiva sects and philosophies are more ritualist or spiritualist. Indeed, here too there are differences: In the early Bhakti period, Śaivism was strongly represented; from the seventh century on, the Tamil Śaiva movement was embodied philosophically and poetically especially in the system of the Śaivasiddhānta and the Āgamic texts. In the tenth century, the texts of sixty-three Śaiva Nāyaṉmārs were codified and their compiler acknowledged as an authoritative teacher. From the twelfth century on, the cult group of the Vīraśaiva ("heroic Śivaites") or Liṅgāyat, founded by Basava, arose in Karnataka. Like many—but by no means all—Bhakti movements,[177] the Vīraśaivas rebelled against Vedic-Brahmanic traditions: They did away with sacrifice and temple worship, pilgrimages, acts of penance, and cremations. They rejected the caste system and did not even exclude women from their religious activities. Typical of their image of god, at the initiation a small Liṅga is tied around the believer, and he wears it all his life: Not even a priest can come between the individual and Śiva, although over time a distinction between priests (*jaṅgama*) and lay people has developed. The Aghorīs, an especially extreme ascetic group, graciously worship their founder Kina Rām, the Gorakhnāthīs their Gurus Matsyendranātha and Gorakhnātha, who are all seen as forms of Śiva. The same is true—with qualifications—for Śaṃkara and the Śaṃkarācāryas, the principal Śaiva order (*maṭha*). And finally, it must be noted that many groups that are considered Vaiṣṇava also worship Śiva. The largest ascetic groups that celebrate the Śivarātri festival with mortification of the flesh and pilgrimages are the Vaiṣṇava Rāmānandīs.

More clearly than in so-called Śaivism is the devotionalism with which the goddesses are summoned up, even though, in most treatises on the Bhakti movements this is ignored. Even the worship of the fearsome goddesses is permeated with devotional, obsequious parts,[178] which can hardly be distinguished typologically from Kṛṣṇa devotionalism. There is also a vast number of chants and hymns devoted to the goddesses.

The Grace of the Gods

Despite the multiple orientations of devotionalism, common features can be noted, for example, the religiosity of grace. It assumes a thoroughly different image of god from that of sacrificial ritualism. If the relationship between believer and god in the latter is a kind of contractual relationship, in devotionalism the main god has the highest, sole power, which one submits to and trusts in. In the Bhakti texts, the power of a god is often restricted by atheistic or polytheistic concepts—such as the Śakti idea, the notion of the featurelessness (*nirguṇa*) of the god, or the doctrine of the various manifestations of a god (*avatāra*). But in religious practice and belief, the power of the god that is worshipped is undisputed and all-embracing: He can grant liberation anytime and immediately. This is seen clearly in the Tyāga section of the Rāmānandī ascetics: They pursue the harshest asceticism, and thus are interested primarily in their own self-liberation; but unlike Śaiva ascetics, they do not cut the Sacred Thread. Their reasoning is that only Viṣṇu or Rāma can grant liberation and cut the Sacred Thread off them. Hence, their self-liberation is based not only on ascetic and meditative practice, but also on the grace of god.

The self-sacrifice (*tyāga*) of devotionalism is first of all a complete devotion to the god, an attempt to share (*bhaj*) his omnipotence. At the same time, as in Islam, a submission to the will of the main god is demanded. Therefore, between believer (*bhakta*) and god there is a relation of loyalty or love, which is not seen as an obstacle to liberation—as in many spiritualist doctrines. Especially devoted Bhaktas, such as the ascetic sections of the Rāmānandīs, explicitly call themselves Tyāgīs or Mahātyāgīs (= [great] abandoned ones, submissives"). The love of the (ideal) wife for her husband is the model of this divine love. In certain tradition (such as the Bauls of Bengal), men had to become "women" to be able to worship Kṛṣṇa, and it is said of Caitanya that he was a manifestation of both Kṛṣṇa and Rādhā. Even the dog is a model of submission for Bhaktas.[179]

Hardly anything is as loathsome to devotionalism as rigid, empty sacrifice ritualism. In many texts it is objected to, but so are caste privileges, the dominating priesthood, and the exclusion of women or casteless people from religious life. Typical of this attitude is a famous verse of the seventh-century southern Indian poet-saint Triruñāvukkaracar, called Appar ("Father"): "Why bathe in the Ganges or the Kaveri, / why make a pilgrimage to Kumari's cool, fragrant beach, / why bathe in the ocean's swelling waves? / All this is in vain, if you do not think: / 'The Lord is everywhere.'"[180]

Quite often, the poet-saint himself came from the lower strata: Nāmdev was a tailor, Tukārām was a Śūdra, Kabīr came from a Moslem family of weavers; the Brahmans among them—Jñāneśvara, Rāmānuja, Nimbārka—were often expelled from their subcastes. The saints often opposed the Brahmans, the Veda, Sanskrit, widow-burning, and the ban on remarriage. The Bhakti movements contain a reformation of the elite, priestly Brahmanism, but unlike the Protestant Reformation in Europe, as Robert C. Zaehner notes, it never came "to an open break."[181]

In many sects or traditions, this eventually led to a "counter-reformation" caste ritualism, expressed as the preference of Sanskrit, an inherited priesthood,

19. Rām Kṛṣṇa Dās, an ascetic devoted to the god Rāma in Deopatan, Nepal, who feeds himself only on milk products; on the wall: images of gods and a poster of King Birenda. Photographer: A. Michaels, 1983–1984.

or the exclusion of women from divine worship. In this respect, the movements share the fate of almost all founded religions that have to preserve the heritage or the direct charisma of their founders, and cohesion can often be achieved only through a tight organization, centralization, and normative regulations. The spread of a movement beyond regional borders also leads to a development that runs counter to the original intentions. Thus the Śrīvaiṣṇava movement divided into a southern and a northern school; the latter increasingly used Sanskrit and was less skeptical about caste ritualism. Thus, Tulsīdās demanded not only the acknowledgement of the priority of the Brahmans, but also the "suppression" of women. Thus, the Vīraśaivas acknowledge their own priests (*jaṅgama*), and the Vaikhānasas or Rāmānuja do not absolutely reject the authority of the Veda.

The Bhakti notion of god is extremely anthropomorphic and personal. It is not much connected to independent powers, forces, and ideas as ritualism or spiritualism. In many cases, an emotional, eroticized love of god prevails, whose pattern is seen as the love of the cowherd (Gopī) for Kṛṣṇa. This is why most Bhakti literature also consists of love and bridal mysticism, chants and songs (*kīrtana, bhajana*) or hymns (*stotra, stuti, vacana*), usually connected with music and dance. The believers see themselves as the children of the god or as his servants (*dāsa*), and frequently accept this addition to their names: Tulsīdās, Premdās, Sūrdās (see table 4). They worship the feet of the god (*pādeś-vara*); they organize into voluntary service groups (*sevā*). The form of devotion can go so far that a union with god is sought, a *unio mystica* (*sahaja*) in which every separation is abolished. Pictures and chants in which human suffering is traced back to the separation (*viraha*) from god are widespread. The idea of god as a savior and redeemer, of the savior and "Descender" (*avatāra*), who seeks the proximity of men to support them in their need, is also closely connected with the Bhakti movements.[182] On the other hand, the image of the united lovers, for whom there is no longer a painful, yearning separation, is a favorite metaphor for a successful or desired encounter with god.

God as redeemer and the infinite love of god—connections to Christian theologies are obvious here, and in fact, Bhakti religiosity dominates in the interreligious dialogue between Hindus and Christians, especially since it claims to exclude neither Śūdras nor women from divine worship. The highly emotional part of devotionalism also led to gods being worshipped as children or even babies. Kṛṣṇa and Rāma especially experienced this form of worship, but these days, Śiva also appears in colored pictures with childish features. Mothers of gods or goddesses as mothers also receive a lot of attention. Finally, it is a special characteristic of devotionalism that the god plays. That can go so far that the whole world is interpreted as a game (*līlā*) of the main god.[183] But usually it is a belief in the childishness of the god. To play with him in dancing, singing, and celebrating is therefore a favorite form of divine worship.

Many devotional aspects are also contained in ritualism. When the god is awakened with a hymn, dressed and entertained in a Pūjā, when his name is constantly called, when he is asked lovingly for grace or help, in terms of the forms of religiosity this is also devotionalism. Thus, the fact that Bhakti is seen as an independent religious movement cannot be explained only by the form of religiosity. There were also social and political changes, mainly regionalization and decentralization, as well as the influence of Islam in the fifth epoch, when regional poet-saints acquired high esteem in the vernacular.

The search for fusion with god also represents a variant of the Identificatory Habitus, primarily through the coupling between god and believer (*bhakta*). Even if salvation is seen in abolishing every duality, it is still clear that the wish for fusion is not often fulfilled, not because the Bhakta is incapable of it, but because the identification itself, the linking of the couple, forms the divine experience. The believer can only serve, love, and participate, but he cannot have god or—as in certain forms of asceticism—be god. He strives for symbolic fusion with god, yet remains in constant tension with him. God and man are separate. This is a significant difference from the sacrifice and ascetic ritualism, in which the boundary between god and man is not available in principle and as a result, "self-deification" (Max Weber) is possible. In Bhakti religiosity, on the other hand, man is painfully aware of the separation from god. From his suffering comes the strong yearning of the Bhakta for peace (*śānta*), obedience (*dāsya*), friendship (*sākhya*), affection (*vātsalya*), and passion (*rati*), as the five Bhakti feelings (*rasa*) are called in the poetics.[184]

SPIRITUALISM AND MYSTICISM[185]

By its nature, devotionalism is theistic and usually even monotheistic. But more than in other religions, an atheistic form of religiosity, spiritualism, is widespread in India. Because of the notion shaped by Christianity that religion is linked with ideas of god, this form of religiosity is often treated in books on Indian philosophy. In fact, large parts of Indian scholasticism remain within the circle of Brahman philosophers. But the conversion of the doctrine into a mystical, meditative-spiritual, or ascetic practice had a broader effect. Following Kurt Ruh,[186] it is only this practice or form of religiosity that I call "mystical." Here, the doctrines of the Upaniṣads, the Sāṃkhya-Yoga, and Śaṃkara and Advaitavedānta are chosen as examples. In conclusion, I take up the question of the peculiar characteristics of Indian mysticism and spirituality.

The Identification Doctrine of the Upaniṣads[187]

The literature of the Upaniṣads can be divided into various groups; an often-published collection of 108 Upaniṣads is "canonic," but even today Upaniṣads are still being composed. The older Upaniṣads (see table 3) are composed mainly in prose and are seen as the last part of the Śruti (literally: "the heard") and Veda in the narrow sense. They are part of the so-called forest books (*āraṇyaka*) because they may be heard only outside the settlements. Therefore, the Upaniṣads have acquired the meaning of "secret doctrines," since knowledge of effective connections (*bandhu*) and forces is also involved. One had to know what was hidden behind the visible or the identity-forming "chains of dependence" (Harry Falk). Even though the texts are preserved only fragmentarily and anonymously, a few teachers—Yājñavalkya, Uddālaka Āruṇi, Śāṇḍilya, and others—may have been historical figures. The Upaniṣads were soon known in the West, too. In 1801–1802, A. H. Anquetil Duperron (1731–1805) translated fifty Upaniṣads from Persian into Latin, and the anthology impressed the German philosopher Arthur Schopenhauer, who called it a "consolation of my life and death."

The special character of the older Upaniṣads is that they constitute the first great philosophical text of India in which the relationship of the individual to the world is considered without priestly privileges. It is often overlooked that these texts as secret doctrine—according to Paul Thieme, the verb *upa-ni-ṣad* means "sitting down near or next to someone" or "approaching [a teacher] respectfully"[188]—are nevertheless in a ritual context and are by no means "only" philosophical. The idealistic representation of the Upaniṣadic doctrine by the philosopher Paul Deussen, a follower of Schopenhauer, and the commentary of Śaṃkara played a major role in shaping that attitude.

Clearly, the Upaniṣads represent a turning point in intellectual history. What is new are the doctrines of the transmigration of the soul, the effectiveness of fire, the cycle of nature, the importance of breath for life, the epistemological function of deep sleep, the effective causality of acts, the identity of Brahman and Ātman—in principle no longer bound to the status of birth, being as suffering, the internalization of the sacrifice, and so on. The focus is on questions about the salvation of the soul and liberation, life after death, and immortality, which are treated in the older Upaniṣads, as in the Platonic dialogues, often in a dialogue between a teacher and a student. Questions[189] were also an excellent stylistic means. One Upaniṣad, the Praśna-Upaniṣad, is even called the "Questions-Upaniṣad," and another has a question preposition in the title: Kena-Upaniṣad (*kena* = "how, through whom?"). The question, however, was not only an expression of a thirst for knowledge, but also a profound search for liberation: One who asked (*ati-pṛcch*) too much or wrongly could shatter his head, says the text.

The starting point of the questions is a dogmatic attitude to the world: Life is suffering (*duḥkha*). This view of the world may have to do with deep-seated historical changes or ecological catastrophes, but the ancient Indian thesis of the suffering of existence is basically not world-weariness or pessimism. It is based on radical reflections of time and ephemerality: Everything is ephemeral, even joy and happiness. But what is ephemeral is sorrowful, for it means separation. Therefore, eternity free of suffering can only be beyond joy and suffering. This insight is also part of the basic doctrine of Buddhism. In many other religions, the explanation of suffering leads to the consolation of life in the next world. But the teachers of the early Upaniṣads did not want to take this "way out." The old ideas of re-death in the next world and a return of the deceased were too strong. The solution they offered was, therefore, not theistic, in the form of trusting in the grace of a god, but rather extremely intellectual. Note that the early Upaniṣads directly continued the ancient Indian sacrificial identifications, took over the methodology without the ritual, as it were: The individual was identified with the whole and with immortality. Detached from the sacrificial event, in the Upaniṣads, the identification of the individual soul (*ātman*) with the absolute (*brahman*) became a fundamental doctrine. The consistent application of this doctrine, however, was hardly compatible with a normal life. The Upaniṣads came from sacrifice and led to asceticism.

The whole way of thinking revolved around questions of the conditions and consequences of this Ātman-Brahman identification, expressed among others in the classical sayings of *tat tvam asi* ("That is you") or *ahaṃ brahmāsmi* ("I am the Brahman").[190] As in piling the fire altar, the identification had to lead to complete congruence. Nothing could come between the subject of knowledge and the object of knowledge: Ātman is Brahman, and Brahman is Ātman, but neither Ātman nor Brahman can be for itself. What counts is the identification itself, the nonduality of both of them.

Along with the sacrificial ritual identifications, notions of substance influenced the doctrine of the Upaniṣads. This concerned notions of substances of force, which have a few things in common with Edward B. Tylor's and James George Frazer's ideas of spiritual beings. Thus it was asked which substance of force or essence (*rasa*) is life, and, as in other religions, it was seen in fire or warmth, or in breath;[191] thus in what leaves the body at death. Breath—usually called *prāṇa* in Sanskrit—was thought to be a wind; thus, there must be a relationship between the cosmic wind and bodily winds, including the breath. Breath passes away, but the cosmic wind does not. This is clearly formulated in the Bṛhadāraṇyaka-Upaniṣad: "[When my body falls] may my vital force return to the air [cosmic force], and this body too, reduced to ashes go to the earth."[192] If the relationship between breath and the cosmic wind is produced in terms of identification, then in a way, one *is spiritus sanctus* ("holy spirit"), or the immortal, eternal, cosmic wind. But now wind and breath are again only part of something, for example, of the cosmos. So, the abstraction must be pushed even further, and they came upon the idea that there must be one force behind everything. This force was usually called *brahman,* that force which also guaranteed the effectiveness of the sacrifice.[193] Consequently, the identification was offered between Ātman and Brahman, between soul and All-soul.[194]

A second, subsequent thought was that this fundamental force did not have to be part of something itself, because it would then not be the whole. Instead, it had to be part of the whole. Thus, it could not be possessed, but one could only be it. For possession can get lost, but then the force would not be omnipresent and everlasting. This consideration had effects on the understanding of the self. An ego could not possess the Brahman, the force could not be something that comes and goes, but the ego had to be identified completely with the all in order to be able to be it. "Become what you are," as Hermann Hesse formulated this idea. Then indeed there is no longer the knower of the knowledge, but only knowledge remains.

In the Bṛhadāraṇyaka-Upaniṣad, before the seer Yājñavalka moves into seclusion, he gives Maitreyī an instruction about immortality, in which these thoughts are expressed:

> For when there is a duality of some kind, then the one can see the other, the one can smell the other, the one can taste the other, the one can greet the other, the one can hear the other, the one can think of the other, the one can touch the other, and the one can perceive the other. When, however, the Whole has become one's very self (*ātman*), then who is there for one to see and by what means? Who is there for one to smell and by what means? Who is there for one to taste and by what means? Who is there for one to greet and by what means? Who is there for one to hear and by what means? Who is there for one to think of and by what means? Who is there for one to touch and by what means? Who is there for one to perceive and by what means?
>
> By what means can one perceive him by means of whom one perceives this whole world?
>
> About this self (*ātman*), one can only say "not——, not——." He is ungraspable, for he cannot be grasped. He is undecaying, for he is not subject to decay. He has nothing sticking to him, for he does not stick to anything. He is not bound; yet he neither trembles in fear nor suffers injury.
>
> Look—by what means can one perceive the perceiver?[195]

It is characteristic that the relationship between Ātman and Brahman in the early Upaniṣads—later, under theistic influences, this was seen differently—is hardly called oneness (e.g., *brahmātmaikyam*), but rather nonduality. This shows that "oneness" is an identificatory relation, which must be known, produced, and maintained, but not resolved. The logic of such a concept of salvation can be understood only if the substantive preliminary stages and assumptions are shared. The immortality (of the sacrifice) is given by a substantive, but not coarse material force; is condensed, for example, in the holy syllable *Oṃ*, the meter, the fire, or even the Brahman. These "parts" are the whole force because they are identified with sacrificial knowledge (*veda*) and the sacrificial acts (*karman*), which guarantee immortality: "Whoever in like manner knows It as, 'I am Brahman,' becomes all this [universe]. Even the gods cannot prevail against him for he becomes their self."[196]

The substance of immortality can also be obtained with such identification. For the self is living, thus has a share in the religious eternal substance of "life" and thus of immortality. Human mortality strikes only because man does not know about that part in himself which is the Brahman, which is immortality, or cannot filter it. This part or essence of human immortality is—as we said—called variously *brāhman, ātman, Oṃ, udgītha* (sacred chant), *prāṇa* (breath or life breath), or *puruṣa,* a small soul manikin that is seen in the pupils of the eyes or that resides in the heart. But this is also always about the identification of that part with immortality, which is the whole.

The identifications were thoroughly "epistemological," for they concerned a knowledge that was necessarily in the system and irrefutable because of its truth. This is contained impressively in the conversations of Uddālaka Āruṇi with his son Śvetaketu,[197] in which the method of identification or "substitution method," as Paul Thieme calls it, is learned. Uddālaka Āruni first explains conceptual abstractions with examples: You know what clay is only if you know what a lump of clay is. Similarly—and here, too, I am abbreviating long discussions—you know what the self is only when you have seen that it arises out of what is (eternal) life. The father/teacher illustrates this truth by letting his son divide the fruit of a fig tree until nothing more is to be seen so that he can then state: "The first essence here—that constitutes the self of this whole world; that is the truth; that is the self (*ātman*). And that is how you are [*tat tvam asi*], Śvetaketu."[198] He also lets salt dissolve in water to repeat the same truth. Thus, the goal of all efforts was a spiritualistic search for the self freed from age and death, which is the part in man that is immortal and is thus the Brahman (or a substitute: sacrifice, Veda, etc.). The older Upaniṣads are always dealing with such searches. He who was successful obtained all worlds, his wishes were fulfilled,[199] he was redeemed.

Age is a slow dying. The abolition of time was consequently a prerequisite for the search for immortality. The real self was not to be connected with becoming and passing away. It had to be identified with the everlasting whole and in this way was released from age and death. Only by detachment was salvation possible. This static notion of salvation led to premises for countless Indian systems of philosophy, but also for everyday thought:

1. This world is false knowledge or apparent reality.
2. Striving for acts and their effects can only produce ephemerality. On the other hand, being free of action and abolishing thoughts is liberating, but also acts and thoughts carried out knowing the proper identification.[200]
3. Thoughts, wishes, and feelings are to be understood as active substances of a fine, invisible material.

4. Anyone who lives and thinks "dynamically" of a future produces continuation of life, rebirth, and re-death. Anyone who lives and thinks "statically" in the here and now will not be reborn and does not die.
5. The epistemological boundary between this world and the next cannot be bridged.

These premises are in the equitheism of the concept of god, in the father-son identification, in identifying the sacrificer with the sacrifice and other sacrifice ritual identifications, in the equivalence of the believer with god: the "nonduality without oneness" is always produced with identificatory means.

Another consequence of the radical abolition of time, which I shall come back to in the next chapter, is a doctrine of causality particularly unique to Indian thought, in which cause and effect are equated. This is clearly developed in the Sāṃkhya system, which is one of the six classical systems of philosophy (*darśana*) of Brahmanic-Sanskritic scholasicism, along with Yoga, Vaiśeṣika, Nyāya, Mīmāṃsā, and Vedānta.

The Psycho-Physical Identifications of Sāṃkhya and Yoga

The Sāṃkhya doctrines[201] go back to the older Upaniṣads, even though they were compiled into a system only later. The legendary seer Kapila is considered the founder of the system, even while central to the system, along with fragments in the Mahābhārata (Bhagavadgītā, Mokṣadharma sections), and the Sāṃkhyakārikā of Iśvarakṛṣṇa composed before 500 A.D. Sāṃkhya doctrines were formative for the later philosophies, but also for the general psychology of India. I shall try to develop the causality doctrines of the old Sāṃkhya through its theory of evolution.

The basis of the Sāṃkhya is the dovetailed dualism of—simply put—spirit (*puruṣa*) and (primeval) materiality (*prakṛti*). The Puruṣa is completely unchanging, eternal, omnipresent, pure spiritual light; in short, pure consciousness, sufficient unto itself, but not consciousness of something; its individuations, also called *puruṣa,* are the "parts" of the individual soul capable of salvation. The Prakṛti, on the other hand, is active, unconscious material—eternal, omnipresent, and imperceptibly subtle (*sūkṣma*)—and it is also thought, will, and feeling, for it comprises physical *and* psychical things. It consists of three components (*guṇa*): *sattva* ("goodness, light, purity; state of light, joy, and peace"), *rajas* ("passion, agility, excitement"), and *tamas* ("darkness, heaviness, obstruction"). If these components are not developed, the Prakṛti is in imperceptible balance. The "primeval materiality" is not set in motion and thus into imbalance by an actor or a creator, but by itself. The Sāṃkhyakārikā uses the image of milk for the calf flowing by itself to represent this process: This is also without consciousness and yet flows for a purpose, to nurture the young animal. The Prakṛti unfolds itself for a particular purpose: It instinctively wants to help the individual Puruṣas, the individuations of the Puruṣa, that is, pure spirit. It is the mere proximity of the Puruṣa that evokes the imbalance of the three components and thus stimulates the Prakṛti to unfold itself and inaugurate the process of evolution.

Through stages of twenty-three increasingly gross ontological essences (*tattva*), the Prakṛti develops into the cosmos (see table 25); in the undeveloped condition, it reabsorbs these essences again. So there is a permanent alternation of active evolution (*pravṛtti*) and inactive non-evolution (*nivṛtti*).[202]

In this system, psychic features have a material character and can adhere to other things as subtle, but not gross material substance. Only the Puruṣas are pure spirit, almost *natura naturans,* as Spinoza defined it. They are distinguished from one another by a subtle body (*sūkṣmaśarīra*) or a kind of soul cover, but basically arc thc samc as one another. The Puruṣas, therefore, are not individual souls, distinguished by features, that transmigrate, for the Prakṛti does comprise these psychic and subtle things.

When the Prakṛti is evolved and thus has developed gross bodies (*sthūlaśarīra*) among other things, the Puruṣas unite with Prakṛti, at least ostensibly, and attain individuality. But then the lethargic, inactive, spiritual Puruṣa will only seem to act, and the unspiritual Prakṛti will only seem spiritual; in truth the Prakṛti acts only because the Guṇas, the three components of the Prakṛti, are unbalanced. Thus it is a mistake to grant thoughts, feelings, acts, and individuality to the Puruṣa. It sheds its spiritual light on the essences such as knowing, ego-consciousness, and the like belonging to the Prakṛti, so that the incorrect opinion arises that it is a thinking, feeling, and acting individual soul (*jīva*).

This is an elegant solution to the problem of dualism and causality: That is, the Puruṣa is completely unchanging, pure spiritual light, mere consciousness, sufficient unto itself, and therefore neither consciousness nor cause or effect of anything else. Neither is the Puruṣa dependent on the consciousness of the individual soul nor can the individual soul—mystical-monistic—be united with it. In both cases, the Puruṣa would then be dependent on the ephemerality of the individual soul or could only be incompletely known. This is why both Puruṣa and the individual soul must be independent and must not refer causally to one another, but yet, they must be identical with one another. The difficulty is inherent in the intellectual construction: How can one think something that must not be thought through thoughts? In the Sāṃkhya, the truth of this thought can be learned only nonintellectually—mystically: by the

TABLE 25
The Unfolding of Matter according to the Sāṃkhyarkārikā

Emerging from (1) the primeval materiality (Prakṛti):	
(2) *buddhi:* knowing, decision-making organ	The Buddhi has four possibilities to choose (tending either to *sattva* or *tamas*): between morality and no morality (*dharma/adharma*), knowing and not knowing the difference between Prakṛti and Puruṣa (*jñāna/ajñāna*), renunciation and nonrenunciation (*vairāgya/avairāgya*), and achieving and not achieving glory (*aiśvarya/anaiśvarya*).
(3) *ahaṃkāra:* ego-consciousness, ego-material, ego-maker, sense of self	The Ahaṃkāra allows the emergence of the mistaken belief (*abhimāna*) that there is an acting soul (*jīva*); at the same time, it allows the emergence of the thinking organ (*manas*) with ten sense organs (*indriya,* nos. 5–14) and five pure elements (*tanmātra,* nos. 15–19).
(4) *manas:* thinking organ, thinking stuff	Unlike the Buddhi, Manas is thought connected with the senses.
(5–9) *buddhi-indriya:* (five) knowing or organs of perception, sensory matter	Buddhi-indriyas are face, hearing, smell, taste, and feel; abilities to see, hear, smell, taste, feel; *sattva*-like.
(10–14) *karma-indriya:* (five) organs of action, action matter	The Karma-indriyas are abilities to speak, grasp, go, leave, beget; *tamas*-like.
(15–19) *tanmātra:* (five) subtle elements	The Tanmātras are pure matter of the elements that correspond with the special features of the Buddhi-indriya, namely, smell (corresponds with earth), taste (water), colors and forms (fire), feelings (air/wind), and tone (ether).
(20–24) *mahābhūta:* elements	The Mahābhūtas are earth (*pṛthivī*), water (*āpas*), fire (*jyotis*), air/wind (*vāyu*), and ether (*ākāśa*).

liberated, in deep sleep, or in the epochs of twilight between the four world ages. But if these connections are known, then the binding link between Puruṣa and Prakṛti is also dissolved, then salvation is achieved, then the materiality withdraws back into itself because the Puruṣa sees through its game—as a modest woman withdraws in shame when a strange man looks at her.[203]

The Sāṃkhya had a great influence mainly through its effect on the Yoga system,[204] which, in its early form, tried to transplant ideas of the Sāṃkhya through a polished psychophysical practice of meditation. The system of Yoga is based mainly on a text, the Yogasūtra, which is supposed to have been composed by an author named Patañjali, but which is composed of various fragments and traditions of texts stemming from the second or third century. The first commentary, allegedly composed by Vyāsa, on the aphorisms of the Yogasūtra that are difficult to understand, dates from the fifth century A.D. In between these two texts, there are considerable gaps in the transmission of the tradition.

Whereas the Sāṃkhya forms an analysis of the dualism of idle, pure spirit (Puruṣa) and active materiality (Prakṛti)—a dualism that produces suffering—Yoga has succeeded in removing this suffering in practice. Both systems assume that being is suffering, which has quite a bit to do with notions of ephemerality. Because man tends to take his own (material, ephemeral) soul, and hence his thoughts, feelings, and perceptions, for the pure spirit (Puruṣa)—the relationship between both types of being tempts him to do that—he is aging and mortal, even ephemeral. But, if he has the proper consciousness—according to the salvation message of Upaniṣads, Sāṃkhya-Yoga, Buddhism, Advaitavedānta, and other systems—then he can identify with the everlasting pure spirit and be freed of every material causal bond. A prerequisite for that is an external and internal, moral and meditative preparation. One such technique is offered by Yoga.

First, the five activities of the spirit must be known: true knowledge (*pramāṇa*), erroneous knowledge (*viparyaya*), false notion (*vikalpa*), sleep (*nidrā*), and remembrance (*smṛti*). These can be afflicted (*kliṣṭa*) or not (*akliṣṭa*). They are afflicted by ignorance (*avidyā*), egoism (*asmita*), attachment (*rāga*), dislike or hate (*dveṣa*), or instinctive determination (*abhiniveśa*). The affliction stems from the production of suffering or rebirth material (*karma*). The afflictions can be abolished by efforts (*abhyāsa*) through detachment (*vairāgya*) in the process of eight stages (*aṣṭāṅga*) in three categories (see table 26).

The ethicization of the search for salvation through the first two stages of table 26, which are still lacking in the Maitrī-Upaniṣad,[205] the acceptance of good deeds (*kriyāyoga*) and the theistic orientation through divine worship as part of the second stage, are variable and can be fulfilled in various ways. But

TABLE 26
The Eight Stages of Yoga

	A. Moral Preparation
1. *Yama*	"(external) self control" through practicing nonviolence (*ahiṃsā*), truth (*satya*), honesty (*asteya,* literally: "not stealing"), chastity (*brahmacarya*), and being devoid of possessions (*aparigraha*)
2. *Niyama*	"(internal) self-discipline" through purity (*śauca*), contentedness (*saṃtoṣa*), asceticism (*tapas*), self-study (*svādhyāya*), recitation of the holy syllable *Oṃ,* and divine worship (*īśvarapraṇidhāna*)
	B. Physical Preparation
3. Āsana	"Physical posture": especially sitting position (e.g., the Lotus position, the Lion position); up to eighty-four positions are taught, especially in Haṭhayoga
4. *Prāṇāyāma*	"Breath restraint": restraining the inhalation and exhalation, as well as the frequency of breath
5. *Pratyāhāra*	"Withdrawal (of the senses)": Separation of the sense organs from the sense objects
	C. Spiritual Preparation
6. *Dhāraṇā*	"Retention": concentration on an object in order to bring thoughts to a standstill
7. *Dhyāna*	"Contemplation," meditation: letting go of thoughts
8. *Samādhi*	"Concentration," highest stage of contemplation: experience of the nondistinction of spirit and matter, by releasing the soul

the technique itself is the same in nearly all spiritual traditions. Thus, according to orientation—ritualistic, devotional, or even heroic—various Yogas could be developed over time (*haṭha-rāja-, kriyā-, karma-, mantra-, or jñāna-Yoga*).

Whichever variant is chosen, the goal is the release through knowledge of the oneness in the duality, the equality of spirit and matter, and the differentiation of soul and matter through the identification of the individual soul with immortality.

Śaṃkara's Doctrine of Nonduality

Śaṃkara, the philosopher of the Advaitavedānta or the Advaitavāda, took a somewhat different position in the "doctrine of nonduality." Precisely when Śaṃkara lived is not known, but it is currently thought that his work falls in the second half of the seventh century and the beginning of the eighth. According to Indian tradition, he was born into a Nambudiri Brahman family in Kerala. As a wandering ascetic, he traveled throughout India and founded various monasteries. More than four hundred different works are attributed to Śaṃkara, three of which are part of the "canonic" texts of the Vedānta, that is, his commentaries on the Upaniṣads, the Bhagavadgītā, and the Brahmasūtras, a text that the legendary Bādarāyaṇa was supposed to have written in the fourth century A.D.

In a strict sense, Vedānta, "end of the Veda," denotes the Upaniṣads, understood in some cases as the temporal and textual conclusion of the authoritative Vedic literature (*śruti*), and in others as the completion of thc Vcda. In a broader sense, Vedānta means all philosophical and spiritual schools and masters who referred to the Upaniṣads. Of these, Śaṃkara received special recognition even though he did not establish his own school. His influence was based on his acumen and his charisma as a teacher and master of a loyal circle of close students, including the influential Padmapāda.

Unlike the dualistic Sāṃkhya-Yoga, Śaṃkara represented a monism, even though a precise analysis shows that this characterization is mistaken. For Śaṃkara, the Ātman, the self of the person, is identical with the Brahman, the reality that is at the base of everything and the first cause of everything. So, for him, the Brahman is absolute, without a second (*advaya*), without features, immutable; it is simply being (*sat*), pure consciousness (*cit*), and highest bliss (*ānanda*), but it is also called—weakly theistically—lord or highest lord (*īśvara, parameśvara*) and self (*ātman*) or highest self (*paramātman*). Consequently, everything else is unreal, the world of duality, belonging to many names and forms, which is also developed from Brahman or his creative power (*māyā*), but only in its non-evolved form, thus only in its non-empirical reality. This construction mainly affected the Brahman-Ātman identity: Man is also Brahman, but only in his non-empirical, non-evolved form, of which he must become aware; otherwise, he has to suffer. What is important here is that man cannot *become* Brahman, for then Brahman would not be in him already and he could not experience the oneness; nor can he already be it, for then he would not have to become it anymore. Therefore, the doctrine of nonduality demands what it basically denies: the oneness of Ātman and Brahman. Here, too, the way out leads through two forms of knowledge, for there is duality for man only through ignorance (*avidyā*). The (higher) knowledge, on the other hand, can know and realize the nonduality in itself.

According to Śaṃkara, ignorance is also based on a misunderstanding of language, especially the first person of the personal pronoun, which tempts one to identify always with the ephemeral. With sentences like "I am this" (*aham idam*) or "this is mine" (*mama idam*), one tries to equate oneself with the unspiritual, with psychical and physical forms, with his own body, with character traits, and with physical or emotional conditions. But in this way the "I" is granted an existence, which it cannot have or can have only when it is identified with the only reality, the Brahman. Everything else is superimposition (*adhyāsa*) of unequal quantities and therefore erroneous. The only way to liberation is knowledge (*vidyā, vijñāna*) of the congruence of Brahman and Ātman. Only then can the statement "I am the Brahman" be right, because the I is no longer seen as different from the Brahman and Brahman is no longer an object of the perception of the I.

In Śaṃkara, nonsalvation is embedded in a clear conception of the cycle of rebirth (*saṃsāra*). Salvation is the Brahman-Ātman identification, which can be striven for neither intellectually nor through acts—both belong to the world of the transitory—but which can only be produced by a proper preparation and (a special component of Śaṃkara) through written revelation.[207]

Special Features of Indian Mysticism

From the Upaniṣads to Śaṃkara (and beyond), the spiritualistic form of religiosity has always dealt with identity and identification. Does this constitute a specifically Indian mysticism?

The term *mysticism* is later than every experience called by that name. In the Bible, Greek *mystikos* and related words are not common; in antiquity, mysticism was essentially *mysterium:* that which was kept silent (Greek: *myein*) because it was a secret or mystery cult. "Mysticism" usually means a religious practice that comprises internal and external purifications—such as obliterating yearnings—visions, hearing things, exercises in concentration, meditation, silence, and so on. This practice can, but does not necessarily lead to a normally not experienced state of consciousness, which is described in different and contrasting ways: rest and unrest; experience of timelessness, infinity, or openness; an oceanic feeling; direct experience of god; internal emptiness—in short, *purificatio, illuminatio, unio.* With this multiplicity, it is no wonder that the term *mysticism* is also controversial.[208] Differentiation and precision are necessary to avoid statements that lack all historical or contextual firmness. But it is precisely this "beyond all infinity" (Kurt Ruh) that is obviously what mystics talk—or do not talk—about. This is a basic problem that Ludwig Wittgenstein solved with the closing sentences of his *Tractatus Logico-Philosophicus:* "There are, indeed, things that cannot be put into words. They *make themselves manifest.* They are what is mystical" (6.522). "He must transcend these propostions, and then he will see the world aright" (6.54). "What we cannot speak about we must pass over in silence"(7).[209]

For science, mysticism is never independent of context, but is always given in linguistic or other forms and cannot be separated from them. The question of the truth of a mystical experience, therefore, cannot be answered by science, but can only be formulated as a statement of faith. Thus, there are a great many correspondences between Meister Eckhart's "*Sohnsein*" and Śaṃkara's notion of Ātman, as Rudolf Otto and more recently Annette Wilke have demonstrated.[210] Parallels can also be drawn with Islamic mysticism, the non-being (*fanā̊*), in which one is as one was, as only god was (Annemarie Schimmel). And the Buddhist doctrine of the Non-self (*anātman*), through the doctrine of the Buddha nature, has more in common with the doctrine of the Ātman-Brahman identity than Śaṃkara liked. And yet the differences are almost too great to assume an experience common to all these mysticisms. Eckhart's doctrine of the childhood of god or the soul sparks is bound irrevocably with Trinitarian theology; the Islamic primeval contract between God and man has no correspondence in Christianity (or only a remote one): God made the compact with Israel, not with the individual; the Non-self of Buddhism is linked inseparably with the doctrine of existential constituents; Śaṃkara's notion of Ātman is atheistic. To be able to produce an equivalence, these dogmatic or historic peculiarities had to be overlooked. There would be no problem with this, but if the characteristic of the *tertium comparationis* is precisely that it eludes a comparison, the situation is problematic. As Gershom Scholem says, mysticism is always "mysticism *of* something." It is hard to compress the postulated silence between two book covers, yet the books are full of talk about silence, talk about finger-pointing instead of naming what the finger points to, veiled talk. Silence itself is postulated in Christianity, too, where the divine truth became the Word, the Logos.

Indian mysticism, therefore, is also specific; like every mysticism, at any rate, it permits scientific statements about it. Five special features count as five characteristics:[211]

1. The possibility of identifying the individual with the Absolute or God: In Christianity,[212] such a mysticism was suspected as hybris, self-deification, and thus contempt of Almighty God. In the Vaiṣṇava Bhakti movements a similar critique exists.

2. Atheism: Indian mysticism can also do without notions of god.
3. Escapism: In Christianity, mystical inwardness was often disparaged as quietist self-importance, which diverted from the congregation in the church and good acts, and therefore did not lead to acts of love of thy neighbor (*caritas*) *in maiorem Dei gloriam*. Such criticism also arose in the Hindu religions, but could not win a majority.
4. Redemption during one's lifetime (*jīvanmukti*): The experience *is* already salvation or at least the crucial encounter with it. Therefore, redemption during one's lifetime is, in principle, not excluded—as in Christianity.
5. Psychophysical techniques of identification: the gradual detachment of the spirit from its attachments.

From the substitution doctrine in the Upaniṣads, through the psychophysical techniques of identification of Sāṃkhya-Yoga, to Śaṃkara's doctrine of nonduality and the still-influential Vedānta—the Identificatory Habitus pervades, to think and teach the unthinkable, that man must not first become what he already is: immortal.

HEROISM AND KINGSHIP

Even though heroism—it could be called *vīryamārga*—is not noticed as much,[213] it is just as important as the other three classical paths (*mārga*) to salvation of knowledge, devotion, and acts. It can even be objected that heroism is included in the path of acts and sacrifice (*karmamārga*), since it—as defined by the Bhagavadgītā ethic—demands the fulfillment of caste duties, and heroic acts are part of the duties of a Kṣatriya; but then the path of the devotional participation (*bhaktimārga*) and even the path of knowledge (*jñānamārga*) can also be interpreted as subdivisions of the Karmamārga, for they also assume appropriate acts (Pūjā, studying texts, etc.). Moreover, heroism is not just a form of religiosity for Kṣatriyas. Instead, it encompasses all those acts aimed at salvation, which include violence, protection of family honor, prestige, pride, and self-sacrifice.

Thus, the social meaning of heroism exists not only for warriors and the aristocracy, for heroism forms a high ideal for all classes in southern Asia. The courageous act, whether it is of a "secular" or "religious" nature, is admired and glorified. Gods and spirits are violent, they provoke violence, and often, they can be given what they demand only by violence. Men are "heroes" (*vīra, śūra*) and are called "heroes" when they manage to live with greatness, are daring in battle, pull heavy chariots, undertake difficult pilgrimages to the icy sources of the Ganges, or participate in ritual struggles. Friedhelm Hardy correctly points out that the "great hero" Mahāvīra, the founder of Jainism, and the historical Buddha were Kṣatriyas.[214] In the legends of his birth, Mahāvīra was even brought from the womb of a Brahman woman to that of a Kṣatriya woman, partly to emphasize the heroism of his unique and famous life.[215] Hagiographies are generally full of the heroic acts of the leaders and founders of religions.

Heroism in the military sense is the subject of countless texts, such as the epics—the Mahābhārata and Rāmāyaṇa are monumental reports of war—of the Arthaśāstra, the courtly *cañkam* poetry in southern India, or the royal genealogies (*vaṃśavalī*). Accidental or premature death, heroic death, and religiously motivated suicide, killings, or self-sacrifice can also lead to salvation and deification in the popular religions. Shivaji, the leader of the Marathas in the uprising against the foreign rulers, was deified, since kings are frequently considered gods and thus homage rendered to them is almost equivalent to divine worship.

It is impossible here to do justice to the full scope and significance of heroism. For that, we would have to go into details about the roles of the hero gods, first of all Indra in his heroic struggle against the Vṛtra demon,[216] Rāmaism with its modern radicalizations, the worship of Bhīma or Hanumān with his army of monkeys, and the eternal war between gods and demons in the Purāṇas. There would also have to be a discussion of the Bhagavadgītā ethic; royal cults and festivals,[217] the institution of marriage by abduction; the special worship of the sword in countless rituals; the kind of loyalty characteristic of bhakti, of subordinates to their lords;[218] parts of political Hinduism; the erection of hero stones (*vīrakal*); the "heroic Śaivas" (Vīraśaivas); the rise of Sikhism; and so on.

Nevertheless, I want to present two concrete examples: the religious function of the Ākhāṛās, a special kind of centers of strength, and the position of the king and ascetic as saviors.

Ākhāṛās: Religious Centers of Strength[219]

Indian ascetics, it is widely thought, are saints who have devoted themselves completely to the spiritual study of their self and to the search for salvation. Their military tradition is not so well known. But ever since the seventeenth century, whole groups of ascetics, most of them naked or scantily clad, called "Nāgā," have fought against Moslem and British foreign rule or hostile kingdoms. They were usually recruited by princes and kings from the classes of the so-called casteless and were organized into regiments (Hindī *ākhāṛā, anī*) strictly guided by a leader. Their weapons were often nothing more than the age-old stick granted to ascetics, the trident (*triśūla*) obligatory for Śaiva Nāgās, or a club, the weapon of Hanumān. Yet occasionally they were provided with light firearms; even today ascetics sometimes carry swords. In addition, nearly all ascetics have long fire tongs (Hindī *cimtā*) with which they threaten unwelcome visitors.

One main task of the warrior-ascetics was to keep the streets safe. Until the nineteenth century, the militant ascetics, the Nāgā sections of the Rāmānandīs or Daśanāmīs, or the Khalsās of the Sikhs, guarded most of the inter-urban trade in northern India. On the trade routes threatened by robber castes, they were feared because of their strength and their fearlessness. They could deploy whole armies, which were involved in all kinds of struggles. In 1760, during a pilgrimage celebration in northern Indian Hardwar, more than eighteen thousand people died in a dreadful fight between rival sects. Even today, at such mass festivals, brutal arguments occasionally arise between Śaiva and Vaiṣṇava Nāgās over the order of rank in the procession. The British increasingly disarmed these militant groups of ascetics, but the sects have maintained their heroic traditions to this day.

The regiments of ascetics form a loose compound according to sectarian orientations. The Daśanāmī ascetics often belong to a "regiment," allegedly founded by Śaṃkara. Membership in a Śaiva regiment can sometimes be identified by the way the ascetics have put up their hair: Hair on the left side indicates the Junā Ākhāṛā, in the middle the Nirañjanī Ākhāṛā, and on the right the Nirvāṇī Ākhāṛā. The Vaiṣṇava Ākhāṛās are also subdivided into divisions (*anī*).

Ākhāṛās have always been partly *gymnasia* in the ancient sense of the word, that is, physical training places and centers of strength. Benares was a center for this martial aspect of the ascetics and had several hundred such places. There is not much feeling of the ascetic and meditative search for meaning there, and yet they are also religious sites. Today, many Ākhāṛās no longer belong to sects, but to private or group associations. They have turned into peaceful sites for the cultivation of athletic physical culture, which are attended especially by sons of boat people, milkmen, and craftsmen. Most of them are simple enclosures with a locked room for equipment, a shade tree, and arcades that stand around a quadrangular, roofed sand square where one exercises.

A mythical model for many ascetics and young men is Hanumān, the heroic monkey god, who helps the hero god Rāmā to withstand danger and hostility. In almost every Ākhāṛā is a small shrine with a statue of Hanumān, who is invoked before exercises and is embellished every day. The founder or leader of the Ākhāṛā is also worshiped regularly. Models are famous fighters who

(a)

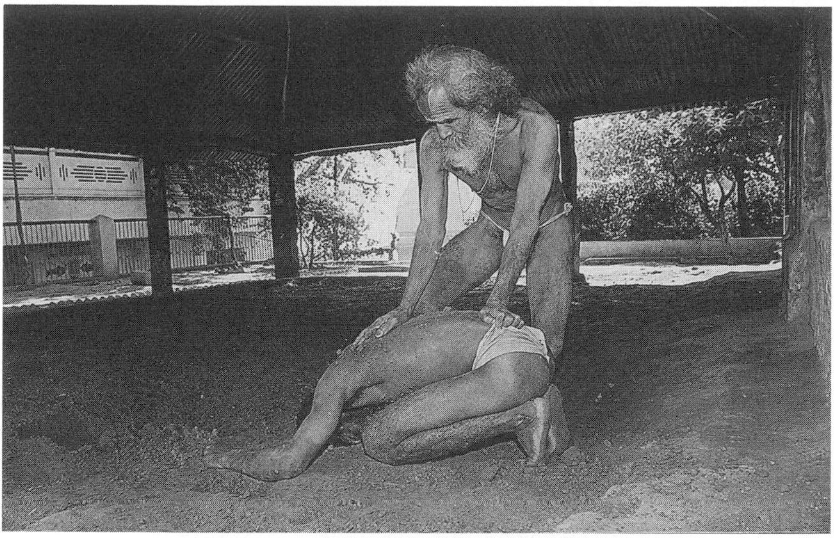

(b)

20. (a and b) Milkmen of the Yādav subcaste in the sand arena of a wrestling place (*ākhāṛā*) at the Tulsīghāṭ of Benares. Photographer: N. Gutschow, 1991.

were awarded medals in countrywide competitions, just as many Nāgās today still wear military orders from past battles.

The boundaries between mere physical exercise and religious claims are fluid. When men wash thoroughly in the Ganges before they go into the arena, that is for both hygienic and religious reasons. When they exercise not only with modern metal weights or stone rings (Hindī *garnāl*), but also with Hanumān's clubs, a stick about one meter long with a stone or steel foot, or with a pair of clubs (Hindī *joṛī*) on which Hanumān and the hero Bhīma are represented, they believe that religious forces strengthen physical ones. The sand (Hindī *miṭṭī*) in the arena is especially holy to them. In Benares, it comes from the holy Ganges and is mixed with Ganges water, mustard oil, and tumeric in order to keep it soft and supple. On special occasions, milk and clarified butter *(ghī)* are also added. The ground must be turned, loosened, and renewed periodically. Only the master (Hindī *ustād*) is allowed to enter the new sand after he has honored it with flowers and incense. The young men not only rub themselves with sand, they also wallow in it. Sand is balm for their heroism.

Power and Authority of the King[220]

In representations of Hindu religions, heroism has generally not been given adequate importance because interest in India is mainly in religion and philosophy. Therefore, the romantic caricature of peaceful India, where there was no violence but only the search for wisdom and redemption, could last a long time. Yet many paths lead to heaven, even in India, and many pass over priest and temple; many merely imply violence. It is primarily the king who both competed and cooperated with the priests since ancient times, and who therefore is also very significant for salvation. According to Jan Heesterman, the sacrificial relationship between the Brahmans and the king was also based on a specific exchange of violence.

It is quite certain that the king does not only stand "under" the priest, as Louis Dumont and the Brahmanic-Sanskritic literature asserts.[221] Dumont assumes this because he starts from an opposition between "pure" and "impure" and thus conceives of purity as a high value, which includes impurity. This construction (which I have presented above) also applies to a special extent to the relation between priest (Brahman) and king: The Brahman is not only in opposition to and competition with the king, he also stands higher than Kṣatriya and king because he embodies purity, a value classified higher than power by everyone. Therefore, according to Dumont, since religious power does not want to be political, the king in India gladly "submits" to the authority of the Brahmans. Dumont has been criticized for this position,[222] primarily for not sufficiently considering the countless counterexamples and for judging the relationship too much from the perspective and literature of the Brahmans.

Arthur Maurice Hocart, with a regicentric instead of a Brahmanocentric theory, is considered Dumont's "opponent."[223] Hocart also sees the king as a guarantor of salvation. The main task of both king and priest is to maintain or increase life, order, safety, and welfare. Therefore, the emergence of religion and the emergence of monarchy go together, like the spread of monarchy and religion. According to his view, monarchy stems from ritual: The king is the direct and legitimate successor of the ritual lord. In a certain sense, the king is then more powerful than the Brahman, not only politically but also religiously. Classical and modern material confirms a great deal of what Hocart says. In traditional Sanskritic literature, too, the king was not only the preserver of public order and the chief warrior, he was also considered as a creator, a savior, and the first and foremost sacrificer, as the protector and embodiment of the Dharma, as god. Coronation was deification and—at least in the Nepalese monarchy[224]—that is still the case. A Rāja is a Deva (god); worship of him is Pūjā (divine service). The king does not produce the Dharma, he implements it; he *is* the Dharma. The king is beyond good and evil, unblemished, undying. Therefore, he has all divine characteristics, and at his death, it is not the "king" who dies, but only the earthly king.

It is important to see that, in this connection, "king" is not a person or a symbol or a metaphor, neither a chosen one nor a son of heaven as in China, but rather a salvational power, which—in principle—everyone has, and can use, but which the anointed king embodies to a special extent. This power is based on heroism, security, and centrality. The religious and social need for a center, for community, for convergence internally and delimitation externally, is expressed in the king. *Pace* Emile Durkheim, it could be said that the king is the "church" of society. But the Brahman and the ascetic are also "churches" of Hindu society. Richard Burghart[225] has correctly indicated that Hindu society has not just *one* center and that, therefore, Brahman-centered or king-centered studies are one-dimensional. Instead, all of them—Brahman, ascetic, and king—are all rulers over different realms and "territories": the Brahman over the organic universe, the ascetic over the temporal universe, and the king over the terrestrial universe. These realms are incongruent and thus superiority is relational. Burghart adds that the king is always aware of how his power is limited by other gods, both divine and human. In India there is neither one religious nor one secular autocrat.

What distinguishes the king from the Brahmans and ascetics and is prominent in a certain respect is not his profanity—that is, assuming a distinction between politics and religion, which traditional India knows only in moderation—but rather his specific power, which is essentially heroic. The king is the epitome of the man of action, and power assimilated with interest in salvation is heroism. Clifford Geertz correctly criticized the reduction of the king to command and power,[226] in order to overcome the opposition of politics and religion; but in India the force of power as far as the king is concerned is in fact specific. Umbrella and stick (*daṇḍa*) are *the* royal symbols for protection and punishment. But the king has legal authority because he has religious authority, not because he possesses the military means to exert pressure. On the other hand, quite often, the secular power of the king consists of little more than royal insignia and declarations of loyalty. The power of the king is also religious, as Hocart says correctly: "The temple and the palace are indistinguishable, for the king represents the gods."[227] He even *is* god.

One specific form of the Indian monarchy has nearly been overlooked because of the sometimes negligible means of compulsion. For a long time, in the social historiography of India, it was assumed that royal states need clearly defined territories and administrations and that communities without such structures are to be counted as tribal. This bias has made the Western scholar direct his attention either to the large empire or to the village. Thus, the village has become a nearly autarchic unity and the village representative, who usually belongs to the dominant subcaste, has become a kind of small king. Louis Dumont, Burton Stein, and Nicholas B. Dirks[228] were the first to explain that within the sphere of influence of larger kingdoms, there were little kingdoms whose strength came primarily from religious motives. Their strength was not composed of military and administrative superiority or the ability to conduct war or repel foes, but rather of the usually inherited charisma of the king and the traditional loyalty of the population to him. It was mainly a privilege of the king to strengthen his rule, by granting titles, orders, lands, and sinecures, but also by establishing imperial temples. In this way, the king was giver and receiver of several gifts, which, according to the system of the hierarchical exchange of gifts, meant both higher rank (vis-à-vis subjects) and dependency (vis-à-vis the bigger kings). Thus, owning land was the crucial criterion. The king was the owner and protector of the land; the distribution of land was his privilege, which he used to create dependencies and to profit economically from the income of the land. In this respect, the king was hardly different from a medieval feudal lord. But what legitimated him was not land ownership, but rather his power, acquired through heroic strength, to protect the land and make it flourish. This power is based above all on religious substance, not on physical or political strength. It is acquired or maintained primarily by religious legitimations. The following example from the Paśupatinātha Temple in Nepal, the national guardian place of worship of the only still extant Hindu kingdom, may help explain this assertion.[229]

King and Ascetic

The traditional duty of the king to protect the land often devolves upon a ruler because he takes care of the "national" gods, either by giving land to the main temple or by appointing priests. This still happens at the Paśupatinātha Temple in Deopatan. Thus, this national place of worship preserves its "royal" strength independent of changing political power relations. It is sustained by the power and splendor of the royal house and yet remains beyond it. In Nepal in 1846, when the Rāṇā family usurped power for a century and the Śāhā kings, who had ruled since 1769, were degraded to shadow kings, the Paśupatinātha Temple suffered no damage. On the contrary, it kept the traditional support of the kings who were seen as divine and received additional extensive donations from the Rāṇās, who tried in this way to legitimate their power religiously, too.

Because power was concentrated in the Kathmandu Valley in the eighteenth century and a national awareness emerged, the Paśupatinātha Temple was used as a place of national identity. Especially when all small kingdoms declined in British India and with the independence of the Republic of India, Nepal was seen increasingly and—despite the democratic constitution of 1990—is still seen as the last Hindu kingdom in the world. This affects the Paśupatinātha Temple because, from time immemorial, it has been a well-known pilgrimage site even in India. The Rāṇā rulers in Nepal, primarily Jaṅga Bahādur Rāṇā, deliberately played this card: By luring ascetics to the Paśupatinātha Temple for a few days for the Śivarātri celebration with travel expenses, money, and free food, they could demonstrate their fidelity to traditional Hindu values—one of which is the king's care for ascetics.[230]

So, even though temple and palace profit from one another, they also endanger each other: If the proximity is too close, if the temple becomes too "secular," the priests can no longer give the king the desired religious legitimation. This mutual suspicion is especially clear in the Hindu religions since the temple priest has a lower status vis-à-vis the domestic priest. The Nepalese king does have his own domestic priests, Rājguru and Rājpurohita, but—because of popular religious reasons, among other things—he needs the temple priests, especially the Bhaṭṭa priests of the Paśupatinātha Temple, who traditionally come from southern India. That is, this temple is above things in a certain respect because of its emphasis on purity and its superregional significance.

Many temples in Nepal that are attended by the king are local sanctuaries, cared for by lower-ranking priests, and worshiped by the local population, often with bloody animal sacrifices. But if such rituals are practiced, if impure castes have free access to the sanctuary, if the myths are focused too much on a limited shrine and claim little validity beyond the local territory, then such a temple is not suited to give power to the king. His visit, in any case, has an integrating function; he gives more than he gets. But if—as in the Paśupatinātha Temple—the Sanskritic divinities of the Great Tradition are in the foreground, the ritual pays special attention to purity, the place is included in the superregional sacred geography, and the temple priests are scholars, then this place is largely released from its local bonds and is especially well suited for national interests and the general welfare.

Nevertheless, this place also remains linked with the locality, and the legitimation, needed both by place and king, is shaped neither by temple nor palace: It resides in the idea of a transcendental life force, available to both king and priest.[231] By being identified with this force through coronation or consecration, priest or king obtain authority—at the price of being no longer of this world: According to Hocart, the ideal king is the dead king,[232] and the "better," ideal Brahman or priest is the ascetic who is "dead" to society. This means that the farther the king, priest, and even holy site are from society, the purer they are, the more they are the religious substance of the life force. The life force is not the prevailing king; he cannot be, because he dies; on the other hand, his power must remain: *Rex non moritur.*[233] The life force is the idea of power over life and of immortality, with which the king is identified in the coronation as the son is in the initiation. Therefore, *pace* Hocart, both the coronation and the initiation can be seen as a ritual killing and also as a rebirth: "The king is dead; long live the king."

But because the power of the king is a religious substance, it is not bound only to the king either. Everyone can possess it or assimilate it. Only if territory is understood as secular land, only if strength is reduced to political or military strength is the king a unique figure in the socioreligious power structure. But if land and power are understood as domains from the start, then monarchy is rule over that area that can be obtained by heroic acts. These acts include heroic achievements, subordination to rulers (god, king, or Guru), privileges of giving and taking, victory over evil forces or over human, demonic, or internal foes, but finally—here, too—victory over death and mortality. The victor (*jina*), as many texts of all forms of religiosity say, is the one who obtains immortality, no matter whether achieved by ritualist, devotionalist, mystic, or heroic methods, and no matter whether he is priest, king, or ascetic.

FROM DESCENT TO TRANSCENDENCE

6. Religious Ideas of Space and Time

The sciences today—except for theology and philosophy—usually respond to epistemological challenges pragmatically or conventionally, but are ultimately goal-oriented.[1] The humanities especially more or less openly assume a naïve realism drawn from the model of empirical sciences: Things are as "reality" professes them. The basis of truth of scientific statements is that they convey "reality" as precisely as possible. But the scientist determines that himself. Moreover, almost all current scientific paradigms are determined by the Aristotelian and mainly Galilean-shaped consensus about truth and reason: The truth of empirically based knowledge rests not on the perception of an individual, but rather on the notion that anyone can verify it under the same conditions. Ever since Galileo—unlike Aristotle—empiricism is no longer bound to a life-world practice, hardly an inductive generalization of this practice, but is rather embedded in a technical practice constructed in experimentation. Thus, empirical knowledge becomes what "is attained with the instrumentation of a physical or technical praxis (often *against* the experiential knowledge of a life-world praxis)."[2]

In such a scientific ambiance, other empirical knowledge is declared unreliable, obsolete, or at best, only subjectively valid. It is an alarming result of modernity that life-world orientation is increasingly degraded and the scientization of everyday life is enhanced. For the exploration of other knowledge orientations this reductionism means that authorship and social or psychological functions are examined only after their historical emergence, but are hardly taken seriously as a basis for a different world understanding for religious and life world orientations.

In this chapter, two forms of this orientation knowledge are grasped in their uniqueness: Hindu religious notions of space and time.[3] In the first section, I start with a hypothesis that I illustrate with four short examples: spheres of existence and spatial directions as sacred powers, sites of pilgrimage and their hierarchy, bodies as divination cards, and the determination of cosmic places for people; in conclusion, I take up again the theoretical challenges of spatial orientations. In the second section, the focus is on the religious awareness of time, illustrated by ancient Indian and Purāṇic cosmogonies, cyclical models of time, particularly the doctrine of the ages of the world, and calendar calculations. Finally, I illustrate the unity and parallelism of religious space and religious time with the example of a festival: the Śivarātri in Nepal.

Time-space orientation knowledge in Hindu religious contexts means that everything that is manifested needs extension and thus a space, but not necessarily a physical space; therefore, according to the Hindu notion, the nonmaterial, nonconcrete, nonpunctual also has a sphere of existence. This hypothesis is contrary to a scientific, physical notion of space with its three-dimensionality and precision of locality.

RELIGIOUS AWARENESS OF SPACE

In Hindu religious thinking, all material and nonmaterial manifestations need a sphere of existence (*loka*): gods, humans, animals, plants, fire, wind, water, language, meters, feelings, thoughts. Yet at the same time, everything that needs a sphere is not lasting, but is ephemeral, and thus not the "true" existence, hence sorrowful. The sphere of existence, Loka,[4] is always specific, but there is no space as such in Hindu religious thought. Humans have their own Loka, animals have another, and so do plants or gods, stars or spirits. But even humans do not have a common life space, or have it only in a nonreligious sense: In Vedic texts, the sphere of the Brahman is the sky (*dyaus*) with the sun (*sūrya*), the Kṣatriya has the space in between (*antarikṣa*) with the wind as his "element," the common person (*viś*) lives on the earth (*pṛthivī*) with the fire as a principle of nourishment, and the ascetic (*saṃnyāsin*) lives in the world of the stars (*nakṣatra*) and of the moon with the principle of immortality.[5] In Hindu religious thought, space represents a field of force, a characteristic of all manifestations. This also applies for nonmaterial manifestations, whose "space" can be felt rather than seen or perceived. Because such spaces are less clearly delineated than volume which is perceived or measured with the eye or sense of touch, grasping the religious concept of space has a special problem of edges and thresholds.[6] I shall discuss this principle with examples.

Spaces and Directions as Sacred Powers

In ancient India, the idea of a common world for everything was not accepted. Instead, different cosmological models[7] of various worlds existed beside one

Table 27
The Seven Worlds

1. Bhūrloka	Earth with seven continents, seven oceans, and seven underworlds—the world of humans, animals, and plants
2. Bhuvarloka	Space between earth and the course of the sun, air space—in-between space for gods, demons, spirits, etc.
3. Svarloka (also Svargaloka)	Space between the course of the sun and pole stars (*dhruva*)—world of the stars and planets
4. Maharloka	1 *koṭi* (= 10^7) *yojana* (1 *yojana* = ca. 3.6 km) high—world of the saints
5. Janarloka	2 *koṭi yojana* high—world of the sons of Brahmā
6. Tapoloka	8 *koṭi yojana* high—world of the Vairāja gods
7. Satyaloka	48 *koṭi yojana* high—world of the gods = Brahmā's world

another. Thus, since the second epoch, there has been the familiar dualism of "heaven" (Dyaus Pitā, masculine: see Zeus, Jupiter) and "earth" (Pṛthivī, feminine), often combined in the dual (Dyāvāpṛthivī) or even tripartite divisions into earth, space in between, and sky; or into underworld, earth, and sky. Similarly, for the Vedic period,[8] a seven-part division of the universe can be shown, consisting of seven rings, each doubled like big continents surrounded by seven oceans of various liquids.

The first continent, Jambūdvīpa, consists, on the other hand, of seven hierarchical worlds (*loka*), which represent the realms of life for various creatures (see table 27). While the first division of seven is horizontal, the second is vertical. Along with it are countless more ideas, as that the world is oval (*brahmāṇḍa*),[9] that it is a disk with the mountain Meru as a world axis, or that it is a round, unmoving ball, surrounded by ether and orbited by heavenly bodies.

Every life space mentioned in table 27 is a force, a power, a kind of feeling of space that is limited not only to visible space determinants. The words for earth express this multiplicity: *Bhū* is not only the world for living things, but also a goddess (Bhūdevī); similarly, *pṛthivī* also indicates the goddess and the religious substance "breadth." The terms are linked inseparably with a specific sense of space. One cannot talk of *the* earth, which has this or that aspect.

Therefore, there is no word for that because there is no such idea. "Sky" and "earth" are not two different spaces, but rather senses of space that can be either in the sky or on the earth. In death, therefore, one only changes one's Loka, the sphere of existence. Similarly, directions are not only coordinates of a geocentric notion of space, but rather—in religious terms—also senses of space.

The word *orientation* originally denoted the alignment of directions by the sunrise (*oriens sol,* "rising sun"). In ancient and present-day India, this is not just a physical-spatial alignment. Directions are not only directions, but also forces (see table 28).[10] As the "(wild) West" is linked with freedom and therefore can be a name or a term for advertising cigarettes, so in India, directions also stand for definite qualities, in this case, religious ones. At any rate, the directions are not a symbol for something; they cannot be abstracted from their substance. Directions are consequently singular, not relative to the location, but absolute: In terms of religion, north is always north because only north has some particular tone. This is why the Kailash Mountain is always in the "north," no matter whether one is south, north, west, or east of it. In the religious context, detaching a place or a position from its substance is hardly possible. Nor is the abstraction of a geographical determination a relation. Every geographical determination is a mixture of basically equal forces and is neither egocentric nor geocentric.

Thus, directions are not only geocentric or astronomical coordinates, but also and primarily powers. Therefore, the tripartite division of the world (see table 27) into earth (*bhū*), in-between space between earth and the course of the sun (*bhuvaḥ,* actually the plural of *bhū*), and the starry sky (*svaḥ*) belongs to the three obligatory ritual expressions (*vyāhṛti*) that a Twice-Born must recite during the morning ritual (*saṃdhyā*) in order to confirm the powers of these life spaces.[11] The powers of these worlds also inhere in their denotations and thus the words *bhū, bhuvaḥ,* and *svaḥ* are detached from directions or spaces. Space and volume are identical, and so are names and what is named.

In the Puruṣa hymn[12] of the Ṛgveda, the emergence of the earth is described with similar ideas of space. It is a late ṛgvedic, but an early cosmogonic myth for Indian intellectual history. The core of the hymn is that creatures emerge from the thousand-headed, thousand-eyed, and thousand-foot Puruṣa ("Manu")—a kind of primeval giant (comparable to the Germanic Ymir)—to whom the gods themselves sacrifice: From his head, the Brāhmaṇa emerge; from his arms, thighs, and feet, the other Varṇas; from him the whole earth is covered and is towered over by a ten-finger breadth; from him are born the wind, moon, and sun, seasons, living creatures, Vedas, meters, and so on. At the same time, various powers were assigned to specific parts of the body: the

TABLE 28
Religious Categories of Space in the Veda

Directions:	East	South	West	North (leftover or mixed category)
Worlds:	Earth (*bhū*) or sky (*svaḥ, svarga*)	Atmosphere (*bhuvaḥ, antarikṣa*)	Sky (*svaḥ, svarga*) or earth (*bhū*)	(Under- or upper-worlds)
Varṇas:	Brāhmaṇa	Kṣatriya	Vaiśya	King or Brahman and Sūdra
Spheres and powers:	*bráhman:* (eternal) life, sacrifice, speech (*vāc*); *sattva*	*kṣatra:* death, violence, sexuality; *rajas*	*viś:* fertility, harvest and feeding, wealth; *rajas/tamas*	*tamas*
Beings, creatures:	Gods	Violent gods, especially Indra, demons	Human, animal, *Viśve Devāḥ*	Animals, demons
Veda:	Ṛgveda	Yajurveda	Sāmaveda	Atharvaveda
Meter:	*gāyatrī*	*triṣṭubh*	*jagatī*	—

sky to the head, the air space to the navel, the earth to the feet. Thus, the world comes from the Puruṣa and yet Puruṣa and world are identical. Because the gods offer the Puruṣa as a sacrifice, the world is also produced by the sacrifice. As the cell has the genetic code of the whole living creature, so the whole (the world) is contained in the part (sacrifice) because of the essential identity of the part and the whole.

Pilgrimage Sites and Their Hierarchy[13]

What is in space is already the whole substance of space. Therefore, *tīrtha* (literally: "ford") means "pilgrimage site" but also "(holy) man" (e.g., Rāmatīrtha), a certain religious "line in the palm" or "(holy) text." Tīrtha is then the holy substance "transition, junction" between worlds that touch and do not touch each other. Here a relationship between religious and scientific thinking of space exists: Just as there are no ideative criteria of space, coordinates in three-dimensional space, homogeneity and the isotropic variety of points "in reality," so there is no holy space as a "real phenomenon." Both spaces are otherworldly, spiritual spaces to a certain extent. As Ernst Cassirer put it: "The whole spatial world, and with it the cosmos, appears to be built according to a definite model, which may manifest itself to us on an enlarged or a reduced scale but which, large or small, remains the same. All the relations of mythical space rest ultimately on this original *identity;* they go back not to a similarity of efficacy, not to a dynamic law, but to an original identity of essence."[14]

The same is true with celebrations of such places. They can take place on various levels and in various, basically equal spaces. Thus, one goes on a pilgrimage to Benares,[15] but also within Benares, one walks around holy places. With every tour (*pradakṣiṇā*), the pilgrim receives the sacred power possessed by the enclosed space. This can be a brief walk around the gods in the temple, but also a five-day procession such as the Pañcakrośīyātrā, the walk around Benares in a radius of five *krośas* (17.5 km), in which 108 sanctuaries, also called *tīrtha,* are visited. Every sanctuary thus encloses other holy sites through its mythology, so that at the end of the procession, the universe is celebrated. But what can be expanded because it is infinite can also be contracted into the one: Identifications can be dilated or compressed. Thus, in Benares, there is the Pañcakrośī Temple with 108 reliefs, which represent the shrines of the procession; there, walking around Kāśī—an ancient name of Benares—can be performed in one place: with a walk around the temple, which brings as much religious merit as the five-day procession. In addition, there is the temple of Kāśīdevī ("goddess Kāśī"), where the sacred power "Kāśī" can be obtained. Because of the identity of the part and the whole, the universe can be in Kāśī, and Kāśī can be in one specific temple or in another place: Several places in southern Asia call themselves a true or secret "Benares."

Thus, a holy site is not only a site within geocentric space coordinates. For then it would not be holy. Just as the king can only be king because he is "dead"—i.e., from another world—so the power "Benares" is bound not only to the geographical place of Benares. In the extreme case, neither effigy nor external ways are necessary: "Benares" is then visited in the mind, in the heart. The pilgrim texts and city eulogies themselves elevate Benares to this transcendent level. Kāśī appears there in bright light, as a field of cosmic forces, as a sacred Maṇḍala enclosing the whole universe as a place of perfect purity, liberation, and redemption. Kāśī is built of pure gold there; it floats in the ether, where the city is supported by Śiva's trident, whose extension forms the Viśvanātha, one of the main temples. Kāśī has the form of a Maṇḍala circle or a Yogic or cosmic body there. Kāśī expands there into the seven concentric rings of the universe listed above, which surround the center like the seven oceans and enclose the holy space. Kāśī appears in the shape of a trident, a disk, a heavenly cart, or a conch there. Kāśī changes and yet remains the same because the sacred power "Kāśī" is singular.

Yet, a pilgrimage site is not only a vague religious feeling. On the contrary, its sacred power can be measured precisely, as illustrated by a category of texts studied by Richard Salomon.[16] The texts are called *tīthapratyāmnāyāḥ* ("pilgrimage sites as [equivalent] substitute [for penance]"). In them, visiting holy sites is balanced against atonement (*kṛcchra, prāyaścitta*), which is stipulated in specific procedures. Thus, pilgrimage sites have a certain atonement value that depends on distance and other factors. An early example for these identifications comes from the Parāśarasmṛti, a legal text: According to this, a pilgrimage of two *yojanas* (about 3.2 km) is considered equal to a Kṛcchra act of penance.[17] In later texts, the holy places themselves are named and listed. For example, a bath in the Ganges corresponds to six years of Kṛccha acts of penance, when one has covered sixty *yojanas* in order to visit the river; since one Kṛccha act of penance needs twelve days and can be carried out only once a month, the bath in the Ganges along with some thirty miles of pilgrimage corresponds to 180 *kṛcchas* altogether. It is also obvious in these equations that the equivalent can be determined only through an abstraction, the sacred value. Spaces and sites can have this value, but it is not connected to them and it can be miscalculated because of its materiality. The religious value of the recitation of a text can also be given precisely: To get a husband, the Rāmarakṣastotra text should be repeated 220 times; for the birth of a child, sixty-four times; in illnesses twelve times, etc.[18] This can be compared to calculating and paying for indulgences in the Roman Catholic church.

(a)

(b)

21. (a) Pilgrims on the walk around Benares that lasts several days. (b) A part of the way can be covered by boat on the Ganges. Photographer: N. Gutschow, 1991.

Like a person, an animal can also be a "holy place," particularly the cow. It is considered a goddess because—among other things–it is identified with the sacred power *śrī* ("wealth, good fortune, abundance"), because it is a part of this substance and thus—since the divine cannot be divided—the substance itself. In India, such thinking is visualized, for example, by painting countless other gods in the picture of the cow. As in the Puruṣasūkta of the Ṛgveda mentioned above, body parts are then linked with gods and their powers, but in this case, only to express the universalism of the whole. Such a divination card can be read in which relations are assigned and produced: Why does one deity reside in the horns, another in the tail, the third in the hooves? In India, however, the individual localities of the gods in the cow are not as important as the expression of abundance represented by the cow. Therefore, the cow is also called Kāmadhenu, the "wish cow" or "wish-fulfilling cow." It is the sacred power "abundance," and an appropriate form of expression for her is that everything is contained in her.

These examples are definitely not only esoteric intellectual games, concocted by priests and myth-makers, without reference to experienced reality, as illustrated by another example from the rural milieu.

Astrology and the Cosmic Place of Man[19]

Ever since the second ("Vedic") epoch, knowledge of the effects of the fixed stars and planets has been part of the basis of Indian scholarship. Astronomy (*jyotiṣa*) forms one of the six classical complementary sciences, the "limbs of the Veda" (*vedāṅga*)—along with phonetics (*śikṣā*), metrics (*chandas*), grammar (*vyākaraṇa*), etymology (*nirukta*), and ritual (*kalpa*). Jyotiṣa is traditionally subdivided into astronomy (*gaṇita, tantra*), as well as astrology (*horā, jātaka*) and divination (*śākhā*). In religious practice, the use of astrological and other divinatory means has always been extraordinarily widespread. Horoscopes, interpretations of signs, soothsaying, and palm reading enjoy great popularity. Almost every Indian has his "position in life" determined in this way.

The ritual of naming (see table 5) is an alignment, even an orientation, to astronomical coordinates. In this ritual, the house of the moon at the time of birth is authoritative for determining the personal name that begins with the syllable attributed to this constellation, so that the life of the child will proceed propitiously. As an example, I have chosen the name Nūtan. According to a customary Nepalese calendar (Pañcāṅga, see below) of 1994–1995, his name falls within the syllable category of *nā-nī-nū-ne*. These are syllables that are connected, among other things, with the following listed traits and powers: Zodiac sign (*nakṣatra*): Anurādha (name of the seventeenth station of the moon); house of the moon: Scorpion; regent: Mars; class (*varṇa*): Brahman; animal category (*yoni*): gazelle; group membership (*gaṇa*): god (*deva*); mount: gander. Note that membership in a class (*varṇa*) is not a question of origin, but of the constellation of the stars at birth. One can be a farmer (Vaiśya), but belong astrologically to the category of Brahmans. One can also have the astrologically defined group category of the gods, but also belong to the animal category of "rats."

These space-time coordinates also form the birth horoscope that remains formative for many events, such as the "matching ceremony" in the betrothal (see table 10): If the woman belongs to the group of the demons (*rākṣasa*) and the man to the group of the gods (*deva*), a marriage does not fall under favorable signs; such a combination is to lead to marital conflict and hostility.[20]

Such calculations are also used for changing places, as Gloria G. Raheja has shown.[21] If someone moves into a new village, he occasionally has an astrologer test whether the place suits him, since otherwise, disaster threatens. In Raheja's example, the syllables of the name of the village and the newcomer are matched with the twenty-eight houses of the moon (*nakṣatra*)[22] and the four parts of the body, i.e., forehead, back, heart, and feet. Raheja demonstrates this with the example of "her" village of Pahansu: *Pa*—the first syllable—corresponds to the house of the moon *uttarā phālguni;* the sequence of the other houses of the moon and the parts of the body are established: seven (beginning with *uttarā phālguni*) fall on the forehead, back, heart, and feet. The same is done with the name of the person in question. If the Nakṣatra of the first syllable of his name falls in the forehead or heart group, place (village) and person are suited to each other, then the stars are favorable, and then he and his family prosper. But if the house of the moon is in the foot group, he should settle somewhere else.

Divination cards and birth horoscopes are therefore regularly used in India.[23] In them, localities are characterized by sacred powers which can be combined into complex systems of orientation and allow the person to determine his respective place in order to use the good forces and eliminate the harmful ones. In every Brahmanic-Sanskritic ritual, the individual must be brought into harmony with a place and time through a specific ceremony (*deśakālasaṃkīrtana*). Only then are there the necessary congruences between the person who commissions the ritual and the sacred powers of the ritual. Only then are such identifications beneficial.

Religious and Scientific Concepts of Space

These examples have illustrated that a physical concept of space is not sufficient to grasp the special quality of the (Hindu) religious systems of orientation.

The same is true for the geography of religion,[24] which is often exposed to the danger of a deterministic evaluation of environmental factors, especially landscape, earth, and climate. This is so when a rather blatant dualism of good and evil in Egypt is linked to the fertile, green Nile Delta and the desert, and thus a clear-cut border between arable land and wasteland; or Shamanism is indicated as an especially characteristic form of religion for the Arctic north; or it is assumed that the Tibetan religion is a religion that suits the high Asian landscape.[25] Such simplifications are not fair to religious ideas.

The environment does influence religious ideas: Visions of paradise and hell are shaped by local facts, vegetation, and climate; the festival calendar is often aligned with the harvest cycle; forms of settlement often have religiously motivated structures: The church is in the center, the casteless live at the edge; the characteristic nature of itinerant monks is based on deeply rooted ideas of the animism of nature and its protection (which is why Indian ascetics are to stay in one place or one monastery during the intensive growing phase of the Monsoon). But the special nature of the religious sense of space is that it cannot be functionalized and reduced because it always also includes the other world: Religious experiences take place *in illo loco* and *in illo tempore.* This is why religious places and sites "in space" or on maps can never be the whole *holy* place. Benares is *eo ipso* no holy place if its religious sense of space is not understood. Here, Emile Durkheim's strict separation between sacred and profane can be perceived in fact. Holy places, then, are holy only when they are *at the same time* the complete other, thus, when man, place, and deity are identical or are identified *ritually.* A stone can be the seat of Śiva today and a simple paving stone tomorrow, but the awareness of the identification must be there—through a *intentio solemnis* (see table 20). The boundaries are abstract-spatial, not "merely" empirical-spatial. But the boundaries can be drawn solid and clear. *Pace* Kurt Hübner, the differences between a scientifically shaped conception of space and a religious (in Hübner, "mythical") sense of space can be characterized as in table 29.[26]

The scientific view of the world is far from the religious one. The religious man does not know similarities of volume, but only identities or distinctions.[27] Every perceivable equivalent is identity. Nor is it merely coincidence for the religious man, or only an externality where something is; instead, there is a binding relation between the object and its position. Objectivity is possible only in radical subjectivity or singularity—in the sense that every religious space is subjective because otherwise it would not be. There cannot be a space "in itself," because what is in itself has no space: It cannot manifest itself and thus needs no sphere of existence.

Table 29
Scientific and Religious Conceptions of Space

Scientific Conception of Space	*Religious Conception of Space*
Space is a medium *in* which objects are found.	Space and what is within the space form a unit. There is no space in itself, only various spaces.
Space consists of a continuous, homogeneous, isotropic multiplicity of points.	Spaces are sacred powers that are felt rather than perceived. Various things can have the same sacred power of space.
Three-dimensional space coordinates lead to topological and metrical conceptions of space.	Places have not only a relative, but also an absolute location, which constitutes their sacred power.
There are norms of measures of length and distances.	Space is not isotropic: it matters in which "direction" something moves, since the directions themselves form absolute powers; it can be compressed and expanded and yet remain the same.
Up and down, right and left; the directions are all relative and dependent on abstract relations: gravitation, geomagnetism, the position of the observer, etc.	Holy space is absolute and thus separated in principle from "profane" space. Up and down, right and left, etc., are not merely conventions, but absolute forces like gods, light, or principles.

Concepts of space are usually[28] relational: A space consists of things at a distance from one another; an object in space can be perceived and located only as distinguished from another object in space. Up-down, left-right, inner-outer, before-behind, are thus relations. But in a religious sense of space, space equals the whole: "Now, here in this fort of *brahman* there is a small lotus, a dwelling-place, and within it, a small space. . . . As vast as the space here around us is this space within the heart," says the Chāndogya-Upaniṣad.[29] And because space is everything, it can be identified with the self (*ātman*). In other words, this space cannot itself be relational, it can itself not be a space thing. There cannot even be space around it so that the internal space is the same as the external.

The example of the world of the ancestors[30] illustrates this feeling of space. One lives with the forefathers, but their world is different from the world of the survivors. But where are the ancestors? They are neither only inside the consciousness of the survivors, nor are they only outside, somewhere above in the sky. When asked about the location of the ancestors, no indicative movement is made, not to the sky, but because of that it should not be said that they have no space. On the contrary, their existence is considered real and so is their space (see table 12), even if these are not to be located with a physical conception of space.

Religious boundaries between places were initially sharper than the profane in human history.[31] *Templum* ("space of observation," Greek: *temenos*) comes from the root *temno* ("cut, separate"), and *con-templari,* the (theoretical) examination and viewing, as Ernst Cassirer notes, is based on the idea of the "defined space." The thresholds of the holy space were marked early, when there were still firm boundaries for private property and ownership of land and places. The singular subjectivity of a space or rather its sacred power can set absolutely trenchant boundaries: In some circumstances, it can be measured where a holy space begins and where it ends; the thresholds mark it and demand a specific ritual relation, such as removing one's shoes. But only the indeterminacy and boundaryless nature of the religious space make such clear boundary interchanges necessary. Nevertheless, it was not the scientific conception of space that was the first to be precise and "objective," but rather the religious conception. Scientific objectivity does not convey the *one,* common reality better, but rather it is usually based on a procedure of trial and error, whose truth depends on use and consent. Nevertheless, hardly anyone says seriously that the current conception of space is better than the previous one unless he *believes* in progress. But that is a belief that cannot be verified.[32]

RELIGIOUS AWARENESS OF TIME

Hindu religious and the general religious sense of space, as I have tried to show, determines sacral space through identification with a non-empirical space—beyond the beyond. Even though this conception of space is abstract and leaves hardly any room for theistic approaches, the Indians have also asked themselves questions that form the major subjects of mythologies in religions:[33] Who created this world and the next world or how did they come into being? How do these worlds pass away? These questions about creation and cosmogony also raise the aspect of time, which I deal with here. But first, I present various cosmological models.

Ancient Indian Cosmogonies[34]

In the second ("Vedic") epoch, no unified cosmogony or a single world creator can be discerned. Instead, images of the emergence of the world were used. The early images show contours of a world creator or a demiurge. Thus, there is the image of building, like the carpenter Viśvakarman,[35] the firstborn of the universe: The worlds are measured out, the earth is held up with stakes, supported by posts. Tvaṣṭṛ is also a divine architect, Brahmaṇaspati is a blacksmith. The idea that something formless must be shaped (molded, cut, woven) is common. These myths and stories talk of creating (*sṛj*), measuring (*mā*), or manufacturing (*takṣ*). Alongside are theogonous images of tools and gestures. The gods produce sun, earth, water, and light, but also themselves; they are *causa sui* (*svayambhū*). Indra produced sky (*dyaus*) and earth (*pṛthivī*), which are considered the heavenly father and mother of nature, and thus it is said of Indra: "From your own person you have generated both mother and father."[36]

On the other hand, in other images, the worlds emerge out of themselves or out of their elements, sprout, evolve, expand. Thus, waters (always plural) produce the world through heat (!): Water is thus primeval material,[37] fire the child or grandchild of water. Associations to the egg and hatching are desirable and explicit. Later in the ṛgveda and then increasingly popular is the idea that the One originally developed out of a primeval material with no beginning and no characteristics, that Prajāpati thinks he would like to be a Second. Thus, god is in everything and there is no Second aside from the One, which manifested itself. The problem of the theodicy is then posed only in a very unconventional form. (I shall return to this question in the conclusion of the book.) It seems as if there is not a Nothing next to the absolute One, no area that is not permeated with the (Divine) One. Thus, god is not the absolutely other, but rather an identification between individual and absolute, which cannot be seen only because of illusion.

How tentatively such questions are posed is shown in a famous hymn of the origin of the world in the Ṛgveda:

> The non-existent was not, the existent was not; then the world was not, not the firmament, nor that which is above [the firmament]. How could there be any investing envelope, and where? Of what [could there be] felicity? How [could there be] the deep unfathomable water? Death was not nor at that period immortality, there was no indication of day or night; That One unbreathed upon breathed of his own strength, other than That there was nothing else whatever. There was darkness covered by darkness in the beginning, all this [world] was undistinguishable water; that empty

> united [world] which was covered by a mere nothing, was produced through the power of austerity. In the beginning there was desire, which was the first seed of mind; sages having meditated in their hearts have discovered by their wisdom the connexion of the existent with the non-existent. Their ray was stretched out, whether across, or below, or above; [some] were shedders of seed, [others] were mighty; food was inferior, the eater was superior. Who really knows? Who in this world may declare it! Whence was this creation, whence was it engendered? The gods [were] subsequent to the [world's] creation; so who knows whence it arose? He from whom this creation arose, he may uphold it, or he may not [no one else can]; he who is its superintendent in the highest heaven, he assuredly knows, or if he knows not [no one else does].[38]

The idea of the demiurge appears hesitantly and relatively late. The unknown creator is asked about,[39] and even in the Puruṣa hymn[40] of the Ṛgveda, the primeval creature is not a creator of the world, but gods, elements, creatures, and the world order emerged from him. The gods who are younger than the universe are awarded the privilege of having created the world only by extension: Through their dance in which things emerged in a cloud of dust,[41] or through their playfulness (*māyā, līlā*). The gods also have limited lifetimes: Brahmā is to live a hundred or a hundred twenty years in every world year, Prajāpati a thousand years. This god—his name means "lord of the creatures"—is the first to have the features of a demiurge. But it says of him, too, that he himself was created; the world emerged from the nonbeing (*a-sat*), the One, the Brahman, the egg, heat, or time (*kāla*). There is a plethora of ideas of the first man (Manu, Yama), but creation is not directed at man: "Man . . . is only one of the many creations the world fulfills, along with horses and cattle, Vedas and poetry meters."[42]

By extension, a myth of incest arose in the early Vedic period[43] and developed in the middle Vedic period, from which the world emerged—in a dangerous act, in which a Third emerged from Two. The idea is widespread that (Prajāpati's) seed is manifested in the multiplicity of the world, so that the One is many and—from an ascetic view—is thus wasted.

In these many different images of creation, a coherent cosmogony can hardly be discerned. Everything and nothing can be extracted from them: a dualistic conception of the world (the world emerged from the tension of chaos and order, light and dark, man and woman, later Puruṣa and Prakṛti) as well as monistic ideas: The One, the primeval material, the seed, the water are all unmanifested (*avyakta*) at the beginning; the world then manifests itself; but theogonic myths can also be seen: Gods such as Puruṣa, Prajāpati, or Viśvakarman created or sired the world. Only one thing is sure: Clearly there is hardly any need to unify and reduce these ideas. The designs of the world—contradictory but equal—stand beside one another.

Creation in Classical Mythology[44]

In the Purāṇas, too, there is no single creation myth or single creator. Instead, various cosmogonic themes return: the creation out of the body of a demiurge, the primeval egg, the quarrel between the gods over creation, incest myths, the duality (of Puruṣa and Prakṛti) that lets everything emerge, and others. But more than in the ṛgveda, it is emphasized that certain gods (Brahmā, Viṣṇu, Śiva) are granted a greater share in the creation. But these gods, too, are often considered self-born or emerging out of themselves. There are countless new cyclical creation myths according to which the world is always re-created. More distinct than in the Veda is also the view that the gods let the world emerge out of their desire for sport (*līlā*).[45] Finally, there are attempts to harmonize the various ideas of creation theistically. A striking example of that is the myth of Viṣṇu's cosmic sleep and Brahmā's birth.[46]

At the end of every Kalpa, Viṣṇu sleeps his cosmic sleep. All three worlds are in darkness; nothing but the ocean remains, not even gods. Only Viṣṇu (as Nārāyaṇa) sleeps in a bed made of the serpent named Śeṣa ("remnant") or Ananta ("endless"). From his divine playfulness (*līlā*), a lotus grows in Viṣṇu's navel. Brahmā appears and asks Viṣṇu who he is. He introduces himself as Nārāyaṇa and says: "Know that I am origin and disintegration. See in me the whole world, the continents with their mountains, the oceans and seven seas, and you too, the grandfather of the worlds." Viṣṇu asks Brahmā who he is and gets the answer: "I am the creator and priest, the self-existing patriarch; in me everything is erected. I am Brahmā who looks in all directions." Then, Viṣṇu enters Brahmā's belly and sees all three worlds with gods, men, and demons. Astounded, he asks Brahmā to come into his (Viṣṇu's) belly now. There, Brahmā finds no end and no way out, for Viṣṇu has closed all doors. Only the navel offers him a way out, where Brahmā then appears on a lotus.

In this myth, Viṣṇu and Brahmā compete for the creation; both have let the whole world emerge (*pravṛtti*) in their bellies (wombs) and have taken it back (*nivṛtti*). The ideal of a uterine state of redemption (sleep, water, darkness) is at the beginning, and the serpent, guardian of water and life energy, is without beginning (*anādī*) or end (*ananta*). Viṣṇu is clearly emphasized vis-à-vis Brahmā, corresponding to the monotheistic character of the Purāṇa. But again, no single creator god is accepted.

In another myth, it is Brahmā from which everything has emerged:[47] In rapture, Brahmā creates gods, demons, ancestors, and humans. First, *tamas* emerges in him, the element of darkness, from which the demons appear. Then Brahmā gives up his body, which has brought forth the demons; this body becomes night. Then, Brahmā takes another body with a great deal of purity (*sattva*). From his mouth, the gods emerge. Since he gleams (*divyatas*), they are known as the gleaming ones (*deva*). Brahmā gives up this body, too, which becomes day; therefore, men worship the gods in the day. Then he takes a body that is all purity (*sattva*). Brahmā thinks of his sons, and thus the forefathers (*pitaraḥ*) emerge between day and night. He leaves this body, which becomes twilight. Therefore, men worship ancestors at dawn and dusk. Finally, Brahmā assumes a body that is all energy (*rajas*). This body becomes moonlight. From his organ of thought men emerge. In a similar way, he creates spirits, animals, and plants, as well as the four Vedas and so on. This myth is clearly modeled on the Puruṣasūkta hymn mentioned above. The world is created from divine bodies, in this case from Brahmā's bodies. But Brahmā is not a sole creator god either. Things get violent when the gods quarrel about their acts, and such a quarrel can take place within one's own family, as illustrated in a myth in which Brahmā curses his son Nārada because he reveals himself as a supporter of Viṣṇu or Kṛṣṇa.[48]

After Brahmā has accomplished the creation to a large extent, he wants to let the sons he created from himself shape the rest of the world. (In another myth, his sons are to continue because Brahmā pursues his self-created beautiful daughter Śatarūpā.)[49] But the sons refuse and Nārada even tells his father that everything Brahmā has created is ephemeral. Why should he get entangled in this illusory world (*māyā*)? Nārada also reveals that he is a follower of Viṣṇu. Brahmā is beside himself: He wants to extinguish Nārada's wisdom, wants to send him fifty lecherous women with whom he has to amuse himself for two hundred years in order then to become only a son of a slave woman. "And then, my child, you will again be my son, and I give you heavenly, eternal wisdom, but only because you belong to the Vaiṣṇavas and through the grace of Kṛṣṇa." Thus, Brahmā recognizes Viṣṇu's superiority, an expression of his diminished authority in the fourth ("Classical") epoch. Nārada weeps and begs his father to restrain his rage:

> That son alone who violates the principles of virtue or transcends the law of morality is cursed by his father. How could you, being a savant, have the face to curse a pious and innocent child, devoted to God? . . . Now be graciously pleased to grant me this boon that whatever life I may take, my faith in Hari may forsake me not and that the name of Hari might always

> afford me satisfaction. . . . O four-faced Brahmā, when you have cursed me (though I am innocent), you ought likewise to be cursed by me in return. . . . by the might of my imprecations, your mystic worship performed with hymns, amulets, and established methods shall disappear from the face of the world. Unquestionably you shall have to pass your days like an ordinary person who does not deserve to be worshiped. And after the lapse of three kalpas, you shall be worshiped in the proper way. O Brahmā, the only things to which you shall be at present entitled are your necessary share in sacrificial offerings and worship in matters relating to vow, etc; the rest of your privileges shall vanish. But the gods etc. shall still adore you.

The creation—as suggested here—goes on. It must continue; it must be renewed. This idea is developed fully in the doctrine of the cyclical destruction of the world and the ages of the world.

The Doctrine of the Ages of the World[50]

The best-known expression of the cyclical image of the world is the doctrine of the four ages of the world (*yuga*).[51] The calculation of time is complex and has not been handed down uniformly.[52] A common calculation is summarized in table 30. According to that, the course of the world consists of the change of unfolding (*sarga, pratisarga*) or creation (*sṛṣṭi*) and dissolution (*pralaya*), presented as day and night in the hundred-year life of the god Brahmā. Such a Brahmā day lasts from creation to the decline of an eon (*kalpa*). And every Kalpa lasts a thousand great ages of the world (*mahāyuga*), corresponding to twelve thousand god years or 4,320,000 human years, which are divided into four ages of the world (*yuga*), and each of them has a tenth long dawn and dusk, in which Brahmā (or Viṣṇu) rests. The whole thing is repeated a thousandfold, a hundred Brahmā years or 311 billion and forty million human years. When this epoch (*para*) is over, the world declines. The coarse material will again become subtle primeval material, in which the constituents are in balance, until they are shaken—either by themselves or by a divine impulse—and the cycle of the emergence and passing away of the world (*saṃsāra*) continues.

According to this calculation, the current age, the Kaliyuga, began on February 18, 3102 B.C. In the Kṛtayuga, all living creatures were satisfied and content; there was no difference between high and low creatures, no classes. Everything lived equally long. There was no hatred, no weariness. Houses were not necessary: One lived in the mountains or in the sea. But with the Tretāyuga, morals began to decline. For the first time, man had to learn duties, to bring sacrifices and appeal to several gods. Rain fell and people had to live in

TABLE 30
The Yuga Calculation of Time

Creation (*sṛṣṭi*)
1 age of the world (*mahāyuga*) = 12,000 god years = 4,320,000 human years divided into four ages (*yuga*) with the following features:

Age (*yuga*)	Kṛta	Tretā	Dvāpara	Kali
God years (including twilight Epochs)	4,800	3,600	2,400	1,200
Human years	1,728,000	1,296,000	864,000	432,000
Metal	Gold	Silver	Bronze	Iron
Guṇa (see table 15)	*sattva*	*rajas*	*rajas* and *tamas*	*tamas*
Color	White	Red	Yellow	Black
Dharma	4/4	3/4	1/2	1/4

x 1,000 years = 1 day of Brahmā (= 12,000,000 god years)
World Dissolution (*pralaya*)
+ 1 night of Brahmā (= 12,000,000 god years): world rests folded up
= 1 age of the world (*kalpa*) (= 24,000,000 god years)
Creation (*pratisarga*)

trees. In the Dvāparayuga, men became greedy, envious, contentious; morality (*dharma*) was only half as great as in Kṛtayuga. And in the current Kaliyuga, the prophetic nature of this doctrine of decadence appears, which supposedly was developed in the third epoch in the Mokṣadharma of the Mahābhārata and was also widespread in Greek antiquity[53] (hence talk of the Golden Age).

In this age, says the Bhāgavatapurāṇa,[54] the rulers are restless; they are strong only in their rage; they enjoy lying and are dishonest; they bring death to women, children, and cows; they take everything; their character is full of darkness (*tamas*), and therefore, their power is short-lived; they are also ambitious and greedy, not virtuous, and they protect the undisciplined barbarians. Under their rule, power is the only definition of virtue, sexual pleasure the only reason for marriage, seduction synonymous with wedding, lust the characteristic of femininity. Money replaces nobility. The lie wins in disputes, boldness and arrogance are synonymous with scholarship, a simple bath becomes purification. Only the poor are still honest, generosity the only virtue. Drought rules the land. Oppressed by politicians, men will hide in valleys and live on honey, vegetables, roots, fruit, birds, flowers, etc.; they will suffer from cold, heat, and rain; no one will be older than twenty-three.

The Revelations of Saint John or Dante's gloomy visions might appear much more about the end of the world, but the Purāṇa apocalypse is also a vision of horror, many of whose criteria seem to have been already realized. The Yuga doctrine may also testify to a shock in the trust in the world. Its emergence may be connected with the crises that erupted with the infiltration of foreigners into northwest India. In any case, there is much evidence of the devaluation of the present and apocalyptic visions in countless other cultures as well (Judaic, Egyptian, Iranian). Moreover, the doctrine need not be understood only as a theory of degeneration. Instead, as Heinrich von Stietencron has indicated,[55] it can also be understood as a justification for a new form of religion and a radical religious change. Its theistic orientation may also be considered evidence for this. Viṣṇu especially, who will appear at the end of the present age as a white horse (Kalkin) and save the good people,[56] is also the creator of the world in most versions:[57] At the end of the world, the earth is almost empty. For one hundred years, drought prevails. Viṣṇu then becomes Rudra, in order to destroy all living creatures and drink up all water, the water of all three worlds. A sea of flames burns up everything in all three worlds. Many different clouds emerge; Viṣṇu blows them away. The torrential rain puts out the fire. The whole world is flooded. Everything drowns in the water. For one hundred years, it rains. Viṣṇu also blows out the wind. The clouds move off and Viṣṇu rests on the serpent in the ocean. Finally, Viṣṇu assumes the form of Brahmā in order to create the world anew.

In this myth, which continues the flood theme, Viṣṇu is destroyer and creator of the world. The inevitable decline is not stopped by him, but is alleviated by the re-creation. Such a doctrine downgrades the Veda and its message of salvation in a certain way. A story of decline becomes a story of salvation, and the new form of religion, devotional religiosity, appears as the basically older—the Veda, it is conveyed, was not yet necessary in the Kṛtayuga—and superior form.

But what about the awareness of time expressed in the Yuga theory? First, it is striking that even the creator gods—either Brahmā, on whom the Yuga calculation of time is based, or Viṣṇu, who may be granted a higher share in the creation—are not free of becoming and passing away. Brahmā lived one hundred god years (or 120, according to another counting), and in the end, Viṣṇu also declines. The gods often have birthdays, but they do not die; their strength wanes and they pass away. Behind this is a deeply rooted cyclical awareness of time, which holds that life consists of an eternal return, of an eternally new expansion and contraction of the world. Thus, the Yuga doctrine is also known as the doctrine of the world cycle (*saṃsāra*). Everything passes away according to these ideas; only change itself is lasting, but only the condition beyond this change brings salvation. In the twilight epochs, when everything rests, there is a condition that corresponds to deep sleep, when something of the state of deliverance can be "experienced." This is articulated clearly in the evolution theory of the Sāṃkhya.

In this regenerative concept of the world and nature, there is hardly any room for the omnipotence of one god or the gods, even if theistic influences of devotionalism are to be noted.[58] There can be no Fall of Man and no Judgment Day either, when heaven or hell is decided. In the cyclical understanding of the world of traditional India, apocalypse, the end of the world, the complete destruction of nature is almost inevitable, but it is the work of neither man nor god, but rather of time itself. It is primeval nature or primeval material itself that expands and contracts, but can be known only through this process.

The polarity of activity and inactivity, movement and stillness, dynamic and static corresponds to the opposition of time and timelessness. Movement (also history and future, time in general) is detrimental to redemption because it brings illusion, the eternal cycle, and thus the eternal return of death. What is good and brings redemption (in Sāṃkhya: Puruṣa/spirit) is static; the disastrous (Prakṛtri/primeval material) is dynamic.[59] So, there is a "time" beyond eternal time, which fosters the sacral time.

Even in the ancient Indian understanding of nature, the distinction "animate/inanimate" depended essentially on the distinction "self-moving/fixed-in-place" (*jaṅgama-sthāvara*) or "moving/unmoving" (*sajiva/jīvat-jaḍa*, literally: "living-numb," Pāli *tasa-thāvara*).[60] This means a gradual distinction in creatures or material with or without awareness. Creatures with awareness will be reborn: Only they have an idea of time because only they are exposed to the cycle.

This awareness of time has already been mentioned a great deal: In the genealogical doctrine of salvation, the linear, natural father-son sequence is broken by the "timeless" father-son substitution, and thus the cycle of becoming and passing away is evaded. Similarly, in the Yuga theory, the sacral history of redemption is not understood as a triumph over human history, in which the end of time—as in Judeo-Christian ideas—is also the original state created by god, the indestructible, eternal paradise, but rather as a continuous repetition of change. Time brings salvation only when it has no direction, neither in a vertical line nor in a cycle. The Judeo-Christian messiah and Kalkin, Viṣṇu's appearance at the end of every Yuga cycle, are thus essentially different: In India, the apocalypse is before you, but it is also behind you. Moreover, it is hardly possible to secularize the Hindu apocalypse and make it irrational, as in the West,[61] with the threat that the decline of the world is no longer an issue for God but for man; because in India, at the end, there is not a new heavenly kingdom, but rather the beginning. Whereas the apocalypse was for a long time in Christianity the promise of redemption, in the Hindu apocalypse—paradoxical as it may sound—is the consolation of its return. Reason has no goal and therefore must remain calm and static, but not be practical or—in India—"*prakṛtical.*" The human being does not have to prove himself to avoid destruction, for this is inevitable, so the human being may identify with homeostatic time or be engrossed in it, for which the various identity forms of Hindu religiosity are open to him. He can try to achieve it spiritually: Meditation strives for timelessness to a large extent; he can strive for it ritually: The various substitutions in the sacrifice and rites of passage were constant identifications with immortality; or he can try devotionally or heroically to obtain the timelessness granted conditionally by the gods if they allow him a place in heaven or if he is deified himself. The homeostatic awareness of time is also expressed in everyday life: in the widespread habitus that everything always was—"from the beginning (*ādi*)" is a standard answer to historical questions—or that everything returns.

Cyclical and Linear Time: The Calendar[62]

Every awareness of time rests on basic experiences of time: on the one hand, on the experience of the linear time of the age, which flows into the doctrine of the stages of life (*āśrama;* see table 8); and on the other hand, on the experience of cyclical time, as expressed in the change of the day and the seasons and the stars. The awareness of temporality and thus mortality comes at the beginning of religions and their notions of redemption,[63] both of which are affected by notions of time.[64]

The significance for salvation of linear time is shown especially clearly in the ideas of creation and descendance, which are always linked to the primeval beginning—the patriarch, the ṛṣis, the ancestors—or in individual ideas of deliverance, in which liberation (*mokṣa, mukti*) represents the end without return. In these ideas, time means change, and change means death, which must be stopped by identification, managed, "defeated," by striving for a redemptive time (*in illo tempore*) beyond all change.

Soteriologically, the cyclical awareness of time is shaped fundamentally in a similar way, even though it is based on another experience of time. For, in it too, it appears that the dynamic process (Prakṛti) in the Yuga doctrine leads to decay, is apocalyptic, which the static state—in the twilight epochs, in the equilibrium, deep sleep, or cosmic slumber—is not. Perfect rest is immortality and thus highest bliss (*ānanda*). The endless cycle (*saṃsāra*) of the world can also mean salvation—from a theistic perspective: There is no "liberation" for Brahmā in Saṃsāra, only eternal birth and death.[65]

It is tempting to ascribe the linear-genealogical ideas of time of the second ("Vedic") epoch to its half-nomadic, goal-oriented lifestyle and the cyclical ideas of time to the transition to settled agriculture, but experiences of time are too fundamentally anthropological to allow such simple connections to be drawn. It is also misleading to represent cyclical and linear ideas in Indian or Christian cosmology as an expression of a basically different consciousness of time, as has been done since Hegel, by seeing the lack of historiography[66] in India as a sign of a certain attitude toward the world that does not hold (historical) acts in high regard. Soteriologically, conceptions of both time and history concern the abolition or transcendence of temporality. The religious person denies history, either because he regards it only as a divinely created transition stage or a period of probation as in Christianity, or because he seeks an identification with timelessness during his lifetime as in the Hindu religions.

In everyday life, too, cyclical and linear awareness of time are also mixed. The daily routine and stages of life mark the near or distant future on a linear time scale. But life is also oriented toward the change of nature, toward the rhythm of the day and year (see table 31).[67] Measures and calculations of time remain comparatively vague in rural areas, oriented to the sun and the stars. The sun, sand, and water clocks found in history were used only at court and by a few well-to-do merchants. The temporal segmentation of days and months mainly concerned ritual occasions; everyday life has never been strictly standardized temporally. Even today, the almost universal spread of wristwatches has hardly changed this. The simple person in India did not know the number of the year, could not tell you his birthday. That is still the case today in many places.

Change is ritualized especially in the divisions of time: dawn and dusk, the equinox, new and full moon, the change of the moon in a new constellation, the new year, eclipses of the sun and moon. It is not the proliferation of time or its continuum that demand rituals, but rather the interruptions, changes, and transitions.

As in Babylonian and many Indo-European languages, the names of the days are connected with the planets or stars. Every day is ascribed to a regent (*graha*, "grabber"): Sunday (*sūryavāra*) to the sun (*sūrya*); Monday (*somavāra*) to the moon; Tuesday (*maṅgalavāra*) to Mars; Wednesday (*budhavāra*) to Mercury; Thursday (*guruvāra, bṛhaspativāra*) to Jupiter; Friday (*śukravāra*) to Venus; and Saturday (*śanivāra*) to Saturn. Along with the two "demons" (*asura*)

TABLE 31
Seasons and Months

Months	*Seasons*
	>Vasanta (spring)
Caitra (March/April)	
Vaiśākha (April/May)	
	>Grīṣma (summer)
Jyeṣṭha (May/June)	
Āṣāḍha (June/July)	
	>Varṣā (rainy season)
Śrāvaṇa (July/August)	
Bhadrapada (August/September)	
	>Śarad (fall)
Āśvina (September/October)	
Kārttika (October/November)	
	>Hemanta (winter)
Mārgaśīrṣa/Māṅgsīra (November/December)	
Pauṣa (December/January)	
	>Śiśira (cool, pre-spring)
Māgha (January/February)	
Phālguna (February/March)	
	>Vasanta (spring)

Rāhu and Ketu, who are responsible for eclipses (they "swallow" moon or sun), the seven regents of the weekdays form the Navagraha group, which is often worshipped collectively. The Navagrahas have a direct influence on men; they can "seize" them or bring misfortune; for example, nine children's diseases are related to the Navagrahas. Therefore, it is not only important for religious ritual occasions to determine the appropriate day of the week and the time, but also to be favorably in tune with the Navagrahas. As a consequence, several temple gates have Navagraha motifs.

Religious events must not only be determined precisely, they must also be in harmony with the astronomical courses; otherwise they are considered ineffective. Specialists—astrologers, genealogists, or house priests—can be consulted for the precise temporal determination of celebrations, rites of passage, or betrothals. The care concerning calculations thus achieved is impressive, especially since the calendar for religious occasions (Pāñcāṅga) deviates from the calendar for public life, resulting in countless problems of calculation with thoroughly practical effects.

The Indian calendar is luni-solar. In a solar year of 365 days, which begins in mid-April, twelve months each have 29 1/2 days (see tables 31 and 32). The revolution of the moon around the earth is divided into twelve waxing and waning phases of fourteen lunar days (*tithi*), connected with the new or full moon (*amāvāsya* and *pūrṇimā*). Specifications of dates of festivals almost always refer to this light (*śukla*) or dark (*Kṛṣṇa*) half before or after the full moon along with the name of the solar month. Therefore, to keep the spring festival from sometimes falling in the winter in the lunar year which is five days shorter, days or months are periodically added to and subtracted from the lunar calendar according to a complicated calculation. Usually, every thirty months, a leap-month (*malamāsa*) considered disastrous is inserted, usually after Āṣāṣha or Śrāvaṇa, so that these months are then counted twice. Thus, festivals are postponed some days every year, like Easter. As a result, the Holī festival (see table 32) was celebrated on the following days in March: on the twenty-fourth in 1997, on the thirteenth in 1998, on the second in 1999, on the twentieth in 2000, and on the tenth in 2001. The luni-solar divided years are counted in different calculations of time depending on the epoch and region, of which the Vikrama era, which begins in 57 B.C. is the most familiar. But also in India, the Gregorian calendar usually applies to public life.

One example of the complicated calculations is the night of Śiva (Śivarātri),[68] which I shall discuss later in another context: According to the legal texts, every fourteenth day of the dark half of a moon month is a night of Śiva. But only in the month of Phālguna or Māgha, depending on which calendar system (*amānta* or *pūrṇimānta*) is consulted, is this day the great night of Śiva (Mahāśivarātri). In any case, the *tithi*, the lunar day, is crucial for determining the exact time of the festival. Yet, because of the myth, the natural time for Śivarātri must also be considered because a night vigil and fasts are required for this festival. The problem of harmonizing a natural time with one set by the calendar concerned the legal scholars because it is a fundamental problem:

Table 32
Frequently Celebrated Festivals (Selection)

Kp = *Kṛṣṇapakṣa* (dark half of the moon with waning moon)
Śp = *śuklapakṣa* (light half of the moon with waxing moon)

Festival	*Event*
Caitra (March/April)	
Navarātri (Nine Durgā Nights): śp 1–9	Worship of Durgās, Gaurīs, and Aṣṭamātṛkās in their temples
Rāmanavamī (Rāma's Ninth): śp 9	Celebration of Rāma's birthday in Rāma's and Viṣṇu's temples
Meṣasamkrānti (equinox): April 14	Ritual bath
Vaiśākha (April/May)	
Gaṇeśavrata (Gaṇeśa vow): kp 4	Worship of Gaṇeśa with sweets
Buddhajayantī (Buddha's Birthday): śp 15	Thanksgiving celebration in honor of Buddha
Jyeṣṭha (May/June)	
Śītalāṣṭamī (Śītalā's Eighth): śp 8	Worship of the goddess Śītalā
Āṣāḍha (June/July)	
Hariśayanī-Ekādaśī (Viṣṇu's falling asleep): śp 15	Fasting and worship of Viṣṇu, beginning of a four-month period in which weddings are considered unfavorable
Gurupūrṇimā (Full Moon of the Teacher): śp 15	Worship of one's own teacher at home and in the temple
Śrāvaṇa (July/August)	
Navagaurīpūjā (Nine-Gaurī worship): śp 1–9	Worship of the Nine Gaurīs in their temple; fasting, daily bath
Nāgapañcamī (Serpents' Fifth): śp 5	Worship of Nāgas (serpents), ritual cleaning of wells
Rakṣābandhana (binding of the demons): śp 15 (full moon)	Sisters bind a thread around their brothers' wrists to keep evil spirits away from them
Bhādrapada (August/September)	
Gaṇeśacaturthī (Gaṇeśa's Fourth): kp 4	Worship of Gaṇeśa at his shrines and temples
Kṛṣṇajanmāṣṭamī (Kṛṣṇa's Birthday): kp 8	Worship of Kṛṣṇa
Haritālikā Tīj (Haritāla's Third): śp 3	Worship of Pārvatī, Maṅgalāgaurī and other goddesses; fasting of women

(continued)

Table 32
Frequently Celebrated Festivals (Selection) (Continued)

Festival	*Event*
Āśvina (September/October)	
Pitṛpakṣa (month half of ancestors): kp 1–15	Worship of ancestors
Navarātri (Nine Durgā Nights) with Lakṣmīpūjā (on the eighth day): śp 1–9	Worship of the Durgās, Gaurī, and Aṣṭamātṛkās in their temples
Vijayādaśamī/Daśaharā (Victorious Tenth): śp 10	Ritual renewal of the victory of Durgā over the demon Mahiṣa
Kārttika (October/November)	
Hanumānjayantī (Hanumān's Birthday): kp 14	Worship of Hanumān in his temples
Divālī (Dipāvalī): kp 15 (new moon)	Light festival in honor of Lakṣmī, worship of the newly acquired Lakṣmī and Gaṇeśa figures, lighting of oil lamps and fireworks
Prabodhinī (Viṣṇu's Awakening): śp 11	Fasting
Mārgaśīrsa (November/December)	
Dattātreyajayantī (Dattātreya's Birthday): śp 15	Worship of Viṣṇu in his temples; fast day for men
Pauṣa (December/January)	
Pūrṇimā (full moon): śp 15	Processions to the temples of the four Dhāmans (main *tīrthas*)
Māgha (January/February)	
Gaṇeśacaturthī (Gaṇeśa's Fourth): kp 4	Worship of Gaṇeśa at home (with newly acquired clay figures) and in his shrines
Makara-Saṃkrānti: January 14	Winter solstice, ritual bath
Vasantapañcamī (Spring Fifth): śp 5	Worship of Sarasvatī
Phālguna (February/March)	
Mahāśivarātri (Śiva's Great Night): kp 14	Worship of Śiva, fasting, vigil, and bath
Caitra (March/April)	
Holī (color festival): kp 1	(New year's) festival to honor Viṣṇu, Kṛṣṇa, and Rādhā, throwing of bags of colored powder, visit of relatives and friends, burning Holikā figures

A Tithi often comprises two, and sometimes even three, civil or solar days (*dina* or *divāsa*). Therefore, the various measures of time must be aligned. In the case of the Śivarātri, for example, it is necessary to determine on which solar day one is to fast and stay awake. According to the generally accepted rule of connecting the solar with the lunar days (*yugmavākya*), the Tithi, which lasts until or begins at sunrise, gives the solar day its name or number. However, there are a few special problems with these calculations.

An example from the Nepalese calendar (Pañcāṅga) of the year 2040 of the Vikrama-Saṃvat time calculation may illustrate the point: In this calendar, the sacral Śivarātri day, thus the Tithi, began on Wednesday, February 29, 1984, at noon (precisely: 31 *ghaṭi* and 58 *pala,* corresponding to 12:47 Nepal Standard Time). The sacral Śivarātri day ended on Thursday, March 1, at 14:43. The sacral day thus included two solar days. According to the Yugmavākya, one had to fast and stay awake on Thursday, and in fact, in India in that year it did proceed like that. In Nepal, on the other hand, in agreement with the calendar mentioned, the festival was celebrated on Wednesday, and it was also on this day that the king appeared for the traditional worship of the god Paśupati. That means that the festival was carried out when the sacral day had not yet begun, at least partially. Naturally, this example does not deal with a special case either in Nepal or in India. A great deal depends on local stargazers who compile this calendar, and on the question of which part of the night is more highly valued, evening (*pradoṣa*) or midnight.

But the opposition to natural time is represented not only by divided, counted, ritually standardized time, as in calendar calculations, but even more the homeostatic, unconscious, mythical time: for example, the simple duration or the uninterrupted cyclical continuum. This time primarily has the character of salvation, independent of whether it concerns linear or cyclical ideas of time. Because, for the sacredness of a holiday, what is crucial for the best time and its celebration is that it be identified with a mythic, immutable time. Only then is the ritual event also a mythical one.

Unity of Space and Time: Festivals[69]

Hardly a day goes by in India when the music of celebrations is not heard in the narrow streets of the old cities or in the backyards, that does not smell of torches, oil lamps, and incense: India is a country of festivals (see table 32).[70] Many celebrations have to do with the harvest cycle, with the eagerly awaited Monsoon, with sowing and rice cultivation. And the borders and identity of a city or a neighborhood must also be reinforced by processions and rituals. On other days, the dead and ancestors must be pacified or family ties have to be reinforced. Rites of passage can assume the character of a big festival. The gods' birthdays must be celebrated. Pilgrimages to temples bring religious merit for the individual and his extended family.

Every festival is a complex space-time unity and must be understood in terms of its historical, mythological, socio-ritual, and performance references. Only then does the "meaning" of the event appear, which cannot be separated from its mythical references and those who perform, celebrate, organize, or pay for the festival. Neither myth alone nor its history or social function can explain the festival. I shall try to illustrate this with the example of the above-mentioned Night of Śiva by concentrating on the celebration at the Nepalese Paśupatinātha Temple in Deopatan in Kathmandu.[71]

The myth of Śivarātri is pan-Indian, handed down especially in various Purāṇa texts. In almost all versions, a hunter clings to a bilva tree at night in the jungle for fear of wild animals. There he stays awake all night, and from time to time, lets a few drops of water and a few bilva leaves fall—onto a Śivaliṅga covered with foliage. So, unaware and inadvertently, this lower-caste man worships Śiva by fasting, vigil, leaves, and water. This pleases Śiva so much that he offers the hunter liberation or a place near him. He thus frees the hunter from his profane life limited by death.

But, as so often, the highly traditional myth is not the motive for celebrating the festival. Among some 350 pilgrims I asked about this and other subjects during the Śivarātri in 1987, not a single one knew the story of the hunter and his unwitting worship of Śiva. Instead it was said that on this day, Śiva married Pārvatī or that Śiva was born in the Śivarātri, even though, as far as I know, no birthday for Śiva is handed down in the Purāṇic high tradition.

Thus, the content of the textual high traditional myth is not a critical motivation to celebrate the Śivarātri, at least in Nepal. Many festivals are also based on a vow (*vrata*) or are linked with a vow. Several texts determine when and in what form the celebrations are to be held. This is also true for the Śivarātri. The main subject of these ritual texts is the proper behavior of the believer. Corresponding to the myth, the Śivarātri vow refers to three central acts: vigils, fasts, and worshipping Śiva. And yet, myth and vow do not agree: In the myth, everyone, but especially—like the hunter—non-Hindus or lower-caste people or casteless people can worship Śiva; this seems to be the very core of the myth. But in the Brahmanic-Sanskritic conception of a vow, only the Twice-Born are allowed. Moreover, in the myth, the focus is on the accidental, unconscious, and inadvertent worship of Śiva; but a vow is ineffective without a previously explicit, thus intended decision (*saṃkalpa*). A contradiction may be seen here between theological claim and ritual practice; vow and myth may be seen as different, but that would be wrong: Both happen to have a share in the mythical substance of the Śivarātri, that is, the worship of Śiva at a mythically marked time and at a mythically marked place. That is the reason for the departure, for pilgrimage and vow.

Externally, the festival at the Paśupatinātha Temple is not noted for being based substantially on an individual vow. Instead it appears as a popular festival. For days before, pilgrims come here on foot, in buses, or in trucks from far away, even outside India, to worship Paśupati (Śiva). For weeks, Deopatan has been preparing for this day. The pilgrim inns are readied to accept the influx. Almost all festivals are accompanied by such a *melā,* a mixture of market and fair. Stands with all kinds of articles are erected, itinerant traders extol their wares. Everything the pilgrim needs and wants is sold, especially images of the gods or small plates for sacrificial offerings. Beggars, storytellers, ascetics, and traveling entertainers enliven the colorful and loud scene.

A pilgrimage is distinguished from the everyday worship of a deity mainly by the joys and efforts of a pilgrimage, which is made valuable and meritorious by the *darśana,* the beneficial view of a deity, in a pilgrimage site, as opposed to the *darśana* of the village and house deity, which are easier to get to. On the other hand, only in exceptional cases do pilgrims fast and they do not stay awake all night, like the hunter in the Śivarātri myth and as prescribed in the traditional texts.

Although the Śivarātri festival is in many ways a popular festival with masses of pilgrims, it basically remains a vow of the individual. It is merely the accumulation of people that lends the event the appearance of a communal celebration. Everyone comes for himself; hardly anything is celebrated in common. In any case, *Communitas* as defined by Victor Turner,[72] the experience of brotherhood and group solidarity, in contrast to the normal everyday world, appears cumulative. Common features emerge through participation in the mythical place and moment.

In the Paśupatinātha Temple, which is closed to non-Hindus, southern Indian priests and Nepalese temple assistants worship the main shrine, a five-faced Liṅga with a Pūjā that is only slightly changed from everyday worship (see table 22). Thus, conforming to vow stipulations, they worship Paśupati and other gods, not only morning and evening, but on every quarter-day and -night (*prahara*). On that day, Paśupati also receives no cooked food. It seems as if the god himself carries out a vow of fasting. Finally, the doors of the main temple remain open during the night, as an exception, as if Paśupati did not lie down to sleep.

The formal decision (*saṃkalpa*) for the temple ritual must be made by the king. In addition, a priest usually sets out for the palace to fetch the decision. Since Paśupati is the tutelary deity of Nepal, from this perspective, the festival becomes a vow of the king to keep protecting the land. In the late afternoon, the king then appears with his retinue at the Paśupatinātha Temple. During his worship, only chosen persons may remain in the area of the main temple. These also include the ascetics who have been summoned to Kathmandu to this festival by the Rānā princes in order to legitimate their rule.

Even if these factors are combined—myth, vow, the intentions of the pilgrims, the king, the Rāṇā aristocracy, and the ascetics—it is clear that they themselves are not enough to understand the "whole" significance of the festival. Only the common belief that time and place are steeped in an equal power brings the individual components together. The meeting point is not in the Paśupatinātha Temple in Deopatan and not in the night of Śiva, but rather in the fact that myth, time, place, and participants find themselves in the mythical substance of "Śivarātri," which is not a usual night since it belongs to the *other* world and the *other* time. This also applies for saints, kings, and pilgrims, but also for the site of the pilgrimage and the time of the festival.

Religious and Scientific Ideas of Time

Kurt Hübner, to whom I am indebted here too (see table 28) for basic insights,[73] introduces his book *Die Wahrheit des Mythos* with a relevant quotation from Hölderin: "It is near / And hard to grasp the god." This is precisely the problem of a religious event. If the manifestation of a god in space and time means ephemerality, then despite all closeness, the god can be grasped only with difficulty. He can be near only because he is far from the occurrence, and the occurrence brings him near only because it has itself eluded space and time. *One* means for this is the eternal return, the cyclical celebration. In myth and in mythic events, thus in festival or ritual, the immutable, eternal sameness is repeated. Not that a mythic occurrence is repeated, but rather, as Hübner says, it is "again iterated"; it is not a new edition, but rather is always the same as what constitutes its truth, the religious power. Only externally are myth, time, place, and participants different; internally, they are identical, and festivals and rituals are what produce this identity.

It is precisely the static nature of time, its non-ephemerality or in any case its sameness in return, its unmeasurability, or its mythic divisibility that guarantees the redemptive character of the ephemeral events. Timelessness, eternity, and immortality have no point in time, so that festivals can be holy only when they do not take place, but rather are always already or always again and thus do not come and go, but endure.

Pace Ernst Cassirer, Kurt Hübner, and what was said previously about the religious awareness of space, distinctions can again be determined between a religious and a scientific understanding of time: The religious notion of time admits no points of time in a time continuum, but rather only duration without the flow of time; it knows only prototypes or archetypes. It has no historical time because history means ephemerality, and only unique events. It will have no abstractions of time, only discrete events of time. Measuring time, then, is a religious segmentation only when the units themselves are singular, but not when they are equal on an abstract plane.

The religious awareness of time of the Hindu religions can with complete justification be called identificatory—and indeed from time immemorial: When the Brāhmaṇa texts say that Prajāpati was the year, this identification says only that there is no difference between god and eternal time, assuming that the year is understood as always the same year. In this understanding of time, festivals do not take place in a time, but are testimony of the one, eternal, and thus imperceptible time, which knows no end and no death.

7. Immortality in Life

ASCETICISM: LIFE IN TRANSCENDENCE[1]

Asceticism means celibacy, physical self-torture, wandering, begging, and a special diet. It is a ritualized form of climbing to transcendence and climbing out of society through a systematic control of body, spirit, and speech, with a soteriological goal aimed at the Next World. The motives and reasons why a man (rarely a woman) leaves home and family, renounces posterity, and devotes himself to a sparse life of castigation vary from one religion to another. Christian asceticism is sustained mainly by the *imitatio* of the life of Jesus and the idea of *caritas*. Something similar applies to some forms of Buddhist asceticism and the Bodhisattva ideal. The asceticism of the Hindu religions (*saṃnyāsa, tapas*), on the other hand, is directed primarily at the spiritual goal of self-liberation from rebirth or achieving "magical" powers (*siddhi*), and is usually connected to a teacher.

Asceticism is a key to understanding the Hindu religions. It was initially a peripheral phenomenon, but was increasingly integrated into the Brahmanic-Sanskritic Hindu religion or developed its own religious communities, which kept producing crucial reform impulses. The early Vedic religion did not yet know escapist asceticism, but a reform movement began in the late Vedic phase that objected to the Vedic rituals and had predominantly ascetic features. The historic Buddha Śakyamuni with his supporters or Mahāvīra, the founders of Jainism, were opposed to the Brahmans and their sacrifice ritual, and thus also to the Veda and the house fire. The reasons for ascetic reformism are controversial:[2] Internal reasons (the escapism from the sacrifice ritual and its internalization) were advanced along with acculturation processes (the clash of Indo-Aryan cultures with indigenous vagabond saints), serious socioeconomic factors (transition to settlement, agrarian surplus, city and state formation), or ecological catastrophes (famines, epidemics). Asceticism probably emerged from a mixture of Brahmanic development and non-Brahmanic influences.[3]

I shall first discuss ascetic practice and sects before I try to define the relationship of asceticism and sacrifice and thus the relationship of Brahman, priest, and ascetic.

Ascetic Practice and Sects[4]

Indian types of ascetics are extraordinarily prolific (*saṃnyāsin, yogin,* Hindī *bābā, sādhu*). Corresponding to the forms of Hindu religiosity, there are ritualist, devotionalist, mystical-spiritual, and heroic types (see table 33):[5] hermits who seek salvation, fending completely for themselves in the wilderness or in the Himalayas; begging ascetics who move from one holy place to another in organized groups; monks and nuns living in inns or monasteries (*maṭha, āśrama*); priest ascetics who perform divine worship at temples; armed, militant ascetics (*nāgā*), who had an important political function, especially in the nineteenth century; spiritual masters, teachers, and advisers (*guru, svāmī*) who behave more or less ascetically; beggar-ascetics who mortify their flesh more for show; and so on.

The ascetic who tortures himself physically attracts great attention, yet his contortions and exercises[6] have been criticized in India from the start: The historic Buddha tried them on himself, but rejected them and promulgated the middle way instead. Among the ascetics themselves, there are various views about the harshness of asceticism. They too hold physical self-mortification in high esteem: performing all eighty-four Hathayoga positions (*āsana,* fig. 22); maintaining a certain position for years, such as holding up an arm or standing on one leg, until their limbs become atrophied; crouching permanently under a dripping water pail in order to copy Śiva, who caught the Gaṅgā in his hair; sitting on beds of nails or in a thorn bush; measuring a holy stretch with one's own body for kilometers. But ascetic practices such as wandering, fasting, or monodiets (drinking only milk or eating only fruit) are also considered difficult. Ascetics pay the highest respect to the vow of silence that forbids even inner speech for years. Celibacy is considered even more difficult because it also includes avoiding lustful thoughts, sexual dreams, and nocturnal emissions. The life of the ascetic has always been concentrated on these practices, whose declared goal is one's own liberation (*mokṣa, mukti*). It concerns controlling body and mind, and withdrawing as far as possible from the normal world. Only thus is dispassion and indifference (*vairāgya*), a prerequisite for liberation, to be achieved.

The motives for an ascetic life are hard to determine. But conversations with ascetics indicate that a personal crisis was often the immediate cause: family problems, a social crisis, an exclusion from the extended family, crimes.

Table 33
Groups and Sects of Ascetics

Group/Subgroup	*Founder*	*Identifying Signs, Special Features*
Daśanāmī (Saṃnyāsī, Brahmacārī)	According to traditional understanding: Śaṃkara	Ten subdivisions: Giri, Purī, Bhārati, Vana, Āraṇya, Pārvata, Sāgara, Tīrtha, Āśrama, and Sarasvatī
Daṇḍī		Carries a stick, Brahmanic; no ordination of women
Paramahaṃsa		Scholar, Brahmanic; rare ordination of women
Nāgā		Organized in Ākhāṛās (regiments), naked, militant
Gorakhnāthī, Nātha, Aughar; Kānphaṭā	Gorakhnātha (between the ninth and thirteenth centuries)	Worshipper of Bhairava; ring in the ear
Nimbārkī	Nimbārka	Worshipper of Rādhā-Kṛṣṇa
Rāmānandī (Bairāgī)	Rāmānanda (thirteenth/ fourteenth century?)	Wear a Sacred Thread
Tyāgī, Mahātyāgī		After ash initiation (*khākdiksā*)
Nāgā, Khalsā		Naked, militant
Kābīrpanthī	Kabīr (fifteenth century)	Syncretic: worship Rāma and Allah
Gauḍīyā, Caityanites	Caitanya (1485–1533)	Kṛṣṇaite ascetics and "lay people" (Gosvāmī); occasionally transvestites
Udāsī (Nānakputra)	Śrīcandra (sixteenth century)	Worship Granth Sahib and Hindu gods
Aghorī	Kina Rāma (eighteenth century)	Use skulls as begging bowls, live on cremation squares; Kapālimukhas are considered predecessors

(a)

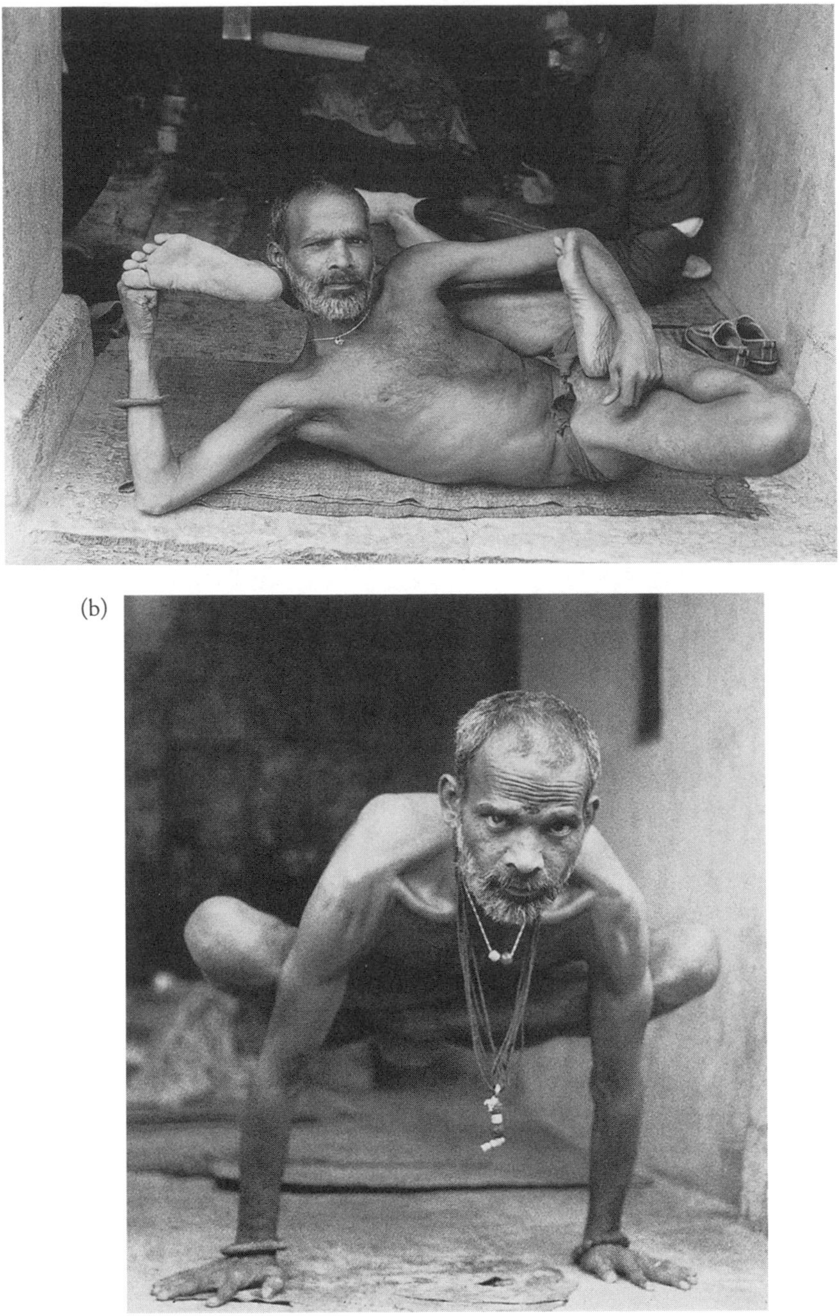

(b)

22. (a and b) The Aghorī ascetic Pāgalānanda (literally: "whose bliss is madness") in two of eighty-four yoga positions on the cremation place in Deopatan, Nepal. Photographer: A. Michaels, 1983–1984.

Now and then, fear of an arranged marriage was also hinted at. Finally, the ascetics themselves usually present spiritual reasons: the search for salvation and liberation, the desire to be near god or his charismatic leader, the Guru. Nevertheless, socioeconomic factors should not be underestimated: for members of lower castes or the poorest of the poor, belonging to a sect often forms a chance to survive and to gain social mobility. For in India, ascetics are still respected, especially when they are said to have spiritual powers, and are feared because people are afraid of being cursed. This helps the ascetics endure the malice to which they are occasionally exposed.

Ascetics are usually members of a sect. But in the Indian context, the word *sect* does not denote a split or excluded community, but rather an organized tradition, usually established by a founder, with ascetic practices. In India, there are various words for *sect:*[7] *pantha* ("way"), *saṃpradāya* ("tradition"), *saṅga* ("community"), or *samāj* ("society"). Thus, Indian sects do not focus on heresy, since the lack of a center or a compulsory authority makes that impossible—instead, the focus is on adherents and followers. Therefore, if the term *sect* is derived from the Latin *sequi* ("accompany, follow, pursue") instead of the Latin *secare* ("cut, separate"), it is acceptable. Accordingly, there is also no unified word for the places where ascetics live or sojourn; the common ones are: *maṭha* ("ascetics' inns," originally "hermits' huts"), *āśrama* ("hermitage"), *sthāna* ("place"), *vihāra* ("monastery"), and Hindī *ākhāṛā* ("gymnasium, regiment").

In the fourth ("classic") epoch, ascetics living alone were still clearly to be found more often than later on. In the texts, various ascetic groups are named, but this has more to do with the classifications of ascetic forms of life, which concern accepting food, walking sticks, emblems, etc., than with organized communities. From the fifth ("Sectarian") epoch on, organized ascetic groups guided by leaders (*mahant*) increase (see tables 33, 18, 23, and 24). They are distinguished by founders, teachers, sect signs, the colors of the garment, and ritual paraphernalia such as chains or beggar's bowls. Moreover, they each have different names and ritualized forms of greetings. If, for example, one person says "*Jaya* [greetings to] Sītā-Rāma," the other person knows that he is dealing with a Rāmānandī. Guru, age, ascetic practice, and site of the sect are crucial for determining the hierarchy in the sects. The two best-known and biggest groups of ascetics are the Śaiva Daśanāmīs and the Vaiṣṇava Rāmānandīs.

The Daśanāmīs ("followers [of the order with the] ten names"), who refer to Śaṃkara as a founder, are traditionally divided into ten sections; hence their name. Moreover, the Śaiva ascetics, who are also called "Saṃnyāsīs" or "Sannyāsīs," are distinguished by their form of asceticism. The largest groups of the Daśanāmīs are the shorthaired Daṇḍīs, who carry sticks granted only to Brahmans (*daṇḍa*) as a sign of their rank. They accept only male Brahmans—

including highly respected scholars—into their order. The shorthaired Paramahaṃsas are distinguished from the Daṇḍīs because they do not carry sticks and occasionally also allow women into their ranks. In the ascetic literature, mythical birds are called *paramahaṃsa,* who can filter out the water in milk with their beaks, and thus can distinguish between truth (milk) and lies (water). But "Paramahaṃsa" is also a kind of title that ascetics of other sects can bear.

The most radical form of asceticism of the Daśanāmīs is pursued by the longhaired, "heroic" Nāgās (literally: "naked ones"). In the sixteenth century especially, they quarreled with Moslem fakirs, and in the twentieth century achieved significance in the war of independence against the British. Even today, they appear naked at big festivals, with only spear, shield, and occasionally military orders. Their regiments (Hindī *ākhāṛā*), named after the original training sites, are strictly organized; they have several branches, some of which derive wealth from landowning and property from a previous trade in silk and other goods.

Even more radical than the Nāgās are the Aghorīs, who are understood as the followers of the historical Kāpālikā (see table 18), but whose current sect probably dates back to the founder Kina Rāma, who lived in the eighteenth century.[8] The Aghorīs express their overcoming of the world with an especially extreme behavior. They are still said to eat parts of corpses or excrement, drink alcohol and urine, cook their food on remnants of cremation wood, and smoke marijuana. In speech and manner, they appear deliberately "crazy," excessive, and exhibitionistic. The Gorakhnāthīs[9] are named after their founder Gorakhnātha, who was to supposed to have lived between the ninth and the thirteenth centuries. They are also called "Nātha" or "Nāthīs"; an important subgroup is called "Kānphaṭās," who are marked by piercing an ear at their second initiation (prior to that, neophytes are called "Aughars").

The major external sign distinguishing the Vaiṣṇava ascetics from the Śaiva ascetics is that the former paint their sect signs horizontally (*tripuṇḍra*) on their forehead and not vertically (*ūrdhvapuṇḍra*). Distinct from Śaṃkara's doctrine and referring to Rāmānuja's qualified nondualism, they teach that the highest essence (*brahman*) appears as god (*īśvara*) and that salvation during one's lifetime is not possible, but can be strived for only through a mystical-devotional union with god. Thus, salvation is mainly an act of grace of god, not just a matter of the right knowledge. This is why Vaiṣṇava ascetics usually do not deliberately take off the Sacred Thread. The worship of a god (Viṣṇu, Rāma, Kṛṣṇa) with or without their companions is intense; therefore, most Vaiṣṇava ascetics bear the name Dās ("servant"). The sect tradition of the Vaiṣṇava distinguishes four trends (*saṃpradāya*) with minor deviating doctrines, but the individual sects are known rather by the names of their founders.

23. A Rāmānandī ascetic during the long night of Śiva (Śivarātri) in Deopatan, Nepal: Wrapped in a leopard skin, he sits meditating in the middle of a "fire" of cow dung; in the foreground, an altar with the image of Śiva. Photographer: A. Michaels, 1983–1984.

The Rāmānandīs[10] (also called Bairāgīs) form the biggest group of Indian Sādhus in northern India. Their founder, Rāmānanda, is supposed to have lived in Benares in the thirteenth or fourteenth century and to have been a teacher (according to another tradition, a scholar) of the poet-saint Kabīr; but the Rāmānandī sect developed their current significance only in the eighteenth century. The Rāmānandīs have a few things in common with the Śaiva Daṇḍīs and Nāgās, such as rigid organization in regiments (Hindī *akhāṛa*) and divisions (*anī*), with which they appear in big pilgrimage festivals, arranged hierarchically and by their sacred banners. They are subdivided into wandering ascetics (*khalsā*), militant ascetics (*ākhāṛāmalla, nāgā*), ascetics rubbed with ashes (*tyāgī, mahātyāgī*), and ascetics who stay in inns (*sthānadbhārī*), with divergent forms of initiation and practices. They accept members from all castes, but in festivals, ascetics from the Śūdra caste sit in a separate row. Unlike the Daśanāmi-Nāgās, the Nāgās of the Rāmānandīs, who are subdivided into temporary residents of Tyāgīs and always-itinerant Mahātyāgīs, are never completely naked.

Along with the Daśanāmīs and Rāmānandīs, there is also a barely visible multitude of other, frequently syncretic sects. The larger groups include the Udāsīs, who worship the five main Hindu gods (*pāñcāyatana*) as well as the holy scripture of the Sikhs, the Gurugranhta; their sect is supposed to have been established by Guru Nānak (1459–1539), the founder of the Sikh religion, but the Udāsīs are supposed to have split from the Sikhs under Nānak's son, Śrīcandra. The Kabīrpanthīs[11] are also significant, especially in Benares, where their founder, Kabīr, was allegedly born in the fifteenth century as the son of a Muslim weaver. Kabīr objected to every caste limitation and worshipped both Rāma and Allah.

In many other sects, lay people dominate. In general, they are recognized as "ascetics" only by the sign of the sect on their forehead or by their behavior during certain special occasions. Most of these sects have no or hardly any caste limitations, and many are open to women. Many of them are marked by devotionalism; a few practice a distinct transvestism. Among the Nimbārkīs (also called Nimāvats), who refer to the southern Indian founder Nimbārka (twelfth century) and preach a divine love for Kṛṣṇa-Rādhā, women are even the majority, at least in Benares. Similar to them are the Vallabhācārīs, named for the founder Vallabha (ca. 1479–1531), who was born in Benares; and the Gauḍīyās, who claim the Bengali mystic Caitanya (1486–1533) as their founder.

Asceticism and Sacrifice[12]

Asceticism is self-sacrifice. This applies to ancient Indian asceticism in a direct sense in reference to the actual sacrifice: The Vedic ritual was designed essentially to achieve immortality by a way that identifies with sacrifice. To perform the ritual, it was first obligatory to be married.[13] This bond of the "immortality" of the sacrifice with the mortality of the human could be dissolved only by eliminating the "mortality" of the human or his biological origin (descendance), and thus linear time, becoming, and passing away. This happened in the ritual substitution of the son for the father during the initiation, in the substitution of the husband's for the wife's line of descent in marriage, but also by the internalization of the sacrifice in the sacrificer himself.

Immortality was not to be exposed to becoming and passing away. Thus, people began to ask themselves, why are man *and* wife, why are descendants needed for the immortality of the sacrifice? "The ancient sages, it is said, did not desire children [thinking], 'What shall we achieve through children, we who have attained this Self, this world.' They, it is said, renounced their desire for sons, for wealth, and for the worlds, and lived a mendicant's life,"[14] says the Bṛhadāraṇyaka-Upaniṣad. By uniting sacrifice and sacrificer in themselves, the Self of the ascetics became "ageless" and "deathless," as the Ātman is often called in the Upaniṣads. The tension between the finite nature of all human activities, including the sacrifice, and the goal of immortality promised by the sacrifice ritual had become unbearable for people whose search for salvation was serious. Every infant means a new death for them. As they see it, man has fallen into debt (*ṛṇa*) to gods, men, and forefathers simply by his birth, not only by his personal conduct. Rebirth and heaven are for the Twice-Born; immortality and deliverance are for us, the ascetics told themselves. Life at home with a house fire, a wife, children, and ancestors could no longer be their life; they wanted to light their internal fire in the wilderness.

Since that time, ascetics have considered their bodies mere shells, filled with blood and excrement, a sign of infirmity, age, and death. They must overcome this obstacle on the way to deliverance, and they can do this by identifying the physical body with the religious "substances" of immortality or by placing their bodies in clear opposition to the bodies of "normal" people: Thus, their hair is shaved off completely or is not cut; rubbing oneself with ashes, cow urine, or Ganges mud is considered a seat of supernatural forces. Only "normal" people have haircuts or clothing; the ascetic, on the other hand, runs around naked (*nāgā, digambara,* literally: "clad in air") or dressed only in a loincloth. The man in life eats meals, prepared with others or by others, but the ascetic takes only what he gets. As a "dead" man, he really needs no nourishment, and in fact Jaina monks are always starving to death. Other ascetics do not eat "normally," but rather fast or subsist on a monodiet; they take begging bowls of calabash or even human skulls as "plates"; they obtain their livelihood not through work, but rather by begging; they have as their "home" eternal wandering, interrupted only by the rainy season—old regulations even forbid the ascetic to go begging in the village where he was born. The rules for the ascetic in the Dharmaśāstras and Saṃnyāsa-Upaniṣads are extremely detailed: He is to take what is given him; he is not to eat with his hands, but rather, like a cow, with his mouth; he is not to go back to a house where he got a lot of good food to eat.[15]

The ascetic is in fundamental opposition to the domestic (fire) ritual. The authority to light the sacred fire is achieved through initiation, through the Second Birth. As a result of his criticism of the sacrifice, the ascetic must give up this authority and everything that has to do with the sacrifice: fire tools, cooking utensils, Vedic mantras, especially the Gāyatrī.[16] This is why, from the Brahmanic perspective, noninitiated Śūdras and women cannot be ascetics; they have nothing they can give up. An old term for ascetics is "fireless" (*anagnin*). Śaiva ascetics sometimes demonstrate giving up the authority to perform sacrifice by cutting off the tuft of hair (*śikhā),* the sign of the patrilinear descendance, and cutting the Sacred Thread in half. The medieval discussion about fire, tuft of hair, Sacred Thread, and walking stick thus touches on the basic problems of Hindu religious asceticism, which are still meaningful.[17] However, the Vedic sacrifice can also be substituted and internalized.[18] Thus, the ascetic's acceptance of food is explained as the obligatory morning and evening fire ritual:[19] Since the ascetic himself is the fire—*tapas* is the familiar expression for heat and fire as well as for asceticism—food is the sacrifice offering burned by his internal heat. Breath is also explained as the internal fire of the ascetic.[20] The sacrifice becomes self-sacrifice.

Despite all criticism, even today, Hindu ascetics spend most of the time at the fire, doing ascetic exercises, in which they sit in the middle of four fires and look at the sun as a fifth (*pañcatapas*), or sit with bowls full of hot coals on their head. The sacrifice fire is indeed given up, but another fire (Hindī *dhunī*) remains the center of ascetic life: both home and temple.[21] Therefore, the ashes (*vibhūti*) with which many ascetics demonstratively rub themselves, are holy; occasionally, they give them to lay people as redemptive gifts (*prasāda*) or even aphrodisiacs.

Ascetics die a social and ritual death.[22] As a sign of that, certain members of the Daśanāmī sect have to lie on the bier at their ordination. The marriage of an ascetic is considered dissolved; many legal scholars even allow the wife to remarry. The possessions the ascetic left behind are distributed as an inheritance, yet ascetics themselves are no longer entitled to inherit. They are even released from the duties to the ancestors. In a certain respect, they are treated as Pretas (see tables 12–13), the liminal deceased, whose souls have not yet found their place.[23] During his lifetime, the ascetic moves up in the tripartite group of the forefathers (*pitaraḥ*) and thus lets the great-grandfather rise into the group of the generalized deceased (*viśve devāḥ*). The Saṃnyāsa-Upaniṣads even say that an ascetic saves sixty generations before and after from disaster.[24]

These examples show how radically a large part of Hindu asceticism tries to eliminate the natural and mortal. Ascetics have to and want to put their claim outside of society, but not to be involved in family discord and group rivalries. Max Weber correctly called this asceticism otherworldly in comparison with the Protestant innerworldly asceticism of work. Indian ascetics hardly work. They are occasionally temple priests, organize chanting and festivals, maintain social institutions, gymnastic exercise sites, or schools, and are asked now and then to help with medical, psychological, sexual, or even financial problems; but most ascetics beg and live on the economic surplus of others. Nevertheless, Indian ascetics contribute indirectly to society, precisely because they stand in that other world that fosters their charisma.

As Jan Heesterman has explained, the ascetic way corresponds to the internal logic of the ancient Indian sacrifice. Under changed socioeconomic relations, this must necessarily lead to the substitution of the sacrifice, its individualization and internalization: "The point I want to stress is that the institution of renunciation is already implied in classical ritual thinking. The difference between classical ritualism and renunciation seems to be a matter rather of degree than of principle. The principle is the individualization of the ritual, which could not but lead to its interiorization."[25] In fact, only by substituting self-sacrifice for sacrifice, by purifying the search for redemption of all social aspects, primarily descendance, and also in some cases of the gods, could man be identified wholly with the religious substance of immortality, self-deification succeed, and immortality be possible not only in the Next World, but right here on earth.[26]

THE SALVATION OF IDENTIFICATIONS[27]

What links rites of passage, norms of purity, criteria of hierarchy, forms of religiosity, and notions of the Other World in the Hindu religions? In the preceding sections, I repeatedly emphasized the salvation reference of descent and the Identificatory Habitus as cornerstones primarily of the Brahmanic-Sanskritic Hindu religion. It is time now to pull the threads together. In this concluding part, I develop the following summarizing trains of thought: *Pace* Louis Dumont, my premise is that the Hindu religious society is characterized mainly by the social system of the extended family and subcastes. Membership in these groups is determined by kinship criteria, primarily by the ideal of a "pure" patrilinear origin. Throughout great economic changes, this criterion of descent is maintained because it forms the crucial reference to salvation as a justification for sacrifice. This results in (purity) norms concerning contact of the individual and the extended family with other extended families. Since the status of the extended family acquired by birth can be endangered by wrong or excessive contacts, there is an ideal of the autonomy of extended families, which leads to the avoidance of interfamily contact. By making it possible to substitute, individualize, and internalize the sacrifice ritual descent, because of internal religious and socioeconomic changes, not only did Hindu religious asceticism develop, but so did the Hindu religions and the Identificatory Habitus that shapes their culture.

In this summarizing analysis, I return to the notion of god, on the one hand because it represents the most clearly defined difference from ideas shaped by Christianity; and on the other, to raise the question of how Hindu religions have contributed to a "culture of humanity."

The Socioreligious Function of Norms of Purity

The most important feature of Hindu religious society is the caste system, whose norms mainly concern contact between subcastes and extended families. There are duties of the extended family and the subcaste, but there are hardly any general duties. In ethical terms, a man is a tanner, a cloth merchant, a Brahman, a member of his extended family, but hardly a "mere person."[28] Even before the gods, not everyone is equal; and despite a few Hindu theological tractates that do claim this, socioreligious acts (entrance to the temple, selection of priests, etc.) say something else. An extended family, with its socioreligious forms and norms of conduct, primarily the rules of marriage that are strictly oriented to patrilinearity, and the conformity of the ritual, cannot be determined. Thus, the stylization or ritualization of everyday life shaped by norms of purity is striking. In many ways, food is regulated by dietetics, the acceptance of food by norms of commensality, work by professional norms specific to castes.

Such deep-seated standardization, stylization, and discipline of everyday life, which are codified in the Brahmanic-Sanskritic Hindu religion, are reminiscent of the "civilizing process" that Norbert Elias and Rudolf zur Lippe elaborated for the West.[29] Elias traced this transition from constraint by the other to constraint by the self to the centralization of power. In India, too, stylization with respect to life begins at the end of the second epoch, especially in the centralized monarchies of the fourth epoch. In India, too, the process of civilization is a process of individualization, of advancing boundaries of shame and embarrassment, an internalization of social boundaries. But in India, to this day, the norms of purity have also remained as strategies of demarcating extended families. Thus, only to a small extent can the individual determine whether he personally feels impure by greetings, touches, or feedings. And yet, pollution is not external, but rather a bodily change or a mental and physical quality. Even love, grief, or hatred can happen to the individual and thus the extended family (and therefore must be given away with impure gifts)—through one's own misbehavior but even more as a happenstance. Anyone who pollutes must not purify himself, but the polluted person; not to feel pure, but rather to be pure for his extended family. Purity, therefore, is defined mainly in collective terms.

Moreover, it can get lost, so one must strive to preserve it. Only to a small extent is the social status of purity—through the Karma doctrine—the merit of the individual; it is primarily obtained and passed on by birth. In this life, one cannot essentially improve it but can only preserve it. One gets rid of received impurity by purifying acts and by gifts that take away impurity. Many high-caste people begin the day with a ritual bath, personal hygiene, and prayers, to protect against the possibly of polluting the day with contacts. Many bathe when they come home, not only to get rid of the dirt of the street, but also to be pure again for meals.[30] The status of purity is best preserved by avoiding the contact that endangers it. This is done most extensively by ascetics, since they rise out of social life and therefore claim the purest status. Ascetics should go on wanderings alone, be indifferent to everything, not greet anyone, and not ask for alms.[31] "Those who are the least worldly remain the most pure—they avoid contact with other castes, restrict the foods that they eat, are, ideally, sexually continent, and spend much time worshipping gods while in a state of ritual purity," writes Edward B. Harper.[32]

Contact brings pollution; avoiding contact brings purity. This principle has led to placing the Brahman ascetic, the escapist, on the highest rung of the socioreligious hierarchy. Declan Quigley notes that the Brahman is supreme only when he floats in a "cloud of transcendent ethereality," and he intends this comment as a criticism of Dumont.[33] But Declan Quigley overlooks the point that is grasped precisely by Edmund Leach:[34] Only when the Brahman becomes depersonalized is his own ideal—graphically clear in the father-son substitution of the initiation—of "embodying" immortality or the Brahman realized concretely. The ambiguity of the position of the Brahmans—scholars or Veda authorities or priests on the one hand, ascetics on the other—is that they claim this ideal of immortality, but cannot live either as (ideal) Brahmans or as ascetics. They remain mortal men, but their ideal of immortality is not affected by that. Even if various boxing associations compete for the title of world champion, the ideal of the best boxer remains intact. Similarly, the fact that very different social groups (from scholars to death priests) call themselves Brahmans confirms the ideal of the Brahman. But for most of society, this ideal exists only when it is no longer linked to a category of persons, thus when it is abstracted and biological origin is removed, when *it* (not he, the Brahman) is floating in the "clouds of transcendental heavenliness." The Brahman, as *he*, is not the Brahman, as *it,* even when he bears the charisma of the Brahman—as Max Weber would say. Confusing these two ideals is one of the most disastrous errors of Indian sociology influenced by Dumont.

Thus, the definition of purity is that nothing is mixed. That applies to the Varṇas, the subcastes, the extended families, but also to the whole physical and mental world, the universe, the gods, even trees and stones. Mixing happens through contact (touching, feeding, greeting, and so on) and through temporal and spatial changes, alterations, or transitions. Contact and change are detrimental to purity. Or vice versa: Impurity is best avoided through lack of contact and statics, through an identification with the unmixed, unchanged, and therefore immortal Vedic sacrifice. This basic idea of the Brahmanic-Sanskritic Hindu religion has had a lasting influence on Hindu society; it can be seen on many levels, as in the Guṇa theory of Sāṃkhya philosophy: The primeval material (*prakṛti*) loses its state of highest purity by going into motion. It goes into motion because it comes in contact with individual souls of spirits or individuations (*puruṣa*) and thus receives names and shape, although it itself is amorphous and has no features. If it is static and without contact, it is pure; if it is in motion, it is mixed and thus no longer pure. Therefore all manifestations are explained as mixtures of three features (*guṇa*): (1) *sattva* ("pure, true, good, virtuous, happy, white"); (2) *rajas* ("dusty, passionate, violent, egoistic, red"); and (3) *tamas* ("dark, gloomy, fearful, black"). This is a system of categories widespread in Hindu religions; it is found in rules of food, in the Varṇa system, where the Brahmans are characterized by *sattva,* the Kṣatriyas by *rajas,* the Vaiśas by *rajas* and *tamas,* the Śūdras only by *tamas,* or in the assessment of the age of the world (see table 30). Typically, only in the creator god Brahmā and the absolute (*brahman*) are the features unmoving and thus unknowable, but even the other gods have features through their contacts and are thus no longer wholly pure.

Thus, impurity is mixture; purity is the preservation or reproduction of the condition of nonmixture.[35] Purity happens with water (the clear, unmixed liquid) and fire, but also with ashes (the end product of the eternal fire of the sacrifice and ascetic) and the products of the holy cow, especially with a mixture of milk, sour milk, clarified butter, cow urine, and dung (*pañcagavya*). In addition, the ideal is to be able to filter the unmixed out of a mixture by digestion or like the Paramahaṃsa ascetics, who have the ability to separate water out of milk. Or physical gates are separated: The mouth is sealed for vows of silence and fasts, the Sacred Thread is renewed, the head is shorn. Or purity happens in the sacrifice ritual by the identification with the unmixed sacrifice or Veda in the prayer, mantra, or vow. Radical avoidance of contact means celibacy and renunciation of intimate contact. Reproduction, on the other hand, means sexual mixture and thus a far-reaching contact, which is why marriage is especially to be regulated ritually. In many religions, biology and sexuality are debased. But often the religious solution to that is to view purity as a matter of transcendence, which is not possible in this world; life is then only a preparation for the condition of purity in the Next World, where contacts are no longer necessary. Therefore, purity must be free of everything ephemeral, secular, mortal. The solution that India has to offer is special: In the Hindu religions, especially in Brahmanic-Sanskritic Hinduism, there is complete purity also during one's lifetime, since man can overcome his human existence through a complete identification with purity.

Descent and Autonomy

Thus, Hindu society is a caste society and a caste society means specific norms of purity for extended families. The purity status the individual receives at birth must be protected because it relates to a salvation ideal of the autonomy of the extended family. Why does this ideal exist? Why is it still so significant today?

In the second epoch, descent formed the basis of solidarity, as is usually the case in stateless but already segmented clans and tribes.[36] For this period, it is not the totem animal that is sacred, but rather the ancestor. It is he who establishes the sacred community of tribe and extended family. Such a community, as was plausibly represented by Emile Durkheim and which can also be shown for India, resembles a legal community favored by one of the gods or by the respective Dharma. On the other hand, a violation of the norms of this community means a violation of its holiness. The social meaning of many acts is aimed simply at maintaining the norms and thus the stability of the extended family, but not of the society as a whole. *There is no one common heaven for everyone.*

Descent conceived as patrilinear fixes the community at the time of its founding, at the patriarchs, and at the origin of their emergence. The ancestors, the forefathers, and prehistoric times are the community point of reference and produce the feeling of belonging together. The prominent significance of the strictly patrilinear and sometimes genealogical and fictive descent took shape in Vedic times, when no institutions yet protected life, when survival was hardly possible without belonging to such an often autarchic group. *The way to heaven leads through the forefathers.*

The Arthaśāstra of the Kauṭilya clearly formulated the extent to which the relative Dharma and the ideas of salvation are based on origin: The paterfamilias should live according to his own Dharma (*svadharma*) and within his class, but should marry outside his line of descent (*gotra*); what are considered general obligations are "only" ethical norms, such as not wounding human creatures, (love of) truth, or decency (*śauca*), but these do not lead to heaven and infinity (*anantya*); what does lead to heaven is only performing relative and contextual duties according to social membership, while disregard for this commandment means doom.[37] The sacral texts of the second ("vedic") epoch deal intensively with achieving heaven, winning life, and eliminating death from the ritual. Immortality is thus overcoming the biological aspects of man, and ultimately also descent. *The Laws of Manu* says clearly: "The offerings into the fire for the embryo, the birth rites, the ceremonial haircut and the tying of the belt of rushes, wipe away from the twice-born the guilt of the seed and the guilt of the womb. By the study of the Veda, by vows, by offerings into the fire, by acquiring the triple learning, by offering sacrifices, this body is made fit for ultimate reality."[38] *Heaven means victory over mortality (of origin).*

The significance for salvation of descent continues even during the great changes of the second to the fourth epoch, as social relations become increasingly reified. Once again, I list the key terms: contact with the indigenous population, settlement, cities, monarchies, bureaucracy, government institutions, agrarian surplus, division and specialization of labor, interregional trade and production of goods, greater individualism, and religious freedom of choice. Why did descent remain so important to achieve heaven or immortality?

The answer is not simple, especially since the religious cannot merely be reduced to the nonreligious without losing something essential. For Indo-Aryan extended families, clearly only one way remained between extremes: either ghettoization with the danger of isolation and economic stagnation or assimilation with the danger of dissolving the socioreligious compound. In any case, the cohesion of the former tribal bands was considered inalienable despite altered economic conditions, clearly because it constituted the crucial part of social identity. (This is comparable to [modern] strategies of demarcation such as racism, apartheid, ethnicity, or racially based nationalism, which also propagate ideologies of purity to maintain an identity that is usually already lost.) Along with socioeconomic changes came a reinforcement of the socioreligious demarcations vis-à-vis the other, usually indigenous population groups: The four-stage Varṇa ideology and the Second Birth arose as ritual fault lines, along with descent in the initiation, Gotra transference in marriage, professional demarcations in social stratification, and purity demarcations in social contact—in short, the so-called caste system. The religion of the Vedic clans and tribes developed into a religion and ideology of the elite and the upper classes.

Despite these epochal socioeconomic upheavals, the prominent significance of the genealogical reference to salvation remained and was extended, as illustrated by a few examples: It is a persistent idea that the ancestors were dangerous to the survivors if the Varṇas, subcastes, and extended families were mixed improperly: "To hell does this confusion bring the family and those who slay it; for when the ritual offerings of rice and water fail, their Fathers fall degraded," says the Bhagavadgītā.[39] Because of the genealogically constructed ideal of salvation, there is considerable pressure to produce a son. For the primary marriage, whose main social obligation is the birth of this son, a Brahman priest is required in any case, because this is the only way the paternal line remains preserved; for other rituals, the "lower" subcastes do not always call on a Brahman. Finally, in practice, caste exclusion occurs rather seldom, a procedure is usually handled discreetly or is silenced, and there are countless means for purification; but when a pregnancy occurs after the death of the husband and endangers the descent, this almost always leads to caste exclusion.[40]

The question still remains of how a genealogical goal of salvation oriented toward an ancient ideal of origin could continue to exist, even though social conditions have not supported it for some time. Buddhist, Jain, and other reform movements have radically attacked descent as a prerequisite for all salvation and thus provided proof that religious development in India could have taken a different direction. With these religious alternatives, a profound critique of the ancient ideal of salvation connected with biological origin soon arose: Descent in the sense of biological origin does not overcome mortality, but rather produces (new) birth and (new) death; genuine salvation, on the other hand, means immortality or eternal life, in which there is never (re)birth or (re)death. Yet, the reference to salvation of descent in Hinduism proved to be so strong that it could fend off these attacks to a certain extent. How was that possible? My answer is: only because biological descent was replaced by a fictive one through the method of identification practiced by the sacrifice ritual.

Those who deal professionally with immortality, priests and theologians, have the highest authority in these questions. Eschatology and soteriology, assurance of salvation and order of salvation are their domain, and even kings must bow. The way to salvation offered by the Vedic priests was bound up with descent and belonging to the clan; it was inherited. Only by gradually substituting biological descent ritually with a fictive one could the Brahmans maintain their influence and yet preserve their socioreligious superiority vis-à-vis other religious messages. One way was to abolish the difference between sacrifice and the sacrificer in self-sacrifice. The sacrifice does not remain a communal, congregational event of the clan, but rather becomes a private matter between priest (Brahman) and sacrificer (*yajamāna*). According to ancient doctrines, only Brahmans can have the salvation of the sacrifice; it is personal knowledge, the Veda, handed down in priestly extended families. Others could participate only if they also became Brahmans, if they received initiation, if they were identified with the Veda in the Second Birth and were integrated into the Brahman line of descent. With this identification, however—according to the principle—descent was removed by autonomy.

Thus what may be the only dogma known to the Hindu religions, that is, the genealogical reference to salvation, was solved on a "higher," abstract level, and yet remained preserved—as an identificatory maxim. From the end of the second ("Vedic") epoch, salvation could no longer remain reserved for only one descent group, but other means to obtain heaven, the Other World, or immortality were hardly available—to the Brahmans. Consequently, what remained were only the substitution of descent and the ritual identification of other strata with the Brahmans, ultimately only the method of equivalence itself.

The Logic of the Identifications[41]

Thus, since the end of the second epoch, it can be said that the true Brahman is not the born Brahman, but rather—depending on the form of religiosity—an honest, ascetic, knowing, god-fearing, brave man. For, since the true Brahman must no longer be a born Brahman, the rigid birth reference of the Varṇa—and Gotra system—is broken, but need not be given up entirely. Thus, the salvation-related, sacrifice-identificatory goal of equating oneself with the Brahman could be replaced by wisdom that casts doubt on descent itself. It became a freely available method of identification with salvation. On the other hand—as in early Buddhism—ignorance (*avidyā*) was responsible for becoming and passing away, for mortality. Finally—at the high abstract level—descent was replaced by knowledge about immortality on earth.

Knowing about salvation itself and the changed socioreligious framework conditions penetrated the independence of identifications and therefore made it easier to replace genealogically determined Brahmans with abstract "Brahmans." It led almost necessarily to internalization. Even the ancient Brāhmaṇa texts assumed the premise of the sacrifice ritual that man is the sacrifice. This recurring equivalence is based among other things on the recognition that only man is not sacrificed, but rather sacrifices himself;[42] everything else could be a sacrifice offering. In the substantive thinking of that time, there also had to be a common feature between sacrifice and man: a substance, "immortality," which is neither the sacrifice nor only man, but which makes man and sacrifice identical. The substance, "sacrifice"—always stated explicitly—is immortality because it is the settled order or Dharma (derived from the verbal root, *dhṛ*, "to hold, support"), opposed to life and death, becoming and passing away. Man is immortal because he has a self that survives the mortal remains. As Jan Heesterman puts it: "In Vedic-Brahmanic thinking, this order is the sacrifice which represents the dynamic of emerging and passing away, life and death as a cyclical process, and which is identified with the self of all living creatures and all gods. Therefore, sacrifice and soul are closely connected."[43] Since the self could be identified with the sacrifice and the sacrifice with the substance "immortality," both the self and the sacrifice had to be withdrawn from the mortal world. The paradox of the mortality of immortality allows only two ways out: (a) the real, immortal self (or sacrifice) is basically another self (or sacrifice), for example, the All, the Brahman, or immortality; or (b) the real, immortal self is a nonself. The first way follows Brahmanism, the second follows Buddhism.

The first way is clearly articulated in the early Upaniṣads: "In the beginning this world was only *brahman,* and it knew only itself (*ātman*), thinking: 'I am *brahman.*' As a result, it became the Whole. Among the gods, likewise, whosoever realized this, only they became the Whole. It was the same also among the seers and among humans. . . . This is true even now. If a man knows 'I am *brahman*' in this way, he becomes this whole world. Not even the gods are able to prevent it, for he becomes their very self (*ātman*). So when a man venerates another deity, thinking, 'He is one, and I am another,' he does not understand. As livestock is for men, so is he for the gods."[44]

Belief becomes knowledge, the self becomes deity, the gods are deprived of power, mortality is dealt with purely intellectually. Once detached from a sacrifice ritual context and the demand of descent, the method of substitution was abstracted and finally became customary, and thinking and acting in a certain way developed into ritual, spiritual, devotional, and heroic methods of identification with immortality. It entered the triumphal procession as an Identificatory Habitus, as I have tried to show in the previous chapters: in the father-son substitution and the fictional descent during the initiation: "The father is the same as the son, and the son is the same as the father";[45] in the Gotra substitution of the wife in marriage; in the oceanic feeling of life—which could be said to level everything; in the sacrifice ritual substitution practice and its chain of identification (father = son = Veda = sacrifice = fire = verse meter = father . . .); in "connections" (*bandhu*) and "appropriateness" (*sāmānya, sammita*) of the sacrifice,[46] and of the sacrifice symmetry and isometry of the altars (man as measure of all things); in the "secret" Upaniṣad doctrines, whose center is shaped by equivalences and substitutions;[47] in the nondualism of spiritualism with the emphasis on the Brahman-Ātman identity; in the equitheistic notion of god with its collective (inclusivist) identification of "foreign" gods; in the equivalences of gods' names; in the "avoidance" of history through the homochronic notion of time, its eternal cyclicalism; in the substitution of pilgrimage for penance in the awareness of space; in the means of equalizing a "failed" or wrong, i.e., unbalanced, identification through religious gifts; in the ascetic man-god identification with the paradox of the mortality of immortality.[48]

The many forms of the Identificatory Habitus and the typical cognitive patterns of the Hindu religion can be schematized as in table 34.

Cases 1 through 9 are balanced, equal identifications; they lead to salvation. On the other hand, numbers 10 and 11 are lopsided identifications that mean disaster, hierarchy, defect, or impurity. "Identity" and "identification" are also to be distinguished; the first term indicates a relation (*bandhu, nidhāna, sāmānya, saṃpad, saṃkhyāna,* etc.); the second is the operation derived from it. The term *identifying* is not used in this context because of its psychological undertone.

The form and context of the equivalence established are crucial. According to Ludwig Wittgenstein, in the extreme case, A = A is tautological, and A = B is contradictory.[49] In fact, it depends on the scope and form of the agreement. In Wittgenstein, this leads to conceptual "family resemblances,"[50] as they are known in every dictionary: The German word *Heimat* means the same thing as the English *home* only in some cases. Nevertheless, the equation *Heimat* = *home* fills a function. A logical identity inheres only in few "is" sentences, that is, when (a) the copula "is" can be replaced by "is the same as"; (b) both sides of the equation can be exchanged without changing the meaning ([A = B] = [B = A]); and (c) one side of the equation is a singular (proper name, demonstrative noun, pronoun, etc.).[51]

Logical identities are the exceptions in religious texts. Instead, there are equivalences that are inferred only when (a) the secret or sacral connections are known; (b) the religious premise that the part is the whole is respected; and (c) the performative part of the sentences (the emphasis, the sacrifice context, the speaker, etc.) is included. In such a context, the sentence "Indra is a bull" means neither that Indra is called "bull" nor that he is like a bull, but that Indra and bull have the religious substance of "strength." Thus, they are not like each other—Indra is not as strong as a bull—but rather, in this context (!), they are in fact identical; which is why, if it is known, the religious substance of "strength" can be used ritually. Similarly, the Chāndogya-Upaniṣad says that one eats "heat" (not hot food), which becomes a third speech, which is why the equation speech (*vāc*) = heat (*tejas*) is valid.[52]

TABLE 34
Variants of Identifications

Number	*Formula*	*Operation*	*Example*
1.	$A = B$	(Defining) identification, equivalence	The sacrifice is (means) the man; the sacrifice is equal to the man.
2.	$A \approx B$	Analogy	The sacrifice is similar or equal to the man.
3.	$(B) = A$	Cryptic identification	The man is basically the sacrifice.
4.	$A = B = C$	Serial identification	The sacrifice is the man, the man is the Veda. . . .
5.	$a = [A = B]$	Inclusivist identification	The sacrifice is everything and thus also the man.
6.	$A \supset B$	Substitutive identification	The sacrifice can be replaced by or in the man.
7.	$a = A$	Expanded identification	The sacrifice is everything.
8.	$A = a$	Compressed identification	Everything is in the sacrifice.
9.	$A + B$	Paired identification	The sacrifice and the man necessarily belong together.
10.	$A \nearrow B$ $A \searrow B$	Hierarchical identifications	The sacrifice is bigger (smaller) than the man.
11.	$A = A_1, A_2$	Dismembered identification	The sacrifice is the sum of its parts.

The schematizations of table 34 are no doubt suggestive and so simple or abstract that they can be proved almost everywhere. Lucien Lévy-Bruhl, Arthur M. Hocart, Ernst Cassirer, Kurt Hübner, and others[53] have also referred to the logic and function of such religious identifications, analogies, and equivalents. Lévy-Bruhl spoke of the essential identity between reproduction and model—"the Bororós *are* Araras" is a famous standard example taken from Karl von der Steinen[54]—that leads him to his "Law of Participation" (*loi de participation*). Hocart saw the ritual as working only because it was considered possible that one was equal with something else and thus affected it: "By effecting this equivalence men are enabled to control whatever has been allotted to them."[55] Influenced by Lévy-Bruhl, Cassirer[56] also says that "for myth every perceptible similarity is an immediate expression of an identity of *essence*," that "All the relations of mythical space rest ultimately on this original *identity* [of big and small]."[57] He also refers to analogy magic that is often proved in ethnography. Hübner, influenced in turn by Cassirer,[58] talks of "substantial units" in mythical thinking and a "principle of analogy."[59]

What is common to all these authors is that they emphasize the distinction between identificatory (magic, analogous) and symbolic thought:[60] B is not expressed by A, B is not represented by A—B is consequently not a symbol of A—but rather A *is* B, in a very real sense.[61] This identity is based on the religious principle that the *tertium quid* itself cannot be known or produced because it belongs to another, numinous world, to which there are no epistemological bridges. This also applies to the Hindu religions: The sacrifice is the man because both share the same common substance, which itself is neither only man nor only sacrifice. "The sacrifice is the man" is therefore a (ritual) program and method, which is based less on experience or even revelation than on a (secret) knowledge of (secret) identities. If it is known of the sun that it basically does not go down, the person who knows can produce this identification and use it for himself: "In fact the sun never sets. Nor does it set for him who has such knowledge. Such a one becomes united with the sun, assumes its form, and enters its place,"[62] so that he does not set either.

The analogies, equivalents, and identifications have often been demonstrated for India—from Sylvain Lévi and Hermann Oldenberg, through the debate on inclusivism, to Jan Heesterman, Michael Witzel, Brian K. Smith, and Albrecht Wezler. The early authors, influenced by the ethnological material of James George Frazer or Edward B. Tylor, tended to see the ancient Indian sacrifice identifications as elaborated variants of the archaic and magic analogy of homeopathy,[63] if they did not deny them all coherence anyway. They misunderstood that the ancient Indian ritual—aside from explicit damage rites (*abhicāra*) of the Atharvaveda—is hardly performed to affect another person or thing, but rather to construct a world that is identical with the (world of) immortality.

Influential, but theoretically overestimated in Indology, is the discussion of inclusivism triggered by Paul Hacker,[64] which he defines thus: "Inclusivism means that one declares that a central idea of a foreign religious or ideological group is identical with one or another central idea of the group to which one belongs oneself. Usually inclusivism includes the explicit or implicit statement that the foreigner who is declared identical with one's own, is subordinate or inferior in some way. Moreover, proof of that is that the stranger who is identical with one's own is usually not taken in."[65] Hacker has also said that inclusivism can be "a special identification with a special intention," and thus, in short, cites the "Vedic practice of identification" as an example.[66] In the same volume, Albrecht Wezler pointed to the clear parallels between Vedic identifications and Hacker-ite inclusivism.[67] He thus characterized the inclusivist form of thought as "a nonmarginal element of the continuity of the Vedic time in later India,"[68] as I too draw a big arc from the sacrifice ritual identifications to the still currently tangible Identificatory Habitus. Indeed, Wezler—continuing Paul Thieme's study of *ādeśa* (substitution, substitute)[69]—does not want to talk of identifications but of substitutions; in another place, he proposes the term *substantialism.*[70] In conceptual preferences, I can follow neither Hacker nor Wezler. The Vedic texts generally produce only equivalents; depending on context and practice, the concern is thus with the forms of identifications listed in table 34, including inclusivist (number 5) and substitutive (number 6) forms. *Identification* is the generic term, and like most equations in the sacrifice texts, relates to acts; therefore it is preferable. Moreover, there are still equivalents as metaphors and metonymies, which are largely omitted.

More recently, Michael Witzel and Brian K. Smith have pointed out the significance of Vedic identifications.[71] Their merit is to have taken seriously the significance of the connections and homologies and to disprove the long-prevailing opinion that these were wild fantasies (Max Müller: "Their chief content is prattle and—what is worse—theological prattle").[72] Yet, neither of these authors proves the concept of identity or identification as rigorously as Wezler did with scientific theoretical and philological arguments.[73] Moreover, Smith also commits the error of trying to win a solid point where only method itself counts. Thus, in *Classifying the Universe*, he takes the category of the original tripartite *varṇa* scheme as a hub of all Vedic identifications referring to fauna, flora, time, and space; such a claim has to founder since the material is too heterogeneous and—because of the various Vedic schools—too contradictory. Smith wants to understand the identifications as resemblances and explicitly rejects the notion of identity.[74] But he fails to understand that the Vedic identifications are hardly derived from observation of nature or from experience, and thus do not try to convey views of reality or to grasp "reality," but rather produce them. It is not identities that are desired, but rather identifications.

Thus, neither causality nor experience is the key concept for understanding the Vedic chain of identification, but rather transcendence and immortality. No one has elaborated this as convincingly as Jan Heesterman in a review of

Brian K. Smith's *Reflections on Resemblance, Ritual, and Religion* (1989).[75] In that review, Heesterman explains again why the prevailing identifications and references in the Vedic ritual are independent and shaped precisely by the permeability of Hinduism. Religion, according to Heesterman, breaks out of real life in order to create its own world. Only in a ratiocinative construction of equivalences is it possible to produce identities with that world. Therefore, the Vedic identifications are not a mystery, but rather explicit equivalences that can be known, taught, and learned.[76] This knowledge was detached from society in an axial breakthrough (not dated by Heesterman), because the identification with the immortal world becomes more problematic the more it is carried out in the mortal world. In addition, the knowledge was individualized and was no longer a matter of the community—so much so that it was not even necessary anymore to carry out the sacrifice: "It is only required to be known."[77] The central figure was no longer the sacrificer, but rather the expert on the identifications, "the one who knows (such things)"—a standard formula in early and middle Vedic texts—who had the wisdom, the Veda. Heesterman adds that this construction almost necessarily had to lead to pushing the initiate out of the world, too, to becoming an ascetic, since uniting worldly immanence and otherworldly transcendence in oneself was an insoluble problem that applies more to people in the world, the Brahmans as priests. With the radical internalization of the search for salvation, with their breaking out of society, with their individualization—Louis Dumont also saw individual religious realization in India as possible only outside of society[78]—it was understandable how "transcendent Vedic ritualism could permeate Hindu society,"[79] and why the Hindu religions neither could nor would define themselves with clear boundaries.

With the concept of the Identificatory Habitus, I go a step further than Heesterman, since I let knowledge "break out" not only from society, but also from the Brahmanic-Sanskritic Hindu religion. Heesterman and Smith limit a general form of thought to the Veda and thus construct a kind of canonization of Hinduism, whose existence they also challenge.[80] But the form of thought is a general one: Infinity cannot be expressed with finite means, immortality through mortality. Or in the worlds of Raimon Panikkar, whom I will discuss soon: "Inasmuch as man *is,* God is not; insofar as God is, man is not. . . . The relation between the temporal and the eternal cannot be expressed in terms of being."[81]

Indeed, in India, no one tries to solve the paradox of the mortality of immortality; it is rather to be gotten around, and identification itself remains only because it enables the *tertium quid,* which does not even emerge in the equation. Thus, what India does especially in the use of religious-ritual analogies and identifications is adhere explicitly to the relation itself. Duality, not the One, is at the beginning and at the end. Duality becomes nonduality when both sides of the equation are identified with one another, but not when one of the two is denied, devalued, or dissolved. It requires at least twoness, a connection, not the one, the in-dividual, but rather the di-vidual (McKim Marriott), which is equated through the so-called identificatory means. Thus, in India there cannot be only *one* god, but there must be several, even if these can be seen as identical. Not monotheism, polytheism, or henotheism, but rather homotheism or equitheism is an appropriate expression for the ideas of god of the Hindu religions. Another example comes from A. K. Ramanujan, who points out the contextuality and reflexivity of the Hindu worldview. For example, the Dharma cannot be defined without temporal, spatial, and social factors, but always only as the Dharma of a group or region.[82] Western thought, on the other hand, tends toward context-free abstractions.

Salvation in India has also been grasped and described as unique: The Other World and time are eternal and cannot be divided; they are described with adjectives such as *sanātana* ("perpetual"), *nitya* ("fixed, eternal, unchanging"), *acala* ("unmoving"), *sthānu* ("solid"), and *sarvagata* ("ubiquitous").[83] But at the same time, almost without exception, the premise is valid that what is in this world belongs to that world and may not be different from that world—"the sacred is the uniquely unalterable," says Max Weber;[84] in order to produce or protect equality, there are various identificatory ways. This premise entails additional religious principles:[85] The whole and the part (space and volume, time and point in time, god and reproduction of god, etc.) are identical. Material and thoughts or feelings, if they relate to transcendence, are also identical; divine, redeeming features do not cling to the "dead" material, but are themselves material. Because of the indivisibility of the other world, every equality of parts means reciprocal identity.

India has formulated these principles on an abstract level. Thus, the Śivadṛṣṭi, a Śaiva philosophical text, says: "Through his strength, Śiva lives in [every] concrete form, just as [vice versa] everything [concrete] exists in formlessness. The equality of all [manifestations] is obvious."[86] As early as the Chāndogya-Upaniṣad, this way of thinking can be seen clearly: There, breath (*prāṇa*), speech, eyes, ears, and thought organ (*manas*) fight about which of them is the best sense organ. One after another, speech, eyes, ears and Manas leave the body, but every time it can get help. On the other hand, when the breath prepares to leave, the other senses acknowledge its higher rank and say approximately: If I can be only through you, then my features are also yours, then we are also breath, for "only breath becomes all these [senses]."[87] The part is the whole and vice versa, produced by the false conclusion *post hoc, ergo propter hoc* ("after this, therefore because of it"). But, in terms of religion, because of the indivisibility of the whole, this conclusion is not a false syllogism but rather a premise.

Building on such premises, all "great" offers of salvation of India are more or less identificatory: the way of knowledge, participation in divinity and the ritual or heroic act, the doctrine of immortality and timelessness in sacrifice ritual, Upaniṣads, and other texts, ritualistic identifications, speculations of deep sleep, after-death identifications, the significance for salvation of the cosmological equilibrium. But the soteriological thought that has become the habitus is also expressed in "small," everyday identifications: "All mothers, gods, religions, or even car factories are equal," "In every pebble, Śaṃkara (or Śiva) sits" (a proverb), "The beginning (*ādī*) was already the present"—these are sentences that can be heard nearly every day. Big and small identifications, as Pierre Bourdieu and Jan Assmann have described, enter the social sense or the cultural memory of India through processes.[88] They are indeed "only" a habitus, custom, something to protect and not to forget. Yet, the Identificatory Habitus is not an innate way of thinking and communicating, a thought that is immutable for all time. It is no more and no less than *one* way of interpreting the world and acting in it acquired in childhood and preserved by cultural traditions. It forms the social sense of many (religiously motivated) acts in the Hindu religions.

The Identificatory Habitus is based on a genealogical and sacrifice ritual principle that was once important for survival, from which it freed itself when socioeconomic assumptions and internal logic allowed. But it is also based on an intellectual stringency, which does not depend so much on historical and social factors. The doctrines of identity are not radical thoughts confined only to India, but their methodical and habitual permutation is uniquely consistent in the Hindu religions. Like love in Christianity, the mightiness of Allah in Islam, the Non-Self in Buddhism, so, "self-deification" (Max Weber) or, more precisely, the uncompromising identification of man with immortality, the radical individualization of the search for salvation, and the Identificatory Habitus that developed from it, are the special features of the Hindu religions. It led to a special form of religious composure and a culture of serenity, which has been criminally misjudged in the West as fatalism.

The "Theology" of the Hindu Religions: Identity of God and Man

For Christians and Moslems, the Hindu religious concept of immortality during one's lifetime (*jīvanmukti*) is a provocation. Both consider the possible equality of god and man as disrespect for Almighty God. And yet, the concept

24. Worship of a girl as a goddess (Kumārīpūjā) in Kathmandu. Photographer: A. Dietrich, ca. 1984.

is not as impudent as it may seem. Raimon Panikkar explained this in chapter 3 ("Myth of Prajāpati") of *The Return to Myth*,[89] emphasizing that it was precisely in this regard that the Hindu religions had something to teach. My final question about the contribution of the Hindu religions to interreligious and intercultural questions of the present relates to his considerations.

Theodicy is a basic problem of all religions: Why is there suffering if there is an Almighty God? The modern age says that there is no god, and thus it does not have to deal with the problem of theodicy. "Fate" is the answer of the modern age. Christianity, as we know, posited original sin as an answer to the tedious question about the reason for suffering: The first man was sinful and lost the identity with God; therefore he must suffer. "Man falls, not God," says

Panikkar.[90] But the question does remain: How can man sin, offend God, if he is His work? Either God wanted it that way and then He is not a good, gracious God; or He did not want it, and then He is not almighty. Christianity has put a value on suffering itself as salvation as a way out of this dilemma: "The myth of pain becomes the mystery of pain."[91]

India has found a fundamentally different answer to the problem of theodicy. In the Hindu religions—as in all religions—the separation of God and man must be explained, as well as why men are mortal but God is not. India has considered the problem a logical one and thought the incompatibility of god (eternity) and man (mortality) so radically to the end that it has even sacrificed "god."

In the cosmogonic myths of the Veda, when the world emerges out of a demiurge or primeval creature (Brahmā, Prajāpati, Puruṣa), through this act, the god himself becomes "mortal." The dismemberment of his body, from which the creation emerges, means that the god sacrifices himself. But, basically, in his very own, highest form, god is the only purely spiritual reality. That is said countless times in the cosmogonic myths, whether of Śiva, Viṣṇu, or a goddess. These gods are always being asked by others to show themselves, grant an insight (*darśana*) into their real form. And when this happens, a chain of identifications usually follows: "I am the lord, Brahmā, the stars, the sun . . . everything." But precisely because the god shows himself, he is no longer in his highest form. This is why the texts quite often say: "Not by study of the Vedas nor by yoga, chanting, austerity, or sacrifice can you see this form in any way, without my favour. It was then, I grant it because of my mercy, it was then, you too, believer, are like me."[92] But for whom does the god sacrifice himself if, at the beginning, there is no one except himself? The myths give various answers: There is the wish for offspring, or the reluctance to be alone, or pure playfulness. And as always, by creating the world out of himself, the god exposes himself to mortality. Otherwise, there would be no reason to want to be something twice, something that is not the One, which is immortality. God himself, says Panikkar, is guilty for the problem of theodicy: "God is dead from having created; he has immolated himself so that his creature might be; the world is nothing else but God sanctified, immolated."[93] So God becomes "mortal" by performing the creation.

The criticism hits the "sore" point of every Hindu religious theology: An old Upaniṣad says that the gods keep man in a state of ignorance because they want to and must get sacrifices.[94] But when, in asceticism, the sacrifice becomes self-sacrifice, the duality dissolves in the desired nonduality of god and man. He who "only" achieves heaven by producing Karma as defined by rituals and (good) deeds, remains in the state of ignorance and thus of mortality.[95] One can fall out of heaven, but not out of equality with god.

In Christianity, from the start, theodicy amounts to separating dualism: God and man confront each other. In India, god and man form a dualistic unity. If man only knew the identity and the right identifications! In terms of the Hindu religions, it is hardly comprehensible that a religion such as Christianity, in which God becomes man, creates more distance between man and God precisely because it does not allow the reversal and thus the identity of both: Eckhart's son-being of man was as God-being and is not really accepted in Christianity to this day,[96] and the image of God is not considered in its full scope.

Man is not responsible for his suffering. Instead it is God Himself. But can evil be attributed to a god? Is god then not godless? Can guilt and suffering in fact come from a god? Is there "a certain act of God that is not divine?"[97] In fact, that is how it is seen in India, yet not as personal guilt or as an evil, punitive act, but rather as a grace, negligence, or error of god. The god plays, is bored, yearns, becomes "human" and—almost unexpectedly—the world arises. "He goes out of himself, he falls in love, he commits the fault of creating the creature. In brief: we are God's fault."[98]

Panikkar has seen and "felt" what is essential. He has described in theological terms what I have called identificatory thinking: "God dies, so to speak, in creating his creature; there is no room for two at this level."[99] Thus, man must compose god in order to be able to have immortality. That happens in various ways: in sacrifice, in recognizing the identity of part and whole, in the *unio mystica.* But in the Hindu religions, god and man are not basically separated. They are not only dependent on one another, they are also both parts of the ephemeral creation: God is man as man becomes god, God's act of creation is his humanity, which is not to be separated from his existence. What lies beyond that is no longer god *because* it is not divisible.

In this place, the whole personality dissolves in the Hindu religions, both for god and for man; and abstract doctrines of identity intervene, which Buddhism formulated much more radically by denying not only god and man, but also the self. Richard Gombrich says correctly that the Upaniṣads opened the equation 1 = 1 because they assume a single essence (*ātman, brahman, oṃ, udgītha, prāṇa*) or, in my words, religious substance, even if it has various names. On the other hand, the Buddha also denies this essence, so for him, the equation 0 = 0 is appropriate.[100] In fact, the "logic" of Buddhism also grows from the ground of such equations. An essential difference is that—as Gombrich also emphasizes—this identification does not find an end, is not static, but is a process, an activity; it leads to asking no longer what man is, but how man is—and ultimately to making the doctrine ethical.[101] Each in its own and corresponding way, Buddhism and the Brahmanic-Sanskritic Hindu religions "solve" the insoluble problem of the identification of the finite with the infinite, man with "god," but the Hindu religions remain in the socioreligious structure of the relative Dharma, the Svadharma.

The Hindu religions have seen the connection between god and man itself as—ultimately—sorrowful, but at least the gods are not freed from their guilt for suffering. Instead, they have seen a salvation beyond This World and the Next World, in order to avoid every contingency, guilt, or separation, which may be neither this nor that. Instead, it had to be the once achieved (static) or permanently maintained (dynamic) connection itself: identification, equation, substitution. These ideas of salvation developed out of simple but lasting sentences such as: "Everything is the one, the one is everything," "You are you," or "The sacrifice is the man," and long texts such as the recent Maitreya-Upaniṣad, which is a single sequence of identifications of the following type: "I am I, but also the other. I am Brahman, I am the source. I am the teacher of the whole world. I am the whole world. I am he [Śiva]. . . . From honor and dishonor and from qualities I am free. I am Śiva! From oneness and duality and from opposites I am free. I am he!"[102]

Such sentences are more than well-formulated thoughts; they are an attitude toward the world and god—and they are an expression of a habitus. Perhaps this voice of India is heard in all apocalyptic calls of modern times: the recognition that the new is also the old, that the future is also the past, that man and animal are one, that god is also man, but man is also god, that the part, the singular, the individual, is the whole, that This World is the Next World and the Next World is This World. Thus, in the inevitable fusion of cultures and religions, India brings its sympathetic pledge: the wise, smiling habitus of serenity and courage for equations in which the self—not the yearning and egotistic I—is identical with friend and foe, animals and plants. Perhaps it is this serenity that ultimately is good for a godless world where savings are more important than salvation.

Notes

PREFACE

1. Older literature is covered, e.g., by Gonda 1960–1964; an introduction to popular religious and anthropological literature is offered by Fuller 1992:271–282.

CHAPTER 1: THEORETICAL FOUNDATIONS

1. See Doniger 1991:519, and B. K. Smith 1989:6ff., for more proofs.
2. Hacker 1957:172.
3. See B. K. Smith 1996:120, and Inden 1990:86.
4. Eck 1985:25.
5. Main figure in Kālidāsa's drama *Abhijñānaśakuntala.*
6. Marquard 1981.
7. See Inden 1990:130.
8. The term, *Hindu religions,* introduced by Stietencron 1992:288ff., is explained below.
9. Thus, Kolenda (1978:4): "The constant feature in caste is its kinship or descent-group."
10. E. Bloch 1978:360.
11. Weber 1968.
12. *Devī* [or *Mā*] *sab ek hī hai.*
13. See Weber 1968 and Bourdieu 1977 and 1990.
14. Bourdieu 1980:101.
15. Bourdieu 1980:191.
16. Durkheim 1966:13.
17. Assmann 1997:29–160.
18. Assmann 1997:140.
19. The following is taken partly from Michaels 1998.
20. See Trawick 1990:xvii–xix and 136ff.; Fuchs 1988.
21. Berger 1979.
22. See Auboyer 1965; Edwards 1969.

23. E. Gellner 1988:12.

24. See Goetz 1993.

25. Kippenberg 2002:1.

26. See Schluchter (ed.) 1984 and Fuchs 1988 for more proofs.

27. Inden 1990; see the similarly titled essay by J. Z. Smith 1982.

28. Trawick 1990:139.

29. See W. C. Smith 1978:63ff.; Larson 1995.

30. Küng et al. 1987:25–26; similarly Frykenberg 1989:29; or Nehru 1960:63.

31. The legal text is reproduced, among others, in Derrett 1957:app. III, 319f. And see A. Sharma 1986, and Conrad 1995:323ff.

32. Census of India 1881 Panjab, p. 101 (quoted from Glasenapp 1922:11); however, see Cohn 1987:243ff. for the questionable methodology of this census.

33. See Stietencron 1989 and Frykenberg 1989.

34. The German sources for the history of the reception of India in early modern times have been elaborated by Dharampal-Frick 1994.

35. For the following, see D. Gold 1992; Horstmann 1994; Klostermaier 1994:32; as well as the articles in *Religion* 26.2 (April 1996) by J. G. Lochtefeld, B. K. Smith, M. Juergensmeyer, and N. Smart, with additional references.

36. V. D. Sarvarkar, *Hindūtva,* Bombay 1969, p. 1 (quoted in D. Gold 1992:549).

37. M. S. Gowalkar, *Spotlights: Guruji Answers,* Bangalore, 1974, p. 51; D. Gold 1992:167.

38. Source: The Organizer of February 11, 1979; see Lochtefeld 1996:107.

39. Kane 1968–:I.1; Lingat 1973:3–17; Flood 1996:51–74.

40. For a discussion, see Stietencron 1997:13ff.

41. See Surah 3, 17: *al-dīn ʿinda ʾllāh* ("religion with Allah").

42. "The Greeks even had just as few special words for 'rite' as for 'religion' " (Kerényi 1950:16).

43. Already in the *Bhagavadgītā* 1.40; see Hacker 1965 and Horstmann 1995.

44. Hacker 1978:512; and see Halbfass 1981:chapter 17.

45. *Āpastambadharmasūtra* 1.20.6.

46. *Bhagavadgītā,* 3.35.

47. *Āpastambadharmasūtra* 1.20.6–8; and see Wezler 1985.

48. See, e.g., *Bhagavadgītā,* 2.31; the textbook of the art of thievery (*Ṣāṇmukhakalpa*) or the *Kamasūtra.*

49. *Philosophy of World History,* part 1, section 2.

50. Gombrich 1988:66–69 and 1996:51–52.

51. Gombrich 1996:51.

52. Zaehner 1962:6.

53. Eliade 1958c:3.

54. Küng et al. 1987:25f.; Stietencron 1989 and 1997:6ff.

55. See Spiro 1966.

56. See B. K. Smith 1989:3–29; Halbfass 1991:1–22; Heesterman 1997 with additional proofs; for the Veda in a very controversial legal decision, see Derrett 1986:51 and Derrett 1957:76ff.

57. B. K. Smith 1989:13–14 [italics in the original].

58. Thieme 1966a:27; and Baldissera/Michaels 1988:17; and see B. K. Smith 1989:22.

59. 2.62.10; see chapter 3.

60. See *Bhagavadgītā* 2.41–46.

61. B. K. Smith 1989:26.

62. Stietencron 1997:7–10.

63. Sanderson 1988:699.

64. See D. Gellner 1992:73–104.

65. Gokhale 1980:72–73.

66. See Schneider 1989:5.

67. Brunner-Lachaux 1977:553.

68. Stietencron 1995:66.

69. See also Halbfass 1991:54–55.

70. Unlike Sontheimer 1989, I separate tribal and folk religions, since the boundaries between tribe and caste or local populations are not clear.

71. See especially Babb 1975 and Fuller 1992 (with a survey of the literature).

72. For the problem of the concept of "sect," see chapter 7.

73. Hardy 1994:92–93.

74. According to McDaniel (1989:86ff.), the Śākta traditions in Bengal are Yogic, devotional, and Tantric.

75. See *Baudhāyanadharmasūtra* 1.18.2–5.

76. *cf. Āpastambadharmasūtra* 1.1.4–5.

77. See Biardeau 1989:156; and below, chapter 5.

78. McDermott 1996.

79. Srinivas 1952; Redfield/Singer 1954; and for the discussion, see Staal 1963; Singer 1972; Fuller 1992:24–28.

80. Parry 1985a; Wezler 1985; Sontheimer 1989.

81. Also Ramanujan 1988:189; and Fuller 1992:26.

82. Srinivas 1952; Staal 1963.

83. Hacker 1983.

84. Marriott 1955.

85. Bhandarkar 1913; Gonda 1960–1964: vol. 2.

86. See Thapar 1978:1–25; for the question of whether the transference of these period divisions is ethnocentric to India, see Kulke 1982.

87. Kane 1968–:V:1622: "there has been an unbroken religious tradition from the Vedic times almost to the present day. Vedic mantras are still employed [. . .]."

88. For this problem, see Erdosy (ed.) 1995.

89. Thus Southworth 1995.

90. See Klostermaier (1994:33) for the consequences of this thesis in Gowalkar's definition of Hinduism as well as Biardeau 1989:2–3 and 15.

91. Eliade 1959: 100, 135, 156.

92. Sachau, Edward C. (trans.), *Alberuni's India,* 1910:19–20.

93. Eliade 1958c.

94. More examples in Gonda 1965:16ff.

95. Mensching 1959:79.

CHAPTER 2: HISTORICAL FOUNDATIONS

1. Kulke/Rothermund 1986; Rothermund 1986; Schwartzberg (ed.) 1992.
2. Erdosy (ed.) 1995 and Flood 1996:23–30.
3. For the latest state of research, see Fairservis 1992 and Parpola 1994.
4. Srinivasan 1975–1976 and 1984; Hiltebeitel 1978.
5. For this problem complex, see Gonda 1965:19ff.
6. Thus Thieme 1938; however, the etymology is controversial: see Erdosy (ed.) 1995:3, fn. 4. "Indo-Aryans" indicates the speakers of a subgroup of the Indo-Iranian branch of the Indo-European language family.
7. In the early Vedic time, when only small iron implements (nail files, butcher knives, pots) were used, and later also the *vajra,* an arrow with barbs (see Rau 1974:3–4; and 1986:228–229). *Áyas,* the black metal, is mentioned first in the *Atharvaveda*(11.2.7.9.5.4).
8. Rau 1983:36.
9. For the state of research, see Rau 1983 and especially Erdosy (ed.) 1995.
10. Kennedy 1995:60–61.
11. Renfrew 1987:192.
12. Shaffer 1984:88.
13. See *Ṛgveda* 1.104.2.
14. For the structural stratification of the *Ṛgveda,* see Witzel 1995.
15. See *Ṛgveda* 10.75.5.
16. Rau 1983:35.
17. A drink of fly mushroom or ephedra; see Falk 1989, Kashikar 1990 (with the review by Oberlies 1995) as well as the article by Parpola and Nyberg in Erdosy (ed.) 1995.
18. Rau 1983:38–39.
19. Rau 1957; Mylius 1970; Witzel 1989.
20. Oldenberg 1919; Schayer 1925.
21. Bronkhorst 1993.
22. Erdosy 1988:125–126.
23. E. Gellner 1983:8.
24. For the delineations, see Ritschl 1997.
25. For the following, see also Gombrich 1988:78–86 and Olivelle 1992:29ff. and 1993:58ff.
26. Weber 1958:104
27. Basham 1951.
28. See *Baudhāyanadharmasūtra* 2.6.31–4; *Āpastambadharmasūtra* 1.32.21; Olivelle 1992:38–39.
29. Rau 1975:6–7.
30. Renou 1953:47.
31. See Bayly 1983.
32. See Rothermund (ed.) 1995:104.

33. For detailed treatments of literature, see Winternitz 1996, Glasenapp 1961, and Gonda et al. (Mylius 1983, eds.) 1973; and Bechert/v. Simson (eds.) 1979. All dating in table 2 is to be understood as approximate, rather cautiously fixed, and referring only to the first emergence of a new form or genre of literature, including the assumption of a final redaction of the work. Relatively reliable dating or discussion of the dating problem is offered by the volumes of the *History of Indian Literature* by Jan Gonda et al. (1973) and for Vedic texts, see Mylius 1970 and Witzel 1989; for philosophical texts, see Potter et al. (eds.) 1979–1987; for legal texts, see Kane 1968–. For additional references to special areas, see Bechert/von Simson 1979. For linguistic changes, see Hinüber 1986 and Witzel 1989.

34. Bechert 1986:180.

35. See above, n. 3.

36. See Falk 1993; Hinüber 1990.

37. For the overall problem, see especially Witzel 1989.

38. Hinüber 1990; Falk 1993; Salomon 1995.

39. See Rocher 1986.

40. Gonda 1977:164.

41. Gonda 1977:54.

42. Goudriaan/Gupta 1981:22.

43. For dating, see Kane 1968–:I.2; and Derrett 1973.

CHAPTER 3: STAGES OF LIFE AND RITES OF PASSAGE

1. See Wach 1947:30–33.

2. S. Stevenson 1920:27–45; Gonda 1965:315ff. and 1980; N. N. Bhattacharya 1968; Pandey 1969:112–152; Kane 1968–:II.1:268–415; B. K. Smith 1986 and 1989:91–104; Bennett 1983:59–71; Kaelber 1989.

3. *Manu* 2:148: *satya.*

4. *Āpastambadharmasūtra,* 1.1.18; and see *Manu* 2.174 and 2.169–170.

5. See Beattie 1964:93–94.

6. Gonda 1985:315–462.

7. Lingat 1973:39–40.

8. *Pañcaviṃśabrāhmaṇa* 17.1.2: *hīna.* For the Vrātyas, see the (controversial) study of Hauer (1927) and Heesterman 1962.

9. See *Baudhāyanadharmasūtra* 1.3.6; *Manu* 2.39–40 and 172.

10. Cf. *Gautamadharmasūtra* 2.1.

11. Haradatta on *Gautamadharmasūtra* 1.6 calls the *upanayana* the main rite (*pradhāna saṃskāra*); and see B. K. Smith 1989:93.

12. S. Stevenson 1920:27.

13. For the *saṃskāra,* see Gonda 1980:364; and B. K. Smith 1986:66 and 1989:86–87 and 91.

14. B. K. Smith 1989:91–92.

15. *Manu* 2.146.

16. *Puruṣo vai yajñah: Śatapathabrāhmaṇa* 1.3.2.1 et passim.

17. *Maitrāyaṇīsaṃhitā* 3.6.7; and see *Jaiminīya-Upaniṣadbrāhmaṇa* 3.14.8; *Śatapathabrāhmaṇa* 11.2.1.1; *Āitareyāraṇyaka* 2.5; B. K. Smith 1989:102; Olivelle 1993:39

18. Elizarenkova 1995:291.

19. *Ṛgvedasaṃhitā* 5.4.10; see *Taittirīya-Brāhmaṇa* 1.5.5.6

20. Olivelle 1992:23ff.

21. See *Manu* 2.28.

22. See Leach 1976.

23. For the Hindu initiation in Nepal see Michaels 1986a; for Buddhist initiation see Locke 1975; Bennett 1983:59–71; D. Gellner 1988.

24. I am grateful to G. B. Kalikote and his family for allowing me to observe all phases of the initiation of his son. For comparison, I participated in eight other initiations in Nepal, which were less detailed.

25. Time: May 22, 1983; place: Kathmandu; family of the initiate: Khaḍga (Kṣatriya); priest: Bhaṭṭarāi-Brahman.

26. *Manu* 2.37; *Āpastambadharmasūtra* 1.1.10.20–21.

27. According to B. K. Smith 1986:69–70, supplemented by *Vratabandhapaddhati*, *l.c.*, and Pandey 1969:126ff.

28. See Kaelber 1978:69, n. 92.

29. *Manu* 2.171; see *Viṣṇusmṛti* 28.38; *Yājñavalkyasmṛti* 1.39.

30. *Manu* 2.35; Kane 1968–:II:260–265; Pandey 1969:94–101; S. Stevenson 1920:20–23.

31. *Yajurvedasaṃhitā* 3.6.3.

32. For the interpretation of the tonsure as a process of individuation, see Kakar 1978:250.

33. Pandey 1969:98–99.

34. *Suśrutasaṃhitā* (Śarīrasthāna) 6.83; Pandey 1969:101.

35. See Kane 1968–:II:264.

36. See J. Z. Smith 1987:109.

37. S. Stevenson 1920:23.

38. Kane 1968–:II:164–165.

39. See Olivelle 1986:I:29–35; Michaels 1994a.

40. *Kaṭhaśruti-Upaniṣad* 34.4; Olivelle 1992:131.

41. See Toffin 1984 and D. Gellner 1992.

42. For a discussion of such oppositions, see T. Turner 1984 and Bell 1992:101.

43. *Manu* 2.148

44. Lévi 1898, Eliade 1958b:53–57; and see Lommel 1955.

45. Gonda 1965:323ff.

46. The *Atharvaveda* has the verb root *nī* with the prefix *upa*, from which the term *upanayana*, "initiation," is formed.

47. *Atharvaveda* 11.5.3; and see *Śatapathabrāhmaṇa* 6.6.2.16, 10.4.10.1–2, 11.1.2.2, 11.5.40.12–16, 12.5.1.13.

48. As opposed to Kaelber's (1978:67–68) statement, the new birth symbolism is also preserved in the modern Hindu initiation.

49. See *Manu* 2.69; *Gautamadharmasūtra* 2.1–4; *Mitākṣara* on *Yājñavalkyasmṛti* 1.1.

50. Pandey 1969:128.

51. *Pāraskaragṛhyasūtra* 2.2.6; *Hiraṇyakeśigṛhyasūtra* 1.2.5.2; *Jaiminīyagṛhyasūtra* 1.12; *Gautamagṛhyasūtra* 2.10.21.

52. *Manu* 2.150.

53. Gonda 1965:231.

54. *Manu* 11.55.

55. *Śatapathabrāhmaṇa* 7.3.1.46.

56. *Śatapathabrāhmaṇa* 7.3.1.28ff.; and see *Taittirīyāraṇyaka* 1.5.5.6; *Āitareyāraṇyaka* 2.5; Olivelle 1993:42–44 (with additional references).

57. Stietencron 1979:53.

58. See *Śāṅkhāyanāraṇyaka* 6.11; *Bṛhadāraṇyaka-Upaniṣad* 2.18; B. K. Smith 1989:82ff.; M. Davis 1976; Weiss 1980:98ff.; Trawick 1990:159; and Filippi 1996: 37–61.

59. See *Manu* 2.16; but also 2.27.

60. *Manu* 9.69; Jolly 1896:70–72.

61. Harīta in *Saṃskāratattva,* quoted by Kane 1968–II:192; and see *Manu* 2.27–28.

62. *Manu* 3.45–50.

63. Stietencron 1979:53–54.

64. Dumont (1980:112) talks of "endorecruiting."

65. *Śatapathabrāhmaṇa* 7.3.1.46; *Aitareya-Upaniṣad* 2.1–4; Stietencron 1979:54.

66. *Manu* 2.147–148; *Viṣṇusmṛti* 30.45–46.

67. *Manu* 10.4; *Baudhāyanagṛhyasūtra* 1.7.1; *Vaikhānasagṛhyasūtra* 1.1; *Gautamadharmasūtra* 10.50.

68. *Śatapathabrāhmaṇa* 11.2.2.5.

69. See *Bhagavadgītā* 2.10; Kaelber 1978:69.

70. See *Śvetāśvatara-Upaniṣad* 1.7.

71. B. K. Smith 1989:92.

72. *Śatapathabrāhmaṇa* 6.2.2.7. Quoted from B. K. Smith 1989:103.

73. *Śatapathabrāhmaṇa* 3.1.3.18, 1.1.1.4, 1.1.2.17; *Bṛhadāraṇyaka-Upaniṣad* 1.3.28.

74. *Viṣṇusmṛti* 30.45–46; *Manu* 2.147–148.

75. Olivelle 1986:29ff. The following section partially continues Michaels 1994a.

76. *Āpastambadharmasūtra* 1.2.39–41.

77. Details in Kane 1968–II:287ff.

78. Cf. *Manu* 2.42–44.

79. Oldenberg 1917:467.

80. See H. D. Sharma 1939:35.

81. *Manu* 4.257, 6.35.

82. Thus the Vaidyas in West Bengal (Monier-Williams 1899: *yajñopavīta*); see also the mass donning of the Sacred Thread among the casteless and untouchables in the Ārya Samāj (Brockington 1981:180).

83. See Michaels 1994a:337–342.

84. *Brahma-Upaniṣad* 85; translation from *Saṃnyāsa-Upaniṣads.*

85. See B. K. Smith 1989:88–89.

86. For the stick, see Gonda 1969a:22 (with references); as well as the discussion of the ascetics in Olivelle 1986:I:35–54.

87. See *Āśvalāyanagṛhyasūtra* 3.8.1.

88. See Gonda 1969a:22.

89. See Glaser 1912:14ff.

90. Winternitz 1926; Olivelle 1993: chapter 3; and Jolly 1896:148; Lingat 1973:45–51.

91. Winternitz 1926; Sprockhoff 1981–1984; Olivelle 1993.

92. *Ṛgvedasaṃhīta* 3.62.10 (my translation—A. M.).

93. *Manu* 2.170.

94. *Āpastambadharmasūtra* 1.2.11–16.

95. *Manu* 2.77.

96. See S. Stevenson 1920:218ff.

97. See *Manu* 2.78.

98. *Manu* 2.40.

99. See Steinmann 1986.

100. See *Bhāgavatapurāṇa* 7.15.26; and *Manu* 2.153.

101. See Olivelle 1993:58.

102. Textual examples and other comments are in Michaels 1986a.

103. In what was certainly a rare case of hardship in Nepal, I observed how the rite was "used" in fact to expel two youths from their village: Michaels 1986a:208–214.

104. See Ariès 1981; Gnilka 1972; Erikson 1968; Thomas 1976.

105. See also *Bṛhadāraṇyaka-Upaniṣad* 6.4.26, where a secret name is bestowed with the phrase: "You are the Veda."

106. Masson 1980 is such a case: See Michaels 1982.

107. For a critique of that, see Sen 1993:452ff.

108. See *Bhāgavatapurāṇa* 10.12.32 and 41.

109. *Garuḍapurāṇa.* See Abegg 1921:17.

110. *Baudhāyanadharmasūtra* 1.3.6; *Gautamadharmasūtra* 2.1; Lingat 1973:45.

111. See Chaudhuri 1951:42–61; Michaels 1986b:57.

112. Cormack 1953; Dube 1955; Carstairs 1957; Kakar 1978, 1979, and 1981; Petzold 1986:169–221; Roland 1988; Trawick 1990; Kurtz 1992 (with a literary review). Some of this section takes up material from Michaels 1986b:52–71 and Wiemann-Michaels 1994:99–104; the works of Trawick and Kurtz have provided a more critical view of Kakar's still impressive theory (see Michaels 1982).

113. See *Mahānirvāṇatantra* 8.45–47; *Arthaśāstra* 1.17.6; Carstairs 1957:64–65; Kakar 1978:88–89 and 1981:87; Roland 1988:249; Kurtz 1992:62.

114. Ruben 1944:80.

115. Kakar 1979:34.

116. Cormack 1953:21.

117. Kurtz 1992:60ff.

118. Cormack 1953:21.

119. Kurtz 1992:69.

120. Kurtz 1992:84–86.

121. Kakar 1981:85.

122. See Kakar 1978:104.

123. Quoted in Kakar 1981:87.

124. Kakar 1981:86–87.

125. Kurtz 1992:88–89.

126. Cormack 1953:23; Carstairs 1957:155–159; Ramanujan 1972; Kakar 1978:79–139; Goldman 1978; Roland 1988:266–268; Obeyesekere 1990:71–139; Trawick 1990:140 and 161.

127. Gough 1956:835.

128. Chaudhuri 1951:143.

129. *Manu* 2.225–237; Winternitz 1920:19–20 (with more evidence); Steinmann 1986:36ff.

130. Kakar 1978:108–109.

131. Wiemann-Michaels 1994:104.

132. Kakar 1978:107.

133. Kurtz 1992:101.

134. First described by Trawick 1990:156–157.

135. Kurtz 1992:104 (with proofs).

136. Bennett 1983:173.

137. See Wiemann-Michaels 1996.

138. First in Kakar 1974; elaborated in Kakar 1978.

139. Trawick 1990:165–166.

140. Freud got the concept of the "oceanic feeling" from India through Romain Rolland; see Masson 1980:chapters 2–4.

141. Trawick 1990:242ff.

142. Goldman 1978; Sprockhoff 1979; Stietencron 1979; Olivelle 1993:41ff.; Gonda 1985; Steinmann 1986:46ff.

143. *Taittirīyabrāhamaṇa* 1.5.5.6; see Olivelle 1993:43 (with additional evidence).

144. *Taittirīyasaṃhitā* 6.3.10.5; Malamoud 1977:11–12; Olivelle 1993:46–53.

145. *Śatapathabrāhmaṇa* 11.5.60.6–7; *Taittirīya-Āraṇyaka* 2.10.1; Olivelle 1993:53 (with more evidence).

146. *Śatapathabrāhmaṇa* 1.7.2.1.

147. *Śatapathabrāhmaṇa* 14.4.13.25ff. (my translation—A. M.). Cf. Bṛhadāraṇyaka-Upaniṣad 1.5.17–20. Sprockhoff 1979:385ff. grasped these transference rites; see also Stietencron 1979; Olivelle 1993:41–46.

148. *Āitareyāraṇyaka* 7.12.12 (my translation—A. M.).

149. *Śatapathabrāhmaṇa* 12.4.3.1.

150. Geldner 1928:66: "under the guardianship of the son"; Sprockhoff 1979:390: "to live (actually to sojourn with his son; *putrasyaiśvarye pitā vaset*)."

151. *Kauṣītaki-Upaniṣad* 2.14.

152. *Āpastambadharmasūtra* 1.14.25; *Manu* 2.135.

153. *Chāndogya-Upaniṣad* 4.4.1.

154. See Trawick 1990:163.

155. *Manu* 9.107.

156. Stietencron 1979:57.

157. *Mahābhārata* 1.68.47.

158. *Hiraṇyakeśigṛhyasūtra* 1.2.5.11; for the wedding, see *Pāraskaragṛhyasūtra* 1.8.8; Steinmann 1986:52.

159. Cormack 1953:121–148; Kapadia 1955:167–197; Dumont 1966; and the literature listed in notes 112 and 126.

160. Trawick 1990:153.

161. See, among others, Goody 1983; Ariès 1985.

162. Ariès 1985.

163. *Manu* 3.12; Bennett 1983:71.

164. *Manu* 3.20–34; *Yājñavalkyasmṛti* 1.58–61; *Nāradasmṛti*12.38–44; *Viṣṇusmṛti* 24.17–28; Jolly 1896:§16; Pandey 1969:158–170.

165. Devala, quoted in Pandey 1969:171.

166. Winternitz 1892 and the literature listed in notes 112 and 159.

167. Gough 1955; Allen 1982; Lienhard 1986; Good 1991.

168. For the age of marriage and child marriage, see Jolly 1896:59; Winternitz 1920:27–38; Pandey 1969:182–191.

169. For the forms of marriage, see Dumont 1980:114ff.

170. Dumont 1980:114ff.

171. *Āpastambadharmasūtra* 2.11.17; *Gautamadharmasūtra* 8.16.

172. See *Manu* 3.6–7 and 3.17; or *Yājñavalkyasmṛti* 1.52–55; Pandey 1969: 191–199.

173. Time: autumn 1980; place: Hārutī region (Rajasthan); caste: Rājput; priests: Brahmans. According to Agarwala 1982:17–75; references were to Babb 1975:81–90, as well as Kane 1968–:II.1:427ff.; and Pandey 1969:199–233; S. Stevenson 1920:46–95; and Bennett 1983:71–92. Abbreviations: H. = Hindī; all other words: Sanskrit.

174. *Saral Vivāha Paddhati* by Pandit Dharnidhar Shastri (Kishangarh, 1973), a text that essentially follows the *Pāraskaragṛhyasūtra.*

175. Dumont 1980:117; Trautmann 1981; Raheja/Gold 1994:chapter 3 and the literature listed in note 199, below.

176. Raheja/Puri 1995:27.

177. See Dumont 1980:138.

178. See Trautmann 1981:26.

179. For the invisible or visible gain (*adṛṣṭaphala, dṛṣṭaphala*), see *Kṛtyakalpataru,* pp. 5–6; and Trautmann 1981:45, 280.

180. *Manu,* 3. 51–54.

181. Jolly 1896:71ff.

182. *Nāradasmṛti* 12.19.

183. *Manu* 3.12.

184. See Fürer-Haimendorf 1966:30–31; Bennett 1983:16.

185. Vatuk 1975.

186. Winternitz 1920:25; Parry 1979:213ff.

187. Pandey 1969:175.

188. Brough 1946–1947; Tiemann 1970; Trautmann 1981:238ff.

189. *Śatapathabrāhmaṇa* 14.5.2.6.

190. Fick 1920.

191. Jolly 1896:63.

192. *Manu* 10.24ff.; Brinkhaus 1978.

193. Bennett 1983:74.

194. Trawick 1990:179.

195. Raheja 1994:56.

196. Parry 1979:223; Trawick 1990:131–135.

197. Dumont (1980:112): "the group reproduces itself by itself from generation to generation, is endorecruiting."

198. See Kapadia 1955:130.

199. Winternitz 1920; Cormack 1953; Altekar 1956; Wadley 1977; Jacobson/Wadley 1977; Bennett 1983; Mies 1986; Wichterich 1986; Raheja/Gold 1994; Kumar (ed.) 1994; Harlan/Courtright (eds.) 1995.

200. Agarwala 1982; Raheja 1994; Raheja/Gold 1994.

201. See Kumar (ed.) 1994:1ff.

202. Raheja 1994:57.

203. Raheja 1994:71.

204. See Trawick 1990:180.

205. See Winternitz 1920:38.

206. *Manu* 9.31–56; Jolly 1896:49.

207. Raheja 1994:72.

208. *Aitareyabrāhmaṇa* 7.13.8; Winternitz 1920:21–22.

209. Lewis 1958:195.

210. See Weiss 1980.

211. See Pandey 1969:60ff.

212. See Miller 1981; Wichterich 1986:61–62.

213. *Manu* 3.55–62 and 9.25–29; for the murder of girls, see Winternitz 1920:25.

214. Bennett 1983:168. For myths and rituals about "shattered" wives, see Trawick 1990:167.

215. Raheja 1994.

216. See Trawick 1990:170–178, 181; Bennett 1983:246–252.

217. See *Taittirīyasaṃhitā* 6.1.8.5; *Śatapathabrāhmaṇa* 5.2.1.10.

218. Apffel-Marglin 1984; Yocum 1984; and below, table 19.

219. Hershman 1977:276.

220. In general, see: Hertz 1907; Ariès 1981; Bloch/Parry (eds.) 1982; Metcalf/Huntington (eds.) 1991; Cederroth/Corlin/Lindström (eds.) 1988; Oberhammer (ed.) 1995; Schömbucher/Zoller (eds.) 1999.

221. Gladigow 1985:121.

222. Caland 1896; S. Stevenson 1920:135–192; Abegg 1921; Pandey 1969:234–274; Kane 1968–:IV:179–266; Knipe 1976; Parry 1985b and 1994; Evison 1989; Müller 1992; Filippi 1996:91–178 (with reproductions).

223. Taken from a death ritual in Benares with the aid of Müller 1992; Parry 1985b and 1994; Evison 1989:appendix; and Kaushik 1976. See Gutschow/Michaels 1993: 175–185; and Michaels 1999.

224. The death ritual is treated in the Uttarakhaṇḍa section of the *Garuḍapurāṇa,* which has only a loose and allegedly late connection with the "real" *Garuḍapurāṇa;* this section is also known as Pretakalpa or Pretakhaṇḍa ("Section on the Dead"), of which there are several versions and a compendium, *Naunidhirāmas Sāroddhāra* (Abegg 1921).

225. *Garuḍapurāṇa, Uttarakhaṇḍa* 3.11 (Abegg 1921:12).

226. *The Garuḍapurāṇa Sāroddhāra* 9.14; *Garuḍapurāṇa, Uttarakhaṇḍa* 19.18–19 (Abegg 1921:20).

227. *Garuḍapurāṇa, Uttarakhaṇḍa* 24.12 (Abegg 1921:22).

228. *Garuḍapurāṇa Sāroddhāra* 10.61, with note 1.

229. *Garuḍapurāṇa Sāroddhāra* 1.33.

230. *Garuḍapurāṇa Sāroddhāra* 9.36; see S. Stevenson 1920:139.

231. *Garuḍapurāṇa Sāroddhāra* 10.64; see Müller 1992:29.

232. *Garuḍapurāṇa Sāroddhāra* 10.67–87; *Antyeṣṭipaddhati* 57; Müller 1992:27.

233. For *aśauca,* see especially Kane 1968–:IV:267–268.

234. *Antyeṣṭipaddhati* 57; see Müller 1992:99.

235. *Manu* 5.84; *Viṣṇusmṛti* 22.48; *Garuḍapurāṇa Sāroddhāra* 12.23.

236. *Garuḍapurāṇa Sāroddhāra* 13.6–7.

237. Harper 1964.

238. Harper (1964:167): "Āme, the pollution that results from a birth, is in many ways like sūtaka [death pollution]." See S. Stevenson 1920:157.

239. *Garuḍapurāṇa, Uttarakhaṇḍa* 14.1.3 (Abegg 1921:16).

240. Sontheimer 1977:20ff.

241. Filippi 1996:41.

242. Parry 1985b:622.

243. Knipe 1976.

244. See *Garuḍapurāṇa, Uttarakhaṇḍa* 30.21–34 (Abegg 1921:25).

245. *Garuḍapurāṇa Sāroddhāra* 10.9ff., 12.57–59; *Garuḍapurāṇa, Uttarakhaṇḍa* 5.27–29 (Abegg 1921:13); Parry 1985b:616.

246. Parry 1985b:616.

247. According to the *Pretamañjari;* for another division, see *Garuḍapurāṇa* 1.50–54.

248. *Garuḍapurāṇa Sāroddhāra* 12.21ff.

249. *Garuḍapurāṇa Sāroddhāra* 1.56–2.86.

250. Babb 1975:96–97.

251. See Michaels 1994c:154.

252. Parry 1985b:620–621.

253. *Garuḍapurāṇa, Uttarakhaṇḍa* 16.10 (Abegg 1921:17); Parry 1985b:622; S. Stevenson 1920:185–186.

254. *Manu* 9.186; *Garuḍapurāṇa, Uttarakhaṇḍa* 25.6–7 (Abegg 1921:23).

255. *Antyeṣṭipaddhati* 25; Müller 1992:102; Filippi 1996:148–149.

256. Müller 1992:46.

257. *Manu* 3.150–166.

258. Parry 1985b.

259. *Garuḍapurāṇa, Uttarakhaṇḍa* 3.16 (Abegg 1921:12).

260. *Āpastambadharmasūtra* 2.16.1.

261. *Manu* 3.284.

262. Parry 1985b:622.

263. *Manu* 9.137; and see *Yājñavalkyasmṛti* 1.78; *Viṣṇusmṛti* 15.56.

264. Knipe 1977; Müller 1992:86 and 96.

265. Caland 1896:172–174; V. Das 1982:95ff.; Müller 1992:85–86.

266. *Garuḍapurāṇa Sāroddhāra* 1.45.

267. Sprockhoff 1985; and see Schmithausen 1995:49.

268. See *Viṣṇusmṛti* 20–32.

269. See Thapar 1981; Blackburn 1985.

270. Krick 1982:116ff. discusses the various ways of death for this ritual.

271. For these and other forms of funerals, see Filippi 1996:167–178.

272. *Garuḍapurāṇa, Uttarakhaṇḍa* 10.100 (Abegg 1921:150).

273. *Garuḍapurāṇa Sāroddhāra* 10.92.

274. *Baudhāyanadharmasūtra* 1.11.5–8; Winternitz 1920:15, with more proofs of women in the death cult.

275. The section on the death sacrifice in *Caturvargacintāmaṇi*, for example, is 1,717 pages long; in Jolly (1896:153–154), the ancestor ritual is treated in only a half page; in Pandey 1969, it is mentioned only marginally. Only Kane (1968–:IV:334–551) devotes the necessary detail to the subject; see the detailed description of a modern *śrāddha*, pp. 485ff. A comprehensive documentation and analysis is still lacking. The unpublished dissertation of Evison 1989, and Müller 1992 are only a beginning.

276. According to Kane 1968–:III:737; and see Bennett 1983:92ff.

277. Köhler 1973.

278. See Kane 1968–:IV:335

279. Parry 1985b:615.

280. Kane 1968–:IV:503.

281. Evison 1989:422.

282. The following section in some cases expands on Michaels 1992b, 1993b, and 1994b; see the literature listed there and Abegg 1921:140, note 1; *Garuḍapurāṇa* 10.34–55; Courtright 1995; Hawley 1996; Weinberger-Thomas 1999; Fisch 1998.

283. Sprockhoff 1979:423 (with proofs).

284. E.g., in the *Mahābhārata;* see Kane 1968–:II.1:626.

285. Michaels 1993b and 1994b.

286. See Garzilli 1997.

287. Michaels 1994c:41 (fig. 9).

288. *Garuḍapurāṇa, Uttarakhaṇḍa* 16.34 (Abegg 1921:18).

289. Alsdorf 1961; Dumont 1980:146–151; Schmidt 1968: Chapple 1993; Wezler (ed./ms.).

290. See Derrett 1979.

291. See Michaels 1997b and 1998.

292. See Rau 1957:34–35.

293. Quoted in Alsdorf 1961:34–35; see Mahābhārata 13.116.29: *yajñārthāni hi sṛṣṭhāni.*

294. *Manu* 2.85.

295. Horsch 1971; O'Flaherty (ed.) 1980 and 1993; Keyes/Daniel (eds.) 1983; Neufeldt (ed.) 1986; Tull 1989; Oberhammer (ed.) 1995; Michaels 1995a.

296. Kramer 1978:16.

297. See Oldenberg 1917:523–565; Keith 1925;252ff, 454ff, and 581–591.

298. Bodewitz 1996.

299. *Chāndogya-Upaniṣad* 5.9–10; see the schematic representation of A. Etter in Michaels 1995a:168.

300. Long in O'Flaherty (ed.) 1980:40.

301. The following section partially expands on Michaels 1999 and see M. Bloch 1992:48.

302. See Heesterman 1995:39–42.

303. *Garuḍapurāṇa Sāroddhāra* 11.8.

304. Cassirer 1955:37.

305. See *Bhagavadgītā* 2.22; *Bṛhadāraṇyaka-Upaniṣad* 4.4.4; Kane 1968–:IV:335.

306. Parry 1985b.

307. *Garuḍapurāṇa* 10.100.

308. Weber 1958:222.

CHAPTER 4: THE SOCIAL SYSTEM

1. Attached: a selection of the best-known names of castes.

2. Senart 1930:13; O'Malley 1941:357 and 1932:19.

3. Dumont 1980:46.

4. Collective representations: J. N. Bhattacharya 1896; Ketkar 1909; Risley 1908; Senart 1930; O'Malley 1932; Ghurye 1950; Hutton 1946; Kolenda 1978. Bibliographies: Srinivas et al. 1959; Fürer-Haimendorf 1958–1964; Kantowsky/Kulke/Rösel 1968; Pfeiffer 1974. And Mandelbaum 1970; L. Dumont 1980 and in *Bibliography of Asian Studies.*

5. See Quigley 1993:1.

6. Mandelbaum 1970:29; and see Klass 1980:20ff.

7. Senart 1930:103–104.

8. See Rösel 1982; Dirks 1989.

9. Quigley 1988 and 1993:12–20; Inden 1990:56ff.

10. Dumont 1980.

11. Yule/Burnell 1886: see "caste."

12. Pitt-Rivers 1971.

13. See the commentator Kullūka on *Manu* 10.4, where the mule (*aśvatara*) is introduced as a comparison for the "species" of the mixed caste.

14. Pitt-Rivers 1971:234; and see Klass 1980:27.

15. *Indikē* 11–12.

16. McCrindle 1877:198; see Klass 1980:21ff.

17. Al-Bīrūnī, trans. Strohmaier, 160–162.

18. In Al-Bīrūnī, *jātaka* is used incorrectly instead of *jāti.*

19. See *Manu* 10.6–40; *Arthaśāstra* 1.3.15; *Bhagavadgītā* 1.41–44; Brinkhaus 1978; Tambiah 1973a.

20. *Manu* 3.239; *Chāndogya-Upaniṣad* 5.10.7; *Mahābhārata* 1.79.13: *paśudharmin,* more evidence in Halbfass 1981.

21. See *Manu* 12.43.

22. J. N. Bhattacharya 1896:15.

23. Oldenberg 1917:2.

24. The well-known compendia and gazetteers include: J. N. Bhattacharya 1896; Blunt 1931; Crooke 1896; Enthoven 1920–1922; Ibbetson 1916; Iyer/Najundaa 1928–1935; Nesfield 1885; Risley 1891; Russell/Lal 1916, *The Imperial Gazetteer of India* 1907–1909; Thurston/Rangachari 1909.

25. Risley 1908:111.

26. Risley 1908:29; see Dumont 1980:28; Inden 1990:61.

27. Risley 1908:275.

28. Weber 1958:123.

29. See Zilm 1997.

30. Lingat 1973:36.

31. Dumont 1980:39, 43.

32. Bouglé 1971.

33. Dumont 1980; Heesterman 1985:180ff. and 194ff.; B. K. Smith 1994 is one of the most conspicuous examples of this thesis.

34. The most important village studies with maps are in Mandelbaum 1970 and Schwartzberg, ed., 1992; and see Dube 1955; Lewis 1958; Marriott 1955.

35. Summarized in Kolenda 1978:40–41.

36. The following is based partly on Michaels 1986b:chapter 3.

37. Modified according to Kolenda 1978:fig. 1.3., p. 19. The Indian terms can overlap. Thus, *kula* can mean the extended family, the race in the sense of *gotra,* or a lineage in the sense of *vaṃśa.*

38. Dumont 1980:62–63; Milner 1994:269.

39. Leach 1960:5; see especially Dumont 1980:39–42.

40. Trautmann (1964:198) suggests "order" and "estate" as translations of *varṇa;* see Dumont 1980:67 ("'estates,' in the sense the word had in France in the Ancient Régime"); B. K. Smith 1994:26ff.

41. See B. K. Smith 1994.

42. See *Manu* 1.87–91; Kane 1968–:II.1:50–179; above, table 8.

43. See Rau 1957:§42.

44. *Arthaśāstra* 1.30.5–8.

45. See the convincing critique of Dumézil by Malamoud 1982b (1996:109–129).

46. See Lingat 1973:29–45.

47. And detailed, if also controversial, B. K. Smith 1994:26ff; and see Dumont 1980:66ff.

48. *Ṛgvedasaṃhitā* 10.90; see Schneider 1989:36–60; B. K. Smith 1994:67–68.

49. *Ṛgvedasaṃhitā* 10.90.12.

50. Details in Rau 1957 and Witzel 1997.

51. Quigley 1993:18–19.

52. Thus, Hocart (1938:23): "The four-caste system is a pure figment"; see Dumont 1980:67.

53. Milner 1994:73.

54. Senart 1930:114ff.; Ghurye 1932:19; Hutton 1963:64; Dumont 1980:61ff.; Klass 1980:90; B. K. Smith 1994:317; Milner 1994:63–79.

55. See Brinkhaus 1978; Tambiah 1973a.

56. Milner 1994:67.

57. Even though the difference is known, Weber (1958), Ketkar (1909), Hocart (1935) (see above, note 52), and many others (most recently Becke 1996:48ff.) translate *varṇa* as "caste."58. Mayer 1960:5.

59. Dumont 1980:57–58.

60. In the early Dharmaśāstra, *jāti* denotes caste in the sense given here: *Manu* 10.4; see Lingat 1973:32.

61. See the discussion in B. K. Smith 1994:317–319, with evidence.

62. Thus also Kolenda 1978:10–11; the term was probably introduced by Senart (Mayer 1960:5). Dumont (1980), Quigley, Milner, and others use the term *subcaste*, but do not define it.

63. Klass 1980:92–93.

64. The term *extended family* that I have chosen corresponds to what has been called *birādarī* by Blunt (1931:10); subcaste by Ghurye (1950:20) and Dumont (1980); *jāti* group by Mandelbaum (1970:17); kindred of recognition or *biradan* by Mayer (1960); sub-clan or *birādari* by Parry (1979:136); and marriage-circle by Klass (1980:93).

65. Sontheimer 1977.

66. Hutton 1963:121; and especially Dumont 1980.

67. Weber 1968:411.

68. Bourdieu 1977.

69. Glaser 1912; Kane 1968–:II.1:334ff.; Michaels 1997a with more evidence.

70. Jolly 1896.

71. *Manu* 12.1–11.

72. Cf. *Āpastambadharmasūtra* 1.14.6ff.

73. Atri in *Devaṇṇabhaṭṭa's Smṛticandrikā,* p. 38.

74. *Āpastambadharmasūtra* 1.5.16.

75. *Devaṇṇabhaṭṭa's Smṛticandrikā*, p. 39.

76. Bhaviṣyapurāṇa according to *Devaṇṇabhaṭṭa's Smṛticandrikā*, p. 37.

77. Gennep (1960) interprets the return greeting as a rite of affiliation.

78. Harper 1964:158.

79. There is a detailed analysis in Bennett 1983:150–164.

80. See Michaels 1994c:118, with evidence.

81. Harper 1964; Marriot 1976 and 1990 (introd.); Marriott/Inden 1973 and 1977; see Michaels 1986b:73–91.

82. Douglas 1966:121.

83. See *Manu* 5.135; *Viṣṇusmṛti* 22.81; *Atrismṛti* 5.31.

84. Douglas 1966:121.

85. See Mandelbaum 1970:192–193; Das 1985.

86. Harper 1964:161.

87. Harper 1964:158–159.

88. *Gautamadharmasūtra* 14.30.

89. See Dumont 1980:131–137; Moffat 1979.

90. Harper 1964; Dumont 1980:130–145; Marriott 1968a and 1990 (introd.); Marriott/Inden 1977; Eichinger Ferro-Luzzi 1977; Dumont 1980:137ff.; Khare/Rao 1986.

91. Jolly 1896:157; Harper 1964:157.

92. Parry 1985b:613.

93. See Dumont 1980:83ff.; Parry 1985b:613. Table taken from Wiemann-Michaels 1994:86 (table 19).

94. Dumont 1980:146–151.

95. Mandelbaum 1970:188; Kolenda 1978:80.

96. Harper 1964:158.

97. H.N.C. Stevenson 1954; Dumont/Pocock 1959; Harper 1964; Dumont 1980:46ff. and 130ff.; Marriott 1959, 1960, 1968a, 1968b, 1969, 1976; Marriott/Inden 1977; Kolenda 1978:62–85; Quigley 1993; Milner 1994:106–123.

98. For these and the following examples, see O'Malley 1941:366ff.

99. Harper 1964:176.

100. *Garuḍapurāṇa* 9.14.

101. Parry 1979.

102. Douglas 1966; see Durkheim/Mauss 1903.

103. Douglas 1966:36.

104. Marriott 1959, 1960, 1968a; Mahar [Kolenda] 1959; and see Dumont 1980:89ff. and Kolenda 1978:62ff.

105. Höfer 1979:45.

106. Berremann 1971; Freed 1963; Mahar [Kolenda] 1959; Marriot 1959 and 1960; Dumont 1980:65ff.; Burghart 1978; Höfer 1979.

107. Quigley 1993:20.

108. Heesterman 1964; Dumont 1980:66ff. et passim; Veer 1989; Quigley 1993:54–87, and the literature listed in note 124 below.

109. Heesterman 1964:1–31, slightly revised in 1985:26–44.

110. Dumont 1980:47.

111. Weber 1958:131.

112. Kane 1968–:II.1:105–153; Shulman 1984; Stietencron 1985.

113. Kane 1968–:II.1:136.

114. See Gombrich 1996:20, 29, 42.

115. See Dumont's neglected postscript to the German translation of *Homo Hierarchicus*, and the symposium: "The Contributions of Louis Dumont," *Journal of Asian Studies* 35 (1976).

116. Dumont 1980:61.

117. Dumont 1980:240.

118. Dumont 1980.

119. Dumont 1980:66 and 1975.

120. Dumont 1975.

121. Dumont 1980:245; see Fuchs 1988:320.

122. Dumont 1980:66ff. and appendix B.

123. The most violent critics of Dumont and especially his Brahman-centrism are Berreman 1971; Delfendahl 1973:114; Lynch 1977:248ff.; Fuchs 1988:402ff.

124. Heesterman 1964:27; Derrett 1976:602; Parry 1979 and 1980; Fuller 1979:462 and 1984:49–71; Raheja 1988; Veer 1989; Quigley 1993:54ff. For Brahmanic classifications of Brahmans, see Kane 1968–:II.1:130–132.

125. Kolenda 1978, with evidence.

126. Quigley 1993:44–45.

127. See Gokhale 1980.

128. Shulman 1984:108–109.

129. See the list of Schreiner 1996:166–167.

130. Dumont 1980:58.

131. Gould 1967.

132. Dumont 1980:47.

133. Dumont 1980:72; Derrett 1976:603; Shulman 1985:110–111 and 149–151.

134. Dumont 1975.

135. See the justified objections of Fuchs 1988:403.

136. But see Kolff 1990.

137. Marriott 1968b; Raheja 1988; Kolenda 1978.

138. See the model of Raheja 1988:243.

139. Burghart 1978.

140. Rau 1957:§ 41; Witzel 1997:36.

141. *Chāndogya-Upaniṣad* 4.4.1ff. (my translation—A. M.).

142. Wiser 1936; Beidelman 1959; Harper 1959; Gould 1967; Dumont 1980:92–108; Commander 1988; Kolenda 1985:46ff.; Raheja 1988:93–101; Fuller 1989; Quigley 1993:69ff.; Milner 1994:80–96.

143. Marriott 1968a:145.

144. Milner 1994:90.

145. Raheja 1988:1.

146. See Rahaja 1988:25 and Quigley 1993:114–141.

147. Parry 1979:72; Raheja 1988:26.

148. Especially Commander 1988 and Fuller 1989.

149. See Kölver 1988.

150. Kolenda 1976:48–52.

151. The following section follows Michaels 1997a; and see Kane 1968–:II.2:chapter 25; Gonda 1965:198–228; Malamoud 1980; Trautmann 1981:279ff.; Parry 1986; Nath 1987; Raheja 1988; Gellner 1992:121–124.

152. Mauss 1990.

153. Hierarchies of merit of a *dāna* are found, e.g., in *Agnipurāṇa* 209.34ff.

154. *Manu* 10.102.

155. Trautmann 1981:279n. 42 and 282n. 46; Parry 1986:461; and see Fuller 1984:196 and Raheja 1988:250.

156. Heesterman 1985:28.

157. *Manu* 9.1–6, 4.192–200, 3.128–137, 7.85–86; Kane 1968–:II.2:845.

158. *Manu* 4.247–250; *Agnipurāṇa* 109.29–33; *Bhagavadgītā* 17.20–22; *Caturvargacintāmaṇi* (Dānakhaṇda) 13–14.

159. *Kṛtyakalpataru*, pp. 5–6; see Trautmann 1981:45, 280.

160. See Kolenda 1976:82.

161. Raheja 1988:37ff.

162. "Dān is always given to those who are seen as 'other' (*dūsre*) precisely in order to 'move away' (*hatanā*) the inauspiciousness afflicting the jajmān." (Raheja 1989:88).

163. Gellner 1992:123.

CHAPTER 5: RELIGIOSITY

1. Feyerabend 1981:56.

2. Marquard 1989:105.

3. See MacDonell 1897; Hopkins 1915; Oldenberg 1917; Hillebrandt 1980; Gonda 1960–1964: vol. 1; O'Flaherty 1975; Daniélou 1985:63–148.

4. This is a selection; only the most conspicuous features of the divinities are mentioned.

5. Hübner 1985:111–112 *et passim.*

6. Weber 1968: 216.

7. *Ṛgvedasaṃhitā* 4.42, 7.82.2, 7.83.9, 7.85.2, 7.86.

8. *Ṛgvedasaṃhitā* 6.61.

9. Oldenberg 1917:98.

10. *Atharvaveda* 11.2.28; *Ṛgvedasaṃhitā* 8.100.3; Gonda 1978/I:29.

11. Weber 1968:254.

12. Gonda 1960–1964:I:29.

13. *Aitareyabrāhmaṇa* 2.31.2.

14. *Jaiminīya-Upaniṣadbrāhmaṇa* 1.283.

15. *Śatapathabrāhmaṇa* 1.1.4.1.

16. *Atharvaveda* 11.8.20.

17. *Śatapathabrāhmaṇa* 7.4.1.39; see Gonda 1960–1964:I:30.
18. See Gonda 1965; Daniélou 1985:20.
19. Hübner 1985:112–113 and chapter 9.
20. *Bṛhadāraṇyaka-Upaniṣad* 1.40.9–15; 3.70.3–23; 2.80.7–12; 3.90.1–9.
21. *Bṛhadāraṇyaka-Upaniṣad* 3.9.1.
22. *Bhāgavadgītā* 11.15–16.
23. *Bhāgavadgītā* 9.23.
24. *Cakṣur hi vai satyam* (*Bṛhadāraṇyaka-Upaniṣad* 5.14.4).
25. *Ṛgvedasaṃhitā* 1.164.46; see *Mahābhārata* 13.17.7.
26. See below, and Michaels 1994c:88–91, with appendix 24.
27. Oldenberg 1919:3.
28. Winternitz 1996:506–507.
29. Cassirer 1955:7.
30. See Daniélou 1985:8–11.
31. Gonda 1960–1964:236ff. and 1970b.
32. Hacker 1960; Gonda 1968; Schneider 1989:105ff.
33. See Dhavamony 1982:chapter 2.
34. *Bhāgavatapurāṇa:* 1.3.27–28.
35. *Bhagavadgītā* 4.1–9.
36. See *Mahābhārata* 12.326.61; *Bhagavadgītā* 4.14, 9.11, 15.14.
37. See *Bhagavadgītā* 7.24ff.
38. See *Bhagavadgītā* 9.18.
39. *Bhagavadgītā* 4.14, 7.25.
40. *Bhagavadgītā* 7.4.
41. *Aṣṭādhyāyi* 4.3.98.
42. Wilke 1996:279.
43. See Fuller 1988.
44. See Flood 1996:118.
45. Bhandarkar 1913; Gonda 1960–1964/I:254–255 and 1970b; O'Flaherty 1973; Kramrisch 1981.
46. Sanderson 1988; Flood 1996:155.
47. Sanderson 1988:660.
48. Modified from Sanderson 1988 and Flood 1996:152.
49. "In India the god that is loved is Viṣṇu-Nārāyaṇa-Vāsudeva-Kṛṣṇa, while the god that is feared is Rudra-Śiva" (Bhandarkar 1913:106).
50. *Ṛgvedasaṃhitā* 1.43, 1.114, 2.33, and 7.46.
51. See *Śatapathabrāhmaṇa* 1.7.4.3.
52. Bhandarkar 1913:104.
53. *Taittirīyasaṃhitā* 4.5.1.
54. See above, chapter 2.
55. Zaehner 1962:21–22.
56. *Mahābhārata, Anuśāsanaparvan,* fourteenth chapter.
57. See *Vāyupurāṇa* 23.115ff.; *Kūrmapurāṇa* 1.51.10.

58. Leach 1976.

59. O'Flaherty 1973:41.

60. Michaels 1994c:66ff.

61. Gutschow/Michaels 1993:65ff. and 84ff.

62. Michaels 1992a and 1993a.

63. Courtright 1985; Grimes 1995; on the miracle (with regard to Sai Baba), see also Fuller 1992:178–179.

64. *Ṛgvedasaṃhitā* 2.23.1, 10.112.9; *Aitareyabrāhmaṇa* 1.21.

65. Courtright 1985:11.

66. Kinsley 1986; Hawley/Wulff 1982 and 1996; Pintchman 1994; Michaels/Vogelsanger/Wilke 1996:introduction.

67. See Michaels 1994c:191–240.

68. See Michaels/Vogelsanger/Wilke 1996:21–22.

69. From Michaels 1993a:177–178 and 1994c:table 17; see Michaels/Vogelsanger/Wilke 1996:table 1.

70. See Michaels 1994c:92; and Michaels/Sharma 1996.

71. Babb 1975:15–32; D. Gellner 1992:73ff.; see Michaels/Vogelsanger/Wilke 1996:22.

72. Heiler 1932; Dhavamony 1982:206–242.

73. Heiler 1932:358–362.

74. *Śatapathabrāhmaṇa* 1.4.4.2.

75. Padoux 1990:77.

76. Gonda 1977; Bühnemann 1984 and 1986.

77. Gonda 1963; Bharati 1965; Alper 1989; Staal 1989; Padoux 1990; Elizarenkova 1995.

78. Alper 1989:11.

79. Bharati 1965:102.

80. See *Bṛhadāraṇyaka-Upaniṣad* 5.14; *Maitreya-Upaniṣad* 6.7; see above, chapter 3.

81. *Māṇḍūkya-Upaniṣad* 1.1 (my translation—A. M.).

82. *Chāndogya-Upaniṣad* 1.10.2–3; see Thieme 1966b:11–18.

83. Gonda 1970a; Stietencron 1975; Vandana 1996.

84. Cassirer 1955:41.

85. Wilke (ms.).

86. Stietencron 1975:59.

87. Gonda 1969b; Eck 1981.

88. Kane 1968–:II.2:chapter 26.

89. Halbfass 1981:296ff.

90. Maloney 1976 has collected an abundance of material.

91. S. Stevenson 1920:14.

92. S. Stevenson 1920:13.

93. S. Stevenson 1920:113.

94. Trawick 1990:93.

95. Eck 1981:9.

96. Baldissera/Michaels 1988:52.

97. Maloney 1976:124–125.

98. Eck 1981:6; see Fuller 1992:59–61.

99. Masilamani-Meyer 1996.

100. O'Flaherty 1975:158.

101. Hopkins 1915:135; O'Flaherty 1973:247; Shulman 1980:133; Trawick 1990:95.

102. Gonda 1969b:9.

103. *Bṛhadāraṇyakā-Upaniṣad* 5.15.5; similarly *Aitareyabrāhmaṇa* 1.6.11.

104. This section follows Michaels 1997d, where I have treated the subject in greater detail.

105. Bühnemann 1988:114.

106. Humphrey/Laidlaw 1994:89.

107. See Humphrey/Laidlaw 1994:120.

108. V. Turner 1964:19 and 1969.

109. Durkheim 1995.

110. Malinowski 1967:29.

111. S. Stevenson 1920:210–225; Srinivasan 1978; Kane 1968–:II.1:312–321; Einoo 1993.

112. S. Stevenson 1920:210–211; Kane 1968–:II.1:648.

113. *Manu* 4.45–52; see Kane 1968–:II.1:649.

114. Kane 1968–:II.1:312ff. treats the *saṃdhyā* as part of the initiation!

115. Einoo 1993:198; the origin of this *mantra* is unknown.

116. S. Stevenson 1920:214.

117. *Yājñavalkyasmṛti* 1.19; *Viṣṇusmṛti* 62.1–4; *Baudhāyanadharmasūtra* 1.50.14–18; see Bühnemann 1988:104–105, with figs. 5–6.

118. *Baudhāyanadharmasūtra* 3.1.26; see Kane 1968–:II.1:651–652 for *śauca* and 656ff. for *snāna.*

119. *Taittirīya-Āraṇyaka* 6.25.

120. See chapter 3.

121. *Ṛgvedasaṃhitā* 10.190; see chapter 6.

122. Kane 1968–:II.1:313.

123. Kane 1968–:II.1:672ff.

124. For the history of the Saṃdhyā, see Einoo 1993:206ff.; Kane 1968–:II.1:314–315; for *agnihotra,* P.-E. Dumont 1939; Bodewitz 1976; Witzel 1986.

125. Bühnemann 1988:49–51.

126. Bühnemann 1988:49.

127. Thieme 1939; Brunner-Lachaux 1963, 1969, and 1977; Kane 1968–:II.2:705–740; Babb 1975:31–68; Tachikawa 1983; Bühnemann 1988:29, 43ff.; R. H. Davis 1991; Fuller 1992:66–82; Gutschow/Michaels 1993:91–101; Einoo 1996.

128. Thieme 1939:121–122; Eichinger Ferro-Luzzi 1981:709–710.

129. See Bühnemann 1986:no. 10.

130. Summary in Bühnemann 1988:34–42; and see Goudriaan 1970.

131. Edited by Michaels 1994c:appendix A 13.

132. Fuller 1992:61.

133. For a description of an inner vision during meditation, see Preston 1980:53.

134. See Gonda 1970b:186; Fuller 1992:67; Kane 1968–:II.2:729. Table reprinted from Michaels 1994c. table 3.

135. Kane 1968–:II.2:739–740.

136. See Eichinger Ferro-Luzzi 1981.

137. Babb 1975:56; see Wezler 1978.

138. Fuller 1992:78.

139. Babb 1982:310; and see D. Gellner 1992:107.

140. Babb 1982:307.

141. Hillebrandt 1897 and 1921; Lévi 1898; Hubert/Mauss 1964; Oldenberg 1917; Gonda 1960–1964:I:104–173; Mylius 1973; Thite 1975; Biardeau/Malamoud 1976; Fuller 1992:83–105; Heesterman 1993.

142. See *Taittirīyasaṃhitā* 1.8.4.11; *Viṣṇusmṛti* 3.50: *dehi me dadāmi te.*

143. See the survey of Drexel 1993 (with bibliography).

144. See Heesterman 1995.

145. *Śatapathabrāhmaṇa* 2.3.1.5.

146. Frauwallner 1973.

147. And *Manu* 3.76.

148. Michaels 1978:48–50.

149. Heesterman 1997:58.

150. *Taittirīya-Upaniṣad* 3.10.6.

151. For Soma, see above, chapter 2.

152. See Staal 1983; Witzel 1986; Tachikawa (1993).

153. *Taittrīyasaṃhitā* 1.7.9.

154. *Taittrīyasaṃhitā* 2.5.2.1; *Śatapathabrāhmaṇa* 1.6.3.10 and 1.7.3.19.

155. See especially Heesterman 1997.

156. Michaels 1978; Krick 1982; Staal 1983.

157. *Taittrīyasaṃhitā* 4.1.10.5; *Śatapathabrāhmaṇa* 6.7.2.6.

158. Eggeling, introduction to *Śatapathabrāhmaṇa,* vol. 4, p. xxiv.

159. *Śatapathabrāhmaṇa* 3.6.3.1.

160. The following is from Michaels 1978:40ff. and 1995b; and see Mylius 1973:477ff.

161. *Śatapathabrāhmaṇa* 3.1.4.3, 9.4.3.11.

162. Hillebrandt 1921:796.

163. Schayer 1925.

164. *Taittrīyasaṃhitā* 5.5.20.1–2 (my translation—A. M.).

165. See Panikkar 1992:81ff.; I discuss this in the conclusion of the fourth section of chapter 7.

166. Keith 1925:445; see Olivelle 1993:37.

167. See Michaels 1986b:106ff.; B. K. Smith 1989:54ff.; Olivelle 1993:37ff.

168. Heesterman 1978:36–37.

169. *Śatapathabrāhmaṇa* 8.6.1.10, 14.3.2.1.

170. *Śatapathabrāhmaṇa* 1.3.2.1.

171. *Jaiminīya-Upaniṣadbrāhmaṇa* 3.14.8.

172. *Manu* 4.25.

173. *Manu* 11.60.66; *Gautamadharmasūtra* 15.16.

174. The symbol ⊃ denotes a substitutive identification: see table 34.

175. Gonda 1960–1964:II; Hardy 1983 and 1994; Thiel-Horstmann (ed.) 1983; Eck (ed.) 1991; Fuller 1992:153–181; Werner 1993.

176. Lorenzen 1996.

177. See Fuller 1992:158.

178. See especially McDermott 1996.

179. Zaehner 1962:132 (with reference to Yudhiṣṭhira's dog).

180. Peterson 1989.

181. Zaehner 1962:146.

182. See Biardeau 1997:74–76.

183. Bäumer 1969.

184. See Dhavamony 1982:234–240.

185. Frauwallner 1973; Oberhammer (ed.) 1978; Schmithausen 1973; Küng et al. 1986; Vetter 1994.

186. Ruh 1990–1996.

187. Translations: Deussen 1997; Hillebrandt 1923; Geldner 1928; Thieme 1966b; Bäumer 1994; Olivelle 1996. Studies: Oldenberg 1991; Keith 1925; Frauwallner 1973; Zimmer 1973:319ff.; Hanefeld 1976.

188. Thieme 1996c:83; but see also Falk 1986 and Olivelle 1996:liii.

189. *Bṛhadāraṇyaka-Upaniṣad* 3.6.1, 3.9.26; see Bäumer 1994:37 and 59.

190. *Chāndogya-Upaniṣad* 6.8.7ff; *Bṛhadāraṇyaka-Upaniṣad* 1.4.10.

191. Oldenberg 1991; Frauwallner 1973; Bäumer 1994:47; see Kohl 1997:52–53.

192. *Bṛhadāraṇyaka-Upaniṣad* 5.15 (my translation—A. M.).

193. For *bráhman*, see Thieme 1952.

194. See *Bṛhadāraṇyaka-Upaniṣad* 1.40.20–22.

195. *Bṛhadāraṇyaka-Upaniṣad* 4.5.15.

196. *Bṛhadāraṇyaka-Upaniṣad* 1.4.22 (my translation—A. M.).

197. *Chāndogya-Upaniṣad* 6; Thieme 1966c:43ff.; Frauwallner 1973; Hamm 1968–1969:149–159; Vetter 1994:177ff.; Hanefeld 1976:116ff.

198. *Chāndogya-Upaniṣad* 6.12.3.

199. *Chāndogya-Upaniṣad* 8.7.1.

200. *Manu* 12.88–90.

201. Fundamental are Garbe 1917; Keith 1918; Strauss 1924; Frauwallner 1973 (whose terminology I have adopted to a large extent); and see Frauwallner 1958; Larson 1969; Potter et al. 1979–1987: vol. 4. My description is based on the *Sāṃkhyakārikā* and follows Michaels 1995a:163–165 or 1996b:827–831.

202. Bailey 1985.

203. *Sāṃkhyakārikā* 63.

204. Woods 1914 and 1927; Frauwallner 1973; Eliade 1958c; Hauer 1958; Schreiner 1979. And see the literature on the Sāṃkhya system above.

205. *Maitreya-Upaniṣad* 6.18.

206. Deussen 1912; Potter 1979–1987: vol. 3 (lit.); Vetter 1979; Halbfass 1991:205–242; Isayeva 1993; Wilke 1995.

207. See Wilke 1995:357–358.

208. Haas 1986.

209. Wittgenstein 1961:73–74.

210. Otto 1932; Wilke 1995.

211. See Vetter 1994.

212. See Küng et al. 1986.

213. Hardy 1994:102ff.; Bollée 2003.

214. Hardy 1994:120.

215. See Bollée (ms.).

216. Hiltebeitel (ed.) 1989; *vīra and śūra* appear in Vedic literature as epithets mainly referring to Indra: Bollée 2003.

217. See Brückner 1995.

218. Hardy 1994:114.

219. Farquar 1925; Lorenzen 1978; Corre 1989; Alter 1992; Hartsuiker 1993:31ff. and 51–52; the following section is based on studies of Ākhāṛas in Benares: see Gutschow/Michaels 1993:207–210.

220. Rau 1957:84–128; Losch 1959; Schlerath 1960; Dumont 1962; Lingat 1973:207ff.; Gonda 1969a; Derrett 1976; Richards (ed.) 1978; Heesterman 1985:108–157; Shulman 1985; Kolff 1990; Inden 1978 and 1990:162–212; Fuller 1992:106–127; Kulke 1993.

221. Dumont 1962 (1980:290) and 1980:74–75.

222. See Inden 1990:201–202.

223. Hocart 1927 and 1936 (with a foreword by R. Needham); and Schnepel 1988, 1996, and 1997:59–63; Quigley 1993:114–141.

224. Witzel 1987.

225. Burghart 1987:194.

226. Geertz 1980:121.

227. Hocart 1950:68.

228. Dumont 1980:154ff.; Stein 1980; Dirks 1987; Berkemer 1993; Schnepel 1997.

229. See Michaels 1994c:312–313.

230. Michaels 1994c:272ff. and 1996c.

231. See Hocart 1936:244.

232. Hocart 1954:77; Schnepel 1988:184.

233. See Kantorowicz 1957.

CHAPTER 6: RELIGIOUS IDEAS OF TIME AND SPACE

1. See Mittelstrass 1974:56ff.
2. Mittelstrass 1974:66.
3. In general, see Mandal 1968 and Vatsyayan (ed.) 1991.
4. Gonda 1966.

5. *Śatapathabrāhmaṇa* 11.6.3.6; see table 13.

6. Instructive for this is volume 3 of Hermann Schmitz, *System der Philosophie* (1967, 1969, and 1978).

7. Kirfel 1920; Sircar 1967; Gombrich 1975; Klaus 1986; Schwartzberg 1992.

8. *Taittirīya-Āraṇyaka* 10.27–28; Kirfel 1920:57; Schwartzberg 1992:337.

9. *Chāndogya-Upaniṣad* 3.19.1.

10. Selection from B. K. Smith 1994:125–170, especially 156.

11. *Manu* 2.78.

12. *Ṛgvedasaṃhitā* 10.90; Gonda 1960–1964:I:173; Schneider 1989:36–51; O'Flaherty 1973:27–28.

13. Bharati 1963; Bhardwaj 1973; Morinis 1984; Veer 1988; A. G. Gold 1989; Fuller 1992:204–223.

14. Cassirer 1955:II:89.

15. Gutschow/Michaels 1993:14ff. and 102ff.

16. Salomon 1979.

17. *Parāśarasmṛti* 12.64; Salomon 1979:102–103.

18. Bühnemann 1984:86.

19. Thibaut 1899; Kaye 1924; Kane 1968–:I:chapter 14ff.; Billard 1971; Türstig 1980.

20. Kane 1968–:II:515.

21. Raheja 1988:52–53.

22. Corresponding to the length of the lunar month, the heavenly spheres are divided into twenty-seven or twenty-eight constellations (*nakṣatra*).

23. For more examples, see Schwartzberg 1992:349 (fig. 16.12).

24. See Sprockhoff 1964:108.

25. Examples from Sprockhoff 1964:108.

26. From Hübner 1985:163ff.

27. For the following, see Cassirer 1955:79ff. and 108ff.; and Panikkar 1991.

28. For exceptions, see Wassmann 1994.

29. *Chāndogya-Upaniṣad* 8.1.1 and 3.

30. Panikkar 1991:12.

31. Cassirer 1955:83–94.

32. See Michaels 1997f.

33. See Mann 1982; Eliade 1959 and (ed.) 1964.

34. Jacobi 1911; Brown 1942; Gombrich 1975; Kuiper 1983; Klaus 1986; Pfeiffer 1994.

35. *Ṛgvedasṃmhitā* 10.81 and 82.

36. *Ṛgvedasaṃhitā* 10.54.3; see Oldenberg 1917:277.

37. *Ṛgvedasaṃhitā* 10.127.7, 10.129.3.

38. *Ṛgvedasaṃhitā* 10.129.1–7; see Thieme 1966b:66–67 with explanations.

39. *Ṛgvedasaṃhitā* 10.121.

40. *Ṛgvedasaṃhitā* 10.90.

41. *Ṛgvedasaṃhitā* 10.72.

42. Oldenberg 1917:280.

43. *Ṛgvedasaṃhitā* 10.61.5–7, 3.31.1; O'Flaherty 1973:326 and 313.

44. Dimmitt/Buitenen 1978:16ff.; Pfeiffer 1994; Biardeau 1997:120–173.

45. Bäumer 1969.

46. Reprinted in *Kūrmapurāṇa* 1.90.6–29; see Dimmitt/Buitenen 1978:30–31.

47. Reprinted in *Brahmāṇḍapurāṇa* 1.2.80.1–61; see O'Flaherty et al. 1988:65; and O'Flaherty 1973:no. 9.

48. *Brahmavaivartapurāṇa* 1.8.1.30, 37–53, 62–68; O'Flaherty 1973:no. 11.

49. *Matsyapurāṇa* 3.1.

50. Kirfel 1920:91ff., 180–207, and 1927; Abegg 1928:5–39; Frauwallner 1973; Huntington 1964; Church 1971; O'Flaherty 1976:15ff.; Stietencron 1986; Biardeau 1981 and 1997:120–173; Wessler 1995:123ff. The following is based partly on Michaels 1995a and 1997e.

51. *Bhāgavatapurāṇa* 12.1–3; *Kūrmapurāṇa* 1.29; *Mahābhārata* 3.148 and 188–189.

52. See Frauwallner 1973.

53. See Roth 1860.

54. See *Bhāgavatapurāṇa* 12.2.

55. Stietencron 1986:148–149.

56. *Viṣṇupurāṇa* 4.240.25–29; O'Flaherty 1973:236; Dimmitt/Buitenen 1978:41.

57. *Viṣṇupurāṇa* 6.30.14–41, 4.1–10; Dimmitt/Buitenen 1978:41ff.

58. Stietencron 1986:145–147.

59. Huntington 1964:38; O'Flaherty 1976:18. For a comparison of the cosmological evolution of the world in the *Purāṇas* and *Upaniṣads* with the emanation process of the Sāṃkhya system, see Biardeau 1997:120ff.

60. See Thieme 1971a:376ff.; Schmithausen 1985:123; Halbfass 1991:chapters 8–10; Slaje 1993.

61. See Böhme 1988:380ff.

62. S. Stephenson 1920:252–342; Underhill 1921; Freed/Freed 1964; Merrey 1982; Wessler 1995:15–32.

63. Basically (but controversially) in Eliade 1951 and 1959; and Brandon 1965.

64. See Kramer 1978:16.

65. Biardeau 1997:126.

66. See Kulke 1979 and 1982; Halbfass 1981:chapter 18; Kölver 1993; Wessler 1995.

67. See Sprockhoff 1964:136–137.

68. See Michaels 1994c:255–264.

69. Underhill 1921; Glasenapp 1928; Gonda 1960–1964:II:271ff.; Holland 1979; B. N. Sharma 1978.

70. From Gutschow/Michaels 1993:168–174.

71. In more detail in Michaels 1994c:241–175 and 1996c.

72. V. Turner 1969 and 1974.

73. Hübner 1985:142–158.

CHAPTER 7: IMMORTALITY IN LIFE

1. H. D. Sharma 1939; Eliade 1958c; Bhagat 1976; Sprockhoff 1976 and 1981–1984; Rüping 1979; Olivelle 1986 and 1992:19–112; Olson 1997.

2. Bronkhorst 1993.

3. Also Olivelle 1992:20ff.

4. Oman 1903; Ghurye 1964; Gross 1979; Veer 1988; Hartsuiker 1993. The following section, which is based on investigations of and conversations with ascetics in Deopatan (Nepal) and Benares, refers literally in some cases to Gutschow/Michaels 1993:144–155.

5. Selection of the bigger groups; see tables 4, 18, 23, and 24.

6. See Hartsuiker 1993 with remarkable photos.

7. McLeod 1978.

8. Parry 1994.

9. Briggs 1938; Unbescheid 1980.

10. Gross 1979; Burghart 1996:chapters 4–6.

11. Lorenzen 1996.

12. Heesterman 1964; Dumont 1960; Kaelber 1989; Olivelle 1992:23ff.; as well as the literature mentioned above in note 4.

13. *Śatapathabrāhmaṇa* 12.8.2.6; *Taittirīyabrāhmaṇa* 2.2.2.6.

14. *Bṛhadāraṇyaka-Upaniṣad* 4.4.22 (my translation—A. M.).

15. Olivelle 1992:103–105.

16. *Āruṇi-Upaniṣad* 6.

17. See Olivelle 1986:I:29ff.; Michaels 1994a.

18. See Heesterman 1995; Kaelber 1989; Olivelle 1992:86–89.

19. *Kaṭhaśruti-Upaniṣad* 39; Olivelle 1992:134.

20. Olivelle 1992:68.

21. Hartsuiker 1993:95.

22. Olivelle 1992:89ff.

23. Olivelle 1992:93.

24. *Bṛhatsaṃnyāsa-Upaniṣad* 251; Olivelle 1992:243.

25. Heesterman 1964:27.

26. For the concept of salvation during one's lifetime (*jīvanmukti*), see Oberhammer 1994 and Fort/Mumme (eds.) 1996.

27. Part of this section was the core of my inaugural lecture at the University of Heidelberg on June 17, 1998.

28. See Dumont 1975.

29. Elias 1978, 1982; Lippe 1974.

30. Dumont 1980:53–54.

31. See *Manu* 6.42ff.

32. Harper 1964:173.

33. Quigley 1993:83.

34. Leach 1976.

35. See Harper 1964:153; Dumont 1980:51.

36. See Kramer 1978.

37. *Arthaśāstra* 1.3.9 and 13–16.

38. *Manu* 2.27–28.

39. *Bhagavadgītā* 1.42.

40. Harper 1964:172.

41. Lévi 1898; Oldenberg 1919:110–123; Hillebrandt 1921:796; Schayer 1925; Heesterman 1985:79–80; Witzel 1979; Falk 1986; B. K. Smith 1989; Wezler 1996; and see Mylius 1976 and 1977.

42. *Śatapathabrāhmaṇa* 14.3.2.1.

43. Heesterman 1995:31.

44. *Bṛhadāraṇyaka-Upaniṣad* 1.4.10; and see the place of the *Maitreya-Upaniṣad.*

45. *Śatapathabrāhmaṇa* 12.4.3.1.

46. See B. K. Smith 1989:30–38.

47. Olivelle 1992:lii and 348.

48. The list of examples can be continued: through the linguistic-philological discussions of the dualistic Dvaṇḍva compound, the soteriological significance of equilibrium in the Sāṃkhya system, the philosophizing or equality (*sāmānya*) in the Vaiśeṣika system or about division and duality (*bheda, dvaita*), the mythological dismemberment of a primeval creature or creator (Puruṣa, Prajāpati) whose limbs are identified with the whole, the *membra disiecta* (see below).

49. Wittgenstein 1961:4.46.

50. Wittgenstein: 1958:§67.

51. See *A Dictionary of Philosophy,* ed. J. Speake, New York, 1984; and see Wittgenstein 1961:4.241ff. and 1958:§558.

52. *Chāndogya-Upaniṣad* 6.5.3.

53. See, e.g., Weber 1968:230.

54. Lévy-Bruhl 1984.

55. Hocart 1936:58; and see also p. 45 ("If you cannot act on A by acting on B there can be no ritual."); and Schnepel 1988:171–175.

56. See Cassirer 1955:64 *et passim.*

57. Cassirer 1955:67 and 89.

58. See Hübner 1985:63ff. and 166.

59. Hübner 1985:112–113, or 257.

60. See Schnepel 1988:177.

61. Witzel 1979:6.

62. *Aitareyabrāhmaṇa.* 3.44.

63. Also Schayer 1925; for "analogical ways of thinking," see also Tambiah 1973b.

64. Hacker 1983; Oberhammer (ed.) 1983.

65. Hacker 1983:12.

66. Ibid.

67. Wezler 1983:77ff.

68. Wezler 1983:80.

69. Thieme 1968 and 1966c:43ff. (on p. 83, Thieme himself uses the term *identification*).

70. Wezler 1978:114 and 1996:517.

71. B. K. Smith 1989 and 1994.

72. Quoted from Winternitz 1996; and see Keith 1925:483 ("world of fancy").

73. Wezler 1996:491–497.

74. B. K. Smith 1989:47.

75. Heesterman 1990–1991; more detailed in Heesterman 1993 and 1995.

76. Heesterman 1990–1991:300.

77. Heesterman 1990–1991:302.

78. Dumont 1960:42 and 1980:272, 286.

79. Heesterman 1990–1991:304.

80. See Heesterman 1990–1991:305 ("Vedic ritualism did indeed lay the foundation and as such continued as a 'canon,' but it does not answer the human predicament"); and Heesterman 1997:49. For Smith's definition of Hindusim, see chapter 1.

81. Panikkar 1992:105.

82. Ramanujan 1990:47.

83. See *Bhagavadgītā* 2.24.

84. Weber 1968.

85. See Cassirer 1955:II:60ff.

86. Translation: Mayer-König 1996:90.

87. *Chāndogya-Upaniṣad* 5.1.15.

88. Assmann 1997:48ff.

89. Panikkar 1992.

90. Panikkar 1992:86.

91. Panikkar 1992:87.

92. *Devīgītā* 4.2; see Bühnemann 1986:37.

93. Panikkar 1992:93.

94. *Bṛhadāraṇyaka-Upaniṣad* 1.4.10.

95. See Olivelle 1992:41.

96. See Wilke 1995.

97. Panikkar 1992:101.

98. Panikkar 1992:101.

99. Panikkar 1992:105.

100. Gombrich 1996:33.

101. Gombrich 1996:62ff.

102. *Maitreya-Upaniṣad* 120 and 125 (Olivelle 1992:165–169).

Glossary

Advaitavedānta — Philosophical system: Knowledge of the identity of the individual self (*ātman*) with the universal self (*brahman*) brings salvation; most prominent representative: Śaṃkara

ākhāṛā — "Regiment" of ascetics, gymnastic center

agni — "Fire," god of the fire

ahiṃsā — Ban on harming living creatures

āraṇyaka — "Wilderness text," supplements to the Brāhmaṇas with esoteric interpretations of the sacrifice rituals; related to the Upaniṣads

ār(a)tī — Evening ceremony in temple worship, especially with oil lamps

Arjuna — One of the five Pāṇdava brothers in the Mahābhārata, who in the Bhagavadgītā is taught by Kṛṣṇa about the path to salvation

ārya — "The hospitable," self-description of the Indo-Iranian tribes that invaded southern India in the second millennium B.C.

Aśoka — Indian ruler (ca. 273–236 B.C.), who created the first big Indian empire and professed faith in Buddhism

Atharvaveda — "Knowledge of the [magic spells of the] Atharvans [and Aṅgiras]," collection (see *saṃhitā*) of formulas and hymns for warding off demons and disaster

ātman — Self, core of being, soul

avatāra — "Descent," manifestation of Viṣṇu and other gods

Āyurveda — Traditional Indian art of healing

Bhagavadgītā — "Song of the Glorious [Kṛṣṇa]," part of the Mahābhārata in which Kṛṣṇa teaches Prince Arjuna about the ways that lead to salvation

Bhairava — "Atrocious, terrifying," form of the god Śiva.

bhakta — Person who practices Bhakti

bhakti — "Participation, devotion," devotional form of religion

Bhīma — One of the five Pāṇḍava brothers in the Mahābhārata, who are distinguished by immense strength

bhūta — "Essence, spirit"

bodhisattva — "Enlightenment being," Buddhist saint who renounces his salvation to help other beings to salvation

Brahmā — One of the three main gods (along with Śiva and Viṣṇu), creator god

bráhman — All-souls, absolute, highest spiritual principle, Veda word

brāhmaṇa — Genre of texts that connect with the Saṃhitās and contains prescriptions for carrying out and explaining sacrificial rituals

Brahman — Member of the priest and scholar professional class (*varṇa*)

Bṛhadāraṇyaka-Upaniṣad — "Big-Wilderness-Upaniṣad," belonging to the Śatapathabrāhmaṇa, pre-Buddhist

Chāndogya-Upaniṣad — Upaniṣad of the Chāndogya school, belonging to the Sāmaveda, pre-Buddhist

dāna — Religious "gift"

Deopatan — City in northeastern Kathmandu with the national shrine of Paśupatinātha (= Śiva)

Devanāgarī — Northern Indian syllabary; used today for Sanskrit, Hindi, and Nepālī, among others

devī — "Goddess," collective term for (local) goddesses

dharma — (a) Divine order; (b) law and morality, ritual and social norms that are cut to fit a certain group—gods, animals, men (particularly for those who wear the Sacred Thread), women, inhabitants of a region, etc.

dharmaśāstra — (a) Legal text, in which prescriptions for everyday life are codified for various groups from the brahmanic perspective; (b) the Brahmanic-Sanskritic legal system

Durgā — Manifestation of the goddess (*devī*) that defeats the various demons

Gaṇeśa — Elephant-headed god, son of Śiva and Pārvatī; considered the god who clears obstacles out of the way

Gāyatrī — Also called Sāvitrī: Verse from the Ṛgveda (3.62.10), which is considered as (sometimes divine) essence of the Veda

gotra — Line of descent of a mythical seer (*ṛṣi*), which originally represented a sacrificial community; members of the same Gotra may not enter into marriage according to the Dharmaśāstra

gṛhyasūtra — Genre of texts that include prescriptions for domestic rituals

Hanumān — Monkey god, hero in monkey form in the Rāmāyaṇa, with whose help Rāma frees Sītā

harijan — "Child of the god (Hari = Viṣṇu)," used by Mahatma Gandhi to characterize the casteless

haṭhayoga — Strict form of physical asceticism within the philosophy of Yoga
Indra — War god and king god
jaina — Supporters of the ascetic reform movement of Mahāvīra, the founder of Jainism
Kālī — Manifestation of the goddesses (*devī*) in their destructive form
karman (and *karma*) — "Act, sacrifice," effect of an action that had been committed in another life
Kaunteya — "Son of the Kuntī," another name for Arjuna
Kṛṣṇa — Manifestation of the god Viṣṇu
kṣatriya — Member of the warrior professional class (*varṇa*)
Lakṣmī — Goddess of beauty and wealth; consort of Viṣṇu
liṅga — Phallus-shaped emblem and sign of Śiva
Mahābhārata — "Great India," comprehensive epic that describes the quarrel of two princely families, the Kauravas and Pāṇḍavas
Mahārāja — "Great king."
maṇḍala — "Circle," spiritual sketch or drawing that serves as an object of meditation
mantra — Ritual and spiritually effective formula
Manu — Presumed author of the influential Mānavadharmaśāstra, "The Law Book of Manu"
Maurya Empire — Indian empire (ca. 320–185 B.C.).
Nāṭyaśāstra — Dance textbook from the second to third century A.D.
Nevārī — Tibetan-Burmese language of the Newar population in Nepal
Nyāya — Philosophical system of logic
oṃ — Mystical syllable in which the whole universe is contained
Pāli — Middle Indian language
Pāli canon — Buddhist canon written in Pāli
Paraśurāma — "Rāma with the axe," sixth manifestation of the god Viṣṇu
Pārvatī — Śiva's consort
Pāśupata — Śaiva ascetic group
Paśupatinātha — Form of the god Śiva worshiped in Kathmandu, Nepal.
pitaraḥ (pl.) — "Forefathers"
Prajāpati — "Lord of creation," creator-god
prasāda — (Food) gift for gods, part of which the giver retains
Prākrit — Collective term for middle Indian languages or dialects
prakṛti — "Nature," in the philosophy of the Sāṃkhya consists of primal material of three qualities (*guṇa*) from which the word develops
preta — "The Passed-Away," spirit of the dead
puṇya — Religious merit
pūjā — Ritual worship, mainly of a divinity

purāṇa — Genre of texts with mainly mythological content
puruṣa — "Person, man"; in the ṛgveda primeval man from whom the world emerges; in the philosophy of the Sāṃkhya: spirit and inner core of essence of man
Puruṣasūkta — Creation myth in the Ṛgveda (10.90), in which the emergence of the world through the sacrifice of the primal man Puruṣa is described
Rādhā — Kṛṣṇa's consort
rāja — "King"
rājput — "King's son," member of the Kṣatriya professional class in Rājasthān
Rāma — Seven manifestations of the god Viṣṇu
Rāmāyaṇa — Epic about the life of Rāma with the robbery and recovery of his consort Sītā
Rāvaṇa — Demon in the Rāmāyaṇa, who abducts Sītā to Laṅkā
Ṛgveda — "The wisdom existing in verses," collection of appeals to gods and hymns; oldest of the Sāṃhitās
ṛṣi — "Seer," mythical sage, saint
śaiva — Worshiper of the god Śiva
Śaivasiddhānta — Spiritualistic trend of Śaivism
Śakuntalā — Leading figure of a Sanskrit drama by the poet Kālidāsa
śākta — Worship of the goddesses
śakti — Strength, energy, especially from goddesses, sometimes also deified
saṃkalpa — Formal decision to hold a ritual
Sāmaveda — "The wisdom (existing) in melody," Vedic Saṃhitā, with instructions for the correct singing of the Veda hymns at sacrificial acts
saṃdhyā — Brahmanic morning and evening ritual
saṃhitā — "Collection" of verses, hymns, and prose compiled into a Veda; each of the four Vedas (Ṛg, Sāma, Yajur, and Atharvaveda) forms a Saṃhitā
Śaṃkara — Teacher and saint (seventh to eight century A.D.), main representative of the Advaitavedānata
Sāṃkhya — Philosophical system: The recognition of the difference of individual consciousness and deep core of essence brings salvation
saṃsāra — World cycle
saṃskāra — "Perfecting," rite of passage
Sanksrit — Classical Indian language, standardized by the grammatician Pāṇini (fifth century B.C.)
Śatapathabrāhmaṇa — "The Brāhmaṇa of the hundred paths," the most comprehensive, but not the oldest Brāhmaṇa
Sāvitrī — Gāyatrī
Sikhs — Followers of the doctrine of the Guru Nanak, Islamic-influenced reform movement

Sītā — Rāma's consort
Śiva — Hindu divinity
Śivarātri — "Night of Śiva," festival in February/March
smṛti — "The remembered," the handed-down Veda
soma — Narcotic drink in Vedic time
śrāddha — Ancestor ritual
śruti — "The heard," the revealed Veda
stūpa — Buddhist shrine with relics of the Buddha or a Buddhist saint
śūdra — Member of the servant professional class (*varṇa*)
sufi — Member of an order of Islamic myticism
sūrya — Sun, sun god
sūtra — "Leading thread," as Vedāṅga in the widest sense is counted among the Vedic literature, a rule book (e.g., for philosophy, ritual, grammar)
Tantrism — A form of Hinduism and Buddhism determined by the opposition between feminine and masculine forces
tīrtha — "Ford," place of pilgrimage, holy place
tithi — Lunar day
Trikāya Doctrine — Doctrine of the three bodies of the Buddha
upanayana — Initiation of the Twice-Born
upaniṣad — Text genre with mainly (nature) philosophical and mystical content
Vaiśeṣika — Philosophical system
vaiṣṇava — Worshipper of the god Viṣṇu
vaiśya — Member of the merchant and farmer professional class (*varṇa*)
varṇa — "Color," professional class; mythical concept, with which Indian society is divided into priests, warriors, merchants, and servants
Veda — "Knowledge," holy texts; in the narrow sense, the Saṃhitās; in the broader sense, the totality of texts considered directly revelatory
vedāṅga — "Limb of the Veda," six complementary sciences of the Veda in the narrow sense: astronomy (*jyotiṣa*), phonetics (*śikṣā*), metrics (*chandas*), grammar (*vyākaraṇa*), etymology (*nirukta*), and ritualistics (*kalpa*)
vedāntin — Follower of the Advaitavedānta
Viṣṇu — Hindu divinity
viśve devāḥ — "All gods"; ancestors who have achieved heaven
vrata — Religious vow
Yajurveda — "Knowledge of the ritual sayings," handed down in two versions (black and white Yajurveda), Vedic Saṃhitā with instructions for the sacrificial ritual
yakṣa — Spirit

yantra — Holy, power-charged diagram
yātrā — "(Holy) journey," pilgrimage, procession
Yoga — Philosophical system that teaches an eight-step, ascetic path to salvation
yuga — World period

References

TEXT EDITIONS AND TRANSLATIONS

Agnipurāṇa. Ed. Rājendra Lāl Mitra. Calcutta: Asiatic Society of Bengal, 1876.

Agnipurāṇa. Trans. Manmatha Nāth Dutt Shastrī. Varanasi: Chowkhamba Sanskrit Series Office, 1967.

Aitareyabrāhmaṇa. Trans. A. B. Keith, *Rigveda Brāhmaṇas*. Cambridge, Mass.: Harvard University Press, 1920.

Aitareyabrāhmaṇa. Ed. and trans. (German) M. Haug. Bombay: Government Central Book Depot, 1931.

Āitareyāraṇyaka. Ed. and trans. A. B. Keith. Oxford: Clarendon Press, 1909.

Aitareya-Upaniṣad. Trans. P. Olivelle, *Upaniṣads*. Oxford: Oxford University Press, 1996.

Al-Bīrūnī. Fī tahqīq mā li'l Hind. Ed. E. Sachau. London, 1887.

Al-Bīrūnī. In den Gärten der Wissenschaft. Ausgewählte Texte aus den Werken des muslimischen Universalgelehrten, trans. G. Strohmaier. Leipzig: Reclam, 1991.

Ancient India as Described by Megasthenes and Arrian. Trans. J. W. McCrindle. Calcutta: Thacker, Spink and Co.; London: Trubner and Co., 1877.

Antyeṣṭipaddhati of Nārāyaṇabhaṭṭa. Ed. Vāsudeva Paṇaśīkara. Bombay, 1915.

Āpastambadharmasūtra. 2 vols. Bombay: Nirṇaya Sāgara, 1892–1894.

Āpastambadharmasūtra. Trans. P. Olivelle, *Dharmasūtras: The Law Codes of Āpastamba, Gautama, Baudhāyana, and Vāsiṣṭha*. Oxford: Oxford University Press, 1999.

Āpastambagṛhyasūtra. Ed. U. C. Pandey. Varanasi: Chowkhamba Sanskrit Series Office, 1971 (Kashi Sanskrit Series 59).

Āpastambagṛhyasūtra. Trans. H. Oldenberg, *The Grihya Sutras*. Oxford: Oxford University Press, 1886.

Arthaśāstra. Ed. and trans. R. P. Kangle, *The Kauṭilīya Arthaśāstra*. 2 vols. Bombay: University of Bombay, 1970–1972.

Āruṇī-Upaniṣad. See *Saṃnyāsa-Upaniṣads*.

Aṣṭādhyāyī. Ed. and trans. O. Böthlingk, *Pāṇini's Grammatic*. Kyoto: Rinsen Book Company; reprint of Leipzig, 1887.

Aśvalāyanagṛhyasūtra. Ed. and trans. (German): N. N. Sharma. Delhi: Eastern Book Linkers, 1976.

Aśvalāyanagṛhyasūtra. Trans. H. Oldenberg. See *Āpastambagṛhyas*ūtra.

Atharvaveda. Ed. V. Bandhu. Hoshiarpur: Vishveshvarnand Vedic Research Institute, 1960–1962.

Atharvaveda. Trans. W. D. Whitney, *Atharvaveda Saṃhitā.* 2 vols. Cambridge, Mass.: Harvard University Press.

Atrismṛti. Ed. and trans. Manmatha Nath Dutt, *The Dharma Śāstra Texts.* Calcutta: M. N. Dutt, 1908.

Baudhāyanadharmasūtra. Ed. E. Hultzsch. Leipzig: Brockhaus, 1922.

Baudhāyanadharmasūtra. Trans. P. Olivelle. See *Āpastambadharmasūtra.*

Baudhāyanagṛhyasūtra. Trans. H. Oldenberg. See *Āpastambagṛhyasūtra.*

Bhagavadgītā. Trans. S. Radhakrishnan. London: George Allen and Unwin, 1949.

Bhāgavatapurāṇa. Ed. S. Pāṇḍuraṅga. Bombay: Nirṇayasāgara Press, 1950.

Bhāgavatapurāṇa. Trans. G. V. Tagare et al., *The Bhāgavata Purāṇa.* 5 vols. Delhi: Motilal Banarsidass.

Brahmāṇḍapurāṇa. Trans. J. L. Shastri. Delhi: Motilal Banarsidass, 1973.

Brahma-Upaniṣad. Ed. F. O. Schrader, *Saṃnyāsa-Upaniṣads.* Madras: Adyar Library and Research Centre, 1912.

Brahma-Upaniṣad. Trans. P. Olivelle, See *Saṃyāsa-Uupaniṣads.*

Brahmavaivartapurāṇa. Ed. V. Śāstrī Rānade. Poona: Ānandāśrama Press, 1935.

Brahmavaivartapurāṇa. Trans. Rajendra Nath Sen. Allahabad: Panini Office, 1919–1922 (Sacred Books of the Hindus 24); reprint, New York: AMS Press, 1974.

Bṛhadāraṇyaka-Upaniṣad. Ed. V. P. Limaye and E. D. Vadekar, *Eighteen Principal Upaniṣads.* Poona: Vaidika Saṃśodhana Maṇṣala, 1964.

Bṛhadāraṇyaka-Upaniṣad. Trans. P. Olivelle, *Upaniṣads.* Oxford: Oxford University Press, 1996.

Bṛhatsaṃnyāsa-Upaniṣad. See *Sāṃnyāsa-Upaniṣads.*

Caturvargacintāmaṇi of Hemādri. Ed. Yogeśvara Bhaṭṭācārya and Kāmākhyānātha Tarkaratna. Calcutta: Asiatic Society of Bengal, 1879.

Chāndogya-Upaniṣad. Trans. P. Olivelle. See *Bṛhadāraṇyaka-Upaniṣad.*

Devaṇṇabhaṭṭa's Smṛticandrikā (Āhnikakāṇda). Ed. J. R. Gharpure. Bombay: Law College, 1914–1918.

Devaṇṇabhaṭṭa's Smṛticandrikā. Trans. Poona, 1946.

Devīgītā. Ed. and trans. Satyananda Saraswati. Napa, Calif., and Delhi: Devi Mandir Publications and Motilal Banarsidass, 1991.

The Garuḍa Purāṇa. Ed. and trans. E. Wood and S. V. Subrahmanyam. Allahabad: Panini Office, 1911; reprint: Sacred Books of the Hindus 9.

Garuḍapurāṇa. Trans. (German) E. Abegg, *Der Pretakalpa des Garuḍa-Purāṇa (Naunidhirāma's Sāroddhāra). Eine Darstellung des hinduistischen Totenkultes und Jenseitsglaubens.* Berlin: Vereinigung wissenschaftlicher Verleger (Walter de Gruyter & Co), 1921.

Garuḍapurāṇa, Uttarakhaṇḍa. Ed. J. Vidyāsāgara. Calcutta, 1890.

Gautamadharmasūtra. In *Āṣṭādaśasmṛtayaḥ*, ed. Khemarāja Srīkṛṣṇadāsa. Bombay: Veṅkateśvara Sṭīma Yantrālaya, n.d.

Gauṭamadharmasūtra. Trans. P. Olivelle. See *Āpastambadharmasūtra.*

Gautamagṛhyasūtra. Ed. Chintamani Bhattacharya. Calcutta: Metropolitan Printing and Publishing House, 1936.

Gautamagṛhyasūtra. Trans. H. Oldenberg. See *Āpastambagṛhyasūtra.*

Gorkhā Thar Gotra Savāi. Banares: Dudhvinayak, n.d.

Hiraṇyakeśingṛhyasūtra. Trans. H. Oldenberg. See *Āpastambagṛhyasūtra.*

Indikē. Trans. J. W. McCrindle, *Ancient India as Described by Megasthenes and Arrian.* Calcutta: Thacker, Spink and Co. London: Trubner, 1877.

Jaiminīyagṛhyasūtra. Ed. and trans. W. Caland. Lahore: Motilal Banarsidass, 1922; reprint: Delhi, 1984.

Jaiminīya-Upaniṣadbrāhmaṇa. Ed. and trans. H. Oertel. *Journal of the American Oriental Society* 16 (1896): 79–260.

Kaṭhaśruti-Upaniṣad. See *Saṃnyāsa-Upaniṣads.*

Katha-Upaniṣad. Trans. P. Olivelle. See *Bṛhadāraṇyaka-Upaniṣad.*

Kauṣītakī-Upaniṣad. See *Bṛhadāraṇyaka-Upaniṣad.*

Kṛtyakalpataru (Dānakhaṇḍa) of the Lakṣmīdhara. Ed. K. V. Rangswami Aiyangar. Baroda: Oriental Institute, 1942 (Gaekwad's Oriental Series 98).

Kūrmapurāṇa. Ed. Anand Swarup Gupta; trans. Ahibhushan Bhattacharya et al. Varanasi: All-India Kashi Raj Trust, 1972.

Mahābhārata. The Mahābhārata: Text as Constituted in Its Critical Edition. 4 vols. Poona: Bhandarkar Oriental Research Institute, 1971–1976.

Mahānirvāṇatantra, The Great Liberation. Trans. Arthur Avalon. Madras: Ganesh, 1971.

Maitrāyaṇīsaṃhitā. Ed. L. von Schroeder. Leipzig: F. A. Brockhaus, 1883–1886.

Maitreya-Upaniṣad. See *Saṃnyāsa-Upaniṣads.*

Māṇḍūkya-Upaniṣad. Trans. P. Olivelle. See *Bṛhadāraṇyaka-Upaniṣad.*

Manu. The Laws of Manu. Trans. W. Doniger with B. K. Smith. Harmonsworth: Penguin, 1991.

Matsyapurāṇa. Trans. by various scholars, ed. B. D. Basu. Allahabad: Pānini Office, 1916 (Sacred Books of the Hindus, 17).

McCrindle. See *Ancient India as Described by Megasthenes and Arrian.*

Nala und Damayantī: Eine Episode aus dem Mahābhārata. Trans. A. Wezler. Stuttgart: Reclam, 1965.

Nāradasmṛti. Trans. J. Jolly. Oxford: Clarendon Press, 1889 (Sacred Books of the East 33).

Pañcaviṃśabrāhmaṇa. Ed. P. A. Cinnaswami Sastri and P. Pattachirama Sastri. Benares: Kashi Sanskrit Series Office, 1935 (Kashi Sanskrit Series 105).

Pañcaviṃśabrāhmaṇa. Trans. W. Caland. Calcutta: Asiatic Society of Bengal, 1931 (Bibliotheca Indica 225).

Paraśārasmṛti. Ed. M. Chandrakantha Tarkalankara. Calcutta: Asiastic Society, 1883; (reprint, 1974).

Pāraskaragṛhyasūtra. Ed. M. G. Bakre. Bombay: Gujarati Printing Press, 1917; reprint Delhi, 1982.

Pāraskaragṛhyasūtra. Trans. H. Oldenberg. See *Āpastambagṛhyasūtra*.

Ṛgvedasaṃhitā. Ed. F. M. Müller. Varanasi: Chowkhamba Sanskrit Series Office, 1972.

Ṛgvedasaṃhitā. Trans. H. H. Wilson. Delhi: Parimal Publications, 1997.

Ṛgvedasaṃhitā. German trans. K. F. Geldner, *Der Rig-Veda*. 4 vols. Cambridge, Mass.: Harvard University Press, 1951–1957 (Harvard Oriental Series 33–36).

Sacred Books of the East, 50 vols. Oxford: Clarendon Press.

Sāṃkhyakārikā des Iśvarakṛṣṇa. Commentary on *Yuktidīpikā*, ed. S. S. Suryanārāyaṇa Sāstrī. Madras. 1930.

Sāmkhyakārikā. English translation. See Larson 1969.

Saṃnyāsa-Upaniṣads. Ed. F. O. Schrader. Madras: Adyar Library, 1912.

Saṃnyāsa-Upaniṣads: Hindu Scriptures on Asceticism and Renunciation. Trans. P. Olivelle. New York: Oxford University Press, 1992.

Śāṅkhāyanāraṇyaka. Ed. Bhim Dev. Hoshiarpur: Vishveshvaranand Vedic Research Institute, 1980.

Ṣāṇmukhakalpa. Ed. and trans. D. George. Berlin: Dietrich Reimer Verlag, 1991.

Saral Vivāha Paddhati, by Pandit Dharnidhar Shastri. Kishangarh, 1973.

Śatapathabrāhmaṇa. Ed. A. Weber. Berlin: Ferd. Dümmler's Buchhandlung; London: Williams and Norgate, 1849.

Śatapathabrāhmaṇa. Trans. J. Eggeling, 5 vols. Oxford: Clarendon Press, 1882–1900.

Smṛticandrikā. See *Devannabhatta's Smṛticandrikā*.

Somaśambhupaddhati. Ed. and trans. H. Brunner-Lachaux. 3 vols. Pondichérry: Inst. Français d'Indologie, 1963, 1969, 1977.

Suśrutasaṃhitā. Ed. Yadavaśarma Trivikrama Acarya. Varanasi, Delhi: Chaukhambha Orientalia, 1980.

Śvetāśvatara-Upaniṣad. Trans. P. Olivelle, *Upaniṣads*. Oxford: Oxford University Press, 1996.

Taittirīya-Āraṇyaka. Ed. A. Mahadeva Sastri and K. Rangacarya. Delhi: Motilal Banarsidass, 1985.

Taittirīyabrāhmaṇa. 3 vols. Poona: Ānandāśrama, 1979 (Ānandāśrama Sanskrit Series 37).

Taittirīyasaṃhitā. 8 vols. Paona: Ānandāśrama, 1978 (Ānandāśrama Sanskrit Series 42).

Taittirīyasaṃhitā. Trans. A. B. Keith, 2 vols. Cambridge, Mass: Harvard University Press, 1914 (Harvard Oriental Series 18–19).

Taittirīya-Upaniṣad. Trans. P. Olivelle. See *Bṛhadāraṇyaka-Upaniṣad*.

Tattvakaumudi of the Vācaspati Miśra. Ed. S. A. Srinivasan. Hamburg: deGruyter, 1967.

Vaikhānasagṛhyasūtra. Ed. W. Caland. Calcutta: Asiatic Society of Bengal (Bibliotheca Indica 242).

Vāsiṣṭhadharmasūtra. Trans. P. Olivelle. See *Āpastambadharmasūtra*.

Vāyupurāṇa. Ed. Rajendra Lal Mitra. 2 vols. Calcutta: Asiatic Society of Bengal.

Viṣṇusmṛti. Ed. V. Krishnamacharya. 2 vols. Madras: Adyar Library, 1964 (Adyar Library Series 93).

Viṣṇusmṛti. Trans. J. Jolly, *The Institutes of Vishnu*. Oxford: Clarendon Press, 1880 (Sacred Books of the East 7).

Vratabandhapaddhati. Ed. Kṛṣṇa Prasāda Bhaṭṭarāi. Kathmandu: Nepāla Rājakīya Prajñā-Pratiṣṭhāna, V.S. 2030.

Yājñavalkyasmṛti with Vijñeśvara's *Mitākṣara*. Ed. W. Laxman Shāstrī Pansīkar. Bombay: Nirṇaya Sāgara, 1918.

Yajurvedasaṃhitā. Ed. and trans. R. H. Griffith. Delhi: Nag Publishers, 1990 (reprint).

Yogasūtra. Ed. J. H. Woods. 2 vols. Cambridge, Mass.: Harvard University Press, 1914 and 1927.

ANTHOLOGIES, MONOGRAPHS, AND ARTICLES

Abegg, Emil (1921). *Garuḍapurāṇa*. See under Text Editions and Translation.

———(1928). *Der Messiasglaube in Indien und Iran*. Berlin: de Gruyter.

Agarwala, Atul Kumar (1982). *Marriage Songs in Harauti*. Dissertation, University of Kiel.

Allen, Michael (1982). "Girls' Pre-Puberty Rites amongst the Newars of Kathmandu Valley." In Michael Allen and S. N. Mukherjee, eds., *Women in India and Nepal*. Canberra: Australian National University Publications 179–210.

Alper, Harvey P. (1989). *Understanding Mantras*. New York: State University of New York Press.

Alsdorf, Ludwig (1961). *Beiträge zur Geschichte von Vegetarismus und Rinderverehrung in Indien*. Mainz: Akademie der Wissenschaften und der Literatur in Mainz.

Altekar, A. S. (1956). *The Position of Women in Hindu Civilization*. New Delhi: Motilal Banarsidass.

Alter, Joseph S. (1992). *The Wrestler's Body: Identity and Ideology in North India*. Berkeley: University of California Press.

Apffel-Marglin, Frédérique (1984). "Types of Sexual Union and Their Implicit Meanings." In Hawley/Wulff, eds., 298–315.

Ariès, Philippe (1962). *Centuries of Childhood*. Trans. Robert Baldick. New York: Vintage Books.

———(1981). *The Hour of Our Death*. Trans. Helen Weaver. New York: Knopf.

———(1985). "The Indissoluble Marriage." In P. Ariès and A. Bejin, *Western Sexuality: Practice and Precept in Past and Present Times*. Trans. Anthony Forster. Oxford: B. Blackwell.

Assmann, Jan (1997). *Das kulturelle Gedächtnis, Schrift, Erinnerung und politische Identität in frühen Hochkulturen*. Munich: C. H. Beck.

Auboyer, Jeannine (1965). *Daily Life in Ancient India from Approximately 200 BC to AD 700*. London: Weidenfeld and Nicholson.

Babb, L. A. (1975). *The Divine Hierarchy: Popular Hinduism in Central India*. New York: Columbia University Press.

———(1982). "The Physiology of Redemption." *History of Religions* 22: 293–312.

Bailey, Greg (1985). *Materials for the Study of Ancient Indian Ideologies: Pravṛtti and Nivṛtti*. Turin: Pubblicazioni dei Indologica Taurensia.

Baldissera, Frabrizia, and Axel Michaels (1988). *Der Indische Tanz.* Cologne: DuMont.

Bareau, André, Walther Schubring, and Christoph von Fürer-Haimendorf (1964). *Buddhismus, Jinismus, Primitivvölker.* Stuttgart: Kohlhammer (*Die Religionen Indiens,* vol. 3). See Gonda (1960–1964).

Basham, A. L. (1951). *History of the Doctrines of the Ajīvikas.* London: Lucac (reprinted: Delhi: Motilal Banarsidass, 1981).

Bäumer, Bettina (1969). *Schöpfung als Spiel: Der Begriff līlā im Hinduismus, seine philosophische und theologische Bedeutung.* Dissertation, University of Munich.

———(1994). *Upanishaden: Befreiung zum Sein. Innere Weite und Freiheit aus den indischen Weisheitslehren.* Selected and translated by B. Bäumer. Munich: Heyne.

Bayly, C. A. (1983). *Rulers, Townsmen and Bazaars: North Indian Society in the Age of British Expansion.* Cambridge: Cambridge University Press.

Beattie, John (1964). *Other Cultures: Aims, Methods and Achievements in Social Anthropology.* London: Routledge & Kegan Paul.

Bechert, Heinz (1986). *Die Lebenszeit des Buddha—das älteste feststehende Datum der indischen Geschichte?* Göttingen: Vandenhoeck & Ruprecht.

———, ed. (1991). *The Dating of the Historical Buddha.* Vol. 1. Göttingen: Vandenhoeck & Ruprecht.

Bechert, Heinz, and Georg von Simson, eds. (1979). *Einführung in die Indologie.* Darmstadt: Wissenschaftliche Buchgesellschaft (second revised edition, 1993).

Becke, Andreas (1996). *Hinduismus zur Einführung.* Hamburg: Junius.

Beidelman, Thomas O. (1959). *A Comparative Analysis of the Jajmani System.* Locust Valley, N.Y.: Augustin.

Belier, Wouter W. (1994). "Arnold van Gennep and the Rise of French Sociology of Religion." *Numen* 41: 141–162.

Bell, Catherine (1992). *Ritual Theory, Ritual Practice.* New York: Oxford University Press.

Bennett, Lynn (1983). *Dangerous Wives and Sacred Sisters: Social and Symbolic Roles of High-Caste Women in Nepal.* New York: Columbia University Press.

Berger, Hermann (1966). "Hochsprache und Volkssprache in Indien." *Jahrbuch des Südasien-Instituts der Universität Heidelberg* 1966: 24–34.

Berger, Peter (1979). *The Heretical Imperative: Contemporary Possibilities of Religious Affirmation.* Garden City, N.Y.: Anchor Press.

Berkemer, Georg (1993). *Little Kingdoms in Kaliṅga. Ideologie, Legitimation und Politik regionaler Eliten.* Stuttgart: Franz Steiner Verlag.

Berreman, Gerald D. (1971). "The Brahmanical View of Caste." *Contributions to Indian Sociology* n.s. 5: 16–23.

Bettelheim, Bruno (1954). *Symbolic Wounds: Puberty Rites and the Envious Male.* Glencoe, Ill.: Free Press.

Bhagat, M. G. (1976). *Ancient Indian Asceticism.* Delhi: Munshiram Manoharlal.

Bhandarkar, R. G. (1913). *Vaiṣṇavism, Śaivism and Minor Religious Systems.* Varnasi: Indological Book House (reprint, 1965).

Bharati, Agehananda (1963). "Pilgrimage in the Indian Tradition." *History of Religions* 3: 135–167.

———(1965). *The Tantric Tradition.* London: Rider and Co. (reprint, 1970).

Bhardwaj, Surinder Mohan (1973). *Hindu Places of Pilgrimage in India: A Study in Cultural Geography.* Berkeley: University of California Press.

Bhattacharya, Jogendra Nath (1896). *Hindu Castes and Sects.* Calcutta: Thacker, Spink & Co.

Bhattacharya, N. N. (1968). *Indian Puberty Rites.* Calcutta.

Biardeau, Madeleine (1981). *Cosmogonies purāṇiques.* Paris: Publications de l'Ecole Française d'Extrême Orient.

———(1989). *Hinduism: The Anthropology of a Civilization.* Delhi: Oxford University Press.

———(1997). "Some Remarks on the Links between the Epics, the Purāṇas and Their Vedic Sources." In Oberhammer, ed. (1997), pp. 69–177.

Biardeau, Madeleine, and Charles Malamoud (1976). *Le sacrifice dans l'Inde ancienne.* Paris: Presses Universitaires de France.

Billard, Roger (1971). *L'Astronomie indienne.* Paris: Publications de l'Ecole Française d'Extrême Orient.

Blackburn, Stuart (1985). "Death and Deification: Folk Cults in Hinduism." *History of Religions* 24: 253–273.

Bleeker, C., ed. (1965). *Initiation.* Leiden: E. J. Brill.

Bloch, Ernst (1978). *Tendenz—Latenz—Utopie.* Frankfurt/M: Suhrkamp.

Bloch, Maurice (1992). *Prey into Hunter: The Politics of Religious Experience.* Cambridge: Cambridge University Press.

Bloch, Maurice, and Jonathan Parry, eds. (1982). *Death and the Regeneration of Life.* Cambridge: Cambridge University Press.

Blunt, E.A.H. (1931). *The Caste System of Northern India with Special Reference to the United Provinces of Agra and Oudh.* London: Oxford University Press.

Bodewitz, W. W. (1976). *The Daily Evening and Morning Offering (Agnihotra) according to the Brāhmaṇas.* Leiden: E. J. Brill.

———(1996). "Redeath and Its Relation to Rebirth and Release." *Sudien zur Indologie und Iranistik* 20 [Festschrift for P. Thieme]: 27–46.

Böhme, Hartmut (1988). *Natur und Subjekt.* Frankfurt/M: Suhrkamp.

Bollée, W. B. (2003). "A Note on the Birth of the Hero in Ancient India." In Heidrun Brückner, Hugh van Skyhawk, and Claus Peter Zoller, eds., *The Concept of Hero in South Asia in Indian Culture.* Heidelberg: South Asia Institute, 1–33.

Bouglé, Célestine (1971). *Essays on the Caste System.* Trans. D. Pocock. Cambridge: Cambridge University Press.

Bouillier, Véronique (1985). "Preliminary Remarks on Bāljogīs or Ascetic Children." In K. Seeland, ed., *Recent Research on Nepal.* Cologne: Weltforum Verlag.

Bourdieu, Pierre (1977). *Outline of a Theory of Practice.* Trans. Richard Nice. Cambridge: Cambridge University Press.

———(1980). *Sozialer Sinn. Kritik der theoretischen Vernunft.* Frankfurt/M.: Suhrkamp, 1993.

Brandon, Samuel George F. (1965). *History, Time and Deity: A Historical and Comparative Study of the Conceptions of Time in Religious Thought and Practice.* New York: Barnes & Noble.
Briggs, George Weston (1938). *Gorakhnāth and the Kānphaṭa Yogīs.* Delhi: Motilal Banarsidass (reprint, 1982).
Brinkhaus, Horst (1978). *Die altinischen Mischkastensysteme.* Wiesbaden: Franz Steiner Verlag.
Brockington, J. L. (1981). *The Sacred Thread: Hinduism in Its Continuity and Diversity.* Edinburgh: Edinburgh University Press.
Bronkhorst, Johannes (1993). *The Two Sources of Indian Asceticism.* Bern: Peter Lang.
Brough, John (1946–1947). "The Early History of the Gotras." *Journal of the Royal Asiatic Society* 1946: 32–45, and 1947: 76–90.
Brown, W. Norman (1942). "The Creation Myth of the Rigveda." *Journal of the American Oriental Society* 62: 85–98.
Brucker, Egon (1980). *Die spätvedische Kulturepoche nach den Quellen der Śrauta-, Gṛhya- und Dharmasūtras. Der Siedlungsraum.* Wiesbaden: Otto Harrassowitz.
Brückner, Heidrun (1995). *Fürstliche Feste: Texte und Rituale der Tuḷu-Volksreligion an der Westküste Südindiens.* Wiesbaden: Otto Harrassowitz.
Brunner-Lachaux, Hélène. See *Somaśambhupaddhati* in Text Editions and Translations.
Bühnemann, Gudrun (1984). "Some Remarks on the Structure and Application of Hindu Sanskrit Stotras." *Wiener Zeitschr. für die Kunde Süd- und Südostasiens* 27: 75–104.
———(1986). *Stotramālā. An die Götter.* Wichtrach: Institut für Indologie.
———(1988). *Pūjā: A Study in Smārta Ritual.* Vienna: Institut für Indologie der Universität Wien.
Burghart, Richard (1978). "Hierarchical Models of the Hindu Social System." *Man* n.s. 13: 519–536.
———(1987). "Gifts to the Gods: Power, Property and Ceremonials in Nepal." In Burghart 1996, 193–225.
———(1996). *The Conditioning of Listening: Essays on Religion, History and Politics in South Asia.* Delhi: Oxford University Press.
Caland, Willem (1896). *Die Altindischen Todten- und Bestattungsgebräuche.* Amsterdam: Koninklijke Akademie van Wetenschappen (reprint, Wiesbaden: Sändig, 1967).
Carstairs, Morris (1957). *The Twice Born.* London.
Cassirer, Ernst (1955). *The Philosophy of Symbolic Forms*, vol. 2: *Mythical Thinking.* Trans. Ralph Manheim. New Haven, Conn.: Yale University Press.
Cazeneuve, J. (1971). *Sociologie du Rite.* Paris: Presses Universitaires de France.
Cederroth, S., C. Corlin, and J. Lindström, eds. (1988). *On the Meaning of Death: Essays on Mortuary Rituals and Eschatological Beliefs.* Stockholm: Almquist & Wiksell.
Chapple, Christopher Key (1993). *Nonviolence to Animals, Earth and Self in Asian Traditions.* New York: State University of New York Press.
Chaudhuri, Nirad C. (1951). *The Autobiography of an Unknown Indian.* Bombay: Jaico Books.

Church, Cornelia D. (1971). "The Purāṇic Myths of the Four Yugas." *Purāṇa* 13: 151–159.

Classen, Annette (1988). *Kann die Gupta-Kunst Kālidāsas Werke illustrieren?* Berlin: Dietrich Reimer Verlag.

Cohn, B. S. (1987). *An Anthropologist among Historians*. Delhi: Oxford University Press.

Commander, S. (1988). "The Jajmani System in North India: An Examination of Its Logic and Status across Two Centuries." *Modern Asian Studies* 17: 283–311.

Conrad, Dieter (1995). "The Personal Law Question and Hindu Nationalism." In Dalmia/von Stietencron, eds., 306–337.

Cormack, Margaret (1953). *The Hindu Women*. Westport, Conn.: Greenwood Press (reprint, 1974).

Corre, L. (1989). "Akhara and naubatkhana." In P.-D. Couté and J.-M. Léger, eds., *Bénarès. Un Voyage d'Architecture*. Paris, 141–149.

Courtright, Paul B. (1985). *Gaṇeśa: Lord of Obstacles, Lord of Beginnings*. New York: Oxford University Press.

———(1995). "Satī, Sacrifice, and Marriage: The Modernity of Tradition." in Harlan/Courtright, eds., 184–203.

Crooke, William (1896). *Tribes and Castes of the North-Western Provinces and Oudh*. 4 vols. Calcutta: Office of the Superintendent of Government Printing.

Dalmia, Vasudha, and Heinrich von Stietencron, eds. (1995). *Representing Hinduism: The Construction of Religious Traditions and National Identity*. New Delhi: Sage Publications.

Daniel, E. Valentine (1984). *Fluid Signs: Being a Person the Tamil Way*. Berkeley: University of California Press.

Daniélou, Alain (1985). *The Myths and Gods of India*. New York: Bolligen (reprint, 1991).

D'Aquili, E. (1983). "The Myth-Ritual Complex: A Biogenetic Structural Analysis." *Zygon* 18: 247–269.

D'Aquili, E., Charles D. Laughlin, and John McManns, eds. (1979). *The Spectrum of Ritual: A Biogenetic-Structural Approach*. New York: Columbia University Press.

Das, Veena (1982). *Structure and Cognition: Aspects of Hindu Caste and Ritual*. Delhi: Oxford University Press.

———(1985). "Paradigms of Body Symbolism: An Analysis of Selected Themes in Hindu Cultures." In R. Burghart and A. Cantlie, eds., *Indian Religion*. London: Curzon Press; New York: St. Martin's Press, 180–207.

Davis, Marvin (1976). "A Philosophy of Hindu Rank from Rural West Bengal." *Journal of Asian Studies* 36: 5–24.

Davis, R. H. (1991). *Ritual in an Oscillating Universe: Worshipping Shiva in Medieval India*. Princeton N.J.: Princeton University Press.

Delfendahl, Bernard (1973). *Le clair et l'obscur: Critique de l'anthropologie savante—défense de l'anthropologie amateur*. Paris: Editions anthropos.

Derrett, John Duncan M. (1957). *Hindu Law: Past and Present*. Calcutta: A. Mukherjee.

———(1968). " 'Hindu': A Definition Wanted for the Purpose of Applying a Personal Law." *Zeitschrist für vergheichende Reechtswissenschaft* 70: 110–128.

———(1973). *Dharmaśāstra and Juridical Literature.* Wiesbaden: Otto Harrassowitz.

———(1976). "Rājadharma." *Journal of Asian Studies* 35.4: 597–609.

———(1979). "Die Rechtsideen in Indien (Hinduismus)." In John Derrett, G.-D. Sontheimer, and G. Smith, *Beiträge zu indischern Rechtsdenken.* Wiesbaden: Otto Harrassovwitz, 1–16.

———(1986). *Religion, Law and the State in India.* London: Faber and Faber.

Deussen, Paul (1906). *System der Philosophie,* vol. 2: *Das System der Upaniṣaden.* Kiel.

———(1912). *The System of the Vedanta according to Badarayana's Brahmasutras and Cankara's Commentary Thereon Set Forth as a Compendium of the Dogmatics of Brahmanism from the Standpoint of Cankara.* Trans. Charles Johnston. Chicago: Open Court Publishing.

———(1997). *Sixty Upanishads of the Veda.* Trans. V. M. Bedekar and G. B. Palsule. Delhi: Motilal Banarsidass.

Dharampal-Frick, Gita (1994). *Indien im Spiegel deutscher Quellen der Frühen Neuzeit (1500–1750): Studien zu einer interkulturellen Konstellation.* Tübingen: Niemeyer.

Dhavamony, Mariasusai (1982). *Classical Hinduism.* Rome: Università Gregoriana Editrice.

Dimmitt, Cornelia, and J.A.B. van Buitenen (1978). *Classical Hindu Mythology: A Reader in the Sanskrit Purāṇas.* Philadelphia: Temple University Press.

Dirks, Nicholas B. (1989). "The Invention of Caste: Civil Society in Colonial India." *Social Analysis* 25: 42–51.

———(1993). *The Hollow Crown: Ethnohistory of an Indian Kingdom.* Ann Arbor: University of Michigan Press.

Doniger, Wendy, et al. (1991). "Hinduism." In *Encyclopedia Britannica. Macropaedia.* fifteenth edition, vol. 20, pp. 519–558.

Douglas, Mary (1966). *Purity and Danger: An Analysis of the Concepts of Pollution and Taboo.* New York: Praeger.

Drexel, Josef (1993). *Die Illusion des Opfers. Abriss der Opfertheorien.* Munich: Akademischer Verlag.

Dube, S. C. (1955). *Indian Village.* London: Routledge & Kegan Paul.

Dumont, Louis (1960). "World Renunciation in Indian Religions." *Contributions to Indian Sociology* 4: 33–62.

———(1961, 1964, 1966). "Marriage in India." *Contributions to Indian Sociology* 5: 75–95, 7: 77–98, and 9: 90–104.

———(1962). "The Conception of Kingship in Ancient India." *Contributions to Indian Sociology* 6: 48–77.

———(1975). "Société, religion et pensée." In *La civilisation et nous.* Paris: Armand Colin.

———(1980). *Homo Hierarchicus: The Caste System and Its Implications.* Trans. Mark Sainsbury, Louis Dumont, and Basia Gulati. Chicago: University of Chicago Press.

Dumont, Louis, and David Pocock (1959). "Pure and Impure." *Contributions to Indian Sociology* 3: 9–39.

Dumont, Paul-Emile (1939). *L'Agnihotra. Description de l'agnihotra dans le rituel védique d'après les Śrautasūtras.* Baltimore: Johns Hopkins University Press.

Durkheim, Emile (1966). *Rules of Sociological Method.* Trans. Sarah A. Solovay and John H. Mueller, ed. George E. G. Catlin. New York: Free Press.

———(1995). *Elementary Forms of Religious Life.* Trans. Karen E. Fields. New York: Free Press.

Durkheim, Emile, and Marcel Mauss (1903). *Primitive Classification.* London: Cohen and West (reprint, 1963).

Eck, Diana L. (1981). *Darśan: Seeing the Divine Image in India.* Chambersburg, Penn.: Anima Books (Second edition, 1985).

———, ed. (1991). *Devotion Divine: Bhakti Traditions from the Regions of India. Studies in Honour of Charlotte Vaudeville.* Groningen: Forsten.

Edwards, Michael (1969). *Everyday Life in Early India.* London: B. T. Batsford.

Eichinger Ferro-Luzzi, Gabriella (1977). "The Logic of South Indian Food Offerings." *Anthropos* 72: 529–556.

———(1981). "*Abhiṣeka,* the Indian Rite That Defies Definition." *Anthropos* 76: 709–742.

Einoo, Shingo (1993). "Changes in Hindu Ritual: With a Focus on the Morning Service." *Senri Ethnological Studies* 36: 197–237.

———(1996). "The Formation of the Pūjā Ceremony." *Studien zur Indologie und Iranistik* 20: 73–87.

Eliade, Mircea (1951). "Le temps et l'éternité dans la pensée Indienne." *Eranos-Jahrbuch* 20.

———(1958a). *Birth and Rebirth: The Religious Meanings of Initiation in Human Culture.* Trans. Willard Trask. New York: Harper.

———(1958b). *Rites and Symbols of Initiation.* New York: Harper 8 Row.

———(1958c). *Yoga: Immortality and Freedom.* Trans. Willard R. Trask. New York: Pantheon Books.

———(1959). *Cosmos and History: The Myth of the Eternal Return.* Trans. Willard Trask. New York: Harper.

———(1965). "Initiation." In *Religion in Geschichte und Gegenwart.* Tübingen: Thieme.

———(1969). "Initiation und die moderne Welt." In *Die Sehnsucht nach dem Ursprung.* Vienna (reprint, 1973).

———(1971). *La Nostalgie des Origines.* Paris: Gallimard.

———(1974). *Gods, Goddesses, and Myths of Creation.* New York: Harper & Row.

———, ed. (1964). *Schöpfungsmythen.* Einsiedeln: Benziger.

Elias, Norbert (1978, 1982). *The Civilizing Process.* Trans. Edmund Jephcott. New York: Pantheon Books.

Elizarenkova, Tatyana J. (1995). *Language and Style of the Vedic ṛṣis.* Albany: State University of New York Press.

Elsas, Christoph (1975) *Religion: Ein Jahrhundert theologischer, philosophischer, soziologischer und psychologischer Interpretationsansätze.* Munich: Kaiser Verlag.

Enthoven, R. E. (1920–1922). *The Tribes and Castes of Bombay,* 3 vols. Bombay: Government Central Press.

Erdosy, George (1988). *Urbanization in Early Historic India.* Oxford: B.A.R.

———, ed. (1995). *The Indo-Aryans of Ancient South Asia: Language, Material Culture and Ethnicity.* Berlin: de Gruyter.

Erikson, H. Erik (1968). *Identity: Youth and Crisis.* New York: Norton.

Evison, Gillian (1989). "Indian Death Rituals: The Enactment of Ambivalence." Dissertation, Oxford University.

Fairservis, Walter A. (1992). *The Harappan Civilisation and Its Writing: A Model for the Decipherment of the Indus Script.* Leiden: E. J. Brill.

Falk, Harry (1986). "Vedisch *upaniṣád.*" *Zeitschr. d. Deutschen Morgenländischen Gesellschaft* 136: 80–97.

———(1989). "Soma I and II." *Bulletin of the School of Oriental and African Studies* 52: 77–90.

———(1993). *Die Schrift im alten Indien. Ein Forschungsbericht mit Anmerkungen.* Tübingen: Gunter Narr Verlag.

Farquar, J. N. (1925). "The Fighting Ascetics of India." *Bulletin of the J. Rylands Library* 9: 431–452.

Feil, Ernst (1995). "Zur Bestimmungs- und Abgrenzungsproblematik von 'Religion.' " *Ethik und Sozialwissenschaften* 6.4.: 441–514 [with a discussion by C. Colpe et al.].

Feyerabend, Paul (1981). "Irrationalität oder: Wer hat Angst vorm schwarzen Mann?" In H.-P. Duerr, ed., *Der Wissenschaftler und das Irrationale,* vol. 2. Frankfurt/M: Syndikat.

Fick, Richard (1920). *The Social Organization in North-East India in Buddha's Time.* Trans. Shishirkumar Maitra. Calcutta: University of Calcutta Press.

Filippi, Gian Guiseppe (1996). *Mṛtyu: Concept of Death in Indian Traditions.* New Delhi: D. K. Printworld.

Fisch, Jörg (1998): *Tödliche Rituale. Die indische Witwenverbrennung und andere Formen der Totenfolge.* Frankfurt/M: Campus.

Flood, Gavin (1996). *An Introduction to Hinduism.* Cambridge: Cambridge University Press.

Fontaine, J. S. (1985). *Initiation: Ritual Drama and Secret Knowledge across the World.* Hammondsworth: Penguin.

Fort, Andrew O., and Patricia Y. Mumme, eds. (1996). *Living Liberation in Hindu Thought.* Albany: State University of New York Press.

Frauwallner, Erich (1958). "Zur Erkenntnislehre des klassischen Sāṃkhya-Systems." *Wiener Zeitschrift für die Kunde Süd- und Ostasiens* 2: 54–157.

———(1973). *History of Indian Philosophy.* Trans. V. M. Bedekar. Delhi: Motilal Banarsidass.

Freed, Ruth S., and Stanley A. (1964). "Calendars, Ceremonies and Festivals in a North Indian Village." *Southwestern Journal of Anthropology* 20: 67–90.

Freed, Stanley A. (1963). "An Objective Method for Determining the Collective Caste Hierarchy of an Indian Village." *American Anthropologist* 65: 879–891.

Frykenberg, Robert (1989). "The Emergence of Modern 'Hinduism' as a Concept and as an Institution." In Sontheimer/Kulke, eds., 29–49.

Fuchs, Martin (1988). *Theorie und Verfremdung: Max Weber, Louis Dumont und die Analyse der indischen Gesellschaft.* Frankfurt/M: Peter Lang.

Fuller, Christoph (1979). "Gods, Priests and Purity: On the Relation between Hinduism and the Caste System." *Man* n.s. 14: 459–476.

———(1984). *Servants of the Goddess: The Priests of a South Indian Temple.* Cambridge: Cambridge University Press.

———(1988). "The Hindu Pantheon and the Legitimation of Hierarchy." *Man* n.s. 23: 19–39.

———(1989). "Misconceiving the Grain Heap: A Critique of the Concept of the Indian Jajmani System." In J. Parry and M. Bloch, eds., *Money and the Morality of Exchange.* Cambridge: Cambridge University Press, 33–63.

———(1992). *The Camphor Flame: Popular Hinduism and Society in India.* Princeton, N.J.: Princeton University Press.

Fürer-Haimendorf, Christoph von (1966). "Unity and Diversity in the Chetri Caste of Nepal." In *Caste and Kin in Nepal, India and Ceylon.* Bombay: Asia Publishing House, 1–63.

Fürer-Haimendorf, Elisabeth von (1958–1964). *An Anthropological Bibliography of South Asia.* 3 vols. Paris: Mouton.

Garbe, Richard (1917). *Die Sāṃkhya-Philosophie: eine Darstellung des indischen Rationalismus.* Leipzig: Haessel.

Garzilli, Enrica (1997). "First Greek and Latin Documents on Sahagamana and Some Connection Problems." *Indo-Iranian Journal* 40: 205–243, 339–365.

Geertz, Clifford (1980). *Negara: The Theatre-State in Nineteenth-Century Bali.* Princeton, N.J.: Princeton University Press.

Geldner, Karl F., trans. (1928). *Vedismus und Brahmanismus.* Tübingen: J.C.B. Mohr (Paul Siebeck) (*Religionsgeschichtliches Lesebuch,* ed. A. Bertholet, no. 9).

Gellner, David (1988). "Monastic Initiation in Newar Buddhism." In R. F. Gombrich, ed., *Indian Ritual and Its Exegesis.* Oxford: Oxford University Press, 42–112.

———(1992). *Monks, Householder, and Tantric Priest: Newar Buddhism and Its Hierarchy of Ritual.* Cambridge: Cambridge University Press.

Gellner, Ernest (1983). *Nations and Nationalism.* Oxford: Basil Blackwell.

———(1988). *Plough, Sword, and Book.* Chicago: University of Chicago Press.

Gennep, Arnold van (1960). *The Rites of Passage.* Trans. Monika B. Vizedom and Gabrielle L. Caffee. Chicago: University of Chicago Press.

Ghurye, G. S. (1932). *Caste and Race in India.* London: Kegan Paul.

———(1950). *Caste and Class in India.* Bombay: Popular Book Depot (revised edition of Ghurye 1932).

———(1964). *Indian Sadhus.* Bombay: Popular Prakashan.

Gladigow, Burkhard (1985). "Naturae deus humanae mortalis. Zur sozialen Konstruktion des Todes in römischer Zeit." In Stephenson, ed., 119–133.

———(1988). "Religionsgeschichte des Gegenstandes—Gegenstände der Religionsgeschichte." In H. Zinser, ed., *Religionswissenschaft: Eine Einführung*. Berlin: Dietrich Reimer Verlag, 6–37.

Glasenapp, Helmuth von (1922). *Der Hinduismus: Religion und Gesellschaft im heutigen Indien*. Munich: Kurt Wolf.

———(1928). *Heilige Stätten Indiens—Die Wallfahrtsorte der Hindus, Jainas und Buddhisten, ihre Legenden und ihr Kultus*. Munich: Georg Müller.

———(1961). *Die Literaturen Indiens*. Stuttgart: Kröner.

Glaser, Karl (1912). "Der indische Student. Auf Grund der Dharmaśāstra- und Gṛhyasūtraliteratur bearbeitet." *Zeitschrift der Deutschen Morgenländischen Gesellschaft* 66: 1–37.

Gnilka, Christian (1972). *Aetas Spiritalis: Die Überwindung der natürlichen Altersstufen als Ideal frühchristlichen Lebens*. Bonn: Hanstein.

Goetz, Hans-Werner (1993). *Life in the Middle Ages: From the Seventh to the Thirteenth Century*. Trans. Albert Wimmer. Notre Dame, Ind.: University of Notre Dame Press.

Gokhale, Balkrishna Govind (1980). "Early Buddhism and the Brahmanas." In A. K. Narain, ed., *Studies in the History of Buddhism*. Delhi, 67–80.

Gold, Ann Grodzins (1989). *Fruitful Journey: The Way of Rajasthani Pilgrims*. Delhi: Oxford University Press.

Gold, Daniel (1992). "Organized Hinduisms: From Vedic Truth to Hindu Nation." In M. E. Marty and R. S. Appleby, eds., *Fundamentalisms Observed*. Chicago: University of Chicago Press, 531–593.

Goldman, R. P. (1978). "Fathers, Sons and Gurus: Oedipal Conflict in the Sanscrit Epics." *Journal of Indian Philosophy* 6: 325–392.

Gombrich, Richard (1975). "Ancient Indian Cosmology." In C. Blacker and M. Lowew, eds., *Ancient Cosmologies*. London: George Allen & Unwin, 110–142.

———(1988). *Theravada Buddhism: A Social History from Ancient Benares to Modern Colombo*. London: Routledge & Kegan Paul.

———(1996). *How Buddhism Began: The Conditioned Genesis of the Early Teachings*. London: Athlone Press.

Gonda, Jan (1960–1964). *Die Religionen Indiens*. 3 vols. Stuttgart: Kohlhammer. Vol. 1: *Veda und ältester Hinduismus*, 1960; vol. 2: *Der jüngere Hinduismus;* vol. 3: see Bareau et al. (1964). (Second edition, 1978).

———(1963). "The Indian Mantra." *Oriens* 16: 244–297.

———(1965). *Change and Continuity in Indian Religion*. The Hague: Mouton.

———(1966). *Loka: The World and the Heaven in the Veda*. Amsterdam: N.V. Noord-Hollandsche Uitgevers Maatschappij.

———(1968). "Hindu Trinity." *Anthropos* 63: 212–226.

———(1969a). *Ancient Indian Kingship from the Religious Point of View*. Leiden: E. J. Brill.

———(1969b). *Eye and Gaze in the Veda*. Amsterdam: North-Holland Publishing Company.

———(1970a). *Notes on Names and the Name of God in Ancient India.* Amsterdam: North-Holland Publishing Company.

———(1970b). *Viṣṇuism and Śivaism: A Comparison.* London: Athlone Press.

———(1977). *Medieval Religious Literature in Sanskrit.* Wiesbaden: Otto Harrassowitz.

———(1980). *Vedic Ritual: The Non-Solemn Rites.* Leiden: E. J. Brill.

———(1985). *Fatherhood in the Veda.* Turin: Pubblicazioni di Indologica Taurinensia.

Gonda, Jan, et al., eds. (1973). *A History of Indian Literature.* Wiesbaden: Otto Harrassowitz.

Good, Anthony (1991). *The Female Bridegroom: A Comparative Study of Life-Crisis Rituals in South India and Sri Lanka.* Oxford: Clarendon Press.

Goody, Jack (1983). *The Development of the Family and Marriage in Europe.* Cambridge: Cambridge University Press.

Goudriaan, Teun (1970). "Vaikhānasa Daily Worship." *Indo-Iranian Journal* 12: 161–215.

Goudriaan, Teun, and Sanjukta Gupta (1981). *Hindu Tantric and Śākta Literature.* Wiesbaden: Otto Harrassowitz.

Gough, E. Kathleen (1955). "Female Initiation Rites on the Malabar Coast." *Journal of the Royal Anthropological Institute* 85: 45–80.

———(1956). "Brahmin Kinship in a Tanjore Village." *American Anthropologist* 58: 826–853.

Gould, Harold (1967). "Priest and Contrapriest: A Structural Analysis of Jajmani Relationships on the Hindu Plains and the Nilgiri Hills." *Contributions to Indian Sociology* n.s. 1: 26–55.

Grimes, John A. (1995). *Gaṇapati: Song of the Self.* Albany: State University of New York Press.

Gross, Robert (1979). *Hindu Asceticism: A Study of the Sadhus of North India.* Berkeley: University of California Press.

Gutschow, Niels, and Axel Michaels (1993). *Benares: Tempel und religiöses Leben in der heiligen Stadt der Hindus.* Cologne: DuMont.

———, eds. (1987). *Heritage of the Kathmandu Valley: Proceedings of an International Conference in Lübeck 1987.* Sankt Augustin: VGH Wissenschaftsverlag.

Haas, Alois (1986). "Was ist Mystik?" In K. Ruh, ed., *Abendländische Mystik im Mittelalter. Symposium Kloster Engelberg.* Stuttgart: Metzler, 319–341.

Hacker, Paul (1957). "Religiöse Toleranz und Intoleranz im Hindusmus." *Saeculum* 8: 167–179.

———(1958). "Der Dharma-Begriff im Neuhinduismus." *Zeitschrift für Missions- und Religionswiss.* 42: 1–15.

———(1960). "Zur Entwicklung der Avatāra Lehre." *Wiener Zeitschrift für die Kunde Süd- und Südostasiens* 4: 47–70.

———(1965). "Dharma im Hinduismus." *Zeitschrift für Missions- und Religionswissenschaft* 49: 92–106.

———(1978). *Kleine Schriften.* Ed. L. Schmithausen. Stuttgart: Franz Steiner Verlag.

———(1983). "Inklusivismus." In Oberhammer, ed. (1983), 11–28.

Halbfass, Wilhelm (1981). *India and Europe: An Essay in Understanding*. Albany: State University of New York Press.

———(1991). *Tradition and Reflection: Explorations in Indian Thought*. Albany: State University of New York Press.

Hamm, Frank-Richard (1968–1969). "Chāndogyopaniṣad VI: Ein erneuter Versuch." *Wiener Zeitschrift für die Kunde Süd- und Südostasiens* 12–13: 149–159.

Hanefeld, Ehrhart (1976). *Philosophische Haupttexte der älteren Upaniṣaden*. Wiesbaden: Otto Harrassowitz.

Hardy, Friedhelm (1983). *Viraha Bhakti: The Early History of Kṛṣṇa Devotion in South India*. Delhi: Oxford University Press.

———(1994). *The Religious Culture of India: Power, Love and Wisdom*. Cambridge: Cambridge University Press.

Harlan, Lindsey, and Paul B. Courtright, eds. (1995). *From the Margins of Hindu Marriage: Essays on Gender, Religion and Culture*. New York: Oxford University Press.

Harper, Edward B. (1959). "Two Systems of Economic Exchange in Indian Village." *American Anthropologist* 61: 760–778.

———(1964). "Ritual Pollution as an Integrator of Caste and Religion." *Journal of Asian Studies* 23: 151–197.

Hartsuiker, Dolf (1993). *Sādhus: Holy Men of India*. London: Thames and Hudson.

Hauer, J. W. (1927). *Der Vrātya*. 2 vols. Stuttgart: Kohlhammer.

———(1958). *Der Yoga—Ein indischer Weg zum Selbst*. Stuttgart: Kohlhammer.

Hawley, John Stratton, and Donna Maria Wulff, eds. (1982). *The Divine Consort: Rādhā and the Goddesses of India*. Delhi: Motilal Banarsidass (reprint, 1984).

———(1996). *Devī: The Goddesses of India*. Berkeley: University of California Press.

Heesterman, Jan C. (1962). "Vrātya and Sacrifice." *Indo-Iranian Journal* 6: 1–37.

———(1964). "Brahmin, Ritual, and Renouncer." *Wiener Zeitschrift für die Kunde Süd- und Südostasiens* 8: 1–31.

———(1978). "Vedisches Opfer und Transzendenz." In Oberhammer, ed. (1978), 29–44.

———(1985). *The Inner Conflict of Tradition: Essays in Indian Ritual, Kingship, and Society*. Chicago: University of Chicago Press.

———(1990–1991). "Hinduism and Vedic Ritual." *History of Religions* 30: 296–305.

———(1993). *The Broken World of Sacrifice: Essays in Ancient Indian Ritual*. Chicago: University of Chicago Press.

———(1995). "Feuer, Seele und Unsterblichkeit." In: Oberhammer, ed. (1995), 27–42.

———(1997). "Vedism and Hinduism." In Oberhammer, ed. (1997), 43–68.

Heiler, Friedrich (1932). *Prayer: A Study in the History and Psychology of Religion*. Trans. Samuel McComb. London: Oxford University Press.

Hershman, Paul (1977). "Virgin and Mother." In I. Lewis, ed., *Symbols and Sentiments: Cross-Cultural Studies in Symbolism*. London: Academic Press.

Hertz, Robert (1907). "Contribution à une étude sur la représentation de la mort." *L'Année Sociologique* 10: 48–137.

Hillebrandt, Alfred (1897). *Rituallliteratur.* Strassburg: Karl J. Trübner.

———(1921). "Worship (Hindu)." In *Encyclopedia of Religion and Ethics,* vol. 12, pp. 795–799.

———(1923). *Aus Brāhmaṇas und Upaniṣaden.* Jena: Insel.

———(1980). *Vedic Mythology.* Trans. Sreeramula Rajeswarma Sarma. Delhi: Motilal Banarsidass.

Hiltebeitel, Alf (1978). "The Indus Valley 'Proto-Śiva,' Reexamined through Reflections on the Goddess, the Buffalo, and the Symbolism of *vāhanas.*" *Anthropos* 73: 767–797.

———, ed. (1989). *Criminal Gods and Demon Devotees.* Albany: State University of New York Press.

Hinüber, Oskar von (1986). *Das ältere Mittelindische im Überblick.* Vienna: Verlag der Österreichischen Akademie der Wissenschaften.

———(1990). *Der Beginn der Schrift und frühe Schriftlichkeit in Indien.* Mainz: Akademie der Wissenschaften und der Literatur in Mainz.

Hocart, A. M. (1927). *Kingship.* London: Oxford University Press.

———(1936). *Kings and Councillors: An Essay in the Comparative Anatomy of Human Society.* Ed. R. Needham. Chicago: University of Chicago Press, 1970.

———(1938). *Caste: A Comparative Study.* London: Methuen (reprint, 1950).

———(1954). *Social Origins.* London: Watts.

Höfer, András (1979). *The Caste Hierarchy and the State in Nepal: A Study of the Muluki Ain of 1854.* Innsbruck: Universitätsverlag Wagner.

Holland, Barron (1979). *Popular Hinduism and Hindu Mythology: An Annotated Bibliography.* Westport, Conn.: Greenwood Press.

Homans, G. C. (1941). "Anxiety and Ritual." *American Anthropologist* 43: 164–172.

Hopkins, Washburn E. (1915). *Epic Mythology.* Strassburg: Karl J. Trübner, (reprint, 1979).

Horsch, Paul (1971). "Vorstufen der Seelenwanderungslehre." *Asiatische Studien* 25: 99–157.

Horstmann, Monika (1994). "Entfremdung und fundamentalistische Identitätskonstruktion im zeitgenössischen Indien." *Internationales Asienforum* 25: 315–333.

———(1995). "Towards a Universal Dharma: *Kalyāṇ* and the Tracts of the Gītā Press." In Dalmia/von Stietencron, eds., 294–305.

Hubert, Henri, and Marcel Mauss (1964). *Sacrifice, Its Nature and Function.* Trans. W. D. Halls. Chicago: University of Chicago Press.

Hübner, Kurt (1985). *Die Wahrheit des Mythos.* Munich: C. H. Beck.

Humphrey, Caroline, and James Laidlaw (1994). *The Archetypal Actions of Ritual: A Theory of Ritual Illustrated by the Jain Rite of Worship.* Oxford: Clarendon Press.

Huntington, R. M. (1964). "Avatāras and Yugas: An Essay in Purāṇic Cosmology." *Purāṇa* 6: 7–39.

Hutton, J. H. (1946). *Caste in India: Its Nature, Function and Origins.* Bombay: Oxford University Press (third edition, 1963).

Ibbetson, Denzil Charles Jelf (1916). *Punjab Castes.* Lahore: Government Printing.

The Imperial Gazetteer of India (1907–1909). New ed., 26 vols. Oxford: Clarendon Press.

Inden, Ronald (1978). "Ritual, Authority, and Cyclic Time in Hindu Kingships." In Richards, ed.

———(1990). *Imagining India.* Oxford: Basil Blackwell.

Isayeva, Natalia (1993). *Shankara and Indian Philosophy.* Albany: State University of New York Press.

Iyer, A. K., and H. V. Najundaa (1928–1935). *The Mysore Tribes and Castes.* 4 vols. Mysore: University Press.

Jacobi, Hermann (1911). "Cosmogony and Cosmology (Indian)." In J. Hastings, ed., *Encyclopedia of Religion and Ethics,* vol. 4, pp. 155–161.

Jacobson, Dorane, and Susan Wadley, eds. (1977). *Women in India: Two Perspectives.* Columbus, Missouri: South Asia Books.

Jansen, Michael (1986). *Die Indus-Zivilisation: Wiederentdeckung einer frühen Hochkultur.* Cologne: DuMont.

Jolly, Julius (1896). *Recht und Sitte.* Strassburg: Karl J. Trübner.

Kaelber, Walter O. (1978). "The 'Dramatic' Element in Brāhmaṇic Initiation: Symbols of Death, Danger, and Difficult Passage." *History of Religions* 18: 54–76.

———(1989). *Tapta Mārga: Asceticism and Initiation in Vedic India.* Albany: State University of New York Press.

Kakar, Sudhir (1974). "Indische Kultur und Psychoanalyse." *Psyche* 28: 635–650.

———(1978). *The Inner World: A Psycho-analytic Study of Childhood and Society in India.* Delhi: Oxford University Press.

———(1979). *Indian Childhood: Cultural Ideals and Social Reality.* Delhi: Oxford University Press.

———(1981). "Kindheit in Indien." *Kindheit* 3: 79–91.

Kane, P. V. (1968–). *History of Dharmaśāstra.* Poona: Bhandarkar Oriental Research Institute.

Kantorowicz, Ernst Hartwig (1957). *The King's Two Bodies: A Study in Medieval Political Theology.* Princeton, N.J. Princeton University Press.

Kantowsky, Dieter, Hermann Kulke, and Jakob Rösel (1968). "Bibliographie ausgewählter neuerer sozialwissenschaftlicher Literatur über Indien." In R. König, ed., *Aspekte der Entwicklungssoziologie.* Cologne and Opladen, 626–651.

Kapadia, K. M. (1955). *Marriage and Family in India.* Calcutta: Oxford University Press.

Kashikar, C. G. (1990). *Identification of Soma.* Pune: Shri Balmukund Sanskrit Mahavidyalaya—Tilak Maharashtra Vidyapeeth.

Kaushik, Meena (1976). "The Symbolic Representation of Death." *Contributions to Indian Sociology* n.s. 10: 295–292.

Kaye, G. R. (1924). *Hindu Astronomy.* Calcutta: Archaeological Survey of India.

Keith, Arthur Berriedale (1918). *The Sāṃkhya System: A History of the Sāṃkhya Philosophy.* Calcutta: YMCA Publ. House.

———(1925). *Religion and Philosophy in the Vedas and Upaniṣads.* Cambridge, Mass.: Harvard University Press.

Keller, Carl A. (1994). "Hinduismus." In: U. Tworuschka, ed., *Heilige Stätten.* Darmstadt: Wissenschaftliche Buchgesellschaft.

Kennedy, Kenneth A. R. (1995). "Have Aryans Been Identified in the Prehistoric Skeletel Record from South Asia? Biological Anthropology and Concepts of Ancient Races." In Erdosy, ed., 32–66.

Kerényi, Karl (1950). "Dramatische Gottesgegenwart in der griechischen Religion." *Eranos Jahrbuch* 19: 13–40.

Ketkar, S. V. (1909). *The History of Caste in India.* Ithaca, N.Y.: Taylor & Carpenter.

Keyes, C. F., and E. V. Daniel, eds. (1983). *Karma: An Anthropological Inquiry.* Berkeley: University of California Press.

Khare, R. S., and M.S.A. Rao, eds. (1986). *Food, Society, and Culture: Aspects in South Asian Food Systems.* Durham, N.C.: Carolina Academic Press.

Kinsley, David R. (1986). *Hindu Goddesses: Visions of the Divine Feminine in the Hindu Religious Traditions.* Berkeley: University of California Press.

Kippenberg, Hans G. (2002). *Discovering Religious History in the Modern Age.* Trans. Barbara Harshav. Princeton, N.J. Princeton University Press.

Kirfel, Willibald (1920). *Die Kosmographie der Inder nach den Quellen dargestellt.* Bonn: Schroeder.

———(1927). *Das Purāṇa Pañcalakṣaṇa: Versuch einer Textgeschichte.* Bonn: Schroeder.

Klass, Morton (1980). *Caste: The Emergence of a South Asian Social System.* Philadelphia: Institute for the Study of Human Issues.

Klaus, Konrad (1986). *Die altindische Kosmologie. Nach den Brāhmaṇas dargestellt.* Bonn: Indica et Tibetica Verlag.

Klostermaier, Klaus (1994). *A Survey of Hinduism.* New York: State University of New York Press.

Knipe, David M. (1977). "*Sapiṇḍikāraṇa:* The Hindu Rite of Entry into Heaven." In F. E. Reynolds and E. H. Waugh, eds., *Religious Encounters with Death: Insights from the History and Anthropology of Religions.* University Park: Pennsylvania State University Press, 111–124.

Kohl, Karl-Heinz (1997). "Edward Burnett Tylor." In Michaels, ed., 41–60.

Köhler, Hans-Werbin (1973). *Śrad-dhā- in der vedischen und altbuddhistischen Literatur.* Wiesbaden: Franz Steiner Verlag.

Kolenda, Pauline M. (1978). *Caste in Contemporary India: Beyond Organic Solidarity.* Prospect Heights, Ill.: Waveland Press (2nd ed., 1985).

Kolff, Dirk H. A. (1990). *Naukar, Rajput and Sepoy: The Ethnohistory of the Military Labour Market in Hindustan, 1450–1850.* Delhi: Manohar Publications.

Kölver, Bernard (1988). "On the Origins of the Jajmānī System." *Journal of the Economic and Social History of the Orient* 31: 265–285.

———(1993). *Ritual und historischer Raum: Zum indischen Geschichtsverständnis.* Munich: Historisches Kolleg.

———, ed. (1986). *Formen kulturellen Wandels und andere Beiträge zur Erforschung des Himālaya.* Sankt Augustin: VGH Wissenschaftsverlag.

———, ed. (1997). *Recht, Staat und Verwaltung im klassischen Indien.* Munich: R. Oldenbourg Verlag.

Kramer, Fritz (1978). "Über Zeit, Geneaologie und solidarische Beziehung." In F. Kramer and C. Sigrist, eds. *Gesellschaften ohne Staat,* 2 vols. Frankfurt/M: Syndikat, vol. 2, pp. 9–27.

Kramrisch, Stella (1981). *The Presence of Śiva.* Delhi: Oxford University Press.

Krick, Hertha (1982). *Das Ritual der Feuergründung (Agnyādheya).* Ed. G. Oberhammer. Vienna: Österreichische Akademie der Wissenschaften.

Krishnamachariar, M. (1937). *History of Classical Sanskrit Literature.* Delhi: Motilal Banarsidass.

Krügel, Sybil (1997). "*Dāsá/dā'sa und dásyu im Ṛgveda.*" Seminar Paper, Institut für Religionswissenschaft der Universität, Bern.

Kuiper, F.B.J. (1983). *Ancient Indian Cosmogony.* New Delhi: Vikas Publ. House.

Kulke, Hermann (1979). "Geschichtschreibung und Geschichtsbild im hinduistischen Mittelalter." *Saeculum* 30; 100–112.

———(1982). "Gibt es ein indisches Mittelalter? Versuch einer eurasiatischen Geschichtsbetrachtung." *Saeculum* 33: 221ff.

———(1993). *Kings and Cults: State Formation and Legitimation in India and Southeast Asia.* Delhi: Manohar Publications.

———, ed. (1985). *Regionale Traditionen in Südasien.* Stuttgart: Franz Steiner Verlag.

Kulke, Hermann, and Dietmar Rothermund (1986). *A History of India.* London: Croom Helm.

Kumar, Nita, ed. (1994). *Women as Subjects: South Asian Histories.* Charlottesville: University Press of Virginia.

Küng, Hans, with H. Bechert, J. van Ess, and H. von Stietencron (1986). *Christianity and the World Religions: Paths of Dialogue with Islam, Hinduism, and Buddhism.* Trans. Peter Heinegg. Garden City, N.Y.: Doubleday.

Kurtz, Stanley N. (1992). *All the Mothers Are One: Hindu India and the Cultural Reshaping of Psychoanalysis.* New York: Columbia University Press.

Lanczkowski, Günter (1971). *Begegnung und Wandel der Religionen.* Düsseldorf: Diedrichs.

———(1980). *Einführung in die Religionswissenschaft.* Darmstadt: Wissenschaftliche Buchgesellschaft.

Larson, Gerald (1969). *Classical Sāṃkhya: An Interpretation of Its History and Meanings.* Delhi: Motilal Banarsidass.

———(1995). *India's Agony over Religion.* New York: State University of New York Press.

Laubscher, Matthias (1979). "Angst und ihre Überwindung in Initiationsriten." In H. von Stietencron, ed., *Angst und Gewalt.* Düsseldorf: Patmos, 78–100.

Leach, Edmund R. (1960). "Introduction: What Should We Mean by Caste?" In *Aspects of Caste in South India, Ceylon and North-West Pakistan.* Cambridge: Cambridge University Press, 1–10.

———(1976). *Culture and Communication: The Logic by Which Symbols Are Connected.* Cambridge: Cambridge University Press.

Lévi, Sylvain (1898). *La doctrine du sacrifice dans les Brāhmaṇas.* Paris.
Lévi-Strauss, Claude (1976). *Mythologica.* Vols. 1–4. Frankfurt/M: Suhrkamp.
Levy-Bruhl, Lucien (1984). *How Natives Think.* Trans. Lilian A. Clare. Salem, N.H.: Ayer Co.
Lewis, Oscar (1958). *Village Life in Northern India.* Urbana: University of Illinois Press.
Lienhard, Siegfried (1984). *A History of Classical Poetry: Sanskrit—Pāli—Prakrit.* Wiesbaden: Otto Harrassowitz.
———(1986). "Dreimal Unreinheit: Riten und Gebräuche der Nevars bei Geburt, Menstruation und Tod." In Kölver, ed., 127–154.
Lingat, Robert (1973). *The Classical Law of India.* Trans. J.D.M. Derrett. Berkeley: University of California Press.
Lippe, Rudolf zur (1974). *Naturbeherrschung am Menschen.* Frankfurt/M Suhrkamp.
Lochtefeld, James G. (1996). "New Wine, Old Skins: The Sangh Parivār and the Transformation of Hindus." *Religion* 26: 101–118.
Locke, John K. (1975). "Newar Buddhist Initiation Rites." *Contributions to Nepalese Studies* 2: 1–23.
Lommel, Hans (1955). "Wiedergeburt aus embryonalem Zustand in der Symbolik des altindischen Rituals." In C. Hentze, ed., *Tod, Auferstehung, Weltordnung.* Zurich: Origo.
Lorenzen, David (1978). "Warrior Ascetics in Indian History." *Journal of the American Oriental Society* 98: 61–75.
———(1996). *Praises to a Formless God: Nirguṇī Texts from North India.* New York: State University of New York Press.
Losch, Hans (1959). *Rājadharma: Einsetzung und Aufgabenkreis des Königs im Lichte der Purāṇa.* Bonn: Selbstverlag des Orientalischen Seminars der Universität Bonn.
Lynch, Owen M. (1977). "Method and Theory in the Sociology of Louis Dumont: A Reply." In K. David, ed., *The New Wind: Changing Identities in South Asia.* The Hague: Mouton, 239–262.
MacDonell, Alexander (1897). *Vedic Mythology.* Varanasi: Indological Bookhouse (reprint, 1963).
Madan, T. N., ed., (1982). *Way of Life: King, Householder, Renouncer. Essays in Honour of Louis Dumont.* New Delhi: Vikas.
Mahar [Kolenda], Pauline Moller (1959). "A Multiple Scaling Technique for Caste Ranking." *Man in India* 39: 127–147.
Malamoud, Charles (1977). *Le svādhyāya: à récitation personelle du Veda, Taittirīya-Araṇyaka, Livre II.* Paris: Institut de Civilisation Indienne.
———(1980). "Théologie de la dette dans les *Brāhmaṇas.*" *Puruṣārtha* 4: 39–62.
———(1982a). "Les morts sans visage." In G. Gnoli and J. P. Vernant, eds., *La mort, les morts dans les sociétés anciennes.* Cambridge: Cambridge University Press.
———(1982b). "On the Rhetoric and Semantics of *puruṣārtha.*" In Madan (1982), 33–54.
———(1996). *Cooking the World: Ritual and Thought in Ancient India.* Delhi: Oxford University Press.

Malinowski, Bronislaw (1967). "Die Rolle des Mythos im Leben." In K. Kerényi, ed., *Eröffnung des Zugangs zum Mythos.* Darmstadt: Wissenschaftliche Buchgesellschaft, 177–193.

Mallebrein, Cornelia, ed. (1993). *Die anderen Götter. Volks- und Stammesbronzen aus Indien.* Heidelberg: Edition Braus.

Maloney, Clarence (1976). "Don't Say 'Pretty Baby' Lest You Zap It with Your Eye: The Evil Eye in South Asia." In Clarence Maloney, ed., *The Evil Eye.* New York: Columbia University Press, 102–148.

Mandal, Kumar Kishore (1968). *A Comparative Study of the Concepts of Space and Time in Indian Thought.* Varanasi: Chowkhamba Sanskrit Series Office.

Mandelbaum, David (1970). *Society in India.* 2 vols. Berkeley: University of California Press.

Mann, Ulrich (1982). *Schöpfungsmythen.* Stuttgart: Kreuz-Verlag.

Marquard, Odo (1989). "Praise of Polytheism." In *Farewell to Matters of Principle: Philosophical Studies.* Trans. Robert M. Wallace, with the assistance of Susan Bernstein and James I. Porter. New York: Oxford University Press.

Marriott, McKim (1955). "Little Communities in an Indigenous Civilization." In Marriott, ed., (1955), 171–222.

———(1959). "Interactional and Attributional Theories of Caste Ranking." *Man in India* 39: 92–107.

———(1960). *Caste Ranking and Community Structure in Five Regions of India and Pakistan.* Poona: Deccan College Monograph.

———(1968a). "Caste Ranking and Food Transactions: A Matrix Analysis." In Singer/Cohn, eds., 133. 171.

———(1968b). "Multiple Reference in Indian Caste Systems." In J. Silverberg, ed., *Social Mobility in the Caste Systems in India: Comparative Studies in Society and History.* The Hague: Mouton, 103ff.

———(1969). Review of Louis Dumont's *Homo Hierarchicus. American Anthropologist* 71: 1166–1175.

———(1976). "Hindu Transactions: Diversity without Dualism." In B. Kapferer, ed., *Transaction and Meaning.* Philadelphia: Institute for the Study of Human Issues, 109–142.

———, ed. (1955). *Village India: Studies in the Little Community.* Chicago: University of Chicago Press.

———, ed. (1990). *India through Hindu Categories.* New Delhi: Sage Publications.

Marriott, McKim, and Ronald Inden (1973). "Caste Systems." In *Encyclopedia Britannica, Macropaedia.* Chicago: Helen Hemenway Benton, vol. 3, pp. 982–991.

———(1977). "Toward an Ethnosociology of South Asian Caste Systems." In K. David, ed., *The New Wind: Changing Identities in South Asia.* The Hague: Mouton, 423–438.

Masilamani-Meyer, Eveline (1996). "The Eyes of the Goddess." In Michaels/Vogelsanger/Wilke (1996), 449–482.

Masson, J. M. (1974). "The Childhood of Kṛṣṇa: Some Psychoanalytical Observations." *Journal of the American Oriental Society* 94: 454–459.

———(1980). *The Oceanic Feeling: The Origins of Religious Sentiment in Ancient India.* Dordrecht: Reidel Publishing.

Mauss, Marcel (1990). *The Gift: The Form and Reason for Exchange in Archaic Societies.* Trans. W. D. Halls. London: Routledge.

Mayer, Adrain C. (1960). *Caste and Kinship in Central India.* London: Routledge & Kegan Paul.

Mayer-König, Birgit (1996). *Die Gleichheit in der Unterschiedenheit: eine Lehre des monistischen Śivaismus, untersucht anhand des fünften Kapitels des Śivadṛṣṭi des Somānanda Nātha.* Frankfurt/M: Peter Lang.

McCrindle, J. W. (1877). See *Indikē* in Text Editions and Translations.

McDaniel, June (1989). *The Madness of the Saints: Ecstatic Religion in Bengal.* Chicago: University of Chicago Press.

McDermott, Rachel Fell (1996). "Popular Attitudes towards Kālī and Her Poetry Tradition: Interviewing Śāktas in Bengal." In Michaels/Vogelsanger/Wilke, eds., 383–416.

McLeod, W. H. (1978). "On the Word *Panth:* A Problem of Terminology and Definition." *Contributions to Indian Sociology* n.s. 12: 287–295.

Meisig, Konrad (1996). *Shivas Tanz: Der Hinduismus.* Freiburg: Herder Verlag.

Mensching, Gustav (1959). *Die Religion: Erscheinungsform, Stukturtypen und Lebensgesetze.* Stuttgart: Curt E. Schwab.

Merrey, K. L. (1982). "The Hindu Festival Calendar." In Guy R. Welbon and Glenn E. Yocum, eds., *Religious Festivals in South India and Sri Lanka.* New Delhi: Manohar, 1–25.

Metcalf, P., and R. Huntington, eds. (1991). *Celebrations of Death: The Anthropology of Mortuary Ritual.* Cambridge: Cambridge University Press.

Michaels, Axel (1978). *Beweisverfahren in der vedischen Sakralgeometrie. Ein Beitrag zur Entstehungsgeschichte von Wissenschaft.* Wiesbaden: Franz Steiner Verlag.

———(1982). Review of Kakar 1978 and Masson 1980. *Psyche* 38: 371–376.

———(1986a). "Der verstoβene Sohn. Nepalesische *bālyogis* [Kinderasketen] und der *deśāntara*-Ritus während der Initiation (*upanayana*)." In Kölver, ed. (1986), 189–224.

———(1986b). *Ritual und Gesellschaft in Indien: Ein Essay.* With photos by Niels Gutschow. Frankfurt/M: Verlag Neue Kritik.

———(1992a). "Lukumahādyaḥ—The Hiding Śiva: A Nepalese Stone Deity and Its Cult." In B. Kölver, ed., *Aspects of Nepalese Traditions.* Stuttgart: Franz Steiner Verlag, 193–208.

———(1992b). "Recht auf Leben, Tötung und Selbsttötung in Indien." In B. Mensen, ed., *Recht auf Leben—Recht auf Töten, ein Kulturvergleich.* Nettetal: Steyler Verlag, 95–124.

———(1993a). "Śiva under Refuse—The Hidden Mahādeva (Lukumahādyaḥ) and Protective Stones in Nepal." In H. Brückner et al., eds., *Flags of Fame: Studies in South Asian Folk Culture.* New Delhi: Manohar Publications, 165–200.

———(1993b). "Widow Burning in Nepal." In G. Toffin, ed., *Nepal, Past and Present: Proceedings of the Franco-German Conference Arc-et-Senans, June 1990.* Paris: Editions du Centre National de la Recherche Scientifique, 21–34.

———(1994a). "Die Heilige Schnur und 'hinduistische' Askese." *Zeitschrift der Deutschen Morgenländischen Gesellschaft* 144: 330–344.

———(1994b). "The Legislation of Widow Burning in Nineteenth-Century Nepal: Edition and Translation of the Chapter *Satijānyako* of the Mulukī Ain." *Asiatische Studien* 48: 1213–1240.

———(1994c). *Reisen der Götter. Der nepalische Paśupatinātha-Tempel und sein rituelles Umfeld.* 2 parts. Bonn: VGH Wissenschaftsverlag.

———(1995a). "Reinkarnation—ein morgenländisches 'Dogma'?" *Der Evangelische Erzieher* 47: 159–171.

———(1995b). "Sakralgeometrie, vedische." In J. Mittelstrass et al., eds., *Enzyklopädie Philosophie und Wissenschaftstheorie.* Stuttgart: Metzler, vol. 3, pp. 661–662.

———(1996a). "Das Buch als Fundament von Religionen." In P. Rusterholz and R. Moser, eds., *Die Bedeutung des Buches.* Bern: Haupt, 111–142.

———(1996b). "La nature pour la nature. Naturzerstörung und Naturschonung im traditionellen Indien." *Asiastische Studien* 50: 817–834.

———(1996c). "Śivarātri at Deopatan." In Siegfried Lienhard, ed., *Change and Continuity: Studies in the Nepalese Culture of the Kathmandu Valley.* Turin: Edizioni Dell'orso (CESMEO).

———(1997a). "Gift and Return Gift, Greeting and Return Greeting in India: On a Consequential Footnote by Marcel Mauss." *Numen* 44: 242–269.

———(1997b). "The King and the Cow: On a Crucial Symbol of Hinduization." In D. Gellner, J. Pfaff-Czarnecka, and J. Whelpton, eds., *Nationalism and Ethnicity in a Hindu Kingdom: The Politics of Culture in Contemporary Nepal.* Amsterdam: Harwood Academic Publishers, 79–100.

———(1997c). "Le rituel pour le rituel? Oder wie sinnlos sind Rituale?" *Unimagazin. Die Zeitschrift der Universität Zürich* 1. 98: 10–12.

———(1997d). "Religionen und der neurobiologische Primat der Angst." In F. Stolz, ed., *Homo naturaliter religosus. Gehört Religion notwendig zum Mensch-Sein?* Bern: Peter Lang, 91–136.

———(1998). "Wissenschaftsgläubigkeit." In P. Rusterholz and R. Moser, eds., *Bewältigung und Verdrängung spiritueller Krisen: Esoterik als Kompensation von Wissenschaft und Kirchen.* Bern: Peter Lang, 29–55.

———(1998/ms.). "Kuhschützer und Kuhesser: Gesetzliche Verbote der Rindertötung in Nepal." In A. Wezler, ed. (ms., forthcoming).

———(1999). "Ancestors, Demons and the Ritual Impossibility of Death in Brahmanical Hinduism: Bālā's Fourteenth in Deopatan (Nepal)." In: Schömbucher/Zoller, eds. (1999), 112–134.

———, ed. (1997). *Klassiker der Religionswissenschaft: Friedrich Schleiermacher bis Mircea Eliade.* Munich: C. H. Beck.

Michaels, Axel, with Nutan Sharma (1996). "Goddess of the Secret: Guhyeśvarī in Nepal and Her Festival." In Michaels/Vogelsanger/Wilke, eds., 303–342.

Michaels, Axel, Cornelia Vogelsanger, and Annette Wilke, eds. (1996). *Wild Goddesses in India and Nepal.* Bern: Peter Lang.

Mies, Maria (1986). *Indische Frauen zwischen Unterdrückung und Befreiung.* Frankfurt/M: Europäische Verlagsanstalt.

Miller, Barbara D. (1981). *The Endangered Sex: Neglect of Female Children in Rural North India.* Ithaca, N.Y.: Cornell University Press.

Milner, Murray (1994). *Status and Sacredness: A General Theory and Analysis of Indian Culture.* New York: Oxford University Press.

Mittelstrass, Jürgen (1974). *Die Möglichkeit von Wissenschaft.* Frankfurt/M: Suhrkamp.

Moffat, Michael (1979). *An Untouchable Community in South India: Structure and Consensus.* Princeton, N.J.: Princeton University Press.

Monier-Williams, Monier (1899). *Sanskrit-English Dictionary.* Oxford: Oxford University Press.

Moore, Sally F., and Barbara G. Myerhoff, eds. (1977). *Secular Ritual.* Assen: van Gorkum.

Morinis, Alan E. (1984). *Pilgrimage in the Hindu Tradition: A Case Study of West Bengal.* Delhi: Oxford University Press.

Müller, Klaus-Werner (1992). *Das brahmanische Totenritual nach der Antyeṣṭipaddhati des Nārāyaṇabhaṭṭa.* Stuttgart: Franz Steiner Verlag.

Mürmel, Heinz. "Bemerkungen zur Kastenkozeption in der 'Durkheimgruppe,'" *Ethnographisch-Archäolische Zeitschrift* 30; 22–35.

Mylius, Klaus (1970). "Zur absoluten Datierung der mittelvedischen Literatur." In: Horst Krueger, ed., *Neue Indienkunde: Festschrift Walter Rubem zum 70. Geburtstag.* East Berlin: Akademie Verlag, 421ff.

———(1972). "Das geographische Milieu der mittelvedischen Literature." *Mitteilungen des Instituts für Orientforschung* 17.3: 369–382.

———(1973). "Die gesellschaftliche Entwicklung Indiens in jungvedischer Zeit nach den Sanskritquellen. [Appendix:] Das vedische Opferritual." *Ethnographisch-Archäolische Zeitschrift* 14: 475–498.

———(1976). "Die vedischen Identifikationen am Beispiel des *Kauṣītakī-Brāhmaṇa.*" *Kilo* 58: 145–166.

———(1977). "Die Identificationen im *Kauṣītakī-Brāhmaṇa.*" *Altorientalische Forschungen* 5: 237–244.

———(1983). *Geschichte der indischen Literatur.* Leipzig: Philipp Reclam, Jr.

Nath, Vijay (1987). *Dāna: Gift System in Ancient India: A Socio-economic Perspective.* Delhi: Munshiram Manoharlal.

Nehru, Jawaharlal (1960). *The Discovery of India.* Garden City, N.Y.: Doubleday.

Nesfield, John C. (1885). *Brief View of the Caste System of the North-Western Provinces and Oudh.* Allahabad: North-Western Provinces and Oudh Educational Department.

Neufeldt, R. N., ed. (1986). *Karma and Rebirth: Post-Classical Developments.* New York: State University of New York Press.

Oberhammer, Gerhard (1994). *La délivrance dès cette vie (jīvanmuktiḥ).* Paris: de Boccard.

———, ed. (1978). *Transzendenzerfahrung, Vollzugshorizont des Heils: Das Problem in indischer und christlicher Tradition.* Vienna: Institut für Indologie der Universität.

———, ed. (1983). *Inklusivismus: Eine indische Denkform.* Vienna: Institut für Indologie der Universität.

———, ed. (1995). *Im Tod gewinnt der Mensch sein Selbst: Das Phänomen des Todes in asiatischer und abendländischer Religionstradition.* Vienna: Verlag der Österreichischen Akademie der Wissenschaften.

———, ed. (1997). *Studies in Hinduism: Vedism and Hinduism.* Vienna: Verlag der Österreichischen Akademie der Wissenschaften.

Oberlies, Thomas (1995). Review of Kashikar 1990. *Wiener Zeitschrift für die Kunde Süd- und Südostasiens* 139: 135–138.

Obeyesekere, Ganannath (1990). *The Work of Culture: Symbolic Transformation in Psychoanalysis and Anthropology.* Chicago: University of Chicago Press.

O'Flaherty, Wendy Doniger (1973). *Asceticism and Eroticism in the Mythology of Śiva.* London: Oxford University Press.

———(1975). *Hindu Myths.* Harmondsworth: Penguin.

———(1976). *The Origins of Evil in Hindu Mythology.* Delhi: Motilal Banarsidass.

———(1993). "Reinkarnation im Hinduismus." *Concilium* 29: 380–388.

———, ed. (1980). *Karma and Rebirth in Classical Indian Traditions.* Berkeley: University of California Press.

O'Flaherty, Wendy Doniger, et al. (1988). *Textual Sources for the Study of Hinduism.* Manchester: Manchester University Press.

Oldenberg, Hermann (1917). *Die Religion des Veda.* Stuttgart: J. G. Cotta'sche Buchh. Nachf.

———(1919). *Vorwissenschaftliche Wissenschaft. Die Weltanschauung der Brāhmaṇa-Texte.* Göttingen: Vandenhoeck & Ruprecht.

———(1991). *The Doctrine of the Upaniṣads and the Early Buddhism.* Trans. Shridhar B. Shrotri. Delhi: Motilal Banarsidass.

Olivelle, Patrick (1986). *Renunciation in Hinduism: A Medieval Debate.* 2 vols. Vienna: Publications of the Nobili Research Library.

———(1992). See *Saṃnyāsa-upaniṣads* in Text Editions and Translations.

———(1993). *The Āśrama System: The History and Hermeneutics of a Religious Institution.* New York: Oxford University Press.

———, trans. (1996). *Upaniṣads.* Oxford: Oxford University Press.

Olson, Carl (1997). *The Indian Renouncer and Postmodern Poison: A Cross-Cultural Encounter.* New York: Peter Lang.

O'Malley, L.S.S. (1932). *Indian Caste Customs.* Cambridge: Cambridge University Press.

———(1941). "The Hindu Social System." In *Modern India and the West.* Oxford: Oxford University Press, 354–388.

Oman, J. Campbell (1903). *The Mystics, Ascetics and Saints of India.* London: T. F. Unwin.

Otto, Rudolf (1932). *Mysticism East and West: A Comparative Analysis of the Nature of Mysticism.* Trans. Bertha L. Bracey and Richenda C. Payne. New York: Macmillan.

Padoux, André (1990). *Vāc: The Concept of the Word in Selected Hindu Tantras.* New York: State University of New York Press.

Pandey, Raj Bali (1969). *Hindu Saṃskāras: Socio-Religious Study of the Hindu Sacraments.* Delhi: Motilal Banarsidass.

Panikkar, Raimon (1991). "There Is No Outer without Inner Space." In Vatsyayan, ed., 7–38.

———(1992). *Rückkehr zum Mythos.* Frankfurt/M.: Insel.

Parpola, Asko (1994). *Deciphering the Indusscript.* Cambridge: Cambridge University Press.

Parry, Jonathan (1979). *Caste and Kinship in Kangra.* London: Routledge & Kegen Paul.

———(1980). "Ghost, Greed and Sin: The Occupational Identity of the Benares Funeral Priests." *Man* n.s. 15: 88–111.

———(1985a). "The Brahmanical Tradition and the Technology of the Intellect." In J. Overing, ed., *Reason and Mortality.* London: Tavistock Publications, 200–225.

———(1985b). "Death and Digestion: The Symbolism of Food and Eating in North Indian Mortuary Rites." *Man* n.s. 20: 612–630.

———(1986). "The *Gift,* the Indian Gift and the 'Indian Gift.' " *Man* n.s. 21: 453–473.

———(1994). *Death in Benares.* Cambridge: Cambridge University Press.

Peterson, Indira Viswanathan (1989). *The Hymns of the Tamil Saints.* Princeton, N.J.: Princeton University Press.

Penner, Hans H. (1985). "Language, Ritual, and Meaning." *Numen* 32: 1–16.

Petzold, Matthias (1986). *Indische Psychologie: Eine Einführung in traditionelle Ansätze und moderne Forschung.* Munich: Psychologie Verlags Union.

Pfeiffer, Martin (1974). "Hinduismus der Gegenwart." *Verkündigung und Forschung* 19: 24–56.

———(1994). *Indische Mythem vom Werden der Welt: Texte—Strukturen—Geschichte.* Berlin: Dietrich Reimer Verlag.

Pintchman, Tracy (1994). *The Rise of the Goddess in the Hindu Tradition.* Albany: State University of New York Press.

Pitt-Rivers, Julian (1971). "On the Word 'Caste.' " In T. O. Beidelman, ed., *The Translation of Culture: Essays to E. E. Evans-Pritchard.* London: Tavistock Publications, 231–256.

Pollack, Detlef (1995). "Was ist Religion? Probleme der Definition." *Zeitschrift für Religionswissenschaft* 3: 163–190.

Potter, Karl, et al. (1979–1987). *Encyclopedia of Indian Philosophies.* Delhi: Motilal Banarsidass. vol. 1: *Bibliography,* 1983; vol. 2: *Indian Metaphysics and Epistemology: The Tradition of the Nyāya-Vaiśeṣika Up to Gaṅgeśa,* 1979; vol. 3: *Advaita-Vedānta*

Up to Śaṃkara and His Pupils, 1982; vol 4: *Sāṃkhya: A Dualist Tradition of Indian Philosophy*, 1987.

Preston, James I. (1980). *Cult of the Goddess: Social and Religious Change in a Hindu Temple.* Delhi: Vikas Publishing House.

Quigley, Declan (1988). "Is Caste a Pure Figment, the Invention of Orientalists for Their Own Glorification?" *Cambridge Anthropology* 13.1: 20–36.

———(1993). *The Interpretation of Caste.* New York: Oxford University Press.

Raheja, Gloria Goodwin (1988). *The Poison in the Gift: Ritual, Prestation, and the Dominant Caste in a North Indian Village.* Chicago: University of Chicago Press.

———(1989). "Centrality, Mutuality and Hierarchy: Shifting Aspects of Inter-Caste Relationships in North India." *Contributions to Indian Sociology* n.s. 23: 79–101.

———(1994). "Women's Speech Genres, Kinship and Contradiction." In Kumar, ed. (1994), 49–81.

Raheja, Gloria Goodwin, and Ann Grodzins Gold (1994). *Listen to the Heron's Words: Reimagining Gender and Kinship in North India.* Berkeley: University of California Press.

Raheja, Neeta, and Adishwar Puri (1995). *How to Arrange a Wedding.* New Delhi: UBSPD.

Ramanujan, A. K. (1972). "The Indian Oedipus." In *Indian Literature: Proceedings of a Seminar.* Simla: Indian Institute of Advanced Study.

———(1988). "Where the Mirrors Are Windows: Toward an Anthology of Reflections." *History of Religions* 28: 178–216.

———(1990). "Is There an Indian Way of Thinking? An Informal Essay." In Marriott, ed. (1990).

Rau, Wilhelm (1957). *Staat und Gesellschaft im Alten Indien—nach den Brāhmaṇa-Texten dargestellt.* Wiesbaden: Otto Harrassowitz.

———(1974). *Metalle und Metallgeräte im vedischen Indien.* Mainz: Akademie der Wissenschaften und Literatur in Mainz.

———(1975). *Indiens Beitrag zur Kultur der Menschheit.* Wiesbaden: Franz Steiner Verlag.

———(1983). *Zur vedischen Altertumskunde.* Wiesbaden: Akademie der Wissenschaften und Literatur in Mainz.

———(1986). *Naturbeobachtung und Handwerkskunst im vorislamischen Indien.* Stuttgart: Franz Steiner Verlag.

Raynal, Guillaume, and Denis Diderot (1775). *The Sentiments of a Foreigner on the Disputes of Great Britain with America.* Translation of an extract of *Histoire Philosophique et Politique des établissements et du commerce des Européens dans les deux Indes.* Philadelphia: James Humphreys, Jr.

Redfield, Robert, and Milton B. Singer (1954). "The Cultural Role of Cities." *Economic Development and Cultural Change* 3; 53–73.

Reik, Theodor (1931). *Ritual: Psycho-analytic Studies.* Trans. Douglas Bryan. London: L. and Virginia Woolf at the Hogarth Press and the Institute of Psycho-Analysis.

Renfrew, Colin (1987). *Archaeology and Language: The Puzzle of Indo-European Origins.* London: Jonathan Cape.

Renou, Louis (1953). *Religions of Ancient India.* London: Athlone Press (Jordan Lectures 1951).

Richards, J. F., ed. (1978). *Kingship and Authority in South Asia.* Madison: University of Wisconsin Press.

Ries, Julien, and Henri Limet, eds. (1986). *Les rites d'initiation. Actes du colloque de Liège et de Louvain-la-Neuve 20–21 novembre 1984.* Louvain-la-Neuve: Centre d'histoire des religions de l'Université de Liège.

Risley, Herbert (1891). *The Tribes and Castes of Bengal.* 4 vols. Calcutta: Bengal Secretariat Press.

———(1908). *The People of India.* Calcutta: Thacker & Spink.

Ritschl, Eva (1997). "Überlegungen zu *aṭavī* und andern Gruppen der *Anārya*-Bevölkerung im alten Indien nach Sanskritquellen." In Kölver, ed. (1997): 241–247.

Rocher, Ludo (1986). *The Purāṇas.* Wiesbaden: Otto Harrassowitz.

Roland, Alan (1988). *In Search of Self in India and Japan: Towards a Cross-Cultural Psychology.* Princeton, N.J.: Princeton University Press.

Rösel, Jakob (1982). *Die Hinduismusthese Max Webers. Folgen eines kolonialen Indienbildes in einem religionssoziologischen Gedankengang.* Munich: Weltforum-Verlag.

Roth, R. (1860). *Der Mythos von den fünf Menschengeschlechtern bei Hesiod und die indische Lehre von den vier Weltaltern.* Tübingen.

Rothermund, Dietmar (1986). *Indische Geschichte in Grundzügen.* Darmstadt: Wissenschaftliche Buchgesellschaft (third edition, 1991).

———, ed. (1995). *Indien. Kultur, Geschichte, Politik, Wirtschaft, Umwelt—Ein Handbuch.* Munich: C. H. Beck.

Ruben, Walter (1944). *Krishna. Konkordanz und Kommentar der Motive seines Heldenlebens.* Istanbul (Istanbuler Schriften, vol. 17).

Rudolph, Kurt (1971). "Das Problem einer Entwicklung in der Religionsgeschichte." *Kairos* 13: 95–118.

Ruh, Kurt (1990–96). *Geschichte der abendländischen Mystik.* Munich: C. H. Beck.

Rüping, Klaus (1979). "Zur Askese in indischen Religionen." *Zeitschrift für Missionswissenschaft* 2: 81–98.

Russell R. V., and R. B. Hira Lal (1916). *The Tribes and Castes of the Central Provinces of India.* 4 vols. London: Macmillan.

Salomon, Richard (1979). "*Tīrtha-pratyāmnāyāḥ:* Ranking of Hindu Pilgrimage Sites in Classical Sanskrit Texts." *Zeitschrift d. Deutschen Morgenländischen Gesellschaft* 129: 102–128.

———(1995). "On the Origin of Early Indian Scripts: A Review Article." *Journal of the American Oriental Society* 115: 271–279.

Sanderson, Alexis (1988). "Saivism and Tantric Traditions." In St. Sutherland et al., eds., *The World's Religions.* London: Routledge, 660–704.

Scharban, Carl Anders (1932). *Die Idee der Schöpfung in der vedischen Literatur: Eine religionsgeschichtliche Untersuchung über den frühindischen Theismus.* Stuttgart: Kohlhammer.

Schayer, Stanislaw (1925). "Die Struktur der magischen Weltanschauung nach den Brāhmaṇas." *Zeitschrift für Buddhismus* 4: 259ff.

Schlerath, Bernfried (1960). *Kas Königtum im Rig- und Atharvaveda.* Wiesbaden: Franz Steiner Verlag.

Schluchter, Wolfgang, ed. (1984). *Max Webers Studie über Hinduismus und Buddhismus: Interpretation und Kritik.* Frankfurt/M: Suhrkamp.

Schmidt, Hanns-Peter (1968). "The Origins of Ahiṃsā." In *Mélanges d'Indianisme à la mémoire de L. Renou.* Paris: Boccard, 625–655.

Schmithausen, Lambert (1973). "Spirituelle Praxis und philosophische Theorie." *Zeitschrift für Missions- und Religionswissenschaft.* 51: 161–186.

———(1985). "Buddhismus und Natur." In R. Panikkar and W. Strolz, eds., *Die Verantwortung des Menschen für eine bewohnbare Welt im Christentum, Hinduismus und Buddhismus.* Frieburg: Herder Verlag, 100–133.

———(1995). "Mensch, Tier und Pflanze und der Told in den älteren Upaniṣaden." In Oberhammer, ed. (1995), 43–74.

Schmitz, Hermann (1967, 1969, and 1978). *System der Philosophie.* Vol. 3: *Der Raum.* Part I: *Der leibliche Raum;* part II: *Der Gefühlsraum;* part IV: *Das Göttliche und der Raum.* Bonn: Bouvier Verlag Herbert Grundmann.

Schneider, Ulrich (1989). *Einführung in den Hinduismus.* Darmstadt: Wissenschaftliche Buchgesellschaft.

Schnepel, Burkhard (1988). "In Quest of Life: Hocart's Scheme of Evolution from Ritual Organization to Government." *Archives Européennes de Sociologie* 29: 165–187.

———(1996). "The Hindu King's Authority Reconsidered: Durgā-Pūjā and Dasarā in a South Orissan Jungle Kingdom." In A. Boholm, ed., *Political Ritual.* Göteborg: Institute for Advanced Studies in Social Anthropology.

———(1997). *Die Dschungelkönige: Ethnohistorische Aspekte von Politik und Ritual in Südorissa/Indien.* Stuttgart: Franz Steiner Verlag.

Schömbucher, Elisabeth, and Claus-Peter Zoller, eds. (1999). *The Meaning of Death in South Asia.* Heidelberg: Südasien-Institut; New Delhi: Manohar Publications.

Schrader, F. Otto (1930). *Der Hinduismus.* Tübingen: J.C.B. Mohr (Paul Siebeck), (Religionsgeschichtliches Lesebuch, ed. A. Bertholet, no. 14).

Schreiner, Peter (1979). *Yoga. Grundlagen, Methoden, Ziele. Ein bibliographischer Überblick.* Cologne: commissioned by E. J. Brill.

———(1996). *Im Mondschein öffnet sich der Lotus: Der Hinduismus.* Düsseldorf: Patmos Verlag.

Schuman, Hans Wolfgang (1996). *Die grossen Götter Indiens. Grundzüge von Hinduismus und Buddhismus.* Munich: Diederichs.

Schwartzberg, Joseph (1992). "South Asian Cartography." In J. B. Harley and D. Woodward, eds., *Cartography in the Traditional Islamic and South Asian Societies.* Chicago; University of Chicago Press.

———, ed. (1992). *A Historical Atlas of South Asia.* Oxford: Oxford University Press.

Sen, Amartya (1993). "Economics and the Family." In Uberoi, ed. (1993), 452–463.

Senart, Emile (1930). *Caste in India: The Facts and the System.* London: Methuen.

Shaffer, J. G. (1984). "Indo-Aryan Invasions: Myth or Reality?" In J. R. Lukacs, ed., *The People of South Asia: The Biological Anthropology of India, Pakistan and Nepal.* New York: Plenum Press.

Sharma, Arvind (1986). "What Is Hinduism? A Sociological Approach." *Social Compass* 23: 177–183.

Sharma, B. N. (1978). *Festivals of India.* New Delhi: Abhinav Publications.

Sharma, Har Dutt (1939). *Contributions to the History of Brāhmaṇical Asceticism (Saṃnyāsa).* Poona: Oriental Book Agency.

Shulman, David Dean (1980). *Tamil Temple Myths: Sacrifice and Divine Marriage in the South Indian Śaiva Tradition.* Princeton, N.J.: Princeton University Press.

———(1984). "Die Integration der hinduistischen Kultur durch die Brahmanen." In Schluchter, ed., 104–148.

———(1985). *The King and the Clown in South Indian Myth and Poetry.* Princeton, N.J.: Princeton University Press.

Singer, Milton (1972). *When a Great Tradition Modernizes: Text and Context in the Study of Hinduism.* New York: Praeger Publishers.

Singer, Milton, and Bernhard S. Cohn, eds. (1968). *Structure and Change in Indian Society.* Chicago: Aldine Publishing Company.

Sircar, D. C. (1967). *Cosmography and Geography in Early Indian Literature.* Calcutta: D. Chattopadhyaya on behalf of Indian Studies: Past and Present.

Slaje, Walter (1993). "Merkmale des Lebendigen: Zu einer naturphilosophisch begründeten Biologie in Bhāskarakaṇṭhas *Cittānubodhaśāstra.*" *Journal of the European Āyurvedic Society* 3: 250–281.

Smith, Brian K. (1986). "Ritual, Knowledge, and Being: Initiation and Veda Study in Ancient India." *Numen* 38: 65–89.

———(1989). *Reflections on Resemblance, Ritual, and Religion.* New York: Oxford University Press.

———(1994). *Classifying the Universe: The Ancient Indian Varṇa System and the Origins of Caste.* Oxford: Oxford University Press.

———(1996). "Re-envisioning Hinduism and Evaluating the Hindutva Movement." *Religion* 16: 119–128.

Smith, Jonathan Z. (1982). *Imagining Religion: From Babylon to Jonestown.* Chicago: University of Chicago Press.

———(1987). *To Take Place: Toward Theory in Ritual.* Chicago: University of Chicago Press.

Smith, William Cantwell (1978). *The Meaning and End of Religion.* San Francisco: Harper & Row.

Sontheimer, Günther Dietz (1977). *The Hindu Joint Family: Its Evolution as a Legal Institution.* New Delhi: Munshiram Manoharlal.

———(1989). "Hinduism: The Five Components and Their Interaction." In Sontheimer/Kulke, eds., 197–212.

Sontheimer, Günther Dietz, and Hermann Kulke, eds. (1989). *Hinduism Reconsidered.* New Delhi: Manohar Publications.

Southworth, Franklin C. (1995). "Reconstructing the Social Context from Language: Indo-Aryan and Dravidian Prehistory." In Erdosy, ed., 258–277.

Spiro, Milford E. (1966). "Religion: Problems of Definition and Explanation." In M. Banton, ed., *Anthropological Approaches to the Study of Religion*. London: Tavistock Publications.

Spratt, Philip (1966). *Hindu Culture and Personality: A Psycho-analytic Study*. Delhi: Delhi Printers Prakashan (reprint, 1977).

Sprockhoff, Joachim Friedrich (1964). "Religiöse Lebensformen und Gestalt der Lebensräume. Über das Verhältnis von Religionsgeographie und Religionswissenschaft." *Numen* 9: 85–146.

———(1976). *Saṃnyāsa—Quellenstudien zur Askese im Hinduismus*. Vol. I: *Untersuchungen über die Saṃnyāsa-Upaniṣads*. Wiesbaden: Otto Harrassowitz.

———(1979). "Die Alten im alten Indien." *Saeculum* 30: 374–433.

———(1981–1984). "Āraṇyaka und Vānaprastha in der vedischen Literatur: Neue Erwägungen zu einer alten Legende und ihren Problemen." *Wiener Zeitschrift für die Kunde Südasiens* 25: 19–90; and 28: 5–43.

———(1985). "Die feindlichen Toten und der befriedende Tote: Die Überwindung von Leben und Tod in der Entsagung." In Stephenson, ed., 263–284.

Srinivas, M. N. (1952). *Religion and Society among the Coorgs of South India*. Bombay: Asia (reprint, 1965).

Srinivas, M. N., et al. (1959). *Caste: A Trend Report and Bibliography*. Oxford: Blackwell.

Srinivasan, Doris (1973). "Saṃdhyā: Myth and Ritual." *Indo-Iranian Journal* 15: 161–178.

———(1975–1976). "The So-called Proto-Śiva Seal from Mohenjo Daro: An Iconological Assessment." *Archives of Asian Art* 29: 47–58.

———(1984). "Unhinging Śiva from the Indus Civilization." *Journal of the Royal Asiatic Society of Great Britain and Ireland* 1984: 77–89.

Staal, J. F. (1963). "Sanskrit and Sanskritization." *Journal of Asian Studies* 22: 261–275.

———(1979). "The Meaninglessness of Ritual." *Numen* 26: 2–22.

———(1983). *Agni: The Vedic Ritual of the Fire Altar*. 2 vols. Berkeley: University of California Press.

———(1989). *Rules without Meaning: Ritual, Mantras and the Human Sciences*. New York: Peter Lang.

Stein, Burton (1980). *Peasant State and Society in Medieval India*. Delhi: Oxford University Press.

Steinmann, Ralph Marc (1986). *Guru-Śiṣya-Sambandha: Das Meister-Schüler-Verhältnis im traditionellen und modernen Indien*. Wiesbaden: Franz Steiner Verlag.

Stephenson, Gunter, ed. (1985). *Leben und Tod in den Religionen*. Darmstadt: Wissenschaftliche Buchgesellschaft.

Stevenson, H.N.C. (1954). "Status Evaluation in the Hindu Caste System." *Journal of the Royal Anthropological Institute* 84: 45–65.

Stevenson, Sinclair (1920). *The Rites of the Twice-Born*. New Delhi: Munshiram Manoharlal (reprint, 1971).

Stietencron, Heinrich von (1975). "Name und Manifestation Gottes in Indien." In Heinrich von Stietencron, ed., *Der Name Gottes.* Düsseldorf: Patmos, 50–65.

———(1976). "Vom Tod im Leben und vom Leben im Tode. Bemerkungen zur hinduistischen Auffassung von Tod." In J. Schwartländer, ed., *Der Mensch und sein Tod.* Göttingen: Vandenhoeck & Ruprecht, 146–161.

———(1979). "Die Rolle des Vaters im Hinduismus." In H. Tellenbach, ed., *Vaterbilder in den Kulturen Asiens, Afrikas und Ozeaniens,* Stuttgart: Kohlhammer, 51–72.

———(1985). "Brahmanen als Integratoren und Interpreten von Regionaltraditionen." In Kulke/Rothermund, eds., 23–56.

———(1986). "Kalkulierter Religionsverfall: Das Kaliyuga in Indien." In H. Zinser, ed., *Der Untergang von Religionen.* Berlin: Dietrich Reimer Verlag, 135–150.

———(1989). "Hinduism: On the Proper Use of a Deceptive Term." In Sontheimer/Kulke, eds., 11–27.

———(1992). "Hinduismus/Hindu-Religionen." In *Lexikon der Religionen.* Ed. Hans Waldenfels. Freiburg: Herder Verlag, 288–296.

———(1995). "Religious Configurations in Pre-Muslim India and the Modern Concept of Hinduism." In Dalmia/von Stietencron, eds., 51–81.

———(1997). *Hindu Religious Traditions and the Concept of "Religion."* Amsterdam: Royal Netherlands Academy of Arts and Sciences (Gonda Lecture 1996).

Strauss, Otto (1924). *Indische Philosophie.* Munich: Ernst Reinhardt.

Tachikawa, Musashi (1983). "A Hindu Worship Service in Sixteen Steps, Shoḍaśa-Upacāra-Pūjā." *Bulletin of the National Museum of Ethnology* 8: 104–186.

———(1993). "*Homa* in Vedic Ritual: The Structure of the Darśapūrṇamāsa." *Senri Ethnological Studies* 36: 239–267.

Tambiah, Stanley J. (1973a). "From Varṇa to Caste through Mixed Unions." In J. Goody, ed., *The Character of Kingship.* Cambridge: Cambridge University Press, 191–230.

———(1973b). "Meaning of Magical Acts: A Point of view." In Robin Horton and Ruth Finnegan, eds., *Modes of Thought.* London: Faber and Faber.

Thapar, Romila (1966). *A History of India.* Vol. 1. London: Penguin.

———(1978). *Ancient Indian Social History: Some Interpretations.* New Delhi: Longman.

———(1981). "Death and the Hero." In S. C. Humphreys and H. King, eds., *Mortality and Immortality: The Anthropology and Archaeology of Death.* London: Academic Press, 293–315.

Thibaut, George (1899). *Astronomie, Astrologie und Mathematik.* Strassburg: Karl. J. Trübner.

Thiel-Horstmann, Monika, ed. (1983). *Bhakti in Current Research, 1979–1982: Proceedings of the second International Conference on Early Devotional Literature in New Indo-Aryan Languages, St. Augustin, 19–21 March 1982.* Berlin: Dietrich Riemer Verlag.

———(1991). "On the Dual Identity of the Nāgās." In D. L. Eck, ed., *Devotion Divine: Bhakti Traditions from the Regions of India. Studies in Honour of Charlotte Vaudeville.* Groningen: Forsten, 255–271.

Thieme, Paul (1938). *Der Fremdling im Rigveda: Eine Studie über die Bedeutung der Worte ari, arya, aryaman und ārya.* Leipzig (Abhandlung für die Kunde des Morgenlandes, vol. 23, no. 2).

———(1939). "Indische Wörter und Sitten. 1. pūjā." *Zeitschrift der Deutschen Morgenländischen Gesellschaft* 93:105–124.

———(1952). "Bráhman." *Zeitschrift der Deutschen Morgenländischen Gesellschaft* 102: 91–129.

———(1966a). "Das indische Theater." In H. Kindermann, ed., *Fernöstliches Theater.* Stuttgart: Alfred Kröner, 21–120.

———(1966b). *Gedichte aus dem Rig-Veda.* Stuttgart: Reclam.

———(1966c). *Upanischaden. Ausgewählte Stücke.* Stuttgart: Reclam.

———(1968). "*ādeśa.*" In *Mélanges d'Indianisme à la mémoire de Louis Renou.* Paris, 715–723.

———(1971a). "Beseelung in Sprache, Dichtung und Religion." In Thieme 1971b, vol. 1, pp. 374–385.

———(1971b). *Kleine Schriften.* 2 vols. Ed. G. Buddruss. Wiesbaden: Franz Steiner Verlag.

Thite, Ganesh Umakant (1975). *Sacrifice in the Brāhmaṇa-Texts.* Poona: Poona University Press.

Thomas, Keith (1976). "Age and Authority in Early Modern England." *Proceedings of the British Academy* 62 (Raleigh Lecture on History).

Thurnwald, Richard (1939). "Primitive Initiations- und Wiedergeburtsriten." *Eranos-Jahrbuch* 1939: 321–398.

Thurston, F., and K. Rangachari (1909). *Castes and Tribes of Southern India.* 7 vols. Madras: Government Press.

Tiemann, G. (1970). "The Four-Gotra-Rule among the Jat of Harayana in Northern India." *Anthropos* 65: 166–177.

Toffin, Gérard (1984). *Société et Religion chez les Néwar du Népal.* Paris: Editions du Centre National de la Recherche Scientifique.

Trautmann, Thomas (1964). "On the Translation of the Term *Varṇa.*" *Journal of the Economic and Social History of the Orient* 7: 196–201.

———(1981). *Dravidian Kinship.* Cambridge: Cambridge University Press.

Trawick, Margareth (1990). *Notes on Love in a Tamil Family.* Berkeley: University of California Press.

Tull, Herman W. (1989). *The Vedic Origin of Karma: Cosmos as Man in Ancient Indian Myth and Ritual.* Albany: State University of New York Press.

Turner, Terence (1984). "Dual Opposition, Hierarchy and Value." In J.-C. Galey, ed., *Différences, valeurs, hiérarchie: Textes offerts à Louis Dumont.* Paris: Ecole des Hautes Etude en Sciences Sociales, 335–370.

Turner, Victor (1964). "Betwixt and Between: The Liminal Period in Rites des Passage." In *The Forest of Symbols.* New York.

———(1969). *The Ritual Process: Structure and Anti-Structure.* London: Routledge & Kegan Paul.

———(1974). *Dramas, Fields, and Metaphors: Symbolic Action in Human Society.* Ithaca, N.Y.: Cornell University Press.

———(1982). *From Ritual to Theater: The Human Seriousness of Play.* New York: Performing Arts Journal Publications.

———(1985). *On the Edge of the Bush: Anthropology as Experience.* Ed. L. B. Turner. Tuscon: University of Arizona Press.

Türstig, Hans-Georg (1980). *Jyotiṣa. Das System der indischen Astrologie.* Wiesbaden: Franz Steiner Verlag.

Uberoi, Patricia, ed. (1993). *Family, Kinship and Marriage in India.* Delhi: Oxford University Press.

Unbescheid, Günther (1980). *Kānphaṭā—Untersuchungen zu Kult, Mythologie und Geschichte śivaitischer Tantriker in Nepal.* Wiesbaden: Otto Harrassowitz.

Underhill, M. M. (1921). *The Hindu Religious Year.* London: Oxford University Press.

Vandana, Mataji (1995). *Nama Japa: The Prayer of the Name.* Delhi: Motilal Banarsidass.

Vatsyayan, Kapila, ed. (1991). *Concepts of Space: Ancient and Modern.* New Delhi: Indira Gandhi National Centre for the Arts.

Vatuk, Sylvia (1975). "Gifts and Affines." *Contributions to Indian Sociology* n.s. 5: 155–196.

Veer, Peter van der (1988). *Gods on Earth: The Management of Religious Experience and Identity in a North Indian Pilgrimage Centre.* London: Athlone Press.

———(1989). "The Concept of the Ideal Brahman as an Indological Construct." In Sontheimer/Kulke, eds., 67–80.

Vetter, Tilmann (1979). *Studien zur Lehre und Entwicklung Śaṃkaras.* Vienna: Institut für Indologie.

———(1994). "Gedanken zu einer Geschichte der indischen Mystik." *Zeitschrift für Missions- und Religionswissenschaft.* 78: 175–190.

Wach, Joachim (1947). *Sociology of Religion.* London: Kegan Paul.

Wadley, Susan S. (1977). "Women and the Hindu Tradition." In Jacobson/Wadley, eds., 113–139.

Wagner, Falk. (1986). *Was ist Religion? Studien zu ihrem Begriff und Thema in Geschichte und Gegenwart.* Gütersloh: Gütersloher Verlagshaus Mohn.

Wassmann, Jürg (1994). "The Yupno as Post-Newtonian Scientists: The Question of What Is 'Natural' in Spatial Description." *Man* n.s. 29.3: 645–666.

Weber, Max (1958). *The Religion of India: The Sociology of Hinduism and Buddhism.* Trans. and ed. Hans H. Gerth and Don Martindale. Glencoe, Ill.: Free Press.

———(1968). *Economy and Society: An Outline of Interpretive Sociology.* New York: Bedminster Press.

Weinberger-Thomas, Cathérine (1999). *Ashes of Immortality: Widow-Burning in India.* Trans. Jeffrey Mehlman and David Gordon White. Chicago: University of Chicago Press.

Weiss, Mitchell G. (1980). "*Caraka Saṃhitā* on the Doctrine of Karma." In O'Flaherty, ed., 90–115.

Werner, Karel (1993). *Love Divine: Studies in Bhakti and Devotional Mysticism.* Richmond, Surrey: Curzon Press.

Wessler, Heinz Werner (1995). *Zeit und Geschichte im Viṣṇupurāṇa.* Bern: Peter Lang.

Wezler, Albrecht (1978). *Die wahren "Speiseresteesser" (Skt. vighasāśin).* Mainz: Akademie der Wissenschaften und Literatur in Mainz.

———(1983). "Bemerkungen zum Inklusivismusbegriff Paul Hackers." In Oberhammer, ed. (1983), 61–92.

———(1985). "Dharma und Deśadharma." In Kulke/Rothermund, eds., 1–22.

———(1996). "Zu den sogenannten Identifikationen in den Brāhmaṇas." *Studien zur Indologie und Iranistik* 20: 485–522.

———, ed. (ms). "Die indische Idee der Gewaltlosigkeit. Zur Beziehung zwischen Mensch und Nature in Indien." Hamburg (forthcoming).

Whiting, J.W.M., R. Kluckhorn, and A. Anthony (1958/1971). "The Function of Male Initiation Ceremonies at Puberty." In Jonathan L. Freedmann, ed., *Readings in Social Psychology.* Engelwood Cliffs, N.J.: Prentice Hall: 359–370.

Wichterich, Christa (1986). *Stree Shakti: Frauen in Indien: Von der Stärke der Schwachen.* Bornheim-Merten: Lamuv Verlag.

Wiedenmann, Rainer E. (1991). *Ritual und Sinntransformation.* Berlin: Duncker & Humbolt.

Wiemann-Michaels, Annette (1994). *Die verhexte Speise. Eine ethnopsychosomatische Studie über das Depressive Syndrom in Nepal.* Frankfurt/M: Peter Lang.

———(1996). "Multiple Mutterschaft und Depression. Neue psychoanalytische Theorien für Indien." *Curare* 19: 323–329.

Wilke, Annette (1995). *Ein Sein—Ein Erkennen: Meister Eckharts Christologie und Śaṃkaras Lehre vom Ātman: Zur (Un-)vergleichbarkeit zweier Einheitslehren.* Bern: Peter Lang.

———(1996). "Mythos in Bewegung. Die Große Göttin in Symbolsystem, Kultus und Alltag." *Zeitschrift für Missions- und Religionswissenschaft* 80: 265–283.

———(ms.) "Nomen est Numen. Götternamen und Namensritual im Hinduismus."

Winternitz, Moritz (1892). *Das altindische Hochzeitsrituell nach dem Āpastambīya-Gṛhyasūtra und einigen anderen verwandten Werken [. . .].* Vienna: Kaiserliche Akademie der Wissenschaften.

———(1920). *Die Frau in den indischen Religionen.* Part I: *Die Frau im Brahmanismus.* Leipzig: Verlag von Curt Kabitzsch.

———(1926). "Zur Lehre von den Āśramas." In W. Kirfel, ed., *Beiträge zur Literaturwissenschaft und Geistesgeschichte Indiens. Festgabe Hermann Jacobi.* Bonn, 215–227.

———(1996). *History of Indian Literature.* Trans. V. Srinivasa Sarma. Delhi: Motilal Banarsidass.

Wiser, William H. (1936). *The Hindu Jajmani System.* Lucknow: Lucknow Publishing House (reprint, 1969).

Wittgenstein, Ludwig (1958). *Philosophical Investigations.* Trans. G.E.M. Anscombe. Oxford: Basil Blackwell.

———(1961). *Tractatus Logico-Philosophicus.* Trans. D. F. Pears and B. F. McGuinness. London: Routledge & Kegan Paul.

Witzel, Michael (1979). *On Magical Thought in the Veda.* Leiden: Universitaire Press.

———(1985). "Regionale und überregionale Faktoren in der Entwicklung vedischer Brahmanengruppen im Mittelalter." In Kulke/Rothermund, eds., 37–76.

———(1986). "Agnihotra-Rituale in Nepal." In Kölver, ed., 155–188.

———(1987). "The Coronation Rituals of Nepal—With Special Reference to the Coronation of King Birendra (1975)." In Gutschow/Michaels, eds., 415–468.

———(1989). "Tracing the Vedic Dialects." In C. Caillat, ed., *Dialects dans les Littératures Indo-Aryennes.* Paris: Collège de France, Institut de Civilisation Indienne, 97–264.

———(1995). "Ṛgvedic History: Poets, Chieftains and Polities." In Erdosy, ed., 307–352.

———(1997). "Early Sanskritization: Origins and Development of the Kuru State." In Kölver, ed., 29–52.

Woods, James Haughton (1914 and 1927). See *Yogasūtra* in Text Editions and Translations.

Yocum, Glenn E. (1984). "Comments: The Divine Consort in South India." In Hawley/Wulff, eds., 278–281.

Young, Frank W. (1965). *Initiation Ceremonies: A Cross-Cultural Study of Status Dramatization.* Indianapolis: Bobbs-Merrill.

Young, Katherine K. (1987). "Hinduism." In A. Sharma, ed., *Women in World Religions.* New York: State University of New York Press, 59–103.

Yule, Henry, and A. C. Burnell (1886). *Hobson-Jobson: A Glossary of Colloquial Angloindian Words and Phrases.* Calcutta: Rupa (reprint, 1986).

Zaehner, R. C. (1962). *Hinduism.* Oxford: Oxford University Press.

Zilm, Astrid (1997). *Das Kastensystem in der Rechtsordung Indiens.* Frankfurt/M.: Peter Lang.

Zimmer, Heinrich (1973). *Philosophie und Religion Indiens.* Frankfurt/M.: Suhrkamp.

Index